Lecture Notes of the Institute for Computer Sciences, Social Informatics and Telecommunications Engineering 608

AF172939

The LNICST series publishes ICST's conferences, symposia and workshops.
LNICST reports state-of-the-art results in areas related to the scope of the Institute.
The type of material published includes

- Proceedings (published in time for the respective event)
- Other edited monographs (such as project reports or invited volumes)

LNICST topics span the following areas:

- General Computer Science
- E-Economy
- E-Medicine
- Knowledge Management
- Multimedia
- Operations, Management and Policy
- Social Informatics
- Systems

Alexander Kocian · Paolo Milazzo ·
Ana Lúcia Henriques Martins · Mirco Nanni ·
Luca Pappalardo
Editors

Intelligent Transport Systems

8th International Conference, INTSYS 2024
Pisa, Italy, December 5–6, 2024
Revised Selected Papers

 Springer

Editors
Alexander Kocian (iD)
University of Pisa
Pisa, Italy

Paolo Milazzo (iD)
University of Pisa
Pisa, Italy

Ana Lúcia Henriques Martins (iD)
ISCTE-IUL
Lisbon, Portugal

Mirco Nanni (iD)
ISTI-CNR
Pisa, Italy

Luca Pappalardo (iD)
Institute of Information Science
and Technologies (ISTI)
Pisa, Italy

ISSN 1867-8211   ISSN 1867-822X (electronic)
Lecture Notes of the Institute for Computer Sciences, Social Informatics
and Telecommunications Engineering
ISBN 978-3-031-86369-1   ISBN 978-3-031-86370-7 (eBook)
https://doi.org/10.1007/978-3-031-86370-7

This Springer imprint is published by the registered company Springer Nature Switzerland AG
The registered company address is: Gewerbestrasse 11, 6330 Cham, Switzerland

If disposing of this product, please recycle the paper.

Preface

It is our great pleasure to present the proceedings of the 8th International Conference on Intelligent Transport Systems 2024 (INTSYS 2024) from the European Alliance of Innovation (EAI), a premier forum for researchers, practitioners, and industry experts to share and explore the latest advancements in intelligent transport technologies and systems. The conference took place at the Congress center *"Le Benedettine"* at the University of Pisa, Italy, on 5–6 December 2024.

In today's rapidly evolving world, intelligent transport systems play a critical role in addressing global challenges such as urban congestion, sustainability, and safety. Through this conference, we aimed to foster innovation, collaboration, and the exchange of ideas to drive progress in this transformative field.

The technical program of INTSYS consisted of 21 full papers in the regular track as well as 4 full papers within a workshop. Specifically, the conference tracks were: Track 1 – Smart technologies; Track 2 – Traceability; Track 3 – Traffic forecasting and control; Track 4 – Road safety; Track 5 – Regulations and policies; Track 6 – Autonomous vehicles; and the Workshop Track – Model-based analysis for cooperative transportation under uncertainty and threats by Cinzia Bernardeschi and Gloria Gori. On top of that, the technical program comprised a panel discussion on *"The Human Mobility ecosystem in the era of AI"* organized by Anna Monreale. The technical program also featured two keynote speeches: Simona Pepe, *"Advancing Electromobility: A Holistic Approach to Battery Innovation"*, and Vittorio Loreto, *"New scenarios for inclusive and sustainable cities"*.

We express our heartfelt gratitude to the University of Pisa for sponsoring this event. Furthermore, we thank all the authors, reviewers, and session chairs for their valuable contributions to making this event a success. It was a great pleasure to collaborate with the outstanding organizing team at EAI, whose efforts were instrumental in the success of the INTSYS 2024 conference. In particular, we extend our heartfelt gratitude to Veronika Kissova and Ly "Stella" Dao for their unwavering support across all aspects of the event.

We hope that the research and insights presented in these proceedings will inspire further advancements and collaborations in the field of intelligent transport systems, contributing to a more sustainable, efficient, and safe future for global mobility.

December 2024

Alexander Kocian
Paolo Milazzo
Ana Lucia Martins
Mirco Nanni
Luca Pappalardo

Organization

Steering Committee

Alexander Kocian	University of Pisa, Italy
Ana Lúcia Henriques Martins	Iscte – University Institute of Lisbon, Portugal
João Carlos Ferreira	Iscte – University Institute of Lisbon, Portugal

Organizing Committee

General Chairs

Alexander Kocian	University of Pisa, Italy
Paolo Milazzo	University of Pisa, Italy

TPC Chair and Co-chairs

Ana Lucia Henriques Martins	Iscte – University Institute of Lisbon, Portugal
Mirco Nanni	CNR-ISTI, Italy
Luca Pappalardo	CNR-ISTI and Scuola Normale Superiore, Italy

Sponsorship and Exhibit Chair

João Carlos Ferreira	Iscte – University Institute of Lisbon, Portugal

Local Chair

Paolo Milazzo	University of Pisa, Italy

Workshops Chair

Alessio Vecchio	University of Pisa, Italy

Publicity and Social Media Chairs

Giuliano Cornacchia   CNR-ISTI, Italy
Giovanni Mauro   University of Pisa and Scuola Normale Superiore,
                             Italy

Publications Chair

Luca Pappalardo   CNR-ISTI and Scuola Normale Superiore, Italy

Web Chair

Silvia Torsi   University of Pisa, Italy

Panels Chair

Anna Monreale   University of Pisa, Italy

Technical Program Committee

Alexander Kocian   University of Pisa, Italy
Ana Lúcia Martins   Iscte – University Institute of Lisbon, Portugal
Carlos Sousa   Molde University College, Norway
Cristiano Landi   University of Pisa, Italy
Luís B. Elvas   Iscte – Instituto Universitário de Lisboa, Portugal
Fabio Pinelli   IMT School for Advanced Studies Lucca, Italy
Frederica Gonçalves   University of Madeira, ITI/LARSyS, Portugal
Gabriele Barlacchi   CNR-ISTI, Italy
Giovanna Maria Dimitri   University of Siena, Italy
Giovanni Mauro   University of Pisa and Scuola Normale Superiore,
                             Italy
Giuliano Cornacchia   CNR-ISTI, Italy
Chiara Pugliese   CNR-ISTI, Italy
Chiara Renso   CNR-ISTI, Italy
Joao C. Ferreira   Iscte – Instituto Universitário de Lisboa, Portugal
Kamil Smolak   Wrocław University of Environmental and Life
                             Sciences, Poland
Luca Pappalardo   CNR-ISTI, Italy
Marzio Di Vece   Scuola Normale Superiore, Italy
Mirco Nanni   CNR-ISTI, Italy
Özge Öztürk Hacar   Yildiz Technical University, Turkey

Paulo Pereira	Iscte – Instituto Universitário de Lisboa, Portugal
Paolo Milazzo	University of Pisa, Italy
Roberto Pellungrini	Scuola Normale Superiore of Pisa, Italy
Salvatore Citraro	CNR-ISTI, Italy
Stefano Chessa	University of Pisa, Italy
Tuomo Kujala	University of Jyväskylä, Finland
Ulpan Tokkozhina	Iscte – Instituto Universitário de Lisboa, Portugal
Vitor Monteiro	University of Minho, Portugal
Vitoria Albuquerque	NOVA IMS, Portugal
Yaqin Shaheen	Palestine Technical University, Palestine

Workshop Technical Program Committee Members

Adriano Fagiolini	University of Palermo, Italy
Alessandro Fantechi	University of Florence, Italy
Davide Basile	CNR, Italy
Federico Rossi	University of Pisa, Italy
Francesco Flammini	SUPSI, Switzerland
Christian Quadri	University of Milan, Italy
Laura Carnevali	University of Florence, Italy
Stefania Santini	University of Naples, Italy
Vittoria Nardone	University of Molise, Italy

Contents

Autonomous Vehicles

Model-Based Analysis for Cooperative Transportation under Uncertainty and Threats

Smart Technologies

Beat Trustfully: The Correlation Between Heart Rate and a Multi-dimensional Trust Questionnaire

Saeedeh Mosaferchi⬤, Rosaria Califano⬤, Giuseppe Pica, Luca Orlando, Francesco Villecco⬤, and Alessandro Naddeo^(✉) ⬤

University of Salerno, Via Giovanni Paolo II, 132, 84084 Fisciano, SA, Italy
anaddeo@unisa.it

Abstract. Background: Both industries and academia are paying deep attention to the concept of trust in automation since it is significant that creates people's desire to use and buy autonomous cars.

Objectives: Regarding the previously introduced trust questionnaire by our research team, this study was conducted to present more objective insights of this questionnaire to show its convergent validity based on the physiological data.

Methods: Using a dynamic driving simulator, the 8-step experiment was performed on 29 min with 21 participants. The steps provided building, improvement, destruction, and re-building of trust. The experiment contained both manual and autonomous driving. Subjects completed stress and trust scales regarding the experience they performed. Finally, they answered to the trust questionnaire; their heart rate was acquired throughout the experiment.

Results: The Mean ± SD of participants' trust score was 139 ± 5.76. Self-driving car's unsafe behaviors were accompanied by a rise in the individuals' heart rates (objective metrics of stress). Throughout the two phases of fastest and riskiest parts of the scenario, people felt the highest stress (6 out of 10) and the least trust (4.33 out of 10), that were obtained from the mentioned one question scale.

Conclusion: Regarding the results, the mean score of people's trust from our multi-dimensional questionnaire is far from the desired score, which is 235. Objective (heart rate) and other subjective data (stress and trust) confirmed that the participants' trust in an autonomous vehicle was low. So, it can be claimed that there is a consistency between subjective and objective data with the results of our comprehensive trust questionnaire.

Keywords: Autonomous vehicles · Trust · Heart Rate · Stress · Multi-dimensional questionnaire

1 Introduction

The number of autonomous cars on the road is predicted to rise quickly as more people adopt automated driving, particularly with the advent of partially automated systems like level-1 and level-2 [1]. People who are reluctant to give up control are more likely

A. Kocian et al. (Eds.): INTSYS 2024, LNICST 608, pp. 3–15, 2025.
https://doi.org/10.1007/978-3-031-86370-7_1

to have to rely on conventional vehicles to some extent even as they continue to share the road. People who are uncomfortable with autonomous systems may feel more pressured as a result of this separation, which could make utilizing self-driving cars more stressful [2]. Gaining trust in self-driving cars is essential to putting this automation technology into practice and maximizing its benefits, although the public trust in these sophisticated vehicles is still lacking [3, 4]. The literature, however, suggests that trust can improve and ease human-autonomous vehicle interaction [3, 5]. Due to the critical role that trust plays in individuals' acceptance and willingness to use these vehicles, it has garnered significant attention and discussion among scholars in recent years [6, 7]. On the other hand, various studies have highlighted a direct and positive correlation between trust and perceived comfort levels in self-driving vehicles [8]. Increasing trust in self-driving cars has been shown to improve people's comfort levels and make travel more pleasant [9, 10]. So far, various tools have been constructed to assess individuals' trust in autonomous vehicles from different perspectives, contributing to the exploration of this crucial topic [11–13]. Referring to the multidimensional questionnaire that was developed by the authors for trust in self-driving cars [14], in the present study the consistency between subjective and objective data was investigated to demonstrate the convergent validity of the questionnaire based on the physiological data. In order to accomplish this, some driving tests were conducted to assess the relationship between the trust questionnaire and people's heart rates.

2   Methods and Materials

Briefly, the steps are mentioned in the following table and contain building (1a, 1b, 1c), improvement (2), destruction (3), further destruction (4), and re-building (5a, 5b) of trust in an autonomous vehicle (Based on Shahrdar et al. [15]). In addition to the traffic condition and car aggressiveness (risk number), some other features like driving location (city/highway) and time (day/night) changed during the experiment. The first two phases consisted of manual driving in a city on a sunny day, with low and high traffic occurring in sequence to build trust. To reach the goal, the car drove safe and slowly to make trustworthy situation, and in some cases (phases 2, 3 and 4) it increased the speed and created some dangerous maneuvers with one light crash that had not any damages or stop for the car (4). All steps are shown in Table 1 in details.

2.1   Participants

Twenty-six people were recruited at the experiment, but only 21 of them completed the test (11 males, 9 females); their ages ranged from 19 to 27 years (M = 23.19, SD = 2.82), with an average of 3.9 years of driving experience. Other 5 persons did not complete the test due to simulator sickness, however, the indoor temperature was kept around 19–21 °C using the air conditioner to prevent motion sickness symptoms. In addition to different educational background, they were from various countries such as Spain, Italy, Poland, Colombia, Algeria, etc., while all of them had been living in Italy since at least 4 months before the experiment date. Only 2 out of 21 participants didn't have driver's licenses. The majority of them were students, although some worked in Italian industries. Just 14.28% of respondents had never heard of autonomous vehicles.

Table 1. Driving scenario features

Features	Phase Number							
	Phase 1a	Phase 1b	Phase 1c	Phase 2	Phase 3	Phase 4	Phase 5a	Phase 5b
Trust	+	+	+	+	−	−	+	+
Stress	−	−	−	+	+	+	−	−
Driving Type	Manual	Manual	Automatic	Automatic	Automatic	Automatic	Automatic	Automatic
Driving Time	Sunny Day	Sunny Day	Sunny Day	Sunny Day	Sunny Day	Night	Night	Sunny Day
Driving Location	City	City	City	City	City	Highway	Highway	Highway
The amount of traffic	Low	High	Low	High	High	High	High	Low
Risk Number	0.3	0.3	0.3	0.45	0.6	0.6	0.3	0.3
Driving Duration (min)	4	4	4	4	4	4	2.5	2.5

- Trust description: Positive mode states that the step was designed to build, increase, or rebuild participants' trust. Negative sign shows it has developed for destroying their trust.
- Stress description: Positive mode states that the step was designed to make a stressful condition. Negative sign shows it has developed to decrease stress.
- Risk number: The lowest value of "risk number" on the software is 0.3, the highest is 0.9.

2.2 Apparatus

The experiment was conducted in a dynamic driving simulator in a closed space that has been created inside the laboratory of Human Centered Design and Vehicle Design by Simulation at the University of Salerno in Italy (UNISA). The virtual predefined roads were projected on three displays (size 65 inches, Hisense brand) that created a 120° horizontal field of view; the simulator is equipped with an adjustable seat, a steering wheel, pedals for gas and brake, and surrounding sound equipment. For driving simulation, BeamNG software was utilized [16]. The whole scenario took 29 min including straight and curved roads with traffic, traffic signals and signs, and other cars, except pedestrians, under different situation (e.g., risk number, ego speed, the amount of traffic, mentioned in Table 1). In the software, southern Italian roads were selected to control their stress as a confounding factor. In this way, they were familiar with the driving route and expended less mental effort on analyzing the road.

2.3 Procedure

First, the research team explained the study goals and procedures to all volunteers, who were free to withdraw from the experiment at any point, even during its course. After signing on a consent form, participants filled out a demographic questionnaire, then they started 2–3 min warm-up driving to become more familiar with the system. Participants would announce their readiness to start the experiment. The scenario consisted of 8 steps, two first stages were manual, while the remaining 6 steps were full-autonomous driving without any human input. Between each step, participants responded to stress and trust 10-point Likert scales by a tablet, regarding the stage they passed. At the end of the experiment, in order to avoid the probable simulator sickness, the participants were invited to leave the simulator seat and answer the trust questionnaire [14] while seating on a comfortable seat in a relaxed posture. Furthermore, their heart rate was collected using the chest strap, Polar H10 [17], throughout the whole experiment, since it is a suitable objective indicator to investigate people's stress and anxiety [18, 19]. Worth mentioning that participants could percept all vibration feedback received from the road such as road bumps, as well as hearing the environmental sounds with 2 speakers. Participants were free to do each kind of non-driving related task during autonomous phases, but after following up the road and the car behaviors, using their cell phones was the most preferred activity they performed but for short times (Fig. 1).

Fig. 1. Driving experiment using the dynamic simulator

2.4 The Questionnaires

As mentioned before, a demographic questionnaire, the trust questionnaire (Appendix A), which was developed by UNISA research team, and two 10-point Likert scales of trust and stress were responded. The trust questionnaire contains 3 dimensions (Personal, technical, and social), 21 sub-dimensions, and 47 questions with 5-answer options (1 = completely disagree, 5 = completely agree). 24 out of 47 questions were designed negatively, indeed the scores must be reversed (5 = completely disagree, 1 = completely agree). Thus, the minimum and maximum achievable scores are 47 and 235, respectively.

3 Results

Regarding autonomous driving sections, participants experienced highest stress (Mean = 6) during phase 4 that was full-autonomous driving with the most dangerous behaviors of the car, while the least stressful stage (Mean = 3.90) belongs to phase 5b which was planned to rebuild their trust in the AV. Figure 2 shows their stress graph during the experiment.

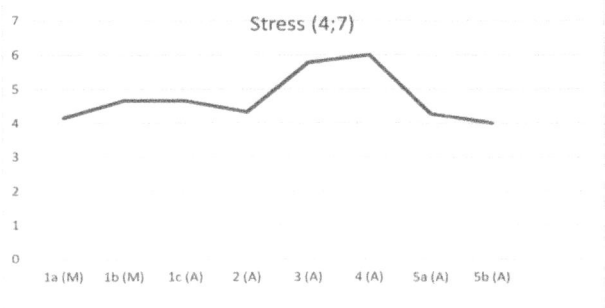

Fig. 2. Participants' stress means during 8 steps of the experiment.

The Mean ± SD of participants' trust score from the main questionnaire was obtained 139 ± 5.76 (maximum possible score = 235). Likert scales' results showed 4.33 out of 10 as the minimum amount of trust which belonged to phase 4 (the riskiest step). Moreover, phase 3 with 5.28 stands as the second unpleasant step from trust point of view. Step 1c was the most trustworthy part of the study with trust mean score of 6.76 out of 10. In this part the car started safe and smooth full autonomous driving with the lowest speed and risk number, in a low traffic city during a sunny day. Worth mentioning that the mean score of the trust scale in two last parts (5a and 5b) increased to 5.95 and 6.42 and reached values that were close to the highest obtained level.

The analysis yielded a sample mean of 139 with a standard deviation of 5.76, derived from a sample of 21 observations. The 95% confidence interval for the population mean was calculated to range from 136.38 to 141.62. This interval suggests that, with 95% confidence, the true mean of the population falls within this range, reflecting the reliability and precision of the sample data (Fig. 3 and Fig. 4).

The average of participants' heart rate for the whole experiment was 71.83 bpm (minimum 57 and maximum 80 bmp), but the highest heart rate was experienced in the phase 3 with 84.58 bmp (when dangerous maneuvers began). It is notable that the usual resting heart rate typically falls between 60 and 100 beats per minute [20] (Fig. 5).

Furthermore, 2 questions about participants' perceived comfort and motion sickness were asked using 10-point Likert scales. They reported low motion sickness (3.23 out of 10) and a moderately comfortable state (4.90 out of 10).

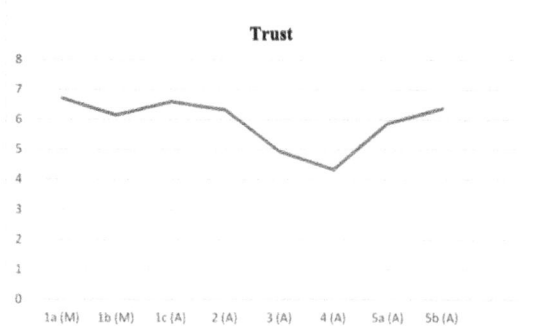

Fig. 3. Participants' trust means during 8 steps of the experiment.

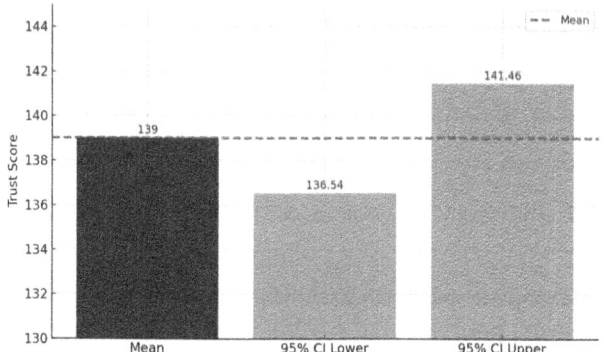

Fig. 4. Mean trust score with 95% confidence interval.

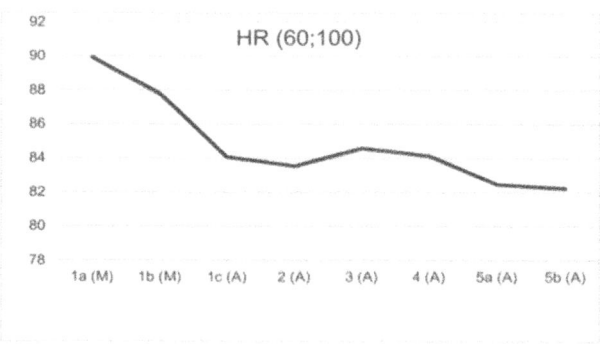

Fig. 5. Participants' heart rate means during 8 steps of the experiment.

4 Discussion

The current study was conducted to explore the consistency between subjective and objective data with the multi-dimensional trust questionnaire that was developed by this research team before. Using a dynamic driving simulator, the authors tried to create a driving environment to achieve more real output. Given the extensive use of the correlation between heart rate and trust in self-driving vehicles across various research studies [21–23] and acknowledging that heart rate consistently serves as a significant indicator reflecting individuals' stress levels [24, 25], we opted to utilize heart rate as a reliable metric to gauge individuals' levels of trust and stress towards the self-driving vehicle. Concerning the outcomes, it's pertinent to note that the average trust score obtained from our multi-dimensional questionnaire falls considerably below the target level of 235. Furthermore, the convergence of objective metrics, such as heart rate data, with subjective evaluations of stress and trust, underscores a consistent pattern indicating a lack of trust among participants toward autonomous vehicle technology. Consequently, a coherent alignment emerges between the subjective perceptions and the empirical data, affirming the conclusions drawn from our comprehensive trust assessment questionnaire.

5 Limitations

It is essential to affirm certain limitations inherent in the study, notably the relatively small number of participants involved. Additionally, the diverse range of nationalities represented among participants may introduce variability stemming from differences in technological landscapes across nations, potentially impacting the study's findings. In future investigations, addressing these limitations will necessitate not only expanding the participant pool but also ensuring a more balanced and homogeneous composition in terms of nationality and gender. Moreover, conducting experiments using driving simulators saves considerable costs and time, executing all these stages with a real self-driving vehicle may potentially provide superior and more realistic results. Lastly, heart rate was evaluated as a physiological indicator of either increased or decreased trust. Even though the literature has demonstrated that heart rate is a reliable indicator and the most effective physiological index for evaluating acute stress in driving simulator studies, further measurements can be included in future investigations. For instance, using measurements like electroencephalography (EEG) or galvanic skin response can offer a more thorough comprehension of the physiological dynamics at work.

6 Conclusions

In summary, our study findings provide compelling evidence supporting the robust correlation between heart rate data, serving as a reliable index for stress and fear, and the trust questionnaire regarding self-driving cars. These results not only validate the questionnaire's reliability in accurately gauging individuals' trust levels in autonomous vehicles but also emphasize its potential as a valuable tool for researchers in related fields. Thus, this study contributes to the growing body of knowledge and underscores the questionnaire's versatility for future research endeavours, affirming its utility in advancing our understanding of trust in autonomous vehicle technologies.

Acknowledgements. Authors are deeply grateful to all who contributed to this study. Their support and warm involvement were invaluable.

Appendix A

(See Table 2).

Table 2. Trust in autonomous vehicles questionnaire developed by Mosaferchi et al.

Personal/Human-Related Dimension

Num	Sub-Dimensions	Questions	Completely disgree	Disagree	No difference	Agree	Completely Agree
1	Knowledge	I'm able enough to take over the driving control from an AV in emergency/dangerous situations					
2		I need to learn about an AV continuously to use it efficiently *					
3	Personality	An AV is attractive for me to use					
4		I'm curious about functions/features of an AV					
5		I'm not afraid of using an AV					
6		I can control my stress when I expose with a dangerous situation in an AV					
7	Duration of the trip	I prefer to use an AV just for short trips (less than 20 min), not long trips *					
8	Companionship	I feel less stress in an AV when I'm not alone *					
9		I'm not worried if my children use an AV alone					
10	Situation Awareness	During the trip with an AV, I don't need to pay a lot of attention					
11		I can analyse surrounding information that I receive in an AV					

(continued)

Table 2. (*continued*)

Personal/Human-Related Dimension							
12	Expectations	If an AV doesn't behave based on my expectations, I'll use it again without any problem					
13	Deskillization	I believe that my driving skills won't decline because of using an AV					
14	Meaningfulness Attitude	The pleasure of driving will increase by using an AV					
15		I would enjoy the AV more if I could drive it myself sometimes					

Social Dimension							
Num	Sub-Dimensions	Questions	Completely disagree	Disagree	No difference	Agree	Completely Agree
16	Governmental considerations/support	I use an AV if some specific lanes are reserved for AVs in cities and highways *					
17		I'll buy an AV if the government gives us good financial support *					
18		I prefer AVs to use as public services like buses, more than personal cars *					
19	Brand	If I want to buy an AV, I prefer famous brands more than others *					
20	Development level of countries	I believe that people who live in advanced countries like Japan, can trust in an AV more *					

Technical Dimension							
Num	Sub-Dimensions	Questions	Completely Disagree	Disagree	No difference	Agree	Completely Agree
21	Personalized design	I prefer to connect my smartphone with the AV to experience a personalized trip					
22	Car Appearance	I prefer to ride with a big AV, rather than a small AV*					

(*continued*)

Table 2. (*continued*)

Personal/Human-Related Dimension

23	Safety	I prefer to use an AV with more sensors than an AV with less sensors *					
24		I prefer to ride in low speeds with an AV than high speeds *					
25		I would like to have an emergency button inside the AV *					
26		I would like to receive information about pedestrians, bicyclists, and other vehicles from the AV					
27		I trust an AV with some technical confirmations of valid organizations like Euro NCAP (The European New Car Assessment Program) *					
28		I prefer to use an AV just during the day, rather than night *					
29		I prefer to use an AV just in cities, not highways *					
30	Internal Interfaces	I prefer to use a mechanical system to manage the AV *					
31		I prefer to use touch screens in the AV to set some features					
32		I prefer to receive information from the AV vocally (by playing sound effects)					
33		I prefer to receive information from the AV visually (by reading a text on the monitor or on my smartphone/smartwatch)					
34	Transparency	I prefer to be informed about technical problems in real-time *					
35		I prefer to be informed about traffic condition by the AV *					

(*continued*)

Table 2. (*continued*)

Personal/Human-Related Dimension							
36		I prefer to be informed about the next behavior of the AV before happening *					
37	Security	I believe that AVs can't be attacked like all technical systems (Cyber-attack) and my data will be kept safely					
38		I believe that AVs need an anti-virus like all computers *					
39	Technical support	I believe that technical support is an important part of after sales services *					
40		I believe that a real time customer service is necessary for an AV *					
41	Possibility of Interventions	I prefer not to drive myself in dangerous situations instead of the AV, because an AV can manage dangers better than me					
42		I prefer to drive myself in some cases instead of the AV, just for fun *					
43	Complexity	I can communicate with an AV with a simple appearance and features better, rather than a complex one *					
44	Usability	I'm sure that an AV will drive very well					
45		I believe that an AV can save our time, energy, and costs					
46		I believe an AV is easy to use					
47		I believe that an AV will send me useful feedback on all situations					

-Questions marked with an asterisk (*) should be reversed for scoring. (5=completely disagree, 4=disagree, 3=No difference, 2=agree, 1=completely agree).

References

1. De Cet, G., Orsini, F., Meneguzzer, C., Gastaldi, M., Saljoqi, M., Rossi, R.: Do we trust automated vehicles? A driving simulator study. Transp. Res. Procedia **78**, 174–181 (2024)
2. Morris, D.M., Erno, J.M., Pilcher. J.J.: Electrodermal response and automation trust during simulated self-driving car use. In: Proceedings of the Human Factors and Ergonomics Society Annual Meeting, vol. 61, no. 1, pp. 1759–1762. SAGE Publications, Los Angeles (2017)
3. Yu, B., Bao, S., Zhang, Y., Sullivan, J., Flannagan, M.: Measurement and prediction of driver trust in automated vehicle technologies: an application of hand position transition probability matrix. Transp. Res. Part C: Emerg. Technol. **124**, 102957 (2021)
4. Zhang, Z., Tian, R., Duffy, V.G.: Trust in automated vehicle: a meta-analysis. In: Human-Automation Interaction: Transportation, pp. 221–234. Springer, Cham (2022)
5. Yi, B., et al.: How can the trust-change direction be measured and identified during takeover transitions in conditionally automated driving? Using physiological responses and takeover-related factors. Hum. Factors 00187208221143855 (2023)
6. Seet, M., Harvy, J., Bose, R., Dragomir, A., Bezerianos, A., Thakor, N.: Differential impact of autonomous vehicle malfunctions on human trust. IEEE Trans. Intell. Transp. Syst. **23**(1), 548–557 (2020)
7. Wu, M., Wang, N., Yuen, K.F.: Can autonomy level and anthropomorphic characteristics affect public acceptance and trust towards shared autonomous vehicles? Technol. Forecast. Soc. Chang. **189**, 122384 (2023)
8. Paddeu, D., Parkhurst, G., Shergold, I.: Passenger comfort and trust on first-time use of a shared autonomous shuttle vehicle. Transp. Res. Part C: Emerg. Technol. **115**, 102604 (2020)
9. Fereydooni, N., Scott-Sharoni, S.T., Walker, B.N., Lenneman, J.K., Austin, B.P., Yoshida, T.: The impact of content temporality and modality in automotive user interface on trust and comfort. In: Proceedings of the Human Factors and Ergonomics Society Annual Meeting, vol. 67, no. 1, pp. 1971–1976. SAGE Publications, Los Angeles (2023)
10. Bellem, H., Thiel, B., Schrauf, M., Krems, J.F.: Comfort in automated driving: an analysis of preferences for different automated driving styles and their dependence on personality traits. Transport. Res. F: Traffic Psychol. Behav. **55**, 90–100 (2018)
11. Nordhoff, S., Stapel, J., He, X., Gentner, A., Happee, R.: Perceived safety and trust in SAE Lev-el 2 partially automated cars: results from an online questionnaire. PLoS ONE **16**(12), e0260953 (2021)
12. Ayoub, J.: Modeling, measuring, and predicting trust in autonomous vehicles. Doctoral dissertation (2022)
13. Jian, J.Y., Bisantz, A.M., Drury, C.G.: Foundations for an empirically determined scale of trust in automated systems. Int. J. Cogn. Ergon. **4**(1), 53–71 (2000)
14. Mosaferchi, S., Califano, R., Naddeo, A.: How personality, demographics, and technology affinity affect trust in autonomous vehicles: a case study. Hum. Factors Transp. **95**(95) (2023)
15. Shahrdar, S., Park, C., Nojoumian, M.: Human trust measurement using an immersive virtual reality autonomous vehicle simulator. In: Proceedings of the 2019 AAAI/ACM Conference on AI, Ethics, and Society, pp. 515–520 (2019)
16. Birchler, C., Mohammed, T.K., Rani, P., Nechita, T., Kehrer, T., Panichella, S.: How does simulation-based testing for self-driving cars match human perception?. In: Proceedings of the ACM on Software Engineering, vol. 1, no. FSE, pp. 929–950 (2024)
17. He, S., Du, Z., Han, L., Jiang, W., Jiao, F., Ma, A.: Unraveling the impact of fog on driver behavior in highway tunnel entrances: a field experiment. Traffic Inj. Prev. **25**(5), 680–687 (2024)
18. Chalmers, T., et al.: Stress watch: The use of heart rate and heart rate variability to detect stress: a pilot study using smart watch wearables. Sensors **22**(1), 151 (2021)

19. Lin, Q., Li, T., Shakeel, P.M., Samuel, R.D.: Advanced artificial intelligence in heart rate and blood pressure monitoring for stress management. J. Ambient. Intell. Humaniz. Comput. **12**, 3329–3340 (2021)

20. Chirakanphaisarn, N., Ganmol, P.: The sleeping positions that affect the heartbeat signal for normal subjects. In: 2021 International Conference on Engineering and Emerging Technologies (ICEET), pp. 1–6. IEEE (2021)

21. Ayoub, J., Avetisian, L., Yang, X.J., Zhou, F.: Real-time trust prediction in conditionally auto-mated driving using physiological measures. IEEE Trans. Intell. Transp. Syst. (2023)

22. Sheng, S., et al.: A case study of trust on autonomous driving. In: 2019 IEEE Intelligent Transportation Systems Conference (ITSC), pp. 4368–4373. IEEE (2019)

23. Waytz, A., Heafner, J., Epley, N.: The mind in the machine: anthropomorphism increases trust in an autonomous vehicle. J. Exp. Soc. Psychol. **52**, 113–117 (2014)

24. Taelman, J., Vandeput, S., Spaepen, A., Van Huffel, S.: Influence of mental stress on heart rate and heart rate variability. In: 4th European Conference of the International Federation for Medical and Biological Engineering: ECIFMBE 2008, 23–27 November 2008, Antwerp, Belgium, pp. 1366–1369. Springer, Heidelberg (2009)

25. Attar, E.T., Balasubramanian, V., Subasi, E., Kaya, M.: Stress analysis based on simultaneous heart rate variability and EEG monitoring. IEEE J. Transl. Eng. Health Med. **9**, 1–7 (2021)

Detecting and Locating Stress in Urban Settings with ChillIn

Daniel Namaki Ghaneh, Emanuele Respino, Gianmaria Saggini,
Niccolò Settimelli, Maurizio Palmieri⬤, and Alessio Vecchio⁽✉⁾⬤

Department of Information Engineering, University of Pisa, Pisa, Italy
{d.namakighaneh,e.respino1,g.saggini1,n.settimelli}@studenti.unipi.it,
{maurizio.palmieri,alessio.vecchio}@unipi.it

Abstract. In modern society, stress has become one of the main issues
affecting both mental and physical health. The ability to detect stress
can help people to improve their daily life. This work proposes ChillIn,
a mobile application designed to track and localize stress in an urban
environment. The application is based on a single wearable device and
its sensors to track stress within urban environments, correlating the
data acquired with geographic locations, and highlighting areas of a city
that tend to induce stress. Preliminary tests show that ChillIn can help
in understanding which are the urban areas where citizens are more
stressed, for example to understand if traffic or transportation modes
play a role from this point of view. ChillIn has a small impact on the
battery duration of the wearable device and runs on a commercially
available smartwatch.

Keywords: urban stress · wearable sensors · well-being · stress
detection

1 Introduction

Stress is one of the principal causes affecting the quality of life in urban areas [13].
The urban context often exposes individuals to stressors, originating from factors such as traffic, noise pollution, and social or economic pressure [2]. Effective stress detection can significantly improve mental and physical health outcomes. An effective means of detecting stress is represented by wearable devices, which can unobtrusively collect physiological signals and users' behavior. Locating where stress is concentrated in an urban area is particularly important, as it provides information useful to possibly identify the sources of stress and then act

Work supported by the European Union - Next Generation EU, in the context of
The National Recovery and Resilience Plan, Investment 1.5 Ecosystems of Innovation, Project Tuscany Health Ecosystem (THE), ECS00000017. Spoke 3. CUP:
I53C22000780001 and by the Italian Ministry of Education and Research (MUR) in
the framework of the FoReLab project (Departments of Excellence).

A. Kocian et al. (Eds.): INTSYS 2024, LNICST 608, pp. 16–25, 2025.
https://doi.org/10.1007/978-3-031-86370-7_2

to mitigate the problem. For example, suppose many pedestrian citizens experience stress when walking along a road characterized by high levels of vehicular traffic. In that case, city authorities can make informed decisions when planning changes to vehicular routes, or an alternative and more pedestrian-friendly route could be suggested by navigation apps. The relationship between stress and urbanicity has been extensively studied in the past, but only recently the availability of biosensing technologies made it possible to capture and quantify geolocated markers of stress in an urban setting. An interdisciplinary research area, neurourbanism, has been called for studying the relationship between mental wellbeing and urbanisation [1]. Collecting biosignals can be useful together with narrative data, collected for instance through interviews, to better understand causal relationships and highlight relevant information, going beyond a purely quantitative estimation [10].

This work proposes ChillIn, an application to visualize stress hotspots on a map. ChillIn exploits commercially available wearable devices to collect physiological data. A remote server is used to offload the estimation of the possible stress level experienced by the user starting from the raw data. As the physiological data is collected using battery-operated wearable devices, the proposed method has been designed to be energy-efficient.

The remaining of this work is organized as follows: Sect. 2 summarizes the most significant related work, Sect. 3 shows the details of the proposed application, Sect. 4 shows the results of preliminary analysis, and finally Sect. 5 concludes the paper and discusses potential future directions.

2   Related Works

The relationship between cyclists and stress was studied in [21]. In particular, the impact of cycling infrastructure, such as the presence of segregated cycling paths or intersections, was evaluated by measuring stress biomarkers using an experimental smartband for collecting skin conductivity and temperature. The level of pedestrian stress was also the focus of studies, such as in [10] where stress was evaluated by collecting interviews. The results showed that attributes of physical infrastructure and traffic conditions influenced stress levels. In [11], the level of stress was monitored by collecting Galvanic Skin Response (GSR), also known as ElectroDermal Activity (EDA), and skin temperature values using an Empatica E4 wristband; experimental results showed the relationship between stress and urban walkability, cycling lanes, and commuting. The stress of cyclists in different road environment was also studied using Heart Rate Variability (HRV) [6]. The relationship between noise, transportation mode, and stress was studied in [24], where the involved subjects self-reported the stress levels experienced during transportation.

A review of measurement approaches for physiological stress monitoring is available in [8], while [20] proposes an exhaustive review on stress detection with wearable devices. Obtaining physiologic data is one of the most important tasks for stress detection. Information useful to detect stress, as already mentioned,

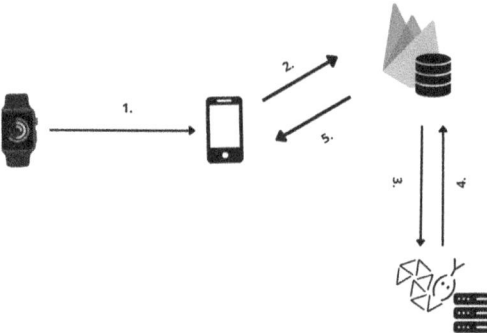

Fig. 1. Flow of data between the main components of the ChillIn app.

includes EDA [12,15] and heart rate [17]. Other approaches have been based on using infrared cameras [7] and speech analysis [22]. Even the way users type on their smartphones, measured with an accelerometer, can be used as a stress detector [19].

A significant research body tries to address the problem of detecting stress when working, as its reduction is expected to have a relevant economic impact on companies. For example, in [18] an approach is proposed to monitor stress during work hours by combining information from a wearable device and the interaction between the subjects and their computers. In [14], face position, sleep habits, and eating/drinking behavior are used for stress detection. A system for improving work productivity that includes human factors, such as stress, is tested in [5] exploiting a sensor-equipped T-shirt for body signals acquisition.

Our work differs from the previously mentioned ones because it involves an urban setting where the users freely move according to their daily habits. The final goal is the detection of the urban areas that are characterized by higher stress levels, to drive urban planning and transportation strategies according to stress-relieving policies. The system has been implemented using commercial smartwatches, to ease the transition from research to real-world applications of urban stress monitoring. Commercial devices also allow a more naturalistic approach, since users are not forced to wear medical, and more cumbersome, acquisition systems.

3   ChillIn Architecture

The system comprises four components: the wearable device, the handled device, the remote service, and the database. The flow of data among the components, shown in Fig. 1, is the following:

1. The wearable device collects the sensed data and sends them to the handheld device through a synchronization channel.
2. The handheld device sends the raw data to a database hosted in the cloud.

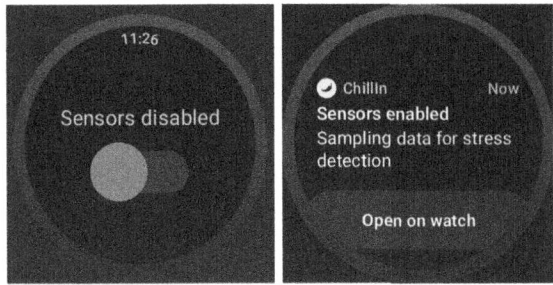

Fig. 2. User interface on the smartwatch.

3. A remote service gets the raw data from the database and analyzes the data to estimate the stress level.
4. The remote service stores the information about the stress level and related positions in the urban area in the database.
5. The handheld device retrieves information about the geolocated stress level from the database and shows it to the user.

3.1   Wearable Device Application

The wearable device, a smartwatch, collects data from three sensors: skin temperature, heart rate, and EDA. The latter undergoes low-pass filtering and high-pass filtering phases to extract the phasic component of the signal, which is the fundamental part of stress detection. These data are saved with a frequency of 1 Hz to reduce battery consumption and extend the usage of the application. Moreover, the wearable device aggregates 30 samples into a single message sent to the handheld device to further optimize battery consumption, as sending a single message with a larger payload is generally less expensive than sending many small messages (because of the overhead introduced by the layers of the communication stack and the transceiver operational states [3,4,23]). The data for stress detection is paired with the location of the user, acquired with the GPS sensor of the wearable device. The frequency of the location acquisition changes dynamically, adapting to the current speed of the user: if the user is moving at high speed (e.g. the user is driving a car), the location is collected with high frequency, on the contrary, if the user is not moving, the location is collected with a lower frequency. More precisely, the device evaluates the time required to cover 100 m with the current speed of the user and sets this time as the interval between two subsequent location updates. A maximum value of 60 s for the sampling period is used if the user moves too slowly. The wearable device relies on the Google Wearable Data Layer APIs to communicate with the paired smartphone. The app running on the smartwatch provides a simple user interface, shown in Fig. 2, with a single button that enables/disables the sampling of the sensors, in order to allow users to avoid being monitored for instance when involved in privacy-related activities.

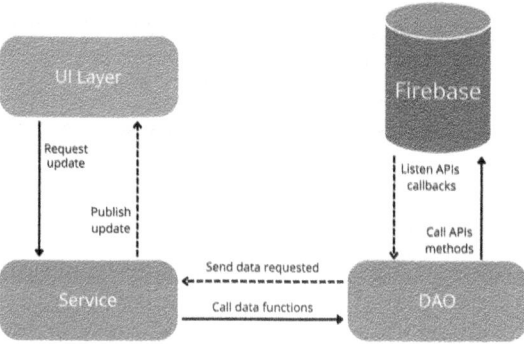

Fig. 3. Scheme of the communication between the App and Firebase.

3.2 Handheld Device App

The handheld device App is structured following the *Model-View-ViewModel and Service* (MVVMS) pattern. The service module manages the App logic and the communication with the Firebase database while a Data Access Object (DAO) manages data access operations. Figure 3 shows the adopted scheme for communication between the App and the Firebase database.

The user interface on the smartphone is divided into 3 submodules:

- *Splash module*: it implements the initial splash screen.
- *Access module*: it implements the login, registration, and password recovery functionalities.
- *Home module*: it implements the main functionalities of the App when the user is logged in.

In particular, the *Home* module is composed of two screens: the *Stress Monitor*, and the *Map*. The *Stress Monitor* screen displays the graphs associated with the physiological data of the user, visualizing a report of the data sensed and the stress level computed on a day-by-day basis, allowing the user to check their current state and history. Data is aggregated in 5-minute intervals to avoid excessive load on the UI and to achieve low response times. The *Map* screen shows a heatmap of the stress level at different hours and days in the urban area under analysis. The map is based on the *Google Maps SDK* for Android.

An example related to preliminary data acquired in Pisa (Italy) during the testing phase is shown in Fig. 4.

3.3 Cloud-Based Data Storage

The system relies on Google Firebase for data management. *Firestore DocumentDB* serves as the database for storing both raw data collected from the wearable device and stress levels evaluated by the remote service. The database contains one data collection for each user account and a public collection for real-time updates and visualization of the heatmaps. *Real-Time Key-Value Firebase*

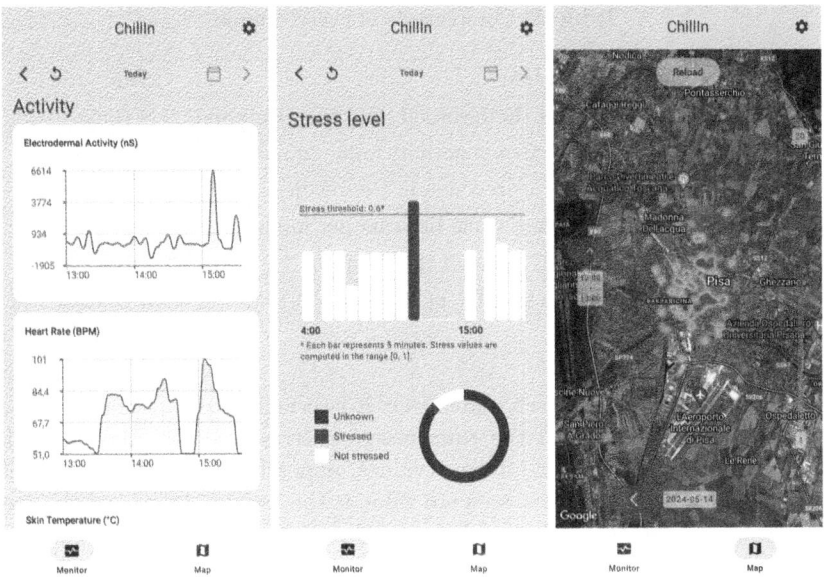

Fig. 4. Smartphone user interface.

DB integrates Firestore to handle the exchange of information with the handheld device. Data is organized into two buckets, one to temporarily store the 30 samples periodically acquired from the wearable device and one to store the stress levels associated with different geographical positions. Moreover, the Firebase database is used to store the information related to the user accounts, namely username and password, and to ensure secure access control.

3.4   Remote Service

The remote service implements two stress detection algorithms in Python. The remote service extracts the raw data stored on Firebase, estimates the presence of stress, and stores back the results onto the cloud. The first algorithm is a Range-Based Algorithm that takes as input the heart rate and checks if it falls within the range that represents the *no-stress* condition. Our algorithm is an adaptation of the algorithm proposed in [9] to continuously monitor the heart rate of the user, using a sliding window to dynamically estimate the *no-stress* range every time new data is received. In particular, the no-stress range is based on a Gibbs sampling approach, and it iteratively estimates the mean and variance of the data.

The second algorithm is a Rule-Based Algorithm that takes as input the EDA and the skin temperature and applies the five rules derived from [11] to detect and quantify moments of stress (MOS). The five rules concern i) the EDA amplitude increase, ii) the skin temperature decrease, iii) the rising time of EDA, iv) the slope of EDA response, and v) the minimum distance between two MOSes.

Table 1. Components of every sample.

Name	Description	Size
Timestamp	Time of the recorded data in milliseconds	8 Bytes
Eda	Electrodermal activity value in nanoSiemens	4 Bytes
Temperature	Temperature value in Celsius degree	4 Bytes
Heart Rate	Heart rate value in beats per minute	4 Bytes
Latitude	Latitude value of the location	8 Bytes
Longitude	Longitude value of the location	8 Bytes

Except for the fifth rule, which states that it is possible to experience only one MOS every 10-s window, all the rules assign a stress score to the input data with 0, 0.5, and 1 as possible output values, depending on specific conditions and thresholds. The overall stress score value is the weighted mean of the scores produced by the four rules, with 0.6 as the threshold to identify an MOS.

4   Preliminary Tests

The preliminary tests consisted of using the application while traveling the urban contexts of Pisa both by car and afoot. The application was tested using a *Redmi Note 8 Pro* (Android 11) smartphone and a *Google Pixel Watch 2* (WearOS 4.0) smartwatch. Each data sample collected by the smartwatch consists of 36 bytes as detailed in Table 1, resulting in the sending of 1 message every 30 s to the smartphone. The message contains the 30 samples collected with a frequency of 1 Hz and its payload is 1080 bytes (30 samples × 36 bytes).

The metric used for assessing the capability of the stress detection algorithms is the comparison between the stress level displayed by ChillIn and the perceived stress of the user that has been annotated during the preliminary trial. This metric provides a qualitative evaluation of the capabilities of the adopted algorithms.

The metric used for evaluating the impact of ChillIn on power consumption is the difference between the battery percentage before and after the trial. This metric provides a quantitative evaluation of the power consumption of the devices while running ChillIn.

Figure 5 shows the *Map* screen after a car trip from Pisa to the countryside (San Piero a Grado onto the map). The MOSes displayed on the map match the stress perceived by the user during the trip. The battery level displayed on the device dropped by 16% during a task of roughly 3 h. This drop is consistent with the daily usage of the smartwatch.

Fig. 5. Example of heatmap resulting after a trial.

5   Conclusions and Future Work

This ongoing work represents a step forward in addressing the pressing issue of stress management in modern society, in particular in urban areas. Thanks to a wearable device, the proposed application, ChillIn, allows users to monitor their stress levels in real time, providing useful insights into the impact of the urban environment and transportation modes on mental well-being. Indeed, the real improvement offered by the application is the ability to correlate stress data with geographical location providing a better understanding of stress triggers for the user and discovering stress hotspots within cities. Overall, ChillIn has the potential to be useful in several fields, from public health and personal wellness to urban planning and community development, as it could also be included in employer wellness programs. Preliminary tests showed promising results for stress detection and power consumption. The code of the application is available according to an open-source license at the following repository: https://github.com/Gianma23/ChillinApp.

We planned to perform a larger and more structured test campaign, to soundly assess the performances of ChillIn. The evaluation campaign will include different types of users (e.g. in terms of age), transportation systems, and devices (in particular smartwatches, as they are responsible for the collection of physiological data). From a usability perspective, the application could be extended to support a larger range of operating systems. Currently, the data layer limits the platform to Wear OS. A Swift version of the mobile application could support also iOS devices. From a more research-oriented point of view, the study of techniques useful to limit the impact of malicious users and/or improper data is a relevant challenge.

References

1. Adli, M., et al.: Neurourbanism: towards a new discipline. Lancet Psychiatry **4**, 183–185 (2017). https://doi.org/10.1016/S2215-0366(16)30371-6
2. Bartoskova Polcrova, A., Dalecka, A., Szabo, D., Gonzalez Rivas, J.P., Bobak, M., Pikhart, H.: Social and environmental stressors of cardiometabolic health. Sci. Rep. **14**(1), 14179 (2024). https://doi.org/10.1038/s41598-024-64847-2
3. Caiazza, C., Giordano, S., Luconi, V., Vecchio, A.: Edge computing vs centralized cloud: Impact of communication latency on the energy consumption of LTE terminal nodes. Comput. Commun. **194**, 213–225 (2022). https://doi.org/10.1016/j.comcom.2022.07.026, https://www.sciencedirect.com/science/article/pii/S0140366422002730
4. Caiazza, C., Luconi, V., Vecchio, A.: Measuring the energy of smartphone communications in the edge-cloud continuum: approaches, challenges, and a case study. IEEE Internet Comput. **27**(6), 29–35 (2023). https://doi.org/10.1109/MIC.2023.3279438
5. Donati, M., Olivelli, M., Giovannini, R., Fanucci, L.: Ecg-based stress detection and productivity factors monitoring: the real-time production factory system. Sensors **23**(12) (2023). https://doi.org/10.3390/s23125502
6. Fitch, D.T., Sharpnack, J., Handy, S.L.: Psychological stress of bicycling with traffic: examining heart rate variability of bicyclists in natural urban environments. Transp. Res. Part F: Traffic Psychol. Behav. **70**, 81–97 (2020). https://doi.org/10.1016/j.trf.2020.02.015, https://www.sciencedirect.com/science/article/pii/S1369847819304073
7. Gioia, F., Greco, A., Callara, A.L., Scilingo, E.P.: Towards a contactless stress classification using thermal imaging. Sensors **22**(3) (2022). https://doi.org/10.3390/s22030976
8. Iqbal, T., Elahi, A., Redon, P., Vazquez, P., Wijns, W., Shahzad, A.: A review of biophysiological and biochemical indicators of stress for connected and preventive healthcare. Diagnostics **11**(3) (2021). https://doi.org/10.3390/diagnostics11030556, https://www.mdpi.com/2075-4418/11/3/556
9. Iqbal, T., et al.: Stress monitoring using wearable sensors: a pilot study and stress-predict dataset. Sensors **22**(21) (2022). https://doi.org/10.3390/s22218135
10. Jessica Pykett, T.O., Resch, B.: From urban stress to neurourbanism: how should we research city well-being? Ann. Am. Assoc. Geograph. **110**(6), 1936–1951 (2020). https://doi.org/10.1080/24694452.2020.1736982
11. Kyriakou, K., et al.: Detecting moments of stress from measurements of wearable physiological sensors. Sensors **19**(17) (2019). https://doi.org/10.3390/s19173805
12. Liu, Y., Du, S.: Psychological stress level detection based on electrodermal activity. Behav. Brain Res. **341**, 50–53 (2018). https://doi.org/10.1016/j.bbr.2017.12.021
13. Montanari, A., Wang, L., Birenboim, A., Chaix, B.: Urban environment influences on stress, autonomic reactivity and circadian rhythm: protocol for an ambulatory study of mental health and sleep. Front. Public Health **12** (2024). https://doi.org/10.3389/fpubh.2024.1175109
14. Morshed, M.B., et al.: Advancing the understanding and measurement of workplace stress in remote information workers from passive sensors and behavioral data. In: 2022 10th International Conference on Affective Computing and Intelligent Interaction (ACII), pp. 1–8 (2022). https://doi.org/10.1109/ACII55700.2022.9953824

15. Raju, A.R., Ramadevi, R., Babu, P.R., D, V.: Galvanic skin response based stress detection system using machine learning and IoT. In: 2023 Second International Conference on Augmented Intelligence and Sustainable Systems (ICAISS), pp. 709–714 (2023). https://doi.org/10.1109/ICAISS58487.2023.10250663

16. Rodriguez-Valencia, A., Ortiz-Ramirez, H.A., Simancas, W., Vallejo-Borda, J.A.: Level of pedestrian stress in urban streetscapes. Transp. Res. Rec. **2676**(6), 87–98 (2022). https://doi.org/10.1177/03611981211072804

17. Salai, M., Vassányi, I., Kósa, I.: Stress detection using low cost heart rate sensors. J. Healthc. Eng. **2016**(1), 5136705 (2016). https://doi.org/10.1155/2016/5136705

18. Sanchez, W., Martinez, A., Hernandez, Y., Estrada, H., Gonzalez-Mendoza, M.: A predictive model for stress recognition in desk jobs. J. Ambient. Intell. Humaniz. Comput. 1–13 (2018). https://doi.org/10.1007/s12652-018-1149-9

19. Sukma Darmawan, A., et al.: Tree-based ensemble learning for stress detection by typing behavior on smartphones. In: 2021 International Conference on Software Engineering & Computer Systems and 4th International Conference on Computational Science and Information Management (ICSECS-ICOCSIM), pp. 394–398 (2021). https://doi.org/10.1109/ICSECS52883.2021.00078

20. Taskasaplidis, G., Fotiadis, D.A., Bamidis, P.D.: Review of stress detection methods using wearable sensors. IEEE Access **12**, 38219–38246 (2024). https://doi.org/10.1109/ACCESS.2024.3373010

21. Teixeira, I.P., et al.: Does cycling infrastructure reduce stress biomarkers in commuting cyclists? A comparison of five European cities. J. Transp. Geogr. **88**, 102830 (2020). https://doi.org/10.1016/j.jtrangeo.2020.102830, https://www.sciencedirect.com/science/article/pii/S0966692319307185

22. Tomba, K., Dumoulin, J., Mugellini, E., Abou Khaled, O., Hawila, S.: Stress detection through speech analysis. In: ICETE (1), pp. 560–564 (2018). https://doi.org/10.5220/0006855803940398

23. Vecchio, A., Nocerino, R., Cola, G.: Gait-based authentication: evaluation of energy consumption on commercial devices. In: 2022 IEEE International Conference on Pervasive Computing and Communications Workshops and other Affiliated Events (PerCom Workshops), pp. 793–798 (2022). https://doi.org/10.1109/PerComWorkshops53856.2022.9767367

24. Wang, A.L., Bista, S., Can, A., Chaix, B.: Personal noise exposure during daily commutes and subjectively reported stress: a trip stage level analysis of mobilisense data. J. Transp. Health **30**, 101612 (2023). https://doi.org/10.1016/j.jth.2023.101612, https://www.sciencedirect.com/science/article/pii/S2214140523000488

Traceability

Interoperable Traceability in Supply Chains: A Use Case in Agritech

Giovanni Farina[8], Gianluca Brunori[1], Stefano Chessa[1],
Alexander Kocian[1(✉)], Maria Bonaria Lai[1], Daniele Nardi[2],
Claudio Schifanella[3], Susanna Bonura[4], Nicola Masi[4],
Fiorenzo Ambrosino[5], Angelo Mariano[5], Lucio Colizzi[7],
Giovanna Maria Dimitri[6], Marco Gori[6], Franco Scarselli[6],
and Silvia Bonomi[2]

[1] University of Pisa, Pisa, Italy
{gianluca.brunori,stefano.chessa,alexander.kocian}@unipi.it,
mariabonaria.lai@agr.unipi.it
[2] Sapienza University of Rome, Rome, Italy
{nardi,bonomi}@diag.uniroma1.it
[3] Computer Science Department, University of Turin, Turin, Italy
claudio.schifanella@unito.it
[4] Engineering Ingegneria Informatica S.p.A, Rome, Italy
{susanna.bonura,nicola.masi}@eng.it
[5] ENEA Italian National Agency for New Technologies, Energy and Sustainable
Economic Development, Rome, Italy
{fiorenzo.ambrosino,angelo.mariano}@enea.it
[6] DIISM, University of Siena, Siena, Italy
{giovanna.dimitri,marco.gori,franco.scarselli}@unisi.it
[7] Dipartimento di Informatica, Università degli Studi di Bari, Bari, Italy
lucio.colizzi@uniba.it
[8] Department of Engineering, Niccolò Cusano University, Rome, Italy
giovanni.farina@unicusano.it

Abstract. In the agri-food sector, traceability is essential to ensure the quality, safety, and transparency of supply chains, where transportation companies are key stakeholders in the overall movement of goods. The multitude of actors involved in supply chains makes it challenging to achieve the above mentioned objectives: each company usually uses its own information system, which is mainly aimed at tracking all relevant information of the single company and is rarely able to interact with other information systems. In addition, when multiple information systems need to exchange data, it is essential to have full control over what data is exchanged and who has access to it.

This study was carried out in part within the Agritech National Research Center and received funding from the European Union Next-Generation EU (PIANO NAZIONALE DI RIPRESA E RESILIENZA (PNRR) - MISSIONE 4 COMPONENTE 2, INVESTIMENTO 1.4 - D.D. 1032 17/06/2022, CN00000022). This manuscript reflects only the authors' views and opinions, neither the European Union nor the European Commission can be considered responsible for them.

In this work, we introduce the concept of *interoperable traceability*. We have developed an innovative model that enables the seamless integration of data from IoT devices, data management software, and distributed ledgers into a newly designed "data space". We provide an implementation of this concept that maps to a practical use case and provides a demonstrator that facilitates the secure transfer of traceability data between existing systems. This gives stakeholders a whole new way to manage and review data with greater transparency and efficiency.

Keywords: International Data Space · Blockchain · Internet of Things · Machine Learning · Intelligent Transport Systems · Agrifood

1 Introduction

Agri-food supply chains are logistic networks with particular constraints, such as the perishability and seasonality of goods, that require highly reliable information, communication, and transportation systems. Along with goods, a variety of information is stored and exchanged, and traceability in this sector is essential to reduce some of the associated potential health risks. *Traceability* is defined in [17] as the ability to access any or all information on a product considered throughout its life cycle by recording identification. Traceability, which promotes the culture of sustainability through the responsibility of all actors, becomes a key open-handed transparency of the Agri-Food System (AFS). Transparency provides a common understanding among stakeholders who can access product information without loss, noise, or distortion [20]. AFS benefits from a transparent supply chain in several ways, including improving market efficiency, enhancing information sharing among all supply chain stakeholders, promoting food quality communication, supporting product differentiation, and improving optimization of logistics activities and business processes [20]. Today, the traceability of agri-food products has become an increasingly interesting topic within the technological field. Digital technologies can play an important role in improving traceability and transparency by ensuring the collection of comprehensive, consistent and reliable data along the food supply chain, together with real-time tracking, easy aggregation, integration, analysis and sharing of data [7]. To establish a traceability system along the food supply chain, it is necessary to be aware of a broader ecosystem of actors and infrastructures and to establish a set of agreements with the actors involved [4]. The concept of "Food traceability 4.0" was recently proposed by Hassoun [10] and refers to the implementation of a smart traceability system from farm to fork using Industry 4.0 technologies, specifically blockchain, Internet of Things (IoT), Artificial Intelligence (AI), and big data analytics [11]. The same technologies are beneficial and should be integrated in intelligent transportation systems, which are fundamental actors in supply chains: there is often a co-presence of a multitude of companies, each usually with its own information system to support the business, and there is a need to make this data available by having the ability to control what data is made available and who can access it [16].

This paper presents a unified federated data lake that integrates data from IoT devices, data management software, and distributed ledgers. Product information is shared in an *interoperable fashion* across different systems and platforms, ensuring consistent and transparent data exchange throughout the supply chain. The proposed model enhances the seamless exchange and verification of traceability data, improving transparency and efficiency across the supply chain. The implementation of this concept is demonstrated through the METRIQA platform, which supports the digitization of agri-food processes by providing a secure and interoperable environment for data exchange. The platform's architecture includes components for data storage, decision support, and user interfaces, leveraging technologies such as blockchain, AI, and big data analytics. Three use cases illustrate the practical applications of interoperable traceability in wine production, automated data sensing, and cattle tracking, highlighting the benefits of improved data integration and fraud prevention. Although the use cases described focus primarily on goods producers and transformers, the solution presented can be extended to any actor in the supply chain, including transport companies.

2   Background and State-of-the Art

Supply chain traceability has become an important area of research due to increasing global complexity, regulatory requirements, and consumer expectations for transparency. It involves tracking the flow of goods, materials, and information across multiple stages of production, transportation, and distribution. With the advent of Industry 4.0, many disruptive technologies have been successfully deployed in traceability systems across different sectors. Many of these approaches have been proposed in the agri-food sector, given the high demand for transparency and safety not only from customers, but also from companies in the supply chain who want to increase the perceived value of their products.

Internet of Things (IoT) plays a key role in capturing real-time data across the supply chain, including environmental conditions, location tracking, and product handling information. By integrating IoT with other technologies, supply chains can achieve end-to-end traceability [15,18]. Blockchain and distributed ledger technology (DLT) enable transparency, security, and certification of supply chain information: they allow all stakeholders in a supply chain to verify and trust data without the need for a central certification authority. The effectiveness of the role of DLT in traceability systems has been demonstrated in several works [2,19]. Artificial intelligence, and more generally machine learning, can detect patterns and inefficiencies, predict problems, and suggest corrective actions [1]. Data analytics enables the analysis of big data generated by modern traceability systems, enabling data-driven decision making.

Blockchain technology has emerged as a revolutionary tool in various sectors, including agri-food chains, by offering unparalleled traceability and transparency. Today, blockchain applications are focused on improving interoperability across different platforms to ensure seamless data exchange and integration. Moreover blockchain immutability ensures that data cannot be altered or deleted, preventing fraudulent activities such as mislabeling, counterfeiting, or product substitution. Its decentralized nature and use of cryptography provide enhanced security against various cyber-attacks. This security protects the interests of all stakeholders, from farmers to retailers. Furthermore, blockchain technology enables the sharing of accurate real-time tracking information throughout the supply chain. Recent advances have seen the development of decentralized platforms that not only facilitate secure data sharing, but also enable the integration of Internet of Things (IoT) devices and smart contracts, further enhancing the traceability and efficiency of supply chains. In addition, efforts are being made to standardize blockchain protocols to enable smoother interoperability between different systems, addressing one of the key challenges to widespread adoption in the agrifood sector.

Data spaces are a rapidly evolving data sharing concept introduced in 2005 by [8]. The concept of data spaces introduces a drastic change to the systematic and centralized perspective of databases, relying instead on decentralized collections of heterogeneous data. According to the recent European Strategy for Data[1], the creation of a single market for data in Europe will ensure Europe's global competitiveness and data sovereignty, and a key point is the creation of Common European Data Spaces. We refer the interested reader to [6] for a comprehensive presentation of data spaces. More specifically, we focus on an emerging specification for data spaces, namely the *International Data Space (IDS)* [13]. This specification responds to requirements of data sovereignty, trustworthiness, and monetization, and it supports the implementation of different business models centered on data exchange, by enabling data sharing through data spaces characterized by uniform rules, certified data providers and recipients and trust among partners guaranteed by certified components and secure interactions. To define a minimum viable data space, the IDS specification defines a limited set of components: two or more IDS connectors with data source and data provider functionality for data exchange; a Certificate Authority (CA) that provides X.509 certificates to ensure the integrity and authenticity of data exchange; and a Dynamic Attributes Provisioning Service (DAPS) for access control and data security. Details on the implementation of IDS can be found here [13].

IoT, sensors, and computer information systems strongly support the traceability processes of individual supply chain actors, i.e. keeping track of all information relevant to their business. In most cases, these traceability systems are not designed to interoperate with external systems; their primary goal is to store and make available the information to a single stakeholder. In particular, proprietary systems and ad hoc data formats are often used. In other words, the main barriers to full supply chain traceability are the variety of ways data

---

[1] https://digital-strategy.ec.europa.eu/en/policies/strategy-data.

is encoded or transmitted, motivating the need for integration technologies to support interoperability, such as distributed ledger technologies and data spaces.

3 METRIQA Digital Information Platform

The METRIQA (MEasurements, TRaceabilIty, and Quality in Agri-food Chains) platform has been developed within the Italian National Research Center for Agricultural Technologies (AGRITECH). The latter is a national implementation of the European Green Deal, to achieve climate neutrality by 2050.

METRIQA supports the digitization of the agrifood sector in Italy in two ways. On the one hand, the platform offers services to research in agri-food by supporting the entire chain of data and information production, storage, and analysis typical of an intelligent environment. Experimental data sets are generated by IoT sensors as well as by researchers during on-site experiments. These data are stored in a distributed fashion and processed by AI tools, to create innovative decision support systems. On the other hand, METRIQA provides a seem-less web-like access to data and services. Additionally, METRIQA offers an open infrastructure for collaboration and innovation in the agrifood sector.

The METRIQA reference architecture, depicted in Fig. 1, is composed of three layers: Storage, Components, and Applications [3,5]. Starting with the Storage layer, METRIQA implements a message broker and a data lake for the (research) data generated by the project partners. At the Components layer, METRIQA introduces a decision support mechanism that facilitates web-based data retrieval services, including a natural language question-answering system. It also incorporates decision support modeling notebooks that utilize scripting languages like Python for data exploration. Additional features include metadata enhancement, Software as a Service (SaaS), Platform as a Service (PaaS), and containerized support for decision support systems crafted by Spoke researchers. At application layer, there are all the User Interfaces (UIs) allowing the end-user to access and interact with the platform. The Application Programming Interfaces (APIs) streamline the data exchange between providers and consumers.

The Blockchain, Security and Data Space components are cross-layer components. Specifically, the blockchain is used in combination with traceability services, and the data space component provides all the elements that support the functioning of the data space according to the International Data Spaces (IDS) specifications [13].

4 Interoperable Traceability and Use Cases

The key objectives - and related performance indicators - of traceability processes are related to the fluidity and accuracy of information flows between the actors that populate the supply chain. The main barriers to these objectives are related to the diversity of the ways in which data are codified or transmitted, as actors follow their own codifying rules and use their technologies. This problem is addressed through the concept of *interoperability*, which can be defined as

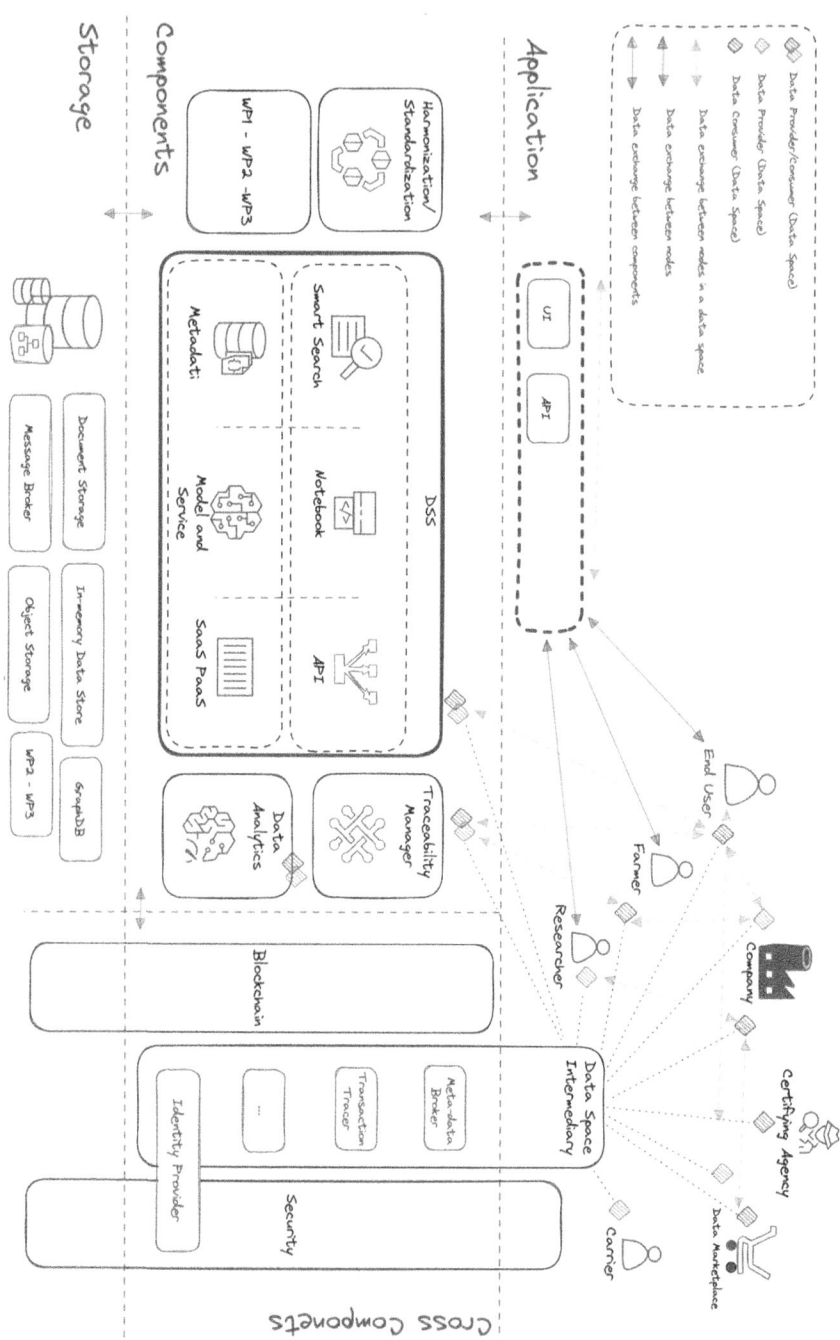

Fig. 1. The reference architecture of METRIQA

the ability of systems to exchange and use information, that encompasses multiple dimensions, including legal organizational, semantic, and technical aspects [12]. Although internally for a company the process to achieve interoperability can be based on the power of the hierarchy, when traceability involves independent actors, interoperability requires the development of governance systems. Strongly coordinated supply chains are more likely to have interoperable traceability systems than loosely coordinated ones, as the chain leader can impose its traceability systems and technologies. For smaller firms, the adoption of the chain leader's traceability system could imply a loss of autonomy, as the shift to another customer could imply a switch to different traceability systems.

The concept of Interoperable Traceability aims at addressing this problem. We aim at building a bundle of technologies, namely data spaces, blockchain, IoT, and AI to respond to the needs of interoperability. In this regard, we propose a model that enables the integration of data from IoT devices, data management software, and distributed ledgers into a data space—specifically, an instance of the International Data Space [13] suitable for the agrifood sector—that allows anyone with the appropriate access rights to use, integrate, enhance, and transfer traceability data into their own traceability systems.

To illustrate how the development process aligns with user needs, improves communication, guides design and testing, and manages project scope, consider three use cases that cover different aspects of interoperable traceability.

Use case 1: *Enabling Interoperability in Wine Supply Chain Traceability Systems* - A wine producer intends to sell wine with data quality to any wine center.

Suppose a wine producer that records various aspects of the wine production process in its information system to ensure quality, authenticity, and traceability. This includes data related to the vineyard, harvest, winery level, packaging, bottling, etc. The sales of its products to different wine distributors, each with its own supply chain management (SCM) system, implies the need to connect to each of these SCM to exchange any relevant information related to traceability along all these supply chains. The lack of interoperability between these systems may become cumbersome for the wine producer, as the technical solutions to implement such a connection imply the development of ad hoc solutions, such as the use of ad hoc middleware for data transformation and APIs for real-time data exchange and/or adaptation to different data formats. The concept of interoperable traceability would instead provide a seamless way to connect these systems, resulting in increased efficiency and reduced costs.

Use case 2: *Automatically sensed data to support supply chain traceability* -
Automated data sensing increases the reliability and visibility of supply chain operations, making it easier to track and verify the quality, origin, and handling of products, increasing consumer confidence and operational efficiency. Artificial intelligence transforms this data into product quality information for the consumer.

Consider a field equipped with a number of IoT nodes to accurately monitor critical soil and crop substrate parameters in real time to optimize water and fertilizer use. The quality of the data collected by these sensors, which measure key variables such as soil moisture, temperature, nitrogen, phosphorus, potassium, and pH, is critical. These real-time measurements are transmitted to a back-end system, where they are stored in a database and certified through a blockchain system for greater transparency and data integrity. The accuracy and security of this data is critical, as decisions throughout the supply chain depend on it. Consider for example the case of fertigation: when its cycles are managed using high-quality real-time soil and crop data, water and nutrients are applied in optimal amounts at the right time, avoiding inefficiencies and potential over fertigation. The latter, especially with nitrogen-based fertilizers, can lead to the accumulation of nitrates in the soil. These nitrates are absorbed by the plants and can eventually be transferred to the final product, compromising its quality. High nitrate levels in crops are undesirable as they pose a risk to both product safety and consumer health. Therefore, accurate data ensures that irrigation and fertigation cycles are not only efficient, but also safe, keeping nutrient levels balanced and within acceptable limits. As a result, manufacturers who use high-quality data can deliver healthier products with less environmental impact, adding value to their products and building trust with consumers and retailers. Machine learning transforms raw sensor data into traceability information by analyzing and interpreting patterns within the data to gain key insights such as the product's origin, handling conditions, and journey. This traceability information is then presented in a consumer-friendly format, enabling transparency and trust in the quality and authenticity of the product.

Use case 3: *Interoperable cattle traceability for parts of the food supply chain with fraud prevention* - From Use Case 1 and Use Case 2, the question arises of how to properly combine interoperable traceability with fraud prevention mechanisms.

Consider, as an example, a typical cow grazing in an alpine pasture, equipped with a smart collar that collects position data stored in the farmer's information system, with the purpose of providing traceability data about the animal's pasture location once it enters a given supply chain. Note that in this process, the GPS data can be exchanged in an interoperable manner by connecting to the appropriate data space of the specific supply chain, and that the GPS data can go through a data analysis process to produce information in a consumer-friendly format, as already explained in the previous use cases. Finally, the user accesses information about the origin of the product (say, a steak) through a QR code on the consumer product. However, in this context, the livestock farmer may fraudulently claim ownership of other people's cattle and sell them as his own; or falsely claim compliance with feeding standards (e.g., hay instead of high alpine grass). Thus, in addition to the issues already discussed in use cases 1 and 2, there is also the issue of fraud prevention. To deal with this case, we need to ensure that the GPS data generated by the collar and stored in the farmer's information system is not altered, and this can be achieved by combining the use of a tamper-proof collar with an integrity code of the GPS data that the collar should be able to store in the blockchain through a channel outside the farmer's control. This latter channel can be achieved, for example, when the cow passes through the hands of the next actor in the supply chain, who can read the integrity code of the collar and store it in an appropriate smart contract in the blockchain, along with the certification of this exchange of the cow.

5 Design and Development of a Live Demo for Interoperable Traceability

5.1 Overview

In this section, we present the demonstrator based on Use Case 3 of Sect. 4 that we are currently developing to illustrate the concept of interoperable traceability. We resemble parts of the food supply chain. Specifically, we focus on the transition from production to processing (and slaughter) of a typical cow in Italy. The functional blocks of the demonstrator are outlined in Fig. 2 and detailed in the following.

We start with the data producer, the cattle farmer. The key components are a *IoT collar* equipped with a GPS sensor connected to an IoT client. Raw location data and its hashes, as well as the ID of the owner and the particular cow, are stored in a local database, the *Farm System*. Suppose that the cattle farmer intends to sell one of his cows to slaughter in the (interoperable) food supply chain. The slaughter opens a dedicated application on the cellular phone and reads out the QR code on the collar. Three types of data flow will occur: *i)* the time series of (hashed) GPS data is sent to the federated dataspace component (described in Subsect. 5.4); *ii)* the daily hashed GPS data is sent to the *Blockchain* smart contract (described in Subsect. 5.3); *iii)* In Italy, the change of ownership of cattle must be reported to the national database (Banca Dati Nazionale - BDN), but this transaction is outside the scope of this demo.

The federated data space component of the METRIQA platform enables secure data exchange between connectors within the AGRITECH Data Space. The process involves deploying core components, ensuring communication between participants, and validating data transfer scenarios. The connector to the data space facilitates data exchange while ensuring data sovereignty.

The data consumer, that is, the *Big Data Analytics* (BDA) component cleans, organizes, and explores historical data before applying machine learning algorithms. The *Machine learning* block tracks the movements of the cow and sets a flag in case the cow was not grazing where it was supposed to be. Similarly, the *Consistency check* performs blockchain-based continuous data integrity checking and sets a flag in case of error. Finally the *Traceability system* block collects all relevant information from the *Machine learning* block as well as the *Consistency check* block via *API Gateway*, in order to be capable of replying to the consumer upon product request via another QR code.

All components of the system operate in real time, except for the cow's movements in space and time. To facilitate reproducibility, the latter has been realized as a theoretical mathematical model.

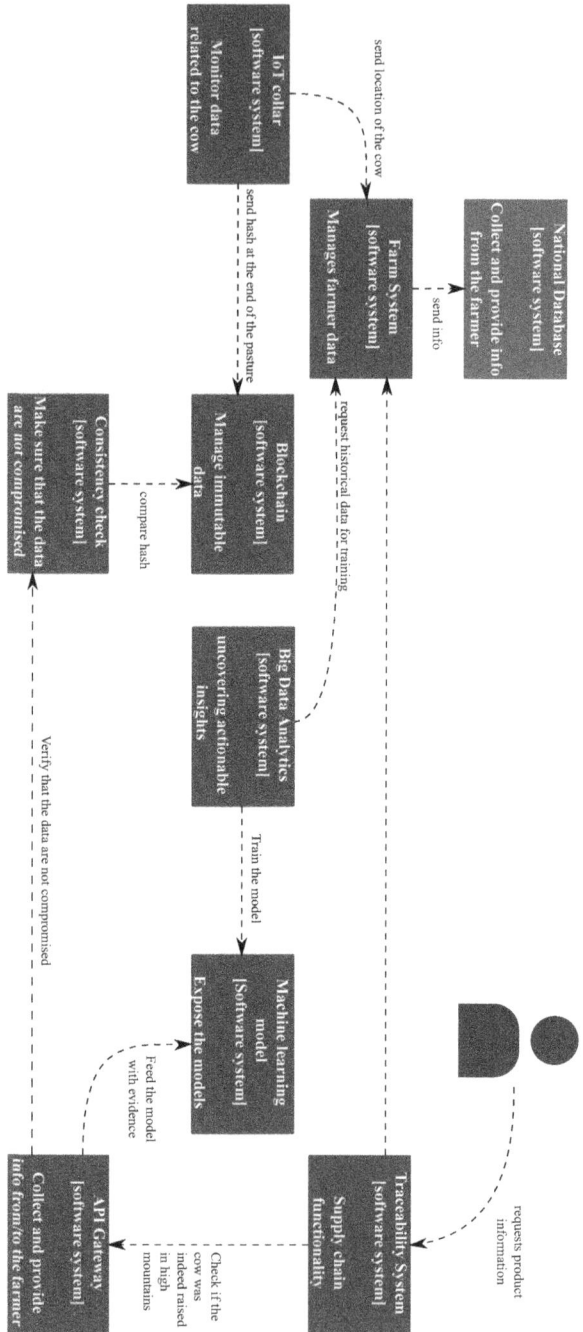

Fig. 2. System architecture of our live demonstrator, comprising IoT client, private Ethereum Virtual Machine, a connector to the International Data Space and tools for data analytics and Machine learning

5.2   The METRIQA IoT Support for the Live Demo

To get accurate location data, we could simply equip the cow with a smart collar with GPS connectivity. The GPS data is collected periodically, say every 15 min, and recursively hashed (SHA-256). The result is sent to the dataspace API (see Sect. 5.4). At the end of the day, the GPS history of the cow, along with the identifying information of the cow as well as the farmer, i.e. the production data, is embedded in another hash (SHA-256), the transaction is signed with the private key and recursive length prefix (RLP) encoded in binary format. The result is sent to the cloud node where the smart contract resides (see Sect. 5.3).

To make the sensed data reproducible, we decided to emulate the IoT client, i.e., we rely on Markov chain models to simulate the evolution of GPS positions (such as shelter, exploration, foraging) according to [9,14].

5.3   The METRQIA Blockchain for the Live Demo

The METRIQA platform integrates a cross-layer blockchain, which provides a programmable decentralized ledger, and a data space component, which regulates the exchange of information between data producers and consumers. Given the nature of the two METRIQA components, by default, the blockchain component should only store data that can be permanently available to all blockchain participants, while the Data Space component should regulate the exchange of all other data.

The blockchain implementation considered for the use case example is *permissioned*, meaning that its access is limited to authorized participants (i.e., accounts) with defined roles, each of which is associated with an identified *entity* (a user, a device, etc.). This is necessary to ensure the authenticity and non-repudiation of the stored data. Each entity is provided with a credential that allows only its owner to perform operations on behalf of the entity. The accounts allow for *pseudo-anonymity* of the entities that interact with the blockchain. This means that the entity associated with each account is not stored in the blockchain by default, but all its interactions with the DLT are auditable. The association between accounts and entities can be made available or not, but it is required for the considered use case. The DLT implementation consists of 3 Hyperledger Besu nodes; this blockchain is compliant with the Ethereum Virtual Machine and uses the Clique consensus mechanism, that is based on proof of authority.

The objectives of the considered use case are pursued through the definition of a *smart contract*, namely a software defined on top of the blockchain network that regulates the ledger updates. More specifically, the smart contract stores data, the *state*, and it exposes a set of interfaces that allow its update, the *functions*. In addition, a smart contract makes it possible to define which accounts can interact with it and how. For the use case under consideration, the smart contract, that is referred to as *Demo-Contract*, keeps track of *1)* a hash (fixed-size string of bytes that is unique to the specific input data) associated with the historical data of each cow's pasture, and *2)* the changes of ownership of a cow. More specifically, the smart contract stores only the hash associated with the cow's pasture data for several reasons: it is not necessary to guarantee the availability of this data, and the amount of data to be stored on a distributed ledger should be minimized; the owner of the cow's pasture data has control over which entity is allowed to access this data. On the other hand, ownership changes are data that must be available to data consumers, motivating its storage in the distributed ledger. Note again that the distributed ledger provides pseudo-anonymity by default; it follows that the association between account and entity (owner) must be made available in order to properly reconstruct all ownership transfers.

The DEMO-contract assigns a *role* to each account that interacts with it. Four roles are defined in order to assign different privileges to different users: *NoPriviledge*, *Administrator*, *Actor*, and *Device*. NoPriviledge is the default role assigned to each account interacting with the DEMO-contract. The Administrator role is assigned to the Contract Deployer (i.e., the account that distributes the smart contract to the DL) and can be extended to other accounts by the initial Administrator. The Administrators in this example have the ability to assign roles to all accounts. The Actor role is the one associated with any account that is controlled by a human. In the DEMO contract, these accounts have the ability to control the devices associated with them and to transfer ownership of the cow they own. The Device role is associated with all IoT devices that interact with the smart contract and are the only ones allowed to register data about the cow's pasture. The DEMO contract state keeps track of 1) the role associated with each account; 2) the ownerships associated with each registered cow; 3) the association between devices, cows, and current owner. Each function can be associated with preconditions, i.e. requirements that must be met in order to execute the functionality. This makes it possible to define access control, i.e. which accounts are allowed to perform certain operations and which state condition must be met in order to update the ledger. More specifically, to name a few examples, the role assignment functionality can only be performed by the administrator account; cow registration and device association can only be executed by the actor account; cow pasture data registration can only be operated by the associated device.

The transfer of ownership functionality requires both the sender and the recipient to acknowledge the transfer, i.e., the transfer is not complete until the recipient confirms the transfer of ownership. Cow pasture integrity data are not stored directly in the states of the contract, but are tracked as events. An *event*, in the context of smart contracts, is a mechanism that allows the contract to communicate that something specific has happened on the blockchain and its occurrence is stored in the DL (outside of the contract state). As a result, all accounts that interact with a smart contract are able to retrieve all events that have been emitted since the contract distribution. This is an alternative mechanism for storing data associated with a Smart Contract and allowing historical data to be offloaded from the contract itself. The DEMO-contract is only responsible for regulating which accounts are allowed to store the cow's pasture-related data and for properly storing a hash associated with a timestamp and a cow.

The software component interacting with the smart contract is responsible for properly generating the data to be stored in the DL.

All requests to update the ledger are made through *transactions*, whose acceptance and execution are governed in a distributed manner by a consensus algorithm. In blockchain terms, a transaction is a signed packet of data that changes the state of the blockchain. It is the primary way to initiate actions on the DL network, especially to interact with a smart contract. To simplify the interaction with the DL and the DEMO-contract, a *Node.js* software component has been developed, which is referred to as *Interaction-Component*. The Interaction-Component provides three main services: it allows to trigger all the functions available on the DEMO-Contract; it simulates the functionality of a smart collar that tracks a cow's pasture data and ensures its integrity (Sect. 5.2); it exposes a remote interface to verify the integrity of the cow's pasture data. The Interaction-Component allows the integrity of the cow's pasture data associated with a specific cow to be remotely verified through a REST API.

5.4   The METRIQA Data Space for the Live Demo

The implementation of data space in METRIQA aligns with the IDS specification, and incorporates all its core components. These data space components have been deployed and tested to validate the communication between participants, implementing the scenario of a farmer as a Data Provider that shares GPS data collected by a IoT device (collar in a cow) and a Data Analytics system (as a Data Consumer) to collect data and train an ML model (as in Use Case 3 presented in Sect. 4).

The components are deployed within a Kubernetes[2] cluster, to achieve application scalability and resilience by automating container orchestration, and by ensuring the optimal utilization of resources and high availability of the METRIQA IDS. The adoption of Kubernetes is also motivated in our case to the need of simplifying our deployment and management processes, and of facilitating the continuous integration and delivery and accelerating development cycles. Within the cluster, Minio[3] is deployed as an object storage solution, enabling connectors to access stored data. In our specific demonstrator, we have deployed two connectors: a provider and a consumer. The provider accesses data from Minio once the Data Owner registers it as an Offered Resource on the connector.

The connector is implemented by the TRUE (TRUsted Engineering) Connector[4], which is an open-source connector developed by ENGINEERING and is also part of the FIWARE catalog. Furthermore, this connector adheres to the latest IDS specifications (e.g., IDS Info Model 4) and can be easily customized to fit a wide range of scenarios due to the internal separation between the Execution Core Container and Data App. It integrates with many existing IDS services

---

[2] https://kubernetes.io/.

[3] https://min.io/.

[4] https://github.com/Engineering-Research-and-Development/true-connector.

(Identity Provider, Clearing House, Metadata Broker, etc.) and is fully configurable in terms of data formats and protocols (HTTP, HTTPS, Web Socket over HTTPS, IDSCPv2). It includes a Data Usage Control App to enforce usage policies and a basic Data App that can be customized to meet specific processing and integration needs.

5.5 Data Analytics of METRIQA in the Live Demo

The Big Data Analytics Platform[5] is a Data Science (DS) and Machine Learning (ML) solution built on advanced frameworks and open-source technologies for designing, deploying, running, and monitoring Big Data Analytics (BDA) workflows in both streaming and batch modes. Its cloud-native architecture allows for scalable computing and storage by leveraging Kubernetes' capabilities for resource management. The platform offers an extensible catalog of BDA services that covers every phase from data ingestion to data preparation, machine learning analysis, and data publishing. The platform supports data processing from various sources, integrates third-party BDA services, and provides a web-based interface to write BDA applications. Users can design workflows for both batch and streaming data scenarios by combining assets such as datasets and models with BDA services. The Big Data Analytics Platforms supports the assembling, deployment and execution of BDA applications through a graphical user interface. Each BDA application is made of one or multiple BDA services. Each BDA service is a containerized OCI-compliant microservice application. Our proposal, named on the Alida platform, is based upon severl open-source technologies:

- **Kubernetes:** as resource orchestrator;
- **Argo Workflows**[6]**:** an open source container-native workflow engine for orchestrating parallel jobs on Kubernetes;
- **Apache Kafka**[7]**:** an open-source distributed event streaming platform;
- **React Flow**[8]**:** a component on which the graphic designer is based in order to design pipelines of BDA services.

6   Discussions and Conclusions

The implementation of interoperable traceability in the agri-food supply chain, as demonstrated by the METRIQA platform, highlights several key advances and challenges in the field.

The integration of IoT, blockchain, and data spaces into a unified system represents a significant technological advancement. This integration ensures real-time data collection, secure data storage, and seamless data exchange, which are

---

[5] https://home.alidalab.it/.
[6] https://argo-workflows.readthedocs.io/en/latest/.
[7] https://kafka.apache.org/.
[8] https://reactflow.dev/.

critical to maintaining the integrity and transparency of the supply chain. In particular, the use of blockchain technology provides an immutable and transparent ledger that increases trust among stakeholders. The ability to track and verify data without a central authority reduces the risk of fraud and increases the reliability of information.

Achieving interoperability between disparate systems and platforms remains a significant challenge. The diversity of data formats, communication protocols, and technology standards requires robust solutions to ensure seamless data exchange. The development of governance systems to manage interoperability is critical. Strongly coordinated supply chains are more likely to achieve interoperability, but smaller companies may face challenges in adopting these systems without losing their autonomy.

The demonstrator effectively showcases the practical applications of interoperable traceability in several scenarios, including wine production, automated data collection, and cattle tracking. These use cases highlight the benefits of improved data integration, such as increased operational efficiency, improved product quality, and increased consumer confidence. Using machine learning to analyze sensor data and provide actionable insights further enhances the value of the traceability system. By transforming raw data into meaningful information, stakeholders can make informed decisions that improve the overall efficiency and sustainability of the supply chain. The combination of tamper-proof IoT devices and blockchain technology provides a robust solution for fraud prevention. By ensuring the integrity of the data collected and stored, the system can effectively prevent fraudulent activities such as mislabeling and counterfeiting. The ability to verify the authenticity of products using QR codes increases consumer confidence and trust in the supply chain.

The study shows that interoperable traceability is a viable and effective solution to improve transparency, efficiency, and trust in agrifood supply chains. The METRIQA platform, with its integration of IoT, blockchain, and data spaces, provides a comprehensive framework for achieving these goals. Key conclusions of the study include:

- **Enhanced Transparency and Efficiency:** Seamless integration of data from multiple sources ensures that all stakeholders have access to accurate and reliable information, improving the overall efficiency of the supply chain;
- **Improved Consumer Trust:** Providing detailed product information through QR codes and ensuring data integrity through blockchain technology improves consumer trust in the quality and authenticity of products;
- **Scalability and Flexibility:** The use of open source technologies and scalable architectures ensures that the system can be adapted to different scenarios and expanded as needed.

Further research is needed to address interoperability challenges and to develop more robust governance systems. In addition, exploring the integration of other emerging technologies, such as artificial intelligence and big data analytics, could further enhance the capabilities of the traceability system. The model, platform, and solutions extend to all transportation systems, fundamental stakeholders in all supply chains.

References

1. Artificial intelligence in supply chain management: a systematic literature review. J. Bus. Res. **122**, 502–517 (2021). https://doi.org/10.1016/j.jbusres.2020.09.009
2. Agarwal, U., et al.: Blockchain technology for secure supply chain management: a comprehensive review. IEEE Access **10**, 85493–85517 (2022). https://doi.org/10.1109/ACCESS.2022.3194319
3. Bacco, M., et al.: Agricultural data space: the METRIQA platform and a case study in the CODECS project. In: Federated Conference on Computer Science and Information Systems (FedCSIS) (2024)
4. Brunori, G.: Agriculture and rural areas facing the "twin transition": principles for a sustainable rural digitalisation. Ital. Rev. Agric. Econ. **77**(3), 3–14 (2022). https://doi.org/10.36253/rea-13983
5. Chessa, S., Dimitri, G.M., Gori, M., Kocian, A.: WoA: an infrastructural, web-based approach to digital agriculture. In: Novais, P., et al. (eds.) ISAmI 2023. LNNS, vol. 770, pp. 113–122. Springer, Cham (2023). https://doi.org/10.1007/978-3-031-43461-7_12
6. Curry, E., Scerri, S., Tuikka, T.: Data Spaces: Design, Deployment and Future Directions (2022). https://doi.org/10.1007/9783030986360
7. FAO: Feasibility study for application of digital technologies for improved traceability and transparency along the agrifood value chains- Case studies in the Near East and North Africa Region. FAO (2023)
8. Franklin, M., Halevy, A., Maier, D.: From databases to dataspaces: a new abstraction for information management. ACM SIGMOD Rec. **34**(4), 27–33 (2005). https://doi.org/10.1145/1107499.1107502
9. Getz, W.M., Luisa Vissat, L., Salter, R.: Simulation and analysis of animal movement paths using numerus model builder (2020). https://doi.org/10.22360/SpringSim.2020.TMS.001
10. Hassoun, A., et al.: Food traceability 4.0 as part of the fourth industrial revolution: key enabling technologies. Crit. Rev. Food Sci. Nutr. **64**(3), 873–889 (2024). https://doi.org/10.1080/10408398.2022.2110033
11. Hassoun, A., et al.: Implementation of relevant fourth industrial revolution innovations across the supply chain of fruits and vegetables: a short update on traceability 4.0. Food Chem. **409**, 135303 (2023). https://doi.org/10.1016/j.foodchem.2022.135303
12. Hodapp, D., Hanelt, A.: Interoperability in the era of digital innovation: an information systems research agenda. J. Inf. Technol. **37**(4), 407–427 (2022). https://doi.org/10.1177/02683962211064304
13. International Data Space Association: Reference architecture model v.3.0 (2019). https://internationaldataspaces.org/wp-content/uploads/IDS-Reference-Architecture-Model-3.0-2019.pdf. Accessed 11 Sept 2024
14. Marshall, B.M., Duthie, A.B.: abmAnimalMovement: an R package for simulating animal movement using an agent-based model. F1000Research (2022). https://doi.org/10.12688/f1000research.124810.1

15. Misra, N.N., Dixit, Y., Al-Mallahi, A., Bhullar, M.S., Upadhyay, R., Martynenko, A.: IoT, big data, and artificial intelligence in agriculture and food industry. IEEE Internet Things J. **9**(9), 6305–6324 (2022). https://doi.org/10.1109/JIOT.2020. 2998584
16. Oladimeji, D., Gupta, K., Kose, N.A., Gundogan, K., Ge, L., Liang, F.: Smart transportation: an overview of technologies and applications. Sensors **23**(8), 3880 (2023). https://doi.org/10.3390/S23083880
17. Olsen, P., Borit, M.: How to define traceability. Trends Food Sci. Technol. **29**(2), 142–150 (2013). https://doi.org/10.1016/j.tifs.2012.10.003
18. Shoomal, A., Jahanbakht, M., Componation, P.J., Ozay, D.: Enhancing supply chain resilience and efficiency through internet of things integration: challenges and opportunities. Internet Things **27**, 101324 (2024). https://doi.org/10.1016/j. iot.2024.101324
19. Singh, A., Gutub, A., Nayyar, A., Khan, M.K.: Redefining food safety traceability system through blockchain: findings, challenges and open issues. Multimed. Tools Appl. **82**(14), 21243–21277 (2023). https://doi.org/10.1007/s11042-022-14006-4
20. Trienekens, J., Wognum, P., Beulens, A., Van Der Vorst, J.: Transparency in complex dynamic food supply chains. Adv. Eng. Inform. **26**(1), 55–65 (2012). https:// doi.org/10.1016/j.aei.2011.07.007

Treemob: Expressive Mobility Data Representation Through Tree-Based Structures

Marta Fioravanti[1], Eleonora Cappuccio[1,2,3]([⊠]), Salvatore Rinzivillo[2], and Riccardo Guidotti[1,2]

[1] University of Pisa, Pisa, Italy
m.fioravanti6@studenti.unipi.it, eleonora.cappuccio@phd.unipi.it,
riccardo.guidotti@unipi.it
[2] ISTI-CNR, Pisa, Italy
{eleonora.cappuccio,salvatore.rinzivillo,riccardo.guidotti}@isti.cnr.it
[3] Università degli studi di Bari Aldo Moro, Bari, Italy

Abstract. This paper explores expressive representations of personal mobility data, focusing on both informational and user-centered design aspects. The goal is to enable users to access, understand, and gain awareness of their mobility behaviours, assuming that expressiveness is not inherently linked to system complexity. We propose a novel methodology for representing and analyzing mobility data using tree-shaped structures. Additionally, we introduce Treemob, a suite of Python-based tools designed to facilitate mobility analysis. The experiments conducted provide a foundation for further research, offering a flexible framework for exploiting different issues and contexts.

Keywords: Mobility Data Analysis · Individual Mobility Network · Spatio-temporal data visualization

1 Introduction

Nowadays, vast amounts of personal data are generated, including spatio-temporal information about individual mobility. These data offer valuable insights, but their raw form requires organization for effective analysis, especially in the context of Personal Data Analytics [13]. Technologies such as GPS and GSM data enable the study of mobility patterns, contributing to urban planning, traffic analysis and sustainable transportation solutions. For example, Andrienko et al. [2] used visual analytics to identify significant geographic locations from trajectory data, while Larcom et al. [12] observed behavioural changes in response to unexpected travel disruptions. These studies demonstrate the potential of mobility data to uncover behavioural patterns at both the individual and collective levels. Recent work has shifted from global mobility analysis to individual models, which reveal detailed, systematic behaviours.

© ICST Institute for Computer Sciences, Social Informatics and Telecommunications Engineering 2025
Published by Springer Nature Switzerland AG 2025. All Rights Reserved
A. Kocian et al. (Eds.): INTSYS 2024, LNICST 608, pp. 46–63, 2025.
https://doi.org/10.1007/978-3-031-86370-7_4

Studies like Pappalardo et al. [14] identified distinct traveller types-explorers and returners-while Trasarti et al. [17] explored practical applications such as carpooling through personalized mobility analysis. Finally, Landi et al. [10,11] designed novel features extraction methodologies to capture interpretable and highly discriminative mobility patterns to boost trajectory classification models. Individual models not only enhance user-centered data applications but also raise ethical concerns about privacy, necessitating frameworks that allow users to control the sharing of their data. However, individual models requires a suitable level of abstraction to let the user understand their data without overwhelming them with excessive cognitive load.

This research introduces a novel method for summarizing and visualize personal mobility data using hierarchical structures, to bridge the complexity of network-based methods [5,8,20]. We complement this analysis with a visual analytics tool and a Python module that facilitates tree-based mobility data analysis. The objective is to apply unsupervised learning to identify mobility patterns across different cities.

2   Related Work

Mobility data analysis can be performed from collective or personal perspectives. In the collective model, the trajectories of multiple users are aggregated to analyze global patterns, such as traffic flows or congested urban areas. Collective mobility data has been instrumental in fields like urban planning, where understanding the movement of large populations over time helps inform decisions about infrastructure improvements [18]. However, as noted by Trasarti et al. [17], global patterns often fail to capture the diversity of individual behaviours, leading to oversimplifications in complex systems like human mobility.

To address this limitation, personal mobility models have been proposed. One example is the mobility profile extraction pipeline introduced by [17], which identifies user habits by clustering trajectories that are temporally and spatially similar. This method aggregates frequent trips into a set of prototypes, effectively creating a mobility profile that reflects the habitual movement patterns of the user. Another significant approach is the Individual Mobility Network (IMN) [7], which organizes user behaviour into a directed graph structure. In the IMN, vertices represent regular and irregular locations, and edges denote the movements between them. This structure provides a nuanced view of personal travel patterns, distinguishing habitual movements from outlier trips. Combined models, which blend global and personal perspectives, have also emerged to exploit the strengths of both approaches by creating hybrid models.

Visual analytics tools play a crucial role in the exploration and interpretation of mobility data. Andrienko et al. [3] proposed a comprehensive visual analytics methodology to analyze both individual and collective movement behaviors. In this approach, movement data is not only visualized geographically but also in a space-time cube, where the third dimension represents the temporal component. This multi-dimensional representation allows users to observe trajectories over time, identifying patterns that might not be visible in a purely spatial view. Moreover, the authors introduce a transformation that maps movements into an abstract space, where directions and clustering of similar trajectories can be analyzed, providing deeper insights into group and individual behaviors. However, one drawback of this tool is its complexity, which can make it challenging to apply outside of research contexts or for communicating results to non-expert audiences.

In another work, Andrienko et al. [1] addressed privacy concerns in mobility data visualization by proposing an abstract representation that hides sensitive user information. The authors developed a pair of two-dimensional histograms that display probabilities for a user's presence at different locations over time, without revealing precise spatial details. The visual simplicity of this method makes it an effective qualitative tool for summarizing mobility patterns while preserving user privacy. However, the reliance on square area sizes to represent probabilities can make it difficult to compare values accurately, especially for less technical users.

A different approach to visualizing mobility data was introduced by Douieb[1], who focused on representing football passes within a play area. This flow visualization emphasizes spatial patterns by displaying movement paths without focusing on individual players. While this tool is designed for a specialized application, it illustrates the potential for visualizing high-density movement data in other contexts, such as public transportation networks or pedestrian flows in urban environments.

3   Preliminaries and Background

This section reviews the key approaches and methodologies used to represent, analyze, and visualize mobility data, focusing on both personal and collective perspectives, as well as the various techniques employed to simplify and interpret complex trajectory datasets.

3.1   Mobility Data Representation and Analysis

The fundamental element in any mobility dataset is the trajectory, defined as an ordered sequence of points traversed by a user over time. Formally, a trajectory t_s can be defined as a series of spatiotemporal points $t_s = \langle p_1, ..., p_n \rangle$, each of them in the form of a triple $p_i = (lon_i, lat_i, t_i)$ where lon_i and lat_i are respectively the longitude and the latitude of the location traversed, while t_i is the timestamp of the event. A trajectory is chronologically ordered, so $\forall 1 \leq i \leq n : ts_i < ts_{i+1}$; so, the ith point of the trajectory ts is identified as $ts[i]$, while its spatiotemporal coordinates are $ts[i].lon, ts[i].lat$, and $ts[i].t$. Therefore, a mobility dataset can be seen as a set of trajectories $T = \langle t_i, ..., t_m \rangle$.

---

[1] https://observablehq.com/@karimdouieb/all-the-passes.

3.2   Tree and Graph-Based Representation

Graphs and trees are fundamental structures for representing and analyzing mobility data, since they are capable of capturing the relationships of different dimensions of human mobility. For example, the origin-destination matrix of a user can be represented with a **mobility graph**, i.e. a directed graph $G = (V, E)$ where V is the set of nodes representing locations, and E is the set of edges denoting movement paths between those locations. Each edge $e = (v_a, v_b)$ corresponds to a trajectory from location v_a to v_b. The edges may be enriched with additional information, such as weights, to reflect the frequency or importance of these paths.

Another common structure in mobility data analysis is the **prefix tree** typically used to compress large sets of sequences. A prefix tree is a variation of a hash tree and can be defined as $PT = (V, E, root)$ where V represents nodes (locations), E represents edges (paths), and the $root$ is a virtual node not associated with any location. The defining feature of a prefix tree is its ability to group all sequences sharing a common prefix into a single branch. This allows for efficient storage and retrieval of sequences, making it ideal for summarizing user trajectories. In [19], Zhao et al. combined prefix trees with differential privacy techniques to create trajectory representations that maintain the structural integrity of mobility data while ensuring user privacy by adding noise to sensitive information.

Spanning graphs aim to simplify the representation of trajectories by preserving essential paths while reducing complexity. A spanning tree is a subgraph of a weighted graph that retains the shortest paths between nodes with minimal error. In the context of mobility data, spanning trees can be used to focus on frequent connections between locations rather than rare or outlier movements. When applied to personal mobility, maximum spanning trees are particularly useful, as they emphasize the most commonly traversed paths, which are often more relevant for understanding user habits.

4   Problem Formulation

In this section, we formulate the problem of transforming a user's mobility data, represented as a set of trajectories $M_u = \{t_1, \ldots, t_n\}$, into two distinct data structures: a tree $T = \{N, E\}$ and a vector $V(T)$. These transformations allow us to encode both trajectory information and structural characteristics of the mobility data in a compact form. Below, we detail the two approaches: tree-based and vector-based representations.

4.1   Tree-Based Representation

The first step in our formulation is to convert a set of user trajectories into a tree structure $T = \{N, E\}$ where $N = \{n_1, ..., n_p\}$ is a set of nodes corresponding to locations visited by the user, and $E = \{e_1, ..., e_m\}$ is a set of directed edges between these nodes.

Prefix Tree. The prefix tree is an intuitive representation of trajectories, treating each trajectory as a sequence of spatial points. Each point, simplified to contain only spatial data, is represented as a node, and the edges reflect transitions between these points in chronological order. Of course, this approach is a trade-off between completeness of information and accessibility. This level of simplification of real mobility masks certain details to provide an overview and let the analyst focus on specific details. In fact, a prefix tree is a flexible structure that can be dynamically explored to highlight different perspectives.

Specifically, we assign each location $g_i = (lon_i, lat_i)$ a unique identifier $j \in J$, where each $j \in J$ is a unique identifier of a spatial grid, for example a regular grid, a voronoi tessellation or a geohash code. Thus, a trajectory point previously defined as $p_i = (lon_i, lat_i, t_i)$ is now simplified as $p_i = j_i$. The resulting tree will be composed by the nodes $N = <n_1, ..., n_n>$, the labels $L = <l_1, ..., l_n>$, assigned to each node and the edges $E = <e_1, ..., e_m>$. The nodes are artificial structures associated with a unique identifier, and contain the information of the represented location; the same label value can be present in different nodes in various positions in the tree. This approach yields a compact yet powerful representation of the user's movements.

Spanning Tree. The prefix tree requires a set of sequences to be scanned during the growing of the tree. For mobility data a natural choice may be the temporal order of the spatio-temporal observations of each trajectory. However, this naive approach may lead to configurations where the first encountered positions may determine the general shape of the whole tree. For example, if the logging of positions starts from a low relevant point, this choice may raise the corresponding position very in high in the tree. Since we have the mobility graph data structure, we propose the use of a spannign tree algorithm to derive the prefix tree given a mobility graph. In particular we adopted the Kruskal algorithm [9], to find a spanning forest over a mobility graph.

Since we are interested in the most frequent paths, we use as a weighting function the inverse of their frequency to keep the algorithm a minimum spanning tree. The resulting representation synthesises the user's mobility, focusing on the connections between each location. This structures preserves the uniqueness of each location/node, since no repetions are possibile. This creates a more condensed data structure and it also keep into account the relation of each location/node with the mobility graph.

4.2   Vector-Based Representation

The second transformation focuses on representing the mobility data as a vector. The vector representation allows us to encode the structure and patterns of mobility in a form suitable for numerical analysis.

Tree-to-Vector Transformation. To convert the tree structure T into a vector $V(T)$, we employ techniques inspired by information retrieval, specifically the TF-IDF (Term Frequency-Inverse Document Frequency) approach. In this analogy, locations in the mobility data correspond to "terms" and users to "documents". The frequency of visits to locations is treated as the term frequency (TF), and the inverse document frequency (IDF) measures how uniquely a location characterizes the user compared to others. The resulting vector $V(T)$ highlights distinctive locations and paths that differentiate a user's mobility from that of others. This vector representation maintains the focus on the shape of the user's mobility, abstracting away from geographical coordinates while still preserving critical information about movement patterns.

Feature Extraction for Mobility Analysis. Additionally, we propose an alternative method of vector representation by extracting features from the tree structures themselves. By summarizing the properties of the mobility trees-such as the number of branches, depth, or the frequency of node occurrences-we generate feature vectors that can be used in unsupervised learning or other analytical tasks. These vectors enable us to quantify and compare different users' mobility patterns without accessing the raw trajectory data.

In summary, both the tree and vector representations provide powerful tools for analyzing personal mobility data. The tree captures structural and sequential information, while the vector form enables further analysis through numerical methods. Together, these approaches offer a comprehensive solution for representing and studying mobility patterns.

5   Methodology

This section outlines theoretical and technical methods for transforming trees and vectors into semantically meaningful representations, focusing on the role of the root in trees and the relationships encoded in both trees and vectors.

5.1   Tree-Based Methods

A trajectory notation was introduced that adds artificial points ('^' and '$', representing respectively the start and the end of a trajectory) to preserve trajectory direction when organized in prefix trees. For prefix trees, three rotation strategies centred around a root location (the most frequent in the dataset) were evaluated. The chosen structure separates trajectories that touch the root from those that do not, facilitating a clear analysis of movement around the root. For spanning trees, undirected graphs were transformed into rooted trees to focus on spatial relationships around locations rather than movement sequences.

5.2   Vector-Based Methods

Two vectorization approaches were developed to represent mobility data. The first, a TF-IDF-inspired method, weighs locations based on their frequency and proximity to the root, adding semantic meaning to the analysis of mobility. The second, a feature-driven method, extracts nine features from mobility trees (e.g., depth, unique location ratios) to create vectors that allow for clustering and comparison. This vector-based approach provides a more abstract and feature-driven perspective on user mobility, complementing the tree-based analysis.

5.3   Distance Functions

Distance functions were applied to compare trees and vectors derived from mobility datasets, enabling the identification of clusters of similar users. Unlike vectors, tree-shaped structures require specialized distance functions. The edit distance is a dynamic programming method that calculates the minimum number of operations (insertion, deletion, relabeling of nodes) required to transform one tree into another. A variation of this method, which compares branches as unordered sets rather than sequences, offers polynomial-time computation and improves on the standard version's exponential complexity. To further enhance the analysis, an ordering mechanism was introduced where heavier branches, based on frequency, are positioned on the left. This allows for easier comparison of tree structures. Additionally, location labels were removed from the nodes, focusing comparisons on user movement patterns rather than specific locations visited. For vectors, traditional distance measures like Euclidean, Manhattan, and Minkowski were employed, given their suitability for vector-based representations.

5.4   Visual Representation of Mobility Tree

Data visualization is essential for both exploring data and effectively communicating research findings. To achieve this, a visual system was designed using the D3.js library, a widely used tool for interactive data visualization. This system allows for the exploration and representation of mobility trees derived from user data, making the complex structure of personal mobility accessible. By implementing the tool in D3.js, a high level of customization was achieved, enabling the creation of interactive modules that visualize various aspects of user mobility in an intuitive and engaging way.

The visualizations are presented in a hierarchical manner, consistent with Shneiderman's Visualization Mantra [16], where more general and important components are immediately visible, while more detailed information is accessible on demand. The primary output is a node-link layout, which mirrors the underlying data structure. In this layout, nodes represent locations, and links depict the paths between them. Nodes are scaled based on how frequently each location is visited in the user's dataset. To enhance interactivity, hovering over a node highlights all corresponding locations across the tree, allowing the discovery of movement patterns. A variation of this tree layout is also provided, where the lengths of links represent the actual distances travelled, offering a clearer view of travel patterns in terms of spatial distance (see Fig. 1).

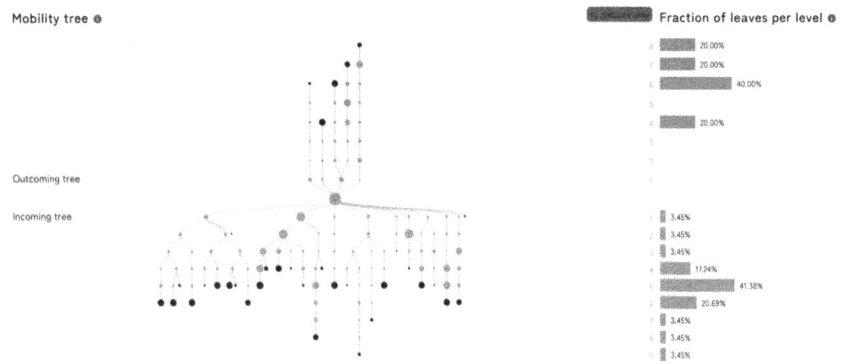

Fig. 1. The mobility prefix tree in the classical shape, accompanied by the bar chart, represents the number of terminal locations for each level.

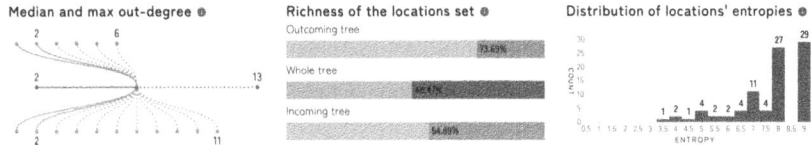

Fig. 2. From left to right: The median and maximum out-degree visualisation; the progress bar representing the ratio between locations and total nodes; the distribution of the locations' entropies.

To complement the tree structure, additional components offer further insights into user mobility. For example, a leaf exploration tool displays the percentage of leaves at different depths, reflecting how far users tend to travel. Barcharts, positioned alongside the tree, represent the richness of location diversity, indicating how often users visit new places versus recurring locations. Out-degree diagrams (Fig. 2) further break down user movements by showing the median and maximum number of connections from each node, revealing the complexity of travel routes around central locations. Another component of the visualization is a progress bar representing the richness of the location set, meaning the proportion between the number of different locations encountered and the number of all the traversed points. The visualization system also includes a histogram displaying the local entropy of locations, which quantifies how much information or variability a location contributes to the user's overall mobility. This is particularly useful for identifying high-entropy locations that play a significant role in the user's travel patterns. The histogram interacts with the main tree visualization, highlighting relevant entropy values when a node is hovered.

We intentionally excluded the use of maps to abstract the geographic layer and protecting user privacy, aligning with ethical considerations in mobility data analysis. The visualization still effectively captures movement patterns and behaviours without relying on geographic context. This choice not only protects privacy but also demonstrates how mobility data can be meaningfully repre-sented through innovative visual strategies. By focusing on user habits and travel patterns, the system offers a comprehensive, anonymized view of personal mobil-ity, providing researchers with a powerful tool for analyzing complex movement data while adhering to privacy standards.

6   Experiments

Mobility Trees offer the feature of summarizing and representing in a concise and ordered way the mobility of an individual. This summarization may enable the identification of groups of individuals with similar mobility patterns and the comparison of different cities to identify distinct movement behaviors. In this section we show the results of the experiments conducted on a dataset of GPS-tracked vehicle movements within two main cities in Tuscany, Italy: Pisa and Florence. For comparison, we used both the Tree-based and Vector-based encodings to identify the most suitable clustering algorithm for the mobility data.

6.1   Preprocessing

To address the extensive number of locations and trajectories typically associated with each user, several data-cleaning techniques were implemented to reduce both computational time and noise that could impact the analysis.

Selection of Locations. For this analysis, two cities, Pisa and Florence, were selected as prototypes. These cities vary in size and user population, provid-ing a solid foundation for detecting potential differences in mobility patterns. From the GPS dataset, a square perimeter surrounding each city was defined, encompassing adjacent areas to account for users residing outside the exact city boundaries.

User and Trajectory Pruning. The preprocessing of each user's dataset involved multiple steps to eliminate outlier trajectories and remove profiles lack-ing sufficient data for comparison. Initially, locations within the defined perime-ter were selected from the seed file. Users whose mobility was predominantly (at least 65%) confined to the city were retained. This percentage was calculated by comparing the size of the user's trajectories within the perimeter to the orig-inal dataset size. This approach ensured that users with limited mobility to a few locations were not penalized, excluding infrequent travels covering extensive locations within the city.

Subsequently, user-specific data cleaning was performed to remove outlier tra-jectories based on length. The distribution of traversed points for each trajectory was analyzed, and outliers were identified and discarded using the interquartile range (IQR) method. Length in terms of traversed locations was prioritized over distance travelled in meters, as data tessellation indicated an average distance of approximately 200 m between adjacent points, providing a reasonable approximation.

Global outlier removal followed, extracting the number of trajectories and median length for each user. After converting these values to a logarithmic scale, the IQR test was reapplied to both distributions, resulting in the exclusion of further outliers.

For the Pisa dataset, the initial count of users was 1,895, which was reduced to 1,636 after the cleaning process. The initial distribution of trajectories per user revealed a mean of 588.79, a median of 387, and a standard deviation of 705.1; after cleaning, these values adjusted to 637.1, 501, and 548.7, respectively. The trajectory length distribution initially exhibited a mean of 29.15, a median of 18, and a standard deviation of 51.02, which changed to 23.73, 17, and 24.5 post-cleaning.

In contrast, the Florence dataset began with 7,155 users, decreasing to 5,762 after cleaning. The original distribution of trajectories per user had a mean of 487.47, a median of 255, and a standard deviation of 841.48, which were adjusted to 553, 386, and 532.697, respectively, after preprocessing. The lengths of trajectories initially had a mean of 25.67, a median of 14, and a standard deviation of 49.42, which changed to 20.468, 14, and 22.795, respectively.

6.2   Tree Extraction

Upon completion of the cleaning process, user-specific mobility trees were generated. Given the volume and complexity of the data, the Ramer-Douglas-Peucker (RDP) [15] algorithm was employed to simplify trajectories. This algorithm approximates paths by removing points that do not significantly differ from preceding and following points in terms of direction. An epsilon value of 0.001 was determined to provide a satisfactory balance between approximation and information retention, as alternative values of 0.005 and 0.0005 yielded similar conceptual results.

From the cleaned data, mobility prefix trees for each user were generated. Due to the computationally intensive nature of clustering algorithms, which require iterative distance calculations between points, a distance matrix between trees was pre-computed using the unordered tree edit distance.

To compare the mobility patterns across different cities, a z-test was conducted to determine whether statistically significant differences existed in the distributions of vector attributes. The attributes examined included the median and maximum depths of both the incoming and outgoing subtrees, the median and maximum out-degrees of the nodes, and the ratio of unique locations to the total number of nodes. The resulting tests are showed in Table 1.

The mobility dataset was preprocessed to remove sensitive information and to generalize movements on a spatial grid determined by a voronoi tessellation. Each movement represented by a sequence of raw GPS points was transformed into a sequence of grid cells. This generalitazion was necessary to protect user privacy and to allow for a more abstract representation of the data. The dataset

Table 1. Pisa's and Florence's distributions

Pisa's and Florence's distributions				
Attribute	Test statistic	P-value	Mean Pisa	Mean Florence
Median depth incoming tree	1.606	0.108	8.0767	7.898
Median depth outcoming tree	−2.531	0.011	1.559	1.699
Max depth incoming tree	0.94	0.347	24.493	24.181
Max depth outcoming tree	1.937	0.053	20.287	19.576
Locations/nodes ratio	−3.946	0.0007	0.15	0.164
Median incoming tree out-deg	0.533	0.594	2	2
Median outcoming tree out-deg	0.571	0.568	1.955	1.952
Max incoming tree out-deg	0.571	0	14.392	12.666
Max outcoming tree out-deg	4.854	0.00001	9.833	9.148

after this phase consists of three primary tables: Seed, which associates grid cells location IDs with their geographic coordinates; *Trajlinks*, which records trajectory information across user IDs; *Trajstats* which store movement attribute distribution, including travel date, duration, and distance.

In the analysis phase, we focused on the prefix tree representation to showcase its potential for summarizing and comparing mobility patterns. By concentrating on this less-explored structure, the experiment aimed to evaluate the feasibility of using tree-shaped data for analysis and to identify potential challenges analysts might encounter when working with such representations. Moreover, the tree analogy provides significant opportunities for effective scientific communication and data storytelling.

6.3   Preliminary Test

Before the main analysis, several feasibility tests were conducted to assess the computational time required for each method. A batch of users from the analysis dataset, particularly those with more trajectories, was selected to have an estimate of the computational cost, allowing for the selection of feasible techniques.

Initial tests showed that the basic operations were computationally efficient. For example, the heaviest tree, containing 681 trajectories, 5428 locations, and an average trajectory length of 84.9 points, was generated in less than half a second. A rotation operation on the tree has the objective of selecting a different root node associated with a different location. Even this operation took no longer than 1.1 s.

Deeper tests on other operations were also performed. Four prefix trees were built for each user based on random samples of 25%, 50%, 75%, and 100% of their trajectories. These tests aimed to evaluate how the data volume impacted performance. The standard tree edit distance was found unsuitable for large-scale real-world datasets, as the tree ordering algorithm took between 103.4 and

Table 2. Completion time of Tree Ordering using different methods: raw ordering, ordered edit distance, unordered edit distance. Completion time expressed in seconds

Percentage of Data	Ordering	Ordered Tree ED	Unrdered Tree ED
25%	103.4099	10.4926	4.3097
50%	204.7914	43.6611	16.0067
75%	256.842	83.3877	26.2233
100%	559.8551	353.147	128.5133

560 s, while the distance function ranged from 10.5 to 353 s. Although optimizing the ordering algorithm might have been possible, reducing the complexity of the distance function remained a challenge (see Table 2).

In contrast, the unordered tree edit distance initially ranged from 4.3 to 128.5 s. However, after optimizing the adjacency matrix structure, the mean computation time on actual data dropped to 0.4 s. This improvement was also supported by data cleaning and selection steps.

Given the large number of techniques hypothesized in the preliminary phase, a choice was made between covering all methods to provide broad but superficial results or focusing on a specific set for a deeper investigation, even if tested methods are incomplete. The decision was made to explore the limits of the tree-shaped representation, with the adopted methodology easily extendable to other scenarios.

Consequently, the prefix tree structure was selected over the spanning tree, and a feature-based vector representation was chosen instead of a TF-IDF approach. The prefix tree architecture was considered more interpretable and suitable for narrative purposes, while the feature-based vector representation provided a complementary perspective within the same analytical framework.

6.4 Clustering Algorithms

The initial choice for clustering algorithms centred on the k-medoids method, primarily due to the need for representative trees for each cluster and the unsuitability of artificial points as centroids for tree data. A grid search was conducted to determine the optimal value of k, measuring the silhouette score for values ranging from 2 to 30 across 30 random initializations of medoids. Additional consideration was given to the sample size within each cluster and the silhouette scores of individual clusters to gain a nuanced understanding of the clustering dynamics. Alternative algorithms, such as DBSCAN [6] and OPTICS [4] for density-based clustering, as well as various hierarchical clustering methods including single, complete, and centroid linkage, were also explored.

Clustering Trees. For both Pisa and Florence, the k-medoids clustering, utilizing the unordered tree edit distance, consistently yielded a predominant cluster characterized by a high average silhouette score (0.71 for Pisa and 0.62 for Florence), alongside sparse and fragmented clusters with negative silhouette scores, regardless of the value of k. The most favourable results were generally achieved with $k = 4$ This trend persisted across different cleaning techniques and varying RDP epsilon values, leading to the retention of the configuration that maximized silhouette scores, as previously detailed in the preprocessing section. The primary cluster for Pisa encompassed an average of 1,481.5 users, while the cluster for Florence averaged 2,552 users, indicating a significant number of individuals with similar movement patterns. To validate these findings, DBSCAN and OPTICS were also employed, revealing similar clustering phenomena. The epsilon parameter for DBSCAN was selected based on a plot of distances to the $i - th$ neighbour, ultimately retaining the distance to the 4th neighbour as recommended by the algorithm's authors; the epsilon values were set at 3000 for Pisa and 2000 for Florence. DBSCAN successfully aggregated 96% of the Pisa samples into a single cluster, while 97% of Florence samples fell into the same category. Similar clustering results were obtained with OPTICS, and all hierarchical clustering techniques tested indicated the emergence of a dominant cluster comprising a substantial subset of the dataset.

Clustering Vectors. Subsequently, the analysis transitioned to clustering the vectorial abstractions of the prefix trees, aimed at uncovering broader patterns in user mobility while disregarding geographical aspects. The k-means algorithm was employed in conjunction with various feature projection techniques. A grid search was performed to identify the optimal number of clusters (k) within a range of 2 to 6, computing the average silhouette for each configuration. This process was repeated for standardized vectors and those projected through independent component analysis (ICA), principal component analysis (PCA) with 2 to 4 features, and multidimensional scaling. For both cities, the best outcomes were observed with a 2-means clustering on the 2-dimensional PCA projection, yielding silhouette scores of 0.45 for Pisa and 0.49 for Florence. However, no meaningful clusters were identified across the configurations tested; even the highest silhouette scores represented divisions within a larger, dense agglomerate of points corresponding to the majority of users. Figure 3 visualizes the results of the clustering for both cities.

Consequently, the second-best result – a 3-means clustering on the 2-dimensional PCA projection – was selected to investigate potential differences within this space and provide three user prototypes, despite the overarching presence of a large and dense group.

The trees closest to each cluster's centroid were analyzed for both cities, and their distinct characteristics are summarized as prototypes P0, P1, and P2 for Pisa, and F0, F1, and F2 for Florence. In Pisa, P0 exhibited a mixture of branches containing both frequently visited and infrequently visited locations, with notable variability in node sizes. P1, on the other hand, was dominated by larger nodes, reflecting a concentration of frequently visited locations with lower location richness and consistent visitation patterns. This regularity was further

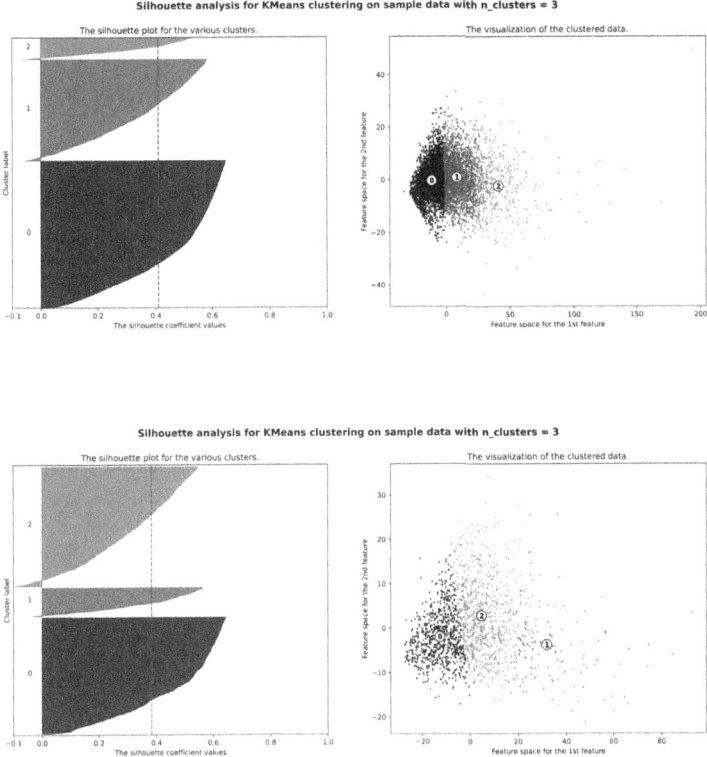

Fig. 3. The results of the 3-means on the vectors projected in two dimensions through PCA.

supported by the limited variation in node sizes, corresponding to higher entropy values. In contrast, P2 consisted predominantly of smaller nodes, indicating a broader and less predictable set of locations, with greater location richness and lower frequency variability. Additionally, P0 featured a prominent branch likely representing the user's regular commute, highlighting a mixed visitation pattern that combined both frequent and rare locations.

In terms of node out-degree, the three prototypes in Pisa exhibited similar characteristics. The visualization mapped against cumulative distances traveled in each path revealed no substantial differences regarding maximum distances traveled in individual trips. All prototypes showed a similar distribution of leaf distances, with the majority of travels concluding within the first seven kilometers. As the distance from the root increased, the frequency of observed travels diminished.

For Florence, the differences in location frequencies were less pronounced, with F0 displaying more variance and a slightly higher maximum entropy value. The prototypes exhibited comparability in terms of location richness and out-degree. The quantity of possible prefixes appeared more discriminative in Florence; F1 exhibited a notably reduced tree, while F0's root had a vast array of successors, indicating significant prefix variety. F2 was larger relative to F1 but smaller compared to F0. An analysis of travel distances revealed greater diversification in Florence users than in Pisa, with the distribution of leaves relative to distance from the root showing less gradation and identifying specific distance ranges frequently traversed.

Another qualitative assessment involved mapping each user's root by cluster within each city's geographical context to explore potential spatial correlations. However, no clear geographical distinction emerged between groups in either Pisa or Florence.

6.5   Results

Further analysis was conducted to compare the characteristics of trees from the two cities. This involved examining the features used to encode the trees into vectors for the previous step and applying a z-test for each dimension after standardization. While the test indicated statistically significant differences in means for certain attributes, the reliability of these results was questionable due to skewed distributions. Table 1 illustrates that differences in means were relatively minor, with the most notable variation occurring in the out-degree of outgoing trees, where differences of approximately two units and 0.15 in median depth were observed. Yet, these differences were not substantial. Contrary to initial expectations, distinct categories of users were not identified within the tree-shaped data or the derived vector representations. However, by examining the most central samples in each cluster for both cities, several distinguishing characteristics emerged. This observation suggests a continuous data space, implying that there are intermediate user types. This hypothesis is reinforced by consistent results across varying preprocessing methods, algorithms, and data structures. Notably, the distinguishing factor appears to be the regularity of users' paths: among the observed users, at least one exhibited equi-probable node usage across branches, while others displayed frequent and rare locations. This characteristic, particularly evident in Pisa, aligns with the "returners" and "explorers" framework proposed by Pappalardo et al. [14]. Additionally, the lack of correlation between users' root positions and their cluster memberships further supports the notion that clustering is not biased by the locations traversed.

7   Conclusion and Future Work

This research explored the mapping of personal mobility data into tree structures, specifically utilizing a variant of prefix trees rotated around the most frequent location. The tree unordered edit distance served as the distance function, enabling effective comparisons of trees irrespective of branch order. Additionally, a vectorial description of the trees was developed to capture their structural characteristics. The analysis focused on the cities of Pisa and Florence, where unsupervised learning was employed to identify distinct user types based on both tree and vector representations. The results consistently indicated the presence of a dominant dense group with minimal noise across all tests. We recognize that the focus on two cities with distinct population sizes and user demographics may limit the generalizability of findings. While these cities offer an initial foundation for exploring mobility patterns, some characteristics-such as infrastructure and population density, may not fully represent the range of mobility dynamics found in diverse urban forms or regions. Consequently, further research will be needed to assess the applicability of tree representations in cities with more complex transportation systems and varied commuting behaviors.

Future research directions include leveraging visualization tools and establishing semantically diverse locations as roots to gain deeper insights into human mobility patterns. This approach could facilitate comparisons of trees generated from distinct data sets belonging to the same individual, such as weekday versus weekend mobility or seasonal variations. Furthermore, examining mobility patterns across different cities in various countries or from alternative modes of transport may yield valuable insights. Another avenue for exploration involves clustering movements within a single tree to uncover recurrent patterns in user behavior. To enhance accessibility and user-friendliness, future work should also consider user-centred design improvements, including user and heuristic usability testing, to ensure that end-users can easily interpret and interact with tree-based mobility data representations. Overall, this work underscores the potential of representing mobility data as trees, reinforcing the findings of [14], which suggest a dichotomy between returners and explorers.

Acknowledgements. This work is partially supported by the EU NextGenerationEU programme under the funding schemes PNRR-PE-AI FAIR (Future Artificial Intelligence Research) - Spoke 1- Partnership Extended PE00000013, PNRR-SoBigData.it - Strengthening the Italian RI for Social Mining and Big Data Analytics - Prot. IR0000013, H2020-INFRAIA-2019-1: Res. Infr. G.A. 871042 *SoBigData++*.

References

1. Andrienko, G., Andrienko, N.: Privacy issues in geospatial visual analytics. In: Advances in Location-Based Services: 8th International Symposium on Location-Based Services, Vienna 2011, pp. 239–246. Springer (2012)
2. Andrienko, G.L., Andrienko, N.V., Hurter, C., Rinzivillo, S., Wrobel, S.: From movement tracks through events to places: extracting and characterizing significant places from mobility data. In: 6th IEEE Conference on Visual Analytics Science and Technology, IEEE VAST 2011, Providence, RI, USA, 23–28 October 2011, pp. 161–170. IEEE Computer Society (2011). https://doi.org/10.1109/VAST.2011.6102454
3. Andrienko, N.V., Andrienko, G.L., Barrett, L., Dostie, M., Henzi, S.P.: Space transformation for understanding group movement. IEEE Trans. Vis. Comput. Graph. **19**(12), 2169–2178 (2013). https://doi.org/10.1109/TVCG.2013.193

4. Ankerst, M., Breunig, M.M., Kriegel, H., Sander, J.: OPTICS: ordering points to identify the clustering structure. In: Delis, A., Faloutsos, C., Ghandeharizadeh, S. (eds.) SIGMOD 1999, Proceedings ACM SIGMOD International Conference on Management of Data, 1–3 June 1999, Philadelphia, Pennsylvania, USA, pp. 49–60. ACM Press (1999). https://doi.org/10.1145/304182.304187

5. Barth, D., Bellahsene, S., Kloul, L.: Mobility prediction using mobile user profiles. In: MASCOTS 2011, 19th Annual IEEE/ACM International Symposium on Modeling, Analysis and Simulation of Computer and Telecommunication Systems, Singapore, 25–27 July 2011, pp. 286–294. IEEE Computer Society (2011). https://doi.org/10.1109/MASCOTS.2011.57

6. Ester, M., Kriegel, H., Sander, J., Xu, X.: A density-based algorithm for discovering clusters in large spatial databases with noise. In: Simoudis, E., Han, J., Fayyad, U.M. (eds.) Proceedings of the Second International Conference on Knowledge Discovery and Data Mining (KDD-96), Portland, Oregon, USA, pp. 226–231. AAAI Press (1996). http://www.aaai.org/Library/KDD/1996/kdd96-037.php

7. Guidotti, R., Nanni, M.: Crash prediction and risk assessment with individual mobility networks. In: 2020 21st IEEE International conference on mobile data management (MDM), pp. 89–98. IEEE (2020)

8. Jeung, H., Yiu, M.L., Zhou, X., Jensen, C.S.: Path prediction and predictive range querying in road network databases. VLDB J. **19**(4), 585–602 (2010). https://doi.org/10.1007/S00778-010-0181-Y

9. Kruskal, J.B.: On the shortest spanning subtree of a graph and the traveling salesman problem. Proc. Am. Math. Soc. **7**(1), 48–50 (1956)

10. Landi, C., Guidotti, R., Nanni, M., Monreale, A.: The trajectory interval forest classifier for trajectory classification. In: SIGSPATIAL/GIS, pp. 67:1–67:4. ACM (2023)

11. Landi, C., Spinnato, F., Guidotti, R., Monreale, A., Nanni, M.: Geolet: an interpretable model for trajectory classification. In: IDA. Lecture Notes in Computer Science, vol. 13876, pp. 236–248. Springer (2023)

12. Larcom, S., Rauch, F., Willems, T.: The benefits of forced experimentation: striking evidence from the London underground network. Q. J. Econ. **132**(4), 2019–2055 (2017)

13. de Montjoye, Y.A., Shmueli, E., Wang, S.S., Pentland, A.S.: openPDS: protecting the privacy of metadata through safeanswers. PLOS One **9**(7), 1–9 (2014). https://doi.org/10.1371/journal.pone.0098790

14. Pappalardo, L., Simini, F., Rinzivillo, S., Pedreschi, D., Giannotti, F., Barabási, A.L.: Returners and explorers dichotomy in human mobility. Nat. Commun. **6**(1), 8166 (2015)

15. Ramer, U.: An iterative procedure for the polygonal approximation of plane curves. Comput. Graph. Image Process. **1**(3), 244–256 (1972). https://doi.org/10.1016/S0146-664X(72)80017-0

16. Shneiderman, B.: The eyes have it: a task by data type taxonomy for information visualizations. In: Proceedings of the 1996 IEEE Symposium on Visual Languages, Boulder, Colorado, USA, 3–6 September 1996, pp. 336–343. IEEE Computer Society (1996). https://doi.org/10.1109/VL.1996.545307

17. Trasarti, R., Pinelli, F., Nanni, M., Giannotti, F.: Mining mobility user profiles for car pooling. In: Proceedings of the 17th ACM SIGKDD International Conference on Knowledge Discovery and Data Mining, pp. 1190–1198 (2011)

18. Wang, R., Zhang, X., Li, N.: Zooming into mobility to understand cities: a review of mobility-driven urban studies. Cities **130**, 103939 (2022)

19. Zhao, X., Pi, D., Chen, J.: Novel trajectory privacy-preserving method based on prefix tree using differential privacy. Knowl. Based Syst. **198**, 105940 (2020). https://doi.org/10.1016/J.KNOSYS.2020.105940
20. Zhou, H., Hirasawa, K.: Spatiotemporal traffic network analysis: technology and applications. Knowl. Inf. Syst. **60**(1), 25–61 (2019). https://doi.org/10.1007/S10115-018-1225-7

From GPS Traces to Individual Emission Exposure: A Data-Driven Four-Step Process

Gurban Aliyev[1,2]([✉]) [iD] and Mirco Nanni[2] [iD]

[1] University of Pisa, Pisa, Italy
gurban.aliyev@phd.unipi.it
[2] ISTI-CNR, Pisa, Italy
mirco.nanni@isti.cnr.it

Abstract. Vehicular traffic is one of the major sources of air pollution in urban settings, making it essential to clearly understand how much and where vehicle emissions impact residents. Estimating vehicular pollution using GPS trajectories and microscopic models is getting more popular as this method has several advantages compared to other approaches. However, GPS data sources usually cover only a small sample of actual traffic, making current approaches unable to provide emission estimates for the whole road network. Moreover, to understand how much of these emissions reach different locations, a dispersion model should be applied, and quantifying their effect on individuals requires considering where they stay and/or how they move. Therefore, in this paper, we propose a four-step process that elaborates on raw, incomplete emission estimates and (i) first, estimates initial emissions from GPS data, (ii) estimates emission concentrations for the missing road segments, (iii) further processes the emission data to consider air dispersion, and (iv) computes the expected exposure to emissions of individuals in several use cases, involving both public buildings (e.g. schools) and pedestrian mobility. The experiments are based on a sample of vehicular GPS data in two Italian cities.

Keywords: road networks · vehicular emissions · missing data imputation · emission dispersion · emission exposure

1 Introduction

Ambient air pollution is one of the main barriers to the sustainable development of urban areas, which are expanding fast recently [22]. Air pollution is a more serious concern in cities than in rural areas as cities are densely populated. Also, primary sources of anthropogenic emissions, such as energy production and transportation, are concentrated around urban clusters. As a result, the concentration of air pollutants causes low air quality in cities, with more and

A. Kocian et al. (Eds.): INTSYS 2024, LNICST 608, pp. 64–82, 2025.
https://doi.org/10.1007/978-3-031-86370-7_5

more people exposed to air pollution every year. Because of the effects of this problem on public health and the economy, the United Nations calls to reduce the adverse per capita environmental impact of cities [1].

Our focus is on the quantification of vehicular emissions and mitigation of these emissions, as with the number of cars in cities increasing, the total amount of vehicular pollutants rises [12]. Studies using GPS traces offer the best trade-off between highly-detailed human mobility and representative vehicle fleets to estimate car emissions [2]. Recent studies [2,7,23] assess spatial and temporal distributions of vehicular emissions using vehicular trajectories. These studies help to quantify the impact of existing green mobility policies [23], next-generation routing principles for vehicles [7], or electrification of gross polluters [2] in terms of the decrease in emissions.

However, the GPS-data-based approach has some gaps: firstly, most of the currently available trajectory datasets cover only a portion of all vehicles and roads in the road network, while – to have a complete view of spatial and temporal emission patterns – network management requires an inventory of vehicular emissions that represent the whole population. Secondly, works focused on emissions mitigation policies only consider changes in total emissions and ignore the average exposure levels of the population. For example, the air quality in some parts of a city can get worse while total vehicular emissions decrease, thus calling for assessment methods at a more granular scale. Another issue is that most previous studies based on vehicle data assume that emissions generated on one road segment will not affect other segments, or areas outside streets, yielding potentially skewed results. For instance, secondary roads running parallel to large ones (a common setting around highway junctions) might receive emission levels from the other roads comparable to or higher than the endogenous ones. In addition, dispersion estimates beyond the road network are essential to evaluate the actual exposure of people staying in buildings or walking/cycling through the city, as both modes of transportation can go where cars cannot.

In this work, we tackle the main open issues discussed above, providing the following contributions:

- we introduce a 4-step process that covers all required phases of a (big) mobility data-based approach to estimate individual exposure to vehicle emissions;
- we provide a validation of the raw emission estimates against an indirect ground truth measured from the air quality monitoring network in Rome;
- we introduce the emission imputation problem, aimed to infer the emissions on road segments not covered by the input mobility data. Since there is no literature directly addressing the specific problem, we explore existing solutions for general data imputation over graphs and networks, adapting several approaches to our context and identifying the best candidate;
- we implement a standard emission dispersion model efficiently, enabling the computation of a city-scale map of resulting emissions at a fine granularity;
- we introduce a simple approach to individual exposure estimation for static and dynamic settings, presenting one use case for each;
- finally, all steps are applied and evaluated on a dataset of real vehicular GPS data traces covering the city of Pisa, Tuscany (Italy).

In the rest of the paper, we discuss the relevant literature (Sect. 2), introduce our 4-step pipeline describing all its components (Sect. 3), show experimental results assessing performances of imputation and showcase the pipeline on two use cases (Sect. 4), and finally provide conclusive remarks (Sect. 5).

2   Related Work

In this section, we discuss existing approaches related to the three main technical problems involved in the paper: estimating emissions at the road level from mobility traces, inferring emissions on road segments where the information is not available, and measuring the exposure of places/people taking into account actual dispersion of emissions.

2.1   Emissions Inference

Several works in the literature can estimate vehicular emissions by exploiting the spatial precision and relative abundance of mobility data coming from vehicle fleets [23]. Researchers of the last decade [2,22] have proved the usefulness of GPS sensors paired with microscopic emission models to track vehicles' mobility in real-time mode and calculate vehicular emissions. An important parameter used in microscopic models to estimate emissions is the emission factor (EF), which is a functional relation shown as pollutant emitted per kilometer traveled or liter of fuel consumed [12]. EFs are useful in the sense that they can project deviation of speed and acceleration in a small temporal scale and increase the accuracy of emission estimate [10].

However, it is worth mentioning that developed emissions models have been suffering from the lack of validation/calibration methods, and that it is not possible to calculate on-road emissions on many road segments as most of the GPS data sets do not cover the whole road network. Some inference/imputation methods need to be implemented in applications where data scarcity is an issue.

2.2   Validation of Emission Estimates

Methods to quantify vehicular air pollution in cities are increasing with the development of technology and changes in municipal air quality management (AQM). Several studies focus on the validation of on-road estimations by using on-road measurements as ground truth data [9,15,26]. This way is accurate, but not convenient, as on-road measurements are not easily available. Meanwhile, satellite and air quality station data are more accessible.

Remote sensing (including satellites) is a useful method to evaluate measurement results of emission models and provide complementary spatial information [24]. Satellite data is represented by maps and is more useful for large-scale analysis. Meanwhile, an air quality station measures the air quality of a neighborhood it is located in (of a certain radius). Given a network of stations scattered across the city, it is possible to analyze urban-level emission levels.

In terms of measurement accuracy, AQM stations are more advantageous than satellites as they are located close to the car emission sources (roads). Satellites show air quality by returning a value of the lowermost 15 km of the atmosphere ('column amounts'), and they are the least sensitive close to the surface, which is the most important part of calculating emissions [24].

The common problem of remote sensing measurements is that they are not weather-proof [13, 24] as interference of high humidity or other gases can be an obstacle for sensors. Also, remote sensors measure amounts from different sources (transportation, manufacturing, etc.). Nevertheless, vehicles are the only source of some pollutants (such as NO_x) in non-industrial areas of cities. Based on such pollutants, estimated road-link emissions can be linked to station measurements by comparing relative changes, instead of focusing on absolute values.

2.3 Imputation Strategies

Because of the limited amount of data collected, the problem of emission data sparsity on urban roads is common. However, according to recent surveys on traffic-related data imputation [5], there are currently no specific methods to impute missing emission values, while there are various attempts using state-of-the-art [6, 14, 20, 27] approaches to estimate other road features.

Some studies [20, 27] claim that missing traffic data imputation methods should be task-specific to allow the model to learn features better. Among task-specific models, those that are built to estimate intensities of traffic flows [20, 27] can be useful to predict vehicular emissions as traffic flows and vehicular emissions are intuitively correlated. Meanwhile, other studies [6, 14] are task-agnostic and their authors claim that it is possible to create feature embeddings of the input data to use them in any task after fine-tuning [6].

Another classification of existing models is based on a graph representation of road networks. The most natural representation of road networks, where road segments are links and crossroads are nodes, is called a *primal graph*: here, node-related knowledge (location, network metrics, number of various POIs around, aggregated characteristics of road segments linking to the node, etc.) is brought in feature representation. Conversion of original node features into a vector representation is called node embedding. Earlier studies [20, 27] rely on node embedding, while more recent works [6, 14] adopt a *dual graph* representation of road networks, where road segments are transformed into nodes, while crossroads between road segments become links connecting nodes.

2.4 Dispersion and Exposure Models

Studying individual and population exposure to air pollution is important to quantify the effect of changing travel behavior and traffic policies. Initial studies [25] focus only on the assessment of exposure in static locations (workplace, school, and home) using population census data. Later studies [8, 21] use more accurate mobile data to quantify average mobility exposure. More recent studies investigate the impact of travel behavior on traffic-induced emissions and subsequent exposure to traffic emissions [18].

However, these studies have some limitations. Firstly, these works disregard the dispersion of vehicular emissions both vertically and horizontally. There are various dispersion models to be considered, and the main approaches used in these models include Computational Fluid Dynamics (CFD), Gaussian, Lagrangian, and Box models [17,19].

Depending on the dispersion levels, exposure to car emissions on roads and around roads can change. The concentration of on-road vehicular emissions in certain places can increase or decrease depending on different factors, such as weather conditions (temperature, precipitation, etc.) and building profile data. Depending on these factors, one approach or the other can be more appropriate, eventually yielding more accurate results [19].

3   Methodology

In this work, we propose a 4-step pipeline[1] covering all the phases that allow to conversion of raw input GPS traces of (a subset of) vehicles circulating in a city into exposure estimates for individuals residing or moving in the area. The overall process is depicted in Fig. 1, and consists of an emissions estimate for roads covered by the input GPS data, emissions imputation for the remaining ones, modeling dispersion to distribute them on the territory, and finally an exposure estimate of static or moving entities. In the rest of this section, we illustrate the four steps in detail.

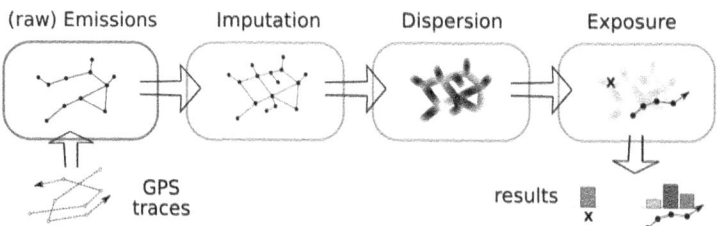

Fig. 1. Overview of the proposed process: estimating initial emissions from GPS data; imputing uncovered roads; simulating dispersion of emissions; computing exposure for static and moving entities.

---

[1] The code that implements the pipeline is available at https://github.com/baygaliyev/eide.

3.1 Raw Emission Estimates

Our work adopts the approach introduced in [2], which makes use of GPS traces of vehicles moving in a city to estimate their contribution to the emissions over the road segments traversed during their trips. Following the microscopic emissions model in [22], instantaneous emissions associated with each trajectory point p are computed through equation:

$$E_p^j = f_1^j + f_2^j v_p + f_3^j v_p^2 + f_4^j a_p + f_5^j a_p^2 + f_6^j v_p a_p \tag{1}$$

where j denotes the pollutant type (in our case $j = CO_2$), and v_p and a_p are the instantaneous speed and acceleration of the vehicle. Emission factors f_i are determined by the type of pollutant and the engine type (petrol, diesel, etc.).

Single point estimates are then aggregated at the level of the road segment to obtain its average emission concentration. Here, the road segmentation provided by OpenStreetMap (OSM)[2] is adopted, assigning each emission point to the closest segment. In Sect. 4.1 we will see – through the comparison against air quality stations data – that this step yields reasonable local estimates. For each road segment, we divided the CO_2 amount assigned by the length of the road segment to normalize pollution amounts (as longer roads will probably have higher CO_2 pollution). As discussed in later sections, the coverage of GPS data can be incomplete, since they usually describe only a sample of the circulating pool of vehicles and the sampling rate is sometimes low (e.g. in our experiments it is around 1 point per minute), thus smaller or lower-traffic road segments might be particularly ill-represented. This calls for the next stage of our process, trying to reconstruct the expected emission concentration in missed segments.

3.2 Imputation

For the missing data imputation (MDI) step we considered all available graph imputation approaches in the literature, selecting those that could fit our use case (though none of them natively addressed emissions imputation) and identifying a subset of representative solutions. The selection also considered the availability of an open-source implementation of the methods.

The simplest approach to graph imputation consists of assigning a fixed and predefined set of features to each entity (node or edge), which encodes into a standard vector representation all its characteristics and relations to other entities deemed relevant. Then, such representation becomes the input for standard prediction models (regression or classification models, depending on the task).

The most sophisticated models for graph imputation are based on computing some intermediate embedding vector representation of the road network, focusing either on nodes embedding or on edges embedding, and applying either generic graph embedding [6,20] or deep graph learning methods, in particular graph convolutional networks [14,27]. In particular, methods that produce edge embeddings typically represent the road network through a dual graph, where

---

[2] https://www.openstreetmap.org/.

nodes represent road segments, thus allowing to adoption of standard node-oriented embedding strategies. As in the basic case of fixed node/edge features, the resulting vectors yielded by generic embedding methods are used as input data for task-specific prediction models. On the contrary, graph convolution methods integrate both steps (embedding and prediction task) in the learning.

Among the existing embedding and deep learning approaches we decided to use two methods: SARN [6], a task-agnostic graph embedding model, which was designed to create embeddings of road segments; and the task-specific convolutional SI-GCN [27], which works with nodes and was originally developed to impute traffic flows – intuitively well correlated with emissions.

Graph Features. Besides being fundamental for the basic fixed-features approach mentioned above, also SARN and SI-GCN can take advantage of features describing, respectively, edges and nodes in the input graph. This information is expected to be extremely important, thus we included some characteristics derived from the road network:

- node features can be grouped in 4 sets with a total of 15 features: i) node coordinates (*latitude* and *longitude*), ii) network measures (*node degree, betweenness, closeness* and *harmonic centralities*), iii) the number of points of interest (POI) around the node, grouped into 6 categories (*cultural, education, food, health, service* and *transportation*), and iv) *the number of road segments connected to the node which have emission data*, aggregations of emissions of the road segments connected to the node (*mean value, standard deviation* of the mean value, *minimum* and *maximum* values).
- edges have the same features with the additions of 4 coordinate features (both of start and end nodes) and 3 features related to roads' physical characteristics (*length, radian, highway class*), making 20 road features in total.

Predictive Models. While SI-GCN directly provides an imputation model that can be applied to road segments with missing target values, the fixed-features approach and SARN's task-agnostic road embeddings are used as input for standard regression models. In particular, we adopt some baseline and state-of-art ones: a basic linear regressor; XGBoost; a support vector machine regressor (SVM); and a multi-layer perceptron (MLP).

A Classification-Regression Approach. An inspection of the different models' behaviors revealed that they typically stringy overestimate low emission amounts and underestimate higher CO_2 amounts. To address this issue, we propose a CO_2 imputation consisting of a two-phase process where we first train a classifier to discriminate highly polluted roads from the others, and then we build a regressor specific for high-emission segments and another one for the others. Notice that the distinction between high and low values depends on a threshold value to be decided during the training phase. Predictions are then performed by applying the classifier to decide which regressor to use, whose output is returned as the final result.

3.3   Dispersion of Emissions

Dispersion models for air pollutants have been studied for many years, yielding several approaches of different complexity that can capture various factors that impact dispersion, such as wind speed, wind turbulent fluctuations, temperature, etc. In this work we selected a basic Gaussian model, in particular, a simplification of the standard Gaussian plume model proposed in [3] and used in several recent works (e.g. [11], which also provides implementations), computing the pollutant concentration in a given position (x, y) relative to the emission location and at height z, and wind direction along the x axis:

$$C\left(x, y, z\right) = \frac{Q}{2\pi u \sigma_y \sigma_z} \cdot e^{-\frac{y^2}{2\sigma_y^2}} \cdot \left[e^{-\frac{(z - H_e)^2}{2\sigma_z^2}} + e^{-\frac{(z + H_e)^2}{2\sigma_z^2}} \right]$$

Besides considering the emission rate Q of the point source and the dispersion coefficients (lateral σ_y and vertical σ_z), the formula can account for wind scalar speed u and its direction (implicit in the x-axis alignment). Yet in our setting (based on long-term aggregates) that is not useful, thus we fixed u and assumed homogeneous wind in all directions.

For each emission source, we estimate its impact on the surrounding area. Each road segment is divided into small chunks (default length is 1 m) which are considered as punctiform sources emitting at a constant rate. Their emission rate is thus computed by normalizing the road raw emissions concentration by the road length and the time interval covered by the dataset:

$$e(c) = \frac{emission(r)}{len(r) \cdot T}$$

for each chunk c of road segment r, where T is the dataset time horizon in seconds (in our experiments, equal to one year). To compute the dispersion of chunk's emissions, we partition the region of analysis into a regular grid of cells having a small size (e.g. in our experiments the default is 5×5 m) and for each cell, we sum up the contributions from all sources.

Efficiency Aspects. The computational complexity of the approach mentioned above is potentially very large. Indeed, it requires applying the dispersion formula for each pair $(chunk, cell)$, whose number is proportional to the total road network length and the surface area of the territory under analysis. In most cases that means a cubic growth w.r.t. the territory size (e.g. the diameter). However, without considering the effects of winds and other location-dependent factors, the dispersion patterns become symmetrical in all directions and with the same shape for all sources, simply rescaled by the emission rate Q specific to the emission location. Moreover, the dispersion patterns vanish beyond large distances (e.g. in our experimental setting, a reasonable threshold appears to be around 250 m), thus a basic dispersion pattern can be computed once for all within a fixed limited spatial range and then applied to each emission source through rescaling. That reduces the computational complexity from $O(n^3)$ to $O(kn^2)$, where n is the territory size (diameter) expressed as several cells, and k is the size of the dispersion pattern discussed above, where typically $k \ll n$. Moreover, computational "constants" are also smaller, since single operations are much cheaper and computable through vectorization.

3.4   Exposure Estimation

The first three steps of the process described above yield a (currently static) mapping of vehicle emission concentrations in all locations within the study area. This allows us to study how much citizens are exposed to emissions in at least two ways, that we will explore and next test in the experiment section: a static location-based one, and a dynamic movement one.

Static location-based studies (e.g., [25]) are the simplest ones, and they consist of comparing the estimated emissions that reach a set of locations, for instance, hospitals, schools, etc., to rank existing places in terms of potential health risk or to identify best candidates for new buildings.

Dynamic movement-based studies (e.g., [18]) consider the movement of individuals and the expected amount of emissions that they absorb while moving. Mathematically speaking, they can be estimated as the integral of the emissions the individual is exposed to in each of the points they visit along their movement trajectory. From a more computational viewpoint, that is obtained by approximating the trajectory T with the sequence S of cells visited and, for each cell $s \in S$, its traversal time $time(s)$, exploiting our cell-based approximation of the emissions' dispersion:

$$exposure(T) = \int_{\bar{x} \in T} e(\bar{x}) d\bar{x} \quad \simeq \quad \sum_{s \in S} e(s) \cdot time(s)$$

Our reference application is estimating exposure for pedestrians in a simplified scenario where the movement speed v_p of pedestrians and their breath intensity are constant – typically true for small and flat cities, while complex scenarios involving hills, stairs, traffic lights, etc. might require a different setting. The first assumption allows us to estimate $time(s)$ as $length(T \cap s)/v_p$, i.e. it is proportional to the length of the trajectory segment contained in the cell. The second one says that the ratio of emissions absorbed by the individual is constant and the overall absorption depends only on the concentration.

4   Experimental Results

In this section, we present experimental results over the four steps of our pipeline, namely raw emission generation, imputation, dispersion, and exposure, each described in a separate subsection. In particular, the first subsection will provide a comparison of raw estimates against air quality data; the second will evaluate the accuracy of various imputation methods; the third will describe the output of the dispersion phase, also showing the impact of imputation on the result; the last one will present two use cases adopting our exposure strategy. Experiments are based on two GPS datasets of private vehicles: one in the area of Rome, Italy (used for raw estimate validation), and one in Pisa, Italy, similar to the one used in [2] and covering respectively ca. 39000 and 11000 vehicles over one year.

4.1 Validation of Model Estimations

The air quality monitoring network of Rome has historical data on several pollutants measured hourly from 1999 (provided by ARPA Lazio[3]). Inside the borders of the municipality of Rome, there are 11 stations (Fig. 2(left)) where traffic is a significant source of emissions. We obtained (mean) daily NO_x concentrations of those stations during the year 2017 (as our emissions estimates are for 2017).

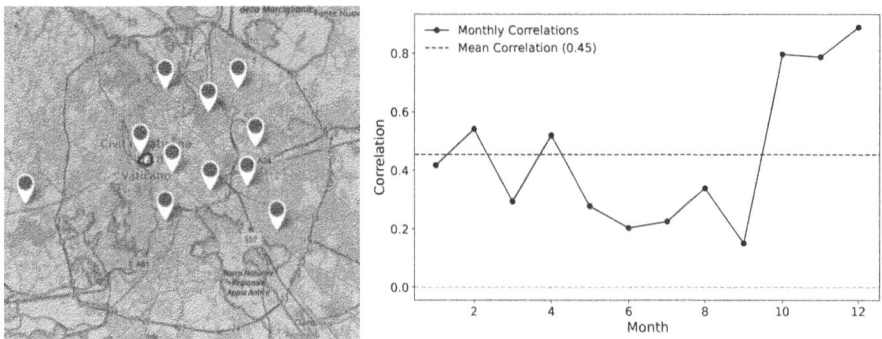

Fig. 2. (left) The air quality monitoring network in the municipality of Rome; (right) Monthly Correlation between CO_2 estimation and NO_x measurements. Correlation values are represented with Pearson's correlation coefficients.

Our validation is based on the comparison between the concentrations measured by the monitoring stations and the emission estimations of our model. More formally, for each station s, day d and week w, we have: i) mean concentrations C_s^d measured by the station (in μ/g^3); ii) aggregated (summed) emissions E_s^w computed by our model (in g). E_s^w is the sum of all the emissions estimated on road segments within a radius r from the monitoring station s during day d. To increase the sample size of cars passing by the stations, we aggregate (summed) road-level emissions by month (E_s^m). Likewise, we aggregate daily station measurements into mean concentration amounts for each month (C_s^m). As a result, we have 11 pairs of estimation-measurement values for each month.

---

[3] https://www.arpalazio.net/main/aria/sci/basedati/chimici/chimici.php.

Since CO_2 emissions are not directly measured by the stations, our estimates are validated against aggregated NO_x values of station measurements. We can conduct this comparison as NO_x and CO_2 are reported in the literature to correlate significantly (especially among gasoline cars) [4]. The radius of 200 m (according to the guidelines of the European Environment Agency [16]) is chosen to aggregate estimated emissions around each air quality station.

Correlation results are shown in Fig. 2(right). The correlation was computed for each month as Pearson's coefficient between our CO_2 estimates over the 11 stations and the corresponding 11 measurements of NO_x. The mean Pearson's coefficient is 0.45, indicating a significant overall correlation. This result exceeds that of a previous study [28], which compared simpler model estimations – proxy emission scores based solely on traffic volume and roadway type – to air quality station data. A seasonal pattern is evident, with the correlation dropping in the warm season (reaching 0.15 in September). The reason for this is an increased number of warm, sunny, and rainy days which leads to more intensive reactions between NO_x and O_3 and thus lower levels of NO_x in the air, heavily affecting correlations with CO_2 emissions. On the opposite, as seen in previous studies [28], the correlation strengthens towards the end of the year, peaking at 0.88 in December, likely due to the accumulation of emitted NO_x gases in colder, more stable atmospheric conditions.

4.2   Accuracy of Emission Data Imputation

As discussed in previous sections, we evaluated the capability of several approaches to infer the emission concentration of road segments that miss it in the input data. In particular, we evaluate the mean average percentage error (MAPE) yielded by SI-GCN and by several standard regression tools applied both to the raw features of road segments and to an embedding computed by the SARN approach. Also, the classification-regression schema proposed in Sect. 3.2 is applied to all basic regressors. In this case, a manual exploration of the training set identified 4.2 g/m as the best threshold to discriminate between the two classes, marking around 85% as low-emission roads.

Table 1 summarizes the results obtained over 10 runs. For classification-regression, we show both the overall MAPE for each configuration (all) and separately the results for test instances classified as low (L) or high (H). For each algorithm and feature subset pair, the results correspond to the parameter configuration that minimizes the MAPE. The first clear observation is the generally poor performances of all models, with MAPE > 100%, highlighting the difficulty of the task as compared to other similar ones treated in literature. Second, performances are not improved by adopting segment embeddings in place of raw features, nor by SI-GCN, signifying that the structural information they can bring is not relevant for emission imputation. Finally, the best approach for overall results is XGBoost within our classification-regression schema, applied over raw features. In particular, we can see that the classification-regression improves XGBoost's MAPE values by 15%–69% over the basic approach – especially for high-emission segments.

Table 1. Imputation results of MDI models over raw features and SARN embeddings. Values represent average MAPE and its standard deviation (in the brackets) over 10 runs.

Model	Inputs	
	Raw Features	SARN Embeddings
SI-GCN	793.40% (−)	−
Direct Regressors:		
Linear Regressor	215.26% (11.85%)	255.51% (16.80%)
XGBoost Regressor	143.25% (5.34%)	185.17% (11.60%)
SVM Regressor	255.57% (7.13%)	217.51% (24.12%)
MLP	198.65% (0.74%)	300.77% (50.82%)
Classification-Regression:		
Linear Regressor	168.91% (all) 173.05% (L) 128.91% (H)	216.19% (all) 198.85% (L) 383.43% (H)
XGBoost Regressor	**129.88% (all)** 130.50% (L) 124.46% (H)	160.85% (all) 156.64% (L) 207.72% (H)
SVM Regressor	186.76% (all) 194.53% (L) 111.60% (H)	181.32% (all) 181.21% (L) 183.42% (H)
MLP	256.41% (all) 267.33% (L) 150.11% (H)	262.89% (all) 268.60% (L) 201.80% (H)

Error Distribution over Road Types. After obtaining final data imputation results, we analyzed MAPE values considering the most important characteristics of road segments, namely the length of the road segment length and the speed limit on it. Prediction errors of CO_2/m grouped by road lengths are reported in Table 2. We can see that the model tends to have larger errors for longer roads with low pollution per meter. The opposite can be noticed for roads with high pollution per meter, where the MAPE across the longest roads (top 20%) goes below 43%. This result supports the intuition that longer segments generally belong to more important and traffic-intensive roads, and vice versa, thus the model makes more mistakes on roads that violate this trend.

We also aggregated errors by the speed limit of roads (Table 3). Results are consistent with Table 2. Indeed, prediction errors are lower (MAPE below 100%) when a road has a low speed limit and low pollution, as shorter roads tend to be located in residential areas and have lower speed limits. The same applies to roads with higher speed limits and higher pollution amounts (a higher speed limit is typical for highways, which are longer than roads in a residential area). It should also be noted that the majority of roads do not have speed limit information (results for such roads are given in the last row of Table 3).

Applying Imputation to the Whole Road Network. After the validation of results, where we identified the classification-regression approach with

Table 2. Performance analysis (average MAPE with the standard deviation) across different road lengths.

Range	Roads		
	Low Pollution	High Pollution	All roads
0%–20%	102.35% (132.20%)	227.74% (303.86%)	103.33% (131.64%)
20%–40%	110.29% (181.97%)	122.18% (171.38%)	126.65% (210.57%)
40%–60%	117.28% (170.33%)	174.71% (231.43%)	111.54% (152.96%)
60%–80%	125.40% (256.94%)	114.28% (186.58%)	127.71% (255.45%)
80%–100%	163.89% (385.46%)	**42.54%** (42.86%)	155.06% (372.81%)
All ranges	123.79% (243.46%)	136.02% (213.69%)	124.82% (241.14%)

XGBoost as the best solution, we applied it to impute the emission data on the 36000 road segments in Pisa that missed that information.

Table 3. Performance analysis (average MAPE with the standard deviation) across different road speed limits.

Limit	Roads				
	All Roads	Low Pollution	Count	High Pollution	Count
10 km/h	287.67% (400.96%)	287.67% (400.96%)	11	–	0
20 km/h	354.91% (302.93%)	354.91% (302.93%)	3	–	0
30 km/h	162.95% (517.46%)	156.54% (513.14%)	151	646.81% (606.09%)	2
40 km/h	107.45% (88.96%)	**97.95%** (75.52%)	36	122.31% (104.93%)	23
50 km/h	**99.77%** (147.56%)	**98.61%** (149.56%)	239	112.95% (121.74%)	21
60 km/h	105.14% (203.50%)	**87.72%** (74.18%)	10	110.59% (229.15%)	32
70 km/h	**73.64%** (83.36%)	**69.57%** (12.71%)	3	**73.97%** (86.59%)	37
80 km/h	**69.36%** (69.02%)	–	0	**69.36%** (69.02%)	11
90 km/h	145.35% (342.12%)	151.09% (347.67%)	25	**1.89%** (–)	1
130 km/h	**83.11%** (–)	–	0	**83.11%** (0.00%)	1
Not Given	126.36% (210.20%)	123.33% (206.90%)	1393	226.69% (281.93%)	42

4.3   Dispersion of Car Emissions

The dispersion approach described in Sect. 3.3 was applied to the central area of the city of Pisa, obtaining a fine-grained map of emissions. Concentrations are log-transformed and they represent accumulated CO_2 emissions over a one-hour period. The results are shown in Fig. 3, where we compare the concentrations obtained using the (incomplete) emissions based only on the original GPS data (left) with those obtained over the data extended through imputation (right).

In both cases, results are rather consistent with common sense, as concentrations are higher around industrial zones (e.g. lower-left and top-right) and some traffic-intensive roundabouts (e.g. on the sides of the rightmost bridge on the river). Yet, the imputed data better captures areas erroneously assigned to very low emissions by the original estimates (in particular in the top-right corner), and some high emissions spots are now slightly more pronounced.

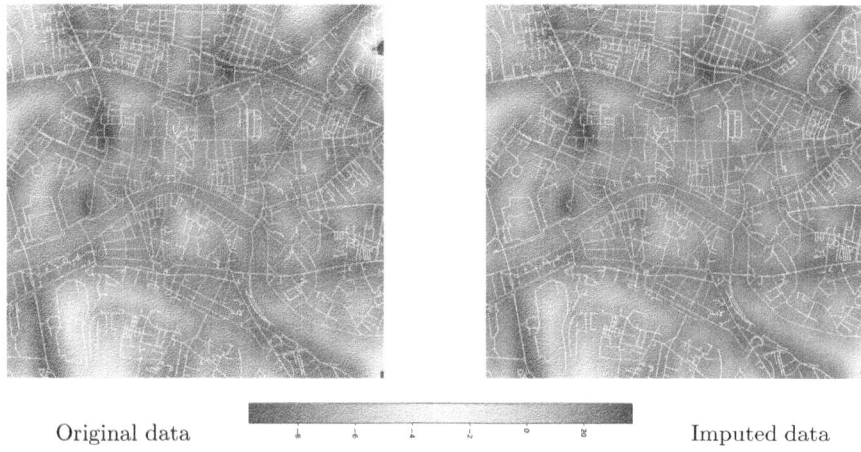

Original data   Imputed data

Fig. 3. Log-transformed vehicular CO_2 concentration in Pisa: Original (left) vs. Imputed Data (right).

4.4 Exposure to Car Emissions

In this section, we describe two use cases that exploit the emission map obtained in the previous steps to infer the exposure of individuals in two settings: 1) exposure from a static place; and 2) exposure while walking. For the first case, we estimated exposure levels at schools in the central area of Pisa. In the second case, we estimated exposure level to emissions while taking several routes to walk from a university building in Pisa to the central train station, which is a very common task for students.

Static Location-Based Exposure in Schools. Estimation of exposure levels at schools is extremely important because children, who are more vulnerable to air pollution, spend a significant part of their day at school. There are 36 schools in the area, all of which are plotted on the map in Fig. 4(left). There is also a table next to the map which shows the school numbers from the map associated with the corresponding concentrations. The values represent the amount of CO_2 emitted by cars that accumulates in the cell where the school is located over the course of one year. These numbers can help us to interpret exposure to traffic emissions at schools.

We can see from the table that the highest concentration level is around school number 7, which is indeed located in via Cisanello, the busiest street in the eastern part of Pisa. The second most exposed school (34) is instead located next to State Highway 1 (via Aurelia) and a factory. Meanwhile, the third most exposed school (3) is next to one of the largest parking areas in the center of Pisa. Interestingly, most schools outside the city walls in the south and southeast (19, 23, 32) are the least exposed ones.

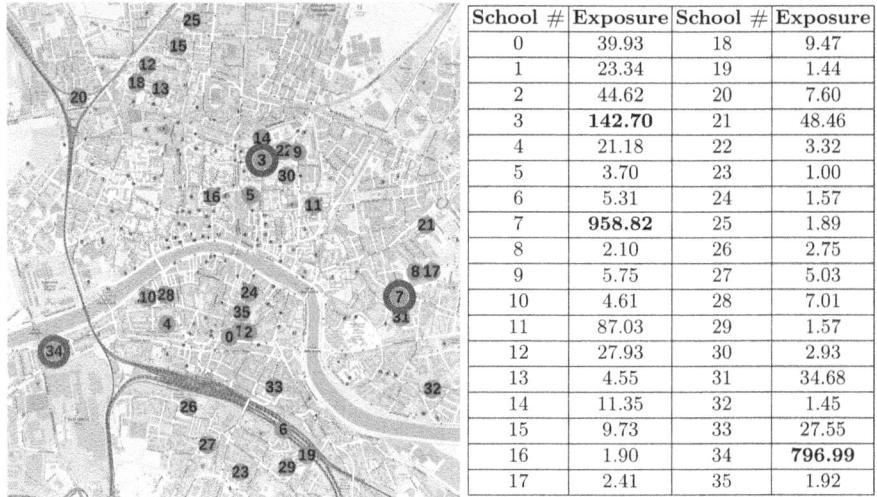

School #	Exposure	School #	Exposure
0	39.93	18	9.47
1	23.34	19	1.44
2	44.62	20	7.60
3	**142.70**	21	48.46
4	21.18	22	3.32
5	3.70	23	1.00
6	5.31	24	1.57
7	**958.82**	25	1.89
8	2.10	26	2.75
9	5.75	27	5.03
10	4.61	28	7.01
11	87.03	29	1.57
12	27.93	30	2.93
13	4.55	31	34.68
14	11.35	32	1.45
15	9.73	33	27.55
16	1.90	34	**796.99**
17	2.41	35	1.92

Fig. 4. Map showing the schools located in the center of Pisa (left) and their annual exposure values (right). The 'top' 3 schools are circled.

Exposure While Walking. The travel between the University and the Central train station is one of the popular commuting activities in Pisa. Therefore, we considered a scenario when a person takes a walk to the train station (in the South) from a relatively close university building (in the North). To simulate realistic paths, we used TomTom's API[4] and got 4 alternatives with the shortest travel times for pedestrians (Fig. 5). Exposure values are calculated considering accumulated CO_2 pollution over a one-hour period.

We can see from the figure that the travel time difference between any two alternative paths is less than 2.5 min or 11%. However, we can see that a pair of routes that pass through the central streets lead to lower exposure. The red route (route 1) passes through pedestrian streets (Borgo Stretto and Corso Italia,

---

[4] https://developer.tomtom.com/.

denoted with a 'pedestrian' sign on the map), consequently having the lowest CO_2 exposure. The blue route (route 2), passes through Borgo Stretto, but not through Corso Italia, which translates to a relatively higher exposure. Most of the travel through Green (route 3) and yellow (route 4) routes pass through driving roads, which results in 2–3 times higher CO_2 exposure compared to the red path. Especially, the yellow route passes through the busiest parts of Pisa after crossing the river: lungarno Fibonacci, piazza Guerrazzi (roundabout sign on the map), and viale Bonaini ('traffic light' sign on the map).

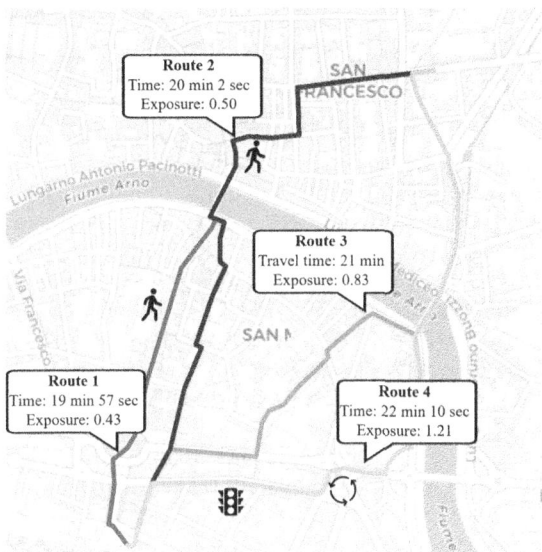

Fig. 5. Alternative walking routes, their travel times and CO_2 exposure amount (mg), from a University building to the Central Train Station of Pisa.

5   Conclusion

In this paper, we introduced a 4-step process to derive estimates of individual exposure to emissions (CO_2 in particular) from raw GPS vehicle data, introducing an imputation phase to account for the limited coverage of GPS data, and exploring existing compatible tools. Finally, emission estimates obtained through a simple dispersion phase are exploited to infer exposure at static locations and along trips with two small use cases.

The proposed pipeline provides the first viable and easy-to-use end-to-end solution for the task under study, yet several issues and open problems emerged, waiting for further studies. First, the best solution for emissions imputation is still far from optimal, suggesting that the problem has peculiarities that call for ad hoc approaches different from other graph-based methods. Also, a factor not considered so far is that we expect low-emission road segments to miss emission data more often than high-emission ones, thus introducing a bias that needs proper treatment. Second, the spatial density of the initial emission estimates might be improved, for computing map-matching with shortest paths between consecutive points, inferring someway the speed and acceleration in reconstructed points. This improved density might allow to have time-dependent estimates, useful to obtain more precise exposure estimates. Finally, more sophisticated dispersion models should be included, for instance taking into account weather data, made possible by time-dependent estimates.

References

1. Transforming Our World: The 2030 Agenda for Sustainable Development. Springer (2018). https://doi.org/10.1891/9780826190123.ap02
2. Böhm, M., Nanni, M., Pappalardo, L.: Gross polluters and vehicle emissions reduction. Nat. Sustain. **5**(8), 699–707 (2022). https://doi.org/10.1038/s41893-022-00903-x
3. Briggs, G.A.: Diffusion estimation for small emissions. Preliminary report (1973). https://doi.org/10.2172/5118833
4. Carslaw, D.C., Beevers, S.D., Tate, J.E., Westmoreland, E.J., Williams, M.L.: Recent evidence concerning higher NOx emissions from passenger cars and light duty vehicles. Atmos. Environ. **45**(39), 7053–7063 (2011). https://doi.org/10.1016/j.atmosenv.2011.09.063
5. Chan, R.K.C., Lim, J.M.Y., Parthiban, R.: Missing traffic data imputation for artificial intelligence in intelligent transportation systems: review of methods, limitations, and challenges. IEEE Access **11**, 34080–34093 (2023). https://doi.org/10.1109/ACCESS.2023.3264216
6. Chang, Y., Tanin, E., Cao, X., Qi, J.: Spatial structure-aware road network embedding via graph contrastive learning. In: Proceedings 26th International Conference on Extending Database Technology, EDBT 2023, Ioannina, Greece, 28–31 March 2023, pp. 144–156. OpenProceedings.org (2023). https://doi.org/10.48786/edbt.2023.12
7. Cornacchia, G., Böhm, M., Mauro, G., Nanni, M., Pedreschi, D., Pappalardo, L.: How routing strategies impact urban emissions. In: Proceedings of the 30th International Conference on Advances in Geographic Information Systems, SIGSPATIAL 2022. Association for Computing Machinery, New York (2022). https://doi.org/10.1145/3557915.3560977
8. Dewuf, B., et al.: Dynamic assessment of exposure to air pollution using mobile data. Int. J. Health Geograph. **15** (2016). https://doi.org/10.1186/s12942-016-0042-z
9. Ekström, M., Sjödin, A., Andreasson, K.: Evaluation of the COPERT III emission model with on-road optical remote sensing measurements. Atmos. Environ. **38**, 6631–6641 (2004). https://doi.org/10.1016/j.atmosenv.2004.07.019
10. Gately, C.K., Hutyra, L.R., Peterson, S., Wing, I.S.: Urban emissions hotspots: quantifying vehicle congestion and air pollution using mobile phone GPS data. Environ. Pollut. **229**, 496–504 (2017). https://doi.org/10.1016/j.envpol.2017.05.091

11. Gavros, A., Karatzas, K.: Air pollution due to central heating of a city-centered university campus. In: Wohlgemuth, V., Naumann, S., Behrens, G., Arndt, H.K. (eds.) ENVIROINFO 2021. Progress in IS, pp. 117–133. Springer, Cham (2022). https://doi.org/10.1007/978-3-030-88063-7_8
12. Huang, Y., et al.: Remote sensing of on-road vehicle emissions: mechanism, applications and a case study from Hong Kong. Atmos. Environ. **182**, 58–74 (2018). https://doi.org/10.1016/j.atmosenv.2018.03.035
13. Huang, Y., et al.: Emission measurement of diesel vehicles in Hong Kong through on-road remote sensing: performance review and identification of high-emitters. Environ. Pollut. **237**, 133–142 (2018). https://doi.org/10.1016/j.envpol.2018.02.043
14. Jepsen, T.S., Jensen, C.S., Nielsen, T.D.: Relational fusion networks: graph convolutional networks for road networks. IEEE Trans. Intell. Transp. Syst. **23**(1), 418–429 (2022). https://doi.org/10.1109/TITS.2020.3011799
15. Kousoulidou, M., et al.: Use of portable emissions measurement system (PEMS) for the development and validation of passenger car emission factors. Atmos. Environ. **64**, 329–338 (2013). https://doi.org/10.1016/j.atmosenv.2012.09.062
16. Larssen, S., Sluyter, R., Helmis, C.: Criteria for EUROAIRNET: the EEA air quality monitoring and information network. Technical Report No. 12, European Environment Agency, Copenhagen, Denmark (1999). https://www.eea.europa.eu/publications/TEC12
17. Leelőssy, Á., Molnár, F., Izsák, F., Havasi, Á., Lagzi, I., Mészáros, R.: Dispersion modeling of air pollutants in the atmosphere: a review. Cent. Eur. J. Geosci. **6**(3), 257–278 (2014). https://doi.org/10.2478/s13533-012-0188-6
18. Li, Q., Liang, S., Xu, Y., Liu, L., Zhou, S.: Assessing personal travel exposure to on-road PM2.5 using cellphone positioning data and mobile sensors. Health Place **75**, 102803 (2022). https://doi.org/10.1016/j.healthplace.2022.102803
19. Liang, M., Chao, Y., Tu, Y., Xu, T.: Vehicle pollutant dispersion in the urban atmospheric environment: a review of mechanism, modeling, and application. Atmosphere **14**(2) (2023). https://doi.org/10.3390/atmos14020279
20. Liu, Z., et al.: Learning geo-contextual embeddings for commuting flow prediction. In: AAAI Conference on Artificial Intelligence (2020). https://api.semanticscholar.org/CorpusID:211037977
21. Nyhan, M., et al.: Exposure track - the impact of mobile-device-based mobility patterns on quantifying population exposure to air pollution. Environ. Sci. Technol. **50**, 9671–81 (2016). https://doi.org/10.1021/acs.est.6b02385
22. Nyhan, M., et al.: Predicting vehicular emissions in high spatial resolution using pervasively measured transportation data and microscopic emissions model. Atmos. Environ. **140**, 352–363 (2016). https://doi.org/10.1016/j.atmosenv.2016.06.018
23. Rahman, M.N., Idris, A.O.: TRIBUTE: trip-based urban transportation emissions model for municipalities. Int. J. Sustain. Transp. **11**(7), 540–552 (2017). https://doi.org/10.1080/15568318.2016.1278061
24. Schneider, P.: Alternative technologies for monitoring urban air quality – from satellites to sensor networks (2019). https://nilu.com/publication/1756394/. Lecture presented at Tekna - Faggruppen for Energi, Industri og Miljø, Oslo
25. de Souza, P., et al.: Quantifying disparities in air pollution exposures across the United States using home and work addresses. Environ. Sci. Technol. **58**(1), 280–290 (2024). https://doi.org/10.1021/acs.est.3c07926

26. Wu, Y., Song, G., Yu, L.: Sensitive analysis of emission rates in moves for developing site-specific emission database. Transp. Res. Part D: Transp. Environ. **32**, 193–206 (2014). https://doi.org/10.1016/j.trd.2014.07.009
27. Yao, X., Gao, Y., Zhu, D., Manley, E., Wang, J., Liu, Y.: Spatial origin-destination flow imputation using graph convolutional networks. IEEE Trans. Intell. Transp. Syst. **22**(12), 7474–7484 (2021). https://doi.org/10.1109/TITS.2020.3003310
28. Yoon, S., Moon, Y., Jeong, J., Park, C.R., Kang, W.: A network-based approach for reducing pedestrian exposure to PM2.5 induced by road traffic in Seoul. Land **10**, 1045 (2021). https://doi.org/10.3390/land10101045

Capacity Vehicle Routing Problem with Time Windows: Simulation Tool for Footprint Network Design

Cosimo Birtolo$^{(\boxtimes)}$ ⓘ, Erica Occhionero ⓘ, and Francesca Torre ⓘ

Digital, Technology and Operations, Poste Italiane, Rome, Italy
{birtoloc,occhio17,torrefr6}@posteitaliane.it

Abstract. The paper focuses on a decision support system designed for logistic experts and aimed at addressing Vehicle Routing Problem that includes multi-vehicles and multi-depot with time constraints and considers the capacities of vehicles and logistic nodes too. The paper proposes a novel solution featuring a three-layer architecture and a system able to simulate the behavior of the network. Therefore, the paper proposes a tool to assess the impact of changes in volumes and capacities on overall delivery times. The integration of information about sorting nodes, delivery nodes, travel distances, and daily item demands is crucial for simulating accurate arrival times at each destination point. Computational experiments are depicted for validating the model and showing its effectiveness and its application.

Keywords: Vehicle Routing Problem · Multi-Depot · Capacity and Time Windows · Digital twin · Logistic Network

1 Introduction

Vehicle Routing Problem (VRP) introduced by George Dantzig and John Ramser in their seminal paper titled "The Truck Dispatching Problem" [1] is still relevant to industries that require efficient organization of its network aimed at guaranteeing the demanding challenges of e-Commerce, such as postal and logistics companies. The evolution of the needs is leading to different scenarios by increasing the alternative delivery endpoints as lockers, post offices, retailers' networks as supermarkets and shopping malls or delivery points at jointly owned buildings. According to a recent literature review on VRP for city logistics [2], the adoption of VRP in urban areas is driven by its ability to reduce congestion and improve the mobility of freight transportation services at minimum cost. Another significant benefit is its positive contribution to the environment and sustainable development [2]. Postal and logistic industries can benefit from novel decision support systems that can solve the problem described by considering the logistic infrastructure required for delivery operations and ensuring working time slots and customers' delivery time windows. Our aim is to model this problem in three-layer delivery architecture from

© ICST Institute for Computer Sciences, Social Informatics and Telecommunications Engineering 2025
Published by Springer Nature Switzerland AG 2025. All Rights Reserved
A. Kocian et al. (Eds.): INTSYS 2024, LNICST 608, pp. 83–97, 2025.
https://doi.org/10.1007/978-3-031-86370-7_6

sorting to middle-mile delivery and to propose a tool able to simulate the delivery time considering volumes, logistics nodes and related capacity being a digital twin of the entire networks. In Sect. 2 we introduce Vehicle Routing Problem (VRP), the related formulation with a review of the state-of-the-art, in Sect. 3 we discuss the foundation of our model and in Sect. 4 the proposed approach for a real-world application. Next, we describe in Sect. 5 experimentation and computational results. Finally, we present our conclusions and some future directions.

2 Literature Review

VRP is a type of transportation problem, which has many applications in real life such as logistics and transportation. This problem is an NP-hard that needs to find an optimal set of routes for serving a set of customers by a fleet of vehicles [1]. It generalizes the Travelling Salesman Problem (TSP) by including different vehicles from the departure point and aims at minimizing the total cost for all the vehicle tours with a solution that consider the shortest path ensuring that each customer is visited exactly once by a vehicle. Christofides' algorithm [3], proposed in 1976, tackle the TSP, but its insights and principles have influenced approaches to solving the VRP when it is reduced to a series of TSP instances. The algorithm consists of four steps: (i) Find a Minimum Spanning Tree (MST) of the graph, (ii) find a minimum weight perfect matching to form a multigraph, i.e., a graph where multiple edges between the same pair of vertices, are allowed, (iii) form a multigraph (a graph where multiple edges between vertices are allowed), and (iv) build a Hamiltonian circuit (a closed tour that visit each vertex once) from the multigraph by skipping repeated vertices.

The goal of Capacity VRP (CVRP) is to determine a set of routes, each starting and ending at the warehouse, while adhering to a limited capacity constraints on each vehicle. In addition, delivery points may include Time Windows (TW) requests: meaning each customer should be visited by only one vehicle during a specified time interval, i.e., CVRPTW problem.

Time Windows constraints have been studied by Solomon and Desrosiers [4] that summarized the routing problems with time windows. On the other hand, for this complex VRP variants such as the VRP with Time Windows in cases where the time windows are relatively loose, adaptations of Christofides' algorithm can be particularly useful in constructing initial feasible solutions that are then improved upon using other optimization techniques as experimented by Ufuk Dereci and Muhammed Erkan Karabekmez [7] for a case study in Turkey. Heuristics and meta-heuristics as Genetic Algorithms [5] and Tabu Search [6] have been proposed in the last decades to solve this class of NP-hard problem. Moreover, the VRP can be Single Depot (SD) or Multi Depot (MD) [8] in case of the departure is a single fixed node or different points.

The focus of this research would be on Multi Depot Capacity Vehicle Routing Problem with Time Windows (MDCVRPTW). For the sake of simplicity, we call it Capacity Vehicle Routing Problem with Time Windows (CVRPTW) with MD. The key objective of MDVRPTW is to minimize the total cost, which can include various factors such as: (i) Total distance or travel time, (ii) Number of vehicles, (iii) Penalties for time window violations, and (iv) combination of costs including operational costs.

Recent research has focused on the MDVRP and optimization of vehicles and routes among multiple depots. Among solution studied, Rapanaki et al. [9] addressed the problem by means of the Artificial Bee Colony (ABC) algorithm, a meta-heuristic approach inspired by the behavior of the real honeybee colony. They compared this approach with other meta-heuristic such as Particle Swarm Optimization and Genetic Algorithms to prove the feasibility. More recently, in December 2023, P. Stodola and J. Nohel [10] explored the adaptation of Ant Colony Optimization (ACO) with Node Clustering. The algorithm was inspired by the behavior of ants in nature when searching for food and it is adopted in conjunction with node clustering for solving the minimization of total costs in MDVRP. Node clustering enhances the algorithm's performance because it is used in the phase of creating a solution when the algorithm searches the next node to be inserted into one of the routes of vehicles (ants).

Goel et al. [11] addresses the stochastic Vehicle Routing Problem with Time Windows which involves uncertainties in customer demands and service times. The authors introduce a mathematical model to estimate potential shortages a vehicle might encounter on its route and to predict the distribution of arrival times at customer locations. They propose an ant colony system-based approach to solve the stochastic VRPTW, noting that optimal solutions for deterministic VRPTW may not be feasible when faced with stochastic variations. Finally, in a previous work [12], we proposed C2VRPTW, a model that assigns capacity to both vehicles and nodes. The variability of time spent at logistic nodes is incorporated into the model to enhance its applicability to real-world scenarios, where logistic nodes in the first mile of the delivery process serve as critical hubs for sorting activities.

Following these research directions, the contribution of this paper is the proposal of a simulation tool based on an overall architecture for first mile and middle-mile delivery tasks for the postal sector and an assessment of impacts on delivery times at varying the size and the fleet of the network.

3 Capacity Vehicle Routing Problem with Time Windows

Every day the items to be delivered are collected at the first mile depots and addressed to the first mile destinations. The connections between nodes indicate the time needed from depot to destination, and the minimization of vehicle is classified as a VRP with multi-depots. The problem falls into the domain of CVRPTW as it requires that node has a fixed time slot to be served and each vehicle has a fixed capacity. Many formulations have been proposed for the CVRPTW. In particular, we refer to the review published by Solomon et al. [4] and the research works of Ursani ed al. [5] and Baldacci et al. [13] which described the problem and its solution, focusing on the state-of-the-art of exact algorithms and meta-heuristics, respectively.

Formally, the CVRPTW with Multi Depots (MD) can be formulated as follows: Let $G = (\mathcal{N} \cup \mathcal{H}, \mathcal{A})$ be a directed graph whose node set is the union of a set $\mathcal{N}$ of customers and a set $\mathcal{H}$ of depots.

Non-negative costs $d_{i,j}$ are associated with each $arc(i, j) \in \mathcal{A}$, representing the travel cost, and $t_{i,j}$ is the travel time to reach $j \in \mathcal{N}$, starting from $i \in \mathcal{N}$, i.e., the difference between the arrival and the starting time of the route.

Each customer $i \in \mathcal{N}$ has a delivery demand q_i, a delivery time window $[a_i, b_i]$ and a vehicle must arrive at the customer before b_i. If it arrives before the time window opens, it has to wait until a_i to service the customer. Moreover, each customer i has a service time s_i^k that expresses the arrival time in the node i, with $k \in \mathcal{K}$ that represents a set of vehicles. Each vehicle has a known capacity $\mathcal{Q}_k \ \forall k \in \mathcal{K}$. In this version of the problem, we assume that all vehicles can be freely associated with any depot: this corresponds to the situation in which the location of the vehicles at the depots is a decision. The vehicles do not necessarily leave their depots at time 0: due to customer time windows, it may delay the departure time to arrive at customer locations within their time windows. According to Solomon et al. [4] formulation, the goal of this problem is the minimization of the total distance travelled by vehicles as described in Eq. (1), where x_{ij}^k expresses whether the vehicle k travelled from node i to node j and it takes the value 0 or 1.

$$\min \sum_{k \in K} \sum_{i \in \mathcal{N}} \sum_{j \in \mathcal{N}, j \neq i} d_{ij} \cdot x_{ij}^k \tag{1}$$

Subject to:

$$\sum_{k \in \mathcal{K}} \sum_{i \in \mathcal{N}, i \neq j} x_{ij}^k = 1 \ \ \forall j \in \mathcal{N} \tag{2}$$

$$\sum_{i \in \mathcal{N}} \sum_{j \in \mathcal{N}} q_i \cdot x_{ij}^k \leq \mathcal{Q}_k \ \ \forall k \in \mathcal{K} \tag{3}$$

$$\sum_{i \in \mathcal{N}} \sum_{j \in \mathcal{N}} q_i \cdot x_{ij}^k \leq \mathcal{Q}_k \ \ \forall k \in \mathcal{K} \tag{4}$$

$$x_{ij}^k \cdot \left(s_i^k + t_{ij} - s_j^k \right) \leq 0 \tag{5}$$

$$a_i \leq s_i^k \leq b_i \ \ \ \forall i \in \mathcal{N}, \ \ \ \forall k \in \mathcal{K} \tag{6}$$

Equations (2) and (3) constrain that each customer can be visited by only one vehicle. Equation (4) ensures that the vehicle capacity is not exceeded. The Eq. (5) establishes the relationship between the vehicle departure time from a customer and its immediate successor. Moreover, constraints in Eq. (6) affirm that the time windows are observed. We assumed that the transportation cost of each vehicle depends on the travelled distance. The transportation network is considered asymmetrical, that is the time spent from node i to reach node j can be different from the time spent from node j to node i.

Capacity constraints are designed to limit the amount of goods or services a vehicle can carry or perform on a single route, ensuring that the solution is feasible in terms of real-world logistics capabilities. In this paper we adopt the formulation described by Birtolo and Torre [12] for a real-world problem where the capacity is assigned to the nodes too, i.e., C2VRPTW with MD. The main goal is to model the first mile sorting scenario, where items and goods are collected in the collection points, addressed to the national sorting centers that have the key task of routing it to destination sorting center. In this scenario the sorting centers act both as depots and customers, according to the goods flow: (i) the sorting center collects the items of its region and routes the items to the national sorting centers according to the destination of the items collected, (ii) the same sorting center receives the items from the other sorting centers for items to be delivered in its region.

4   Simulation Engine for CVRPTW Applied to Real-World Logistic Delivery Problem

4.1   Three Layer Architecture Design

The main depots are the first level of architecture and send and receive items for their networks, in other words they work as pick-up and delivery points. Transshipment nodes are intermediate depots for Delivery Centers, closer to the delivery area than the main depots. And finally, the third level is the delivery centers which are the collection points for customers.

This architecture has been applied to real-world logistic network, as shown in Table 1, where the first-level is the connection among the sorting centers which collect regional items and goods to be delivered and address it to the target sorting center, the second level is the city or the facility acting as a transshipment node for its logistic area to serve, and finally for the third level, each transshipment node address the middle-mile segment to send the item to the target delivery center, the closest to the final addressee.

Table 1. Three level architecture for multi-depot VRP where each first mile sorting centers collects items to send in Italy.

Routing level	Node	Example
Depot	Sorting Center at Origin	Bari
First mile	Sorting Center at Destination	Florence
Intermediate Logistic Node	Transshipment Node	Lucca
Middle-mile end point	Delivery Center	Viareggio

Figure 1 depicts the three layers, i.e., blue circle represents the Origin and Destination of the first level (i.e., multi-depot model), and it is called first mile of the logistic network. This level communicates with the second level of architecture (light blue nodes) in charge of regional distribution of item addressed to the target region. Each intermediate node serves its third level targets that are the delivery centers allocated to each of transshipment node. In the figure, each level relates to direct connection that is not visible in terms of number of vehicles needed for the delivery tasks, that leads to the design of nested VRP problems. In this formulation, we do not consider the time that each vehicles requires to return to the depot because the fleet is managed to avoid the movement of empty vehicles, therefore in our model, each vehicle starts from a depot and there is no need to return to the same depot.

The three-layer architecture describes the routing problem in a flexible way in order to address delivery challenges as the same-day delivery or cost optimization problem. Each layer can be modelled by means of a dedicated VRP formulation as depicted in Fig. 2 and differs for type of operations and vehicle adopted. In a national scenario, the first mile is served by trucks and the sorting machines installed in the node must route the goods and items to the target region and city, for this reason we classify this first level by means of C2VRPTW with MD which extends the capacity constraints to both nodes and nodes [12]. Additional constraints in this level is that each node acting as a depot and at the same time as a customer node, must look for a trade-off between capacity allocated to sorting activities and capacity allocated to delivering received items.

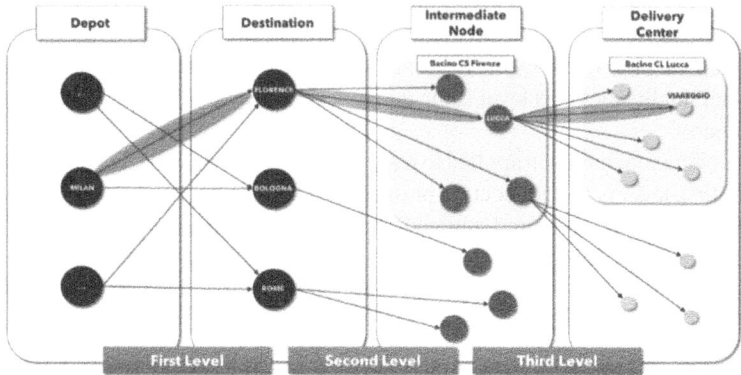

Fig. 1. Three-layer architecture highlighting the direct connections between layers for depot in Milan and destination in Viareggio with a transshipment in Lucca.

The total capacity of each node is allocated: (i) in sorting the items, when the node acts as a depot, and (ii) in routing the received items from the other nodes, when the node acts as a customer of the first level. These constraints have been introduced due to the machine installed in the node that cannot perform the two kinds of operations at the same time.

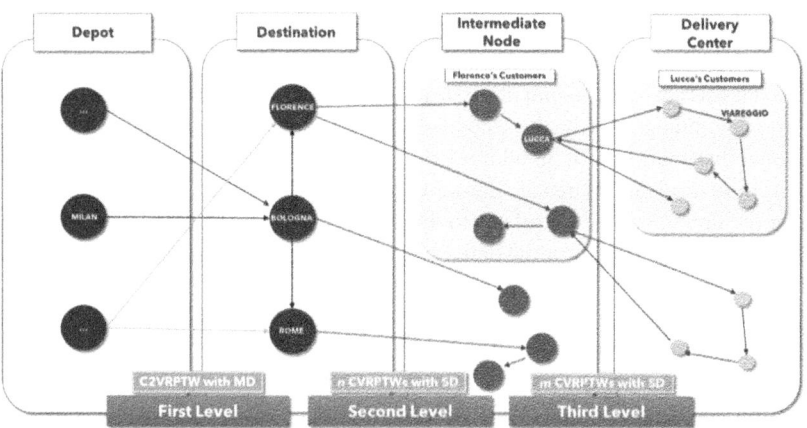

Fig. 2. Mapping of the three-layer architecture with three instances of VRPs.

The second level oversees connection of sorting center, acting as a depot, to the intermediate nodes which are customers without the processing or sorting needs. For this reason, we use for this level a simplified CVRPTW with SD solved by an exact algorithm for the limited number of nodes involved. The last level considers the intermediate nodes as depot and the delivery centers as customers to be served.

The delivery centers have their own time windows, without routing needs and so for this level we can use a CVRPTW with SD. It is a single node because we consider for each intermediate nodes a set of customers to be served with their own vehicle (small tracks or vans). Therefore, the third level is solved by m problems where m is the number of transshipment nodes. In other words, Fig. 2 summarizes the three layers with the adopted VRP formulation: (i) First Layer: long-distance routing between depots and destination hubs, i.e., transportation of goods from depot to key destination hubs, (ii) Second Layer: regional routing from hubs to intermediate nodes, (iii) Third Layer: goods are delivered from intermediate nodes to the end customers or smaller delivery centers (e.g., from Lucca to Viareggio). Each layer of the system ensures a smooth, optimized flow of goods through the hierarchical network, addressing specific constraints and objectives at each stage.

4.2   Simulation Engine for Arrival Time Estimation

We propose a tool for simulating routes and delivery times at varying the network configuration for logistics and delivery route optimization. The system is described in Fig. 3 which outlines the process of retrieving the delivery time per destination and the number of vehicles, routes, and stops. As input the tool requires the number of nodes in the network, a matrix of distances to solve, volumes of collected goods to be delivered in accordance with a fixed service level agreement (e.g., within 2 days), and delivery time windows that is the working time per node.

The Simulator Engine elaborates the results by implementing the following steps: (i) the problem is decomposed by means of the proposed three-layer architecture, (ii) the system starts solving Capacity Vehicle Routing Problem with MD for the first mile and evaluate the arrival time at first level node at destination, (iii) considering the active first level nodes, the system assigns all the second level nodes to a single first level node, (iv) the system solves the resulting Capacity Vehicle Routing Problems with SD and evaluate the arrival time at second level node at destination, (v) considering the active second level nodes, the system assigns all the third level nodes to a single second level node, and (vi) the system solve the resulting VRPs with SD.

4.3   Fitness Function

In order to compare quantitatively the results arising by the different simulation, we propose a fitness function able to look for a trade-off among different criteria as node saturation, estimated arrival time and network cost, providing a score to the logistic experts to compare solutions and extract the optimal one. The fitness is a weighted average of three components: (i) saturation, (ii) delivery time, and (iii) network costs. In the simulations, the best scenario for saturation is to have centers engaged in processing between 60% and 80% (considering 100% as the maximum value, equivalent to 19 working hours). With the aim of minimizing the fitness function, we have conceived a saturation function with: (i) a minimum value if the center operates between 11 and

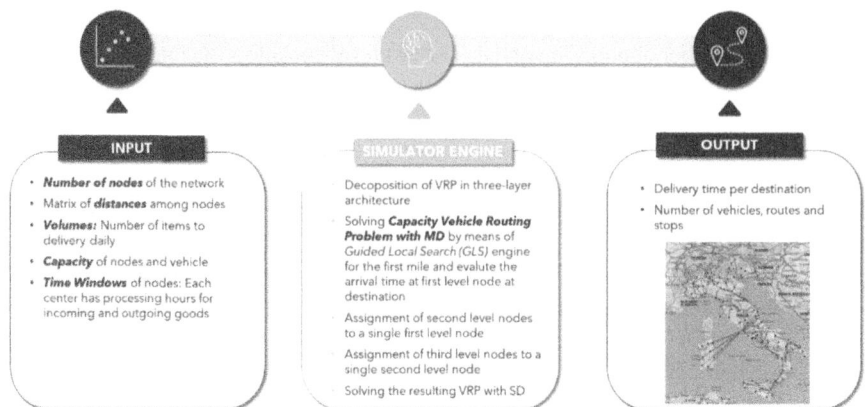

Fig. 3. Simulating routes and expected delivery times at destination

15 h per day (60–80% of its capacity); (ii) a maximum value if the center operates less than 30% of its capacity, e.g., 6 h (strongly undersaturated centers) or if the center is overloaded by working more than 19 h a day (saturated centers).

Figure 4 illustrates the fitness values (y-axis), ranging from 0 (optimal) to 1 (worst), as a function of the saturation level (x-axis). For the entire network assessment, we include in the fitness the average node saturation as the first component.

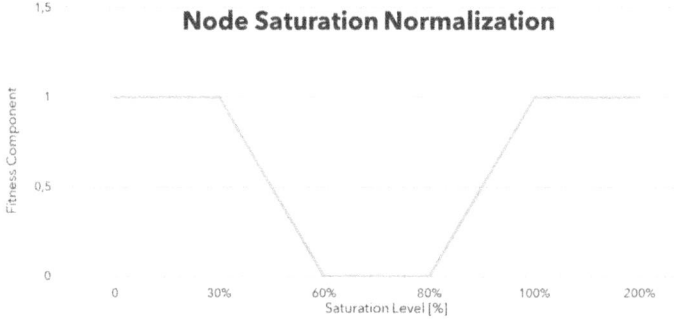

Fig. 4. Fitness Function: Node Saturation Component

The second fitness component keep into account the expected delivery time resulting by addressing the CVRPTW with a fixed number of vehicle and a specified number of active nodes. This addendum considers the average and the maximum elapsed time occurred between a depot and the delivery center closest to the addressee. Finally, the third component simulates the direct cost of the network which is directly proportional to the number of active nodes. Each component has been normalized for providing a value between 0 and 1. Therefore, the simulator provides a fitness value to quantitatively measure the adherence of the proposed solution to the optimal configuration at varying nodes and network parameters.

5   Experimental Results

5.1   Materials and Methods

For our experimentation we consider 3 layers made by 10 sorting centers, 149 intermediate nodes and 715 delivery centers. The sorting center have their own capacity expressed in parcels per hour in sorting activities that is the set of activities performed for routing the items toward other regions and process the item received from the network for the area served. The first layer of architecture is modelled by the proposed C2VRPTW with MD in order to collect in each node the demand and route it to the target nodes. The second layer of architecture is depicted in Fig. 5 where each sorting center is connected to the transshipment nodes. Finally, the last layer of the architecture is modelled by several VRPTWs with SD, one solution per transshipment node that serve a set of customers (i.e., the delivery centers of the logistic network).

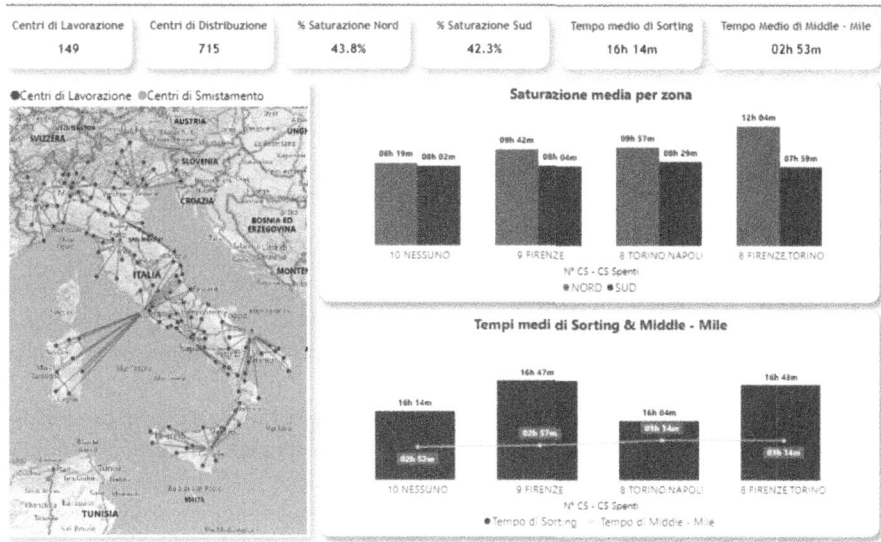

Fig. 5. Power BI Dashboard with sorting centers in yellow and the transshipment node in blue.

5.2   Software

The solution is implemented in Databricks using Python language, while the simulator is realized with Power BI. As computational cluster, we used 8 cores and active memory of 28 GB with Databricks Runtime Version 14.3 LTS that includes Apache Spark 3.5.0, Scala 2.12. Moreover, we integrate Python libraries for the evaluation of distances between nodes and for adapting the VRP solvers, respectively TomTom library and Google OR-Tools [15]. OR-Tools allows executing heuristics and meta-heuristics to solve the VRP and has been developed by Google. CVRPTW is solved by heuristics and meta-heuristics algorithms, respectively. Coordinates, demands (items to be delivered), distance matrix, number and capacities of vehicles, and the sorting centers are inputs of our model. The algorithm implements a solution strategy, i.e., local search option, in order to generate a valid solution. Christofides' algorithm [3] is selected as initial solution strategy and ensures the generation of a feasible solution. Then, Guided Local Search (GLS) option tries to improve initial solution generated by Christofides' algorithm. In our implementation the local search is limited by a fixed number of iteration (avoiding the time limit due to possible reproduction of this experiments in a compute node with different performances) that refers to the maximum number of attempts for algorithm can search for each node.

5.3   Experiment 1: Fixed Nodes and Varying Workload

In this section we focus on the results, the data used in C2VRPTW model and the related constraints. We collected the information related to: (i) the incoming volume i.e., the number of items picked up and delivered from each sorting center (items from origin to destination), (ii) the working time slot per node, (iii) the number and the types of machines installed in each sorting center in order to estimate the related capacity.

To address the real-world logistic capabilities of each center, we estimated the total time requested to process the incoming volume based on machines and human resources. The estimated total time is then directly proportional to the number of items to be delivered (or picked up), to the machine's type used to process them and the number of human resources in the specific sorting center as well.

Once we defined the distance matrix, we developed the first layer using the C2VRPTW model applied to 10 fully connected sorting center. Additionally, we assumed that post offices and local senders collect the items by the 5 pm daily and these items are processed by each sorting center from 6 pm daily. The solution provides the routes and the arrival time in the network for each depot.

To deal with logistic constraints related to the non-parallelization of processing activities within the sorting centers, mainly due to a limited number of machines handling sorting jobs and the available human resources, we did not allow processing job into sorting centers when they are engaged in processing items coming from sorting center within the network. In other words, the time slot allocated to collecting the items and send them to the entire networks differs from the working time allocated for processing the incoming volume.

The model also allows the monitoring of sorting centers' working time, aiming at identifying centers where a volume increase may lead to delivery time increases. For this purpose, we run the model in three different scenarios: (i) a standard load, (ii) volumes with 20% of increase per each segment, and (iii) volumes increased of 50% compared to the annual average daily load. If we consider that a sorting center can perform sorting operations maximum 19 h per day (leaving 5 h for maintenance or administrative tasks), Fig. 6 shows that if the volume increase by 50%, Padova is not able to process them in a single day, resulting in an increase of the delivery times.

Our experimentation is extended to the second and third level of the proposed architecture as described in Sect. 4. As example of application (see Fig. 7), we run the

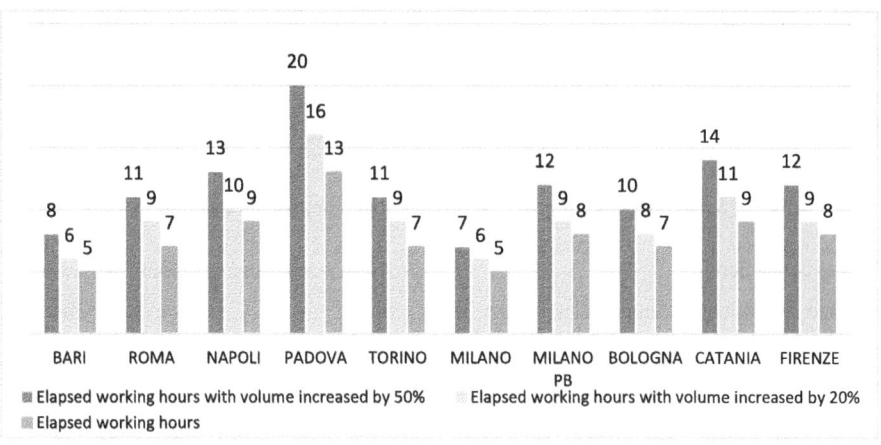

Fig. 6. Sorting centers' working time in three different scenarios

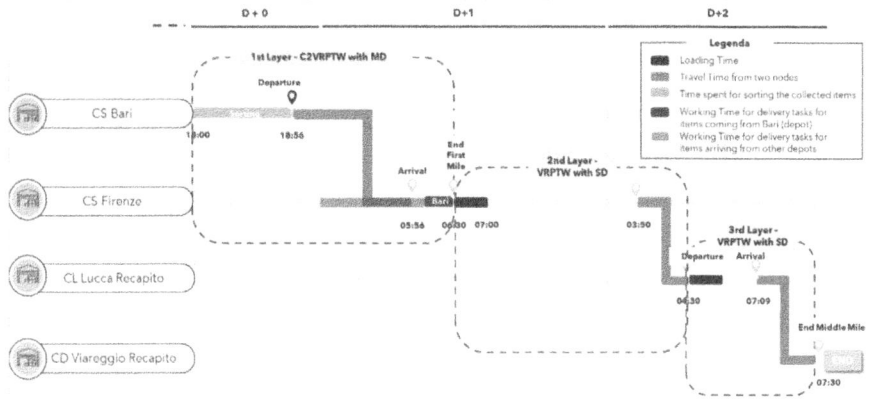

Fig. 7. Analysis of mail flow from Bari (depot) to Viareggio (end customer)

VRPTW instance with SD, because the set of customers is fixed per each sorting center at destination (e.g., Firenze) and each transshipment node (e.g., CL Lucca Recapito).

5.4 Experiment 2: Varying the Number of Sorting Nodes

The tool also provides a mean to compare the different performance when different nodes have been activated. From the one hand, the more the sorting centers are adopted the higher the network costs increase. On the other hand, a reduced network could not satisfy the time constraints and could not lead to a viable routing solution. For this reason, we compare the results obtained with 4 different scenarios by means of the defined fitness function which is described in Sect. 4.3. For the normalization of the fitness components, we consider the maximum allowed sorting and delivery time and we divided the resulting time in order to have a simulated value equals to 1 in this worst case scenario. Similarly for the nodes, we consider as the worst scenario 10 active nodes (maximum value) for cost implications and 8 active nodes as the ideal configuration (minimum value). The VRP does not produce a solution that does not satisfy the specified time constraints.

Table 2. Scenario 1: 10 Sorting Centers - Fitness components and overall value.

Fitness component	Normalized Value	Simulated Value
Average Saturation of Centers (Nord area)	0.38	8 h and 20 min
Average Saturation of Centers (South Area)	0.36	8 h
Number of nodes	1	10 nodes
Average Sorting Time	0.35	16 h and 30 min
Average Delivery Time in middle-mile endpoint	0.14	3 h
Total Fitness Value	**0.44**	

All the scenarios have a standard daily workload but differs for the network configuration: (i) Scenario 1 includes all the 10 sorting centers as depicted in Fig. 6, (ii) Scenario 2 foresees 9 sorting centers (i.e., Firenze is not considered in this daily simulation), (iii) Scenario 3 foresees 8 sorting centers (i.e., Firenze and Torino have not been activated in the daily activities), and (iv) Scenario 4 maintains 8 sorting centers, but deallocates Napoli and Torino, i.e., in the day of the simulation only 8 sorting centers process the national collected workload.

Table 3. Scenario 2: 9 Sorting Centers - Fitness components and overall value

Fitness component	Normalized Value	Simulated Value
Average Saturation of Centers (Nord area)	0.46	9 h and 40 min
Average Saturation of Centers (South Area)	0.36	8 h
Number of nodes	0.5	9 nodes
Average Sorting Time	0.39	17 h
Average Delivery Time in middle-mile endpoint	0.14	3 h
Total Fitness Value	**0.38**	

The results of the first two scenario are depicted in Table 2 and in Table 3 respectively where the benefits obtained by reducing the value of number is only partially mitigated by the increased sorting time for reaching Florence area and the increased saturation of nodes that are replacing the inactive one. The average time needed by sorting centers located in north of Italy increase of 80 min due to deallocation of Firenze in the Scenario 2. The last two scenarios investigate the configuration with 8 nodes at varying the active ones and prove the sustainable benefits of the reduced costs due to the reduction of 2 nodes (from 10 nodes of Scenario 1 to 8 nodes of Scenario 3 and 4). As depicted in Table 4 and in Table 5, the negative impacts are the increased saturation of remaining sorting centers, but the simulator prove the sustainable scenario in term of delivery time and the resulting fitness expresses an optimized solution decreasing from original 0.44 of Scenario 1 to 0.27 value reached in Scenario 4.

Table 4. Scenario 3: 8 Sorting Centers - Fitness components and overall value

Fitness component	Normalized Value	Simulated Value
Average Saturation of Centers (Nord area)	0.60	12 h
Average Saturation of Centers (South Area)	0.36	8 h
Number of nodes	0	8 nodes
Average Sorting Time	0.39	17 h
Average Delivery Time in middle-mile endpoint	0.15	3 h and 10 min
Total Fitness Value	**0.30**	

Table 5. Scenario 4: 8 Different Sorting Centers - Fitness components and overall value

Fitness component	Normalized Value	Simulated Value
Average Saturation of Centers (Nord area)	0.47	10 h
Average Saturation of Centers (South Area)	0.39	8 h and 30 min
Number of nodes	0	8 nodes
Average Sorting Time	0.33	16 h
Average Delivery Time in middle-mile endpoint	0.15	3 h and 10 min
Total Fitness Value	**0.27**	

6   Conclusions and Future Works

In the vehicle routing problem with capacity and time window (CVRPTW), the objective is to minimize the number of vehicles with a fixed capacity and then minimize the total time travelled. In this paper we considered time constraints and the limited capacity of logistic nodes for real-world application in logistic domain. We propose a tool that incorporating information about sorting nodes, delivery nodes, travel distances, and daily demand, allows the simulation of arrival times at each destination point. Computational experiments are presented to demonstrate the effectiveness of the proposed approach. Execution time of each simulation is strongly related to the compute instance of Databricks environment and the specified stopping criteria of Guided Local Search component (i.e., specified number of iterations). This formulation and the proposed solution allow logistic designers to evaluate the impact of volume and capacity changes on the final delivery times at the expected delivery points for the design of same-day delivery services. In our model the distance between nodes of the networks is expressed in time by means an asymmetrical matrix that consider the average travel time between two nodes. As future work, we plan to investigate how the solution varies across different days and times of day. This will be achieved by incorporating a time-of-day-dependent distance matrix to account for potential traffic jams and delays. Moreover, we will propose an optimization engine for the network design by means of Genetic Algorithm approach [14] which provide promising results in optimization problems and can suggest the optimal configuration of the problem parameters.

Disclosure of Interests. The authors declare that they have no known competing financial interests or personal relationships that could have appeared to influence the work reported in this paper.

References

1. Dantzig, G.B., Ramser, J.H.: The truck dispatching problem. Manag. Sci. **6**, 80–91 (1959)
2. Cattaruzza, D., Absi, N., Feillet, D., González-Feliu, J.: Vehicle routing problems for city logistics. EURO J. Transp. Logist. **6**(1), 51–79 (2017)
3. Christofides, N.: Worst-case analysis of a new heuristic for the travelling salesman problem. Carnegie Mellon University (1976)
4. Solomon, M.M., Desrosiers, J.: Survey paper—time window constrained routing and scheduling problems. Transp. Sci. **22**(1), 1–13 (1988)
5. Ursani, Z., Essam, D., Cornforth, D., Stocker, R.: Localized genetic algorithm for vehicle routing problem with time windows. Appl. Soft Comput. **11**(8), 5375–5390 (2011)
6. Hedar, A., Bakr, A: Three strategies tabu search for vehicle routing problem with time windows. Comput. Sci. Inf. Technol. **2**(2), 108–119 (2014)
7. Dereci, U., Erkan Karabekmez, M.: The applications of multiple route optimization heuristics and meta-heuristic algorithms to solid waste transportation: a case study in Turkey. Decis. Anal. J. **4** (2022)
8. Bettinelli, A., Ceselli, A., Righini, G.: A branch-and-cut-and-price algorithm for the multi-depot heterogeneous vehicle routing problem with time windows. Transp. Res. Part C: Emerg. Technol. **19**(5), 723–740 (2011)
9. Rapanaki, E., Psychas, I., Marinaki, M., Marinakis, Y.: An artificial bee colony algorithm for the multiobjective energy reduction multi-depot vehicle routing problem. In: Matsatsinis, N., Marinakis, Y., Pardalos, P. (eds.) Learning and Intelligent Optimization. LION 2019, LNCS, vol. 11968. Springer, Cham (2020)
10. Stodola, P., Nohel, J.: Adaptive ant colony optimization with node clustering for the multidepot vehicle routing problem. IEEE Trans. Evol. Comput. **27**(6), 1866–1880 (2023)
11. Goel, R., Maini, R., Bansal, R.: Vehicle routing problem with time windows having stochastic customers demands and stochastic service times: modelling and solution. J. Comput. Sci. **34**, 1–10 (2019). https://doi.org/10.1016/j.jocs.2019.04.003
12. Birtolo, C., Torre, F.: C2VRPTW: Assigning capacity to vehicles and nodes in a Vehicle Routing Problem for real-world delivery application. In: Proceedings of the 18th Learning and Intelligent Optimization Conference, 9–13 June 2024, Ischia, Italy (2024)
13. Baldacci, R., Toth, P., Vigo, D.: Exact algorithms for routing problems under vehicle capacity constraints. Ann. Oper. Res. **175**(1), 213–245 (2010)

14. Troiano, L., Birtolo, C.: Genetic algorithms supporting generative design of user interfaces: examples. Inf. Sci. **259**, 433–451 (2014)
15. Furnon, V., Perron, L.: OR-Tools Routing Library v9.8. Google (2023). https://developers.google.com/optimization/routing/

Chain of Portable Health Folders: A Systematic Literature Review

Duarte Mateus[1]([envelope]) [iD], Ana Lúcia Martins[1] [iD], and Ricardo Correia[2] [iD]

[1] Iscte – University Institute of Lisbon (Iscte-IUL), Business Research Unit (BRU-IUL),
Lisbon, Portugal
dnrgm@iscte-iul.pt, almartins@iscte.pt
[2] BioGHP – Global Health Platform, Lisbon, Portugal
ricardo@bioghp.com

Abstract. The rise of Information Technologies' influence during the 3rd industrial revolution led to the development of Digital Health Records, with Electronic
Health Records (EHRs) and Personal Health Records (PHRs) beginning patient
empowerment. Today, Health Wallets (HWs), leveraging technologies like Fast
Healthcare Interoperability Resources (FHIR) and Blockchain, represent the next
step in this evolution, focusing on patient-centric health management, and the
growing need for availability, transparency, privacy, and reliability. The paper,
henceforth, will conduct a Systematic Literature Review, following the PRISMA
framework, with the aim of exploring the characteristics of existing patient information platforms, the advantages and limitations of their use, and gaps in the current solutions. An initial search yielded 850 articles, of which 36 were included
in the analysis. The results show that healthcare professionals generally support
the integration of HWs into practice, with accelerated research and implementation following the COVID-19 pandemic. These platforms aim for secure data
management, although challenges persist, particularly in terms of interoperability,
and data protection. Benefits include Patient empowerment, better treatment, and
cost reduction as well as operational efficiency. Despite some resistance due to
established routines and patient eHealth literacy, key issues are mitigated by key
technologies such as FHIR, Blockchain, Role Based Access Control (RBAC), and
Bidirectional Communication. Research should focus on the ability of Health Wallets to integrate seamlessly with existing systems to avoid additional complexity,
enhance privacy, enhance user experience, and improve healthcare efficiency.

Keywords: Digital Wallet · Healthcare Folder · Systematic Literature Review

1 Introduction

Since the 1950s, the 3rd industrial revolution paved the way for an economy driven by
information technology. The healthcare sector was first impacted by the development
of both Electronic Medical Records (EMRs) and Electronic Health Records (EHRs)
[8], which manifested in a shift from paper-based documentation to digital records,

A. Kocian et al. (Eds.): INTSYS 2024, LNICST 608, pp. 98–122, 2025.
https://doi.org/10.1007/978-3-031-86370-7_7

revolutionizing how healthcare data is accessed and stored. These early digital systems helped not only to simplify processes in hospitals and clinics, but also assist in the prevention of the loss of information while aiding with both communication of data and information and efficiency in the access of data.

These investments were primarily provider-centric, focusing on the needs of healthcare providers rather than the patients. However, as these naturally developed, technologies such as the Personal Health Records (PHRs) [9] appeared, allowing for the beginning of patient empowerment, and facilitating a more active role in managing their own health data. This empowerment was further guaranteed by the expansion of Wearable [10] technologies and Over-the-counter (OTC) [11] health records, generating vast amounts of data and emphasizing the need for systems that provide patients access and control. This growth in patient participation saw its rhythm accelerated from the Covid-19 pandemic, requiring an increase in health literacy [12, 13] (with prophylactic measures put into practice). Social distancing also put an emphasis on technological literacy. eHealth literacy grew in importance as patients grew in awareness.

Despite these advancements, significant challenges remain in how health data is managed and shared across different platforms and made visible to its users and owners. The growth in data visibility and availability was not accompanied by management capabilities and operation efficiency or standardization methods, hence the pressing issue of data fragmentation. Interoperability problems not only persist but increase exponentially with the growing amount of information available, as well as, with different healthcare systems using incompatible formats and standards, a hurdle in data exchange, affecting the continuity of care [14]. Additionally, with the continuous usage of informatic means [15, 16], concerns about privacy and security have grown.

In response to these challenges, Health Wallets (HWs) have emerged as a promising solution. These are portable health record management systems, similar to folders but that allow for information transactions, representing the next step in the evolution of digital health records, as a parallel to the wallets increasingly used for payments [17]. HWs are secure, portable digital tools that allow individuals to manage, access, and share their health data across various healthcare settings. Unlike traditional health records, HWs are user-centric, giving patients full control over their data alongside the possibility for value co-creation, a bigger intervention, and cooperation in the processes [18].

With its ability to leverage modern technologies like Blockchain and Fast Healthcare Interoperability Resources (FHIR), health wallets aim to address issues related to data privacy, interoperability, and patient empowerment. While Blockchain ensures that sensitive data remains secure and immutable, allowing for Access Control and Selective Parameter Sharing, FHIR facilitates the smooth exchange of information across different healthcare systems, creating formalized methods of exchanging information and guaranteeing a reduction of constant manual handling [2, 17, 18].

The importance of Health Wallets (HWs) has only grown in recent years due to several key trends in healthcare: the continuous shift towards a patient-centered care model, the rise of telemedicine, and remote healthcare services —accelerated by the COVID-19 pandemic—which emphasized the critical need for secure, accessible health data management [19, 20]. In this evolving landscape, HWs are uniquely positioned to bridge significant gaps in digital health systems, aiming to offer a secure way to integrate and manage the vast amounts of health data generated by wearables, mobile apps, and healthcare providers—data that remains vulnerable in current systems.

Despite their potential, research on HWs remains limited and fragmented. There is a critical lack of consolidated investigations into the specific benefits, challenges, and adoption of these technologies. Crucially, the diminishing marginal returns of introducing yet another tool in an already crowded healthcare technology landscape have not been explored, nor have the effects of eHealth literacy on adoption and continuous usage. Additionally, the essential requirements for effectively integrating HWs into existing healthcare processes are still unclear.

Today, several studies are addressing Health Wallets, their technicalities, benefits and limitations however, none was found that consolidates and compares them. This research aims to address this gap by comparing the current Health Wallet solutions. In doing so, it will answer the following research questions (RQ): 1) Are current developments and solutions in Health Wallet technologies sufficient to overcome existing challenges in healthcare?; 2) What are the key requirements for sustainable usage of a Health Wallet?; and 3) Are all requirements linked with a technology?;

This study resorts to a Systematic Literature Review, examining the state of technology integration in healthcare, identifying key benefits and challenges, and analyzing the conditions that influence HW adoption and sustained use.

The remainder of the article is organized as follows: it will begin by disclosing the Systematic Literature Review (SLR) pathway; then it will address the findings from the SLR and discuss them, leading to the identification of gaps in the current knowledge.

2 Systematic Literature Review

2.1 Search Strategy

To identify relevant articles, a Systematic Literature Review was conducted. Following the Preferred Reporting Items for Systematic Reviews and Meta-Analysis (PRISMA) framework, searches were conducted in 3 Databases – IEEE Xplore, Scopus (main collection), and PubMed, and 5 distinct keywords ("Health Wallet", "Digital Health Wallet", "Personal Health Wallet", "Healthcare Wallet", "Medical Wallet") were used, joined by closely related words and/or synonyms. The closely related words used next to "Wallet" were "Folder" and "App", since these may approach the matter at hand from different perspectives.

The search relied on Boolean operators (AND, OR, NOT) in all databases – "Health Wallet" OR "Digital Health Wallet" OR "Personal Health Wallet" OR "Medical Wallet" AND "Healthcare Wallet" NOT "Financial Wallet". Filters were applied in relation to the used language, allowing English or Portuguese.

2.2 Selection Process

The selection process was conducted systematically and in alignment with the PRISMA framework and guidelines (see Fig. 1). The selection process was carried out independently by the researchers and the compared. Whenever the classification (inclusion or not) was different, discussion followed until a consensus was reached. This input was instrumental in ensuring a holistic and comprehensive review. The studies were selected through content analysis, i.e., excluding papers that did not showcase either of the intervenient perspectives (Physician or Patient side). Topics such as Management, Technology Management or Innovation Management were also prioritized.

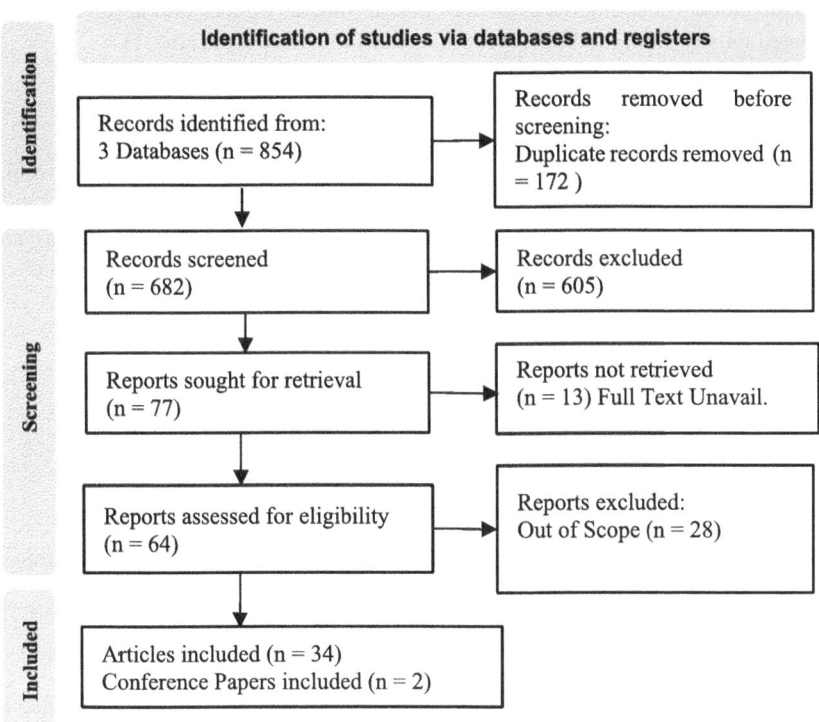

Fig. 1. PRISMA Diagram

2.3 Search Results

Out of 854 records identified from three databases (122 from IEEE Xplore, 391 from PubMed, and 342 from Scopus), 173 duplicates were removed through the usage of Mendeley, ensuring 682 distinct records for screening. From the title and abstract, 605 were excluded since they were irrelevant to this research. 77 records were sought for full-text retrieval. 64 were obtained, since 13 reports were excluded due to the unavailability of their full documents. Post retrieval, upon fully analysing the reports, 28 records were excluded as they were out of scope. Decision made from the apparent lack of attention to the medical professional's side of the interchange required in a Wallet, with ultimately their input being disregarded.

Consequentially, 36 studies were included in the systematic review for analysis. Of these 34 were peer-reviewed academic journal articles, and 2 were conference papers. This inclusion was deemed necessary to capture the rapid developments in the field.

Of the identified studies, only 4 were published before 2017, and since then, there has been a clear tendency to increase the number of publications on the topic per year (See Fig. 2). The final selection of 36 studies encompasses research from various regions across the globe, reflecting the growth of health folders, wallets, and apps. The studies originated mostly from the USA, Australia, and India (See Appendix 1).

2.4 Study Categorization

Groups. After a first content analysis of the collected literature, five distinct groups of articles emerged, based on recurring themes, objectives, and focus areas found across the papers. The group creation process identified patterns in how the articles approached the integration of technology in healthcare, as well as how they tackled related benefits, challenges, and specific features.

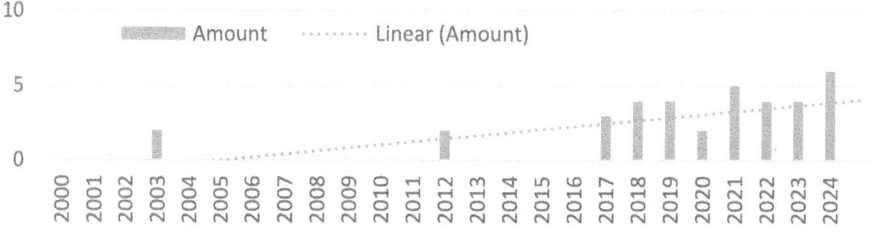

Fig. 2. Studies per Year of Publication

Many studies took a broader view of how digital tools are used and integrated into healthcare systems, forming a category that connected health wallets to overall technology adoption in healthcare. Conversely, several studies balanced advantages and challenges specific to HW/PHR introduction into the sector. There were however others that focused on narrower, more specific aspects, such as requirements from HWs and issues with eHealth literacy. While most studies focus on introducing a technology, there were some, that analyzed post-implementation usage, i.e., continuous intention to use a tool.

Accordingly, the articles were split into five: "Benefits and Challenges in a Health Wallet", "Continuous Intention to Use a Health Wallet", "eHealth Literacy", "Requirements from the Health Wallet", and "Technology Integration in Healthcare Systems" (See Tables 1, 2, 3, 4, and 5).

– Benefits and Challenges in a Health Wallet: This category includes studies that examine both the advantages and obstacles of implementing health wallets or similar technologies. Key topics include data security, user reluctance (both from medical professionals and patients), interoperability, and innovation culture/resistance to change.

- Continuous Intention to Use a Health Wallet: This category focuses on studies that explore post-implementation usage, examining what is most important for users and exploring both ongoing use and long-term retention.
- eHealth Literacy: Studies in this category address not only users' ability to use technology but also how literacy impacts adoption and effective use. These studies look at the influence of users' familiarity with health-related technologies.
- Requirements from technologies: This category encompasses studies that focus on essential features, technologies, and functionalities that users need from a wallet.
- Technology Integration in Healthcare Systems: Studies under this category assess the broader landscape of technology in healthcare, how the system has adapted to these changes, and how previous technologies were implemented.

Categories. The groups built above showcase the topics approached by the paper when discussing HWs' implementation. However, there can be a parallel categorization made from the major conclusions achieved, i.e., if the paper relies on specific technologies, benefits, challenges, or requirements to justify the addition (or not) of the tool - what technologies should be used, what benefits should be sought after, what challenges should a possible implementation prepare to face and what users require from the tool for it to add value to their value-creation.

The Technology Integration category became vital to understand what previous technologies have been used in the healthcare systems, how they were implemented, what can be built upon them, and what challenges they have faced. From this need, all papers will be divided into 4 key research concerns, according to which they address:

- Technologies either used or with the intent to use;
- Benefits either felt or foreseen;
- Challenges felt after the introduction of the technology or foreseen, and;
- Requirements from a tool, for it to add value to its users.

Table 1. Categories per Group - Benefits & Challenges in a HW

	Technology	Benefits	Challenges	Requirements
Equey et al. (2024)	x	x	✓	x
Galetsi et al. (2023)	✓	x	✓	✓
Khodadad-Saryazdi (2021)	✓	✓	✓	✓
Zhang et al. (2024)	✓	✓	✓	✓
Zhou et al. (2019)	✓	x	✓	✓

Table 2. Categories per Group - Continuous Intention to Use a HW

	Technology	Benefits	Challenges	Requirements
Chiu et al. (2020)	x	x	✓	x
Daragmeh et al. (2021)	x	x	✓	✓
Yadav et al. (2022)	x	x	✓	x

Table 3. Categories per Group - eHealth Literacy

	Technology	Benefits	Challenges	Requirements
Elgamal (2024)	x	x	✓	✓
Estrela et al. (2023)	x	x	✓	✓

Table 4. Categories per Group - Requirements from Technologies

	Technology	Benefits	Challenges	Requirements
Baek et al. (2018)	✓	✓	✓	✓
Birkmeyer et al. (2021)	✓	✓	✓	✓
Esmaeilzadeh & Sambasivan (2017)	✓	✓	✓	✓
Keshta & Odeh (2021)	✓	✓	✓	✓
Martínez-Pérez et al. (2015)	✓	✓	✓	✓
Schroeder et al. (2024)	✓	✓	✓	✓
Sengupta et al. (2024)	✓	✓	✓	✓
Sreejith & Senthil (2023)	✓	✓	✓	✓

3   Results

3.1   Group Analysis

Requirements. For a successful implementation and continuous usage of the Health Wallet (See Table 7), Interoperability (n = 15), Access Control mechanisms (n = 13), User-friendly (n = 13), having Patient Management systems (n = 13), allowing for Parameter Sharing (n = 12), maintaining a Privacy Policy (n = 12) and a Connection with Medical Professionals (n = 12) are seen as vital for at least a third of all papers.

These requirements were consistently identified as essential for ensuring correct integration and usability, not just for HWs but for most technology integration in healthcare - allowing for improved coordination, enhanced outcomes, and greater efficiency in healthcare delivery. By meeting these requirements, HWs can facilitate data sharing

Table 5. Categories per Group - Technology Integration into Healthcare

	Technology	Benefits	Challenges	Requirements
Alamri et al. (2021)	✓	✓	✓	✓
Ali et al. (2021)	✓	✓	✓	✓
Belfiore et al. (2022)	✓	✓	x	x
Beratarrechea et al. (2014)	✓	✓	x	✓
Fotiadis et al. (2018)	✓	✓	✓	✓
ICACCS (2019)	✓	✓	✓	✓
ICTAS (2019)	✓	✓	✓	✓
Karadas et al. (2023)	✓	✓	x	✓
Kebodeaux (2019)	✓	✓	✓	✓
Kharrazi et al. (2012)	✓	✓	✓	✓
Morton et al. (2021)	✓	✓	✓	✓
Motta & Furuie (2003)	✓	✓	✓	✓
Patel (2017)	✓	✓	✓	✓
Ranjan et al. (2018)	✓	✓	✓	✓
Tully et al. (2020)	✓	✓	x	x
Ueckert et al. (2003)	✓	✓	✓	✓
Utsha & Morshed (2024)	✓	✓	✓	✓
Van Der Storm et al. (2023)	✓	✓	✓	✓

between users with the correct authentication, making them easier, more secure, accessible, and able to cooperate with multiple organizations without human intervention. Still relevant and shown in several studies, Health Data collection, Authentication, and Minimizing time and Cost, which should also be prioritized in HW design. Not all features developed in the studies are associated with HWs, video calls, and feedback mechanisms (only referenced in 4 studies), e.g., indicate that, while useful, there is no apparent need to prioritize them in the design of HWs.

Technologies. Across the studies, a diverse range of technologies were discussed as an integral part of both the development and the operation of HWs. EHR/EMR (n = 22) and Cloud-based solutions (n = 14), emerged as the most frequently mentioned technologies for their key roles in data storage and accessibility. Equally important, PHRs, Role Based Access Control (RBAC), and Telemedicine were also highlighted, usually approached given their importance in security, patient management, and remote care. It becomes clear that any tool introduced in healthcare must assure the correct management and transmission of information, reducing dissemination, and preventing loss, while aiming to increase patient participation in the process.

Lesser-known technologies such as Selective Sharing (n = 7), Wearable Devices (n = 7), FHIR (n = 5), and Blockchain (n = 5) were shown in some of the most recent

Table 6. Categories: Topics Approached per Study

	Technology	Benefits	Challenges	Requirements
Alamri et al. (2021) [2]	✓	✓	✓	✓
Ali et al. (2021) [21]	✓	✓	✓	✓
Baek et al. (2018) [22]	✓	✓	✓	✓
Belfiore et al. (2022) [19]	✓	✓	x	x
Beratarrechea et al. (2014) [23]	✓	✓	x	✓
Birkmeyer et al. (2021) [24]	✓	✓	✓	✓
Chiu et al. (2020) [25]	x	x	✓	x
Daragmeh et al. (2021) [15]	x	x	✓	✓
Elgamal (2024) [12]	x	x	✓	✓
Equey et al. (2024) [2626]	x	x	✓	x
Esmaeilzadeh & Sambasivan (2017) [1]	✓	✓	✓	✓
Estrela et al. (2023) [13]	x	x	✓	✓
Fotiadis et al. (2018) [27]	✓	✓	✓	✓
Galetsi et al. (2023) [28]	✓	x	✓	✓
ICACCS (2019) [2929]	✓	✓	✓	✓
ICTAS (2019) [30]	✓	✓	✓	✓
Karadas et al. (2023) [31]	✓	✓	x	✓
Kebodeaux (2019) [11]	✓	✓	✓	✓
Keshta & Odeh (2021) [5]	✓	✓	✓	✓
Kharrazi et al. (2012) [32]	✓	✓	✓	✓
Khodadad-Saryazdi (2021) [33]	✓	✓	✓	✓
Martínez-Pérez et al. (2015) [34]	✓	✓	✓	✓
Morton et al. (2021) [35]	✓	✓	✓	✓
Motta & Furuie (2003) [36]	✓	✓	✓	✓
Patel (2017) [18]	✓	✓	✓	✓
Ranjan et al. (2018) [17]	✓	✓	✓	✓
Schroeder et al. (2024) [37]	✓	✓	✓	✓
Sreejith & Senthil (2023) [14]	✓	✓	✓	✓
Sengupta et al. (2024) [4]	✓	✓	✓	✓
Tully et al. (2020) [10]	✓	✓	x	x
Ueckert et al. (2003) [9]	✓	✓	✓	✓
Utsha & Morshed (2024) [38]	✓	✓	✓	✓
Van Der Storm et al. (2023) [39]	✓	✓	✓	✓
Yadav et al. (2022) [16]	x	x	✓	x
Zhang et al. (2024) [40]	✓	✓	✓	✓
Zhou et al. (2019) [41]	✓	x	✓	✓

Table 7. Number of references per Category of Requirements

	Main Groups	Categories	N°	References
Main Requirements	Data Management & Sharing (R1)	Interoperability	15	[1, 2, 5, 17, 18, 22, 24, 27–29, 32, 33, 37–39]
		Parameter Sharing	12	[5, 9, 11, 18, 21, 22, 24, 27, 29, 32, 37, 38]
		Health Data Collection	11	[1, 5, 11, 14, 24, 27, 28, 32, 34, 38, 41]
		Real-time Data Updates	7	[1, 2, 9, 18, 28, 35, 38]
		Limited Data Retention	8	[1, 5, 28, 30, 36, 38, 39, 41]
	Access & Privacy Control (R2)	Access Control	13	[1, 2, 5, 11, 17, 18, 28–30, 32, 36, 38, 41]
		Privacy Policy	12	[1, 2, 5, 17, 18, 28, 30, 32, 35, 36, 39, 41]
		Authentication	10	[1, 2, 5, 17, 18, 28, 32, 35, 39, 41]
	User Experience & Efficiency (R3)	User-Friendly	15	[9, 11–15, 17, 22, 24, 27, 32, 34, 35, 38, 40]
		Minimize Time & Cost	10	[2, 4, 5, 9, 15, 17, 24, 28, 38, 39]
		Digitaliz. of Processes	9	[1, 5, 14, 18, 27, 29, 30, 32, 33]
		Feedback Mechanisms	4	[14, 22, 32, 33]
		Diagnostic Assisting	8	[1, 4, 11, 24, 28, 31, 32, 37]
	Patient Physician Interaction (R4)	Patient Management	13	[2, 4, 5, 11, 18, 24, 28, 32–35, 37, 41]
		Connect. w. Physicians	12	[1, 5, 18, 21, 24, 28, 31–33, 37–39]
		Video Call	1	[28]
		Remote Monitoring	9	[4, 9, 21, 23, 24, 31, 32, 38]

studies and highlighted for their enhancements on interoperability, data security, and patient engagement, i.e., following the same thought process, increasing the difficulty for non-cleared access of records and doubling down on patient intervention.

Finally, there were also niche solutions like Facial Recognition, Chatbots, Natural Language Processing, and Image Matching that, while less frequently highlighted, showcase a standardization of AI and growing interest in introducing AI-driven tools to support patient care. This trend may also indicate the beginnings of automation in the sector, introducing more advanced tools with minimum human intervention, therefore allowing for more time put into treatment and patient relations (Table 8).

Benefits. The studies revealed several key benefits associated with the implementation of HWs (Fig. 6). The most frequently mentioned advantages included Higher Efficiency (n = 19), Patient-centric Approaches & Empowerment (n = 18), and Better Treatment (n = 12). By Centralizing data, HWs enhance treatment quality, empower patients, and optimize workflows.

Table 8. Number of references per Category of Technology

	Main Groups	Categories	N°	References
Main Technologies	Health Data Management & Systems (T1)	EHR/EMR/HIE/OTC	22	[1, 2, 4, 5, 9–11, 17, 18, 21, 22, 24, 27–29, 31–33, 36, 38, 39, 41]
		PHR	11	[1, 2, 5, 9, 10, 18, 30–32, 36, 38]
		Cloud-based	14	[5, 9, 18, 19, 21, 23, 24, 28–31, 34, 40, 41]
	Security & Access Control (T2)	RBAC	9	[1, 5, 11, 17, 18, 29, 30, 36, 39]
		Selective Sharing	7	[1, 5, 10, 11, 18, 31, 38]
		Electronic Consent	3	[1, 17, 39]
		Blockchain	5	[2, 17, 18, 29, 40]
		Facial Recognition	1	[28]
	Patient Monitoring & Interaction (T3)	Wearable Devices	7	[5, 10, 14, 21, 22, 24, 39]
		Patient Monitor. Devices	4	[14, 31, 34, 35]
		Chat-bot	1	[28]
		Telemedicine	9	[4, 5, 10, 19, 24, 28, 33, 34, 40]
	Data Analytics & Processing (T4)	Machine Learning	5	[19, 27, 28, 34, 38]
		AI	4	[19, 28, 38, 40]
		Natural Lang. Processing	1	[28]
		Image Matching	1	[28]

Cost Reduction (n = 13) and Easier Access to Care (n = 10) are closely linked, as HWs reduce administrative burdens and accelerate access to patient records, leading to faster, more affordable care. This also supports Faster Orientation (n = 4) for healthcare providers who benefit from having readily available patient information, guaranteeing the possibility for a holistic analysis and therefore, better treatment – showcasing how most of the shown benefits are, in fact, interconnected.

Security-related benefits, such as Safety and Security of Information (n = 6), Transparency (n = 4), and Completeness & Accuracy of Data (n = 4), ensure HWs foster greater confidence in digital systems. It should be pointed out that Security is seen as a hurdle, a challenge, in older studies, with more recent analyses considering these tools trustworthy enough to publicize it as a benefit. However, this is not so black-and-white, as the overall research is still split on the ability to protect users.

Benefits such as Promoting Process Flow (n = 9) and Lower Manual Handling (n = 5) emphasize the reduction of administrative tasks, while Scalability (n = 3) and Fewer Hardware Components (n = 3) highlight the long-term sustainability and flexibility of HWs in Healthcare as well as featuring the importance of interoperability in a system (Table 9).

Challenges. Out of the 4 Groups, there are distinctively more joint mentions for Requirements (167) and Challenges (164) than the remaining categories, with Benefits (115) and technologies (109) being less prominent. This, however, only validates the need of the sector to maintain order, standardize, mitigate current problems, and prevent future issues related to a possible introduction of a tool, i.e., confirming the rigidness of the sector.

Table 9. Number of references per Category of Benefits

	Main Groups	Categories	N°	References
Main Benefits	Operational Efficiency (B1)	Higher Efficiency	19	[1, 5, 10, 11, 18–24, 29, 30, 32–34, 36–38, 40]
		Promote Flow of Process	9	[4, 17–19, 23, 32–34, 40]
		Lower Manual Handling	5	[22, 27, 33, 37, 40]
		Faster Orientation	4	[4, 17, 32, 33]
	Scalability & Resource Optimization (B2)	High Scalability	3	[21, 23, 27]
		Less Hardware Comp	3	[17, 23, 27]
		Cost Effective	13	[1, 10, 17, 21–24, 31–34, 45]
	Patient-centric & Empowerment (B3)	Patient-centric & Empower	18	[1, 2, 5, 9, 11, 14, 17, 18, 22–24, 26, 31–33, 37, 38, 40]
		Easier Access to Care	10	[1, 4, 5, 22, 23, 31–33, 35, 38]
		Better Treatment	12	[1, 10, 11, 18, 24, 31–35, 38, 40]
		Better Communication	5	[1, , 2414, 32, 38]
	Patient – Physician Interaction (B4)	Completeness of Records	4	[1, 21, 38, 39]
		Transparency	4	[1, 18, 26, 27]
		Security of Information	6	[1, 18, 24, 27, 29, 36]

The main challenges identified are not unique to HWs, but reflect broader issues related to the use of technology in healthcare (See Fig. 7). Challenges were discussed in 32 of the 36 studies, with the most prominent being Privacy and Confidentiality (n = 22) and Security and Encryption (n = 21), both critical concerns in managing sensitive data. Other significant challenges include Trust and Reliability (n = 15), Interoperability (n = 14), and Literacy and Health Consciousness among users (n = 12).

While other categories are more focused, the 'Challenges' section is notably more dispersed, with 18 distinct challenges identified. This diversity highlights the complexity of integrating HWs into healthcare systems. Rather than diminishing the value of HWs, these challenges underscore the need for further research to address these issues as the technology becomes gradually more well-known (Table 10).

Standards and Regulations. To introduce the technology into existing European healthcare systems, the HW must ensure compliance with current regulatory frameworks and must adhere to various legal and technical standards, such as the General Data Protection Regulation (GDPR), ISO 13485 for medical devices, ENISA guidelines on cybersecurity, and the Cyber Resilience Act. These standards provide guidelines for data protection, security, and overall resilience in health technologies. The table (See Table 2) presents a mapping of these regulatory requirements, outlining how each set of standards applies to the development and deployment of health wallets (Table 11).

Table 10. Number of references per Category of Challenges

Main Groups	Categories	N°	References
Data Security & Privacy (C1)	Privacy & Confidentiality	22	[1,2,5,9,11,14,15,17,18,22,24,28,30,32,34-39,41]
	Security & Encryption	21	[1,2,5,9,11,14,15,17,18,22,24,28,30,32,34,35,37-39,41]
	Ethical Issues & Consent	8	[1,5,11,26,28,29,36,39,41]
	Trust & Reliability	15	[1,2,5,14,18,25,28,30,32-34,37,39-41]
Interoperability & Information Sharing (C2)	Interoperability	14	[1,2,11,17,18,21,23,26,28,31,32,36,37,40]
	Sharing Restrictions	10	[1,5,9,11,17,18,21,26,36,37]
	Incomp./Incorrect Storing	8	[1,5,9,11,17,18,27,39]
	Cooperation	7	[1,11,13,22,26,33,39]
Adoption & User Engagement (C3)	Literacy & Health Consc.	12	[1,12,1113,22,24-26,33,39]
	User At. & Self-efficacy	8	[1111,13,15,18,22,24,33,40]
	Resistance from Profess.	9	[1,4,5,26,33,35,37,39,40]
	Innovation Culture	2	[33,40]
System Usability & Impact on Care (C4)	Depersonalize of Care	6	[1,4,33,35,39,40]
	Intrusiveness	6	[1,5,11,14,36,41]
	Staff Overloading	1	[33]
	Accessibility	5	[1,11,13,24,30]
Cost & Policy Constraints (C5)	High Cost of Health IT	5	[25,35,37,40,41]
	Policies	4	[11,26,33,39]

(Left margin: Main Challenges)

3.2 Result Grouping

The shown data (See Table 2, 3, 4, 5 and Table 6), as mentioned in each article, is further grouped into 4 or 5 main topics. 2 dimensions should be evaluated. Firstly, not all technologies are implemented in today's healthcare landscape so, which ones were implemented, which ones are required, and what's the degree of adoption? Secondly, it becomes clear that several of these groups are related, with technologies often overlapping in purpose, addressing common challenges, or complementing each other to fulfill broader service needs.

4 Discussion

4.1 Relationship Between Groups

Through the analysis of the results, it becomes possible to create a few propositions:

The proposition suggests that obstacles encountered in healthcare can be directly mapped to certain requirements, i.e., manifest as requirements in technologies. *P1*

Table 11. Standards & Regulatory Requirements for HW Compliance

Regulation/ Standard	Category	Requirement	Description/Objective	Relevant Section
GDPR [4244]	Data Privacy & Protection	Content & Data Processing	Requires explicit user consent for Data Collection and Processing	Article 6, 7, 9
	Data Security	Encryption	Protects data through anonym. And encryption	Article 32
ISO 13485 [45]	Medical Device Quality	Quality Management System	Requires a quality management system for medical device manufacturers	Section 4.1, 4.2
	Risk Management	Risk assessment and Hazard Analysis	Focuses on evaluating risks related to the usage of devices	Section 7.1
ENISA [46]	Cybersecurity	Network & Information Security	Establishes security measures for network and information systems	Section 3, ENISA Guidelines
	Incident Response	Incident Notification & Breach Response	Requires creation of breach response procedures	Section 6
Cyber Resilience Act [47]	Security of Digital Products	Security by design	Digital products must integrate security measures from the outset	Section 5.1, 5.2
	Market Surveillance	Continuous Monitoring	Manufacturers must maintain and update Security measures	Section 6.3

implies that understanding present challenges allows for the development of requirements necessary to successfully integrate technologies.

$$P1 \ = \ Challenges\,(C)\ can\ be\ translated\ into\ specific\ Requirements\,(R) \qquad (1)$$

Once the requirements are identified, they can be addressed through the application of appropriate Technologies. For instance, access control requirements can be met with RBAC, while interoperability issues can be mitigated with standards like FHIR and OpenEHR. P2 showcases the role that the right solutions play in addressing defined requirements, bridging challenges, and the solution.

$$P2 = Requirements(R)\ can\ be\ fulfilled\ using\ appropriate\ Technologies\ (T) \quad (2)$$

The third proposition, P3, supports the ability to achieve significant benefits once the proper technologies are implemented to meet established requirements.

$$P3 = Using\ Appropriate\ Technologies\ (T)\ leads\ to\ significant\ Benefits\ (B) \quad (3)$$

Building upon the previous propositions, the final one combines all elements to suggest a comprehensive framework. It proposes that challenges arising from healthcare processes can be systematically targeted by translating them into actionable requirements. These, when met with the appropriate solutions, ultimately yield meaningful benefits. The interconnection between these categories ensures a link between problem identification to problem resolution.

$$P4 = Challenges\ (C),\ identified\ in\ healthcare\ settings\ are\ effectively$$
$$addressed\ through\ their\ translation\ into\ specific\ requirements\ (R),$$
$$which,\ when\ fulfilled\ using\ appropriate\ technologies\ (T),$$
$$lead\ to\ significant\ Benefits\ (B) \quad (4)$$

This shows a connection between groups and between categories - that technology usage in healthcare follows a similar path to other sectors. The alignment of these elements suggests that the integration of Health Wallets into healthcare is not only feasible but could follow a clear and structured approach that mirrors successful technology adoption in other fields.

There are also links more complete than this first linear connection. For instance, using new technologies can originate new challenges, which themselves would require new technologies to fix. Since achieving benefits may restart the process of redefining requirements, we are therefore debating continuous improvement, where the evolving needs of healthcare and technological advancement demand an ongoing process of refinement and adaptation, rather than a static solution.

These categories are therefore not only related but interdependent. Technology will not be introduced without a requirement, or it will not add value. Value is the difference between benefits and challenges, which can both come from the usage of a new technology.

The Venn Diagram (See Fig. 4) showcases how all groups interact with each other.

The combined efforts of all groups create an ecosystem, i.e., state-of-the-art, how everything works in a living organization, in this case, in the healthcare sector. The development and future introduction of a HW should aim to seamlessly enter this system. Introducing technology, answering challenges, creating benefits, and working efficiently and effectively, like a cogwheel in a machine.

The introduction of the Wallet itself will bring new challenges in need of defining into requirements, will involve technologies within the processes for it to function as intended, and will take x amount of time until showcasing its benefits (depending on the learning curve and inertia to learning, e.g.) (Fig. 3).

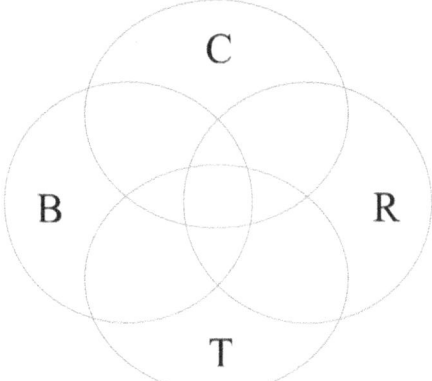

Fig. 3. Links between Categories

This required fluidity aims for future scalability and adaptation to new challenges and requirements that will appear. Tools such as FHIR make the HW scalable and ready to integrate emerging tools, guaranteeing its long-term value and viability. From this knowledge, an iterative approach should be preferred, i.e., the process should position itself as agile development, where improvements are based on real usage and require regular feedback from all stakeholders.

4.2 Technologies Implemented in the Healthcare Sector

In addition to exploring requirements and challenges, the level of adoption of key technologies, such as Blockchain, FHIR, and RBAC, has been analyzed to understand the feasibility of implementing Health Wallets; these have different levels of value-added, ease of usage, and standardization.

Their introduction differs in the time of attempted implementation and in the challenges it created. Equally, their evaluation is vital since it is from past introductions that a future one should be based, i.e., understanding what worked and what did not. From content analysis as well as the number of papers mentioning each one, it is also possible to evaluate the adoption and the life cycle stage at which each technology finds itself (Table 12).

While technologies such as EHRs or Cloud-based systems, showcase widespread adoption in healthcare, Blockchain is still in the early stages of integration. As a parallel, PHR, FHIR, OTC, and Blockchain are still in their early stages of market introduction which makes it difficult to confidently predict issues during implementation.

These technologies' value requires their joint effort, interdisciplinary, i.e., the more of these technologies the healthcare system uses the bigger their benefit, with each one promoting a certain requirement and building on top of the others. Combining them would grant the tool interoperability (from FHIR), between Information Systems (EHR), protected and confidential (Blockchain), with selective and minimum access to the tools (from Selective Sharing and RBAC), available for the patient (PHR, OTC), empowering them to access, store and manage their healthcare data.

Table 12. Implementation Status and Challenges from Technology

Technology	Level of Adoption	Technology Lifecycle Stage
AI	Low	Growth
Blockchain	Low	Growth
Cloud-based	High	Maturity
EHR/EMR/HIE	High	Maturity
FHIR	High	Growth
OTC	Low	Growth
PHR	Moderate	Early Growth
RBAC	High	Maturity
Selective Sharing	High	Maturity
Telemedicine	High	Maturity
ZKP	Pilot-Stage Use	Early Growth

It is only thanks to this coordination that the Health Wallet would be able to be correctly and efficiently implemented into today's healthcare sector.

FHIR and Blockchain in Achieving Interoperability. Both FHIR and Blockchain are transformative for interoperability in healthcare, as each focuses on unique secure, and seamless data exchange. FHIR creates standardized protocols that allow health records to be easily exchanged between EHR systems, reducing redundant data entry, improving data accuracy, and enabling real-time data sharing. This interoperability is crucial for data sharing without manual handling of information and, therefore, the risk of data mismanagement, loss, or manipulation.

Blockchain enhances this data exchange by providing a decentralized, secure ledger where patient information is stored in immutable blocks. Each time data is updated or accessed, a new block is added to the ledger, allowing for the creation of a secure trail that ensures data integrity and prevents tampering. This distributed structure also allows patients to control data access directly, aligning e.g. with patient-centred care models.

In Estonia, a comprehensive eHealth system integrates FHIR and Blockchain to facilitate secure data exchanges within the healthcare sector. Patients access their medical records through a patient portal, enhancing data transparency, accessibility, and continuity of care. Similar initiatives are underway in several other countries. In Australia, Blockchain is used to ensure data integrity across healthcare systems, supported by FHIR for compatibility between these systems.

Blockchain's Role in Privacy. Blockchain's distributed architecture is particularly suited for safeguarding patient privacy [2]. Its cryptographic techniques ensure that once data is entered, it can be neither deleted nor tampered with, providing a secure and transparent record. However, the public nature of Blockchain networks, if not managed carefully, could expose patient data to unauthorized access, making not only robust encryption but also access management essential for any health-related applications.

Regulatory Compliance Frameworks. Any development of the HW should, firstly, acknowledge the need to fulfill any legal requirements, such as the GDPR [42–44] (or HIPAA in the U.S.), ENISA [46], Cyber Resilience Act [47], as well as the ISO 13485 [44, 45]. If its definition does fall into the Medical Device spectrum, it must also follow the Medical Device Regulation (MDR) [48].

HWs that use technologies such as Blockchain must comply with these standards. GDPR mandates explicit consent for data processing, stringent encryption, and data anonymization – requiring only the minimum data to be stored, the least amount of people to access it, and for the shortest time possible - while HIPAA focuses on protecting identifiable health information. To meet these regulatory demands, Blockchain systems can incorporate Zero-Knowledge Proofs (ZKPs), enabling the verification of data without revealing its contents. With ZKPs, e.g., patients could be granted limited access to parts of their records without exposing the full content. These techniques, alongside end-to-end encryption, key management, and advanced access controls.

A notable example of ZKPs in Europe is in the European Self-Sovereign Identity Framework (ESSIF), an initiative under the European Blockchain Services Infrastructure (EBSI)[49], aimed at providing a cross-border blockchain infrastructure to enhance the efficiency and trustworthiness of public services across EU member states. This approach allows individuals to authenticate aspects of their identity to access government or private services without exposing their entire identity, e.g., confirming residency without sharing an address. Although this usage aligns with GDPR's emphasis on data exposure minimization, its widespread implementation is limited.

4.3 The Health Wallet

All of the suggested requirements and technologies, uncovered through content analysis, will work together to achieve the objective of this paper: present a consolidated review of the state of technology integration in healthcare as well as being able to confidently showcase, from their combined efforts, an ideal Health Wallet.

Firstly, any aim at technology introduction in healthcare should have a seamless integration into already existing processes as one of the major outcomes of the development process [17, 44]. This emphasis is vital to the implementation and usage of the Health Wallet to not add to the already present issues in the sector, overcrowding systems, and unnecessarily complicated processes.

The uncovered requirements were introduced following these necessary legal compliances, being a vital part of a Privacy Policy [41]. This Policy also requires an Access Control, which, could be secured, through the usage of RBAC [36], for both minimum dissemination of information and maximum privacy and confidentiality. For additional security, recent studies mention the importance of Blockchain.

Interoperability [22, 29], through the usage of both FHIR (for information transactions between organizations) [6, 14] and OpenEHR (for information transactions within the organization) [9, 21], aims for efficiency from the reduction in manual handling of information, which directly impacts the loss of information as well as requiring additional time and effort on the behalf of the physicians [27].

Patient's trust should be fostered, with their willingness to adopt and consistently use such a tool depending on their trust in data security and the sense of control it provides over their health information, even more so for users with lower digital know-how, hence why user-friendliness should also be prioritized by the developers [12]. UI/UX mechanisms should be put into place, given the existing lack of eHealth literacy [12, 13], easing the learning curve for both medical professionals and patients, aiding in their collaborative value creation, with better Health Data Collection and Parameter Sharing [39].

Continuous Intention to use HWs and other similar tools depends on the users' self-efficacy as well as perceived usefulness, improved by more accessible architectures [15, 16, 25]. Patient-facing features must be designed with inclusivity in mind, considering various demographics, including older adults, those with disabilities, and individuals with limited eHealth literacy.

Varying degrees of eHealth literacy on both patients and healthcare providers will surely hinder adoption and effective use. To overcome this, HW developers should prioritize intuitive, accessible user interfaces (UIs) designed for diverse digital fluency levels. Simplified interfaces with guided onboarding can help ease patients into the systems.

Other than the developers, management has a role in adoption, through which educational initiatives are key. These could include interactive workshops or tutorials that explain the functionalities and usage of HWs. Another approach is integrating HWs with telehealth services, where healthcare professionals can actively engage with patients and directly help them in using it for data sharing and their own health management.

The way to guarantee real value creation and usage is through co-designing for end-users, creating feedback loops, and introducing their input in product development. Studies show that co-designing health platforms during development phases significantly improves usability, accessibility, effectiveness, and overall user satisfaction.

HWs face several implementation barriers, especially in real-world settings where healthcare infrastructure varies significantly. A central limitation lies in their effectiveness which itself is strained by data fragmentation and lack of a standardized approach for data management.

Maintaining a connection with physicians should therefore be central to the tool's implementation. Telemedicine practices help achieve this objective with their focus on accessibility [33]. It should be noted that establishing this connection requires more than the correct tool implementation; it requires time and effort, being vital to the well-being and correct treatment of the patient. Although technologies help with physical proximity, they're not substitutes for the physician-patient relationship and should not be treated as such [28].

Although medical personnel are open to the introduction of these technologies, inertia to change always occurs and, as it seems to be the case with physicians, may be higher for this sector, where older ways of processing information still come about, even with the digitalization of processes [24]. Henceforth, all potential added value depends on the effective involvement of both management and physicians. While Management plays a crucial role in supporting the strategic implementation of the HW, ensuring both the necessary resources and infrastructure, Physicians, will have a profound impact on the day-to-day use of HWs – making their endorsement critical to any and all introductions

[4044]. Catering to its users, and conditioned by Physician's perceptions, feedback loops should be created between developers, management, and medical professionals.

Ultimately, the added value of the Health Wallet lies not only in its architecture and legal frameworks it adheres to, but research also makes it viable to ensure it creates a system that genuinely enhances the delivery of care, aiming to maintain and encourage trust in information technology in healthcare, with the collaboration of medical staff and patients alike, the joint value creation empowers both parties. Hence the ultimate goal, patient empowerment and improved healthcare outcomes, is achieved through a combination of technology, legal frameworks, and the collaboration of all stakeholders.

4.4 Limitations and Future Research

Other than limitations and future research ideas mentioned afterward, the paper may showcase the limitations usual to a Systematic Literature Review, with other possible words or manners of research leading to other articles. The sudden growth in articles around the topic may lead to a surge of new papers not included. Health Wallets can be named or categorized differently which might consist of another limitation.

Currently, as of the time of writing, there seem to be gaps in the literature, especially concerning the diminishing value of introducing another tool in the healthcare sector as well as the relationship between these added tools, the perceived challenges and benefits, and continuous improvement. There is, at this time, a diverse array of papers seeing technology as a stressor for both medical professionals and users with digital tools often leading to frustration, anxiety, and information overload, marking the importance of this future research.

Current solutions value privacy and patient empowerment while seeing value in technology introduction. However, there is not a joint solution, through a tool, using a selection of technologies, that consolidates the concerns and wishes of both patients and medical professionals. The existing Wallets and Folders are found to be lacking from either the medical or patient perspectives, inadequately ambitious, and/or without valued features.

These limitations suggest a need for focused efforts to integrate HWs seamlessly within diverse healthcare environments as well as an increase in education initiatives for improved results, and consequentially, better app usage. Future work should aim to assess the specific needs and pain points of the specific healthcare stakeholders catering to their needs and tailoring solutions. Furthermore, it will be important to find out what initiatives improve eHealth Literacy across different demographics and support higher adoption and engagement with health platforms and apps. Understanding these limitations and building specific solutions around them is crucial for the next stages of HW research.

5 Conclusion

This research highlights the potential of Health Wallets, as well as the status of health-care technology introduction, persisting challenges, and difficulties against sought-after technologies and benefits. The key requirements for successful implementation, such as interoperability, privacy, user-friendliness, and secure data sharing, are supported by emerging technologies and frameworks such as FHIR, Blockchain, and RBAC. Despite the significant benefits, challenges related to privacy, security, and user adoption and retention may persist. Addressing these challenges through targeted development solutions is critical to maximizing the impact of HWs and ensuring their seamless integration into existing healthcare systems. It has been shown that co-designing would be a possible way forward for the tool, catering to specific needs and aiming for as much value as possible for all stakeholders.

The sought-after objective was achieved with some difficulties arising from the novelty of the topic, given the existence of multiple gaps in research, even more so for a unified approach that balances both the needs of patients and healthcare professionals. Equally important to note are the relationships established during the creation of this paper. From the literature analysis, not only were HWs presented and debated, but the healthcare sector as a whole was evaluated. The trade-off of exploring yet another tool against the better usage of persisting tools remains underexplored.

Acknowledgement. This work is supported by the project Blockchain.PT (PRR – RE-C05-i01.02: AGEN-DAS/ALIANÇAS VERDES PARA A INOVAÇÃO EMPRESARIAL).

Appendixes

Appendix 1. Origin of Content

(See Table 13).

Table 13. Authors' Continent of Origin

Continent of Origin	N.º of different origins	Percentage
Africa	1	2,3%
Asia	10	22,6%
Europe	12	27,3%
Oceania	5	11,4%
North America	14	31,8%
South America	2	4,6%
TOTAL	44	100%

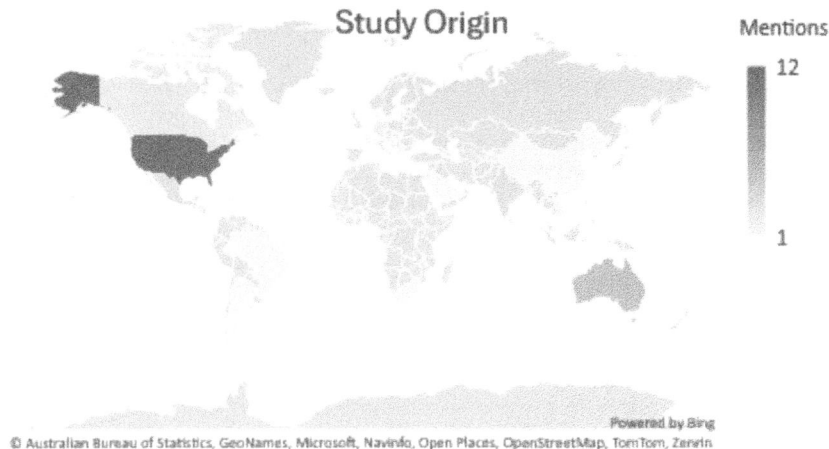

Fig. 4. Country of Origin for Publication

References

1. Esmaeilzadeh, P., Sambasivan, M.: Patients' support for health information exchange: a literature review and classification of key factors. BMC Med. Inform. Decis. Mak. **17**(1) (2017). https://doi.org/10.1186/s12911-017-0436-2
2. Alamri, B., Javed, I.T., Margaria, T.: A GDPR-compliant framework for IoT-based personal health records using blockchain. In: 2021 11th IFIP International Conference on New Technologies, Mobility and Security, NTMS 2021, 19 April 2021. https://doi.org/10.1109/NTM S49979.2021.9432661
3. PRISMA Diagram & Checklist - Systematic Reviews - Research Guides at University of Guelph-Humber (libguides.com). Accessed 06 June 2024
4. Sengupta, A., Sarkar, S., Bhattacherjee, A.: The relationship between telemedicine tools and physician satisfaction, quality of care, and patient visits during the COVID-19 pandemic. Int. J. Med. Inform. **190** (2024). https://doi.org/10.1016/j.ijmedinf.2024.105541
5. Keshta, I., Odeh, A.: Security and privacy of electronic health records: concerns and challenges. Egypt. Inform. J. **22**(2), 177–183. Elsevier B.V. (2021). https://doi.org/10.1016/j.eij. 2020.07.003
6. Office of the National Coordinator for Health Information Technology, T. (n.d.). What Is FHIR®? http://www.hl7.org/fhir. Accessed 12 July 2024
7. BioGHP. (2024). Global Health Platform. Retrieved from BioGHP. Accessed 12 June 2024
8. Overview of openEHR. (2006). http://www.who.int/classifications/icd/en/.4.Primarycareclassificatoin http://www.globalfamilydoctor.com/. Accessed 12 June 2024
9. Ueckert, F., Goerz, M., Ataian, M., Tessmann, S., Prokosch, H.U.: Empowerment of patients and communication with health care professionals through an electronic health record. Int. J. Med. Inform. **70**(2–3), 99–108 (2003). https://doi.org/10.1016/S1386-5056(03)00052-2
10. Tully, J., Dameff, C., Longhurst, C.A.: Wave of wearables: clinical management of patients and the future of connected medicine. Clin. Lab. Med. **40**(1), 69–82 (2020). https://doi.org/ 10.1016/J.CLL.2019.11.004

11. Kebodeaux, C.D.: Prescription and over-the-counter medication record integration: a holistic patient-centered approach. J. Am. Pharm. Assoc. **59**(2), S13–S17. Elsevier B.V. (2019). https://doi.org/10.1016/j.japh.2018.10.002

12. Elgamal, R.: Meta-analysis: eHealth literacy and attitudes towards internet/computer technology. Patient Educ. Counsel. **123** (2024). https://doi.org/10.1016/j.pec.2024.108196

13. Estrela, M., Semedo, G., Roque, F., Ferreira, P.L., Herdeiro, M.T.: Sociodemographic determinants of digital health literacy: a systematic review and meta-analysis. Int. J. Med. Inform. **177**. Elsevier Ireland Ltd. (2023). https://doi.org/10.1016/j.ijmedinf.2023.105124

14. Sreejith, R., Senthil, S.: Smart Contract Authentication assisted GraphMap-Based HL7 FHIR architecture for interoperable e-healthcare system. Heliyon, **9**(4) (2023). https://doi.org/10.1016/j.heliyon.2023.e15180

15. Daragmeh, A., Sági, J., Zéman, Z.: Continuous intention to use e-wallet in the context of the covid-19 pandemic: Integrating the health belief model (hbm) and technology continuous theory (tct). J. Open Innov. Technol. Market Complex. **7**(2) (2021). https://doi.org/10.3390/joitmc7020132

16. Yadav, R., Giri, A., Chatterjee, S.: Understanding the users' motivation and barriers in adopting healthcare apps: A mixed-method approach using behavioral reasoning theory. Technol. Forecast. Soc. Change **183** (2022). https://doi.org/10.1016/j.techfore.2022.121932

17. Ranjan, P., Soman, S., Ateria, A.K., Srivastava, P.K.: Streamlining payment workflows using a patient wallet for hospital information systems. In: Proceedings - IEEE Symposium on Computer-Based Medical Systems, 2018-June, pp. 339–344 (2018). https://doi.org/10.1109/CBMS.2018.00066

18. Patel, M.: Blockchain approach for smart health wallet. IJARCCE **6**(10), 131–135 (2017). https://doi.org/10.17148/ijarcce.2017.61022

19. Belfiore, A., Cuccurullo, C., Aria, M.: IoT in healthcare: a scientometric analysis. Technol. Forecast. Soc. Chang. **184** (2022). https://doi.org/10.1016/j.techfore.2022.122001

20. Bhuyan, S., et al.: Privacy and security issues in mobile health: current research and future directions. Health Policy Technol. **6**(2), 188–191. Elsevier B.V. (2017). https://doi.org/10.1016/j.hlpt.2017.01.004

21. Ali, H., Naing, H. H., Yaqub, R.: An iot assisted real-time high cmrr wireless ambulatory ecg monitoring system with arrhythmia detection. Electronics (Switzerland) **10**(16) (2021). https://doi.org/10.3390/electronics10161871

22. Baek, H., et al.: Enhancing user experience through user study: design of an mHealth tool for self-management and care engagement of cardiovascular disease patients. JMIR Cardio **2**(1) (2018). https://doi.org/10.2196/cardio.9000

23. Beratarrechea, A., Lee, A.G., Willner, J.M., Jahangir, E., Ciapponi, A., Rubinstein, A.: The impact of mobile health interventions on chronic disease outcomes in developing countries: a systematic review. Telemedicine e-Health **20**(1), 75–82 (2014). https://doi.org/10.1089/tmj.2012.0328

24. Birkmeyer, S., Wirtz, B.W., Langer, P.F.: Determinants of mHealth success: an empirical investigation of the user perspective. Int. J. Inf. Manag. **59** (2021). https://doi.org/10.1016/j.ijinfomgt.2021.102351

25. Chiu, W., Cho, H., Chi, C.G.: Consumers' continuance intention to use fitness and health apps: an integration of the expectation–confirmation model and investment model. Inf. Technol. People **34**(3), 978–998 (2020). https://doi.org/10.1108/ITP-09-2019-0463

26. Equey, C., Priftis, A., Trabichet, J.P., Hutzli, V.: Designing a digital citizen-centered service. Technol. Forecast. Soc. Chang. **202** (2024). https://doi.org/10.1016/j.techfore.2024.123280

27. Fotiadis, D.I., Penders, J., Wang, M.D., Jafari, R.: Biomedical and Health Informatics and the Body Sensor Networks Conferences : 4-7 March 2018, Treasure Island Hotel - Las Vegas, Nevada, USA (2018). IEEE

28. Galetsi, P., Katsaliaki, K., Kumar, S.: Exploring benefits and ethical challenges in the rise of mHealth (mobile healthcare) technology for the common good: an analysis of mobile applications for health specialists. Technovation **121** (2023). https://doi.org/10.1016/j.techno vation.2022.102598

29. ICACCS : 2019 5th International Conference on Advanced Computing & Communication Systems : 15–16 March 2019, Coimbatore, India. (2019). Institute of Electrical and Electronics Engineers

30. 2019 Conference on Information Communications Technology and Society (ICTAS): proceedings : Durban, South Africa, 6, 7 and 8 March 2019. (2019). IEEE

31. Karadas, B., et al.: Pregnancy outcomes following maternal favipiravir exposure: a case series. Neurotoxicol. Teratol. **98**, 107213 (2023). https://doi.org/10.1016/j.ntt.2023.107213

32. Kharrazi, H., Chisholm, R., VanNasdale, D., Thompson, B.: Mobile personal health records: an evaluation of features and functionality. Int. J. Med. Inform. **81**(9), 579–593 (2012). https://doi.org/10.1016/j.ijmedinf.2012.04.007

33. Khodadad-Saryazdi, A.: Exploring the telemedicine implementation challenges through the process innovation approach: a case study research in the French healthcare sector. Technovation **107** (2021). https://doi.org/10.1016/j.technovation.2021.102273

34. Martínez-Pérez, B., de la Torre-Díez, I., López-Coronado, M.: Privacy and security in mobile health apps: a review and recommendations. J. Med. Syst. **39**(1). Springer Science and Business Media, LLC (2015). https://doi.org/10.1007/s10916-014-0181-3

35. Morton, E., Torous, J., Murray, G., Michalak, E.E.: Using apps for bipolar disorder – an online survey of healthcare provider perspectives and practices. J. Psychiatr. Res. **137**, 22–28 (2021). https://doi.org/10.1016/j.jpsychires.2021.02.047

36. Motta, G.H.M.B., Furuie, S.S.: A contextual role-based access control authorization model for electronic patient record. IEEE Trans. Inf. Technol. Biomed. **7**(3), 202–207 (2003). https://doi.org/10.1109/TITB.2003.816562

37. Schroeder, T., et al.: Perception of middle-aged and older adults towards mHealth apps: a comparative factor analysis between Australia and Germany. Int. J. Med. Inform. **189** (2024). https://doi.org/10.1016/j.ijmedinf.2024.105502

38. Utsha, U.T., Morshed, B.I.: CardioHelp: a smartphone application for beat-by-beat ECG signal analysis for real-time cardiac disease detection using edge-computing AI classifiers. Smart Health **31** (2024). https://doi.org/10.1016/j.smhl.2024.100446

39. Van Der Storm, S.L., Jansen, M., Meijer, H.A.W., Barsom, E.Z., Schijven, M.P.: Apps in healthcare and medical research; European legislation and practical tips every healthcare provider should know. Int. J. Med. Inform. **177**, 1386–5056 (2023). https://doi.org/10.1016/j.ijmedinf.2023.105141

40. Zhang, X., Shen, K.N., Xu, B.: Double-edged sword of knowledge inertia: overcoming health-care professionals' resistance in innovation adoption. Technovation **133** (2024). https://doi.org/10.1016/j.technovation.2024.103011

41. Zhou, L., Bao, J., Watzlaf, V., Parmanto, B.: Barriers to and facilitators of the use of mobile health apps from a security perspective: mixed-methods study. JMIR MHealth UHealth **7**(4) (2019). https://doi.org/10.2196/11223

42. 2019 IEEE International Conference on Healthcare Informatics (ICHI). (2019). IEEE. Accessed 23 July 2024

43. Council of the European Union. (s.d.). The general data protection regulation. Obtido de What is the GDPR: https://www.consilium.europa.eu/en/policies/data-protection/data-protec tion-regulation/#gdpr. Accessed 06 June 2024

44. I (Legislative acts) REGULATIONS REGULATION (EU) 2016/679 OF THE EUROPEAN PARLIAMENT AND OF THE COUNCIL of 27 April 2016 on the protection of natural persons with regard to the processing of personal data and on the free movement of such data, and repealing Directive 95/46/EC (General Data Protection Regulation) (Text with EEA relevance). (n.d.). Accessed 22 July 2024

45. ISO. (2016). Obtido de ISO 13485 Medical Devices: https://www.iso.org/iso-13485-medical-devices.html. Accessed 16 Aug 2024

46. ENISA. (2023). European Union Agency for Cybersecurity. Retrieved from NIS Directive. https://www.enisa.europa.eu/topics/cybersecurity-policy/nis-directive-new. Accessed 24 July 2024

47. Cyber Resilience Act Requirements Standards Mapping. (n.d.). https://doi.org/10.2760/905934. Accessed 28 June 2024

48. Regulation - 2017/745 - EN - Medical Device Regulation - EUR-Lex (europa.eu). Accessed 12 Aug 2024

49. European Blockchain Services Infrastructure (EBSI) and the eSSIF | Verifiable Credentials and Self Sovereign Identity Web Directory. Accessed 11 Oct 2024

Integrating Metro Infrastructure in Circular Food Supply Chains: A Model for Decentralized Quito's Food Bank Network Redesign

Ariadna Sandoya[1]($\boxtimes$) (ID), Jorge Chicaiza-Vaca[2,3] (ID), Fernando Sandoya[4,5] (ID), and Benjamín Barán[6] (ID)

[1] College of Engineering and Applied Sciences, Stony Brook University, New York, NY, USA
ariadna.sandoya@stonybrook.edu

[2] L3E – Logistics Living Lab–Ecuador, Ecuadorian Freight Transportation and Logistics Chamber, Quito 170512, Ecuador
investigacion@ceet.ec

[3] Posgraduate Faculty, Universidad de las Américas UDLA, Quito 170124, Ecuador

[4] ESPOL Polytechnic University, Vía Perimetral km 30.5, Guayaquil, Ecuador
fsandoya@espol.edu.ec

[5] Universidad de Guayaquil, Av. Delta s/n y Av. Kennedy, Guayaquil, Ecuador
fernando.sandoyas@ug.edu.ec

[6] Comunera University, Dr. Juan Eulogio Estigarribia, Asunción, Paraguay
bbaran@cba.com.py

Abstract. Food waste and food insecurity are pressing global challenges. This study presents a novel approach to optimizing the food bank network redesign (FBNR) by leveraging the Quito Metro system to create a decentralized food bank network. We propose positioning lockers at metro stations for convenient food donations, which are then transported using the metro's spare capacity to designated stations for collection by charities. A blockchain-based traceability system with smart contracts serves as the core data management system, ensuring secure and transparent traceability of donations. Additionally, we develop a multi-objective optimization model aiming to minimize food waste, reduce transportation costs, and increase the social impact of food distribution. A mixed-integer linear programming (MIP) model further optimizes the allocation of donations to ensure efficient distribution. By integrating these models with the blockchain system, we offer a comprehensive solution to the FBNR, promoting a more sustainable and equitable food system.

Keywords: Multi-criteria Decision Making in Smart Transportation Systems · smart logistics · Integrated Passenger Freight Transportation · Blockchain · Food banks

© ICST Institute for Computer Sciences, Social Informatics and Telecommunications Engineering 2025
Published by Springer Nature Switzerland AG 2025. All Rights Reserved
A. Kocian et al. (Eds.): INTSYS 2024, LNICST 608, pp. 123–141, 2025.
https://doi.org/10.1007/978-3-031-86370-7_8

1 Introduction

Food waste and food insecurity are global challenges that necessitate innovative and effective solutions. Each year, a substantial amount of food is lost or wasted throughout the supply chain, contributing to hunger, malnutrition, and environmental degradation [1]. Food banks play a crucial role in mitigating these issues by rescuing and redistributing surplus food to those in need [2,3].

Traditionally, food banks operate within centralized networks where recovered food is stored and distributed from central locations. The supply chain operates with products being transferred by both donors and the food bank itself. The distribution of these products is then handled internally using the food bank's dedicated fleet of vehicles; however, this model often leads to logistical inefficiencies, limited reach, and accessibility issues, particularly in large urban areas. Studies highlight the need for improved logistics, transportation, and real-time tracking to mitigate food waste and enhance crisis preparedness [4–6]. To increase efficiency and expand the reach of food banks, it is essential to explore decentralized approaches that leverage existing and accessible infrastructure such as public transportation networks.

Recent research has increasingly focused on integrated passenger-freight transportation models, which leverage the unused capacity of public transportation to reduce urban congestion and improve efficiency [7]. These models, primarily studied in Europe and Asia, often focus on buses, metros, and trains as transportation modes, and shared vehicles as the most prevalent integration type. Given these advancements in transportation models, there is potential to apply similar strategies to improve food bank operations in urban environments.

Quito, the capital of Ecuador, faces significant socioeconomic challenges, with nearly 30 % of its 2.7 million residents living in poverty, experiencing high rates of underemployment and chronic malnutrition. This study focuses on the Quito Food Bank (QFB), a non-profit, which aims to combat hunger and reduce food waste by collecting surplus food from various sources and redistributing it to vulnerable population. Currently, the food bank operates a centralized distribution model. Given these inequitable conditions, optimizing food distribution is vital to ensure that marginalized groups receive adequate support.

The Food Bank Network Redesign (FBNR) problem can be optimized by leveraging the Quito Metro system, which commenced operations in December 2022, to create a decentralized food bank network. The proposed model involves installing food donation lockers at metro stations for convenient drop-offs, using the metro's spare capacity to transport food to designated stations for collection by charities. To enhance logistics and transparency, a blockchain-based traceability system is implemented, improving data flow and coordination among stakeholders.

The linear sequence of stations, including key sites that serve as collection points, facilitates efficient distribution and improves accessibility to impoverished areas. Furthermore, businesses in the Hotels, Restaurants, and Cafes (HORECA) sector near metro stations are identified as potential donors, strengthening the food bank's capacity to serve those in need. The diverse objectives of stakeholders must be considered to minimize food waste, reduce transportation costs, and enhance the social impact of food distribution, ultimately contributing to a more sustainable and equitable food system. The FBNR provides not only a potential solution for Quito but also a scalable framework that can be replicated in other metropolitan areas facing similar challenges.

2   Related Work

Addressing food waste and food insecurity through innovative strategies has garnered significant attention in recent years. Several studies have explored various aspects of food bank operations, optimization of food distribution, and the use of public transportation networks in logistics. Food waste is a critical issue with far-reaching implications for both the environment and society. Globally, an alarming one-third of food intended for human consumption is lost or wasted [8]. This not only represents a substantial economic loss but also contributes to environmental degradation and greenhouse gas emissions. As noted in [9], reducing food waste is crucial for enhanced food security and sustainability. They argue that effective food rescue and redistribution systems can play a pivotal role in achieving these goals.

The critical role of food banks in mitigating food waste and addressing food insecurity has been well-documented. In research by Davis et al. [10], they emphasize the importance of optimizing food bank operations to maximize their impact. The authors suggest that the efficiency of food banks can be significantly improved through better logistics and supply chain management practices. Similarly, [11] discuss the challenges faced by food banks, including the need for adequate infrastructure and resources to handle large volumes of food donations. Utilizing public transportation networks offers a novel approach to enhance food bank logistics.

Marinov et al. [12] highlight the benefits of using public transportation for urban freight, particularly in reducing traffic congestion and emissions. Likewise, Behiri et al. [13] demonstrate the potential for public transport to improve the efficiency and sustainability of urban logistics. Research shows that decentralizing food manufacturing and distribution can enhance resilience and flexibility during disruptions [14]. Integrating public transportation into this decentralized model further supports resilience by providing a reliable logistics framework.

Optimization models are widely used to address challenges in food distribution and supply chain management. Laporte et al. [15] provide a comprehensive overview of optimization techniques relevant to allocating food donations in this study. The effectiveness of MIP models in minimizing costs and improving service levels is explored by [16]. Several studies on food bank network redesign propose innovative approaches to improve food distribution efficiency and effectiveness. Beheshtian et al. [17] present a MO optimization model for designing food bank networks, focusing on transportation costs, food quality, and service coverage. The findings underscore the importance of balancing multiple objectives to achieve optimal solutions in complex logistical networks.

The redesign of a multi-echelon food bank network for collecting and distributing donations has been discussed [18]. Strategic decisions included opening new food banks, determining storage and transport capacities, and potentially closing or expanding existing ones. They proposed a MIP model that integrates economic, environmental, and social sustainability objectives, validated through a computational study on the Portuguese Federation of Food Banks network. [19] introduced three decompose-and-fix heuristics for the multi-period, multi-product FBNR, focusing on several objectives. Each heuristic simplifies the problem by breaking it into two Multi-Objective Mixed Integer Programming (MO-MIP) problems, significantly reducing computation time. These heuristics reduce Central Processing Unit (CPU) time by 80 % to 97 % compared to exact methods and can be adapted for other large MO problems.

Reusken et al. [20] presented an optimization model designed to allocate investment budgets to increase the number of beneficiaries served by food banks. They prioritize investments with the largest social impact and account for real-world challenges like decentralized organizations, data limitations, and varying transport and storage capacities. The Dutch Food Banks Association has applied these findings in practice, recommending targeted investments that could increase capacity and serve approximately 32 % more beneficiaries.

Suarez et al. [21] propose a novel multi-objective, multi-product, and multi-period model to address the challenge of allocating perishable food items in food bank warehouses. The model aims to ensure food safety, meet nutritional needs, and minimize shortages while adhering to a first expired-first out policy. The effectiveness of the model is demonstrated using real-world data from the Diakonia Food Bank in Guayaquil-Ecuador. Optimization models are critically dependent on the accuracy and reliability of their underlying data management systems. As food bank networks increase in complexity and scale, conventional data management approaches may prove insufficient in providing the necessary monitoring across decentralized networks.

Blockchain systems, such as those outlined by Musamih et al. [22] and IBM Food Trust [23], offer a decentralized and tamper-resistant ledger that significantly enhances data transparency and traceability within supply chains. These systems can leverage smart contracts to automate regulatory compliance and maintain data integrity. Such frameworks can be adapted to address the specific needs of food bank networks. When integrated with public transportation systems, blockchain technology can complement robust optimization models to foster more efficient and resilient food bank operations.

3   Information Management in Food Bank Logistics

Conventional approaches to food bank supply chain traceability are often centralized and opaque, despite growing demand for greater transparency from consumers and stakeholders [24]. The sector's unique characteristics and the integration of multiple stakeholders, from donors to beneficiaries, amplify these challenges. Adopting digital technologies, such as blockchain, can further enhance traceability and transparency [25].

Blockchain is particularly well-suited for traceability in a decentralized food bank network due to its inherent characteristics that align with the needs of such system, improving decision making and operational efficiency. Central to this approach is the concept of a Traceable Resource Unit (TRU) [26], which is key for tracking a food item's journey from donation to distribution, ensuring comprehensive transaction history and real-time monitoring. In the proposed FBNR model, donors pack food in uniquely identifiable *boxes*, that serve as TRUs, which balance detailed tracking with efficient management across the blockchain.

3.1   Blockchain-Enhanced Traceability in FBNR

The proposed system utilizes blockchain technology to improve traceability within the food bank supply chain. By employing a smart contract (SC), stakeholders interact securely and transparently, enabling real-time tracking, maintaining data integrity, and ensuring transparent transactions through decentralized storage. A SC is a self-executing agreement where the terms are encoded directly written into lines of code, this provides an immutable and decentralized environment, enhancing trust and regulatory compliance, which in turn improves the overall reliability of the supply chain.

A high-level system architecture of the proposed food bank traceability system includes stakeholders and their interactions with the SC (see Fig. 1). Stakeholders will use software devices to interact with the SC and other resources through a user interface layer provided by a Decentralized Application (DApp). This DApp connects to the SC and storage systems via application programming interfaces (APIs). Stakeholders will be able to execute and access authorized functions, data files from decentralized storage, Interplanetary File System (IPFS) hashes, and transaction details from on-chain resources.

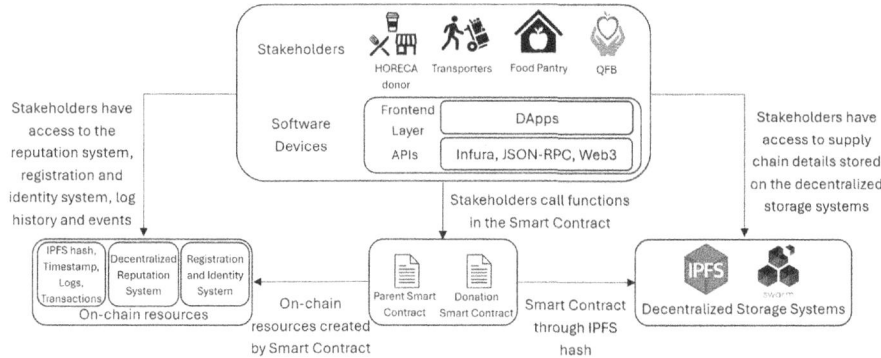

Fig. 1. High-level system architecture for the food bank blockchain-based solution

An event in this context is a distinct action or occurrence within the supply chain that triggers the execution of predefined functions within the SC. Each stakeholder in the supply chain is assigned specific roles and permissions within the SC, ensuring transparency and accountability throughout the process. The SC records every transaction and status update related to the donations, providing real-time traceability to all participants. Each transaction is authenticated, verifiable, and safely logged, further ensuring the integrity and reliability of the system. Details of the donation or other identification techniques such as the images, can be uploaded to IPFS, which will then provide a hash to the SC during each event. The Supply Chain events are as follows:

– *Donation Initiation:* The HORECA donor will request the initiation of the donation process to QFB. Once the request is approved, an event is triggered. The donor will pack the food, drop it off at the metro station locker.
– *Distribution:* The donation is transported via the metro system and the QFB vehicle fleet. Volunteers facilitate the loading of donations from lockers to metro wagons and unloading at destination station from metro wagons to QFB vehicles. The details of the package will be updated at loading and unloading points.
– *Classification and Final Distribution:* Upon arrival at the collection centers, donations are classified. Depending on the classification, donations are either distributed to beneficiaries or sent to composting facilities. Every action is logged, forming a sequence of events, ensuring traceability from donation initiation to final distribution.

3.2 Implementation of Proposed Traceability System

The donor will deploy a SC defining the details of the food donation lot, triggering an event to notify all supply chain participants. New participants can access these events and track the donation's history since the information is stored permanently on the ledger. The donor may also upload an image of the lot to IPFS for visual inspection by participants. The donor will package the lot, drop it off at a secure locker, and announce its availability for transfer via an event. Transporters interested in transferring the lot in the loading and unloading points will use a specialized function. At each step of the transfer, an event will notify participants of the new owner. The approval for the SC deployment is not considered for simplicity.

An Entity-Relationship diagram (see Fig. 2) illustrates the key entities and how they interact with the SC. It considers attributes like *ownerID*, which stores the blockchain address of the current contract owner. The Donation Lot SC can have only one owner at a time. When ownership changes, an event is triggered and recorded on the blockchain, enabling the tracing of the donation lot's origin.

Since the SC represents a specific donation lot, it includes additional attributes like *donationID*, *lockerID*, *numBoxes*, *image*, and *metroWagonID*. There are also five mappings for the authorized entities: donors, transporters,

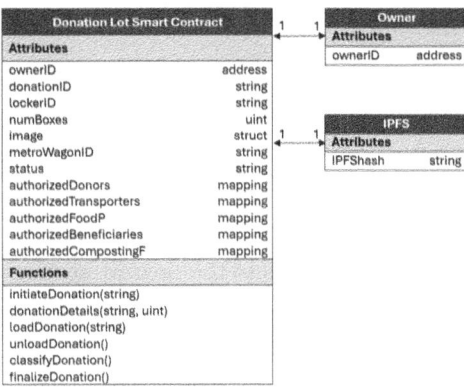

Fig. 2. Entity-Relationship Diagram for Donation Lot Smart Contract

food pantries, beneficiaries, and composting facilities, who have access to certain functions within the contract. Several functions are included to manage the donation process. Donation details, including *donationID* and *numBoxes*, are added through the *donationDetails* function. The SC and IPFS relationship is 1:1, as each donation lot will have one image uploaded to IPFS.

Each HORECA donor declares to participants that the donation lot is available for pick up in the locker via the *initiateDonation* function with *lockerID* as a parameter. An authorized entity intending to load the lot onto the metro wagon invokes the *loadDonation* function, inputting the *metroWagonID*, which subsequently updates the ownership to the designated transporter. Similarly, an entity interested in unloading the lot from the metro wagon executes the *unloadDonation* function, updating the ownership to the food pantry. The pantry then classifies the boxes suitable for consumption, executes the *classifyDonation* which updates the ownership to the composting facilities for the not suitable boxes. The final distribution to the beneficiary is executed with the *finalizeDonation* function, setting the beneficiary as the ultimate owner.

4   Optimization Models for Efficient Donation Distribution

This section delves into the optimization of the donation distribution chain, employing two distinct mathematical models. The first model focuses on the strategic assignment of donors to specific metro stations, aiming to minimize transportation distances and ensure efficient utilization of station capacities. The second model tackles the operational challenge of optimizing the transportation of donations on metro trains, considering factors such as train schedules, loading/unloading times, and storage costs. Both models are designed to address the diverse and sometimes conflicting interests of various stakeholders, including donors, passengers, transportation authorities, and the food bank itself.

4.1   Assignment Model

This model aims to assign donors to the nearest metro station with sufficient capacity to receive their donations, thus minimizing overall travel distance. Station capacity is defined as its ability to handle cargo without impacting passenger service. In scenarios where station i is closest to donor j and possesses the capacity to accommodate the donor's load, this station is designated as the optimal drop-off point (see Fig. 3a and Fig. 3b). However, if station i lacks the necessary capacity, the model dynamically selects the nearest station that can fulfill the capacity requirement (see Fig. 3c).

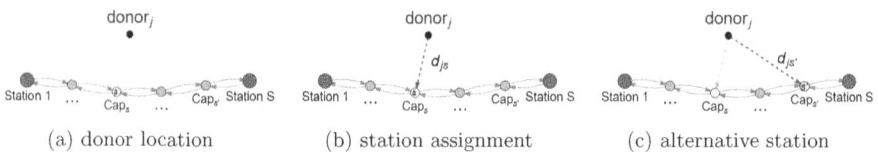

(a) donor location   (b) station assignment   (c) alternative station

Fig. 3. A Donor-Station Allocation Model

Considering the aforementioned factors, a straightforward allocation model incorporating capacity constraints is employed. This leads to the formulation of a MIP model, where the specific elements are detailed in Table 1.

Table 1. Assignment Model

Type	Description
Sets	
$j : 1, ..., J$	Donors
$s : 1, ..., S$	Stations
Parameters	
Cap_s	Donation load capacity at station s
O_j	Donor j's offer
$d_{j,s}$	Unit cost of shipping each unit of donations from donor j to station s
Decision Variables	
$x_{j,s}$	1 If donor j's offer is assigned to station s, 0 otherwise

The model can be formulated as:

$$Min \; Z = \sum_{j=1}^{J} \sum_{s=1}^{S} d_{js} O_j x_{js} \qquad (1)$$

subject to:

$$\sum_{j=1}^{J} x_{j,s} O_j \leq Cap_s, \quad s = 1, 2, \ldots, S \tag{2}$$

$$x_{j,s} \geq 0 \; s = 1, 2, \ldots, S, j = 1, 2, \ldots, J \tag{3}$$

4.2 Storage and Distribution Model

The second model optimizes the food donations transportation from donors to the Metro system's stations, ultimately destined for the food bank's two food pantries at the network's northern and southern ends, as show in Fig. 4. The model considers the loading station ls_i for each donation i, the designated unloading station us_i, and the transportation time ts_s between station s and the next station. The food donations are packaged into standardized boxes as TRUs by the respective donors. The boxes are temporarily stored incurring a storage cost at their assigned stations. Subsequently, these boxes are loaded onto *caddies*, wheeled devices for conveying multiple boxes, and transported via the metro system to their designated destination stations. Upon arrival, each donation is retrieved from the caddies and then transferred to the final food pantry as shown in the Fig. 6.

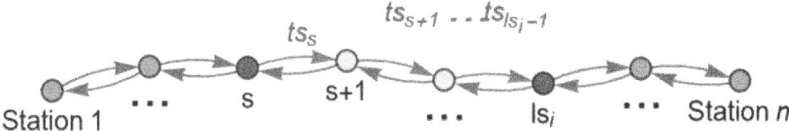

Fig. 4. Schematic Representation of the Donor Load Transportation Model 2

Given these considerations, we formulate the MO optimization model (4)–(22) whose sets, parameters, and decision variables are detailed in Table 2.

$$min \; (Z_1, Z_2, Z_3) \in \mathbb{R}^3 \tag{4}$$

where:

$$Z_1 = \sum_{i=1}^{I} \sum_{j=1}^{J} (G_i - g_i \; x_{i,j,ls_i}) \tag{5}$$

$$Z_2 = \sum_{s=1}^{S} \sum_{i \in II_s} \sum_{j=1}^{J} h_j \; B_i \; x_{i,j,s} \tag{6}$$

$$Z_3 = \sum_{i=1}^{I} P_1 B_i \, (G_i - g_i \,) + \sum_{i=1}^{I} \sum_{f=1}^{F} \sum_{j \in F_f} P_{2,j} B_i \left(E_i - \sum_{s \in I_s} ts_s \right) \tag{7}$$

The objective functions, represented by Eqs. (5), (6), and (7), aim to:

- Minimize Z_1, the total time that donations remain at stations awaiting loading (5).

Table 2. Storage and Distribution Model

Type	Description
Sets	
$i : 1, \ldots, I$	Set of donations
$j : 1, \ldots, J$	Set of trains
$s : 1, \ldots, S$	Set of stations
$f : 1, \ldots, F$	Set of transportation fares
Parameters	
g_i	Time at which donation i is available for transport
ls_i	Departure station for donation i
us_i	Unload station for donation i
P_1	Unit cost of storing a box per time unit at a station
$P_{2,j}$	Unit cost involved in sending a box on train j (\$/box)
F_f	Trains subject to fare f
l_j	Train j's departure time from station 1
ST_s	Storage capacity at station s (boxes)
ts_s	Travel time between station s to the adjacent station
I_s	Set of donations needing to pass by station s on their way
II_s	Set of donations arriving at station s; $s = 1$ or $s = S$
D_i	Set of donations departing from the same station as donation i and ready for departure earlier than i: $D_i = \{k \mid g_k \leq g_i \wedge ls_k = ls_i\}$
V_i	Volume of donation i
W_i	Weight of donation i
BVC	Maximum volume capacity of boxes
BWC	Maximum weight capacity of boxes
B_i	Number of boxes required for donation i
Q_j	Train j's box transport capacity
WT_{max}	Maximum train dwell time at any station s
WT_{min}	Minimum train dwell time at any station s
h_j	Time required to handle (load/unload) one box on train j
M	Sufficiently large number
Decision Variables	
$x_{i,j,s}$	1 if donation i is in train j at station s, 0 otherwise
$u_{k,i}$	1 if k is in D_i and k is not yet loaded when i becomes ready for departure
$C_{j,s}$	Waiting time of train j at station s
G_i	Time at which donation i is loaded (at station ls_i)
E_i	Time at which donation i arrives at its destination station 1 or S

- Minimize Z_2, the total time spent on loading, unloading, and transporting the boxes (6). Note that the in-transit time for boxes is constant regardless of train assignment; thus, only loading and unloading times vary based on the chosen schedule.
- Minimize Z_3, the combined transportation and storage costs from donation arrival at departure stations to delivery at destination stations (7).

Subject to constraints (8)–(22). i.e., subject to:

$$\sum_{j=1}^{J} x_{i,j,ls_i} = 1, \quad i = 1, 2, \ldots, I \tag{8}$$

Equation (8) ensures that each donation is assigned to a single train for transportation, and this assignment occurs precisely once.

$$x_{i,j,s} - x_{i,j,s+1} = 0, \quad \forall\, s \in [ls_i, us_j - 1], i = 1, 2, \ldots, I \tag{9}$$

(9) ensures that once a donation is assigned to a train, it passes through all intermediate stations between its departure and arrival points.

$$\sum_{i \in I_s} x_{i,j,s}\, B_i \leq Q_j, \quad j = 1, \ldots, J,\ s = 1, \ldots, S \tag{10}$$

(10) guarantees that a donation can only be allocated to a metro vehicle that reaches its origin station after the donation's ready time.

$$x_{i,j,ls_i}\, g_i \leq l_j + \sum_{s=1}^{ls_{i-1}} (C_{j,s} + ts_s), \quad i = 1, \ldots, I,\ j = 1, \ldots, J \tag{11}$$

(11) guarantees that a donation can only be assigned to a metro vehicle that reaches its destination station after departing its origin station.

$$C_{j,s} \geq WT_{min}, \quad j = 1, \ldots, J,\ s = 1, \ldots, S \tag{12}$$

$$C_{j,s} \leq WT_{max}, \quad j = 1, \ldots, J,\ s = 1, \ldots, S \tag{13}$$

(12) and (13) guarantee that the waiting time at each station adheres to the specified minimum and maximum limits.

$$C_{j,s} \geq \sum_{i \in II_s} h_j\, x_{i,j,s}\, B_i, \quad j = 1, \ldots, J,\ s = 1, \ldots, S \tag{14}$$

(14) ensures that the waiting time of each train at each station falls within the feasible range.

$$B_i = Max \left\{ \left\lceil \frac{V_i}{BVC} \right\rceil, \left\lceil \frac{W_i}{BWC} \right\rceil \right\} i = 1, \ldots, I \tag{15}$$

Equation (15) is designed to quantify the number of boxes required to pack each donation.

$$G_i \geq l_j + \sum_{s=1}^{ls_i-1} (C_{j,s} + ts_s) - M(1 - x_{i,j,ls_i}), \quad i = 1, \dots, I, \ j = 1, \dots, J \quad (16)$$

(16) establishes the earliest feasible time at which each donation can be loaded onto a train.

$$G_k \leq g_i + M \, u_{k,i}, \ k \in D_i, \ i = 1, \dots, I \quad (17)$$

(17) ensures the logical consistency of variables $u_{k,i}$.

$$\sum_{k \in D_i}^{J} u_{k,i} \, B_k \leq ST_{ls_i} - B_i, \ i = 1, \dots, I \quad (18)$$

(18) enforces the storage capacity limit at each station.

$$x_{i,j,s} \in \{0, 1\}, i = 1, \dots, I, \ j = 1, \dots, J, \ s = 1, \dots, S \quad (19)$$

$$C_{j,s} \geq 0, \ j = 1, \dots, J, \ s = 1, \dots, S \quad (20)$$

$$G_i \geq 0, i = 1, \dots, I \quad (21)$$

$$u_{k,i} \in \{0, 1\}, \ k \in D_i, i = 1, \dots, I \quad (22)$$

(19) to (22) serves to define the nature of the decision variables within the model. It establishes that $x_{i,j,s}$ and $u_{k,i}$ are binary variables. Furthermore, it designates G_i and $C_{j,s}$ as non-negative real variables.

One way to solve the proposed MO model is through the standardization of z_1, z_2 and z_3, so that all objectives are on the same scale and comparable, and then transforming them into a single objective function through a weighted sum of those objectives, as established in [27]. Standardization is achieved by transforming the values of each objective function Z_i into values within the interval $[0, 1]$, for which the largest, Z_i^U, and lowest, Z_i^L, values that Z_i, $i = 1,2,3$ can achieve, are calculated by transforming the MO model represented in Eq. (4) into a weighted single-objective represented in Eq. (23).

$$\min \alpha_1 \frac{(Z_1 - Z_1^L)}{(Z_1^U - Z_1^L)} + \alpha_2 \frac{(Z_2 - Z_2^L)}{(Z_2^U - Z_2^L)} + \alpha_3 \frac{(Z_3 - Z_3^L)}{(Z_3^U - Z_3^L)} \quad (23)$$

where the parameters α_i satisfy the conditions $\alpha_i \geq 0$ and $\sum_i \alpha_i = 1$. By systematically varying the values within the triplet $(\alpha_1, \alpha_2, \alpha_3)$, we can effectively approximate the Pareto front of the MO problem.

The proposed model, solvable using a MIP solver, generates a set of non-dominated solutions and an estimate Pareto front. These results empower food bank managers to assess the trade-offs between competing objectives and select the optimal donation distribution strategy that leverages the metro public transport network. This approach facilitates the minimization of distribution and storage costs while maintaining acceptable service levels for passengers.

5   Quito Metro Case Study: Findings and Insights

Quito, the capital of Ecuador, is nestled within the Andean mountain range. Its urban area is constrained by mountains and gorges to a long, narrow plateau. With a population of 2.7 million, representing 16 % of the national total, Quito faces significant socioeconomic challenges. Notably, nearly 30 % of its residents experience poverty, with 7 % living in extreme poverty and almost 30 % of children under five suffering from chronic malnutrition. Unemployment and underemployment rates stand at 5 % and 40 %, respectively, with poverty concentrated in the city's northern and southern extremities [28] (see Fig. 5a).

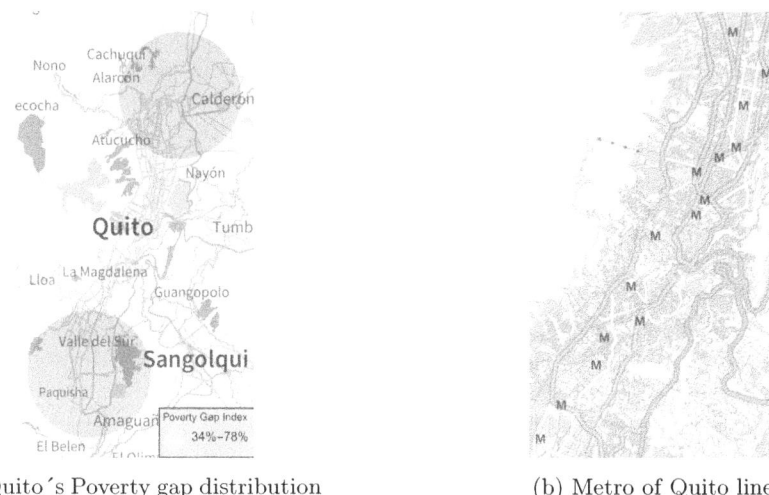

(a) Quito´s Poverty gap distribution   (b) Metro of Quito line

Fig. 5. Mapping Poverty in Quito: A Comparison with Metro Line Coverage

The QFB is a non-profit organization dedicated to fighting hunger and reducing food waste in Quito, Ecuador. Founded in 2003, the bank collects surplus food from various donors, including hotels, restaurants, markets and food producers, and redistributes it to beneficiaries.

Currently, the food bank operates a centralized distribution model, with a central warehouse located in the south of the city. Food donations are collected by the bank's fleet of 3 vehicles and transported to the warehouse for sorting and storage. From there, food is distributed to beneficiary organizations.

The proposed decentralized model leverages the Quito Metro system to create a network of food donation lockers and collection points. Key elements include the installation of secure lockers at strategically chosen metro stations for convenient food donation drop-offs, the use of the spare capacity of metro trains to transport food donations to designated collection points, the development of a data traceability architecture to track and manage the flow of donations, and the implementation of MO-MIP programming models to optimize the allocation and distribution of donations.

This innovative approach is expected to increase the reach of the food bank by leveraging the extensive metro network, reducing transportation costs by decreasing dependency on the food bank's vehicle fleet, improving the efficiency of the logistics process by resulting in more efficient distribution, and enhancing social impact by increasing the volume of food rescued and redistributed, thus benefiting more individuals in need [14]. This supports the Food loss and waste (FLW) law's focus on prioritizing the responsible treatment of food fit for human consumption while also establishing a "culture of donation" [29].

The Quito Metro, an underground public transport network, commenced operations in December 2022. The fully operational line spans 23 km, and serves as the backbone of the Quito Integrated Mass Transportation System (SITM-Q) [30] (see Fig. 5b).

The linear structure of the Quito Metro's first line, featuring a series of stations arranged sequentially, aligns well with the integrated passenger-freight transportation model proposed in [31]. This model serves as a foundation for our proposed food bank supply network design, facilitating the efficient transportation of food to two strategically located food pantries at the northern and southern ends of the city. These nodes are in close proximity to the areas with the highest concentration of poverty, ensuring accessibility for those who would benefit most from the food bank's services.

Within this framework, Quitumbe station (station 1) and El Labrador station (station 15) function as unloading points for food collected at each of the "interior" stations (stations 2 to 14). These interior stations act as loading and unloading points, enabling donors to conveniently deposit food donations, which are then transported along the metro line to the food pantries. This integrated approach optimizes the utilization of existing infrastructure, reduces transportation costs, and streamlines the distribution of food. (see Fig. 6).

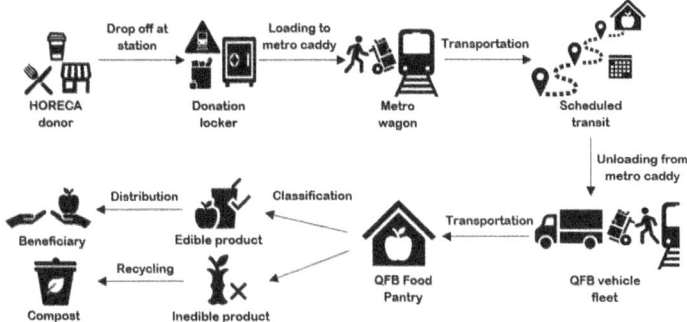

Fig. 6. FBNR Supply chain stakeholders and their relationships

In this study, businesses within the HORECA sector situated in proximity to the Quito Metro network are identified as potential donors. Given the nature of their products, these establishments are well-suited to contribute to the food bank, and their proximity to metro stations facilitates efficient distribution. The spatial distribution of 1,200 such establishments, categorized by type, is illustrated in Fig. 7.

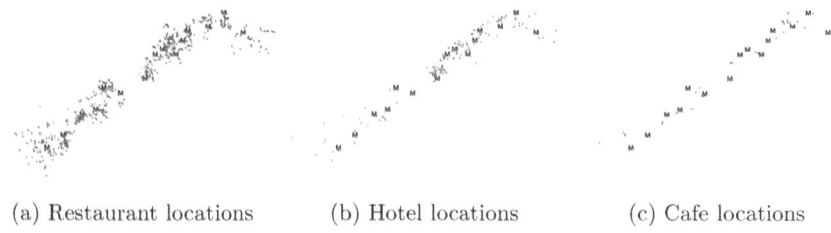

(a) Restaurant locations   (b) Hotel locations   (c) Cafe locations

Fig. 7. Distribution of HORECA establishments near the Quito Metro, by type.

The visualization presented in Fig. 8 illustrates the outcome of the donor-station assignment process, wherein each potential donor within the HORECA sector is allocated to the most suitable metro station for their food donations.

Fig. 8. Spatial Allocation of Donors to Metro Stations in Quito

To showcase the model's real-world applicability, we utilized data from the QFB and potential food donations from HORECA establishments. The MIP model in Eq. (23) was implemented and solved using GAMS [32] for algebraic modeling and the Gurobi solver [33] for optimization. Gurobi's exact methods efficiently determined optimal solutions for various α_i weight combinations. Table 3 presents the values of objective functions z_1, z_2, and z_3 for different α_i combinations, along with their respective computation times. The results underscore the model's computational efficiency in handling real-world scenarios within reasonable time frames. Numerical results reveal conflicts among the considered objectives, highlighting the value of the Pareto front in providing decision-makers with valuable insights for further analysis and decision-making.

Table 3. Values of the objective functions for different combinations of α_i

$(\alpha_1, \alpha_2, \alpha_3)$	Z_1	Z_2	Z_3	Execution time (sec)
(0, 0, 1)	1.175816	1.45778	0.250568	1.2562
(0, 0.5, 0.5)	1.385439	0.1023	1.709063	1.3231
(0.33, 0.33, 0.33)	0.93239	1.04235	1.693897	1.6598
(0, 1, 0)	1.211361	0.05842	0.918517	1.6924
(0.5, 0.5, 0)	1.94141	0.677836	0.10142	1.9335
(1, 0, 0)	0.31225	1.522893	1.23824	1.7226

6 Conclusions

This study proposes the integration of logistics models with public transportation systems to enhance food bank operations in urban environments. The utilization of the unused capacity of mass public transportation, exemplified by the Quito Metro system, represents a promising approach for optimizing food distribution. However, practical implementation of such systems remains limited in Latin America, including Ecuador.

The proposed information management system incorporates blockchain technology to enhance traceability within the food bank supply chain. By defining clear relationships among stakeholders, on-chain resources, and decentralized storage systems, the system facilitates real-time monitoring of donations through unique smart contracts. These contracts trigger events upon ownership changes, with event data accessible to DApp users. This approach aims to improve transparency, reduce human intervention, and minimize delays, by integrating seamless collection, organization, presentation, and utilization of logistics data.

Several limitations are acknowledged, including constraints related to modeling and network topology. The focus on a linear metro structure, rather than more complex configurations with multiple lines and interchanges, restricts the generalizability of the findings. Furthermore, the smart contract was neither implemented nor tested, which limits the ability to assess its practical effectiveness. Future research should address these limitations by exploring more intricate network topologies while conducting security and cost analyses of the proposed blockchain-based solution.

Further investigation is required into the technical infrastructure necessary to support the model, including the design of TRUs, secure lockers and modified subway cars. The operations management associated with the creation and utilization of standardized boxes warrants additional attention. Standardized boxes could enhance automation, sorting, data management, transportation, and regulatory compliance in the food bank network through consistent labeling, uniform dimensions, and simplified inventory management.

Refining these components is essential to optimizing the transportation within the food bank network. Future work should address the design and functionality of these elements to better support the logistics of the food distribution system. Additionally, a comprehensive analysis of the economic, legal, social, and psychological implications of the model is still needed.

Finally, the model must also account for the stochastic nature of the system, including variability in donation volumes and potential delays in transportation. Addressing these unpredictable factors is essential for enhancing the efficiency and effectiveness of the food distribution network.

References

1. Bajželj, B., Quested, T., Röös, E., Swannell, R.: The role of reducing food waste for resilient food systems. Ecosyst. Serv. **45**, 101140 (2020)
2. Garrone, P., Melacini, M., Perego, A.: Surplus food recovery and donation in Italy: the upstream process. Br. Food J. **116**(9), 1460–1477 (2014)
3. Béné, C., Godfrey Wood, R., Newsham, A., Davies, M.: Resilience, poverty and development. J. Int. Dev. **26**(5), 515–534 (2015)
4. Esmaeilidouki, A., Rambe, M., Ardestani-Jaafari, A., Li, E., Marcolin, B.: Food bank operations: review of operation research methods and challenges during Covid-19. BMC Public Health **23**(1), 1783 (2023)
5. Tarasuk, V., et al.: A survey of food bank operations in five Canadian cities. BMC Public Health **14**, 1–11 (2014)
6. Loopstra, R., Lambie-Mumford, H., Fledderjohann, J.: Food bank operational characteristics and rates of food bank use across Britain. BMC Public Health **19**, 1–10 (2019)
7. Chicaiza-Vaca, J., Barán, B., Sandoya, F., Barán, M.: Taxonomy for integrated passenger-freight transportation models as an alternative for urban logistics. In: Martins, A.L., Ferreira, J.C., Kocian, A., Tokkozhina, U., Helgheim, B.I., Bråthen, S. (eds.) Intelligent Transport Systems. INTSYS 2023. LNICS, Social Informatics and Telecommunications Engineering, vol. 540, pp. 210–227 (2024)
8. Gustavsson, J., Cederberg, C., Sonesson, U., van Otterdijk, R., Meybeck, A.: Global Food losses and Food Waste-extent, Causes and Prevention. The Swedish Institute for Food and Biotechnology (2013). https://www.diva-portal.org/smash/get/diva2:944159/FULLTEXT01.pdf. Accessed 1 Aug 2024
9. Buzby, J.C., Hyman, J.: Total and per capita value of food loss in the United States. Food Policy **37**(5), 561–570 (2012)

10. Davis, L.B., Sengul, I., Ivy, J.S., Brock, L.G., III., Miles, L.: Scheduling food bank collections and deliveries to ensure food safety and improve access. Socioecon. Plann. Sci. **48**(3), 175–188 (2014)
11. Bazerghi, C., McKay, F.H., Dunn, M.: The role of food banks in addressing food insecurity: a systematic review. J. Community Health **41**(4), 732–740 (2016). https://doi.org/10.1007/s10900-015-0147-5
12. Marinov, M., et al.: Urban freight movement by rail. J. Transp. Lit. **7**(3), 87–116 (2013)
13. Behiri, W., Belmokhtar-Berraf, S., Chu, C.: Urban freight transport using passenger rail network: scientific issues and quantitative analysis. Transp. Res. Part E: Logist. Transp. Rev. **115**, 227–245 (2018)
14. Barman, A., Das, R., De, P.K.: Impact of COVID-19 in food supply chain: disruptions and recovery strategy. Curr. Res. Behav. Sci. **2**, 100017 (2021)
15. Laporte, G.: Fifty years of vehicle routing. Transp. Sci. **43**(4), 408–416 (2009)
16. Amorim, P., Günther, H.O., Almada-Lobo, B.: Multi-objective integrated production and distribution planning of perishable products. Int. J. Prod. Econ. **152**, 19–36 (2014)
17. Beheshtian, A., Kalantari, M., Jahangirian, M., Rezapour, S.: Multi-objective optimization model for the location and distribution decisions in a food bank network. J. Humanit. Logist. Supply Chain Manag. **8**(2), 182–202 (2018)
18. Martins, C.L., Melo, M.T., Pato, M.V.: Redesigning a food bank supply chain network in a triple bottom line context. Int. J. Prod. Econ. **214**, 234–247 (2019)
19. Martins, C. L., Pato, M. V.: Decomposition heuristics for multiobjective problems. The food bank network redesign case. Int. J. Prod. Econ. **268**, 109121 (2024)
20. Reusken, M., Cruijssen, F., Fleuren, H.: A food bank supply chain model: optimizing investments to maximize food assistance. Int. J. Prod. Econ. **261**, 108886 (2023)
21. Suárez, C.A., Guaño, W.A., Pérez, C.C., Roa-López, H.: Multi-objective optimization for perishable product dispatch in a FEFO system for a food bank single warehouse. Oper. Res. Perspect. **12**, 100304 (2024)
22. Musamih, A.: A blockchain-based approach for drug traceability in healthcare supply chain. IEEE Access **9**, 9728–9743 (2021)
23. IBM Supply Chain Intelligence Suite. Food Trust. IBM (2024). https://www.ibm.com/products/supply-chain-intelligence-suite/food-trust. Accessed 8 Sep 2024
24. Trienekens, J.H., Wognum, P.M., Beulens, A.J.M., van der Vorst, J.G.A.J.: Transparency in complex dynamic food supply chains. Adv. Eng. Inform. **26**(1), 55–65 (2012)
25. Burgess, P., Sunmola, F., Wertheim-Heck, S.: Information needs for transparency in blockchain-enabled sustainable food supply chains. Int. J. Inf. Manag. Data Insights **4**(2), 100262 (2024)
26. Olsen, P., Borit, M.: The components of a food traceability system. Trends Food Sci. Technol. **77**, 143–149 (2018)
27. Ransikarbum, K., Mason, S.J.: Multiple-objective analysis of integrated relief supply and network restoration in humanitarian logistics operations. Int. J. Prod. Res. **54**(1), 49–68 (2014)
28. Quito: Poverty Gap Index. World Economic Forum (2018). https://es.weforum.org/agenda/2018/07/recientemente-la-ciudad-de-quito-ha-logrado-que-los-viajes-al-trabajo-sean-mas-rapidos-y-seguros/. Accessed 31 July 2024
29. FAOLEX Database. Law to prevent and Reduce Food Loss and Waste and to mitigate Hunger in People in Situations of Food Vulnerability. (n.d.) (2022). https://

www.fao.org/faolex/results/details/es/c/LEX-FAOC210684/. Accessed 14 Aug 2024

30. Metro de Quito. https://www.metrodequito.gob.ec/. Accessed 31 July 2024
31. Barán, M., Sandoya, F., Chicaiza-Vaca, J., Barán, B.: Integrated passenger-freight transportation model: metro of quito (Ecuador) as a case study. Lecture Notes of the Institute for Computer Sciences, Social Informatics and Telecommunications Engineering, vol. 486, pp. 215–230 (2023)
32. GAMS Software Gmb. Solvers. https://www.gams.com/products/solvers/. Accessed 5 Sep 2024
33. Gurobi Optimizer. Gurobi Optimization. https://www.gurobi.com/solutions/gurobi-optimizer/. Accessed 5 Sep 2024

Traffic Forecasting and Control

An AutoML Approach for Bike Demand Forecasting and Redistribution

Dimitris Petratos[1], Yannis Poulakis[1], Irene Gimenez Pedralba[2],
Cristina Aragon Garcia[2], and Christos Doulkeridis[1(✉)]

[1] Department of Digital Systems, University of Piraeus, Piraeus, Greece
{dpetr,gpoul,cdoulk}@unipi.gr
[2] Serveo, Barcelona, Spain
{igimenez,cristina.aragon}@serveo.com

Abstract. In this paper we introduce a two-staged pipeline to tackle the
problem of bike redistribution for bike-sharing systems, using Automated
Machine Learning (AutoML) and optimization techniques. Our approach
includes the usage of AutoML for time series forecasting in order to estimate the demand for bikes for each station, along with an optimization
model to efficiently relocate bikes to maximize user satisfaction. In our
study, we used historical data from Barcelona's public bike-sharing system to predict future demand and then used these predictions together
with public data from OpenStreetMap (estimated travel time between
stations) in order to solve the Minimum Cost Flow Problem (MCFP)
and compute the optimal bike redistribution. We demonstrate promising results in terms of accuracy of demand forecasting and reduction
of forecasting time, thus obtaining feasible redistribution strategies and
providing an end-to-end framework to the operator.

Keywords: Bike demand forecasting · time series forecasting ·
AutoML · bike redistribution · minimum-cost flow problem

1 Introduction

During the last decades due to high urbanization rates, large cities face several
challenges in planning and specifically in terms of transportation. The growth
of cities' population has positioned citizens' transportation as one of the most
complex difficulties that policy makers have to overcome. At the same time
the ever increasing pollution from car use, calls for the immediate adoption of
eco-friendly approaches that minimize the energy footprint of transport. Such
solutions include bike-sharing systems (BSSs) that the citizens can use instead
of traditional transportation means such as cars, buses etc. BSSs are highly
adopted from large crowded cities all over the globe and can efficiently satisfy
citizens' transportation needs in a green manner [5]. BSSs can be divided into
two categories. If the bikes are picked up and dropped off at stations in specific

© ICST Institute for Computer Sciences, Social Informatics and Telecommunications Engineering 2025
Published by Springer Nature Switzerland AG 2025. All Rights Reserved
A. Kocian et al. (Eds.): INTSYS 2024, LNICST 608, pp. 145–161, 2025.
https://doi.org/10.1007/978-3-031-86370-7_9

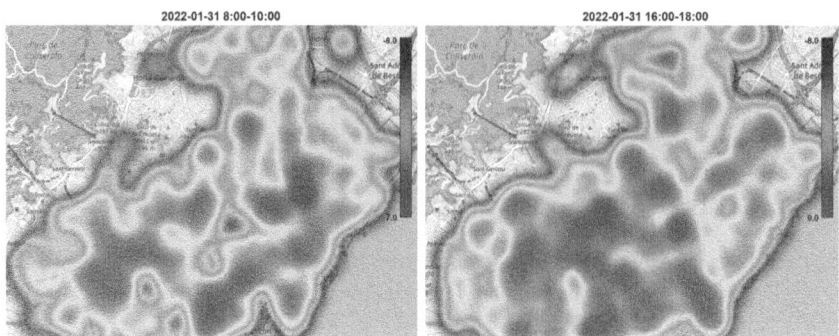

Fig. 1. Bike demand density (of stations) for two different time intervals, 8:00–10:00 and 16:00–18:00 for 31/1/2022. The two intervals illustrate different user behavior. This observation motivates the need for a dynamic redistribution strategy.

geographic locations, the systems are known as *Station-Based* (SB-BSSs). Otherwise, if the users can end their ride and leave the bike at any point to be picked up again for another trip, the systems are known as *Free-Floating* (FF-BSSs).

These systems are greatly affected by the dynamic nature of user behavior. Bike trips are tightly connected to spatio-temporal information, i.e., users are more likely to pick up bikes in urban areas early in the day and drop them off in the same area later in the day. Additionally, bike trips may be affected by events like extreme weather conditions or festivals. This creates imbalances in supply and demand which affects user satisfaction and has economic impact on the organization operating the BSS. To tackle this challenge, BSSs usually include a redistribution strategy to relocate idle bikes where demand is expected to be high. Such strategies can be classified as static and dynamic, namely *Static* (S-BSS) and *Dynamic* (D-BSS), respectively. In the static case, bikes are redistributed at a fixed time in the day, usually at some point in the night when demand is at its lowest, to even out the bike spread over the region for the next day. Contrary to that, in the dynamic approach the redistribution may happen at several points in time in a day, usually at fixed time intervals. While static redistribution has less operational costs associated with, it is incapable of reacting to dynamic changes in bike demand. In Fig. 1 we illustrate the need of a dynamic redistribution approach based on the dataset we used for this paper.

Whatever the BSS operational type, accurate demand prediction is of the essence. Without modeling and predicting the bike demand for a future time period, however good may a redistribution model be, it will fall short as it will fail to meet the actual user activity. In BSSs it is especially difficult, because users do not go through a vehicle request process, which usually takes place in other vehicle systems. Historically, this demand prediction has been of active research as it is necessary for the redistribution process. Motivated by this, in this paper, we address the problem of combined demand prediction and redistribution planning using Automated Machine Learning techniques and in particular

Bayesian Optimization (BO) to tackle the problem of demand prediction, along with redistribution planning based on a linear programming problem defined in the next sections, in order to provide operators with an optimal redistribution strategy.

In summary, we make the following contributions in this paper:

- We cast the problem of demand forecasting for bike-sharing systems as an AutoML-based time series forecasting problem, in order to obtain highly accurate predictions of bike demand.
- We formalize the problem of bike redistribution among the stations of a bike-sharing system based on the Minimum Cost Flow (MCF) problem.
- We present experiments using real-world data from a bike rental operator (Serveo) in Barcelona to evaluate the effectiveness of our approach.

The rest of the paper is structured as follows. Section 2 provides an overview of related work. Section 3 formally defines the problem. Then, in Sect. 4, we present our pipeline for bike demand forecasting and bike redistribution. Section 5 reports the results of the experimental evaluation. Finally, Sect. 6 concludes the paper and points to future research directions.

2   Related Work

The vehicle redistribution problem has been researched under various contexts. One specific area of study is that of empty vehicle redistribution, inspired by the recent traction of autonomous driving vehicles. Some of the recent works [2,10] that focus on this sub-domain, are modeled to include knowledge on passenger wait-time which they model according to proposed utility functions.

Bike-Sharing Systems. Bike redistribution is also being actively researched. In [3,11], a set of mathematical formulations for bike demand and the rebalancing problem are presented. Additionally possible constraints that may be taken into account under different applications are presented. Finally, in the lastly aforementioned work, proposed algorithms and methodologies are benchmarked.

Station clustering has been explored in [6,17]. In [17], the authors use a community detection approach on the graph that represents bike stations (vertices) and bike flows (directed edges). In [6], the bike stations are first classified as supply and demand stations and then are clustered accordingly to create a super-node per cluster. The station matching for bike redistribution is performed upon these produced nodes.

In [12], total station demand is calculated by separately predicting pick up rate and drop off rate for 1h time intervals. The pick up rate is predicted through a weighted KNN that takes into account weather information as well. The drop off rate is predicted based on predicted pick up rate by leveraging a multimodal gaussian distribution to estimate whether picked up bicycles will arrive at their destination at this interval or the next. Rebalancing afterwards is achieved through Mixed Integer Programming on clustered stations to eliminate outliers.

In [15], the authors formulate the BRP in four stages: (1) a demand forecasting model that anticipates inventory levels at different time intervals, (2) station inventory model determines the optimal initial inventory level such that in the next time period system inefficiencies, (3) redistribution needs model that models the redistribution's plan and (4) vehicle routing model that maximizes the utility of redistribution vehicles. Both (1) and (2) are taking advantage of heterogeneous data such as inventory level, traffic and weather and are trained in a dynamic manner (periodically). For (1) the authors use gradient boosting machines and for (2), assuming that departures and arrivals at a station follow a Poisson distribution the authors compute their parameters from historical data. For (3) the authors formulate the redistribution problem as a stochastic linear integer program, whereas for (4) they use an arc and sequence-indexed formulation.

In this paper, we formulate the BRP using real-world historical data to compute the demand and combine this information with real-world traffic information to provide the operator with a redistribution strategy, solving a linear program problem.

AutoML for Time Series. Time series forecasting (TSF) methods can be broadly classified in statistical methods, machine learning methods and deep learning methods. The best performing method depends on various criteria; the application domain, the dataset at hand, the size of historical data, etc. Moreover, each method uses a large number of hyperparameters and finding the optimal values is a time-consuming task, both for the data scientist as well as in relation with the computational resources for evaluation of different setups. To cope with these challenges, a recent trend is to apply Automated Machine Learning (AutoML) [8] techniques in order to automatically detect the best forecasting algorithm and configuration of hyperparameters, without exhaustively testing a huge number of configurations. In the case of BRP where bikes' demand is represented by time series and results' provision needs to be short-termed, AutoML to deal with TSF is essential in order to provide redistribution operators with valid demand predictions very quickly.

AutoARIMA and AutoETS [9] are processes for automating parameter selection for the statistical algorithms ARIMA (Auto-Regressive Intergrated Moving Average) and EST (Exponential Smoothing). Hyndman and Khandakar included these methods for the first time in 2008 in an R package and they are based on the minimization of an information criterion like Akaike's Information Criterion (AIC) or the Bayesian Information Criterion (BIC).

AutoGluon-Time Series (AG-TS) [16] is a Python AutoML library for probabilistic time series forecasting. It contains a variety of forecasting algorithms: statistical, machine learning based and ensembles. It is easy to use and provides to the non-expert end user the ability to perform precise forecasts using a convex combination of forecasted values produced with different forecasters. In this way, AG-TS takes advantage of several predictors.

Auto-Pytorch-TS [4] is an AutoTSF framework for Automated Deep Learning time series forecasting, which was built as an extension of the Auto-Pytorch

[18] package for tabular datasets. The authors introduce a novel Neural Architecture Search (NAS) approach that deals with the joint problem of neural architecture search and data processing hyperparameters' optimization for time series data, taking advantage of BO.

In this paper, we address the AutoML for time series forecasting problem directly, using BO for a predefined number of iterations. In this way, not only we examine different configurations of the search space without human interaction to find the best algorithm's configuration, but we also provide the redistribution operator with the best forecasts in a fast manner.

3 Problem Definition

In this section, we present the problem setting for our work. We identify two subproblems, bike demand forecasting (Sect. 3.1) and bike redistribution (Sect. 3.2). Our approach addresses both of these subproblems, offering an end-to-end solution.

3.1 Bike Demand Forecasting

In this subsection we define the basic concepts of our problem that are connected to the bike demand forecasting problem. Let $S = \{i : i = 1, \ldots, z\}$ denote a set of z stations of bikes, where a station is a fixed-place location of specific capacity (total number of bikes that can be placed there). Users can borrow bikes from a station or return a bike after the trip has been conducted. Supposing that we examine a time interval $[t_{start}, t_{end})$, let a uniform and non-overlapping discretization of n distinct time intervals $T = \{T_1, \ldots, T_n\}$ where $T_i = [t_i, t_{i+1}) \subset [t_{start}, t_{end})$, so that $T_k \cap T_l = \emptyset$, $\forall T_k \neq T_l$ and

$$\delta T = |T_i| = |t_{i+1} - t_i| = \frac{t_{end} - t_{start}}{n}, \ \forall T_i \qquad (1)$$

We define the demand of the i-th station to be the sequence (time series) $\mathcal{D}_i(t)$, that corresponds to the total number of bikes that departs or arrive at station i for a time interval that is denoted by the index t. The bike demand forecasting problem is that of predicting the demand $\mathcal{D}_i(T_j)$ for a station i at the time interval T_j.

3.2 The Bike Redistribution Problem

Here we formulate the so-called Minimum-Cost Flow Problem (MCFP) under the bike redistribution assumptions. Our goal is to redistribute bikes among stations in an optimal manner to cover future demand.

Let a flow network $\mathcal{G} = (V, E)$ be a directed graph with a source node $v \in V$ and a destination node $u \in V$ that represent stations. The source node v represents the station from which we take a number of bikes and redistribute them to the destination node u. Each edge $(v, u) \in E$ carries a *weight* $f(v, u)$

that represents the number of bikes that need to be transported from node v to node u Typically, the $f(v, u)$ weights are the problem's variables which we seek to estimate and they describe the number of bikes that operator has to transfer from station v to station u.

Additionally, each $(v, u) \in E$ has a *capacity* $cap(v, u)$, indicating the maximum number of bikes that the redistribution vehicles can transport. Also, each $(v, u) \in E$ is associated with $cost(v, u)$, a value which indicates the estimated travel time from station v to station u.

Finally, every $v \in V$ has a supply/demand indicator $d(v)$, which suggests whether a node v has surplus or shortage of bikes. More precisely, given $v \in V$ and for a fixed time interval t, $d(v)$ is equal to $\mathcal{D}_i(t)$ (as defined in Sect. 3.1) where v is the node that corresponds to station i.

The bike redistribution MCFP is formulated as a linear programming problem as follows:

$$\min_{\{f(v,u):(v,u)\in E\}} \sum_{(v,u)\in E} cost(v, u) \cdot f(v, u) \tag{2}$$

such that

1. $f(v, u) \leq cap(v, u), \ \forall (v, u) \in E$
2. $\sum_{w\in V} f(u, w) - \sum_{w\in V} f(w, u) = d(u), \ \forall u \in V$
3. $f(u, v) \geq 0, \ \forall (u, v) \in E$

The second constraint illustrates a notion of balance. This means that it enforces the difference of the outgoing flow $\left(\sum_{w\in V} f(u, w) \right)$ minus the incoming flow $\left(\sum_{w\in V} f(w, u) \right)$ of a node u, to be equal with its total demand $d(u)$ and is derived from the general assumptions of MCFP per se.

As mentioned earlier, the solution of MCFP will be the weights $f(v, u), \ \forall (v, u) \in E$ that represent the total number of bikes the operator has to transfer from the station that corresponds to node v to the one of node u (Fig. 2).

4 Proposed Framework

The objective of our approach is to optimize bike redistribution among the stations, in order to maximize bike availability based on the predicted users' demand. The main steps of our approach are briefly described below:

1. **Data Preparation.** We extract a time series of demand from the raw trip data. Each station is associated with a time series of bike demand values for that station for the discretization of time into intervals $\mathcal{T} = \{T_1, \ldots, T_n\}$.
2. **Time series AutoML.** We perform AutoML for each time series to efficiently search the space of forecasting algorithms and hyperparameters. This produces a predicted demand value for each station for the next time interval.

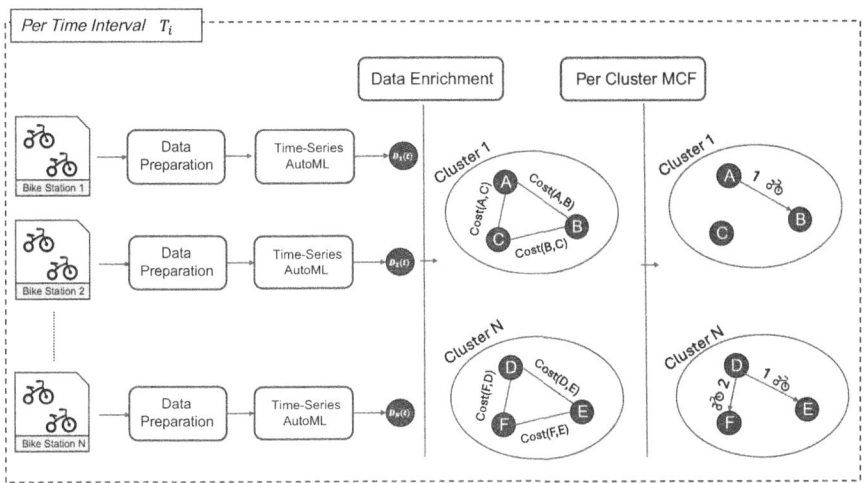

Fig. 2. The end-to-end framework for bike redistribution. For a specific time interval, we create the time series for each station and use AutoML to find the best forecasting algorithm for each station. Then, we predict the demand for each station, and for each cluster of stations, we form the graph that also captures the travel distance between stations. The solution of the MCFP determines the redistribution in each cluster.

3. **Data Enrichment.** The predicted demand values are enriched with the transportation time between stations, obtained from data of OpenStreetMap.

4. **Per Cluster MCF.** Finally, we consider k geographical clusters of stations, and build a graph for each cluster. The stations of each cluster correspond to graph nodes. The capacity is defined as the number of bikes that the operator can load to a redistribution vehicle. The cost between two stations corresponds to the estimated transportation time. Then, we solve the Minimum Cost Flow problem with relaxed constraints for every such graph.

4.1   Data Preparation

The first step is to process raw data of bike trips from one station to another to calculate the historic bike demand for each station. Each record of trips consists of (i) a trip Id, (ii) its Start Time, (iii) its End Time, (iv) the Start Station Id, and (v) the End Station Id. We partition the time into intervals $\mathcal{T} = \{T_1, \ldots, T_n\}$ and we consider the records of each group.

For every station $i \in \mathcal{S}$, we consider two time series $\mathcal{I}_i(t)$ and $\mathcal{O}_i(t)$, $t \in \{T_1, \ldots, T_n\}$, that correspond to the number of incoming and outgoing bikes during time interval t for station i, respectively. Incoming bikes are the bikes that users return to station i during an indexed time interval t, while outgoing bikes are the ones borrowed from station i during t. The time series of demand for station i for an indexed time interval t is the difference between the time series $\mathcal{O}_i(t)$ and $\mathcal{I}_i(t)$:

$$\mathcal{D}_i(t) = \mathcal{O}_i(t) - \mathcal{I}_i(t), \ t \in \{T_1, \ldots, T_n\} \tag{3}$$

Positive values of demand during t indicate that station i had a need for bikes, because the number of trips that considered i as a starting point was greater than the number of trips that considered i as an ending point. On the other hand, negative values of demand during t indicate a surplus of bikes for station i during t. Based on this, the network of stations is considered as a network that can balance itself. Stations with negative predicted demand are used in the redistribution procedure in order to provide bikes to those with positive predicted demand.

4.2   Bike Demand Forecasting

The first problem that we face is the prediction of the demand $\mathcal{D}_i(t)$ for every station i. Since the demand is represented as a time series, we need to employ time series forecasting (TSF) methods. In the literature, one can find many methods for TSF that can be broadly classified in three main categories: i) statistical methods, ii) machine learning methods and iii) deep learning methods. Each TSF method comes along with different hyperparameters, so apart from finding the best performing TSF method, we also need to find the optimal values for its hyperparameters.

AutoML for TSF (AutoTSF) seeks to solve the so-called Combined Algorithm Selection and Hyper-parameter tuning (CASH) for TSF methods. In essence, it seeks to find the TSF method and the values of its respective hyperparameters that minimizes a given error metric. Formally, let the following equation be the one to optimize:

$$\mathcal{A}^* = \arg \min_{m_\lambda} \mathcal{L}(\mathcal{D}_{train}, \mathcal{D}_{val}, m_\lambda) \tag{4}$$

where $(\mathcal{D}_{train}, \mathcal{D}_{val}) \sim \mathcal{D}$ is a train-test split of a dataset $\mathcal{D}$, $m \in \mathcal{M}$ is a TSF method from a collection of available methods $\mathcal{M}$, $\lambda \in \Lambda_m$ is a parametric vector of the hyperparameter search space of method m, m_λ is the method m instantiated with parameters λ and $\mathcal{L}$ is a loss metric function.

In this paper, we deploy Bayesian Optimization (BO) [7] in order to solve the CASH problem. BO is a probabilistic optimization framework that optimizes black-box functions. In detail, for each time series $\mathcal{D}_i(t)$, $t \in \{T_1, \ldots, T_n\}$, we select an index $r \in \{1, \ldots, n\}$ and split the time series in two parts: $\mathcal{D}_i^{train}(t)$, $t \in \{T_1 \ldots, T_r\}$ and $\mathcal{D}_i^{test}(t)$, $t \in \{T_{r+1} \ldots, T_n\}$. We examine two cases:

1. Consider a set of TSF methods $\mathcal{M} = \{m_1, \ldots, m_w\}$ together with the sets of their hyperparameters $\Lambda_{m_1}, \ldots, \Lambda_{m_w}$. In this case, we use the Mean Absolute Error (MAE) as loss metric to solve the optimization problem:

$$m, p = \arg \min_{m_j, p_j} MAE \left(\mathcal{D}_i^{test}, \hat{\mathcal{D}}_i^{test} |_{m_j, p_j} \right) \tag{5}$$

with BO, where $\hat{\mathcal{D}}_i^{test}|_{m_j,p_j}$ is the prediction of $\mathcal{D}_i^{test}|_{m_j,p_j}$ training the algorithm m_j with hyperparameters $p_j \in \Lambda_{m_j}$.

2. Consider a TSF method m together with the set of its hyperparameters Λ_m. In this case, we use the Mean Absolute Error (MAE) as loss metric to solve the optimization problem:

$$p = \arg\min_{p_j} MAE \left(\mathcal{D}_i^{test}, \hat{\mathcal{D}}_i^{test}|_{m,p_j} \right) \tag{6}$$

with BO, where $\hat{\mathcal{D}}_i^{test}|_{m,p_j}$ is the prediction of $\mathcal{D}_i^{test}|_{m,p_j}$ training the method m with hyperparameters $p_j \in \Lambda_m$.

4.3   Data Enrichment

Furthermore, we use the cost of transportation for any pair of stations. Specifically, we retrieve this information from OpenStreetMap [14]. For every pair of geographical points x=(longitude$_1$, latitude$_1$) and $y = $ (longitude$_2$, latitude$_2$) that correspond to two different stations x and y, we retrieve every possible route that connects them. Afterwards, we compute for each pair of stations the shortest route, which is used to finally define $cost(x,y)$ as the cost to travel from station x to y.

4.4   Bike Redistribution

Let $\mathcal{S}$ be a set of stations and $\mathcal{D}_i(t)$, $t = \{T_1,\ldots,T_n\}$, their corresponding demand time series, as defined in Sect. 3. Let also $\hat{\mathcal{D}}_i(q)$ be the predicted demand for every station $i \in \mathcal{S}$ for the time index q that corresponds to the time interval $[t_{end}, t_{end} + \delta\mathcal{T})$, where $\delta\mathcal{T}$ is defined in Eq. 1. We consider a directed graph $\mathcal{G} = (V, E)$, where V is the set of nodes corresponding to stations and E is the set of directed vertices that indicates connections between the nodes of V.

After initializing the graph, we solve the corresponding MCFP, using as demand the values $\hat{\mathcal{D}}_i(q)$ for every node v that corresponds to a station i and by using the costs that were defined in the previous subsection. Under these assumptions, we recommend a redistribution strategy based on the predicted demand, in order to provide the operator with a plan that will cover the future demand.

The second assumption of the MCFP as defined in Sect. 3.2 is very strict, since in real-world applications (like the bike repositioning, the problem we are trying to tackle here) there are no guarantees that the total demand will sum up to zero. What we want to achieve in our case, is that outgoing flow-incoming flow will always cover the station's demand, so we can relax the second constraint as follows

$$\sum_{w\in V} f(u,w) - \sum_{w\in V} f(w,u) \geq d(u), \ \forall u \in V \tag{7}$$

So we end up with the problem's constraints defined below:

1. $f(v,u) \leq cap(v,u),\ \forall(v,u) \in E$

2. $\sum_{w \in V} f(u, w) - \sum_{w \in V} f(w, u) \geq d(u), \ \forall u \in V$

3. $f(u, v) \geq 0, \ \forall (u, v) \in E$

The replacement of the second constraint (from equality to inequality) might create artificial nodes (in the case that the total demand is greater than zero $\sum_{v \in V} d(v) > 0$), but we assume that stations have a surplus of bikes and the operator will always be able to use bikes from stations with negative demand in order to use them during the rebalancing.

Note that one could tackle the MCFP as an Integer Programming (IP) problem. Since IP problems are hard to solve, we chose to treat the MCFP as a Linear Programming (LP) problem. Generally LP problems provide continuous solutions (in our case flows of bikes to be redistributed) and for this reason, as the corresponding flows $f(v, u)$ might be continuous, we perform a rounding in order to make sure that our results are integers.

Additionally, we assume that the available stations are clustered in different subgroups. While this clustering can occur in different ways, in this paper, we utilize clustering based on the geo-location of stations. The clustering is provided by the BSS operator, but other clustering algorithms can be explored as well.

5   Experiments

In this section, we present the results of our experimentation. Our framework is tested using real-world data obtained from the Serveo Bike Sharing System operating in Barcelona for accuracy and efficiency. The framework is implemented in Python and we use the Optuna library [1] to conduct BO and the PuLP [13] library for MCFP optimization.

5.1   Experimental Setup

Dataset. Our data consist of bike trips recorded in January 2022 in the city of Barcelona. Each record consists of the starting and ending station, departure and arrival time and an associated trip id. We partition the trips in 2-h intervals and aggregate incoming and outgoing bikes per interval. There exist 469 bike stations and for each pair of stations we additionally retrieve the cost of transportation, i.e., the estimated travel time of the shortest route, as provided by OpenStreetMap.

Evaluation Methodology. We evaluate our framework in two stages. First, we explore the efficiency of the AutoML solution applied for bike demand forecasting. From the available 469 time series that correspond to each station, we select two of them that significantly differ in terms of volatility and seasonality (shown in Fig. 3), and exhaustively search their hyperparameter space through Grid Search. Additionally, we apply Bayesian Optimization (BO) over the same space, with a budget equal to that of Grid Search and compare the results.

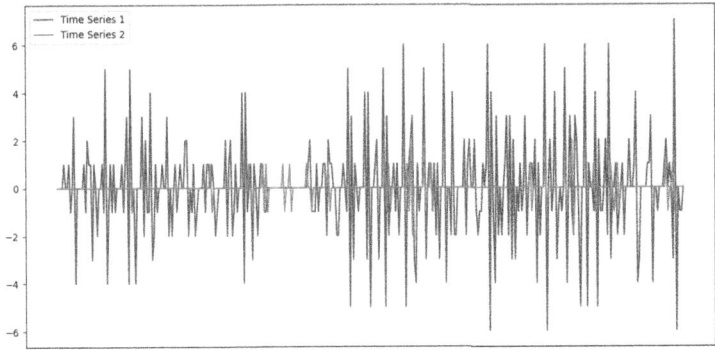

Fig. 3. Demand for two selected time series (1/1/1022–31/1/2022).

For Grid Search, continuous parametric spaces are discretized manually. On the other hand, BO may sample any point in the continuous space.

Moreover, we apply our MCF solution for each cluster of stations. For each station, we apply a narrowed-down version of AutoML based on our findings over the previous experiment. Afterwards, we forecast the demand for each station over the next 2-h time interval, by using the best individual algorithm configuration found. We then report the accuracy of the time series forecasting algorithms, visualize redistribution results and discuss our findings on how per cluster MCF may reduce operational time.

Parameters. For the AutoML in times series forecasting, we considered several types of algorithms including statistical algorithms (ARIMA, Holt Winter's Exponential Smoothing (ES), Holt Exponential Smoothing (H-ES) and Simple Exponential Smoothing (S-ES)), one deep learning algorithm (Multilayer Perceptron, MLP) and a machine learning algorithm (XGBoost Regressor, XGBoost). In Table 1, we show for each algorithm, the number of possible configurations for its hyperparameters, i.e., the size of the search space. We must also highlight, that we do not include to our experimentation other deep learning baselines, such as LSTMs, RNNs etc., due to the fact that their evaluation is empirically more computationally expensive and contradicts the operational time limits we have, even though those approaches have proven to be efficient for time series forecasting tasks.

Table 1. Number of configurations for each algorithm during Grid Search.

Algorithms	ARIMA	ES	H-ES	S-ES	MLP	XGBoost
Cardinality	1000	800	400	20	1600	15,361

Evaluation. In order to evaluate the demand forecasting algorithms, we split the time series for every station i in $\mathcal{D}_i^{train}$ and $\mathcal{D}_i^{test}$ as defined in Sect. 4.2. We keep 80% of the original data for training and the remaining 20% for evaluation. When conducting BO, we additionally split $\mathcal{D}_i^{train}$ again accordingly to use 20% of the training data for optimization. We consider two different evaluations of accuracy on test data, $\mathcal{D}_i^{test}$:

1. n-Steps-Ahead-Forecasting (n-SAF): In this case, we evaluate the forecasting capability of the algorithm m for longer time horizons. For each T_j, $j > r$ we use for the prediction of the corresponding demand value, $\hat{D}_i(T_j)$, the already forecasted demand values of T_k, $r < k < j$. Formally, this is defined as follows:

$$\hat{\mathcal{D}}_i^{test}(T_j) = m\left(\mathcal{D}_i^{train}, \hat{D}_i(T_{r+1}), \ldots, \hat{D}_i(T_{j-1})\right), \forall r < j \leq n \qquad (8)$$

2. 1-Step-Ahead-Forecasting (1-SAF): In this case, we focus on short term predictions. We assume that for every T_j, $j > r$, the demand of $\mathcal{D}_i^{test}(T_k)$ is known $\forall r < k < j$. Formally, this is defined as follows:

$$\hat{\mathcal{D}}_i^{test}(T_j) = m\left(\mathcal{D}_i^{train}, \mathcal{D}_i(T_{r+1}), \ldots, \mathcal{D}_i(T_{j-1})\right), \forall r < j \leq n \qquad (9)$$

Selecting an algorithm according to n-SAF methodology, is useful when we expect operational failures (e.g., stations' power outage, network's lack of communication etc.). On the other hand, algorithms selected according to their 1-SAF capability will likely be more competent but require the actual time series value at each time interval.

Metrics. We use the Mean Absolute Error (MAE), which is the absolute difference between actual and predicted demand for each station averaged over the set of time intervals. Formally it is defined as follows for each station (node) $v \in V$:

$$MAE(v) = \frac{1}{n - r - 1} \sum_{t=r+1,\ldots,n} \left| d(v)_t - \hat{d}(v)_t \right| \qquad (10)$$

5.2   Experimental Evaluation of Demand Forecasting

Our findings over the extensive configuration search on the two selected time series of Fig. 3 are presented in Table 2 and Table 3 for n-SAF and 1-SAF, respectively. Our first observation is that all forecasting algorithms achieve a relatively low error.

In the case of n-SAF, we identify that the best performing algorithm is ARIMA for both time series across both strategies, with the lowest error in terms of MAE being equal to 1.5665 and 0.2133 for the two time series respectively. In the case of 1-SAF, we observe that MLP outperforms both ARIMA and XGBoost, achieving around 14.6% and 17.12% improvement over the other two, respectively. These observations imply that different algorithms may perform best depending on the application scenario.

It is also worth mentioning that some experiments conducted with BO might be slightly better than the respective Grid Search, e.g., for ES and H-ES. This is because of the discretization of the search space of continuous hyperparameters for Grid Search, whereas BO is applicable on continuous variables as such. We also note that for the 1-SAF case we used only the three algorithms that can be used for such types of predictions without the need of refitting the respective algorithms.

Table 2. Comparison of exhaustive search to BO for two time series in terms of MAE for n steps ahead forecast (n-SAF).

	Time Series 1		Time Series 2	
	Grid Search MAE	BO MAE	Grid Search MAE	BO MAE
ARIMA	**1.5665**	1.5671	**0.2133**	**0.2133**
ES	1.6027	**1.6005**	**0.2133**	**0.2133**
H-ES	1.6027	**1.6005**	**0.2133**	**0.2133**
S-ES	**1.6000**	**1.6000**	**0.2133**	**0.2133**
MLP	**1.6375**	1.6384	**0.2173**	**0.2173**
XGBoost	**1.6376**	**1.6376**	**0.2173**	**0.2173**

Table 3. Comparison of exhaustive search to BO for two time series in terms of MAE for one step ahead forecast (1-SAF).

	Time Series 1		Time Series 2	
	Grid Search MAE	BO MAE	Grid Search MAE	BO MAE
ARIMA	**1.5860**	1.5875	**0.2133**	1.0715
MLP	**1.3546**	1.5688	**0.1268**	0.1334
XGBoost	**1.6344**	1.6353	0.2167	**0.2166**

In terms of error, all algorithms showcase smaller MAE for 1-SAF than n-SAF. This result is reasonable due to the fact that in the 1-SAF case, we make the assumption that the ground truth is available, whereas on the other hand in the n-SAF case we use predicted demand. As a result, even though n-SAF may seem as a more practical predictive framework, as highlighted in the Section above, 1-SAF provides more accurate predictions, as such we adopt it in our proposed end-to-end framework.

Focusing on the on the 1-SAF case, we conducted BO only for MLP for both time series, because MLP outperforms both ARIMA and XGBoost for both time series, given a budget of 1600 trials, which is the same as for Grid Search. BO for time series 1 achieved the best MAE value of 1.3674, found in trial 386.

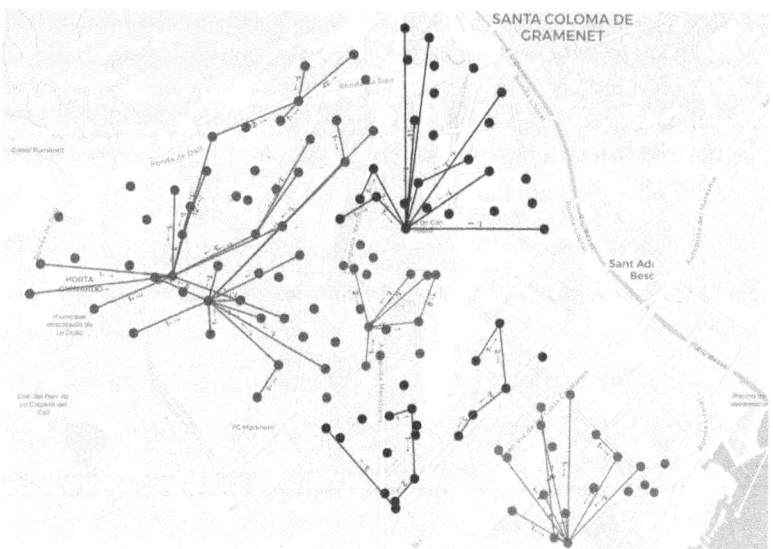

Fig. 4. A sample of redistribution per cluster of stations. Differently colored nodes represent different clusters. Edges represent the number of bikes to be transported between stations.

The respective best MAE value for time series 2 is 0.2225, found in trial 1062. Both results highlight the fact that BO is an effective solution of algorithm optimization, especially when the relative error is higher, as indicated from time series 1. For this reason, we choose to use BO for MLP for the prediction of all stations' demand future moving forward. Considering BO's execution time and in order to align with operational time limits, we chose to conduct BO for all time series using a number of trials that is equal to the 1/3 of MLP's cardinality (533 trials).

We choose to conduct BO for every station separately using MLP, as it is clear from the diverse nature of the given time series, that a single model may not be suitable for every station, so while we use a unique algorithm for all (MLP), we optimize its hyper-parameters, according to the data given.

5.3   Practical Application and Evaluation of MCF

Capitalizing on our findings over the case study on the two time series, we proceed with the evaluation of the MCF model over clusters of stations.

First, we apply for each stations' demand time series BO set to search the configuration space of MLP with a budget of 533 iterations equal to 1/3 of the trials considered in exhaustively searching MLP, based on the results discussed in the previous subsection. We then forecast the demand value for each station over the next 2-hour time interval. In Fig. 5, we showcase a box-plot of the MAE value for each station. We report the average validation MAE across every station to be 1.0964 with standard deviation of 0.7097. Out of 464 stations, we also identify 17 that had an error rate larger than 2.5, which may be accounted to various factors such as unexpected events in the specific time interval, or general forecast difficulty due to the time series specifics. Moreover, we report that BO found the best configuration on trial number 279 on average for every station.

These predictions are afterwards provided along with the estimated duration for each trip among a pair of nodes to our MCF based approach. We identify the station clusters according to their geographic locations, and apply MCF for each of these clusters. The resulting bikes to be transported are then retrieved, as shown in Fig. 4 just for a sample of the available clusters.

Finally, we compare the execution time of the MCF solving algorithm when applied to each cluster against running MCF over all stations (i.e., 1 cluster). We report the average execution time of per cluster MCF to be around 0.38 s. The total execution time for per cluster MCF is 15.64 s, against 8.54 min of execution time when applying MCF over all stations. We note the magnitude of difference between the two approaches, especially since long execution times may be prohibitive when there is need for redistribution in short time intervals.

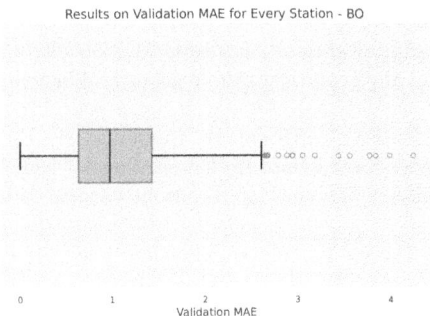

Fig. 5. Best validation MAE achieved for every station after Bayesian Optimization

6   Conclusions and Future Work

In this paper, we proposed an AutoML-based approach for bike demand forecasting and redistribution. To address the first problem of bike demand forecasting, we adopt an AutoML approach that uses Bayesian Optimization in order to find the best time series forecasting method and values of its hyperparameters. Then, the second problem is to determine the process of bike redistribution among stations to cover the predicted demand. To this end, we cast the problem of bike redistribution to the Minimum-Cost Flow Problem to find the optimal solution. Our experiments with real-world data show that careful use of AutoML can indeed find a well performing configuration close to the optimal much faster than traditional approaches, and that a meaningful redistribution can be computed. In our future work, it would be interesting to deploy our redistribution in operational settings to evaluate the improvement of the bike sharing service and user satisfaction. Additionally, future work may include modeling of the demand that is unknown to the system due to the unavailability of bikes in a station, taking also into consideration other validation metrics to align with the robustness of the data.

Acknowledgements. This work has received funding from the Horizon Europe research and innovation programme under the GA 101070416 (project Green.DAT.AI).

References

1. Akiba, T., Sano, S., Yanase, T., Ohta, T., Koyama, M.: Optuna: a next-generation hyperparameter optimization framework. In: Proceedings of SIGKDD, pp. 2623–2631, 2019
2. Babicheva, T., Burghout, W.: Empty vehicle redistribution in autonomous taxi services. EURO J. Transp. Logist. **8**(5), 745–767 (2019). https://doi.org/10.1007/s13676-019-00146-5
3. Dell'Amico, M., Hadjicostantinou, E., Iori, M., Novellani, S.: The bike sharing rebalancing problem: mathematical formulations and benchmark instances. Omega **45**, 7–19 (2014)
4. Deng, D., Karl, F., Hutter, F., Bischl, B., Lindauer, M.: Efficient automated deep learning for time series forecasting. In: Proceedings of PKDD, pp. 664–680, 2022
5. Fishman, E.: Bikeshare: a review of recent literature. Transp. Rev. **36**, 92–113 (2016)
6. Gan, J., Zhang, G., Zhang, Y.: Bike rebalancing: how to find a balanced matching in the k center problem? Eur. J. Oper. Res. **316**, 845–855 (2024)
7. Garnett, R.: Bayesian Optimization. Cambridge University Press, Cambridge (2023)
8. Hutter, F., Kotthoff, L., Vanschoren, J. (eds.): Automated Machine Learning - Methods, Systems, Challenges. Springer (2019)
9. Hyndman, R.J., Khandakar, Y.: Automatic time series forecasting: the forecast package for R. J. Stat. Softw. **27**(3), 1–22 (2008)
10. Karamanis, R., Anastasiadis, E., Stettler, M., Angeloudis, P.: Vehicle redistribution in ride-sourcing markets using convex minimum cost flows. IEEE Trans. Intell. Transp. Syst. **23**, 10287–10298 (2022)
11. Liang, J., Jena, S. D., Lodi, A.: Dynamic rebalancing optimization for bike-sharing systems: a modeling framework and empirical comparison. Eur. J. Oper. Res. **317**, 875–889 (2024)
12. Liu, J., Sun, L., Chen, W., Xiong, H.: Rebalancing bike sharing systems: a multi-source data smart optimization. In: Proceedings of SIGKDD, pp. 1005–1014, 2016
13. Liu, J., Sun, L., Chen, W., Xiong, H.: PuLP: a linear programming toolkit for Python (2011)
14. OpenStreetMap contributors. Planet dump retrieved from, 2017. https://planet.osm.org, https://www.openstreetmap.org

15. Regue, R., Recker, W.: Proactive vehicle routing with inferred demand to solve the bikesharing rebalancing problem. Transp. Res. Part E: Logist. Transp. Rev. **72**, 192–209 (2014)

16. Shchur, O., et al.: Autogluon-timeseries: automl for probabilistic time series forecasting. In: Proceedings of AutoML, pp. 9/1–21, 2023

17. Wang, Y.-J., Kuo, Y.-H., Huang, G.Q., Weihua, G., Yaohua, H.: Dynamic demand-driven bike station clustering. Transp. Res. Part E: Logist. Transp. Rev. **160**, 102656 (2022)

18. Zimmer, L., Lindauer, M., Hutter, F.: Auto-pytorch: multi-fidelity metalearning for efficient and robust autodl. IEEE Trans. Pattern Anal. Mach. Intell. **43**, 3079–3090 (2021)

Adaptive Stop-Skipping Scheduling Approach Using Reinforcement Learning

Perla Hajjar[1,2]([⊠])(iD), Leïla Kloul[2], and Dominique Barth[2]

[1] Communauté d'Agglomération de Saint Quentin en Yvelines, Trappes, France
[2] Laboratoire DAVID/Université Versailles SQY/Université Paris Saclay,
Versailles, France
{perla.hajjar,leila.kloul,dominique.barth}@uvsq.fr

Abstract. To adapt to real-time variations, stop-skipping control has been widely adopted in public transport systems. However, solving the optimal stopping pattern for buses in static bus scheduling problems is challenging due to its combinatorial nature. The complexity of this problem increases exponentially as the number of stations increases, making it difficult to find the best solution in real time. To overcome such a limitation, this paper proposes an adaptive scheduling game model approach using the stop skipping control strategy. The adaptive game model aims to minimize passenger delay by adjusting bus stops, demonstrating the effectiveness of continuous schedule adaptation against a fixed, pre-determined schedule. This game is then solved with Reinforcement Learning (RL) to optimize the bus scheduling sequence based the current system's state. We compare this approach against the Simulated Annealing metaheuristic algorithm in finding a near-optimal schedule. Our results show that the RL-based adaptive scheduling outperforms the schedule found statically and all-stop schedules, reducing waiting, ride, and total trip times.

Keywords: Stop-skipping · Adaptive bus scheduling · Reinforcement Learning · Simulated Annealing

1 Introduction

With the expansion of cities, traditional models of public transport systems struggle to find a balance between frequency of services, time spent in traveling, and operational costs, especially at peak hours when the demand and congestion are highest [1]. Traditional approaches, such as static schedules, struggle to adapt to real-time changes often leading to inefficiencies like increased passenger waiting time or bus bunching.

Solutions have been proposed in the literature such as the increase of the frequency of the bus lines and bus control strategies, such as dedicated bus lanes, traffic signal priority, and vehicle holding [2,7]. However, these solutions require additional infrastructure and operational costs. In addition, while these

A. Kocian et al. (Eds.): INTSYS 2024, LNICST 608, pp. 162–176, 2025.
https://doi.org/10.1007/978-3-031-86370-7_10

strategies are effective in reducing passengers traveling times, they do not address the problem of adapting dynamically to real-time changes in passengers' demand.

The stop-skipping control strategy has gained attraction in recent years. It allows buses to bypass certain stops based on the current demand to improve travel time efficiency and reduce operational costs [4]. However, determining optimal stop-skipping schedules in real-time is a complex combinatorial problem due to fluctuating and unpredictable passenger demand.

In our previous work [13], we adopted the stop-skipping control strategy to solve the optimal scheduling problem in a fixed demand scenario, with the objective of finding a unique global optimal schedule that minimizes passenger delay. Once this schedule was identified, it remained fixed and was applied consistently until all the passengers are served. Our static model successfully learns the optimal bus schedule. However, in real-world scenarios, passengers continuously board at bus stations, which results in changes in the demand matrix. As a result, a pre-calculated static schedule may no longer be the optimal solution as the state of the system changes.

To address this limitation, we propose an adaptive scheduling game model capable of adapting to the current system's state. In this model, we aim to investigate if the generation of a sequence of schedules as the system's state changes may result in improved minimization of passenger delay compared to maintaining a fixed, pre-calculated schedule. Given the demand matrix, our objective is to obtain an optimal bus scheduling sequence that minimizes passengers' delay. In order to enable adaptive stop-skipping decisions based on evolving passenger demand, we suggest the use of Reinforcement Learning (RL) approach that has showed its ability to find a global optimal bus schedule in the static model. The RL allows the system to learn optimal actions through trial and error with the goal of minimizing passenger delay by optimizing the bus schedules. We compare the performance of the RL approach with a traditional metaheuristic approach, specifically Simulated Annealing (SA).

The rest of this paper is structured as follows: Sect. 2 reviews the related literature on stop-skipping control strategies and their limitations. Section 3 defines the problem, providing details on the constraints and objectives of the proposed adaptive scheduling solution. Section 4 introduces the Adaptive Scheduling game model, followed by the proposed learning processes including the RL and SA approaches in Sect. 5. Section 6 provides numerical results and comparative analysis, and Sect. 7 concludes the paper with future directions.

2   Related Works

In recent years, numerous studies have focused on optimizing transit operations by implementing stop-skipping control and on-demand services to improve efficiency and service quality.

The authors in [1] proposed a real-time stop-skipping control strategy in their work that allows passengers to get off at skipped stations. They aim to minimize passenger waiting and in-vehicle travel time using an exhaustive search method. Their approach succeeds in reducing travel time, however, it is unable to adapt to dynamic demand fluctuations. Similarly, [3] developed a bi-level genetic algorithm to find the optimal stooping patterns of buses. Although his proposed model succeeds in reducing the total travel time by 7%, it is difficult to adapt to real time changes as it was based on static demand assumptions.

Autonomous and on-demand transport services have also implemented the stop-skipping control strategy. The authors in [5] proposed a stop skipping autonomous shuttle bus service that adapts to real-time demand. They proposed a deficit function based algorithm to calculate the optimal stop skipping schedules by considering the number of available buses and their capacities. Their results shows a reduction of 1.8% in passenger travel time and 8.1% in the number of used vehicles. However, the deficit function algorithm complexity increases as the network increases which poses challengers in terms of real-time adaptations to demand.

The authors in [6] aims to optimize both the headways and the stopping patterns in a bus rapid transit system. They adopted the genetic algorithm to minimize the costs of the operator and the passengers. Their results shows that the performance of the algorithm depends on accuracy of the demand predictions which may not be reliable during peak hours. The authors in [9] also employed the genetic algorithm to design a limited-stop service that aims to determine the bus's stopping patterns under unbalanced passenger demand. The algorithm aims to minimize both the waiting and in-vehicle times of the passengers while taking into consideration the capacity constraint. Their model succeeds to adapt to demand variations but is limited when it comes to sudden demand fluctuations. The authors in [8] combined the genetic algorithm with Monte Carlo simulations to develop an optimization model to determine the stop-skipping patterns. The Monte Carlo simulation is used to model varying passenger demands and the genetic algorithm is used to adjust the bus's headways and minimize the passengers' waiting times. Although this approach improves the reliability of stop skipping and succeeds in adjusting the headways, but it may be computationally expensive.

Despite the promising results of stop-skipping control and on-demand services, real-time adaptability, scalability and reliance on accurate demand forecasting remain challenging. Therefore, this study proposes an adaptive scheduling game model with Reinforcement Learning method to determine the sequence of buses' stop skipping patterns that can minimize the total travel time for passengers.

3   Problem Definition

In our previous work [13], we introduced a static model where the passenger demand was given at time step $t = 0$. The objective was to find the optimal bus schedule that best serves the passengers with minimum time until the last passenger reaches his/her destination, denoted as delay. We proved the problem to be NP-Hard by considering a polynomial transformation from the Set Partitioning Problem. Thus we introduced a new notion, the schedule *load-delay*, denoted as $LD(Sch)$, that calculates the time, expressed in time steps, needed by the bus having the maximum load to serve its passengers. We have also showed that a correlation exists between the real schedule delay and the schedule *load-delay*. Thus, we focus our optimization on the *load-delay*. However, this static model does not take into consideration the current system's state.

In this paper, we extend our static model by introducing an adaptive scheduling approach. Our aim is to find the optimal bus scheduling sequence while considering the current system's state, such as the number of waiting passengers at stations and the number of passengers onboard of each bus. The main objective is to find the best schedule at each time step t, denoted Sch^t, that minimizes the load-delay $LD(Sch^t)$.

Formally the load-delay of schedule Sch^t, at time step t, is defined as follows:

Definition 1. *Given a transportation system with N slots, K stations, B buses, and the origin-destination demand matrix $M[O, D]^t$, the* load-delay *of schedule Sch^t, noted as $LD(Sch^t)$, is defined as:*

$$LD(Sch^t) = \max_{b_j \in B} \left(\left\lceil \frac{MAXload_j^t}{Cap} \right\rceil \times (N + Stp_j) \right) \qquad (1)$$

where

- $MAXload_j^t$ represents the maximum load of bus b_j on station s_i at time step t, for $i \in \{1...K\}$ and $j \in \{1...B\}$, calculated as:

$$MAXload_j^t = \max_{1 \leq i \leq K} \left(\sum_{\substack{x \neq y \text{ crossing } s_i \\ s.t. \ D_j[s_x]=D_j[s_y]=1}} \frac{M[s_x, s_y]^t}{deg(s_x, s_y)} \right) \qquad (2)$$

It depends on the number of passengers that can board bus b_j at time step t based on its serving vector D_j that determines which stations this bus will stop at, divided by the number of buses serving each origin-destination station pair (s_x, s_y), denoted by $deg(s_x, s_y)$, such as $D_j[s_x] = D_j[s_y] = 1$, for $x, y \in \{1, ..., K\}$ and $x \neq y$.

- $\lceil \frac{MAXload_j^t}{Cap} \rceil$ represents the number of trips needed for bus b_j, having maximum load, to serve its passengers.
- $(N + Stp_j)$ represents the total time bus b_j spends traveling around the ring (N) and stopping at stations (Stp_j), expressed in time steps.

The main objective is to determine the optimal bus scheduling sequence that minimizes the load-delay while taking into consideration the current passenger demand. This requires an adaptive solution that continuously updates the bus schedules based on the current system state.

4   Adaptive Scheduling Game Model

A fixed schedule will not always be the best schedule to serve the passengers over time. To solve this problem, we define an adaptive scheduling game model which takes into consideration the current demand to dynamically calculate a scheduling sequence that best serves the demand.

Similar to the static scheduling game model defined in [13], in this approach we suppose that the stations are the players and the choices of bus stops at each station are the strategies.

4.1   Game Components

The components of the dynamic game include:

- **The environment:**
  - A discrete ring R of N slots, labeled from 0 to N–1. They are used to represent discrete events. Each slot can be occupied only by one bus at a time and it represents the possible position of the bus in the system.
  - The set of B buses serving K stations. We denote by Pos^t_j, $1 \leq j \leq B$, the position of bus b_j at time step t. Each bus b_j serves stations according to its serving vector D_j, where $D_j[s_i] = 1$, $1 \leq i \leq K$, means that bus b_j will stop at station s_i, 0 otherwise.
  - The demand matrix $M[O, D]^t$ which represents the number of passengers at stations with their respective destinations at time step t.
- **The players:** These are the K stations in the network. Each station s_i, $i \in \{1...K\}$, is associated with a slot $Slot_i$ with at most one station per slot.
- **The actions:** The action set A^t_i of each player s_i, $i \in \{1...K\}$, consists of all possible bus stopping patterns, with $|A^t_i| = 2^B$. Each action $a^t_i \in A^t_i$ is a vector of length B, where each element is either 1 or 0. A value of 1 indicates that station s_i has chosen bus $b_j, 1 \leq j \leq B$, to stop at it, $a^t_i[j] = 1$, while 0 means bus b_j will not stop.
- **The strategy profile:** A strategy profile $\pi^t = \{a^t_1, ..., a^t_K\}$ defines a unique schedule Sch^t_π.

4.2   Game Model Parameters

Given the ring R, the number of stations K, the bus fleet B, and the demand matrix $M[O, D]^t$, each station s_i chooses an action $a^t_i \in A^t_i$, for $1 \leq i \leq K$, resulting in schedule Sch^t_π.

Load Calculation: For each schedule Sch^t_π, we define a local station load calculated at time step t for any $s_i, 1 \leq i \leq K$, denoted by SJN^t_i in Eq. 3. This parameter helps to calculate the required time steps to serve the passengers waiting at station s_i at time step t based on the given schedule Sch^t_π. This station load is related to the maximum load of a bus b_j, $1 \leq j \leq B$, stopping at s_i multiplied by the number of slots (N) and stations to stop at (Stp_j), which represents the time steps needed to serve the current demand.

$$SJN^t_i = \max_{j \ s.t \ D_j[s_i]=1} \left(\left\lceil \frac{\sum\limits_{\substack{x \neq y \ crossing \ s_i \\ s.t. \ D_j[s_x]=D_j[s_y]=1}} \frac{M[s_x,s_y]^t}{deg(s_x,s_y)}}{Cap} \right\rceil \times (N + Stp_j) \right) \qquad (3)$$

An upper bound of the *load-delay* for any schedule, denoted as WST, is defined in Eq. 4. This upper bound represents the worst-case scenario and is calculated under the assumption that only one bus serves all the demand. By penalizing schedules that rely heavily on one bus to serve the demand, the model encourages stations to learn and adopt a more balanced and efficient bus stopping patterns by distributing the demand more evenly across available buses.

$$
WST = \left\lceil \frac{\max\limits_{\substack{s_i \\ 1 \le i \le K}} \left(\dfrac{\sum\limits_{\substack{x \ne y \ crossing \ s_i}} M[s_x, s_y]^t}{deg(s_x, s_y)} \right)}{Cap} \right\rceil \times (N + K + 1) \qquad (4)
$$

Cost Minimization: At each time step t, station s_i selects an action $a_i^t \in A_i^t$ that minimizes its cost $C_i^t(a_i^t)$. This cost is defined as:

$$
C_i^t(a_i^t) = \gamma \times TOT - \alpha \times Loc_i \qquad (5)
$$

where $\gamma \ge 1$ and $\alpha \ge 0$ are two tuning parameters of the game indicating the weight of the global (TOT) and the local (Loc_i) loads, respectively. These loads are:

- $TOT = WST$ if Sch_π^t is not feasible, else $TOT = LD(Sch_\pi^t)$
- $Loc_i =$
$$
\begin{cases}
0 & \text{if } \exists\ i', 1 \le i' \le K \text{ such that } M[s_i, s_{i'}']^t > 0 \text{ and } deg(s_i, s_i') = 0 \\
SJN_i^t & \text{if } \exists\ i', 1 \le i' \le K \text{ such that } M[s_i, s_{i'}']^t > 0 \text{ and } deg(s_i, s_i') > 0 \\
TOT & \text{if } \forall\ i', 1 \le i' \le K, M[s_i, s_{i'}']^t = 0 \text{ and } M[s_i', s_i]^t = 0
\end{cases}
$$

We will use this game model as a distributed algorithmic approach to determine a global minimum schedule, at every time step t, that optimally serves passengers by minimizing the schedule *load-delay*, $LD(Sch^t)$.

5   Learning Process

To avoid unnecessary learning while ensuring adaptability to changes in the system, the learning process is initiated whenever a bus is in front of a station whether it is said to stop at it or not. This strategy ensures that learning occurs sufficiently to address system changes without being overly exhaustive at every time step. Once a bus is announced to stop at a station, this decision remains fixed until the bus reaches that station the next turn. This prevents frequent changes and ensures that on board passengers reaches their destination.

More specifically, consider that at time step t, bus b_j is in front of station s_i for $1 \le j \le B, 1 \le i \le K$. We define a slot to be an (i, j)-*milestone* if a bus b_j is in front of station s_i at this slot whether it is stopping at it or not. At every (i, j)-*milestone*, the learning process then runs for T learning steps (or until convergence), taking into consideration the current demand matrix $M[O, D]^t$ and the set of available actions A_i^t for each player s_i.

For the learning process, we propose and evaluate two different strategies for defining the action set of each station:

- The action subset strategy: this means that the stations are only allowed to choose from the subset of actions which allows it to modify its action concerning buses that have not yet been scheduled to stop at it. This strategy implements the learned actions in real-time while limiting the action set to those that are feasible given the current state of the system.
- The full action set strategy: this strategy allows all the stations to choose actions regarding all the buses. However, the action is only applied by the station that has a bus in front of it to ensure that on board passengers reaches their destinations with a minimum delay. This means that all stations learn simultaneously, but their learned actions are applied with a delay.

These strategies define how stations make decisions regarding which bus will stop and how are they applied in real time.

In the following, we present the two learning processes that are used to solve our adaptive scheduling game model: Linear Reward Inaction (LRI) and Simulated Annealing (SA).

5.1   Linear Reward Inaction

Distributed LRI [10] is a reinforcement learning method where stations (players) aim to optimize a common cost through a reward system. Each player s_i, for $1 \leq i \leq K$, has a strategy vector q_i, which is a stochastic vector of potential actions such as $|q_i^t| = |A_i^t|$. Each action $a_i^t \in A_i^t$ for player s_i has an initial probability $q_i^t(a_i^t)$ of being selected. At each time step t, each player s_i randomly selects an action, noted a_i^t, from its strategy vector. The cost of choosing action $C_i^t(a_i^t)$ by station s_i at time step t is calculated based on Eq. 5. After calculating the $C_i^t(a_i^t)$, the next step is to calculate the utility of player s_i. It helps each player to evaluate the effectiveness of choosing action a_i^t and guides it in learning the optimal strategy over time. Hence, we define the utility function for player s_i at time step t as:

$$U_i^t = \frac{C_i^{max}(a_i^t) - C_i^t(a_i^t)}{C_i^{max}(a_i^t) - C_i^{min}(a_i^t)} \qquad (6)$$

with $C_i^{max}(a_i^t)$ (resp. $C_i^{min}(a_i^t)$) being the maximum (resp. minimum) cost impacted to s_i when choosing action a_i^t at time step t. The design of the utility function is critical for the player's learning of optimal stopping pattern. It should be both broad enough to capture the impact of the chosen actions, but specific enough to not cause noise during learning.

After each learning step, the strategy vector is updated using the LRI update rule:

$$\begin{cases} q_i^{t+1}(a) = q_i^t(a) + \eta \times U_i^t \times (1 - q_i^t(a)) & \text{If } a = a_i^t \\[2em] q_i^{t+1}(a') = q_i^t(a') - \left(\dfrac{q_i^t(a')}{1 - q_i^{t+1}(a')} \times \eta \times U_i^t \times (1 - q_i^t(a)) \right) & \forall a' \neq a_i^t \ \& \ a = a_i^t \end{cases}$$

(7)

where:

- η is the learning parameter such that $0 < \eta < 1$.
- $q_i^t(a)$ is the probability that player s_i selects action a at iteration t.
- U_i^t is the utility function.

For the LRI learning process, the definitions of the full action set approach and the action subset strategies are detailed below.

The Full Action Set Strategy: Consider that at time step t, bus b_j reaches station s_i. All stations are allowed to choose simultaneously an action from all the possible available actions. To maintain stability by preserving the previous learned probabilities, the strategy vector q_i^t at the beginning of each learning process for each station s_i is calculated as follows:

$$q_i^t(a_i^t) = q_i^{t-1}(a_i^{t-1})$$

(8)

At the beginning of each learning process, we take into consideration the current demand matrix $M[O, D]^t$ and the schedule found at time step $t-1$, denoted as Sch^{t-1}. For the bus b_j that is in front of station s_i, the action concerning whether this bus will stop at this station or not is initially set to zero. During the learning process, at each learning step, all stations are allowed to choose actions based on their respective stochastic vectors q_i^t, and after calculating the *load-delay*, these values are updated as in Eq. 7.

At the end of the learning process, only the action a_i^t learned by station s_i having the highest probability is considered. A logical OR operation is performed between the previous action a_i^{t-1} and the newly learned a_i^t, yielding the final action for station s_i. For all other stations, their previously learned actions remain unchanged, indicating that the learned actions for these stations are not directly applied until their respective turns.

The Action Subset Strategy: Consider that at time step t, bus b_j reaches station s_i, we set the action considering if b_j will stop at s_i to 0. Then, the LRI algorithm runs for T learning steps (an input parameter), taking into consideration the current demand matrix $M[O, D]^t$, the schedule Sch^{t-1} found at time step $t-1$, and the set of available actions $\overline{A_i^t} \subseteq A_i^t$ for each player such that:

$$\overline{A_i^t} = \{a_i^t \in A_i^t \mid a_i^t[j] = 0 \ \forall j \in \{1, ..., B\}\}$$

This means that station s_i is only allowed to choose from the subset of actions $\overline{A_i}^t$ which only allows it to modify its action concerning buses that have not yet been scheduled to stop at it based on the previously found schedule at time step $t - 1$, Sch^{t-1}. This ensures that once a bus is designated to stop at a station, this decision cannot be reversed until the bus reaches the station.

Since the station is only allowed to choose actions from $\overline{A_i^t}$, then $\overline{q_i^t}$ is a normalized sub-vector of q_i^t where $|\overline{q_i^t}| = |\overline{A_i^t}|$ and the values correspond to respective probability of choosing these actions in the action subset. After all the stations choose simultaneously the appropriate action from $\overline{A_i^t}$, the expected schedule delay is calculated based on previously defined schedule load-delay in Eq. 1. The schedule load-delay in this case determines how many time steps are needed to serve all the passengers if each station sticks to its chosen action until the system is empty. At each learning step, the station's stochastic vectors are updated based on Eq. 7. At the end of each learning process, each station picks the action with the highest probability based on q_i^t, for $1 \leq i \leq K$. All selected actions determines the schedule Sch^t found by LRI at time step t.

5.2   Simulated Annealing

A centralized Simulated Annealing (SA) algorithm is a probabilistic method proposed in [11]. It is used to estimate the global minimum for a function with many variables. This algorithm can produce a good local though not necessarily global optimal solution within a reasonable computing time. Essentially speaking, simulated annealing can be seen as a "randomized variation" of the local search method [12]. The SA algorithm begins with a high temperature, which gradually reduces with time. The temperature is used to control the probability of accepting worse solutions as the algorithm explores the solution space. Higher temperatures permit more exploration, while lower temperatures focus on exploitation.

Consider that at time step t, bus b_j reaches station s_i, for $1 \leq i \leq K$ and $1 \leq j \leq B$. The SA algorithm runs until the temperature reaches 0 or until the number of generated neighbor schedules is equal to the T learning steps of the LRI algorithm. At the beginning of each learning process, the SA runs taking into consideration the demand matrix available at time step t, $M[O, D]^t$, and the schedule Sch^{t-1} found at time step $t - 1$, the previous learning step. At each step of the algorithm, we generate a random neighbor schedule by altering the choice of a bus b_j stopping at s_i. This neighbor schedule generation can be based on either a full action set or an action subset strategy. The current schedule Sch^t found at the (i, j)-milestone, is denoted by V_{Sch^t}, and is the concatenation of the buses binary vectors D_j.

The Full Action Set Strategy: We randomly select a value of i, for $1 \leq i \leq K$, and a value of j, for $1 \leq j \leq B$. If the previous schedule value $V_{Sch^{t-1}}[i][j]$ is 1, it is changed to 0, and if it is 0, it is changed to 1. Then, the schedule *load-delay* is recalculated, and the acceptance criteria are verified. If the new schedule results in a lower load-delay, it is accepted. However, if the new schedule produces a higher load-delay, it can still be accepted with a probability based on the current temperature. As the temperature decreases, the likelihood of accepting a worse schedule decreases, promoting convergence towards the optimal solution. At the end of the learning process, the final schedule at time step t is determined by combining the previous and current schedule decisions using a logical OR operation, denoted as $V_{\mathrm{Sch}^t} = V_{\mathrm{Sch}^{t-1}}[i][j] \vee V_{\mathrm{Sch}^t}[i][j]$. For all other stations, if the previous decision is that bus b_j is to stop at it, then this value can't be changed until b_j reaches s_i. This ensures that only the action related to the bus currently in front of the station is allowed to change its decision regarding the bus stopping at it.

The Action Subset Strategy: We begin by also randomly selecting values for i and j. If the previous schedule value $V_{\mathrm{sch}^{t-1}}[i][j]$ is 0, it is set to 1; otherwise, no changes are made. Then, the schedule *load-delay* is computed, and the resulting neighbor schedule is either accepted or rejected according to the same acceptance criteria defined in the full action set approach. Once the SA learning process is complete, a logical OR operation is performed between $V_{\mathrm{sch}^{t-1}}$ and the updated V_{sch^t}, resulting in the final V_{sch^t}. In this strategy, all the actions that have been learned by the stations are applied collectively.

6   Numerical Results

In this section, we present the results of the proposed adaptive scheduling model.

6.1   The Input Data

To test our proposed adaptive scheduling model, we use real varying data of the one-direction public transport line 414 of the urban community of Saint-Quentin-en-Yvelines, a Paris suburban area. The road is considered as a ring R consisting of $N = 47$ slots numbered from 0 to 46 as shown in Fig. 1. For this line, there are $B = 3$ buses serving $K = 8$ stations.

Passenger Demand: The data set represents a one-direction bus line with the passenger demand defined at the beginning of the simulation. In this scenario, no new passengers enter the system; so the demand matrix decreases based on the passengers boarding the stopping buses. This will allow us to investigate the ability of the learning processes to find the optimal bus scheduling sequence that minimizes the passengers' waiting and traveling time. This scenario considers that there are no new passengers arriving at the stations and the demand $(M[O, D]^t)$ is defined at time step $t = 0$. The demand matrix $M[O, D]^t$ representing the varying demand for every origin destination station, at time step $t = 0$, is provided in Table 1 .

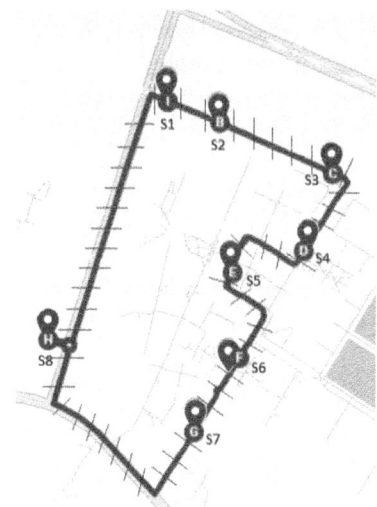

Fig. 1. Bus line 414 in the urban community of Saint-Quentin-en-Yvelines, France

Table 1. Origin-destination demand matrix $M[O, D]^{t=0}$ of line 414

O/D	1	2	3	4	5	6	7	8
1	0	77	34	6	14	3	3	2
2	0	0	55	43	89	17	31	6
3	0	0	0	22	53	20	57	7
4	0	0	0	0	5	4	8	2
5	0	0	0	0	0	6	20	8
6	0	0	0	0	0	0	43	9
7	0	0	0	0	0	0	0	40
8	0	0	0	0	0	0	0	0

LRI Algorithm Parameters: For the LRI algorithm, simulations are executed for $T = 2.5$ million iterations using parameter values that were identified as optimal in the static environment in previous work [13]. For the tuning parameters γ and α in Eq. 5, we set $\gamma = 2$ and $\alpha = 1$ as these values have shown a balance between global load-delay and local station loads. For the learning rate η, the chosen value is 0.00625. Additionally, for θ, the trade-off parameter, we test the value of $\theta = 0$ indicating that we consider the stochastic vectors at the previous learning step.

SA Algorithm Parameters: For the SA algorithm, the initial temperature was set to a high value of 150000, which allows the algorithm to explore a wide range of possible solutions in the early stages as shown in the results of the static system [13]. A cooling rate of 0.98 which ensures slow cooling process was used to gradually decrease the temperature as the algorithm progresses. The algorithm stops when the number of generated neighbor schedules is equal to the number of learning steps (T) used in the Linear Reward Inaction (LRI) algorithm.

6.2   Performance Evaluation of the Adaptive Scheduling Model

We run several simulations of the defined learning processes (LRI, SA) using the SUMO traffic simulator [14] and the TraCI library, a Python library that allows for real-time communication with the SUMO simulator [15]. This setup enables us to model real-time passenger arrival rates and dynamically control bus movements during the simulation.

We compare the performance of LRI and SA with a baseline scenario where buses stop at all stations. This baseline is appropriate since our demand matrix includes passengers traveling from every origin to every destination, thus representing a scenario with maximum service coverage. Additionally, we compare these results with the results of our previous static scheduling model [13], where the optimal bus schedule is well known.

The performance of the LRI and SA algorithms are evaluated based on three key metrics: waiting time, ride time and total trip time of passengers measured in minutes. Tables 2, 3, and 4 provide a summary of the results obtained.

Table 2. Statistics Summary for Waiting Times (in minutes)

Statistics	Static scheduling		Adaptive scheduling				All stops
	SA	LRI	SA Full	SA Sub	LRI Full	LRI Sub	All stops
Min	1.13	1.65	1.73	1.40	1.17	1.32	1.54
Max	13.90	13.05	20.87	14.93	14.75	14.83	14.57
Mean	4.53	5.84	5.62	4.65	4.31	4.46	4.60
Std Dev	3.12	3.00	5.32	3.46	3.29	3.35	3.80

Table 3. Statistics Summary for Ride Times (in minutes)

Statistics	Static scheduling		Adaptive scheduling				All stops
	SA	LRI	SA Full	SA Sub	LRI Full	LRI Sub	All stops
Min	0.25	0.25	0.25	0.25	0.25	0.25	0.25
Max	2.46	2.23	2.67	2.61	2.37	2.45	2.50
Mean	0.77	0.65	0.84	0.75	0.70	0.72	0.80
Std Dev	0.48	0.41	1.55	0.47	0.39	0.42	0.50

Table 4. Summary Statistics for Total Trip Duration (in minutes)

Statistics	Static scheduling		Adaptive scheduling				All stops
	SA	LRI	SA Full	SA Sub	LRI Full	LRI Sub	All stops
Min	1.90	1.90	1.98	1.75	1.42	1.56	1.80
Max	16.36	15.28	23.54	17.12	17.12	17.28	17.00
Mean	5.24	6.49	6.46	5.47	4.96	5.10	5.40
Std Dev	3.40	3.27	5.51	3.81	3.51	3.60	4.23

Results of LRI: Results in the tables show that the LRI full action set strategy outperforms the action subset strategy across all key metrics. These results show also that this strategy can adapt to changes in the system, whereas the action subset strategy converges to a sub-optimal schedule where buses stop at every station.

For most of the metrics, the LRI full action set strategy outperforms the LRI in the static scheduling scenario, except when considering the maximum values, we observe that the performance varies. Indeed, the LRI full adaptive strategy shows an increase of approximately 13.0% in maximum waiting times, an increase of 6.3% in maximum ride times, and an increase of 12.0% in maximum total trip duration compared to the LRI in static scheduling. These differences are due to the difference in how actions are applied in each approach. In static scheduling, all actions are directly applied without constraints, while in adaptive scheduling, even though all actions are available for all players, they are not directly applied which can affect the efficiency.

When comparing the LRI full action set approach with the all stops approach, we can see that this one performs better in minimizing both the maximum waiting time and the maximum total trip time. However, it leads to a slight increase of 5.3% in maximum ride times. This is due to the buses stopping at every stop in the all stops approach which increases the total travel times for on board passengers.

Results of SA. The SA action subset strategy performs better compared to the SA full action strategy in all key metrics. In particular, the SA action subset strategy achieves a 28.5% improvement in maximum waiting times, a 2.2% reduction in maximum ride times, and a 27.3% decrease in maximum total trip duration. This is due to the fact that the SA full action strategy gets stuck on a local minimum with a high *load-delay* value which prevents it from converging to a good local minimum scheduling sequence.

On the other hand, the SA static scheduling strategy succeeds in minimizing all the metrics compared to the SA action subset strategy in adaptive scheduling. This is due to the fact that the SA action subset strategy has a limited action set available after each learning step, which causes it to always converge to a schedule where buses stop at every station.

In addition, when comparing the SA action subset strategy to the all stops approach, we observe that the latter performs better in reducing the maximum of all metrics.

6.3   Discussion Summary

The results show that the SA algorithm performance can vary and its ability to adapt to changes is not always consistent. They also show that the LRI-based adaptive scheduling outperforms the SA-based approaches in both adaptability and minimizing passenger delay.

The LRI full action set strategy shows advantages over the static and the all-stops scenarios, by reducing waiting, ride, and total trip times with lower variability, making it a more reliable choice for real-time bus scheduling. However, while the SA action subset strategy offers some improvements over the full action set, it lacks the consistency and efficiency demonstrated by LRI in adapting to the system's state. Thus, the LRI full action strategy emerges as the more effective algorithm for adaptive bus scheduling in dynamic public transport systems.

In summary, the SA algorithm struggles to find optimal solutions and encounters difficulties during the last stages of the simulation, particularly when the demand begins to decline and certain stations either have no waiting passengers or no passengers needing to travel to them. However, the LRI algorithm with the full action set strategy shows ability to escape local minimums and produces a scheduling sequence that reduces passengers' times while avoiding unnecessary stops.

7   Conclusion

We propose in this research work an adaptive scheduling model game to solve the sequential bus stop-skipping decision problem in a static demand scenario. The goal is to minimize passenger travel time by adjusting bus stops decisions based on current demand. We compared the performance of two proposed learning processes: the Linear Reward Inaction (LRI) and the Simulated Annealing (SA) in adapting to the changes in the system. We also propose two strategies to determine the action sets of the players for each learning process in our game model. The first is the full action set strategy, which allows all players to simultaneously choose an action from all possible actions available in the action set; however, the learned action is applied with a delay. The second is the action subset strategy, which limits the action set available to the players but applies the learned actions in real time.

Results show that the LRI full action set strategy outperforms the SA algorithm approaches by succeeding in minimizing the passengers delays across all key metrics. The LRI full action set strategy also shows better adaptability and ability to find a scheduling sequence that avoids unnecessary stops. In contrast, the SA algorithm frequently converges to a sub optimal schedule.

In future work, we will focus on extending this adaptive game model to handle real time varying passenger demands and more complex networks.

References

1. Sun, A., Hickman, M.: The real-time stop-skipping problem. J. Intell. Transp. Syst. **9**, 91–109 (2005). https://doi.org/10.1080/15472450590934642
2. Liu, Z., Yan, Y., Qu, X., Zhang, Y.: Bus stop-skipping scheme with random travel time. J. Transp. Res. Part C: Emerg. Technol. **35**, 46–56 (2013)
3. Niu, H.: A matheuristic for optimizing skip-stop operation strategies in rail transit lines. Int. J. Transp. Dev. Integr. **3**(4), 306–316 (2011)
4. Black, A.: A method for determining the optimal division of express and local rail transit service. Chic. Area Transp. Stud. **347**, 120–106 (1962)
5. Cao, Z., Ceder, A.: Autonomous shuttle bus service timetabling and vehicle scheduling using skip-stop tactic. J. Transp. Res. Part C: Emerg. Technol. Elsevier (2019)
6. Chen, X., Hellinga, B., Chang, C., Fu, L.: Optimization of headways with stop-skipping control: a case study of bus rapid transit system. J. Adv. Transp. **49**, 385–401. Wiley (2015)
7. Gkiotsalitis, K., Cats, O.: At-stop control measures in public transport: literature review and research agenda. Transp. Res. Part E: Logist. Transp. Rev. **145** (2021)
8. Mou, Z., Zhang, H., Liang, S.: Reliability optimization model of stop-skipping bus operation with capacity constraints. J. Adv. Transp. (2020)
9. Zhang, H., Zhao, S., Liu, H., Liang, S.: Design of limited-stop service based on the degree of unbalance of passenger demand. PLoS ONE **13**(3) (2018)
10. Sastry, P.S., Phansalkar, V.V., Thathachar, M.A.L.: Decentralized learning of Nash equilibria in multi-person stochastic games with incomplete information. IEEE Trans. Syst. Man Cybern. **24**(5), 777–769 (1994)
11. Kirkpatrick, S., Gelatt, C.D., Vecchi, M.P.: Optimization by simulated annealing. J. Sci. **220**, 671–680 (1983)
12. FanRandy, W., Machemehl B.: Using a simulated annealing algorithm to solve the transit route network design problem. J. Transp. Eng. **132**(2) (2006)
13. Hajjar, P., Kloul, L., Barth, D.: Optimal bus scheduling using a distributed game model approach. In: IEEE 26th International Conference on Intelligent Transportation Systems (ITSC), pp. 4571–4576 (2023)
14. Behrisch, M., Bieker-Walz, L., Erdmann, J., Krajzewicz, D.: SUMO - simulation of urban mobility: an overview. In: Proceedings of SIMUL (2011)
15. Wegener, A., Piorkowski, M., Raya, M., Hellbrück, H., Fischer, S., Hubaux, J.P.: TraCI: an interface for coupling road traffic and network simulators. In: Proceedings of the 11th Communications and Networking Simulation Symposium (2008)

Machine Learning Approach for Labeling Undetected Planned Trips in Public Transport Operators

Mohammad Amin Zadenoori[1]([✉]), Marco Calamai[2], Francesca Del Lungo[2], Daria Faucci[2], Andrea Gaffi[2], Lorenzo Sarti[2], and Alessio Micheli[3]

[1] National Research Council (CNR), Pisa, Italy
`mohammadamin.zadenoori@isti.cnr.it`
[2] MAIOR Srl, Pistoia, Italy
[3] Department of Computer Science, University of Pisa, Pisa, Italy
`micheli@di.unipi.it`

Abstract. Accurate labeling of undetected trips in public transportation is critical, as it directly affects operational efficiency, cost savings, and service quality. Undetected trips refer to scheduled trips that were either not completed or inaccurately recorded by Automatic Vehicle Location (AVL) systems. These discrepancies can disrupt resource allocation, hinder operational planning, and compromise financial accountability. If undetected trips are not properly classified, they can cause significant financial losses, misallocation of resources, and lower customer satisfaction due to unaddressed service issues.

This paper presents a machine learning approach to automate the classification of undetected trips in public transit. The model categorizes trips into three types: Operated (successfully completed trips), Lost-Deductible (missed trips within operational limits), and Lost - Non-deductible (missed trips outside operational standards and non-compensable). Automating this process enhances operational efficiency, reduces financial losses, and streamlines claim management. By replacing manual classification with AI-driven automation, transit operators can ensure faster, more accurate trip labeling, ultimately leading to optimized resource use, better decision-making, and higher service standards.

Keywords: Machine Learning · Public Transport · Trip Classification · Random Forest · Model Deployment

1 Introduction

In the realm of public transit, undetected trips are a common occurrence. Undetected trips refer to trips (or parts of them) that are not detected by AVL systems. Public Transport Authorities (PTAs) serve as clients who contract Public Transport Operators (PTOs) to provide mass transit services to the public. The relationship between PTAs and PTOs is contractual and often performance-based, with PTAs holding the authority to impose penalties on PTOs if service

© ICST Institute for Computer Sciences, Social Informatics and Telecommunications Engineering 2025
Published by Springer Nature Switzerland AG 2025. All Rights Reserved
A. Kocian et al. (Eds.): INTSYS 2024, LNICST 608, pp. 177–190, 2025.
https://doi.org/10.1007/978-3-031-86370-7_11

levels do not meet the agreed-upon standards. One essential aspect of this collaboration is the need for operators to report any deviations from the planned service and specify the reason behind such deviations.

Manually categorizing these deviations is both time-consuming and prone to human error. There is a pressing need for an automated solution to address this issue, ensuring that deviations are categorized correctly and efficiently.

Leveraging historical data from a transit operator as our foundational dataset, the primary objective of this work is to develop a machine learning-driven classifier that can analyze trip data and predict the reasons for any undetected trips. In today's landscape, it is crucial for public transport agencies and operators to understand their service levels to optimize transport availability and efficiency, ensuring a high-quality service for the public.

This industrial research was conducted within MAIOR, a global market leader in designing and developing software solutions for strategic service planning, resource scheduling and management for both PTAs and PTOs. The collected data for this work comes from one of MAIOR's customers and serves as the foundation for training and validating the machine learning model. The broader vision of this research is to develop a versatile trip classifier that can be applied across various public transit operators, beyond just the current data source. By doing so, we aim to optimize transit operations, reduce manual workloads, ensure accurate reporting, and pave the way for a more efficient and scalable public transportation system.

In the following sections, this paper explores various aspects of the project. Section 2 presents a Literature Review, focusing on the application of machine learning in public transportation systems. Section 3 details the Project Objectives, outlining the goals and guiding research questions. Section 4 explains the methodology, describing the processes of data collection, feature engineering, model training, and model evaluation. Section 5 offers a thorough discussion of the obtained results, along with the model deployment, including its practical implications for public transit operators and its potential to improve operational efficiency and decision-making. Finally, Sect. 6 concludes the paper by summarizing the research's impact and providing insights for future developments in this area.

2 Literature Review: Machine Learning in Public Transportation

Machine learning (ML) is increasingly pivotal in optimizing public transportation systems, leveraging large-scale data to enhance operations, efficiency, and prediction capabilities. One notable application of ML is in trip classification and anomaly detection. Convolutional neural networks (CNNs) are employed to identify anomalies in scheduled trips by analyzing historical AVL data, significantly improving service reliability [5]. Additionally, hybrid models that combine decision trees and gradient boosting were used to classify trips accurately into categories like "On-Time", "Delayed", or "Missed", helping transportation authorities make timely decisions [6]. Methods such as Random Forests and Extremely Randomized Trees have further improved classification accuracy [1] [3].

ML was also applied to improve operational efficiency. Reinforcement learning models optimize bus routes by analyzing real-time traffic and passenger data, which reduces operational costs and enhances service delivery [7]. Predictive maintenance models, based on sensor data and vehicle health metrics, can forecast when maintenance is required, preventing breakdowns and reducing vehicle downtime [8].

In terms of passenger experience, ML-based recommender systems personalize route suggestions by analyzing commuter preferences and real-time traffic data, leading to more efficient and satisfying travel experiences [6]. Furthermore, ML models are used to manage crowd flow by predicting congestion in transit stations through real-time data integration from sources such as fare gates and CCTV. This helps reroute passengers and prevent overcrowding, improving safety and comfort [9].

In summary, ML is revolutionizing public transportation through examples such as trip classification, operational efficiency improvements, and passenger experience enhancements, offering significant opportunities for future advancements in the management of urban transit networks.

3   Project Objective

The primary objectives of this work are centered around addressing key challenges in public transit operations. These objectives guide the research questions that this work seeks to answer:

Research Question 1: How can a robust machine learning model be developed to accurately classify trips into one of three categories: "Operated", "Lost - Deductible", and "Lost - Non-deductible"?

Research Question 2: How can accurate trip classifications assist in improving decision-making within a transportation company, particularly in identifying potential trip issues and optimizing deductible claims?

Research Question 3: How can the automation of the trip classification process enhance operational efficiency, reduce manual intervention, and streamline public transit operations?

4   Data Modeling

The success of the machine learning model heavily relies on high-quality data gathered from a real public transit operator for the duration of one year (2022). The following steps were taken to collect and prepare the dataset.

Historical trip data was collected from the operator's database, involving both planned and actual trips. The dataset encompasses details about intended trips and actual trips captured using an AVL system. This data includes trip dates, route information, vehicle information, and any incidents or claims associated with each trip.

4.1   Dataset Overview

In the dataset under consideration, three distinct labels have been assigned to various instances: *"Operated"* with a frequency of 75,005, *"Lost - Deductible"* with a count of 53,210, and *"Lost - Non-deductible"* with an occurrence of 45,675.

A 70-30 train-test split was used, allocating 70% of the data for training and 30% for testing. Additionally, 5-fold cross-validation was applied to the training set, cycling through five subsets to improve model reliability and reduce overfitting.

Furthermore, to comprehensively assess the performance of the classifier, an initial evaluation was conducted on the training set using a 5-fold cross-validation approach.

4.2   Features

The features in the dataset were summarized into key categories:

-   **Temporal Features**: Day of the week, type of day (weekday, weekend, holiday).
-   **Route-Related Features**: Line number, pattern, direction.
-   **Operational Features**: Planned number of stops, planned departure and arrival times.
-   **AVL-Related Features**: AVL detection percentages, detection of trip departure and arrival.
-   **Delay Measurements**: Delays at start and end stops.
-   **Contextual Features**: AVL percentages of previous and next trips with the same pattern or vehicle block.

4.3   Description of Trip Categories

Operated Trips
"Operated" trips refer to successfully executed bus journeys within the transportation system. These are instances where buses have completed their scheduled routes and reached their destinations as intended.

Lost - Not Deductible
"Lost - Not Deductible" trips refer to undetected trips that have been deemed lost due to delays or disruptions but are eligible for deductible claims, allowing the transportation company to recover a portion of the financial loss incurred. Causes of Lost - Not Deductible Trips include:

-   **Adverse Weather Conditions**: Heavy rain, snowstorms, or fog causing delays.
-   **Traffic Congestion**: Unexpected road closures, accidents, or high traffic volumes.
-   **Operational Delays**: Route deviations or driver-related issues.

Lost - Deductible

"Lost - Deductible" trips refer to undetected trips that are lost without eligibility for deductible claims, resulting in a direct financial loss for the company. Causes of Lost - Deductible Trips include:

- **Internal Operational Issues**: Delays due to internal inefficiencies without external factors.
- **Schedule Disruptions**: Conflicts arising from poor scheduling.
- **Non-insurable Events**: Incidents not covered by insurance policies.
- **Vehicle Breakdowns**: Mechanical issues disrupting the trip.

4.4 Model Selection and Training

Several machine learning algorithms were evaluated to classify the undetected trips in public transit operations. The models considered include Random Forest, K-Nearest Neighbors (KNN), XGBoost, and Extra Trees.

Random Forest: Random Forest is an ensemble learning method that constructs multiple decision trees and merges them to obtain more accurate and stable predictions. This model is particularly effective in handling both classification and regression tasks, and it mitigates the risk of overfitting compared to individual decision trees [1].

K-Nearest Neighbors (KNN): KNN is a non-parametric, instance-based learning algorithm. It classifies a data point based on the majority label of its nearest neighbors in the feature space. While simple, KNN can be computationally expensive and sensitive to the choice of distance metrics and the number of neighbors, k [2].

XGBoost: XGBoost (Extreme Gradient Boosting) is a powerful gradient boosting algorithm optimized for both speed and performance. It builds sequential trees, where each new tree attempts to correct the errors made by the previous one. Its efficiency and effectiveness make it well-suited for structured data tasks, but it requires careful tuning of hyperparameters to avoid overfitting [4].

Extra Trees: The Extra Trees algorithm (Extremely Randomized Trees) is similar to Random Forest but differs in how it splits nodes. Instead of choosing the optimal split, Extra Trees chooses splits randomly. This randomness often leads to better generalization but can introduce more variance in some cases [3].

Hyperparameter tuning was performed using a grid search strategy. A grid of potential hyperparameters was defined for each model, and an exhaustive search was conducted, varying the parameters in the potential hyperparameter ranges, to identify the best combination of parameters that maximized performance. The models were further evaluated through 5-fold cross-validation to ensure robustness and avoid overfitting.

4.5   Model Classification Performance

The classification performance of four machine learning models-**Random Forest**, **K-Nearest Neighbors (KNN)**, **XGBoost**, and **Extra Trees**-was evaluated based on several metrics. Table 1 presents the comparison of these models in terms of Training Accuracy, Testing Accuracy, Average Cross-Validation (CV) Accuracy with 5 folds, and the Standard Deviation of CV Accuracy.

Table 1. Performance Metrics for Different Models

Metric	Random Forest	KNN	XGBoost	Extra Trees
Training Accuracy	82%	76%	74%	**90%**
Testing Accuracy	**77%**	73%	74%	76%
Average CV Accuracy (k=5)	**76%**	73%	73%	75%
Std. Dev. of CV Accuracy	2.6%	2.6%	**2.5%**	2.6%

From the table, we can observe the following insights:

- The **Random Forest** model demonstrates the highest testing accuracy (77%), which suggests that it generalizes well to unseen data.
- The **K-Nearest Neighbors (KNN)** model has the lowest testing accuracy (73%) and training accuracy (76%), which might suggest that the model struggles with both the training and test sets.
- **XGBoost** shows consistent performance between training (74%) and testing (74%) accuracies, which may indicate that the model is balanced, neither overfitting nor underfitting.
- The **Extra Trees** model shows the highest training accuracy (90%), but with a significant drop to 76% in testing accuracy. This indicates potential overfitting, where the model performs well on the training data but fails to generalize as effectively.

In terms of cross-validation accuracy, all models perform similarly, with averages ranging from 73% to 76%. The standard deviation of cross-validation accuracy is low for all models, indicating that performance is stable across the folds.

Given these results, we choose **Random Forest** as our primary classifier. In addition to its slightly better performance, Random Forest models are known for their interpretability and the ability to provide **feature importance** scores, which are crucial for understanding the underlying patterns in the data. This makes Random Forest not only effective but also valuable for gaining insights into which features most influence the model's decisions.

4.6   Random Forest-Grid Search Hyperparameter Optimization

Here, we present the results of optimizing the Random Forest model using a Grid Search strategy. The objective was to identify the best combination of hyperparameters to enhance the model's predictive performance. The Random Forest algorithm is an ensemble method that constructs multiple decision trees and aggregates their predictions for more accurate and stable outcomes.

During hyperparameter optimization using random search with 5-fold cross-validation, the training data is divided into 5 equal parts (folds). The model is trained on 4 of these folds and validated on the remaining fold. This process is repeated 5 times, with a different fold used as the validation set each time. This ensures that every part of the data is used for both training and validation, helping to avoid overfitting and providing a reliable estimate of the model's performance. For each random combination of hyperparameters, this cross-validation process is repeated, and the best-performing hyperparameter combination across all splits is selected.

Table 2 shows the optimal hyperparameters selected through the Grid Search process. Each parameter is explained below, emphasizing its importance in improving the model's generalization ability and preventing overfitting.

Table 2. Optimized Random Forest Hyperparameters with Modified Parameter Ranges

Parameter	Optimal Value	Range	Description
n_estimators	10	[2, 4, 6, 10]	The number of trees in the forest
min_samples_split	10	[2, 5, 10]	The minimum number of samples required to split an internal node. A value of 10 means a node will only be split if it contains at least 10 samples
min_samples_leaf	2	[1, 2, 4]	The minimum number of samples required to be at a leaf node. Setting this value to 2 prevents the model from creating overly complex trees with too few samples at the leaf nodes
max_features	auto	[auto, sqrt]	The number of features to consider when looking for the best split. When set to auto, the algorithm automatically determines the optimal number of features
max_depth	15	[7, 8, 9, 15, 100, None]	The maximum depth of the tree. A depth of 15 allows the trees to grow relatively deep, capturing more complexity in the data, but it can also increase the risk of overfitting
bootstrap	True	[True, False]	Whether bootstrap samples are used when building trees. When set to True, the model samples with replacement, which helps in creating more robust models

After tuning the model, we evaluated its performance on the test set. The classification report for this dataset is presented in Table 3, summarizing precision, recall, F1-score, and support for each class. The largest number in each column is highlighted in bold to indicate the best-performing metrics.

Table 3. Random Forest Classification Report - Test Set

Class	Precision	Recall	F1-Score	Support
Lost - Deductible	72%	**73%**	72%	10,503
Lost - Non-deductible	**79%**	74%	**77%**	10,691
Operated	78%	**81%**	**80%**	16,021
Accuracy	**77%** (37,215 samples)			
Macro Avg	**77%**	76%	76%	37,215
Weighted Avg	**77%**	**77%**	**77%**	37,215

Explanation of Results

The performance of the model on the test set reveals valuable insights into its classification ability. As shown in Table 3, the model demonstrates its highest precision for the "Lost - Non-deductible" class, reaching 79%. This indicates that the model was most accurate when predicting this class, with fewer false positives compared to the other categories. The highest recall of 81% is observed in the "Operated" class, which means that the model correctly identified the majority of true positive instances within this class, minimizing the number of missed "Operated" samples.

The F1-score, which balances precision and recall, is highest for both the "Operated" (80%) and "Lost - Non-deductible" (77%) classes. This suggests that these two classes exhibit a good balance between identifying positive instances and minimizing false positives, showcasing the model's ability to handle these categories effectively.

Moreover, the overall accuracy of the model on the test set is 77%, calculated across all classes. While this accuracy reflects the model's reasonable performance on unseen data, the difference between the test accuracy and any previously evaluated training performance (not shown here) might indicate slight overfitting or challenges with generalization. Nonetheless, the classification report reveals consistent performance across the three main classes, with similar precision, recall, and F1-scores, highlighting the robustness of the model's predictions for each class.

4.7   Random Forest Feature Importance Analysis

The model's prediction capability is influenced by a set of features, each with varying degrees of significance. Highest importance is **line number** with an importance score of 0.13, underscoring its important role in the model's outcomes. It is closely followed by **number of stops** and **delay at the starting stop**, registering scores of 0.11 and 0.10, respectively.

These top three features potentially reflect the core aspects of transportation patterns, from line-specific dynamics to stoppage patterns and initial delays. mid-tier features such as **pattern** and **avl percentage**, with scores of 0.09 and 0.08 respectively, also retain significant influence. However, as we traverse down the ranking, diminishing importance scores like that of **weekday** at 0.01 and **direction** at 0.01 indicate their lesser contribution to the model's decisions. interestingly, **virtual stops** with a score of 0.00 underscores its negligible or non-existent impact on predictions.

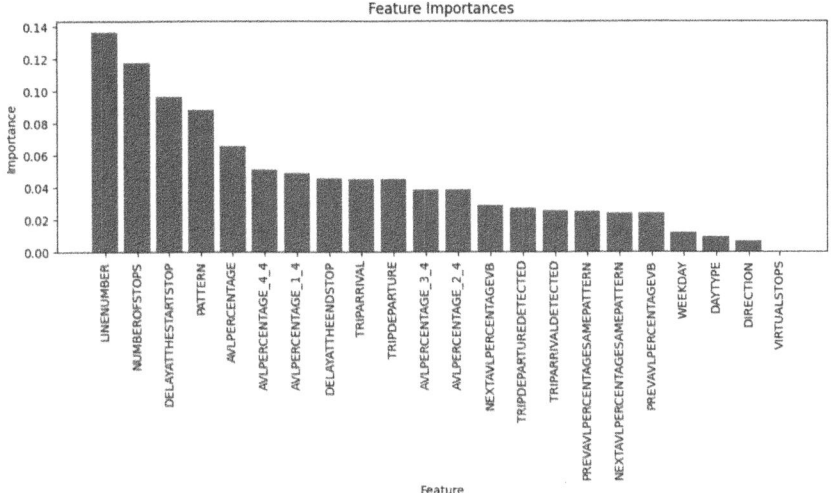

Fig. 1. Feature importance plot showing the relative significance of each feature in the random forest model.

4.8   Insights

As shown in Fig. 1, the *line number* feature emerges as the most influential, indicating that specific transit lines may exhibit unique operational characteristics that significantly affect the overall performance of the system. This could be due to the varying nature of routes, including traffic patterns, ridership levels, or infrastructure quality, which makes this feature critical for accurate trip classification.

Similarly, the *number of stops* and *delay at the starting stop* are highlighted as crucial factors. The *number of stops* directly correlates with the complexity of a trip, while the *delay at the starting stop* is a key indicator of whether the system meets scheduled timetables, which is vital for passenger satisfaction and resource optimization.

Mid-tier features, such as the *pattern* and *AVL percentage*, also play a significant role. These features have relatively high importance scores, reflecting their contribution to the model. The *pattern* represents the predefined route structure, which can influence trip predictability, and the *AVL percentage* indicates the availability of real-time location data, which improves the system's ability to track performance and make informed decisions.

On the other hand, features like *weekday*, *direction*, and *virtual stops* contribute much less, as evidenced by their lower importance scores. Although these features are included in the model, their impact on the classification outcomes is minimal compared to the more dominant features. The *weekday* may introduce some variation in travel patterns, but this effect is relatively minor. Similarly, *direction* and *virtual stops* have limited influence, suggesting they are not as critical in determining the classification of transit trips.

In summary, the model's feature importance rankings provide valuable insights into which aspects of the transit system most influence performance, with operational efficiency and route characteristics emerging as key determinants.

4.9   Confusion Matrix of Random Forest Classifier

The confusion matrix displayed in Fig. 2 represents the performance of the Random Forest classifier on classifying trips into the categories *Lost Deductible*, *Lost Non-deductible*, and *Operated*. Each cell in the matrix corresponds to the percentage of predictions relative to the true labels.

- The classifier correctly identified 69.65% of trips labeled as *Lost Deductible*, while 22.95% were misclassified as *Operated*, and 7.40% as *Lost Non-deductible*.
- For the *Lost Non-deductible* category, 75.44% of the trips were correctly classified, with 12.59% misclassified as *Operated* and 11.97% as *Lost Deductible*.
- In the *Operated* category, the classifier correctly identified 80.50% of trips, while 10.71% were incorrectly classified as *Lost Deductible* and 8.79% as *Lost Non-deductible*.

The confusion matrix highlights that the Random Forest classifier performs reasonably well, particularly in the *Operated* and *Lost Non-deductible* categories. However, there is a noticeable proportion of misclassifications between the *Lost Deductible* and *Operated* labels, which suggests room for improvement in the classifier's ability to distinguish between these categories.

5   Discussion

Based on the results achieved by the Random Forest (RF) classifier, the RF model can be considered to be well-suited for deployment in a real-world application. The RF model demonstrated adequate accuracy during testing, with

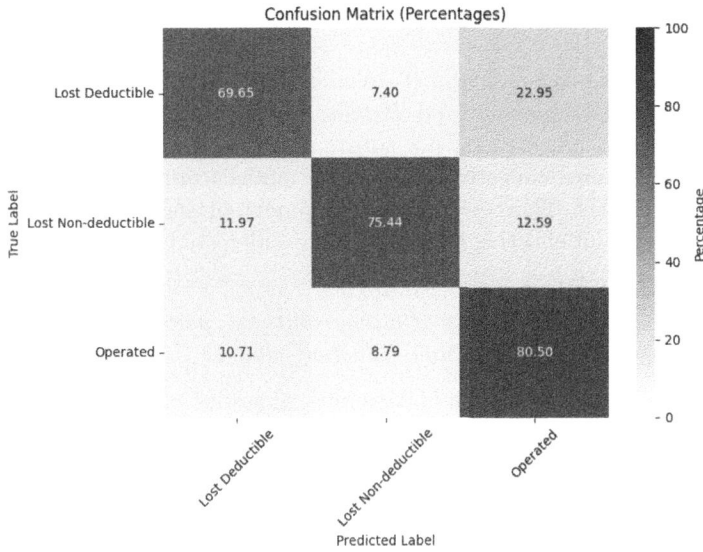

Fig. 2. Confusion Matrix of the Random Forest Classifier (Percentages)

accuracy score of 77%, respectively. This accuracy on testing set indicates that the model can provide reliable predictions on new, unseen data.

Moreover, the RF model's average cross-validation accuracy of 76% and the small standard deviation of 2.6% further validate its robustness and consistency in different data scenarios. The RF model's ability to maintain stable and dependable performance across various data folds increases confidence in its predictive capabilities.

Due to its ability to capture complex relationships in the data, avoid overfitting, and generalize well to new data, the RF model proves to be a powerful and reliable predictive tool. It has demonstrated slightly better performance compared to other classifiers, making it a better choice for model deployment in our application.

5.1   Answering Research Questions Based on Results

Answering RQ1: *How can a robust machine learning model be developed to accurately classify trips into one of three categories: Operated, Lost - Deductible, and Lost - Non-deductible?*

Answer: The Random Forest model demonstrated the slightly better performance among the models tested, achieving high accuracy on both the training (82%), validation (76%), and testing (77%) datasets, with a small standard deviation (2.6%) across cross-validation folds. This suggests that Random Forest can be considered a robust and reliable model for trip classification. The model's ability to generalize well on unseen data highlights its potential to accurately classify trips into the three predefined categories (Operated, Lost - Deductible, and Lost - Non-deductible).

The top five features identified—*NumberOfStops*, *AVLPercentage*, *Delay-AtTheStartStop*, *LineNumber*, and *Pattern*—indicate that specific operational characteristics and patterns have a substantial influence on classification outcomes. These features collectively allow the model to distinguish between the trip types efficiently. Therefore, the development of such a machine learning model is feasible and effective in categorizing undetected trips.

Answering RQ2: *How can accurate trip classifications assist in improving decision-making within a transportation company, particularly in identifying potential trip issues and optimizing deductible claims?*

Answer: Accurate classification of trips into categories such as *Lost - Deductible* and *Lost - Non-deductible* provides critical insights into which trips are eligible for deductible claims and which are not. With Random Forest's reliable predictions, transportation companies can better understand trip performance and quickly identify issues that contribute to deductible losses. For instance, features like *DelayAtTheStartStop* and *NumberOfStops* could be key indicators for identifying trips that need operational interventions.

This capability enables decision-makers to prioritize trips for investigation and streamline the claims process. Furthermore, by understanding the patterns of lost trips, corrective actions can be planned, such as revising scheduling or improving vehicle allocation, thereby optimizing the company's operations and financial outcomes.

Answering RQ3: *How can the automation of the trip classification process enhance operational efficiency, reduce manual intervention, and streamline public transit operations?*

Answer: In this work, we have achieved several industrial milestones, leading to improvements in the efficiency of our processes. These achievements are outlined below:

- We have designed a system that operates effectively in real-world scenarios, managing the labeling of approximately 1500 trips daily.
- The manual labeling process, which previously took 5 to 10 s per trip (amounting to 2 to 4 h each day), has been optimized.
- By implementing an automatic labeling system, the time required per trip has been reduced to an 5 to 10 milliseconds, reducing the total time to merely 2 to 4 s.
- Our model achieves a prediction accuracy of about 76%, ensuring an adequate level of reliability.

Overall, clearly, the new process is much faster, even when considering a final human review for verification.

5.2   Model Deployment with Flask

In this work, Flask serves as the web framework for deploying the machine learning model, allowing seamless integration with MAIOR's transit planning system. By deploying the model as a REST API, the Flask server acts as an intermediary between the model and external systems, efficiently handling requests and delivering predictions [11].

The deployment process involves creating RESTful endpoints that accept data for classification and return the corresponding results. Flask's lightweight nature ensures minimal overhead, while also allowing for easy updates or replacements of the model without disrupting the system's functionality [10]. This modularity ensures that the classifier remains flexible and adaptable to changing needs.

Additionally, Flask supports containerization through Docker, enabling scalable deployment and efficient resource management [12]. This approach ensures that the model is not only operational but also optimized for performance, security, and maintainability within a production environment [13].

6   Conclusions

In conclusion, the application of machine learning for classifying discrepancies in public transit operations is a groundbreaking venture that holds significant promise for the industry. The challenges faced due to manual categorization processes have been met with an innovative, data-driven solution that not only addresses the inefficiencies but also offers scalability across different transit operators. Our efforts, underpinned by the rich dataset from a MAIOR's costumer, have yielded a classifier that can pave the way for more reliable, streamlined, and efficient public transportation systems.

As we reflect on this endeavor, it is evident that machine learning has the potential to revolutionize the way public transit agencies approach operational discrepancies, and we remain hopeful about its transformative impact on the future of transit operations.

Acknowledgement. This research has been carried out as part of the ADDSTRES project, funded by Regione Toscana and MAIOR Srl. Thanks to Prof. A. Frangioni to coordinate the project.

References

1. Breiman, L.: Random forests. Mach. Learn. **45**(1), 5–32 (2001)
2. Altman, N.S.: An introduction to kernel and nearest-neighbor nonparametric regression. Am. Stat. **46**(3), 175–185 (1992)
3. Geurts, P., Ernst, D., Wehenkel, L.: Extremely randomized trees. Mach. Learn. **63**(1), 3–42 (2006)

4. Chen, T., Guestrin, C.: XGBoost. In: Proceedings of the 22nd ACM SIGKDD International Conference on Knowledge Discovery and Data Mining. ACM (2016)
5. Elvas, L., Nunes, M., Francisco, B., Gonçalves, F., Martins, A.L., Ferreira, J.C.: Points of interest in smart cities and visitor behavior (2023)
6. Caroleo, B., et al.: Machine learning methods to forecast public transport demand based on smart card validations (2023)
7. Lozano Pinilla, J.R., Vicente Chicote, C., Sanchez Cordero, I.: Smart-routing web app: a road traffic eco-routing tool proposal for smart cities (2023)
8. Tokkozhina, U., Martins, A.L., Ferreira, J.C.: Blockchain-based solution for charitable supply chains: network proposal architecture for Portuguese tax consignment program (2023)
9. Elvas, L., Nunes, M., Francisco, B., Domingues, N.: City mobility and night life monitor (2023)
10. Grinberg, M.: Flask Web Development: Developing Web Applications with Python. O'Reilly Media Inc, Sebastopol (2018)
11. Flask Documentation, "Flask," (2024). https://flask.palletsprojects.com/. Accessed 03 Oct 2024
12. Docker Documentation, "Docker," (2024). https://docs.docker.com/. Accessed 03 Oct 2024
13. Kruchten, P.: The 4+1 view model of architecture. IEEE Softw. **12**(6), 42–50 (1995)

Reinforcement Learning Algorithms with Graph Convolution Networks for Traffic Signal Control

Shreya Salmalge and Shalabh Bhatnagar[(✉)]

Department of Computer Science and Automation, Indian Institute of Science, Bengaluru, India
shreyas@alum.iisc.ac.in, shalabh@iisc.ac.in

Abstract. Traffic congestion is the root cause of various social and economic problems like longer travel times, increased pollution, and fuel or energy consumption. Addressing the issue is becoming increasingly crucial with rising city traffic and limited road infrastructure. The way we change traffic signals has a significant impact on congestion in road networks. We implement reinforcement learning algorithms for controlling traffic signals adaptive to congestion in incoming roads at junctions. Road networks can be viewed as graphs with intersections as nodes and roads as edges. This motivates us to use graph convolutional networks (GCN) as function approximators in various RL algorithms applied to traffic signal control. We implement Deep Q-learning (DQN), Graph Convolutional Q-learning (GCQN), Graph Convolutional Actor-Critic (GCAC), and individual-DQN models to learn a deterministic policy for adaptive traffic signal control. We also present a comparison of the performances of these models and infer that GCQN models are better suited to work for large road networks. To the best of our knowledge, the Graph Convolutional Actor-Critic model is not used in any existing traffic signal control method. We also compare the GCQN and GCAC models against existing and state-of-the-art approaches. Experimental evaluation shows that our proposed method achieves performance levels comparable to the state-of-the-art techniques.

Keywords: Traffic signal control · reinforcement learning · graph convolution networks · actor-critic and deep Q-network algorithms

1 Introduction

The volume of traffic on the road has steadily increased as population and urbanization have grown over time. This has given rise to increased traffic congestion

This work was supported by a J. C. Bose Fellowship, Project No. DFTM/ 02/ 3125/M/04/AIR-04 from DRDO under DIA-RCOE, the Walmart Center for Tech Excellence at IISc (CSR Grant WMGT-23-0001), and the RBCCPS, IISc.

A. Kocian et al. (Eds.): INTSYS 2024, LNICST 608, pp. 191–208, 2025.
https://doi.org/10.1007/978-3-031-86370-7_12

across traffic networks. Designing traffic lights that change in response to different traffic conditions is an effective way to optimize traffic flow on a road network. Many traffic junctions worldwide currently use fixed signal timings, i.e., periodically cycle through the sign configurations in a round-robin manner. This method is incapable of adapting to changing traffic conditions. Any intelligent traffic signal control system needs data about traffic, such as waiting times of vehicles, queue lengths, the number of vehicles at the junction, etc., to make decisions adaptively. Some signal control systems use past data to determine signal control rules. These methods use the predetermined rules to select a signal configuration based on current traffic at the junction. While these methods perform better than fixed-timing signal control, they assume that traffic patterns will always resemble the past data used.

Traffic Light Control(TLC) has been a well-studied problem, and hence there have been substantial efforts to create models that control traffic lights to reduce congestion in the road network. Many offline traffic signal control techniques have been proposed for generating signal timings using a static optimizer. Several online TLC algorithms based on techniques, such as genetic algorithms [5], stochastic control [31], and dynamic optimization [23], Neural Networks [24] that adapt in real-time have also been proposed.

Unlike model-based methods, RL-based algorithms do not assume any model of the system and can effectively learn the optimal policy through interaction with the environment. Prashanth et al. [21] proposed a Q-learning-based algorithm with linear function approximation to control traffic lights at junctions. Often precise information about queue length and waiting times of vehicles is hard to obtain. Therefore, the method uses certain thresholds to classify queue lengths and waiting times. Another advantage of using thresholds is that it aggregates the state space, making learning easier for the model. Our methods also use these thresholds for queue lengths and maximum waiting times. Authors have also developed an algorithm to set these thresholds optimally [22]. Chenghao Li et al. [11] studied the fairness control of traffic light and propose a deep RL algorithm to optimize the fairness of all drivers' waiting time.

Dongfang Ma et al. [13], used a deep neural network to capture temporal dependencies followed by actor-critic model to control a single junction. Further, Afshin Oroojlooy et al. [18] proposed an attention based method to create universal model for intersections with any number of roads, lanes, phases (possible signals), and traffic flow. There have also been attempts [3,26] to integrate the 'Max pressure theory' into the reward design of RL methods.

Multi-agent RL has also been used as a potential approach to solve the TLC problem. Unlike previous RL approaches where a single agent controls all signals in a centralized road network, [12,20] present a multi-agent setting with an agent per traffic signal. All agents work cooperatively to reduce congestion in the network. Mohammad Aslani et al. [1] compare deep neural network actor-critic methods while also modeling vehicle and pedestrian traffic demands and driver behavior. Shantian Yang et al. [29] introduced the MOA3CG algorithm, which uses Actor-Critic and Coordination Graph algorithms to select traffic light at junctions cooperatively.

There are numerous applications where one needs to work with graphs [6–8,28]. The use of graph convolution networks has become increasingly popular in traffic management applications such as traffic flow prediction [19], Autonomous mobility-on-demand systems [4], etc. The deep neural network, by its design, does not take into account the spatial features of the road network. In other words, there is no specific way for DNN to learn the relation between neighboring traffic signals. Also, for the single-agent DNN method, state space dimensionality increases linearly while action space increases exponentially. As a result, though DNN methods perform well on small networks, they can not perform well on larger road networks. The strength of GCN lies in its convolution mechanism that shares state features between neighboring nodes, which can be used to take cooperative actions at nodes of the graph. We represent the road network as a graph, with intersections in the road network as nodes and the roads as edges in the graph. We then leverage the capabilities of graph convolution networks for effective traffic light control.

Several existing methods have used graph convolution networks with reinforcement learning algorithms for traffic light control [17]. Tomoki Nishi et al. [17] have compared the performance of Q-learning with DNN and with GCNs on a regular grid road network. The state in this method comprises only of the queue length and vehicle speeds, whereas the reward structure consists of waiting times. Gyeongjun Kim et al. [9] proposed an asynchronous update method to train multiple actors with Deep graph Q-network. Hua Wei et al. [27] have used Graph Attention Network to facilitate communication between junctions and traffic lights cooperatively. To the best of our knowledge, no existing traffic light control method implements traffic light control with actor-critic using graph convolution networks using function approximation.

We formulate the traffic signal control problem in the Markov Decision Process (MDP) framework, where state quantifies the level of traffic congestion in the network, and the action of an agent is to select a traffic signal phase at every junction for the next signal cycle. We implement Q-learning and Actor-Critic algorithms with a Graph Convolution network as a function approximator. We call these models GCQN and GCAC, respectively. Using Graph convolution networks, we are able to utilize the graph structure of a road network and leverage neighbor nodes' information while making a decision. All our models select a single greedy action in the current state to maximize the total future reward. That is, these methods are trained to get a deterministic policy. We summarize our key contributions below. We perform implementations of all algorithms using the SUMO platform.

1.1 Our Contributions

1) We consider the problem of adaptive signal control of traffic lights at junctions. The objective is to select a traffic signal phase at each junction such that traffic flows through the network are maximized while congestion levels

are minimized. We propose Q-learning and Actor-Critic algorithms with a Graph Convolution network as function approximator.

2) We implement the GCQN and GCAC algorithms. For the purpose of comparison, we implement two variants of Deep Q-learning for traffic light control - a single DQN to control all traffic lights in the network (DQN) and individual DQNs to control every traffic signal (Ind-DQN).

3) We study the performance of the above models on two road networks: (i) a 2×2 grid network with four traffic signal junctions and (ii) Modified Sioux Falls network with 11 traffic signal junctions. Our experiments demonstrate that Graph Convolution models show promising results for problems of traffic signal control.

4) We compare our proposed models against existing approaches and observe that our proposed method achieves performance levels comparable to the state-of-the-art techniques.

The rest of this paper is organized as follows. In Sect. 2, we describe the traffic light control (TLC) problem as an MDP by identifying states, actions, rewards as well as state-action features. In Sect. 3, we describe the Graph Convolution Neural Networks as well as the Q-learning and Actor-Critic algorithms (GCQN and GCAC, respectively) based on these approximators. Section 4 describes implementation details on the SUMO platform and discusses the experimental results. We present concluding remarks in Sect. 5 and discuss some directions for future work.

2   Adaptive Traffic Light Control

In this section we present a formulation of the adaptive traffic signal control problem in the setting of MDPs with the discounted cost objective.

A Markov decision process comprises of a state space S, an action space A, a stationary transition dynamics with conditional probability distribution $p(s_{t+1}|s_t, a_t)$ satisfying the conditional Markov property, and a reward function $r : S \times A \rightarrow \mathcal{R}$. According to the conditional Markov property, for any states $s_n \in S$ and corresponding actions $a_n \in A$, $n \geq 0$ chosen in those states, we have $p(s_{m+1}|s_0, a_1, ..., s_m, a_m) = p(s_{m+1}|s_m, a_m)$, $m \geq 0$.

In this setting, the agent dynamically interacts with the environment that can be in one of the states at any instant. At time step t, the agent observes the state $s_t \in S$ and takes an action $a_t \in A$. The environment then transitions into a new state s_{t+1} at instant $t + 1$ according to the transition probability p. In addition, the agent gets a single-stage reward $r_t \equiv r(s_t, a_t)$. Suppose we consider episodes of a fixed or random length T. In other words, T can be a number or alternatively can be a random variable with a certain distribution. Then, we define the return from time t as $R_t = \sum_{t'=t}^{T} \gamma^{t'-t} r_{t'}$ where $0 < \gamma < 1$ is the discount factor. By a policy, we mean a decision rule for selecting actions. Policies can be deterministic or randomized. A deterministic policy prescribes the action to be chosen in any state of the environment while a randomized policy prescribes a distribution depending on the state of the environment over the set of feasible actions. For simplicity, we consider all actions to be feasible in every state. In infinite horizon tasks as we consider, it makes sense to consider policies that are stationary or time-invariant.

The goal of the agent is to interact with the environment and learn a policy that maximizes the return. An agent uses a policy to select an action in the given state. We denote a stochastic policy by $\pi : S \to P(A)$ where $P(A)$ is the set of probability measures on A. Further, $\pi(a_t|s_t)$ is the probability of taking action a_t in state s_t. A deterministic policy is denoted by $\mu : S \to A$ where $\mu(s_t)$ corresponds to the action (a_t) chosen in state s_t under policy μ.

Under a given randomized policy π, Q-value function is defined as follows: $\forall s \in S, a \in A$,

$$Q^\pi(s,a) = E\left[\sum_{k=0}^{\infty} \gamma^k r(s_k, \pi(s_k)) \mid s_0 = s, a_0 = a\right]$$
$$= r(s,a) + E\left[\sum_{k=1}^{\infty} \gamma^k r(s_k, \pi(s_k)) \mid s_0 = s, a_0 = a\right]. \tag{1}$$

2.1 Elements of the Underlying MDP

Consider a road network with p junctions, of which m are traffic light junctions, $1 \leq m \leq p$. Each junction has multiple crossroads and a maximum of k incoming lanes. For adaptive traffic light control, we want to find a deterministic policy that takes in the state of congestion in the road network and decides which traffic light phase to turn on at every junction. The state s_t at time t is a vector of queue lengths and elapsed times in all the incoming lanes at the various junctions. The elapsed time on a lane is the maximum time a vehicle has waited in that lane since the signal turned red. This quantity is zero for lanes on which the signal is green, or where no vehicle is waiting in the lane.

Control decisions are made by a controller that receives the state information from the various lanes and makes decisions on which green traffic light phase to turn on at each of the individual junctions. Action a_t comprises the vector of signal phases (each corresponding to the feasible combination of traffic lights to switch on) at each of the m signalized junctions of the road network. Thus, $a_t = (a_1(t), ..., a_m(t))$ where $a_i(t)$ is the signal phase at junction i during the time slot t. We consider the traffic signal cycle time T, which is divided into green phase time T_g followed by yellow phase time T_y. If, at a junction, the controller decides on the same green traffic light phase for two consecutive cycles, then the same green phase is kept on during the yellow phase following the first green phase at that junction. Note that, since the action is taken every T seconds (at the beginning of each traffic light cycle), actions are chosen when the states of the system are s_{nT}, $n \geq 0$.

The reward is the negative of the cost that in turn has two components. The first is the sum of the queue lengths at the individual lanes, while the second component is the sum of the elapsed times on all lanes. The idea here is to regulate the flow of traffic in order to minimize the queue lengths while, at the same time, ensuring fairness so that a certain amount of green time does get allocated to each lane after some intervals of time have elapsed even when the queue lengths there are not high. This will ensure that no lane continues to receive the red light for an inordinately large time interval.

2.2   State Aggregation

As proposed in [21], we use state aggregation to decide state features. This is achieved as follows: Let L_1 and L_2 be two prescribed thresholds for the queue length at each lane with $0 < L_1 < L_2$ and let T_1 be the elapsed time threshold. For an incoming lane j at junction i, suppose the queue length at time t is $q_j^i(t)$ and elapsed time is $w_j^i(t)$. Then the aggregated state features $\sigma_{q_j^i(t)}$ and $\sigma_{w_j^i(t)}$ are given as:

$$\sigma_{q_j^i(t)} = \begin{cases} 0 & \text{if } q_j^i(t) < L_1, \\ 0.5 & \text{if } L_1 \leq q_j^i(t) \leq L_2, \\ 1 & \text{if } q_j^i(t) > L_2. \end{cases}$$

$$\sigma_{w_j^i(t)} = \begin{cases} 0 & \text{if } w_j^i(t) < T_1, \\ 1 & \text{otherwise.} \end{cases}$$

The queue length is thus clustered into three levels - less than L_1 (or low congestion region), more than L_1 but less than $L2$ (or medium congestion region), and more than L_2 (or high congestion region), respectively. Similarly, the elapsed time is clustered into two levels, say, low and high respectively. We follow the same notation for queue length and elapsed time throughout the section.

2.3   Traffic Light Control with DQN

For a given state s, the optimal policy is the one that selects the action a that gives the maximum $Q(s, a)$ value over all actions feasible in state s. While the Q-learning algorithm provides the optimal Q-values in the case of full-state representations making use of the iterative scheme [25], this is not practical to implement in these settings where the number of states and actions is excessive in general. The deep Q-network algorithm, DQN, uses a deep neural network to approximate the Q-function. The detailed characteristics of the algorithm are mentioned in [16].

We use Q_θ to approximate the Q-function where θ denotes the vector of network weights in the Q-learning scheme with neural network parameterization. The input state feature vector σ_{s_t} consists of state features for all incoming lanes at each of the junctions. That is, $\sigma_{s_t} = (\sigma_{q_1^1(t)}, ..., \sigma_{q_k^m(t)}, \sigma_{w_1^1(t)}, ..., \sigma_{w_k^m(t)})$. The output layer gives the Q-values of possible actions a_t for a given input state. Here, for a road network with m junctions and four traffic light phase choices at each junction, the size of the output layer would be 4^m. One output node indicates the Q-value of one action (a combination of phases at all junctions). One typically selects an action with the highest Q-value for a given state.

As mentioned before, the reward $r(s_t, a_t)$ is a real number that is taken as the negative of cost. The cost in turn consists of the sum of the queue lengths and the sum of the elapsed times at the incoming lanes at all junctions.

$$r(s_t, a_t) = - \left(\alpha_i \sum_{i,j} q^i_j(t) + \beta_i \sum_{i,j} w^i_j(t) \right),$$

where we let $\beta_i = 1 - \alpha_i$. For our implementations, we select $\alpha_i = 0.5$ and $\beta_i = 0.5$, respectively. We also maintain target DQN $Q_{\bar{\theta}}$ to calculate the target values. The target network is periodically updated after a fixed number of iterations d. Other implementation details about collecting experience, the architecture of DQN, etc., are provided in Sect. 4.

3   TLC with Graph Convolution Networks

In this section, we discuss about the use of graph convolution networks (GCN) as the underlying neural network based Q-value function approximators. We also discuss two algorithms based on GCN, viz., GCQN and GCAC, respectively.

3.1   Graph Convolution Network

A GCN [10,30] is a multi-layer neural network that can work with graphs and generates embedding vectors of nodes based on the features of their neighborhoods. Formally, consider a graph $G = (V, E)$, where $V (|V| = n)$ is set of nodes and E is sets of edges. Every node is assumed to be connected to itself, i.e., $(v, v) \in E$ for any $v \in V$. Let $X \in \mathcal{R}^{n \times m}$ be a matrix containing all n nodes with their features, where m is the dimension of each feature vector, each row $x_v \in \mathcal{R}^m$ is the feature vector for v. An adjacency matrix A of graph G has diagonal elements set to 1 because of self-loops. The degree matrix D is a diagonal matrix where $D_{ii} = \sum_j A_{ij}$. With one layer of convolution, GCN can capture information about immediate neighbors. With multiple GCN layers stacked, it can integrate information about larger neighborhoods. In an N-layer GCN network, every node can exchange information with up to N-hop neighbors. For a one-layer GCN, the new k-dimensional node feature matrix $L^{(1)} \in \mathcal{R}^{n \times m}$ is computed as $L^{(1)} = \rho(\tilde{A} X W_0)$ where $\tilde{A} = D^{-\frac{1}{2}} A D^{-\frac{1}{2}}$ is the normalized symmetric adjacency matrix and $W_0 \in \mathcal{R}^{m \times k}$ is a weight matrix. Further, ρ is an activation function such as ReLU, in which case, $\rho(x) = max(0, x)$. One can stack multiple GCN layers as follows: $L^{(j+1)} = \rho(\tilde{A} L^{(j)} W_j)$ where j denotes the layer number and $L^{(0)} = X$. The last layer's feature vectors can be passed to linear layers, i.e., layers with no convolution, in order to improve performance. These linear layers act as individual feed-forward networks for every node's last layer feature vectors.

3.2   TLC with GCQN

We use GCN to approximate Q-function that we now call Q_{gc} where gc are network weights. The GCN model consists of stacked graph convolution layers, followed by linear layers. It operates on a road network graph where n junctions are nodes and roads are the edges. Here, the input state feature σ_{s_t} to the GCN input layer is the matrix $X \in \mathcal{R}^{n \times 2k}$, where row $X_i \in \mathcal{R}^{2k}$ is a vector of $\sigma_{q_j^i(t)}$ and $\sigma_{w_j^i(t)}$. The output layer of GCN $Y \in \mathcal{R}^{n \times c}$ denotes Q-values where c is the maximum number of signal phase choices at any junction. Also, $Y_{ij} = Q_{gc}^{i,j}$ denotes the Q-value of turning the jth signal phase on at junction i. Here, action can be taken at each junction by choosing the signal phase with the maximum Q-value for that junction.

Let $r(s_t, a_t) \in \mathcal{R}^n$ denote the reward vector with ith component $r^i(s_t, a_t)$ being the reward accumulated at junction i and given as follows:

$$r^i(t) \triangleq r^i(s_t, a_t) = - \left(\alpha_1 \sum_j q_j^i(t) + \beta_1 \sum_j w_j^i(t) \right).$$

Similarly, the loss (L_{gc}) is also calculated individually at every junction. For traffic light junction i, we have $L_{gc}^i = \left(Q_{gc}^{i,a_t}(\sigma_{s_t}, a_t) - y^i(t) \right)^2$, where, $y^i(t) = r^i(t) + \gamma \max_j Q_{gc}^{i,j}(\sigma_{s_{t+T}}, j)$. For junctions with no traffic light, the loss is set to zero since the model does not have to learn to choose an action there. The total loss for the model is the sum of losses at all nodes. Thus, $L_{gc} = \sum_i L_{gc}^i$ The detailed training procedure is provided in Algorithm 1.

Algorithm 1. Training GCQN in batches with target GCQN

1: Initialize replay buffer B and GCQN Q_ω, target GCQN $Q_{\omega'}$, tuf $= 0, d$
2: For $episode = 1$ to $max\_episodes$
3:     Initialize empty experience replay buffer B
4:     Reset the environment
5:     For step $t = 1$ **to** $max\_episode\_length$
6:         Select action $a_t = (a_t^1, ..., a_t^n)$ according to ϵ-greedy strategy
7:         Execute action a_t and observe r_t, s_{t+1}
8:         Store (s_t, a_t, r_t, s_{t+1}) in B
9:         $s_t = s_{t+1}$
10:         For $epoch = 1$ to max_epochs
11:             Sample a mini-batch S of size s
12:             For $(s_t, a_t, r_t, s_{t+1}) \in S$
13:                 Set $y^i(t) = r^i(t) + \gamma \max_j Q_{\omega'}^{i,j}(\sigma_{s_{t+T}}, j)$ for each of the junctions i
14:                 Set $L_\omega(t) = \sum_i (Q_\omega^{i,a_t}(\sigma_{s_t}, a_t) - y^i(t))^2$
15:             Update ω by minimizing loss $L_{(}\omega) = \frac{1}{s} \sum_t L_\omega(t)$
16:             IF $n\%d = 0$
17:                 Update target network parameters as $\omega' = \omega$
18:             tuf $=$ tuf $+ 1$

A k-layered Graph Convolution leads to sharing of state features, i.e., queue length and waiting time information amongst k-hop neighbors of a traffic light junction. Thus, traffic light at a junction is chosen with some knowledge of congestion at k-hop neighbor junctions. The reward and corresponding loss are calculated separately for each junction. While training the models, the loss at junctions is back-propagated till its k-hop neighbors. GCN learns the right weights to combine state features of neighborhood nodes, that is, it learns the dependencies between neighboring nodes. A well trained graph convolution model can thus take an action at a traffic light junction in a cooperative manner in order to maximise the overall reward and thus minimise the overall congestion in the road network. This is in contrast to using individual DQNs at each junction that tries to maximize the rewards locally, at the junction. This is also confirmed by our experimental evaluations provided in Sect. 5.

3.3   TLC with GCAC

The actor-critic [2] is a widely used architecture that incorporates a combination of policy and value based methods to train the agent. A variant of this approach is the Advantage Actor-Critic (A2C) [15]. A2C consists of two components - an Actor that approximates the policy π_θ with parameter θ and a critic that approximates the value function $V_{\theta'}$ with parameter θ'. A2C uses the Advantage function $A(s, a)$ to calculate the Temporal Difference (TD) Error. The advantage function determines how much better a certain action is than the action chosen as per the given policy. Thus, if $Q^\pi(s_t, a_t) > V^\pi(s_t)$, it is advantageous to select action a_t in state s_t as opposed to selecting an action according to π in that state. Both actor and critic use the advantage function to calculate the loss.

We use GCN to approximate the policy actor π_θ, where θ are the weights of the GCN. Likewise, we use GCN to approximate the value critic $V_{\theta'}$, where θ' are the weights of this GCN. The input to the actor GCN $X \in \mathcal{R}^{n \times 2k}$ is the same as the input to GCQN. The output layer of the actor gives probability distributions over possible actions a_t at every node for a given input state. Formally, for a network with n nodes and c maximum signal phase choices at any junction, the output layer of GCN is $Y \in \mathcal{R}^{n \times c}$, where $Y_{ij} = \pi_\theta^i(j|s_t)$ denotes the probability of turning the jth signal phase on at junction i according to the actor's policy π_θ. Thus, at the ith junction, action is sampled from the distribution π_θ^i.

The input to the critic GCN $X \in \mathcal{R}^{n \times 2k}$ is the same as that to the actor GCN. The output layer of GCN is $Y \in \mathcal{R}^n$, where $Y_i = V_{\theta'}^i(s_t)$ denotes the component of node i in the value of state $V_{\theta'}(s_t)$. The reward $r(s_t, a_t) \in \mathcal{R}^n$ is calculated in the same way as for GCQN.

The actor and critic losses, viz., L_θ^i and $L_{\theta'}^i$, respectively, are also calculated for all nodes. For junctions with no traffic light, the loss is set to zero as before. The total losses of the actor and critic are the sum of respective losses at each node. Thus,

$$A^i(s_t, a_t) = r^i(s_t, a_t) + V_{\theta'}^i(s_{t+T}) - V_{\theta'}^i(s_t) L_\theta(s_t, a_t) = \sum_i L_\theta^i(s_t, a_t)$$

$$= -\sum_i \log(\pi_\theta^i(a_t|s_t) \times A^i(s_t, a_t) L_{\theta'}(s_t, a_t) = \sum_i L_{\theta'}^i(s_t, a_t) = \sum_i (A^i(s_t, a_t))^2.$$

The parameters of actor and critic are updated to reduce the respective losses. The training algorithm is given below, see Algorithm 2.

Algorithm 2. Training GCAC model with A2C algorithm

1: Initialize the actor and critic parameters θ and θ'
2: For $episode = 1$ to $max\_episodes$
3:      Initialize empty experience replay buffer B
4:      Reset the environment
5:      For step $t = 1$ **to** $max\_episode\_length$
6:          Sample action a_t^i from $\pi_\theta^i(\cdot|s_t)$ for all junctions i
7:          Execute action $(a_t^1, ..., a_t^n)$ and observe r_t, s_{t+1}
8:          For junction i
9:              Set $return^i(t) = r^i(s_t, a_t) + V_{\theta'}^i(s_{t+1})$
10:             Set $A^i(s_t, a_t) = return^i(t) - V_{\theta'}^i(s_t)$
11:             Update θ' by minimising the critic loss
                $\sum_i (A^i(s_t, a_t))^2$
12:             Update θ by minimising the actor loss
                $\sum_i (-\log(\pi_\theta^i(a_t|s_t) \times A^i(s_t, a_t))$
13:         Set $s_t = s_{t+1}$

---

4   Experiments and Results

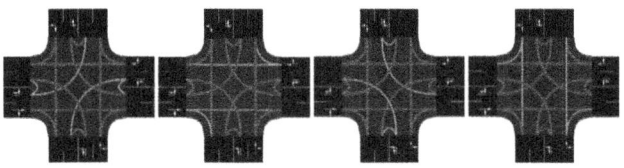

Fig. 1. Four possible green phases of a traffic signal at a junction: Green lines indicate turns that vehicles from corresponding incoming lanes are allowed to take. Each green phase has a corresponding yellow phase with green lines replaced by yellow lines (Color figure online)

We experiment with all methods described in earlier sections for adaptive traffic light control. We use "Simulation of Urban MObility" (SUMO), which is an open-source, highly portable, microscopic, and continuous traffic simulation package.

The GCN models are implemented with the PyTorch Geometric library. We implement TLC methods on two different road networks that we describe below. (i) a 2×2 grid road network with four traffic light junctions and (ii) Modified Sioux Falls road network with eleven traffic light junctions. Sioux Falls network is used in many transportation network studies. We modified it such that no junction has more than four incoming roads. Both networks are shown in Fig. 2. For state aggregation, we choose values of L_1, L_2, T_1 as $7\,m$, $15\,m$, and $13\,s$, respectively, for both these networks. Further, in both of these networks, at every traffic light junction, there are four possible green traffic light phases, as shown in Fig. 5. A traffic light cycle T lasts for $14\,s$. Green phase time T_g is 10 s, and yellow phase time T_y is $4\,s$. In each method we implement for TLC, the controller model selects the next green traffic light phase at each junction at the end of the green phase. If the next selected phase is different from the currently selected phase, then yellow phase corresponding to previous green phase is turned on otherwise green phase continues to be kept on. After T_y duration, the next green phase is turned on for T_g duration. In the 2×2 grid road network, each traffic light junction has eight incoming lanes - 4 incoming roads with two lanes on each road. In every episode, 1,000 vehicles are generated with random source and destination roads. The maximum length of an episode is 5,400 steps (seconds). However, an episode can end before the maximum steps if all vehicles have reached their destination. For every model, we perform training for 800 episodes. A batch of size 100 is sampled from experience collected in that episode. In each episode, the model is trained on 800 such batches. All models are trained with Adam optimizer with an initial learning rate set to 0.001. The discount factor γ is set to 0.75. Further, ϵ is set to 1 at the start of the training and is decreased with a factor of 0.997. The various architectures for all the 2×2 grid road network models used in the algorithms are given below. The input and output layer sizes of these models are calculated as described in (i)–(v) below.

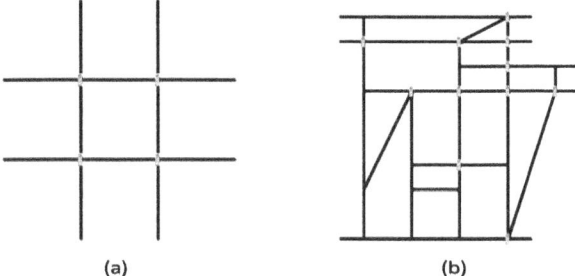

(a)   (b)

Fig. 2. (a) 2×2 Grid road network, (b) Modified Sioux Falls network

(i) Deep Q-learning network (**DQN**): Input layer size of DQN is 64. The output layer size is 256. DQN has three hidden linear layers, each of size 128. The *Relu* activation function follows each hidden layer.

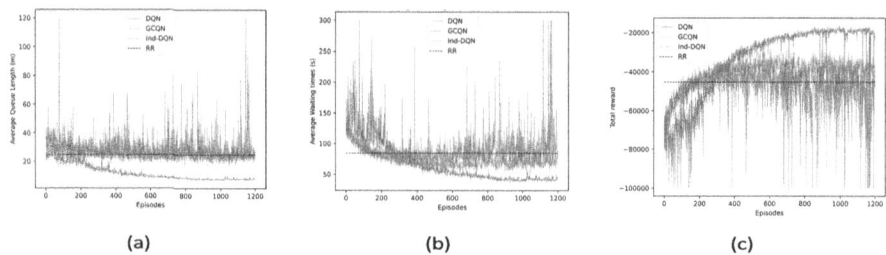

Fig. 3. Average queue length (a), Average waiting time (b) of vehicles and Total reward (c) over training episodes for modified 2×2 grid network

(ii) Graph Convolution Q-learning network (**GCQN**): There are 12 nodes in the network, out of which four are traffic light controlled. GCQN operates on a graph of 12 nodes. The input layer size here is 12×16. There are two stacked convolution hidden layers of size 12×64, each followed by tanh activation functions. These are followed by a linear layer of size 12×64 and tanh activation. This layer is then followed by an output layer of size 12×4.

(iii) Graph Convolution Actor-Critic Network (**GCAC**): The actor-network of GCAC is the same as GCQN, and the output layer is followed by the Categorical distribution layer that gives out a probability distribution over actions. The critic network is also the same as GCQN, except the output layer is of size 12×1.

(iv) Individual DQN networks (**Ind-DQN**): This architecture is similar to GCQN, where linear layers of the same size replace convolution layers. This is equivalent to having a separate DQN at each node of a network.

(v) Round Robin (**RR**): We compare the performance of each of the above networks with round-robin controlled traffic light junctions. In this method, traffic light phases move in cycles in a round robin manner and the same phase at any junction cannot occur consecutively. We keep traffic light cycle time to $T = 30$ seconds with $T_g = 25$ and $T_y = 5$. Since there is no learning involved in RR, it performs roughly the same in every episode. We take the average over a few episodes and use that as a baseline to compare against the other methods.

Figures 3 (a) and (b) show the comparisons of the average queue length at the junction and the average cumulative waiting time of vehicles, respectively. Since there is no training involved in the round-robin method, performance of this method is roughly the same in every episode. We take a single value averaged over 20 episodes for all the comparisons. The best performance for the 2×2 Grid network is achieved by the DQN model, followed by the GCQN model. The GCAC model, however, could not learn for this small road network, and hence result curves are excluded from the figures. The average queue length went down to about 8 m in the DQN model and 24 m in the GCQN model. The Average Cumulative waiting time of a vehicle went down to about 42 s in the DQN model and 72 s in the GCQN model. Figure 3 (c) shows rewards over training episodes.

For a small graph such as a 2×2 network, DQN can perform well. Here, GCQN and GCAC models suffer from a well known over-smoothing problem in GCN. Using a Deeper Graph Convolutional Network (GCN) on a smaller graph leads to the model producing identical node features across the graph that hinders the performance of the model. But as the size of the graph increases, state space increases linearly w.r.t. the number of nodes, while the action space increases exponentially. Hence it becomes infeasible to use DQN for large networks. One way to avoid this could be to use separate DQNs at every junction. But this model cannot take into account congestion levels in neighborhood nodes. As a result, it performs poorly. The GCQN and GCAC models, on the other hand, perform well on larger graphs since these can share congestion information with neighborhood nodes with their convolution mechanism.

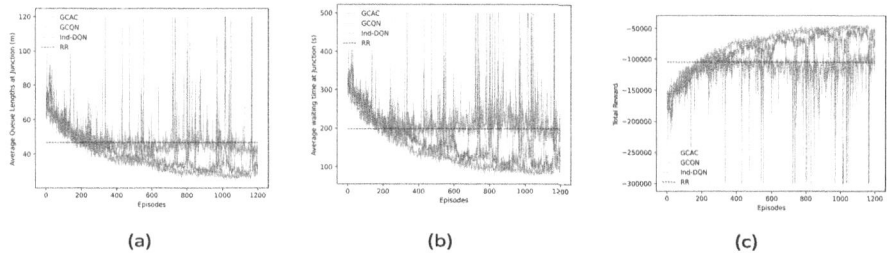

Fig. 4. Average queue length (a), Average waiting time (b) of vehicles and Total reward (c) over training episodes for modified Sioux Falls network

Keeping all the training configurations same, we experiment with different models on a larger road network - the modified Sioux Falls road network. Here one thousand five hundred vehicles are generated in each episode. There are 31 nodes in the network, out of which 11 are traffic light controlled. No junction has more than four incoming roads. Each road has two lanes. Architectures of models are similar to those for 2×2 grid network and are described below:

- Graph Convolution Q-learning network (**GCQN**): Input layer size is 31×16. The number of layers and activation functions is kept the same as for the 2×2 Grid network. Only sizes of layers now become 31×64, and the output layer is of size 31×4.
- Graph Convolution Actor-Critic Network (**GCAC**): The actor-network of GCAC is the same as GCQN, and the output layer is followed by the Categorical distribution layer that gives out a probability distribution over actions. The critic network is also the same as GCQN, except the output layer is of size 31×1.
- Individual DQN networks (**Ind-DQN**): This architecture is similar to GCQN, where linear layers of the same size replace convolution layers. This is equivalent to having separate DQN at every node of a network.

– Round Robin (**RR**): We compare the performance of each of the above networks with round-robin controlled traffic light junctions.

Figures 4 (a) and (b) show the comparisons of the average queue length at the junction and the average cumulative waiting time of vehicles, respectively[1]. Again all RL models are able to achieve better performance than the round-robin method. The best performance for this network is achieved by the GCQN model, followed by the GCAC model. The average queue length went down to about 30 m in the GCQN model and 38 m in the GCAC model. The Average Cumulative waiting time of a vehicle at the junction went down to about 102 s in the GCQN model and 172 s in the GCAC model. Figure 4(c) shows rewards over training episodes.

Table 1. Total Queue length and Total waiting times at the junction in road networks averaged over last 100 episodes of Training

	2 × 2 Grid network		Modified Sioux Falls network	
	Queue Length(m)	Waiting Time(s)	Queue Length(m)	Waiting Time(s)
Round-Robin	24.52	84.43	46.67	198.25
DQN	**7.87**	**42.53**	–	–
Individual-DQN	30.90	115.84	44.19	198.76
GCQN	24.27	72.03	**30.33**	**102.98**
GCAC	36.00	246.13	38.71	172.88

Similar to the 2 × 2 grid, the GCQN model performs better than individual DQN models. GCAC also performs better than individual DQN models. However, towards the end of the training, there are some episodes where the GCAC model shows a sudden increase in queue lengths and waiting times. GCQN model shows more stable behavior as compared to GCAC. The average queue length and waiting time for the various models is given in Table 1.

Additionally, we have benchmarked our GCQN and GCAC models against some state of the art methods. We perform this experiment in the Libsignal framework which provides OpenAI Gym-compatible environments for traffic light control scenarios and collection of baseline models [14]. In our experiments, we used the PressLight [26], MpLight [3] and CoLight [27] models from Libsignal directly, without altering any hyper-parameters. Experiments were conducted on a 4 × 4 grid road network with 16 intersections. We use here an open dataset - 'hangzhou_4 × 4_gudang_18010207_1h' traffic flow data, which is based on camera data in Hangzhou city. It consists of 4,000 vehicles departing in an hour from one of the nodes. We present below performance comparison in terms of Average

---

[1] Queue length values greater than 120 m are set to 120 m while plotting the curve to get proper visualization of performance comparison. Similarly waiting time and reward values are cropped as necessary in the respective graphs.

travel time of vehicles, Average queue length, Approximated delay. More details about experimental setup, traffic flow dataset and evaluation matrices are available in the github repository[2]. Due to lack of space, we do not show plots for the 4×4 grid setting. Due to the complexity of the model, GCAC needs around 200 episodes to converge. Table 2 shows the performance comparisons of all trained models. Here, all models are trained for 100 episodes, except GCAC that is trained for 200 episodes. Although CoLight gives the best performance among all models, GCQN does demonstrate noteworthy performance. In particular, GCQN converges faster than MPLight and PressLight and outperforms these, in terms of Queue length. Even though GCAC doesn't outperform any model, it shows relatively notable performance as well. One can experiment with various training techniques to achieve faster convergence in GCAC. Both GCQN and GCAC show comparable results to the SOTA methods and are worth exploring further for future research.

Table 2. Average Travel time, Queue Length, delay in 4×4 grid road networks with trained models (averaged over 5 episodes)

	Average Travel time	Queue Length	delay
CoLight	333.37	0.152	0.087
MPLight	373.71	0.287	0.096
PressLight	346.66	0.210	0.106
GCQN	347.00	0.195	0.100
GCAC	367.66	0.295	0.131

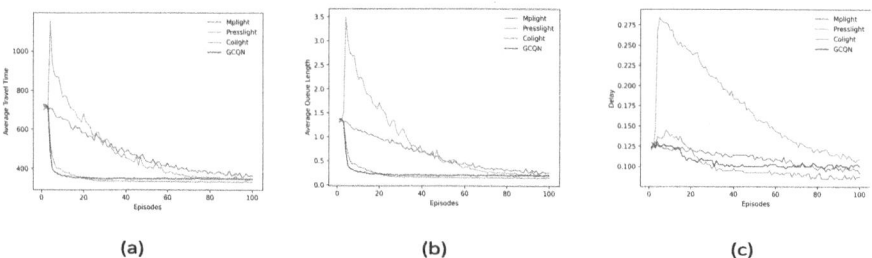

(a)   (b)   (c)

Fig. 5. Average travel time(a), Average queue length(b) and Approximate delay(c) of vehicles over training episodes for 4×4 grid network

5 Conclusion

Designing a traffic management system that adapts to the variation in traffic using traffic light control is a challenging task. Reinforcement learning presents

---

[2] https://github.com/traffic-signal-control/RL_signals.

an interesting paradigm for solving these problems. We have designed and evaluated different models for adaptive Traffic light control. The DQN model works better for small road networks but is unsuitable once the road networks become large. The GCQN model leverages the graph structure for road networks and shows promising results for use in larger road networks. We also proposed the GCAC model, whose results are comparable to GCQN in larger networks but are not as stable as GCQN. We also assess the performance of GCQN and GCAC models against state-of-the-art counterparts, and observe similar levels of performance. However, due to its moderately complex structure, the GCAC model requires more training iterations to converge. Exploring different techniques in training, GCAC may enhance convergence speed.

We analyzed the performance of traffic light control algorithms on waiting times and queue lengths. There is still a need to come up with strategies to handle scenarios (such as accidents) where a certain road is temporarily not in use. Also, it may not be feasible to keep training RL agents on new data too often. Thus, one needs an optimal way to train and update the model.

We used Graph convolution networks in our traffic signal control solutions to capture the spacial relations between nodes of the road network. One can also try GCN layers followed by LSTM layers, which can be better at capturing temporal relations between subsequent states and actions.

References

1. Aslani, M., Mesgari, M.S., Wiering, M.: Adaptive traffic signal control with actor-critic methods in a real-world traffic network with different traffic disruption events. Transp. Res. Part C: Emerg. Technol. **85**, 732–752 (2017)
2. Bhatnagar, S., Sutton, R.S., Ghavamzadeh, M., Lee, M.: Natural actor-critic algorithms. Automatica **45**(11), 2471–2482 (2009)
3. Chen, C., et al.: Toward a thousand lights: decentralized deep reinforcement learning for large-scale traffic signal control. In: AAAI Conference on Artificial Intelligence (2020)
4. Gammelli, D., Yang, K., Harrison, J., Rodrigues, F., Pereira, F.C., Pavone, M.: Graph neural network reinforcement learning for autonomous mobility-on-demand systems. In: 2021 60th IEEE Conference on Decision and Control (CDC), pp. 2996–3003 (2021)
5. Girianna, M., Benekohal, R.F.: Using genetic algorithms to design signal coordination for oversaturated networks. J. Intell. Transp. Syst. - J INTELL TRANSPORT SYST **8**, 117–129 (2004)
6. Guo, Y., Wu, Q., She, H.: A routing optimization policy using graph convolution deep reinforcement learning. In: 2023 IEEE/CIC International Conference on Communications in China (ICCC), pp. 1–6 (2023)
7. Hegeman, T., Iosup, A.: Survey of graph analysis applications. CoRR abs/1807.00382 (2018)
8. Houidi, O., Bakri, S., Zeghlache, D.: Multi-agent graph convolutional reinforcement learning for intelligent load balancing. In: NOMS 2022-2022 IEEE/IFIP Network Operations and Management Symposium, pp. 1–6 (2022)

9. Kim, G., Sohn, K.: Area-wide traffic signal control based on a deep graph Q-network (DGQN) trained in an asynchronous manner. Appl. Soft Comput. **119**, 108497 (2022)
10. Kipf, T.N., Welling, M.: Semi-supervised classification with graph convolutional networks. CoRR, abs/1609.02907 (2016)
11. Li, C., Ma, X., Xia, L., Zhao, Q., Yang, J.: Fairness control of traffic light via deep reinforcement learning. In: 2020 IEEE 16th International Conference on Automation Science and Engineering (CASE), pp. 652–658 (2020)
12. Li, S.: Multi-agent deep deterministic policy gradient for traffic signal control on urban road network. In: 2020 IEEE International Conference on Advances in Electrical Engineering and Computer Applications(AEECA), pp. 896–900 (2020)
13. Ma, D., Zhou, B., Song, X., Dai, H.: A deep reinforcement learning approach to traffic signal control with temporal traffic pattern mining. IEEE Trans. Intell. Transp. Syst. **23**(8), 11789–11800 (2022)
14. Mei, H., Lei, X., Da, L., Shi, B., Wei, H.: LibSignal: an open library for traffic signal control. Mach. Learn., 1–37 (2023)
15. Mnih, V., et al.: Asynchronous methods for deep reinforcement learning. In: International Conference on Machine Learning (2016)
16. Mnih, V., et al.: Playing Atari with deep reinforcement learning. CoRR, abs/1312.5602 (2013)
17. Nishi, T., Otaki, K., Hayakawa, K., Yoshimura, T.: Traffic signal control based on reinforcement learning with graph convolutional neural nets. In: 2018 21st International Conference on Intelligent Transportation Systems (ITSC), pp. 877–883 (2018)
18. Oroojlooy, A., Nazari, M., Hajinezhad, D., Silva, J.: AttendLight: universal attention-based reinforcement learning model for traffic signal control (2020)
19. Peng, H., et al.: Dynamic graph convolutional network for long-term traffic flow prediction with reinforcement learning. Inf. Sci. **578**, 401–416 (2021)
20. Prabuchandran, K.J., AN, H.K., Bhatnagar, S.: Multi-agent reinforcement learning for traffic signal control. In: 17th International IEEE Conference on Intelligent Transportation Systems (ITSC), pp. 2529–2534 (2014)
21. Prashanth, L.A., Bhatnagar, S.: Reinforcement learning with function approximation for traffic signal control. IEEE Trans. Intell. Transp. Syst. **12**(2), 412–421 (2011)
22. Prashanth, L.A., Bhatnagar, S.: Threshold tuning using stochastic optimization for graded signal control. IEEE Trans. Veh. Technol. **61**(9), 3865–3880 (2012)
23. Sen, S., Head, K.L.: Controlled optimization of phases at an intersection. Transp. Sci. **31**, 5–17 (1997)
24. ul Asar, A., Ullah, M.S., Ahmed, J., ul Hasnain, R.: Traffic responsive signal timing plan generation based on neural network. In: 2008 IEEE International Conference on Automation Science and Engineering, pp. 833–838 (2008)
25. Watkins, C., Dayan, P.: Technical note: Q-learning. Mach. Learn. **8**, 279–292 (1992)
26. Wei, H., et al.: PressLight: learning max pressure control to coordinate traffic signals in arterial network. In: Proceedings of the 25th ACM SIGKDD International Conference on Knowledge Discovery & Data Mining, KDD 2019, pp. 1290-1298, New York. Association for Computing Machinery (2019)
27. Wei, H., et al.: CoLight: learning network-level cooperation for traffic signal control. In: Proceedings of the 28th ACM International Conference on Information and Knowledge Management, CIKM 2019. ACM (2019)

28. Xiangyun, Z., Lijun, W., Zhiyuan, L., Yulin, J.: Deep reinforcement learning with graph convolutional networks for load balancing in SDN-based data center networks. In: 2021 18th International Computer Conference on Wavelet Active Media Technology and Information Processing (ICCWAMTIP), pp. 344–352 (2021)
29. Yang, S., Yang, B., Wong, H.-S., Kang, Z.: Cooperative traffic signal control using multi-step return and off-policy asynchronous advantage actor-critic graph algorithm. Knowl.-Based Syst. **183**, 104855 (2019)
30. Yao, L., Mao, C., Luo, Y.: Graph convolutional networks for text classification. CoRR, abs/1809.05679 (2018)
31. Yu, X.-H., Recker, W.W.: Stochastic adaptive control model for traffic signal systems. Transp. Res. Part C: Emerg. Technol. **14**(4), 263–282 (2006)

Optimizing Intelligent Transportation Systems with Multi-agent Reinforcement Learning: A Socio-economic Impact Assessment

Qian Cao[1,3], Jing Li[2], and Paolo Trucco[1(✉)]

[1] Department of Management, Economics and Industrial Engineering,
Politecnico di Milano, Milan, Italy
qian.cao@gsom.polimi.it, paolo.trucco@polimi.it
[2] School of Economics and Management, Tsinghua University, Beijing, China
jing_li@tsinghua.edu.cn
[3] Mogo Co., Beijing, China

Abstract. Rapid urbanization has exacerbated traffic congestion, presenting significant socio-economic and environmental challenges globally. This paper evaluates the socio-economic impact of implementing Intelligent Transportation Systems (ITS) enhanced by a novel Socio-Economic Reinforcement Learning (SERL) framework. We aim to minimize congestion and enhance overall transportation efficiency. The proposed method employs a hierarchical reinforcement learning algorithm specifically designed for complex multi-intersection urban traffic networks, considering socio-economic and environmental factors. Extensive simulations utilizing real-world traffic data assess the impact on travel time, fuel consumption, and emission levels. Experimental results indicate that our approach reduces average travel time by up to 26.67% compared to fixed-time control methods, decreases fuel consumption by 13.99%, and lowers CO_x/NO_x emissions by 20.82% in specific scenarios. These significant improvements over traditional and existing RL-based methods underscore the potential of SERL-powered ITS in promoting sustainable urban development and improving socio-economic outcomes.

Keywords: Traffic Optimization · Multi-Agent Systems · Socio-Economic Impact

1 Introduction

Urbanization has led to increased vehicle usage, resulting in traffic congestion that poses significant socio-economic challenges [4]. Traffic delays lead to economic losses, increased fuel consumption, and elevated emission levels, impacting environmental sustainability and public health.

Urban traffic exhibits highly dynamic and non-linear patterns due to varying demand, incidents, and human behavior. Traditional traffic management

© ICST Institute for Computer Sciences, Social Informatics and Telecommunications Engineering 2025
Published by Springer Nature Switzerland AG 2025. All Rights Reserved
A. Kocian et al. (Eds.): INTSYS 2024, LNICST 608, pp. 209–224, 2025.
https://doi.org/10.1007/978-3-031-86370-7_13

systems lack adaptability to dynamic traffic patterns. Reinforcement Learning (RL), with its ability to learn optimal policies through interaction with the environment, offers a promising solution. However, most existing RL approaches in traffic management are limited by scalability and need more exploration with environmental factors such as fuel consumption and public health risks. Thus, traffic management solutions must consider the broader socio-economic impacts, such as minimizing total travel time and emissions to enhance economic productivity and environmental sustainability. In smart city, effective traffic management requires coordinated control strategies across multiple intersections to prevent bottlenecks and ensure smooth flow. Compared to previous single-agent RL which struggles to adapt in real-time to these fluctuations, coordinating multiple agents (traffic signals) necessitates sophisticated communication and decision-making mechanisms to achieve global objectives without centralized control. And previous work [6] reliance on pressure-based control does not account for socio-economic disparities among different intersections, limiting its applicability in heterogeneous urban environments.

Traditional RL approaches often focus on optimizing immediate rewards without considering long-term socio-economic impacts including ITS and sustainable urban development. To build a more scalable bridge of these issues, this paper presents an innovative RL framework using the Multi-Agent Deep Deterministic Policy Gradient algorithm for ITS with Socio-Economic impact (**SERL**). Our contributions include:

- We propose the **SERL** (Socio-Economic Reinforcement Learning for ITS) framework, a new hierarchical reinforcement learning algorithm tailored for complex urban traffic networks. And we develop a scalable RL model for traffic signal control and route optimization.
- We provide mathematical formulations and proofs of the convergence of our SERL method. This method effectively handles multi-agent coordination and scalability issues.
- Through extensive simulations using real-world traffic data, we evaluate the socio-economic and environmental benefits of the SERL framework, demonstrating significant improvements over traditional RL-based methods.

2   Related Work

This section reviews existing literature relevant to our research, focusing on ITS, the application of RL in traffic management, hierarchical and graph-based RL methods for multi-agent systems, and socio-economic impact assessments in ITS.

2.1   Intelligent Transportation Systems

ITS integrate advanced communication, information, and electronics technologies to improve the efficiency and safety of transportation networks. ITS applications include traffic signal control, incident detection, traveler information systems, and vehicle-to-infrastructure communication [2,9]. Traditional traffic management systems often rely on pre-timed or actuated signal control strategies, which are insufficient to handle the dynamic nature of urban traffic flows. Recent advancements in sensing technologies and data analytics have enabled more sophisticated ITS solutions [13,14,21]. For example, the integration of IoT devices [1,18] allows for real-time data collection, enhancing the responsiveness of traffic management systems. Despite these advancements, there is still a need for more adaptive and scalable approaches capable of handling the complexity of urban traffic networks.

2.2   Reinforcement Learning in Traffic Management

Recent studies have applied RL to ITS, demonstrating improved performance over traditional methods. Early works applied RL to single traffic include Q-learning, Deep Q-Networks, and Proximal Policy Optimization (PPO) [16]. However, challenges remain in terms of scalability and coordination among multiple agents. Multi-Agent Reinforcement Learning (MARL) addresses the coordination among multiple agents (intersections) in traffic networks. Previous works [3,8,10,11,20] applied MARL to traffic signal control using independent learners, but coordination was limited due to non-stationarity in the environment.

2.3   Hierarchical and Graph-Based Reinforcement Learning

Hierarchical Reinforcement Learning (HRL) decomposes the learning task into a hierarchy of sub-tasks, enabling agents to learn policies at different abstraction levels. This approach has been applied in various domains to improve learning efficiency and scalability. Graph Neural Networks (GNNs) have been integrated into RL to handle structured data and capture spatial relationships. Many works [7,22,23] employed GNNs to model traffic networks, enabling the RL agent to consider the influence of neighboring intersections. Combining HRL and graph-based methods offers a promising direction for complex multi-agent systems.

2.4   Socio-economic Impact Assessments in ITS

Traffic congestion leads to significant economic costs due to delays, increased operational costs, and environmental degradation [4]. Assessing the socio-economic impacts of ITS implementations is crucial for understanding their benefits and guiding policy decisions. On the other hand, numerous studies [5,12,17] have documented the socio-economic benefits of intelligent traffic systems, including enhanced productivity and reduced healthcare costs from improved air quality. In this work, we evaluate the economic benefits of reduced travel times, fuel consumption, and emissions. Compared to methods like CoSLight [15] and MonitorLight [6], which emphasize coordination through standard MARL, SERL uniquely incorporates socio-economic considerations, enabling it to optimize traffic flow while addressing broader urban sustainability goals.

3   Methodology

To effectively manage complex urban traffic networks and evaluate their socio-economic impacts, we propose a novel hierarchical graph attention multi-agent reinforcement learning algorithm for ITS, called **SERL**. As shown in Fig. 1, SERL integrates hierarchical reinforcement learning with graph neural networks and attention mechanisms to capture both local and global traffic patterns. We provide a comprehensive mathematical formulation of the problem, describe the hierarchical structure of our RL framework, and present theoretical analyses supporting the convergence and effectiveness of the proposed method. The pseudocode is shown in Algorithm 1.

3.1   Problem Formulation

We model the urban traffic environment as a Hierarchical Socio-Economic Markov Decision Process (HSE-MDP) for multiple agents, where each agent represents a traffic signal at an intersection.

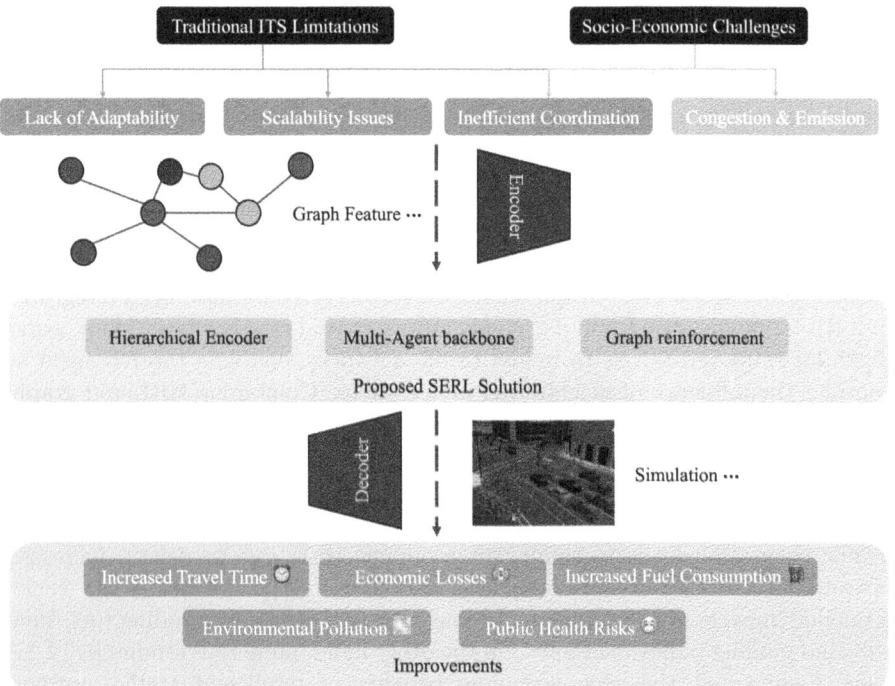

Fig. 1. The whole architecture of SERL and with four key components: (1) Data integration, (2) GAT for spatial relationships, (3) Hierarchical MARL structure, and (4) Socio-economic reward functions. Each component addresses a specific aspect of urban traffic control, from handling data to optimizing traffic flow across various levels.

Agents. Each traffic signal is modeled as an agent. Traffic signals at intersections $i \in \{1, 2, ..., N\}$.

Hierarchy Levels. There are three levels of HSE-MDP and its State Space (S), Action Space (A).

- Level 1 (Local Level): Individual traffic signals control their immediate intersections. Local State (s_i^L): Queue lengths, signal phases, waiting times at intersection i. Local Actions (a_i^L): Switching signal phases at intersection i.
- Level 2 (Regional Level): Groups of signals coordinate within defined regions. Regional State (s_r^R): Aggregated traffic density, average speed within region r. Regional Actions (a_r^R): Adjusting coordination parameters among signals in region r.
- Level 3 (Global Level): Overall traffic flow management across the entire network. Global State (s^G): Overall traffic metrics like total flow, congestion indices. Global Actions (a^G):** Modifying system-wide parameters like signal offsets.

Reward Function (R). We define a composite reward function that integrates socio-economic and environmental factors:

$$R = \sum_i w_i^L R_i^L + \sum_r w_r^R R_r^R + w^G R^G \qquad (1)$$

where R_i^L is local reward considering delay reduction, emission minimization, and economic factors at intersection i. R_r^R is regional reward incorporating regional traffic efficiency and socio-economic benefits. R^G is global reward reflecting overall system performance, economic productivity, and environmental sustainability. The w_i^L, w_r^R, w^G as weighting factors balancing local, regional, and global objectives.

Objective. Each agent aims to maximize the expected cumulative socio-economic reward:

$$\max_\pi \mathbb{E}_\pi \left[\sum_{t=0}^T \gamma^t R_t \right] \qquad (2)$$

3.2 Socio-economic Graph Attention Mechanism

We represent the traffic network as a graph $G = (V, E)$ with socio-economic attributes: Nodes (V) represents Intersections with associated socio-economic data and Edges (E) represents roads connecting intersections, with attributes like traffic flow and environmental impact.

To capture spatial dependencies and socio-economic relationships, we employ Graph Attention Networks (GAT) [19] that consider both traffic dynamics and socio-economic factors. In our GAT-based architecture, each intersection is represented as a node within a socio-economic traffic network graph. Attributes such as traffic density, average income levels, and emission profiles are embedded as node features. During each update, GAT aggregates information from neighboring nodes, weighted by an attention mechanism that considers both spatial relationships and socio-economic similarities. This allows each traffic signal to make data-informed adjustments based on localized and regional economic factors. For each node i, we compute an embedding h_i using attention mechanisms:

$$h_i = \sigma \left(\sum_{j \in \mathcal{N}(i)} \alpha_{ij} W h_j \right) \tag{3}$$

The attention coefficients α_{ij} are computed considering socio-economic similarity:

$$\alpha_{ij} = \frac{\exp \left(\text{LeakyReLU} \left(a^\top [W h_i \| W h_j \| \phi_{ij}] \right) \right)}{\sum_{k \in \mathcal{N}(i)} \exp \left(\text{LeakyReLU} \left(a^\top [W h_i \| W h_k \| \phi_{ik}] \right) \right)} \tag{4}$$

where LeakyReLU means leaky rectified linear unit, ϕ_{ij} represents the socio-economic feature vector between nodes i and j.

3.3   Multi-agent Reinforcement Learning with Socio-economic Policies

In the proposed SERL framework, each traffic signal operates as an autonomous agent employing reinforcement learning to optimize local control policies while considering socio-economic objectives. The agents interact within a hierarchical structure to coordinate actions at the local, regional, and global levels. The policy of each agent is defined as $\pi_i(a_i^L | s_i^L; \theta_i)$, where a_i^L is the local action at intersection i, s_i^L is the local state, and θ_i represents the parameters of the local policy network.

The agents aim to maximize the expected cumulative socio-economic reward:

$$\max_{\theta_i} J_i(\theta_i) = \mathbb{E}_{\pi_i} \left[\sum_{t=0}^{T} \gamma^t R_i^L(t) \right], \tag{5}$$

where $\gamma \in [0, 1)$ is the discount factor, and $R_i^L(t)$ is the local reward at time t incorporating socio-economic factors such as delay reduction, emission minimization, and economic efficiency.

To facilitate coordination among agents, we introduce a centralized critic $Q^{\text{SE}}(s, a; \phi)$, where s is the global state, a is the joint action of all agents, and ϕ represents the parameters of the critic network. The centralized critic evaluates the joint action-value function considering the socio-economic objectives.

The policy gradient for updating the local policy parameters θ_i is given by:

$$\nabla_{\theta_i} J_i(\theta_i) = \mathbb{E}_{s,a \sim D} \left[\nabla_{\theta_i} \log \pi_i(a_i^L | s_i^L; \theta_i) Q^{\text{SE}}(s, a; \phi) \right], \tag{6}$$

where D is the replay buffer storing experiences (s, a, R, s'), and s' is the next state.

3.4   Hierarchical Coordination and Learning

The SERL framework's hierarchical structure integrates three levels—local, regional, and global policies—that interact to achieve socio-economic and traffic management objectives. The local level focuses on minimizing congestion at intersections, while the regional level promotes coordination within defined regions, and the global level aligns overall city-wide traffic management with broader socio-economic goals. Figure 2 provides a visual representation of these interactions, showcasing how decisions at each level influence traffic control strategies. The hierarchical structure in SERL enables effective coordination across different levels:

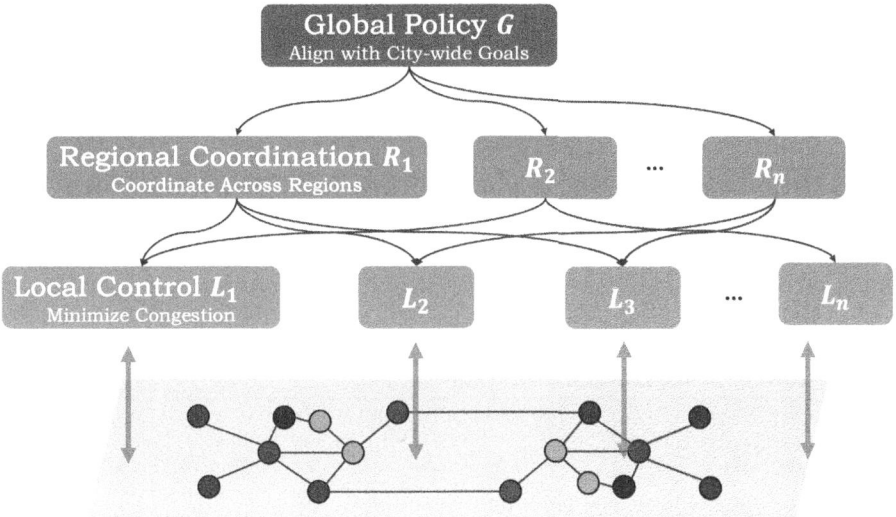

Fig. 2. SERL hierarchical structure integrates three levels—local, regional, and global policies, which represents minimizing congestion at intersections, coordination within defined regions, and overall city—wide traffic management, respectively.

Local Level. At the local level, each agent optimizes its policy to improve traffic flow at its intersection while accounting for immediate socio-economic impacts. The local state s_i^L includes traffic queue lengths, signal phases, waiting times, vehicle occupancy rates, and emission levels. The local reward $R_i^L(t)$ is defined as:

$$R_i^L(t) = -\left(\alpha D_i(t) + \beta E_i(t) + \lambda C_i(t)\right), \qquad (7)$$

where $D_i(t)$ is the average delay at intersection i, $E_i(t)$ is the emission level, $C_i(t)$ is the economic cost (e.g., fuel consumption), and α, β, λ are weighting coefficients.

Regional Level. At the regional level, agents within a region coordinate to optimize regional traffic flow and socio-economic outcomes. The regional policy $\pi_r^R(a_r^R|s_r^R;\theta_r)$ adjusts coordination parameters among local agents. The regional state s_r^R aggregates information from local agents, including average speeds, traffic densities, regional emissions, and economic activity indicators. The regional reward $R_r^R(t)$ is:

$$R_r^R(t) = -\left(\delta D_r(t) + \epsilon E_r(t) + \mu C_r(t)\right), \tag{8}$$

where $D_r(t)$, $E_r(t)$, $C_r(t)$ are the regional average delay, emission level, and economic cost, respectively, and δ, ϵ, μ are weighting coefficients.

Global Level. At the global level, a central policy $\pi^G(a^G|s^G;\theta^G)$ adjusts system-wide parameters to align regional policies with city-wide socio-economic objectives. The global state s^G encompasses overall traffic metrics, total emissions, economic productivity measures, and environmental quality indices. The global reward $R^G(t)$ is defined as:

$$R^G(t) = -\left(\kappa D_{\text{total}}(t) + \eta E_{\text{total}}(t) + \nu C_{\text{total}}(t)\right), \tag{9}$$

where $D_{\text{total}}(t)$, $E_{\text{total}}(t)$, $C_{\text{total}}(t)$ are the total average delay, total emissions, and total economic cost, respectively, and κ, η, ν are global weighting coefficients.

Algorithm 1. SERL Training Procedure

1: Initialize actor and critic networks with random weights
2: Initialize replay buffer D
3: **for** episode $= 1$ to M **do**
4:     Reset environment and obtain initial state s_0
5:     **for** time step $t = 0$ to T **do**
6:         **for** each agent i **do**
7:             Select action a_i^L using policy $\pi_i(a_i^L|s_i^L;\theta_i)$
8:         **end for**
9:         Execute joint action $a = (a_1^L, \ldots, a_N^L)$
10:         Observe reward $R^{\text{SE}}(t)$ and next state s_{t+1}
11:         Store transition $(s_t, a, R^{\text{SE}}(t), s_{t+1})$ in D
12:         **if** time to update **then**
13:             Sample mini-batch from D
14:             Update critic by minimizing loss $L(\phi)$
15:             Update actor using policy gradient $\nabla_\theta J^{\text{SE}}(\theta)$
16:         **end if**
17:         $s_t \leftarrow s_{t+1}$
18:     **end for**
19: **end for**

---

4   Results

4.1   Experimental Setup

Baseline Methods. We compare the performance of the SERL algorithm with several baseline methods and state-of-the-art MARL methods using key performance indicators. The methods included in the comparison are: Fixed-Time Control (FTC): Traditional traffic signal control with pre-determined timing plans, not adaptive to real-time traffic conditions. Adaptive Signal Control (ASC): Traffic signals adjust timing based on real-time traffic data using conventional adaptive algorithms. Independent DQN Agents (IDQN): Each intersection is controlled by an independent Deep Q-Network agent without coordination among intersections. Multi-Agent DQN (MADQN): A multi-agent extension where agents coordinate using standard DQN without hierarchical or socio-economic considerations. MonitorLight [6]: An advanced MARL method focusing on pressure-based control for traffic signals. Cooperative Light (CoSLight) [15]: A state-of-the-art MARL method that utilizes graph convolutional networks for coordination among agents.

Fig. 3. Traffic data sample of a major city, China. The matrix represents the probability distribution of the directional states of different vehicles at multiple intersections.

Hyperparameters and Settings. Key hyperparameters are set as follows, Discount factor $\gamma = 0.99$. Learning rates: $\alpha_\theta = 1 \times 10^{-4}$ for actors, $\alpha_\phi = 1 \times 10^{-3}$ for critics. Replay buffer size: 1×10^6 transitions. Mini-batch size: 64. The models are implemented using PyTorch v2.4.1 (Python v3.10.12) and trained on 8 * NVIDIA GeForce RTX 3090 GPU. The simulations were conducted using the SUMO (Simulation of Urban MObility) platform v1.20.0 integrated with

Python and TensorFlow. The traffic network consisted of 100 signalized inter-sections arranged in a grid topology, divided into 10 regions to reflect varying socio-economic characteristics. Figure 2 shows the traffic data in our private city transportation dataset, a major city area (Hengyang, the second largest city of Hunan Province, China.). The matrix represents the probability distribution of the directional states of different vehicles at multiple intersections. Traffic demand patterns were derived from actual urban traffic data, including peak and off-peak hours. Vehicle compositions included passenger cars, buses, and trucks with different occupancy rates and emission profiles. Regional socio-economic indicators such as average income levels, commercial activity indices, and environmental quality measures were incorporated into the simulation to provide context for the SERL framework.

4.2 Metrics

To assess the performance of the SERL algorithm, we define several key metrics including traffic efficiency metrics, environmental metrics and socio-economic metrics. **Average Travel Time** (A): The mean time taken by vehicles to traverse their routes. **Average Delay** (D_{avg}): The mean delay experienced by vehicles compared to free-flow conditions. **Throughput** (Q): The total number of vehicles successfully traversing the network per unit time. **Total Emissions** (E_{total}): The aggregate emissions of pollutants (e.g., CO_x, NO_x) from all vehicles. **Economic Cost Savings** $(C_{savings})$: The monetary value associated with reduced travel times, fuel consumption, and emissions. **Environmental Quality Index** (E_{qual}): A composite index reflecting the overall environmental impact of traffic operations.

4.3 Quantitative Performance

The results of the simulation experiments are summarized in Table 1. SERL achieved a reduction in average travel time of approximately 26.67% compared to FTC, decreasing from 120 seconds to 88 seconds. Fuel consumption was reduced by 13.99%, and the total emissions decreased by 20.82%. These results demonstrate the efficacy of SERL in improving traffic efficiency while considering socio-economic factors. We also quantified the socio-economic benefits of SERL implementation by calculating economic cost savings and environmental impact reductions in Table 2. The SERL algorithm outperforms baseline methods across all metrics. Specifically, it achieves a 35% reduction in average delay compared to FTC and a 9% reduction compared to MADQN. Emissions and fuel consumption are significantly reduced, leading to substantial economic and environmental benefits. The implementation of SERL leads to significant socio-economic benefits, including substantial cost savings and environmental improvements. These outcomes align with the goals of sustainable urban development.

Table 1. "Overall Performance Comparison of Different Traffic Control Methods"

Method	A (s)	D_{avg} (s)	Q (veh/h)	E_{total} (kg)
FTC	120 ± 5	45 ± 2	1800 ± 50	4800 ± 100
ASC	105 ± 4	38 ± 1.8	2000 ± 60	4300 ± 90
IDQN	95 ± 3.5	34 ± 1.5	2100 ± 55	4100 ± 85
MADQN	90 ± 3	32 ± 1.2	2150 ± 50	4050 ± 80
MonitorLight	88 ± 2.8	31 ± 1.1	2200 ± 48	4000 ± 75
CosLight	87 ± 2.7	30 ± 1.0	2220 ± 47	3980 ± 74
SERL (Proposed)	$\mathbf{88 \pm 2.5}$	$\mathbf{29 \pm 0.9}$	$\mathbf{2250 \pm 45}$	$\mathbf{3950 \pm 70}$

Table 2. Socio-Economic Impact Assessment

Metric	FTC	**SERL**
C_{savings} (\$ million/year)	50.27	**65.91**
Emission Reduction (kg/year)	970,000	**1,050,000**
Fuel Savings (L/year)	96,500	**110,000**
E_{qual} (Scale 0–100)	70.87	**85.03**

To further evaluate the effectiveness of SERL in the context of MARL methods, as shown in Table 3, we compare additional metrics commonly used in MARL research including Convergence Speed (CS), the number of episodes required for the algorithm to converge to a stable policy. Stability (S_t), the variance in performance metrics after convergence. Scalability (S_c), The ability to maintain performance as the network size increases. And Coordination Efficiency (E), which measured by the reduction in total system delay due to coordinated actions among agents.

Table 3. MARL-Related Performance Metrics

Method	CS (episodes)	S_t (variance)	S_c	E (%)
IDQN	5000	High	Moderate	–
MADQN	3000	Moderate	Moderate	10%
CoLight	2500	Low	High	15%
PressLight	2000	Low	High	18%
SERL	**1800**	**Lowest Variance**	**High**	**20%**

To quantify coordination efficiency, we measured the total system delay reduction due to coordinated actions among agents. SERL converges faster than other methods, requiring only 1800 episodes, indicating efficient learning. SERL exhibits the lowest variance in performance after convergence, reflecting consistent and reliable performance.SERL maintains high performance when scaling up to larger networks, demonstrating its applicability to real-world scenarios. SERL achieves the highest coordination efficiency, reducing total system delay by 20% due to effective coordination among agents facilitated by the hierarchical structure and graph attention mechanisms.

4.4   Robustness Study

Scalability Test with Increased Network Size. We evaluated the scalability of SERL by increasing the network size from 10 intersections to 20 and 30 intersections. SERL consistently outperforms even as the network size increases, confirming its scalability and effectiveness in larger urban traffic networks (Table 4).

Table 4. Scalability Test Results

Network Size	Method	A (s)	Q (veh/h)	E_{total} (kg)
10	CoSLight	87 ± 2.7	2200 ± 47	3980 ± 74
	SERL	$\mathbf{88 \pm 2.5}$	$\mathbf{2250 \pm 45}$	$\mathbf{3950 \pm 70}$
20	CoSLight	95 ± 3.0	2100 ± 50	4200 ± 80
	SERL	$\mathbf{93 \pm 2.8}$	$\mathbf{2150 \pm 48}$	$\mathbf{4150 \pm 75}$
30	CoSLight	105 ± 4.6	2000 ± 55	4400 ± 85
	SERL	$\mathbf{102 \pm 3.5}$	$\mathbf{2050 \pm 52}$	$\mathbf{4350 \pm 80}$

Robustness to Traffic Demand Variations. We tested the robustness of SERL under varying traffic demand levels, including peak and off-peak hours, as well as sudden demand surges. SERL demonstrates robust performance across different traffic demand levels, consistently outperforming MADQN. The integration of socio-economic factors enables SERL to adapt effectively to changing traffic conditions (Table 5).

Table 5. Performance Under Different Traffic Demand Levels

Traffic Demand Level	Method	A (s)	D_{avg} (s)	E_{total} (kg)
Low	MADQN	80 ± 2.5	25 ± 0.8	3800 ± 70
	SERL	$\mathbf{78 \pm 2.2}$	$\mathbf{24 \pm 0.7}$	$\mathbf{3750 \pm 68}$
Medium	MADQN	90 ± 3	32 ± 1.2	4050 ± 80
	SERL	$\mathbf{88 \pm 2.5}$	$\mathbf{29 \pm 0.9}$	$\mathbf{3950 \pm 70}$
High	MADQN	110 ± 4	40 ± 1.5	4500 ± 90
	SERL	$\mathbf{108 \pm 3.8}$	$\mathbf{38 \pm 1.3}$	$\mathbf{4450 \pm 88}$

4.5   Socio-economic Analysis

Figure 4 illustrates a comparative analysis of SERL and several baseline methods on two key performance metrics: average travel time and emission reduction. The bar chart displays the average travel time in seconds for each method, while the line chart overlays emission reduction as a percentage, with both metrics using dual y-axes to enable simultaneous comparison. SERL achieves the lowest average travel time (85 s) and the highest emission reduction (26%), highlighting its superior efficiency in alleviating traffic congestion and minimizing environmental impact. Compared to traditional fixed-time control (FTC) and adaptive signal control (ASC), SERL significantly reduces travel times by up to 29.17% and emissions by up to 26%. These results demonstrate SERL's efficacy not only in optimizing traffic flow but also in contributing to broader socio-economic and environmental goals.

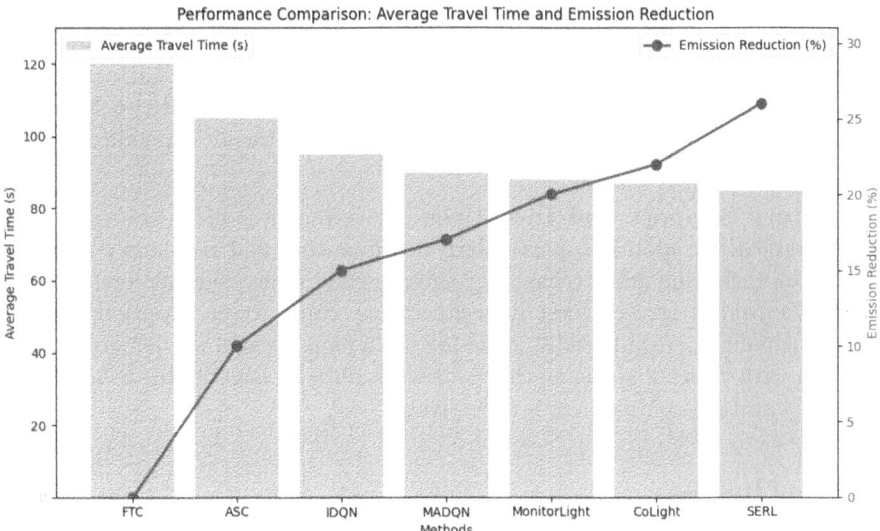

Fig. 4. Performance Comparison of Average Travel Time and Emission Reduction Across Methods.

And in order to evaluate SERL's real-world feasibility, we conducted an economic and financial analysis, examining potential cost savings, return on investment, and broader economic impacts:

Cost-Benefit Analysis (CBA). Implementing SERL requires an initial investment in infrastructure upgrades, data collection systems, and technological deployment. However, the long-term benefits outweigh these costs, as SERL reduces travel times, fuel consumption, and emissions. By alleviating congestion,

SERL can generate substantial annual savings for cities, especially those experiencing severe traffic bottlenecks. This analysis suggests that SERL could lead to an estimated annual savings of up to $65.91 million, factoring in fuel savings, emission reduction, and increased productivity from decreased travel times.

Return on Investment (ROI). The ROI for SERL can be evaluated based on the reduction in travel times and emissions, which have quantifiable economic value. For example, by reducing emissions by 20.82% and travel times by 26.67%, SERL can enhance urban productivity, reduce fuel costs, and improve public health outcomes. Hypothetically, if a city spends $50 million on implementing SERL, the ROI over a five-year period could yield net savings, as demonstrated by our model's reduction in operational costs.

Market Impact and Externalities. SERL's impact on fuel consumption and emissions has broader market implications. By lowering fuel demand, SERL can contribute to price stabilization in energy markets, potentially supporting policies that encourage alternative energy adoption. Additionally, SERL mitigates negative externalities, such as air pollution and associated health costs, which in turn contributes to public health and decreases healthcare expenditures.

Regulatory Support and Incentives. Government policies are critical in supporting SERL adoption, particularly for financing and regulatory support. Policies incentivizing green technology investments, such as grants for ITS solutions or subsidies for eco-friendly technologies, could lower adoption barriers for municipalities. Additionally, emission reduction targets set by policymakers align with SERL's goals, as the framework directly contributes to achieving environmental and public health objectives.

5   Conclusion

Rapid urbanization has intensified traffic congestion, posing major socioeconomic and environmental challenges worldwide. In response, this paper introduces a novel Socio-Economic Reinforcement Learning (SERL) framework tailored for complex urban traffic environments. By embedding socio-economic factors within a hierarchical multi-agent reinforcement learning paradigm, SERL transcends conventional traffic optimization to address a broader range of urban sustainability goals, from reducing emissions to fostering economic productivity.

Our findings demonstrate that SERL significantly enhances traffic flow, reduces emissions, and yields substantial socio-economic benefits, underscoring its potential to drive sustainable urban development. The experimental results illustrate SERL's effectiveness, achieving a 26.67% reduction in travel time, a 13.99% decrease in fuel consumption, and a 20.82% reduction in emissions over traditional methods.

Limitation and Future Work. Despite the promising results achieved by our model, several limitations must be acknowledged. A primary concern is the reliance on the availability and quality of sustainability-related data. In regions where such data is scarce, incomplete, or unreliable, the effectiveness and accuracy of the model may be diminished, potentially hindering its applicability in those contexts. Additionally, while our method demonstrates practical efficacy, it requires further rigorous mathematical analysis and theoretical grounding to solidify its foundational principles. Such analysis would enhance the robustness of the model and provide deeper insights into its performance under various conditions. Exploring the integration of SERL with connected and autonomous vehicle (CAV) technologies can enhance data availability and coordination capabilities. CAVs can provide real-time traffic information and respond more precisely to signal controls, potentially improving overall system performance.

Acknowledgments. We appreciate Mr. Haozhe CHEN's research assistance. The authors sincerely appreciate the anonymous reviewers for their thorough evaluation of this article and for offering valuable suggestions that significantly enhanced its quality. This research was supported in part by the Institute for Industrial Innovation and Finance (IIIF), Tsinghua University. All remaining errors are mine.

Disclosure of Interests. The authors have no competing interests to declare that are relevant to the content of this article.

References

1. Abdel-Aty, M., Zheng, O., Wu, Y., Abdelraouf, A., Rim, H., Li, P.: Real-time big data analytics and proactive traffic safety management visualization system. J. Transp. Eng., Part A: Syst. **149**(8), 04023064 (2023)
2. Bastarianto, F.F., Hancock, T.O., Choudhury, C.F., Manley, E.: Agent-based models in urban transportation: review, challenges, and opportunities. Eur. Transp. Res. Rev. **15**(1), 19 (2023)
3. Chen, D., et al.: Deep multi-agent reinforcement learning for highway on-ramp merging in mixed traffic. IEEE Trans. Intell. Transp. Syst. **24**(11), 11623–11638 (2023)
4. Chen, Y., Zhang, H., Wang, F.Y.: Society-centered and DAO-powered sustainability in transportation 5.0: an intelligent vehicles perspective. IEEE Trans. Intell. Veh. **8**(4), 2635–2638 (2023)
5. Eppenberger, N., Richter, M.A.: The opportunity of shared autonomous vehicles to improve spatial equity in accessibility and socio-economic developments in European Urban areas. Eur. Transp. Res. Rev. **13**(1), 32 (2021)
6. Fang, Z., Zhang, F., Wang, T., Lian, X., Chen, M.: MonitorLight: reinforcement learning-based traffic signal control using mixed pressure monitoring. In: Proceedings of the 31st ACM International Conference on Information & Knowledge Management, pp. 478–487 (2022)
7. Guo, S., Lin, Y., Feng, N., Song, C., Wan, H.: Attention based spatial-temporal graph convolutional networks for traffic flow forecasting. In: Proceedings of the AAAI Conference on Artificial Intelligence, vol. 33, pp. 922–929 (2019)

8. Kolat, M., Kővári, B., Bécsi, T., Aradi, S.: Multi-agent reinforcement learning for traffic signal control: a cooperative approach. Sustainability **15**(4), 3479 (2023)

9. Li, J., Yu, C., Shen, Z., Su, Z., Ma, W.: A survey on urban traffic control under mixed traffic environment with connected automated vehicles. Transp. Res. part C: Emerg. Technol. **154**, 104258 (2023)

10. Liu, Y., et al.: GPLight: grouped multi-agent reinforcement learning for large-scale traffic signal control. In: IJCAI, pp. 199–207 (2023)

11. Mushtaq, A., Haq, I.U., Sarwar, M.A., Khan, A., Khalil, W., Mughal, M.A.: Multi-agent reinforcement learning for traffic flow management of autonomous vehicles. Sensors **23**(5), 2373 (2023)

12. Neverauskienė, L.O., Novikova, M., Kazlauskienė, E.: Factors determining the development of intelligent transport systems. Bus., Manage. Econ. Eng. **19**(2), 229–243 (2021)

13. Njoku, J.N., Nwakanma, C.I., Amaizu, G.C., Kim, D.S.: Prospects and challenges of metaverse application in data-driven intelligent transportation systems. IET Intel. Transport Syst. **17**(1), 1–21 (2023)

14. Oladimeji, D., Gupta, K., Kose, N.A., Gundogan, K., Ge, L., Liang, F.: Smart transportation: an overview of technologies and applications. Sensors **23**(8), 3880 (2023)

15. Ruan, J., et al.: CoSLight: co-optimizing collaborator selection and decision-making to enhance traffic signal control. In: Proceedings of the 30th ACM SIGKDD Conference on Knowledge Discovery and Data Mining, pp. 2500–2511 (2024)

16. Schulman, J., Wolski, F., Dhariwal, P., Radford, A., Klimov, O.: Proximal policy optimization algorithms. arXiv preprint: arXiv:1707.06347 (2017)

17. Tran, C.N., Tat, T.T.H., Tam, V.W., Tran, D.H.: Factors affecting intelligent transport systems towards a smart city: a critical review. Int. J. Constr. Manag. **23**(12), 1982–1998 (2023)

18. Vadivel, G., Hussain, M.J.M., Sangeetha, S.T.: Smart transportation systems: IoT-connected wireless sensor networks for traffic congestion management. Int. J. Adv. Sig. Image Sci. **9**(1), 40–49 (2023)

19. Veličković, P., Cucurull, G., Casanova, A., Romero, A., Lio, P., Bengio, Y.: Graph attention networks. arXiv preprint: arXiv:1710.10903 (2017)

20. Wu, T., et al.: Multi-agent deep reinforcement learning for urban traffic light control in vehicular networks. IEEE Trans. Veh. Technol. **69**(8), 8243–8256 (2020)

21. Zhang, J., Wang, F.Y., Wang, K., Lin, W.H., Xu, X., Chen, C.: Data-driven intelligent transportation systems: a survey. IEEE Trans. Intell. Transp. Syst. **12**(4), 1624–1639 (2011)

22. Zhang, W., et al.: Irregular traffic time series forecasting based on asynchronous spatio-temporal graph convolutional networks. In: Proceedings of the 30th ACM SIGKDD Conference on Knowledge Discovery and Data Mining, pp. 4302–4313 (2024)

23. Zheng, C., et al.: Spatio-temporal joint graph convolutional networks for traffic forecasting. IEEE Trans. Knowl. Data Eng. **36**(1), 372–385 (2023)

Road Safety

A Mobile Application to Secure Pedestrians Interacting with Automated Vehicles

Romain Tessier, Pierre Merdrignac$^{(\boxtimes)}$, Thomas Jacquet, and Natacha Métayer

VEDECOM Institute, 78000 Versailles, France
{romain.tessier,pierre.merdrignac,thomas.jacquet,
natacha.metayer}@vedecom.fr

Abstract. With the increasing deployments of automated vehicles (AVs) in shared environments, many questions arise concerning the safety of interactions between these vehicles and other road users, especially for the most vulnerable. This paper presents 1) a mobile application designed to provide real-time collision risk alerts to pedestrians, leveraging cellular network communication and edge computing for low-latency warnings, and 2) the evaluation of this application by end users after road tests. The system was evaluated through controlled experiments, demonstrating average delays of less than 100 ms for alert notifications. User feedback indicated strong support for such safety technologies, with most participants highlighting the importance of receiving notifications in poor visibility conditions. While some localization challenges led to occasional false positives, the overall user experience and system performance were promising, suggesting this approach as a viable solution to improve VRU safety in smart cities.

Keywords: VRU · Road Safety · automated driving · smartphone application · user assessment

1 Introduction

Cooperative, connected and automated mobility (CCAM) provides innovative technologies for safer, more efficient and more comfortable transportation. CCAM contributes to transform urban transport in smart cities, especially, by relying on automated vehicles (AV) and digital solutions [1]. While AVs offer new alternative for the mobility of persons and goods, ensuring safety is crucial for promoting their adoption [2], in particular when considering interactions with other road users such as pedestrians and cyclists, oftentimes referred as vulnerable road users (VRU). Deb et al. [3] have shown that safety is one of the key factors influencing the willingness of pedestrians to cross in front of an AV. Moreover, with the large adoption of smart devices and the cellular communication, people are always connected to the internet. In addition, recent advancement on the internet of things (IoT) technology enable seamless communication between multiple devices using data brokers. Recent works have investigated alert road users of danger either with direct communications [4, 5] or centralized approaches

A. Kocian et al. (Eds.): INTSYS 2024, LNICST 608, pp. 227–243, 2025.
https://doi.org/10.1007/978-3-031-86370-7_14

[6]. While the direct communication has raised a high interest to ensure low latency communication for warning dissemination, they are limited due to low penetration rate of the technology. Complementary, centralized approach relying on cellular networks are becoming more and more appealing since their performances have been improved with the new generation of mobile networks (5G and beyond). Remaining challenges are to design the communication architecture supporting the vehicular communication in these centralized environments, i.e. developing efficient network services for real time sharing of road hazard and assessing how the solution is understood and accepted by the final users, hence, ensuring technology adoption. Considering the specifications of an automated public shuttle, we have developed an application which can be deployed on top of cellular network to assess collision risks between AVs and VRUs and alert pedestrians through a dedicated application installed in their phone. Our application has been evaluated in an experiment with real participants. The contribution of this work are as follows:

- Design the communication architecture for securing automated driving system and implement VRU protection service for low latency risk warning
- Develop and experiment an application alerting VRUs in the presence of automated vehicles
- Evaluate the technical performance in two separate scenarios
- Assess the solution with external participants in terms of user needs and user acceptance

The rest of the paper is organized as follows. Section 2 addresses the related works and Sect. 3 introduced the proposed system model for VRU warning services. Section 4 presents the methodology for field experimentation and Sect. 5 provides the results. Finally, Sect. 6 concludes the paper.

2 Related Work

Pedestrian decision-making in urban environments relies on infrastructure such as cross-walks, sidewalks, and traffic lights. However, pedestrians also heavily depend on observing vehicle drivers' intentions [7]. Habibovic et al. found that a visual interface could help pedestrians feel safer around automated vehicles [8]. Advances in high-computation hardware improve the detection of VRUs, allowing AVs to respond preemptively before a situation becomes critical [9, 10]. Despite these improvements, current methods do not fully leverage the high density of sensors available in urban environments.

Teixeira et al. developed a method to aggregate data from various sources and alert pedestrians through a smartphone application [11]. External hardware solutions, such as internal audio sensors [12] or radar sensors [13], also aim to protect VRUs. However, these solutions do not consider that predicting an AV's decision-making is generally easier than that of a human driver. Consequently, studies have explored establishing a connection between vehicles and pedestrians to share decision-making processes [4, 14, 15]. These methods, however, often require additional hardware [14, 15] and have limited range and deployment [4].

A centralized solution using cellular connectivity can reduce the need for extensive infrastructure, hardware, and, with the development of new cellular technologies, offer relatively low latency [11]. Our approach focuses solely on AV, which, being connected and operating on predetermined routes, can facilitate edge computing and minimize the required data.

Furthermore, our methodology includes a user-centered approach to include the end user in the design loop as early as possible. Indeed, a user-centric approach is essential when developing a new technological solution. If the proposed solution is accessible and usable but ultimately not useful and does not achieve the user's goals, it will not be adopted [16]. Regarding the use of smartphone applications, Krebs et Duncan [17] the importance of addressing technical features during the requirements gathering phase to ensure that the functionality meets user expectations. By incorporating user insights throughout the development process, developers can create solutions that not only meet technical standards but also deliver real value, increasing overall user satisfaction and adoption.

Although, multiple works studied the requirement and communication architecture for vehicle-to-pedestrian communication during the last decade, most of these studies remain either theoretical or simulation based and few of them have proposed proof-of-concepts. It remains a challenge to deploy such solutions to real world due to environment complexity and diversity of scenarios. By focusing on interactions between automated shuttles and pedestrians in urban condition, our work extends the current state of the art. We propose an architecture relying on edge computing to host VRU protection service where multiple situations, namely hazardous area and collision avoidance, are assessed in parallel to send warnings and messages on a user application. This application has been evaluated with external participants, thus, involving final users in the design and testing to facilitate further adoption.

3   System Modeling and Service Development

3.1   General Architecture

Our work focuses on enhancing communication between an automated shuttle and VRUs. Relying on vehicle-to-everything (V2X) communications protocols, VRUs and AVs share their respective location through cooperative awareness message (CAM) [18].

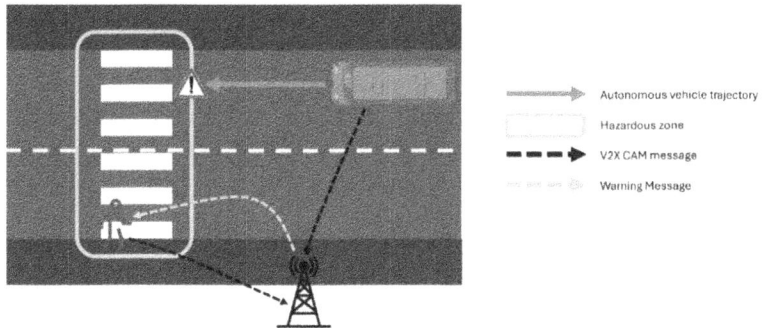

Fig. 1. VRU protection in hazardous zones use case

Unlike conventional vehicles, automated shuttles operate on a predetermined route. This allows the shuttle operator to identify zones with a high risk of interaction between VRUs and the vehicle. By leveraging the shuttle's trajectory, the system can warn VRUs within these high-risk zones when the vehicle is approaching. This constitutes the first use case that the system must address as shown in Fig. 1.

However, VRUs, particularly pedestrians, often exhibit unpredictable behavior in urban environments. Consequently, the system is also equipped with collision detection using the trajectory of both vehicle and VRU. This constitutes the second use case, shown in Fig. 2.

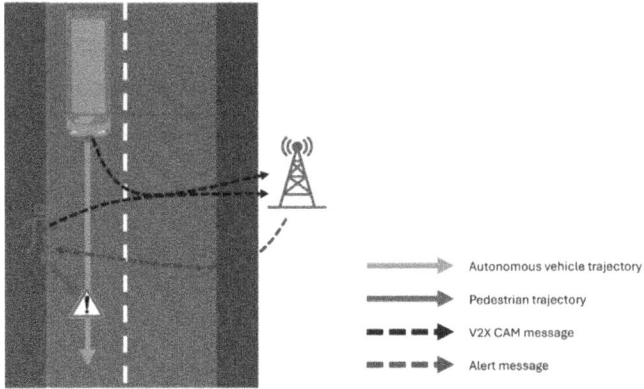

Fig. 2. VRU protection in non-signalised crossing use case

It is crucial to note that both use cases can occur simultaneously. For example, if a pedestrian crosses a sidewalk identified as a hazardous zone, they will first receive a warning for entering a high-risk area as the vehicle approaches. If the pedestrian does not stop, they will also receive a collision detection alert.

3.2   VRU Safety Service

The solution is built around a server that collects data from AVs and VRUs by relying on the Message Queuing Telemetry Transport-(MQTT) protocol, a lightweight messaging protocol ideally suited for IoT applications, as shown in Fig. 3. Periodically, VRUs and vehicles send their location using CAM messages [18] to an MQTT server. The two use cases are handled by two sub-services. One sub-service manages the state of the hazardous zone and triggers warnings if the situation is deemed dangerous, while the collision detection sub-service handles potential intersections between the trajectories of vehicles and VRUs and triggers alerts.

The algorithm, illustrated in Fig. 4 is designed to enhance road safety by processing vehicle and pedestrian messages individually in real time. By updating the dynamic data—such as position and trajectory—of each vehicle and vulnerable road user (VRU), the algorithm proactively assesses risks within hazardous zones. Its primary objective is to provide timely alerts and warnings. The algorithm is divided into two parts: Vehicle

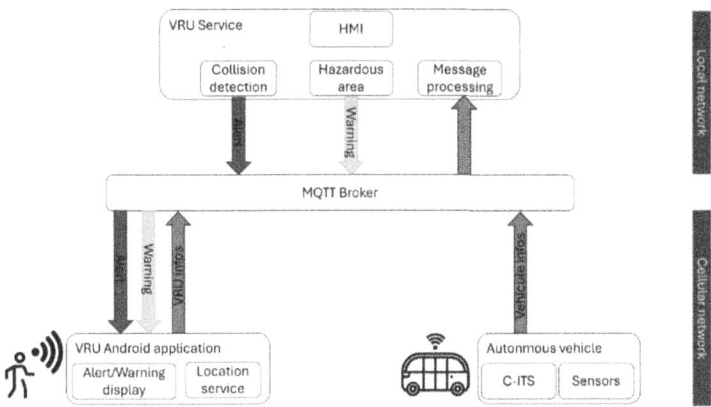

Fig. 3. Architecture of the solution

Message Processing and Pedestrian Message Processing, each responsible for handling interactions within hazardous zones and collision detection from the perspective of either the vehicle or the pedestrian.

Vehicle messages are processed as follows:

1. **Start**: When a vehicle message is received, the server updates the vehicle's last known position and trajectory based on the incoming data.
2. **Update Vehicle Dynamics**: The server processes the message to update the vehicle's dynamic properties, such as speed and direction, ensuring the most current trajectory is used for safety calculations.
3. **Hazardous zone area** – Triggered after vehicle message (case 1):

- The algorithm verifies if the hazardous zone is already marked as dangerous.

   – **Yes**: If the zone is already classified as dangerous, the process ends for this message, as no further action is needed.
   – **No**: If the zone is not yet dangerous, the algorithm proceeds to evaluate potential risks.

- To evaluate the potential risk, the system determines if the vehicle will intersect with a hazardous zone within a certain time threshold.

   – **Yes**: If an intersection is predicted, the system marks the zone as dangerous and sends a first-level warning to any VRU already inside the zone.
   – **No**: If no intersection is expected, the process ends.

VRU message are processed as follows:

1. **Start**: Upon receiving a VRU message, the server updates the pedestrian's last known position and trajectory.

2. **Update VRU Dynamics**: The message data is processed to reflect the VRU's updated dynamics, ensuring accurate tracking within potentially hazardous areas and collision with the vehicle.

3. **Collision Detection** – Triggered after VRU message (case 2):

   - This is the first step after the dynamic update. The system estimates all collision between this VRU and thevehicles based on their last position and trajectory.

     - **Yes**: If an intersection is detected, the system checks if the VRU has already been alerted.

       ○ **Yes**: If already alerted, no further action is required, and the process ends.
       ○ **No**: If not yet alerted, an alert is generated and sent to the VRU

     - **No**: If no intersection is found, the process continues.

4. **Hazardous area** – Triggered after VRU message (case 3).

   - This is the second step, the server checks if the VRU is inside a zone which is marked as dangerous.

     - **Yes**: The system verifies if the VRU has already been warned.

       ○ **Yes**: If they have, no further action is needed, and the process ends.
       ○ **No**: If they have not, a warning is issued

     - **No**: If the zone is not dangerous, the algorithm ends the process.

3.3   End-To-End Delay Minimization

The proposed approach aims to optimize two parameters: latency for VRUs (i.e., alerting the VRU as quickly as possible) and precision (i.e., alerting the VRU only when the situation is genuinely dangerous). Since messages from vehicles and VRUs are not synchronized, making decisions based on a message from a single source may be unreliable. Indeed, as one decision is taken, information from other users may be outdated, thus, affecting precision, or users may be alerted too late, thus affecting latency.

For the collision detection alert case, latency is critical as the situation is immediately dangerous. So, the system concentrates on timely alerting VRUs immediately after the server receives a message from their device. This approach can create false positive as the information of vehicle can be outdated. To minimize such effects, our implementation of hazardous area warning case exploit knowledge on the AV trajectory to anticipate when a situation becomes dangerous and issue a warning to the VRUs. This allows the VRU to be alerted before the situation becomes immediately dangerous, focusing on precision. Consequently, the situation is evaluated after receiving vehicle messages, which may cause a longer latency for the VRU, particularly when they are inside dangerous zone before the AV.

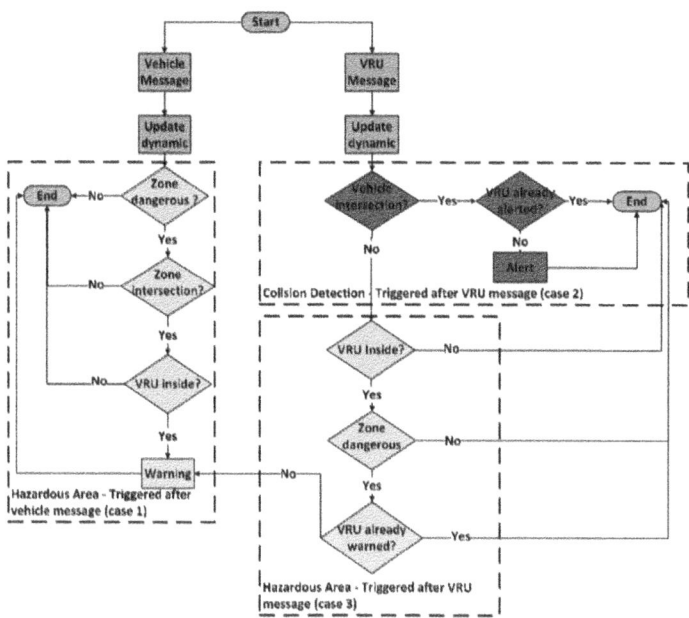

Fig. 4. Algorithm implemented in server for VRU warning and alerting

The analysis of the overall delay to alert pedestrians has been cut out based on the following time instants:

- Ttx_vru: Time of the message transmission from a VRU
- Trx_vru: Time of the message reception from a VRU at the server
- Ttx_av: Time of the message transmission from an AV
- Trx_av: Time of the message reception from an AV at the server
- Tp_start: Time at which processing from the server starts
- Tp_stop: Time at which processing from the server terminates and alert is sent
- Trx_alert: Time at which the alert is received by the VRU

For the pedestrian perspective, the total delay expressed Trx_alert- Ttx_vru and illustrated by the sequence diagram of Fig. 5, comprises several components:

- The communication delay for the last message sent by the VRU
- The computation time for generating the warning/alert at the server
- The communication delay for receiving the incoming alert/warning

In the hazardous area warning case, processing is triggered either at the reception of a message from a VRU or an AV and an alert is triggered when the conditions are met for one of these cases. In the worst case, end-to-end delay is the highest when the pedestrian is already in the alert zone and has send its message before the vehicle, i.e. Trx_vru < Trx_av. In this case, the waiting before processing the VRU message is not null and can be large ($0 <$ Tp_start- Trx_vru < Refresh Rate).

In the collision detection alert, the end-to-end delay between the message issued by the VRU and the reception of an alert is minimized as the processing is necessary triggered at Trx_vru, so that Tp_start- Trx_vru = 0. In this case, the system triggers alert on the fly in the most critical situation where very low latency is required.

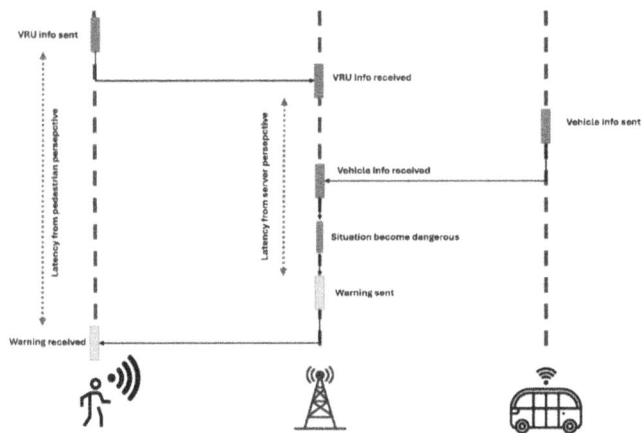

Fig. 5. Sequence diagram including delay for the VRU service

4 Field Experimentation Methodology

4.1 Scenarios

The solution has been tested on relevant scenarios aiming to evaluate the interaction between a user of the smartphone application and one or more automated shuttles. For the experiment, external users are invited to travel along a predefined route and interact with the automated shuttles. Each user is equipped with a smartphone on which the mobile application is installed and experiment the system in two parts:

- Scenario 1: The shuttle runs parallel to the pedestrian, approaching from behind. In this situation, there is no danger to the pedestrian, so they should not receive an alert, but they may be surprised by the sudden presence of a vehicle nearby. This scenario is assessing false positive alerts.
- Scenario 2: The shuttle arrives perpendicular to the pedestrian who is about to cross at a crosswalk. A building obstructs the direct view between the pedestrian and the vehicle. In this scenario, the pedestrian should be alerted to the potential danger. The crosswalk is identified as a hazardous zone and should triggers a warning. Moreover, in certain instances, the system may also emit an alert if the vehicle fails to come to a complete stop while the pedestrian is crossing.

These two scenarios illustrated in Fig. 6 are used to evaluate the benefits of our mobile application compared to a baseline situation where users do not have the application and may be unaware of potential dangers.

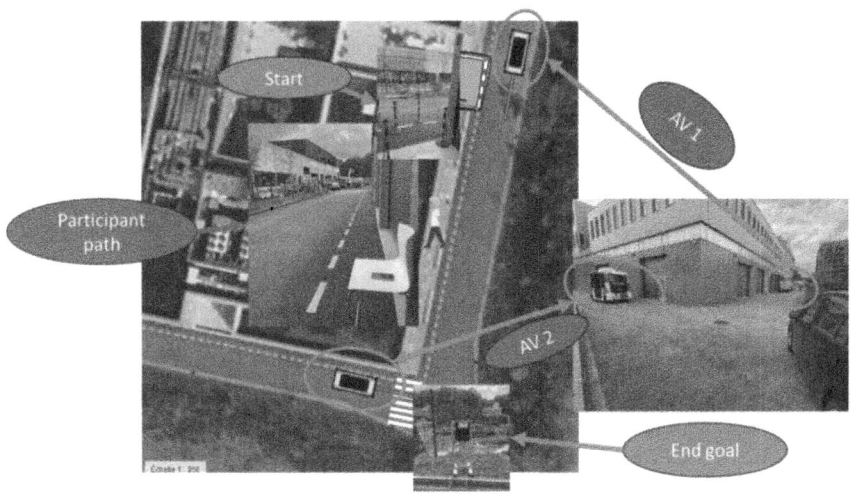

Fig. 6. Experimentation environment

4.2 Mobile Application for Pedestrian Alerting

A mobile application depicted in Fig. 7 was provided to the participants serving two primary functions: transmitting the position and status of the user to the server and alerting the user by displaying alerts or warnings emitted by the server. To closely simulate the V2X environment, the mobile application emits Cooperative Awareness Messages (CAM) at fixed intervals generated using Google's location service, which combines GPS, Wi-Fi positioning, and cell tower triangulation to determine the device's precise location. The alerts and warnings are disseminated using Decentralized Environmental Notification Messages (DENM) [19].

Fig. 7. Snapshot of Android application for VRU warning and alert

Upon receiving DENMs, the application converts them into alerts or warnings based on the cause code and sub-cause code of the event. It also triggers auditory, tactile (vibration), and visual alerts based on whether it's an alert or warning. Additionally, the application includes a database to store both alerts and warnings.

4.3 User Assessment

Participants

44 participants were recruited for the experiment. Experiments took place during the day in good weather conditions (i.e., no rain) and lasted about 15 min. Before the experiment, each participant read the information notes and gave their written informed consent. The experiment was conducted in accordance with the most recent version of the Declaration of Helsinki (1964).

Procedure

Participants were greeted by the experimenter, who first explained that the purpose of the study was to investigate the interaction between pedestrians and AVs. They had to complete a multi-part course with or without the assistance of the mobile application that warned them of the risk of collision with a visual, auditory, and haptic (i.e., vibrating) signal. The course shown in Fig. 6 consisted of exiting a hangar through a door when a light turned green to press a button located approximately 30 m away. To do this, after retrieving a smartphone, they had to walk alongside a building and finally cross a street. The participants were warned about possible encounters with automated vehicles along the way. Before starting, each participant was informed that they would receive a smartphone alert warning them of the risk of a collision with an automated vehicle. Participants completed two rounds and completed several computerized questionnaires at the end of the session. These questionnaires included a rating scale, questions about the importance of receiving warnings about nearby automated vehicles, the timing and intensity of the warnings, and sociodemographic information.

To control order effects, 22 participants used the application first and then did a second round without it, while the other 22 participants did the first round without the application and the second run with it.

Questionnaires

First, participants rated the importance of receiving warnings about AVs operating nearby under three specific conditions: lack of visibility due to obstacles, lack of visibility due to poor weather conditions, and lack of visibility at specific locations (e.g., unsignalized intersections). Ratings were provided on a 4-point scale: 1 (Not at all important), 2 (Somewhat important), 3 (Very important), and 4 (Extremely important). The lack of visibility due to poor weather conditions or at specific locations were not tested directly by the participants, they had to project themselves and indicate their perceptions after testing the application in a situation of lack of visibility due to an obstacle.

Next, they assessed the timing and intensity of the warning signals received through the application. Evaluations were conducted for three modalities: auditory, visual, and haptic. Timing was rated on a scale of 0 (Not perceived), 1 (Much too early), 2 (A little too early), 3 (Ideal), 4 (A little too late), and 5 (Much too late). Intensity was rated on a scale of 0 (Not perceived), 1 (Much too weak), 2 (A little too weak), 3 (Ideal), 4 (A little too strong), and 5 (Much too strong).

Finally, a visual analog scale (0 to 100) was used to measure ease of understanding (0: Difficult to understand, 100: Easy to understand), reliability (0: Not reliable, 100: Reliable), meeting user needs (0: Does not meet my needs, 100: Meets my needs), and future desirability (0: Something I would not want in the future, 100: Something I would want in the future). Participants responded by moving a cursor between the two markers on each scale.

5 Results

5.1 Involved Users

The data collected during our study, involving 44 participants (26 men and 18 women) have published online[1]. The mean age was 33.45 years old ($\pm$11.14). Among the participants, 1 had a baccalaureate degree, 32 had a high level of education, and 11 had a doctorate. Additionally, 13 participants had already interacted with automated vehicles before participating in this experiment (i.e., 29.5% of participants).

5.2 System Performances

Time-to-Collision (TTC), representing the time instant at which a warning or an alert is triggered is presented in Table 1. The results show that the warning is triggered earlier (indicating a larger TTC) because it is easier to determine the intersection of the vehicle's trajectory with an attention zone over longer distances than to compute the intersection between the vehicle's and the pedestrian's trajectories.

Table 1. Time-to-Collision for the different services

	Average	Max	Min	Var	Median
Time-to-Collision for VRU Warning (s)	3,15	4,92	0,97	1,29	2,98
Time-to-Collision for VRU Alert (s)	1,68	2,50	0,87	0,50	1,67

Since there is a timestamp within the message from the android application, computing the delay seems to be straightforward. However, it is important to note that the clocks between the server and the smartphone may not be perfectly synchronized. Therefore, the delay is calculated from the server's perspective, which involves summing the processing delays. To pedestrian latency is then estimated by summing the communication latency to the server's perspective latency.

Table 2 introduces the processing delay on the server side, without the communication delay. It depicts a higher processing time for the VRU warning due to higher variability in the different scenarios:

5. After receiving a pedestrian message when the pedestrian enters an already dangerous attention zone, resulting in a delay similar to the alert.

---

[1] https://zenodo.org/records/14098488.

Table 2. Processing time at the server

	Average	Max	Min	Median
Processing delay for VRU Warning (ms)	33,36	171,2	0,86	5,10
Processing delay for VRU Alert (ms)	1,50	2,50	0,69	1,47

6. After receiving a vehicle message when the pedestrian is inside the attention zone, and the zone transitions from safe to dangerous upon receiving the vehicle message. Thus, the delay between the reception of the last message from the pedestrian and the reception of the vehicle message which generate the warning increase the global delay.

Tests to measure the latency of messages sent and received have been conducted. The results revealed an average round-trip latency of 36.2 ms, with a standard deviation of 17.2 ms, indicating moderate variability in latency. While the majority of messages experienced relatively low latencies, with a minimum of 0.2 ms, outliers were observed, with the maximum latency recorded at 274.1 ms. Notably, the median latency of 32.1 ms suggests a central tendency towards lower latencies. Further analysis revealed that 95% of messages experienced latencies below 59.1 ms, while only 1% of messages encountered latencies exceeding 89.7 ms. Importantly, no packets were lost during the tests, resulting in a packet loss rate of 0.00%, underscoring the reliability of the MQTT protocol.

To summarize, our findings suggest that, from a pedestrian's perspective, the average delays typically range between 70 ms to 100 ms for the warning and approximately 60 ms for the alert notifications. It is noteworthy that the primary contributing factor to latency appears to be the MQTT protocol, which accounts for the majority of the observed delays. TTC and delay metrics tend to correlate, for a warning, the delay may be longer, but the pedestrian is warned earlier (larger TTC). In contrast, for an alert, the pedestrian is alerted later, but the delay is shorter.

Table 3. Succes rate during the scenarios

	Warning Message	Alert Message
Scenario 1	0% (0/44)	14/44 (32%)
Scenario 2	71% (31/44)	14/44 (32%)

Table 3 presents the success rate during the two experiment scenarios. In scenario 1, false positives, i.e. alert messages, are generated by the first vehicle due to inaccuracies in GPS positioning, either of the vehicle or the pedestrian. The fundamental problem lies in the precision of the localization service. In these experiments, the environment resembled an urban setting, situated between two tall buildings, which blocked the direct line of sight to satellites. Consequently, as the pedestrian walked, their position was often inaccurately recorded, sometimes significantly off, until a satellite came into direct view. The inaccuracies also affected the success of the first-level warning in the second scenario. In some cases, the geographical location of the pedestrian was recorded as being outside the hazardous zone, even when their true position was inside it.

The second-level alert was impacted by both inaccuracies of the satellite position system (e.g. GPS) and the experimental setup. For safety reasons, the second vehicle had to stop at a safe distance. As a result, depending on the pedestrian's walking speed, the vehicle might already be stopped or braking sharply when the pedestrian comes in the line of sight of the vehicle, preventing any intersection between the pedestrian's and the vehicle's trajectories.

5.3 User Needs

Participants highlighted the importance of receiving collision risk notifications when visibility is poor. For low visibility due to obstacles, 34% of respondents found warnings extremely important and 39% found them very important, with only two participants finding them unimportant. Similarly, for poor visibility due to bad weather, 41% found warnings extremely important and 32% found them very important, with only three participants finding them unimportant. At specific locations, such as unsignalized intersections, 50% of participants found warnings important and 20% extremely important, with only two participants finding them unimportant (Fig. 8). Notably, women placed greater value on these notifications compared to men, particularly when visibility was limited at specific locations ($p < .001$) or due to weather conditions ($p = .023$).

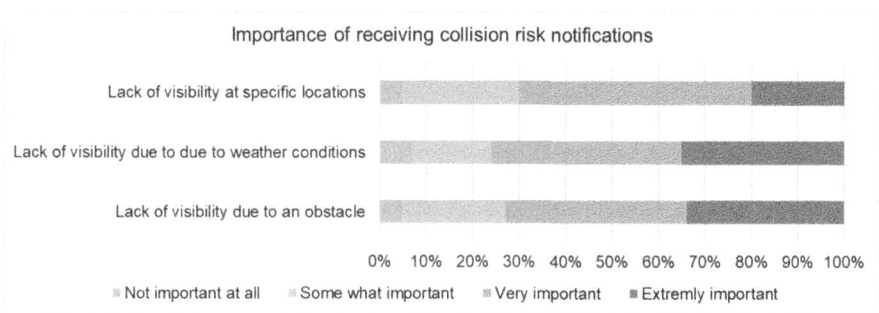

Fig. 8. Evaluation of the important of receiving collision risk notifications

5.4 User Feedback

Participants rated the timing and intensity of alerts from the smartphone application at the end of the experiment. For the auditory modality, 41% of participants found the timing ideal, while 11 participants felt the warning was a little late and three thought it was much too late. Conversely, five participants found the warning a little early, and two found it much too early. Regarding intensity, 43% of participants deemed it a little too weak, 14% found it much too weak, nine participants found it ideal, and six found it a little too strong (Fig. 9 and Fig. 10).

For the visual modality, about half of the participants did not perceive the message. Among those who did, 13 rated the timing as ideal, six as a little too late, one as a little too early, and one as much too early. The intensity was rated a little too low by 14 participants and much too low by seven, with only one finding it ideal. There was a negative correlation between age and intensity perception; older participants found the visual signal less noticeable. Additionally, those who had prior interactions with AVs perceived the visual signal as less intense than those who had never interacted with AVs (Fig. 9 and Fig. 10).

For the haptic modality, 59% of participants perceived the warning as too early, and an additional seven found it much too early. Only four participants found the timing ideal, and one found it a little too late. In terms of intensity, 19 participants rated it as ideal, nine as a little too strong, three as much too strong, five as a little too weak, and one as much too weak (Figs. 9 and 10).

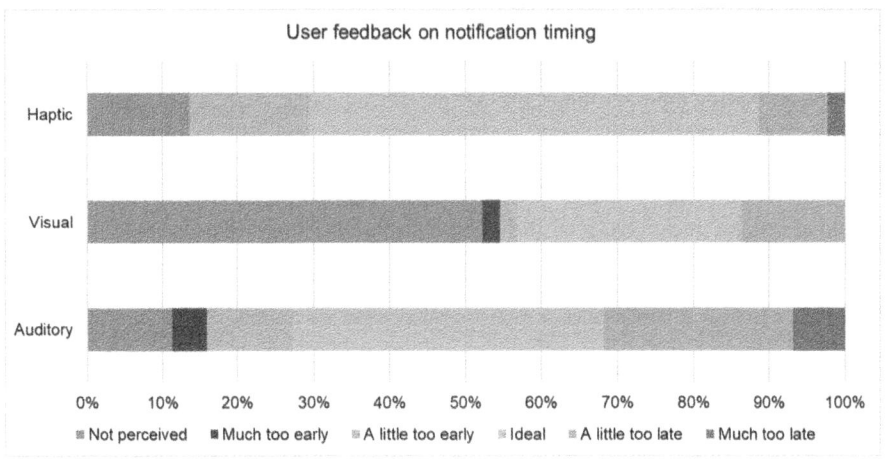

Fig. 9. User feedback on notification timing

5.5 User Acceptance

The application was well understood by most participants, averaging a score of 91/100 ($SD = 13.75$), with 19 participants scoring a perfect 100. However, two participants reported below average understanding. Reliability had a lower average score of 68/100 ($SD = 29.52$), with significant variability; two participants rated it zero, while six found it perfectly reliable. The perceived need for the application scored an average of 58/100 ($SD = 32.84$), showing divergent opinions, and desirability averaged 68/100 ($SD = 29.39$), with nine participants giving a perfect score. There was no significant difference in understanding, need, reliability, or desirability between those for whom the application worked correctly and those for whom it did not (all $p > .10$). Furthermore, no difference appears between men and women ($p > .05$).

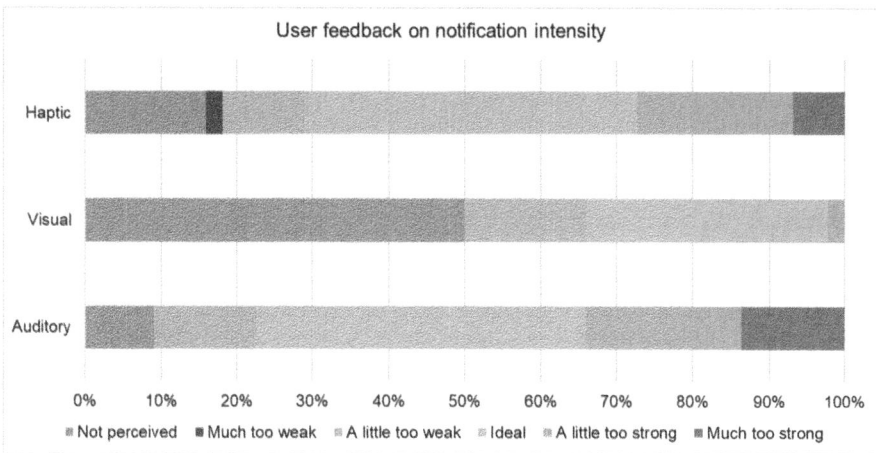

Fig. 10. User feedback on notification intensity

6 Conclusion and Perspectives

In this paper, we demonstrate the technical soundness and user willingness to rely on mobile application combined with cellular communication networks to provide VRU safety alerts in the presence of connected vehicles. The experimental study shows that by running the VRU protection service in an edge environment, the system can provide communication latency below 90 ms in more the 99% with processing time on average of 1.5 ms for alert triggering and 33 ms for hazardous area warning. The main limitation comes from the accuracy of the google localization service resulting in a high false positive rate of the alert (about 32%). To cover such limitations, the use of predefined zones leads to higher detection rates. Thus, increasing location accuracy in urban deployment represents a major challenge which could be solved using infrastructure around hazardous zone and using fusion could be a solution as it has been described in [11]. Participants highlighted the importance of being notified in case of risk of collision with an AV. Interestingly, for women, receiving notifications in this kind of situation was of even greater importance. Although our study did not test this aspect, it could be linked to the fact that women perceive AVs as riskier than men [20] where this higher perception of risk among women is observed in many areas [21]. Moreover, pedestrians' assessments of the application indicated that the messages were delivered at the right time and with appropriate intensity. However, visual messages were often poorly perceived, which may be due to the application's design, as it failed to display visual alerts when users were engaged with other applications on their phones. Although the proposed mobile application solution has been well understood, improvements are still needed to better meet user needs and make it more attractive. This study thus highlighted that the proposed application could be a way to secure interactions between AVs and pedestrians, particularly by using sound and haptic systems, well evaluated in this study, but that further studies are needed to propose a system that meets the needs of users, and it could be interesting to evaluate this kind of application in more challenging situations.

This work has focused on providing information to VRU via their smartphone, however, it is crucial for the VRU to know if the automated vehicle is aware of the dangerous situation. Therefore, it could be beneficial for the safety and reassurance of the VRUs to also transmit the information to the automated shuttle, enabling the shuttle to send a visual or auditory notification, hence, increase the trust and cooperation. Further work can also consider other aspects for large scale deployment such as legal and regulatory challenges.

Acknowledgements. The authors would like to thank the experimental team of VEDECOM, Alexis, Benoit and Émile for their involvement during the experimentation.

The results included in this paper are part of SHOW, a project which received funding from the European Union's Horizon 2020 research and innovation program under Grant Agreement No. 875530.

References

1. Yaqoob, I., Khan, L.U., Kazmi, S.M.A., Imran, M., Guizani, N., Hong, C.S.: Autonomous driving cars in smart cities: recent advances, requirements, and challenges. IEEE Network **34**(1), 174–181 (2020)
2. Prasetio, E.A., Nurliyana, C.: Evaluating perceived safety of autonomous vehicle: the influence of privacy and cybersecurity to cognitive and emotional safety. IATSS Res. **47**(2), 160–170 (2023)
3. Deb, S., Strawderman, L., Carruth, D.W., DuBien, J., Smith, B., Garrison, T.M.: Development and validation of a questionnaire to assess pedestrian receptivity toward fully autonomous vehicles. Transp. Res. Part C: Emerg. Technol. **84**, 178–195 (2017)
4. Anaya, J.J., Merdrignac, P., Shagdar, O., Nashashibi, F., Naranjo, J.E.: Vehicle to pedestrian communications for protection of vulnerable road users. In: IEEE Intelligent Vehicles Symposium Proceedings, Dearborn, MI, USA (2014)
5. American Honda Motor Co., Inc., https://www.prnewswire.com/news-releases/honda-dem onstrates-advanced-vehicle-to-pedestrian-and-vehicle-to-motorcycle-safety-technologies-221495031.html. Accessed 30 Sep 2024
6. Nguyen, Q.H., Morold, M., David, K., Dressler, F.: Car-to-Pedestrian communication with MEC-support for adaptive safety of vulnerable road users. Comput. Commun. **150**, 83–93 (2020)
7. Risto, M., Emmenegger, C., Vinkhuyzen, E., Cefkin, M., Hollan, J.: Human-vehicle interfaces: the power of vehicle movement gestures in human road user coordination. In: Driving Assessment Conference, University of Lowa, USA (2017)
8. Habibovic, A., et al.: Communicating intent of automated vehicles to pedestrians. Front. Psychol. **9** (2018)
9. Islam, M.M., Newaz, A.A.R., Karimoddini, A.: A pedestrian detection and tracking framework for autonomous cars: efficient fusion of camera and LiDAR data. In: IEEE International Conference on Systems, Man, and Cybernetics (SMC), Melbourne, Australia (2021)
10. Alfred Daniel, J., Chandru Vignesh, C., Muthu, B.A., Senthil Kumar, R., Sivaparthipan, C.B., Montenegro Marin, C.E.: Fully convolutional neural networks for LIDAR–camera fusion for pedestrian detection in autonomous vehicle. Multimedia Tools Appl. **82**, 25107–25130 (2023)
11. Teixeira, P., Sargento, S., Rito, P., Luís, M., Castro, F.: A sensing, communication and computing approach for vulnerable road users safety. IEEE Access **11**, 4914–4930 (2023)

12. Xia, S., De Godoy Peixoto, D., Islam, B., Islam, M.T., Nirjon, S., Kinget, P.R.: Improving pedestrian safety in cities using intelligent wearable systems. IEEE Internet Things J. **6**(5), 7497–7514 (2019)
13. Wang, Z., Wan, Q., Qin, Y., Fan, S., Xiao, Z.: Intelligent algorithm in a smart wearable device for predicting and alerting in the danger of vehicle collision. J. Ambient. Intell. Humaniz. Comput. **11**, 3841–3852 (2020)
14. Lewandowski, A., Bocker, S., Koster, V., Wietfeld, C.: Design and performance analysis of an IEEE 802.15.4 V2P pedestrian protection system. In: IEEE 5th International Symposium on Wireless Vehicular Communications (WiVeC), Dresden, Germany (2013)
15. Zhang, C., Wei, J., Qu, S., Huang, C., Dai, J., Fu, P.: Implementation of a V2P-Based VRU warning system with C-V2X Ttchnology. IEEE Access **11**, 69903–69915 (2023)
16. Loup-Escande, E., Burkhardt, J.M., Richir, S.: Anticipating and evaluating the usefulness of emerging technologies in ergonomic design: a review of usefulness in design. Le Travail Humain **76**, 27–55 (2013)
17. Krebs, P., Duncan, D.T.: Health app use among US mobile phone owners: a national survey. JMIR mHealth uHealth **3**(4) (2015)
18. ETSI EN 302 637–2: Intelligent Transport Systems (ITS); Vehicular Communications; Basic set of Applications; Part 2: Specification of Cooperative Awareness Basic Service. v1.4.1 (2019)
19. ETSI EN 302 637–3: Intelligent Transport Systems (ITS); Vehicular Communications; Basic set of Applications; Part 3: Specification of Decentralized Event Notification Service. v1.3.1 (2019)
20. Hulse, L.M., Xie, H., Galea, E.R.: Perceptions of autonomous vehicles: relationships with road users, risk, gender and age. Saf. Sci. **102**, 1–13 (2018)
21. Gustafson, P.E.: Gender differences in risk perception: theoretical and methodological perspectives. Risk Anal. **18**, 805–811 (1998)

A Simulation-Based Security Benchmarking Approach for Assessing Cooperative Driving Automation (CDA) Applications

Mateen Malik[1,2]([✉]) [iD], Behrooz Sangchoolie[1] [iD], and Johan Karlsson[2] [iD]

[1] Dependable Transport Systems, RISE Research Institutes of Sweden,
Gothenburg, Sweden
{mateen.malik,behrooz.sangchoolie}@ri.se
[2] Chalmers University of Technology, Gothenburg, Sweden
{mateenma,johan}@chalmers.se

Abstract. This paper presents our initial contributions toward defining security benchmarks for simulation-based assessment of Cooperative Driving Automation (CDA) applications. A security benchmark is a process or procedure for assessing and validating a system's ability to achieve its operational objectives in the presence of specific security attacks. This work lays the groundwork for developing security benchmarks that assess the robustness of CDA applications against jamming attacks. The *driving scenario* and the *attack model* are the core components of our proposed security benchmark. We used two scenarios *braking* and *sinusoidal* as a stimulus for evaluating the robustness of a platooning application modeled in a simulation framework called Plexe. The platooning application is equipped with a Cooperative Adaptive Cruise Control (CACC) controller. We injected *barrage* jamming attacks into the physical layer of the wireless communication system modeled by the IEEE 802.11p protocol. We demonstrate that jamming attacks can compromise safety, leading to emergency braking and collision incidents among platooning vehicles. Our findings also indicate that the severity of jamming attacks varies with the driving scenario, with the most severe impacts (i.e., collisions) occurring when the attack is injected during vehicle acceleration.

Keywords: Security benchmarks · Cooperative Driving Automation (CDA) · Simulation-based jamming attacks · Platooning system

1 Introduction

Today's road vehicles have transformed into complex interconnected cyber-physical systems, unlocking new possibilities for improved safety, fuel efficiency, driver assistance, and passenger convenience. The advent of vehicle-to-vehicle (V2V) and vehicle-to-everything (V2X) communication technology provides an

© ICST Institute for Computer Sciences, Social Informatics and Telecommunications Engineering 2025
Published by Springer Nature Switzerland AG 2025. All Rights Reserved
A. Kocian et al. (Eds.): INTSYS 2024, LNICST 608, pp. 244–262, 2025.
https://doi.org/10.1007/978-3-031-86370-7_15

important and necessary step towards the introduction of cooperative driving automation (CDA) [1] technologies. Although CDA is expected to increase the safety, efficiency, and reliability of automated automotive transportation systems, more research is needed to tackle the safety and security concerns that naturally occur for systems that depend on sensor data received via a wireless network.

Ensuring that a cooperative driving application is adequately protected against potential security threats is a challenging and costly task that involves many work-intensive activities [2,3]. In this paper, we address an important part of these activities: *simulation-based testing of a cooperative system's ability to cope with security attacks directed toward its wireless communication channel.*

Due to the high cost of proving ground testing and field operational tests, simulation has become the preferred method to study and validate system properties of advanced driver assistance systems (ADAS) [4] and cooperative driving applications such as platooning [5,6]. The work presented in this paper explicitly addresses simulation-based testing of a cooperative system's resilience against *barrage jamming* attacks directed toward the physical layer of the wireless communication system.

Jamming attacks constitute an important class of security threats since they are relatively easy to implement and carry out. The widespread availability of software-defined radio technology [7,8] has enabled the implementation of new types of "intelligent" jamming attacks without costly investments in expensive equipment. Jamming also requires limited knowledge about the targeted system beyond the protocol specifications for the wireless network, which normally are publicly available in open standardization documents. Relevant standards include IEEE 802.11p [9] and C-V2X [10].

This paper introduces and demonstrates a *barrage jamming* attack model for simulations. Barrage jamming is a brute-force approach in which the adversary sends noise-like energy over a broad spectrum of frequencies to block the legitimate signal. According to Lichtman et al., [11], barrage jamming can be classified as *time-uncorrelated* and *protocol-unaware*. This means that barrage jamming is uncorrelated in time concerning the targeted signal and requires no detailed information about the communication protocol. Hence, it is easy to implement and execute.

The work presented in this paper is intended as an initial contribution towards a definition of *security benchmarks* for simulation-based assessment of CDA applications concerning their ability to operate safely in the presence of jamming attacks. A security benchmark is a process or procedure for assessing, validating, or testing a system's ability to achieve its operational objectives in the presence of a given set of security attacks[1]. Work on benchmarks for assessing, testing, and evaluating essential system properties has a history of several decades. Examples include benchmarks for computing performance [12], transaction processing [13,14], dependability [15], and security [16]. In the field

---

[1] The terms security benchmark and security benchmarking are also used in other contexts, e.g., in the security rating of organizations.

of intelligent transportation systems, several papers have addressed simulation-based assessment of the resilience against security attacks for CDA systems, mainly for platooning systems [2,3,17–20]. However, only a few of these papers deal specifically with jamming attacks [20–23] and to the best of our knowledge, no previous paper has discussed the idea of defining security benchmarks, for simulation-based assessment of CDA applications.

To allow a simple and constructive exchange of benchmark definitions and results, we have implemented our attack models in a tool called ComFASE[2], which utilizes well-known and widely used simulation frameworks including Plexe [6], and Veins [24]. We simulate barrage jamming attacks against a platooning system consisting of four vehicles that use a cooperative adaptive cruise controller (CACC) model developed by Segata et al.[3] [6]. We consider two driving scenarios, the *sinusoidal* and *braking* scenarios available in the Plexe framework. In summary, the paper makes the following contributions:

1. A comprehensive study of the impact of barrage jamming attacks on a platooning system equipped with a CACC algorithm developed by Segata et al. [6] using two driving scenarios: *sinusoidal* and *braking*.
2. A detailed analysis of the impact of the parameters of the attack model, including 'attack start time', 'attack duration', and 'attack value', on the outcome of the simulation results.
3. A conceptual discussion and proposals for the future development of security benchmarks for platooning and other CDA systems.

2   Background

2.1   Platooning Application

Platooning is a cooperative driving technology in which a group of vehicles, known as a platoon, travels closely together at high speeds, maintaining a small distance between each other. The vehicles in a platoon are equipped with advanced communication systems and cooperative adaptive cruise controllers that allow them to share information and coordinate their movements.

In the CACC controller investigated in this paper, each vehicle receives information from the lead vehicle and the preceding vehicle in the platoon via the wireless network. This information includes the controller's desired acceleration, the vehicle's actual acceleration, speed, position, and the time at which the data has been measured. Further details about setting the controller parameters, such as engine and driver parameters, can be found in the API section of the Plexe webpage [26].

---

[2] The ComFASE tool has been developed in our research group and is available for download at [27].

[3] In addition to this controller, another three controllers are included in the Plexe simulation environment:'Flatbed' [29], 'Ploeg' [30], and 'Consensus' [31].

2.2   ComFASE: A Fault and Attack Injection Tool

ComFASE [27,32] is an open-source simulation-based fault and attack injection tool built on top of Veins, a network simulation framework [24]. ComFASE injects attacks on the IEEE 802.11p physical layer model in Veins. Moreover, various types of jamming attacks can be modeled in ComFASE, such as *delay attacks*, *denial-of-service (DoS) attacks* [32], *barrage jamming, deceptive* and *destructive interference* [28]. The simulation frameworks that are utilized by the ComFASE simulation environment are *(i)* OMNeT++ *v. 5.6.2* (a network simulator) [33], *(ii)* Veins *v. 5.1* (a vehicular network simulator) to simulate the V2V communication [24], *(iii)* SUMO *v. 1.9.2* (a traffic simulator) to design, simulate traffic, and study traffic behavior [34] and *(iv)* Plexe *v. 3.0a2* (a cooperative driving framework) that enables realistic platooning application simulation [6].

Barrage Jamming Attack Modeling in ComFASE. *Barrage jamming* is a physical layer attack where an attacker continuously transmits noise-like energy across the entire frequency spectrum of the communication channels [35] to reduce the quality of the legitimate signal in terms of Signal to Interference & Noise Ratio (SINR). *Barrage jamming* attacks are categorized as *non-protocol aware jamming* [11] since the attacker does not require any prior in-depth knowledge about the communication protocol to be able to conduct the attacks.

In ComFASE, we model the impact of *barrage jamming* by manipulating the 'noise power' parameter originally used for SINR calculations in the Veins simulator. The noise power parameter is used to model the impact of various sources of *noise* that can affect the received signal, such as channel noise. Our *barrage jamming* attack model targets a broad range of frequencies and simultaneously affects the sending and receiving capabilities of the platooning vehicles. We considered the impact of uniform noise power across all frequencies in a given frequency spectrum, which can be used to model white and broadband noises.

Our model for *barrage jamming* attacks involves injecting equal amounts of noise into all vehicles within a platoon simultaneously. However, the effect of this noise differs among the vehicles due to variations in legitimate signal strength, which is influenced by the distance from each vehicle to the lead vehicle. As a result, the noise can lead to asymmetrical message losses, impacting the communication effectiveness within the platoon. Asymmetric message losses refer to an unequal loss of messages across different vehicles. The distance between each vehicle and the platoon leader varies, leading to differences in how effectively the jamming noise disrupts communication. Apart from distance, other factors, such as interference level, impact the signal strength and could cause asymmetric message losses.

2.3   Related Work

Security Benchmarks. Researchers have proposed security benchmarking frameworks for various cybersecurity domains. Oliveira et al. [16] introduced a two-phase benchmarking framework for web service frameworks (WSFs), focusing on security qualification and trustworthiness assessment. Similarly, Anisetti et al. [36] developed a security benchmark for assessing the security assurance of OpenStack, an open-source cloud infrastructure. Braun et al. also presented NETCARBENCH [37], a benchmark for assessing and comparing techniques and tools used to design in-vehicle communication networks. Despite these advancements, to the best of our knowledge, no previous work has focused on defining security benchmarks for simulation-based assessment of Cooperative Driving Automation (CDA) applications.

Jamming Techniques. Previous studies have explored various jamming techniques capable of partially or entirely disrupting wireless communication. Moser et al. [21] studied the impact of signal cancellation attacks against wireless communication systems such as GPS, where the attacker's signal interferes destructively with the legitimate signal. Mahal et al. [23] designed jammer to emulate the effects of jamming and nulling on the CP (Cyclic Prefix), which involves adding a copy of the end of a signal to the beginning of the signal. In these attacks, the attacker's objective is to partially or entirely cancel the legitimate signal frequency to cause a denial of service. Nulling or cancellation attacks are usually considered challenging and even infeasible to realize, as argued by Lichtman et al. [11]. Clancy et al. studied the performance of wireless transmission under jamming attacks, i.e., *pilot jamming* and *pilot nulling* [22]. Pilot symbols are inserted at specific subcarriers or time slots and help the receiver estimate the channel's frequency response to carry out synchronization and equalization. Our study assesses the impact of barrage jamming, which covers a broader frequency range than other types of jamming, such as pilot jamming and nulling.

Impact of Jamming Attacks on Platoons. Several previous studies have investigated the consequences of jamming attacks on platooning systems. Hu et al. [38] studied the impact of jamming attacks on platoon stability. They used software-defined radios and the Plexe simulator to demonstrate the feasibility of their attacks. Segata et al. [17] simulate jamming attacks using the Plexe simulation framework to demonstrate the effectiveness of fallback and recovery mechanisms that mitigate the impact of communication failures in cooperative driving applications. Van der Heijden et al. [3] proposed a general attack model which they used to evaluate the resilience of three cooperative cruise controllers implemented in Plexe. Alipour-Fanid et al. [5,19] injected jamming attacks in a simulation model of the IEEE 802.11p communication protocol where the string stability and the safety of the CACC controller model is evaluated.

What distinguishes our work from the others presented in this section is the way we modeled jamming attacks. We implemented a more detailed barrage jamming attack model featuring asymmetric message losses. Additionally, the granularity of the attack parameter values in our test campaigns is significantly higher; the step size of our attack model parameters is considerably smaller than those used in comparable studies.

3   Security Benchmarking

In this section, we present the details of our proposed framework for security benchmarking to evaluate the resilience of CDA applications against jamming attacks. We define a security benchmark as a well-defined procedure for assessing, validating, or testing a system's ability to achieve its operational objectives in the presence of a given set of security attacks. This work addresses security benchmarking conducted using simulations where the system under test is subjected to jamming attacks.

In general, the primary motivation for defining benchmarks for computer-based systems is to provide a widely accepted and easy-to-use procedure for evaluating or comparing system implementations, components, or design solutions. When it comes to basic concepts and main objectives, security benchmarking is akin to the closely related field of dependability benchmarking. In their work on dependability benchmarking, Kanoun et al. [39] identified "the main dimensions that are decisive for defining dependability benchmarks and the way experimentation can be conducted in practice". They are *(i)* the target system and benchmarking context, *(ii)* the measures to be evaluated, and *(iii)* the experimental conditions. We believe that these dimensions are also applicable to security benchmarking. Kanoun et al. [39] also give examples of properties that a benchmark must achieve to be successful, such as *repeatability* (at least in statistical terms), *representativeness*, *portability*, and *cost-effectiveness*.

Benchmarking has proven to be pivotal for advancing the state of the art in some fields of computer engineering, such as computer architecture [40]. However, defining a benchmark, or a benchmark suite, is a challenging undertaking that requires involvement and interaction among many groups of researchers, developers, and other stakeholders in the field of interest. Since security benchmarking is a novel topic in the context of CDA systems, we would like to emphasize that our benchmarks are intended as tentative examples of how security benchmarks for assessing the resilience of a CDA system against jamming attacks could be defined. They are not intended as final solutions but rather as a starting point for a wider effort to develop security benchmarks for CDA systems, including benchmarks for other types of security attacks than jamming attacks. In the remainder of this section we discuss the main elements of our benchmarking framework.

3.1   Driving Scenario

A driving scenario comprises specific driving conditions and parameters. The driving scenario includes road and traffic conditions, vehicle driving behavior, and their interaction. Our security benchmarks are based on *sinusoidal* and *braking* scenarios, available in Plexe.

These parameters, as well as the values selected for them, are detailed in Sect. 4.2. The sinusoidal scenario simulates an extreme driving condition and is ideal for testing a platoon's string stability. In contrast, the braking scenario is more representative of real-world situations. Additionally, for both scenarios, a single lane on a highway with no elevation or friction is considered, and no incoming traffic or vehicles that are not a part of the platoon are considered. To further develop our proposed security benchmarking, exploring additional scenarios that reflect real-world traffic conditions would be valuable. This would offer a better evaluation of the system's resilience against the jamming attacks.

3.2   Attack Model

Selecting an appropriate attack model is critical for security benchmarking of CDA applications because it defines the type, scope, and severity of potential jamming attacks. An accurate attack model simulates real-world threats, providing insights into vulnerabilities specific to vehicle communication protocols or decision-making systems.

We implemented a barrage jamming attack model for our proposed framework of security benchmarking. Selecting the attack model parameters that produce correct results is crucial. The key parameters of our attack model include attack duration, attack value, and attack start time. In Sects. 4.1 and 4.2, we provide details about these parameters and the values selected for them.

3.3   Data Collection and Outcome Classification

A key action in creating a security benchmark is to specify the raw data that is to be collected during benchmark experiments. The raw data provides crucial information for understanding the CDA application's performance, safety, and security. It provides the foundational information to analyze vehicle behavior, assess system efficiency, and detect potential vulnerabilities. Key elements of data collection include vehicle performance data (speed, acceleration, braking), sensor data (cameras, radar, LiDAR, and other sensors that help the vehicle perceive its surroundings), communication data (data exchanged between vehicles and with infrastructure, environment data (road conditions, weather, and traffic patterns), and security data (logs of cyber events, anomalies, or intrusion attempts).

The raw data we collect from SUMO include information on vehicle speed, acceleration, deceleration, and collisions. This information can be used for the classification of the outcomes. We have specifically used vehicle acceleration and collision incidents to classify the outcomes.

3.4   Challenges

In this paper, we used two specific scenarios (i.e., *sinusoidal* and *braking*) as a stimulus for evaluating the platooning application equipped with the CACC controller. Other system components influencing the evaluation, such as the wireless communication model, wireless channel model, and the number of vehicles, are kept constant throughout the testing and evaluation process.

One of the primary challenges arises from the number of possible combinations that can be formed using the available system components, such as scenarios and attack models with their various configurations. The permutations of these combinations can be overwhelming, making it difficult to determine which elements should be tested together and how many combinations are necessary for a comprehensive evaluation. Moreover, simulations may not accurately represent all real-world conditions. Factors like unpredictable human behavior and weather conditions can introduce vulnerabilities that might not be captured in a simulated environment.

4 Experimental Setup

4.1 Attack Model

Our attack model for barrage jamming has been designed to enable a simple and constructive exchange of benchmark definitions and results. To this end, we use three basic parameters for the model: *attack start-time*, *attack duration*, and *attack value*. The attack start time defines the time when the attack starts on the timeline of the driving scenario. The attack duration defines the duration while the attack is active. Finally, the attack value defines the severity of the attack, i.e., the amount of noise injected into the communication channel.

To configure the attack injection campaigns, we vary the attack value (i.e., the noise signal power) from 0 to 1×10^{-5} mW, in steps of 0.01×10^{-5} mW, resulting in 100 experiments. We conducted tests that showed little or no difference in the results obtained for noise signal power values above 1×10^{-5} mW.

4.2 Driving Scenarios

We consider two driving scenarios in our simulations, the *sinusoidal scenario* and the *braking scenario*. These scenarios, which are available in Plexe, have been widely used by other researchers in simulation studies of platooning systems.

Sinusoidal Scenario. In this scenario, the vehicles follow a sinusoidal driving pattern where they periodically accelerate and decelerate with a frequency of 0.2 Hz and an amplitude of 5.0 km/h. The lead vehicle's maximum speed is set to 100 km/h. Using a total simulation time of 60 s (see Fig. 1), we vary the attack start time from 17.0 s to 21.8 s in increments of 0.2 s, resulting in 25 attack start times. The selected attack start times allow us to evaluate the vehicle's behavior under different situations (e.g., acceleration and deceleration). For each attack start time, we ran simulations with 30 attack durations ranging from 1 s to 30 s and 100 noise values. Thus, we conducted a total of 75000 (25 *attack start times**30 *attack end times**100 *attack values*) attack simulations for the sinusoidal scenario.

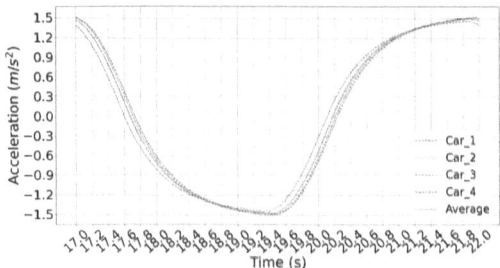

Fig. 1. Sinusoidal scenario: Acceleration profiles of all vehicles in the platoon.

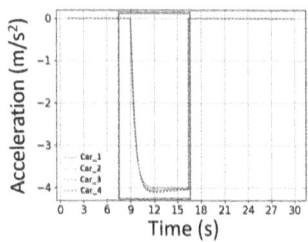

Fig. 2. Braking scenario: Deceleration profiles of all vehicles in the platoon. NB: the solid line marks the period in which the attack start times are selected.

Braking Scenario. In this scenario, the vehicles decelerate with 4 m/s^2 until a complete stop. In the first part of the scenario, the vehicles drive at a constant speed of 100 km/h. In the second part, which starts from 9 s, the vehicles brake until a complete stop.

Using a total simulation time of 30 s (see Fig. 2), we vary the attack start time from 7.0 s to 16.4 s in increments of 0.2 s, resulting in 48 cases. The selected attack start times allow us to evaluate the vehicle's behavior under different situations (e.g., constant speed and hard braking). For each attack start time, we ran simulations with 10 attack durations ranging from 1 s to 10 s and 100 noise values. Thus, we conducted a total of 48000 (48 *attack start times**10 *attack end times**100 *attack values*) attack simulations for the braking scenario.

4.3   Outcome Classification

To classify the outcomes of the simulations, we define four outcome categories based on the vehicles' deceleration profiles and collision events. These four categories are: ***Non-effective:*** The deceleration profiles of the vehicles in a attack simulation run are identical to the ones observed for the golden (attack-free) run. ***Negligible:*** The recorded maximum deceleration of the vehicles in the attack simulation run (RMD_{attack}) is less than or equal to the recorded maximum deceleration in the golden run (RMD_{golden}). ***Benign:*** The RMD_{attack} is greater than the RMD_{golden} and less than or equal to the 'maximum comfortable

Table 1. Test campaign results for sinusoidal (S1) and braking (B1) scenarios.

Campaign	Non-Effective	Negligible	Benign	Severe	Total
S1	3042 (4.0%)	5424 (7.2%)	30788 (41.0%)	35746 (47.8%)	75000
B1	9029 (18.8%)	25827 (53.8%)	2649 (5.5%)	10495 (21.9%)	48000

braking' value. **Severe:** RMD_{attack} is greater than the 'maximum comfortable braking' value, or a collision has occurred.

We selected the, RMD_{golden} to be 1.53 m/s^2 for the sinusoidal scenario, and 4.0 m/s^2 for the braking scenario, while the 'maximum comfortable braking' value for both scenarios was set to 5.0 m/s^2.

5 Experimental Results

We conducted simulations with barrage jamming as described in Sect. 2.2 using the test setups for *sinusoidal* and the *braking* scenarios as presented in Sect. 4.2. The outcomes of these simulations are summarized in Table 1. As described in Sect. 4.3, the outcomes of the attack simulations are divided into four categories: non-effective, negligible, benign, and severe. Severe outcomes represent simulations resulting in collisions or emergency braking, while the other categories represent no to less significant consequences.

Table 1 shows that the outcomes vary considerably depending on the driving scenario. Notably, the severe outcomes are much more prevalent in the sinusoidal scenario than in the braking scenario. The sinusoidal scenario includes periods of acceleration and deceleration, while the braking scenario consists of periods of constant speed and deceleration. Our simulations revealed that collisions are more likely to occur if the attacks coincide with an acceleration period, which explains why severe outcomes are more prevalent in the sinusoidal scenario.

We conducted 75000 simulations in campaign **S1** and 48000 simulations in campaign **B1**. Figure 3 shows the outcomes for all simulations in campaigns S1 and B1, focusing on attack duration (Figs. 3a and 3b), attack start time (Figs. 3c and 3d), and attack (noise) value (Figs. 3e and 3f). Note that the classified results for each attack duration (see Figs. 3a and 3b) include all attack start time and noise value. Similarly, the classified results for each 'attack start time' (see Figs. 3c and 3d) include all attack duration and noise value. Finally, the classified results for each noise value (see Figs. 3e and 3f) include all attack duration and attack start time. We start our analysis by comparing the results presented in Figs. 3a (S1) and 3b (B1).

In **S1**, severe outcomes (indicated by the red bars) are the most prevalent category, comprising 47.8% of all simulations. These severe outcomes show an increasing trend as the attack duration extends. For attack durations longer than 15 s, severe outcomes account for over 50% of the total outcomes in S1.

The second-largest category of outcomes in S1 is benign outcomes (blue bars), which includes cases where the deceleration values fall between 1.53 m/s^2 and

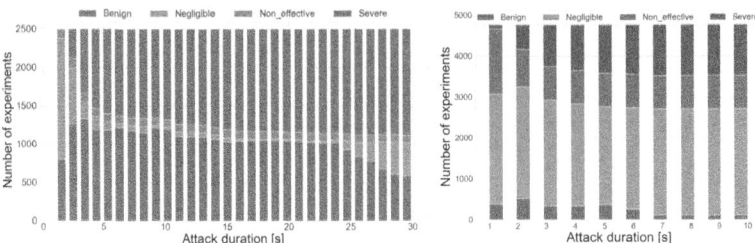

(a) Outcome distribution w.r.t. the attack dura-(b) Outcome distribution w.r.t. the
tion in S1.   attack duration in B1.

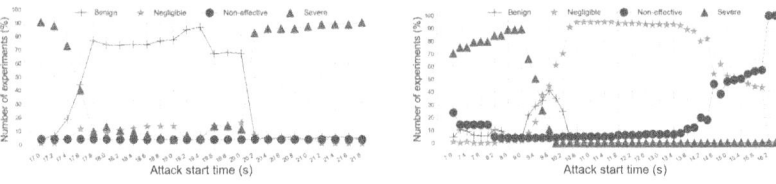

(c) Outcome distribution w.r.t the attack(d) Outcome distribution w.r.t the attack
start times in S1.   start times in B1.

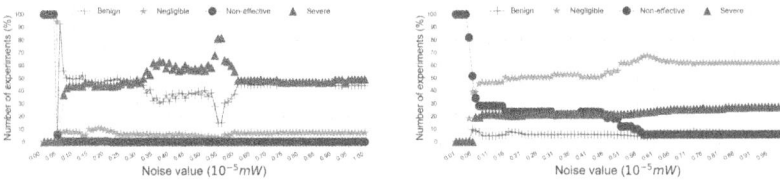

(e) Outcome distribution w.r.t. the noise (f) Outcome distribution w.r.t. the noise
values in S1.   values chosen in B1.

Fig. 3. Outcome distribution for barrage jamming attacks on all vehicles for the sinusoidal and braking scenarios.

5.0 m/s^2, as described in Sect. 4.3. These benign outcomes make up 41.0% of
the total outcomes in S1, and their percentage tends to decrease as the attack
duration increases. Negligible outcomes (orange bars) account for 7.2% of the
outcomes in S1. These outcomes are more prevalent for short attacks lasting
less than 4 s and attacks lasting longer than 25 s. Non-effective outcomes (green
bars) comprise approximately 4% of the outcomes in S1, and their distribution
remains relatively consistent across all attack durations.

Turning to **B1** (Fig. 3b), we observe a different pattern compared to S1
(Fig. 3a). The percentage of severe outcomes is much lower for B1 (i.e., 21.9% and
represented by red bars). In contrast, outcomes with negligible impact (orange
bars) are the most frequent in B1, accounting for 53.8% of all outcomes. Their
occurrence remains relatively constant across all attack durations. In contrast,
B1 exhibits a lower percentage of benign outcomes (blue bars) than S1, while
the percentage of non-effective simulations (green bars) is higher in B1.

There are two noteworthy observations when comparing the outcomes presented in Figs. 3a and 3b. Firstly, the impact of barrage jamming attacks can vary significantly depending on the driving scenarios. Secondly, the percentage of severe attacks (successful attacks from the attacker's perspective) tends to increase with the duration of the attack until a certain point, after which the increasing trend becomes less significant. In the tested driving scenarios, attacks lasting longer than 5 s are comparatively likely to cause severe outcomes.

We now examine the impact of the attack start times on the outcome distributions, as illustrated in Figs. 3c (S1) and 3d (B1). The data depicted in these figures strongly correlate to the acceleration and deceleration profiles of the two driving scenarios shown in Figs. 1 and 2.

In campaign **S1**, the start times range from 17.0 s to 21.8 s, where the intervals 17.0 s to 17.6 s, and 20.4 s to 21.8 s represent acceleration periods, while the interval from 17.8 s to 20.2 s represents a deceleration period. Figure 3c shows that severe outcomes dominate when the attack start times coincide with an acceleration period, as indicated by the red curve.

In contrast, attacks initiated during the deceleration period predominately result in benign outcomes (blue curve), representing around 75% of the outcomes for the attacks initiated during this period. Furthermore, the negligible outcomes (orange curve) account for around 10% of the attacks initiated during the deceleration period, while they represent less than 5% of the outcomes of the attacks initiated during the two acceleration periods. Less than 5% of the attacks in S1 result in non-effective outcomes (green curve). Interestingly, these outcomes are evenly distributed across all attack start times; hence, their percentage appears independent of the acceleration and deceleration periods.

The design of the CACC controller model explains why the platooning system is more vulnerable to attacks during an acceleration period. When utilizing this controller, the lead vehicle periodically sends acceleration and deceleration commands to the platoon's trailing vehicles. If a vehicle loses many messages, it will continue accelerating, decelerating, or keeping a constant speed according to the last received command. Consequently, if a jamming attack begins to block the communication channel during an acceleration period, the affected vehicles will continue to accelerate until the jamming attack ceases and the vehicles receive a deceleration or constant speed command from the lead vehicle, V1.

In campaign **B1**, the start times range from 7.0 s to 16.4 s, where the time interval 7.0 s to 9.0 s represents a period when the vehicles maintain a constant speed. In contrast, the time interval 9.2 s to 16.4 s represents a period when the vehicles reduce their speed rapidly until they have reached a full stop. As shown in Fig. 3d, the most severe outcomes observed in B1 occurred for attacks initiated between 7.0 s and 9.0 s. The high proportion of severe outcomes for attacks initiated in this time interval can be explained by many attacks preventing the target vehicles from receiving deceleration commands that the lead vehicle transmits between 9.0 s and 16.0 s. Thus, these attacks often result in situations where the lead vehicle decelerates while one or several other vehicles in the platoon continue at a constant speed, increasing the risk of collisions.

For attacks initiated in the interval from 10.2 s to 14.2 s, the most prevalent outcomes are those with a negligible impact (indicated by the orange curve). This time interval corresponds to a period in which all vehicles in the platoon rapidly reduce their speed. As shown in Fig. 3d, no severe outcomes (i.e., collisions) were observed for attacks initiated at 10.2 s or later. Furthermore, for attacks initiated at 14.2 s and beyond, we noticed a rapid increase in the percentage of non-effective attacks (represented by the green curve), reaching 100% at 16.4 s, which corresponds to the time when all vehicles in the platoon have come to a complete stop. One important observation we can make from Figs. 3c and 3d is that the platooning system is more vulnerable to attacks initiated during periods of acceleration and also periods of constant speed that precede a deceleration period, compared to attacks initiated during a deceleration period.

Next, we examine how the outcome distributions are affected by the attack value, as illustrated by graphs depicted in Figs. 3e (S1) and 3f (B1). As explained earlier, the attack value represents the power of the interfering noise signal. We simulate barrage jamming attacks by manipulating the noise signal power parameter, which the network simulator uses to calculate the SINR value. As the attack value increases, the SINR decreases, resulting in a complete loss of communication among all vehicles in the platoon.

In Fig. 3e, we observe a negative correlation between the 'severe' (presented by the red curve) and 'benign' (presented by the blue curve) outcomes. In other words, an increase in the percentage of severe cases comes with a decrease in the percentage of benign cases. The graph depicting the negligible outcomes (presented by the orange curve) shows a relatively even distribution across all attack values. Furthermore, for attack values below 0.04×10^{-5} mW, all the attacks are classified as non-effective (presented by the green curve), implying that these attacks do not result in any message losses.

The figure also shows that the percentage of severe outcomes remains relatively constant at approximately 42% for attack values below 0.30×10^{-5} mW and above 0.60×10^{-5} mW. However, for attack values ranging from 0.30×10^{-5} mW to 0.60×10^{-5} mW, the proportion of severe outcomes increases to an average value of approximately 60%. To explain these results, here we present Fig. 4, which illustrates the relationship between 'noise values' and 'collisions' caused by vehicle 2 (represented by the orange curve), vehicle 3 (represented by the green curve), and vehicle 4 (represented by the red curve). We remind the reader that the noise values range from 0.0 to 1.00×10^{-5} mW. To present the results illustrated in this figure, we partition the noise value range into smaller intervals and examine the collisions caused by vehicles within each interval.

Noise Value Range $[0.0 - 0.04] \times 10^{-5}$ mW: No collisions occur, and the platoon operates normally under this low noise level.

Noise Value Range $[0.05 - 0.15] \times 10^{-5}$ mW: Collisions begin to occur, primarily involving vehicle 4. This vehicle is the first in the platoon to be affected by the increasing noise. This is because this vehicle is the farthest away from the lead vehicle, causing the signal's power received, even in the attack-free run, to be the weakest compared to those received by the other vehicles. Therefore,

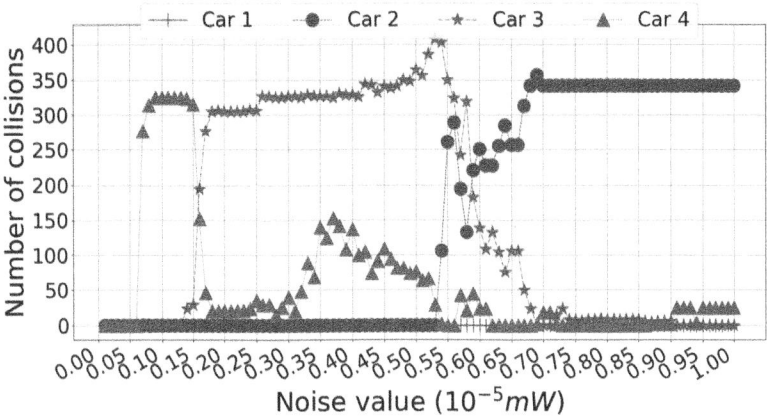

Fig. 4. Number of collisions caused by different vehicles in the platoon for different noise values.

introducing even a small amount of noise in its signals would cause this vehicle to collide. Up to 41% of the injections within this noise range caused collisions.

Noise Value Range $[0.16 - 0.30] \times 10^{-5}$ mW: With the increase in the noise value, vehicle 3 starts to also be affected by the noise interference, adding to the number of vehicles that could potentially cause a collision. Although the total percentage of collisions caused by these two vehicles remains the same as the one observed for the previous range, i.e., $\approx 41\%$ (see Fig. 3e), the majority of the collisions are caused by vehicle 3. This is because now, vehicle 3 is the first vehicle in the platoon to be affected by the increasing noise.

Noise Value Range $[0.31 - 0.55] \times 10^{-5}$ mW: By increasing the noise value further, we observe a larger number of collisions caused by vehicles 3 and 4. This is not surprising as higher noise levels cause more disruptions in communication. In fact, within this range, up to around 60% of the attacks cause either of these vehicles to collide with the vehicle in front.

Noise Value Range $[0.56 - 0.60] \times 10^{-5}$ mW: Within this range, the noise level has reached a point where it disrupts communication of all following vehicles in a platoon. This means that now, vehicle 2, which is the closest vehicle to the lead vehicle, also starts to cause collisions. This dramatically increases the total number of collisions, comprising around 80% of the attacks using the noise values within this range.

Noise Value Range $[0.61 - 1.0] \times 10^{-5}$ mW: The noise levels indicated in this range are so high that as they continue to rise, we observe a complete communication loss of following vehicles with the lead vehicle. Although the initial expectation might be that the complete loss of communication should cause collisions amongst the vehicles, Fig. 3e shows that only about 41% of the injections cause collisions. The reason for this is that for the injection initiated when the vehicles are decelerating, the complete loss of communication does not result in collisions, as the loss happens after the vehicles start to reduce their speed. Figure 4 also shows that almost all collisions are caused by vehicle 2. This is because now, vehicle 2 is the first vehicle to be affected by the increasing noise.

For the braking scenario, Fig. 3f shows that attacks with attack values below 0.04×10^{-5} mW are non-effective and cause no collisions. This is inline with our observation for the sinusoidal scenario in Fig. 3e. For attack values ranging from 0.05×10^{-5} mW to 0.11×10^{-5} mW, there is a significant increase in the proportion of benign, negligible, and severe outcomes with increasing attack values, and an equally significant drop in the non-effective outcomes. As the attack values exceed 0.11×10^{-5} mW, we observe slowly increasing values for the proportion of negligible and severe outcomes with increasing attack values. In contrast, the proportion of benign outcomes remains approximately constant. The proportion of non-effective outcomes decreases in steps until it reaches a constant value of approximately 7% for attack values above 0.61×10^{-5} mW.

In summary, Fig. 3f shows that the distribution of outcomes for the braking scenario tends to become stable (e.g., the total number of severe cases remains unchanged with the increasing noise values) for attack values above 0.61×10^{-5} mW. Our analysis of Figs. 3e and 3f shows that the correlation between the attack value and the proportion of severe outcomes is highly dependent on the number of vehicles experiencing a loss of signal as well as the driving scenario, and may exhibit unexpected and non-linear dependencies, as observed in the sinusoidal scenario.

6 Discussions

6.1 Threats to Validity

Validity refers to how accurately a test method measures its intended purpose. A test is valid when its results are closely aligned with real-world outcomes [41,42]. This section discusses internal and external threats to the validity of our results.

Internal validity can be defined as the degree of confidence that the experimental design parameters are relevant and produce meaningful results. In our benchmarking framework, the key experimental design parameters include: *(i)* the scenario and its parameters, *(ii)* the attack model and its parameters. Inaccurate or inappropriate choices of these parameters would compromise the internal validity, making the results unreliable.

External validity can be defined as the extent to which results from an experimental study can be applied to other situations. The platooning application we evaluated involves a cooperative adaptive cruise controller developed by Segata et al. [6], a sinusoidal scenario where vehicles accelerate and decelerate with a predefined frequency, a braking scenario where vehicles decelerate with a fixed deceleration rate, a wireless channel model called free space path loss (FSPL) and the barrage jamming attack models. Altering any of these potentially yields different outcomes. For instance, consensus-based cooperative adaptive cruise controllers that maintain larger inter-vehicle distances might demonstrate greater resilience to message losses caused by jamming attacks, potentially leading to fewer severe outcomes. Similarly, employing other wireless channel models, such as two-way interference and obstacle shadowing, or scenarios like braking and constant-speed platooning could yield different outcomes. Our results are inherently tied to the experimental design and target application. Even minor variations in them can significantly impact the outcomes. Consequently, generalizing our findings to other contexts is challenging.

7   Conclusion and Future Work

To demonstrate our security benchmarking approach, we used two driving scenarios, *sinusoidal* and *braking*, for assessing the platooning application. Our benchmark approach has the potential for broad adoption. This is primarily because the simulation environment and associated tools are open-source and have already gained wide acceptance in the research for automotive use cases. Our experimental results reveal that the likelihood of a successful barrage jamming attack is notably higher when initiated during acceleration periods of a driving scenario. The attack start time is not the only factor that influences the likelihood of a collision. The attack duration is another factor; longer attacks are generally more likely to cause a collision. However, attack durations longer than a certain threshold do not significantly increase the number of severe outcomes. The higher noise values contribute to greater signal distortion, which can eventually cause communication loss. This loss significantly contributes to collisions when vehicles accelerate. We observe fewer collisions for attacks initiated when the vehicles are braking because the communication loss happens already when the vehicles have started to reduce their speed.

As part of our future work, we intend to use our proposed security benchmarking approach for evaluating other cooperative cruise controllers implemented in the Veins, such as Ploeg [30,43] and Consensus [31,44]. We plan to implement fallback mechanisms in the CACC controller developed by Segata et al. [6] that detect communication losses and activate appropriate responses. We also aim to design and implement real-world testing methodology and tools to validate simulation-based results. This approach will ensure that our simulation-based results are reliable and applicable to real-world scenarios.

Acknowledgments. The work of this paper has been partly done in the context of the SUNRISE project, funded by the European Union's Horizon Europe Research and Innovation Actions under grant agreement no. 101069573.

References

1. Cooperative Driving Automation (CDA) Committee: Taxonomy and Definitions for Terms Related to Cooperative Driving Automation for On-Road Motor Vehicles. SAE Standard J3216_202107. https://www.sae.org/standards/content/j3216_202107/. Accessed 29 July 2024
2. El-Rewini, Z., Sadatsharan, K., Selvaraj, D.F., Plathottam, S.J., Ranganathan, P.: Cybersecurity challenges in vehicular communications. Veh. Commun. **23**, 100214 (2020)
3. Van der Heijden, R., Lukaseder, T., Kargl, F.: Analyzing attacks on cooperative adaptive cruise control (CACC). In: 2017 IEEE Vehicular Networking Conference (VNC), pp. 45–52. IEEE (2017). https://doi.org/10.1109/VNC.2017.8275598.
4. Drechsler, M. F., Seifert, G., Peintner, J., Reway, F., Riener, A., Huber, W.: How simulation based test methods will substitute the proving ground testing? In: 2022 IEEE Intelligent Vehicles Symposium (IV), pp. 903–908. IEEE (2022). https://doi.org/10.1109/IV51971.2022.9827394
5. Alipour-Fanid, A., Dabaghchian, M., Zeng, K.: Platoon stability and safety analysis of cooperative adaptive cruise control under wireless Rician fading channels and jamming attacks. arXiv preprint: arXiv:1710.08476 (2017)
6. Segata, M., Joerer, S., Bloessl, B., Sommer, C., Dressler, F., Cigno, R. L.: Plexe: a platooning extension for veins. In: 2014 IEEE Vehicular Networking Conference (VNC), pp. 53-60. IEEE (2014)
7. Ettus Research: USRP software-defined radio platform. https://www.ettus.com/products/. Accessed 25 July 2022
8. GNURadio: The free and open source software radio ecosystem webpage. https://www.gnuradio.org/. Accessed 25 July 2022
9. Jiang, D., Delgrossi, L.: IEEE 802.11p: towards an international standard for wireless access in vehicular environments. In: IEEE Vehicular Technology Conference, pp. 2036–2040. IEEE (2008). https://doi.org/10.1109/VETECS.2008.458
10. 3rd Generation Partnership Project (3GPP): Study on LTE support for V2X services. Technical Specification (TS) 22.185, Version 17.0.0 (2022). http://www.3gpp.org/ftp/Specs/archive/22_series/22.185/22185-f00.zip
11. Lichtman, M., et al.: A communications jamming taxonomy. IEEE Secur. Priv. **14**(1), 47–54 (2016)
12. Standard Performance Evaluation Corporation. https://www.spec.org/benchmarks.html. Accessed 29 July 2024
13. TPC benchmarking activities. https://www.tpc.org/. Accessed 29 July 2024
14. Gray, J., Reuter, A.: The Benchmark Handbook for Database and Transaction Systems. 2nd edn. Morgan Kaufmann (1993). ISBN: 1-55860-292-5
15. Kanoun, K.: Dependability Benchmarking for Computer Systems. Wiley-IEEE Computer Society Press (2008). https://doi.org/10.1002/9780470370506
16. Oliveira, R.A., Raga, M.M., Laranjeiro, N., Vieira, M.: An approach for benchmarking the security of web service frameworks. Futur. Gener. Comput. Syst. **110**, 833–848 (2020)
17. Segata, M., et al.: Multi-technology cooperative driving: an analysis based on PLEXE. IEEE Trans. Mob. Comput. **22**(8), 4792–4806 (2023). https://doi.org/10.1109/TMC.2022.3154643
18. Fang, W., et al.: Information security of PHY layer in wireless networks. J. Sens. **2016** (2016)

19. Alipour-Fanid, A., Dabaghchian, M., Zeng, K.: Impact of jamming attacks on vehicular cooperative adaptive cruise control systems. IEEE Trans. Veh. Technol. **69**(11), 12679–12693 (2020). https://doi.org/10.1109/TVT.2020.3030251
20. Malik, M., Aramrattana, M., Maleki, M., Folkesson, P., Sangchoolie, B., Karlsson, J.: Simulation-based evaluation of a remotely operated road vehicle under transmission delays and denial-of-service attacks. In: 2023 IEEE 28th Pacific Rim International Symposium on Dependable Computing (PRDC), pp. 23–29. IEEE (2023). https://doi.org/10.1109/PRDC59308.2023.00012.
21. Moser, D., Lenders, V., Capkun, S.: Digital radio signal cancellation attacks: an experimental evaluation. In: Proceedings of the 12th Conference on Security and Privacy in Wireless and Mobile Networks (WiSec 2019), pp. 23–33. Association for Computing Machinery, New York (2019). https://doi.org/10.1145/3317549.3319720
22. Clancy, T. C.: Efficient OFDM denial: pilot jamming and pilot nulling. In: 2011 IEEE International Conference on Communications (ICC), pp. 1–5. IEEE (2011). https://doi.org/10.1109/icc.2011.5962467
23. Mahal, J. A., Shahriar, C., Clancy, T. C.: Emulated CP jamming and nulling attacks on SC-FDMA and two novel countermeasures. In: MILCOM 2015 - 2015 IEEE Military Communications Conference, pp. 275–280. IEEE (2015). https://doi.org/10.1109/MILCOM.2015.7357455
24. Sommer, C., German, R., Dressler, F.: Bidirectionally coupled network and road traffic simulation for improved IVC analysis. IEEE Trans. Mob. Comput. (TMC) **10**(1), 3–15 (2011). https://doi.org/10.1109/TMC.2010.133
25. Rajamani, R., Tan, H.-S., Law, B.K., Zhang, W.-B.: Demonstration of integrated longitudinal and lateral control for the operation of automated vehicles in platoons. IEEE Trans. Control Syst. Technol. **8**(4), 695–708 (2000). https://doi.org/10.1109/87.852914
26. plexe.car2x.org: Plexe Examples - Running Plexe. https://plexe.car2x.org/tutorial/. Accessed 05 Sep 2021. Keywords: Plexe Examples - Running Plexe
27. RISE Dependable Transport Systems: ComFASE GitHub repository for code access. https://github.com/RISE-Dependable-Transport-Systems/ComFASE/. Accessed 27 July 2022
28. Maleki, M., Malik, M., Folkesson, P., Sangchoolie, B., Karlsson, J.: Modeling and evaluating the effects of jamming attacks on connected automated road vehicles. In: 2022 IEEE 27th Pacific Rim International Symposium on Dependable Computing (PRDC), pp. 12–23. IEEE Computer Society, Los Alamitos, CA, US (2022).https://doi.org/10.1109/PRDC55274.2022.00016
29. Ali, A., Garcia, G., Martinet, P.: The flatbed platoon towing model for safe and dense platooning on highways. IEEE Intell. Transp. Syst. Mag. **7**(1), 58–68 (2015). https://doi.org/10.1109/MITS.2014.2328670
30. Ploeg, J., Scheepers, B.T.M., van Nunen, E., van de Wouw, N., Nijmeijer, H.: Design and experimental evaluation of cooperative adaptive cruise control. In: 2011 14th International IEEE Conference on Intelligent Transportation Systems (ITSC), pp. 260–265 (2011). https://doi.org/10.1109/ITSC.2011.6082981
31. Santini, S., Salvi, A., Valente, A.S., Pescapè, A., Segata, M., Lo Cigno, R.: A consensus-based approach for platooning with inter-vehicular communications. In: 34th IEEE Conference on Computer Communications (INFOCOM 2015), pp. 1158–1166. IEEE, Hong Kong (2015). https://doi.org/10.1109/INFOCOM.2015.7218490

32. Malik, M., Maleki, M., Folkesson, P., Sangchoolie, B., Karlsson, J.: ComFASE: a tool for evaluating the effects of V2V communication faults and attacks on automated vehicles. In: 52nd Annual IEEE/IFIP International Conference on Dependable Systems and Networks (DSN2022), pp. 1–12. IEEE (2022)
33. omnetpp.org: OMNet++ Simulation Models and Tools. https://omnetpp.org/. Accessed 14 July 2021. Keywords: OMNet++, Simulation Models and Tools
34. Alvarez Lopez, P., et al.: Microscopic traffic simulation using SUMO. In: The 21st IEEE International Conference on Intelligent Transportation Systems, IEEE Intelligent Transportation Systems Conference (ITSC), pp. 1–12. IEEE (2018). https://elib.dlr.de/124092/
35. Jirjees, A.: Vehicular Ad Hoc networks: growth and survey for three layers. Int. J. Electr. Comput. Eng. (IJECE) **7**(1), 271–284 (2017)
36. Anisetti, M., Ardagna, C.A., Damiani, E., Gaudenzi, F.: A Security benchmark for OpenStack. In: Proceedings of the 2017 IEEE 10th International Conference on Cloud Computing (CLOUD), pp. 294–301 (2017). https://doi.org/10.1109/CLOUD.2017.45
37. Braun, C.: NETCARBENCH: a benchmark for techniques and tools used in the design of automotive communication systems. In: IFAC Proceedings Volumes, vol. 40, pp. 321–328 (2007). https://doi.org/10.3182/20071107-3-FR-3907.00046. ISBN: 9783902661340
38. Hu, Y., Shan, H., Dutta, R.G., Jin, Y.: Protecting platoons from stealthy jamming attack. In: 2020 Asian Hardware Oriented Security and Trust Symposium (AsianHOST), pp. 1–6 (2020). https://doi.org/10.1109/AsianHOST51057.2020.9358269.
39. Kanoun, K.: Dependability benchmarking for computer systems (2008). https://doi.org/10.1002/9780470370506. ISBN: 047023055X
40. Conte, T.M., Hwu, W.-M.W.: Advances in benchmarking techniques: new standards and quantitative metrics. In: Zelkowitz, M., (ed.) Advances in Computers, vol. 41, pp. 231–253. Elsevier (1995). https://doi.org/10.1016/S0065-2458(08)60235-1. Available: https://www.sciencedirect.com/science/article/pii/S0065245808602351
41. Scribbr, "Internal versus External Validity," https://www.scribbr.com/methodology/internal-vs-external-validity/#:~:text=What%20is%20the%20difference%20between,be%20generalized%20to%20other%20contexts. Accessed 06 Sep 2024
42. Baldwin, L.: Internal and external validity and threats to validity. In: Research Concepts for the Practitioner of Educational Leadership, pp. 31–36, Brill (2018)
43. Ploeg, J., Semsar-Kazerooni, E., Lijster, G., van de Wouw, N., Nijmeijer, H.: Graceful degradation of CACC performance subject to unreliable wireless communication. In: 16th International IEEE Conference on Intelligent Transportation Systems (ITSC 2013), pp. 1210–1216 (2013). https://doi.org/10.1109/ITSC.2013.6728397
44. di Bernardo, M., Salvi, A., Santini, S.: Distributed consensus strategy for platooning of vehicles in the presence of time-varying heterogeneous communication delays. IEEE Trans. Intell. Transp. Syst. **16**(1), 102–112 (2015). https://doi.org/10.1109/TITS.2014.2328439

Regulations and Policies

Wireless Interference and Regulatory Frameworks for Frequency Allocation in V2X Communication Systems

James Grow, Nakira Oglesby, Grayson Hatcher, and Billy Kihei$^{(\boxtimes)}$

Kennesaw State University, Marietta, GA, USA
{jgrow1,noglesb5,ghatche3}@students.kennesaw.edu, bkihei@kennesaw.edu

Abstract. Intelligent Transportation Systems (ITS) and Vehicle-to-Everything (V2X) communication technologies are revolutionizing the transportation sector by enhancing traffic efficiency, safety, and overall user experience. However, the performance of these systems can be significantly hindered by various types of interference. This paper provides a comprehensive overview of the regulatory framework for frequency allocation in V2X communication, identifies the types of interference affecting these systems both co-channel and adjacent channel, and explores strategies for managing and mitigating such interference. It includes an overview of current frequency allocations in the USA, EU/United Kingdom, China, Australia, Japan, South Korea, and Singapore, and discusses the implications of interference on ITS/V2X. The findings underscore the need for robust regulatory frameworks to ensure the successful deployment and operation of ITS and V2X communication systems worldwide.

Keywords: V2X · Interference · U-NII-4

1 Introduction

Intelligent Transport Systems (ITS) and Vehicle-to-Everything (V2X) communication technologies are transforming the interaction between vehicles and their surroundings to enhance road safety, traffic efficiency, and overall transportation sustainability. The cornerstone of ITS and V2X functionality is the allocation of spectrum that the designated radio frequencies are essential for wireless communications. Globally, the spectrum allocation varies, with different countries and regions dedicating specific frequency bands according to their unique regulatory environments and technological needs. The primary band for ITS services, including V2X communications, is the 5.9 GHz band, recognized in many parts of the world and specifically in the United States and Europe. Because V2X is supposed to be a globally harmonized technology in the 5 GHz spectrum

Supported by Georgia Department of Transportation RP 23-16.

A. Kocian et al. (Eds.): INTSYS 2024, LNICST 608, pp. 265–278, 2025.
https://doi.org/10.1007/978-3-031-86370-7_16

(except for Japan's 760 MHz technology [19]), the Unlicensed National Information Infrastructure (U-NII) [25] labeling has been adopted for V2X spectrum to standardize nomenclature. U-NII designation is heavily used by various countries to harmonize frequency bands for unlicensed device usage. This band supports both vehicle-to-vehicle (V2V) and vehicle-to-infrastructure (V2I) communications. Additionally, the 5.8 GHz band is utilized in parts of Asia for ITS applications, often serving as a supplementary or overlapping band to the 5.9 GHz allocations. Figure 1 shows the United States U-NII-4 interference from low-cost U-NII-4 devices in Ch. 177. Additionally, the 5.8 GHz band is utilized in parts of Asia for ITS applications, often serving as a supplementary or overlapping band to the 5.9 GHz allocations.

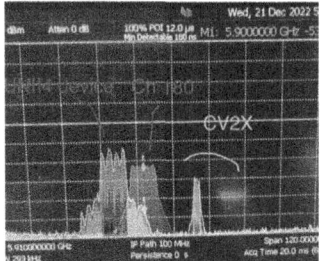 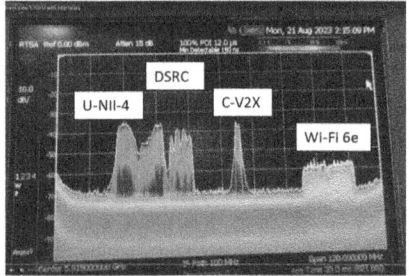

Fig. 1. U-NII-4 Interference on DSRC in the United States.

1.1 EU/United Kingdom 5855–5925 MHz

In the EU/UK, the frequency arrangement is established in 10 MHz blocks. The 5855–5875 MHz frequency band is allocated for non-safety road ITS applications, whereas the 5875–5935 MHz range is reserved for safety-related ITS uses. Within this designated spectrum, the segment 5875–5915 MHz is specifically prioritized for road-ITS, and the 5915–5925 MHz segment is assigned for rail-ITS applications, with the 5925–5935 MHz range exclusively reserved for rail-ITS. Both on-board units (OBUs) and roadside units (RSUs) are allowed to operate under license exemption in these bands. According to the European Commission's Decision (EU) 2020/1426, the 5875–5935 MHz frequency band is dedicated to safety-related Intelligent Transport Systems (ITS/V2x). This decision particularly emphasizes the prioritization of road ITS applications below 5915 MHz, aiming to enhance road safety and traffic efficiency. The 5925–5935 MHz band is mainly allocated for urban rail ITS, allowing shared use and coordination with fixed services to support efficient and safe urban rail operations. Technical specifications set a maximum spectral power density of 23 dBm/MHz and a total transmit power of 33 dBm with a 30 dB transmit power control range. The spectrum in the 5855–5875 MHz frequency range is not protected against interference because it is designated for non-critical uses, such as non-safety related road-ITS and non-specific short-range devices. The updated COMMISSION IMPLE-MENTING DECISION (EU) 2019/1345 of 2 August 2019 [9], amending Decision 2006/771/EC, ensures efficient operation and prevention of interference for short-range devices across the EU [1,10].

As of the COMMISSION IMPLEMENTING DECISION (EU) 2019/1345 of 2 August 2019, amending Decision 2006/771/EC, the European Commission has updated the harmonized technical conditions for the use of radio spectrum by short-range devices. This decision ensures that short-range devices operate efficiently and without causing interference across the EU Short-range devices refer to a category of radio devices designed to operate over short distances at low power this naturally encompass all of V2X/ITS. Member states are not allowed to impose additional technical parameters or usage restrictions beyond those specified in the decision. This prohibition ensures that all short-range devices across the EU follow the same technical standards, preventing discrepancies that could lead to interference or inefficiencies one of the things it dose i regulates the maximum spectral power, density. The density refers to the highest amount of power that can be transmitted per unit of frequency. It is a measure of how much power is distributed across the frequency spectrum by a device. This is important for ensuring that devices do not emit excessive power within any narrow band of frequencies, which could cause interference with other devices operating in the same or adjacent frequencies. However Vehicle-to-vehicle (V2V) communications for road-ITS will be permitted at 5915–5925 MHz once spectrum-sharing solutions for the protection of rail-ITS have been developed at ETSI. In the absence of such sharing solutions for the protection of rail-ITS, the EU permits infrastructure-to-vehicle (I2V) communications for road-ITS at 5915–5925 MHz subject to coordination with rail-ITS [3,18].

1.2   USA 5895–5925 MHz

In the USA, the Federal Communications Commission (FCC) has revised the utilization of the 5.9 GHz radio frequency band, initially designated in 1999 for ITS [26]. The updated policy is (5.895–5.925 GHz) specifically for ITS to support traffic safety functions. This modification was prompted by the growing demand for Wi-Fi, aligning the part of the band now open to Wi-Fi with other frequencies already utilized for similar purposes, thus enhancing the strength and reliability of internet services. Conversely, the segment retained for ITS focuses on promoting vehicle-to-vehicle and vehicle-to-infrastructure communications, crucial for improving road safety and managing traffic effectively. This decision reflects the FCC's intent to balance the imperative needs of robust traffic safety systems with the public's escalating demand for broader and better wireless connectivity. Additionally, the FCC's approach considers international standards, aligning the 30 megahertz reserved for ITS with global practices to standardize technology and minimize costs, thereby preparing for future advancements in traffic safety communication technologies [12].

1.3   Japan 5770–5850 MHz/750–764.5 MHz

In Japan, ITS utilizes specific frequency bands to enhance vehicular communications, thereby improving safety and efficiency in transportation [2]. The spectrum is segmented into two principal parts: the ITS Connect band (755.5–764.5 MHz) supporting V2V, V2I, and I2I communications for safety applications, and the ETC/ETC 2.0 band (5770–5850 MHz) used for Electronic Toll Collection systems, including the advanced ETC 2.0 that integrates additional data services. Seven Frequency Division Duplexing (FDD) channels within the ETC/ETC 2.0 band manage communications at toll booths and support broader ETC 2.0 applications. Notably, in the U.S., the 755.5–764.5 MHz frequency range is not part of the traditional UNII bands and is typically allocated for other services, whereas the 5770–5850 MHz corresponds to the UNII-3 band [27].

1.4   Singapore 5875–5925 MHz

In Singapore, the Infocomm Media Development Authority (IMDA) redefined the framework for ITS in 2017 by allocating specific segments of the 5.9 GHz band (5875 MHz–5925 MHz) for various ITS functions [16]. The spectrum divisions are meticulously categorized: 5875–5885 MHz is earmarked for vehicle-to-vehicle (V2V) safety protocols, 5885–5895 MHz for control communications and WAVE Short Message Protocol (WSMP) operations, and 5895–5905 MHz alongside 5855–5875 MHz are allocated as multifunctional service channels for both governmental and private use. The 5905–5915 MHz range is designated for road pricing initiatives, and 5915–5925 MHz is allocated primarily for long-range communications, mostly for governmental applications. All devices using these bands must strictly adhere to IMDA's specified technical standards, which dictate emission power limits and modifications to the IEEE standards to ensure reliable, swift communications. Furthermore, Singapore's spectrum policy allows vehicular on-board units (OBUs) to operate without licenses, while other installations might require specific licenses, with fees adjusted based on whether the usage is shared or exclusive [5].

1.5   Australia 5855–5925 MHz

In Australia, the regulatory set by Australian Communications and Media Authority (ACMA) for V2X technologies is currently under development, with no specific mandate in effect yet [20]. Guidance and alignment of transport policies across the nation are provided by Austroads, a government advisory body comprising members from all Australian states and New Zealand. The Australian Road Research Board (ARRB) supports these efforts through research aimed at enhancing road safety and efficiency. The Australian Communications and Media Authority (ACMA) has made available radio frequency spectrum in the 5.9 GHz band for use by ITS in Australia through the ITS Class License. The ACMA specifies the use of the 5855–5925 MHz spectrum band for ITS under the Radio communications (Intelligent Transport System) Class License 2017. This spectrum is segmented into seven 10 MHz channels, with 5855–5875 MHz allocated for non-safety ITS applications, 5875–5895 MHz for safety-related applications, and 5905–5925 MHz reserved for future uses. Each ITS station operating within these bands must comply with the ETSI Standard EN 302 571 and adhere to a maximum EIRP of 23 dBm/MHz, allowing some flexibility for minor modifications. This structured yet adaptable approach aids in integrating advanced vehicular communication technologies within Australia's regulatory landscape [5].

1.6   South Korea 5855–5925 MHz

In South Korea, the Telecommunications Technology Association (TTA) documented Dedicated Short-Range Communications (DSRC) in the 5.8 GHz band between Road-Side Units (RSUs) and On-Board Units (OBUs) back in 2006. Building on this foundation, the Ministry of Science and Information and Communications Technology (MSIT) allocated the 5855–5925 MHz band for Cooperative Intelligent Transport Systems (C-ITS) applications in 2016. This strategic allocation was segmented into seven 10 MHz channels to optimize the spectrum for various uses. Specifically, the 5895–5905 MHz segment serves as the Control Channel (CCH), responsible for managing and coordinating communication flows within the C-ITS network. The other channels function as Service Channels (SCH), supporting a mix of safety and non-safety applications. The spectrum policy in South Korea is notably technology-neutral, allowing the use of any radio technology that meets the established standards. The specific allocations within the 5855–5925 MHz range include 5855–5875 MHz for LTE-V2X, 5875–5895 MHz as the guard and experiment band, and 5895–5915 MHz for DSRC. This approach ensures that the spectrum use is efficient and adaptable to various transportation and communication needs [5].

1.7   China 5905–5925 MHz

In China, the frequency spectrum specifically al-located for Intelligent Transport Systems (ITS) comprises 20 MHz in the 5.9 GHz band, focusing on the 5905–5925 MHz range [4]. In 2018, the Bureau of Radio Regulation (BRR), in collaboration with the State Radio Regulation of China (SRRC) and the Telematics Industry Application Alliance (TIAA), undertook comprehensive studies to develop a detailed ITS spectrum policy. Differing from other nations, China has opted for Cellular Vehicle-to-Everything communications C-V2X as the sole technology for ITS safety applications. This decision was solidified after extensive research and trials, leading to the Ministry of Industry and Information Technology (MIIT) regulating this frequency band specifically for the Internet of Vehicles (IoV), utilizing LTE-V2X technology to significantly enhance vehicular communication and safety. The MIIT's Bureau of Radio Regulation (BRR) plays a crucial role in the ongoing planning and evaluation of spectrum needs for ITS services, ensuring the coexistence of various systems and effective spectrum management. This strategic approach facilitates advanced vehicular communications while ensuring compatibility and efficiency across different technological platforms [5].

2   Obscure Technologies Operating in the V2X Band

Each country manages its spectrum differently, allowing for a variety of applications that can coexist within the designated V2X frequency bands. This introduction sets the stage for a detailed country by country discussion, exploring how various regions accommodate these lesser-known uses of the V2X spectrum.

2.1   EU/UK

The frequency band 5855–5935 MHz allocated for V2X communication has obscure technology operating in its band. **Fixed-Satellite Service (FSS)** operate between 5850 MHz–5925 MHz bandwidth. FSS refers to a type of satellite communication service where satellite systems and ground stations (known as Earth stations) are used in fixed locations on the Earth's surface to communicate with satellites in orbit. This service is specifically designated for Earth-to-space communications, meaning it primarily involves transmissions from Earth stations up to the satellites. Guidance for the harmonized use and coordination of **Maritime Broadband Radio (MBR)** systems on board ships and offshore platforms operating within the frequency bands 5852–5872. MBR is where high-speed digital communication and data transfer are essential for effective and safe operations. In addition the Frequencies 5900–5950 kHz has been allocated with additional permissions, meaning it has primary allocations, but other services can also use it under certain conditions. **Fixed Service (in all three ITU Regions)**: This service typically involves communications between fixed points and is allowed globally in this frequency band. **Land Mobile Service (in Region 1)**: This refers to services used by vehicles or portable units on land. **Mobile except Aeronautical Mobile (R) Service (in Regions 2 and 3)**: This covers mobile services excluding aircraft-based communication [13].

2.2   USA

The frequency band 5895–5925 MHz allocated for V2X communication has obscure Technology operating in its band regulations governing the use of certain frequency bands by the **non-Federal Fixed-Satellite Service (FSS)** [15]. With the 5850–5925 MHz (Earth-to-space): This band is used for communications from Earth stations to satellites. Within the 5650–5925 MHz band The military has been given permission to use **Radio Location Service** this is a type of radio service used for determining the position, velocity, or characteristics of objects, by means of the propagation properties of radio waves. Radiolocation involves technologies such as radar and can be utilized for a range of applications including navigation, air traffic control, and maritime vessel tracking [11].

2.3   Japan

In exploring the current utilization of the 5770–5850 MHz and 755.5–764.5 MHz frequency bands, it becomes evident that their usage extends beyond V2X applications. Notably, the **FIXED-SATELLITE (Earth-to-space) services** within these bands are allocated for communications from Earth to satellites. This illustrates the diverse technological implementations within the same frequency spectrum, showcasing a blend of terrestrial and extraterrestrial communication capabilities [27].

2.4   Singapore

In Singapore 5875–5925 MHz frequency bands are predominantly dedicated to ITS and C-V2X technologies. However, there is potential for overlap with **satellite communication services** [1].

2.5   South Korea

In South Korea, the 5855–5925 MHz V2X frequency bands are predominantly dedicated to ITS and C-V2X technologies. However, there is potential for overlap with **satellite communication services**. In addition the applications for this technology is done in a neutral manner, meaning, any radio technology can be used in this spectrum as far as the technology complies with the corresponding regulations [1].

2.6   China

In China 5905–5925 frequency bands are predominantly dedicated to ITS and C-V2X technologies. However, there is potential for overlap with satellite communication services. China has given the allocation of the 6425–7125 MHz frequency band for International Mobile Telecommunications (IMT), which includes 5G/6G [6, 22].

3   Technologies in Adjacent Band that Can Cause Interference on V2X

Adjacent bands are crucial for spectrum management as they can influence or be influenced by the operations within the primary band due to their proximity. Effective management of adjacent bands is essential to prevent interference, ensuring that each service within these bands operates efficiently without disrupting nearby spectrum users. This involves implementing technical measures, such as guard bands or specific transmission limits, to maintain clear and reliable communication channels across different services and technologies.

3.1 EU/UK

In the European Union, the frequency band designated for ITS is 5855 MHz to 5925 MHz. The adjacent bands to this ITS-dedicated spectrum are generally used as follows: Lower Adjacent Band (Below 5855 MHz) 5725–5855 MHz: This band is commonly utilized for **Wi-Fi and other Radio Local Area Network (RLAN) applications** under the regulations for unlicensed use. It supports various wireless communications technologies that require broad bandwidth and are essential for consumer and commercial connectivity. The Upper Adjacent Band (Above 5925 MHz) is 5925–6425 MHz: Recently, this range has been opened up for the new **Wi-Fi 6E** standard in many parts of the world, including the EU. Wi-Fi 6E extends existing Wi-Fi into the 6 GHz band, providing additional spectrum to alleviate congestion in existing bands, offering wider channels, and improving data throughput rates with less interference [3].

3.2 USA

In the lower band the FCC has reallocated the lower 45 MHz 5850–5895 MHz of the 5.9 GHz band for unlicensed uses, such as **Wi-Fi**. This means that this portion of the spectrum can be used for various wireless communications that do not require a license, which includes Wi-Fi networks. The unlicensed operations are allowed indoors with specific power and technical limitations to prevent interference with other services using adjacent frequencies. In the upper band recently, this range has been increasingly considered for **Wi-Fi 6E** deployment, which extends Wi-Fi into the 6 GHz band. The FCC has opened up the lower part of the 6 GHz band (5925–6425 MHz) for unlicensed use, which allows for more robust indoor and outdoor Wi-Fi applications. The spectrum from 6425 MHz up to 7125 MHz is also under consideration for additional unlicensed use as well as other potential future broadband services [8, 21, 24].

3.3 Japan

In Japan, the ITS band is specifically allocated around 5.9 GHz, particularly from 5770–5850 MHz for Electronic Toll Collection (ETC) and related ITS communications and 755.5–764.5 is related to more standard ITS. Here's how the adjacent bands are generally utilized: Lower Adjacent Band (Below 5770 MHz) 5725–5770 MHz: This segment is typically used for applications such as **Wi-Fi and other radio local area network (RLAN) services**. It is part of the spectrum allocated for unlicensed use, supporting various consumer and business wireless applications [27].

3.4 Australia

In Australia, the ITS band allocated from 5855 MHz to 5925 MHz. Lower Adjacent Band (Below 5855 MHz) 5825–5855 MHz: This segment is often used for **wireless access systems and other similar applications**. It may also be allocated for additional wireless communication services, depending on the specific national spectrum plan. Upper Adjacent Band (Above 5925 MHz) 5925–6425 MHz: This range is increasingly being considered for the expansion of Wi-Fi services under the new **Wi-Fi 6E** specifications, which extend Wi-Fi into the 6 GHz band, allowing for more extensive channels and higher throughput with reduced interference. The 5725–5850 MHz and 5925–6425 MHz bands mentioned refer to frequency ranges allocated for Radio Local Area Networks (RLANs) under the IEEE 802.11 series of standards, which include Wi-Fi technologies [14].

3.5 Singapore

In Singapore, the frequency bands adjacent to the 5875–5925 MHz range, used for ITS, are utilized as follows: Lower Adjacent Band (5725–5875 MHz) ISM Band: This band is designated for **Industrial, Scientific, and Medical (ISM) applications**. ISM bands are typically used for various unlicensed purposes that include industrial controls, scientific experiments, and medical equipment. In some regions, this band also supports Wi-Fi networks under specific conditions, such as reduced power limits to minimize interference. Higher Adjacent Band (5925–6425 MHz): **Wi-Fi 6E**. The segment from 5925 MHz onwards is part of the newly allocated spectrum for Wi-Fi 6E in Singapore [7].

3.6 South Korea

In South Korea, the ITS band is allocated in the 5.9 GHz range, specifically from 5850 MHz to 5925 MHz. Lower Adjacent Band (Below 5850 MHz): Typically used for other communication services, which may include additional allocations for **mobile services or fixed satellite services**, depending on South Korea's spectrum planning. Upper Adjacent Band (Above 5925 MHz): Increasingly considered and allocated for expanded Wi-Fi capabilities under the **Wi-Fi 6E** standard, extending into the 6 GHz band. This allows for broader channels and higher throughput with less interference, benefiting both consumer and industrial applications [23].

3.7 China

In China, the adjacent bands to the 5905–5925 MHz segment, which is part of the 5.9 GHz range allocated for ITS, are as follows: Lower Adjacent Band (below 5855 MHz): This range typically includes other communication services, such **mobile services and fixed satellite services**. Specific allocations can vary, often including portions reserved for governmental and military uses, depending on the country's spectrum planning policies. Upper Adjacent Band (above 5925 MHz): This band is increasingly being considered for expanded Wi-Fi capabilities under the **Wi-Fi 6E** standard, which extends into the 6 GHz range. The Wi-Fi 6E standard allows for additional channels at higher frequencies [17].

4   Mitigation Techniques Against U-NII-4 Interference

To address U-NII-4 interference in a realizable way that road authorities could implement immediately, we performed two studies, one that recommends a guard band spacing, another that recommends retrofitting RF in-line hardware.

4.1   Rechannelization/Gaurd Band Spacing

This study investigates the effects of increasing the guard band size of the lower 5.9 GHz DSRC band on the adjacent channel interference from Unlicensed National Information Infrastructure 4 band (U-NII-4) devices and to try and see if there is a significant decrease in the interference level. In this study, two different modes of DSRC communication were used to measure packet reception rate (PRR). The first mode was V2I communication. This was done by using an on-board unit OBU) and having it send dummy packets to a roadside unit (RSU). The second mode of communication used in the study was I2V communication. As opposed to the OBU sending the packets to the RSU, the RSU sent dummy packets to the OBU. Both the RSU and the OBU were controlled from a host computer. The Unlicensed National Information Infrastructure 4 band (U-NII-4) interferes used to cause the interference were all controlled by a custom interference management application (IMA) on the same host computer. Figure 2 shows the in-lab measurements.

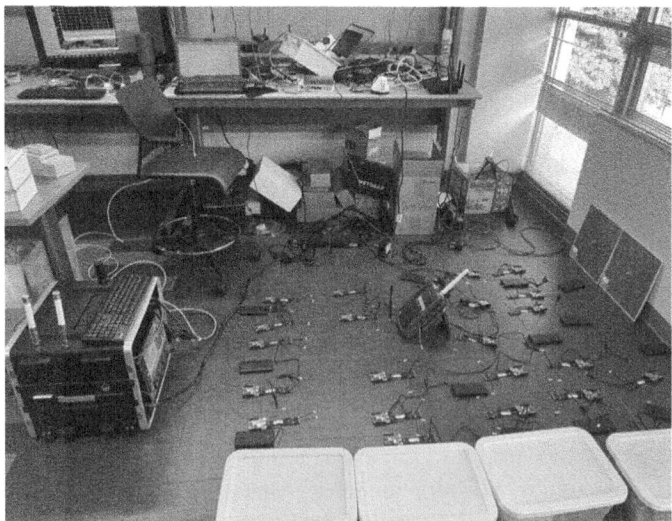

Fig. 2. In lab testing with low-cost U-NII-4 interferers

In the IMA software, the central frequency and bandwidth of the interferer transmissions was able to be manipulated. The results from experimentation

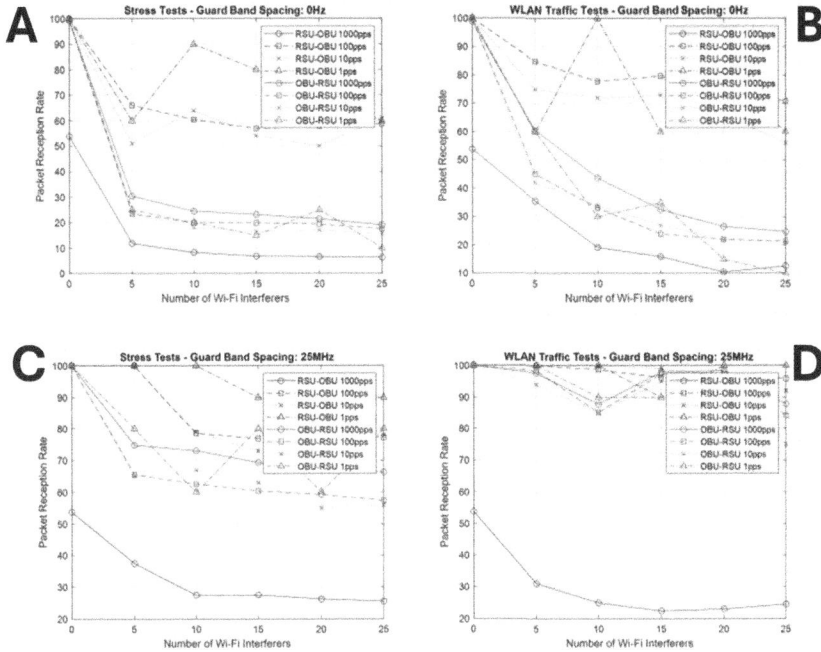

Fig. 3. I2V and V2I PRR when the DSRC band does not have a guard band. (A) Stress Test, (B) Emulated WLAN; I2V and V2I PRR when the DSRC band has a guard band of 25 MHz. (C) Stress Test, (D) Emulated WLAN;

can be shown to support the goal of this study. When comparing the results for the different guard band sizes tested the average packet reception rate is shown to have increased. The minimal guard band size is suggested to be 15 MHz to achieve above 80% PRR. Future works involving this study may focus on increasing the number of U-NII-4 devices used in experimentation or looking at the C-V2X band and trying to mitigate interference there. In Fig. 3 we show our findings.

4.2   In-Line RF Hardware

Past research has proved that interference by adjacent bands can result in thirty percent drop-in Packet Reception Rate (PRR) for I2V, and seventy percent for V2I. This results in less than ideal communication, raising concern for the safety of everyday travel. This study seeks to answer: What measures could be taken, using existing RF Technologies in line with the stock RSU antennas, to restore PRR of both I2V and V2I? This study finds possible solutions through RF filter design, and in-line attenuation techniques. Tested Infrastructure-to-Vehicle (I2V) and Vehicle-to-Infrastructure (V2I). This study finds possible solutions through attenuation integration. Attenuation increases PRR of V2I, while impacting range and I2V PRR. However, circulators can be used to bypass the

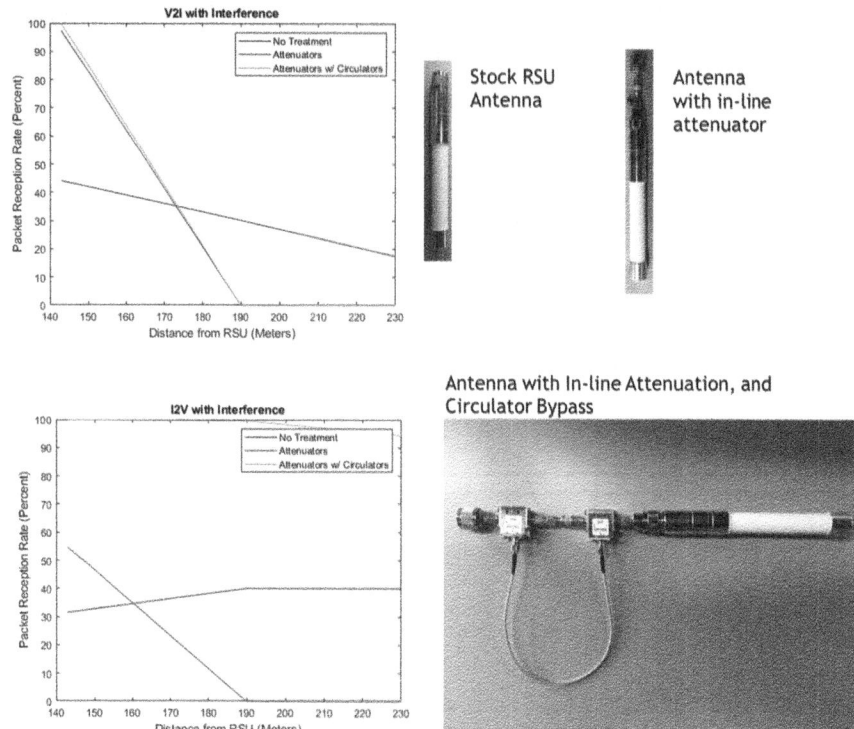

Fig. 4. Field distance measurements for V2I and I2V both with and without RF in-line mitigation treatments.

attenuation and result in higher I2V PRR. Contrary to expectations, V2I benefited from the surrounding interference, having higher PRR ratings. This study finds possible solutions through RF filter design, and in-line attenuation techniques. Future work will search for a cheap to fabricate RF filter solution. In Fig. 4 we show our findings.

References

1. 5GAA: White paper on its spectrum utilization in the Asia pacific region. Technical report, 5GAA (2018). https://5gaa.org/white-paper-on-its-spectrum-utilization-in-the-asia-pacific-region/
2. 5GAA: White paper on its spectrum utilization in the Asia pacific region. Technical report (2018). https://5gaa.org/content/uploads/2018/07/5GAA_WhitePaper_ITS-spectrum-utilization-in-the-Asia-Pacific-Region_FINAL_160718docx.pdf
3. 5GAA: Position paper on European deployment band configuration for C-V2X. Technical report, 5GAA (2021). https://5gaa.org/content/uploads/2021/06/5GAA_S-210019_Position-paper-on-European-deployment-band-configuration-for-C-V2X_final.pdf

4. 5GAA: C-V2X standardization in China. Technical report (2022). https://5gaa. org/content/uploads/2022/10/C-V2X-standardisation-in-China.pdf
5. 5GAA: White paper on its spectrum utilization in the Asia pacific region. Technical report, 5GAA (2023). https://www.5gaa.org/news/white-paper-on-its-spectrum-utilization-in-the-asia-pacific-region/
6. Global Validity Admin: July regulatory newsletter. Technical report, Global Validity (2023). https://globalvalidity.com/july-regulatory-newsletter/
7. Infocomm Media Development Authority: Media factsheet - allocation of 6 GHZ band in Singapore. Techbical report, Infocomm Media Development Authority (2023). https://www.imda.gov.sg/resources/press-releases-factsheets-and-speeches/factsheets/2023/imda-to-allocate-more-radio-frequency-spectrum-for-wi-fi-connectivity-in-singapore
8. U.S. Department of Commerce: United States frequency allocations the radio spectrum. Technical report, U.S. Department of Commerce (2016). https://www.ntia. doc.gov/files/ntia/publications/january_2016_spectrum_wall_chart.pdf
9. European Commission: Commission implementing decision (EU) 2019/1345. Technical report (2019). https://eur-lex.europa.eu/legal-content/EN/TXT/PDF/? uri=CELEX:32019D1345&from=EN
10. European Commission: Commission implementing decision (EU) 2020/1426 of 7 October 2020 on the harmonised use of radio spectrum in the 5 875–5 935 MHZ frequency band for safety-related applications of intelligent transport systems (its) and repealing decision 2008/671/EC. Technical report, European Union (2020). http://data.europa.eu/eli/dec_impl/2020/1426/oj
11. Federal Communications Commission: Federal communications commission. FCC table of frequency allocations. Technical report, Federal Communications Commission (2024). https://docs.fcc.gov/public/attachments/DOC-392207A1.pdf
12. Federal Communications Commission: Use of the 5.850–5.925 GHZ band. Technical report, Federal Register (2021). https://www.federalregister.gov/documents/ 2021/05/03/2021-08802/use-of-the-5850-5925-ghz-band
13. Electronic Communications Committee: The European table of frequency allocations and applications in the frequency range 8.3 KHZ to 3000 GHZ (ECA table). Technical report, Electronic Communications Committee (2023). https://docdb. cept.org/download/4316
14. Australian Communications and Media Authority: Five-year spectrum outlook 2024–29 and 2024–25 work program draft for consultation. Technical report, Australian Communications and Media Authority (2024). https://www.acma.gov.au/ sites/default/files/2024-04/Draft%20FYSO%202024-29.pdf
15. FCC: 47 CFR§ 2.106, NG160. Technical report. https://www.ecfr.gov/current/ title-47/chapter-I/subchapter-A/part-2/subpart-B/section-2.106
16. IMDA: Dedicated shortrange communications in intelligent transport systems. Technical report (2017). https://www.imda.gov.sg/-/media/Imda/Files/ Regulation-Licensing-and-Consultations/ICT-Standards/Telecommunication-Standards/Radio-Comms/IMDA-TS-DSRC.pdf
17. Ministry of Industry and Information Technology: People's Republic of China radio frequency allocation provisions. Technical report, Global Regulation (2014). https://www.global-regulation.com/translation/china/159334/peoples-republic-of-china-radio-frequency-allocation-provisions.html
18. European Telecommunications Standards Institute: Intelligent transport systems (ITS); radiocommunications equipment operating in the 5 855 MHZ to 5 925 MHZ frequency band; harmonised standard covering the essential requirements of article 3.2 of directive 2014/53/EU. Technical report, European Telecommunications

Standards Institute (2017). https://www.etsi.org/deliver/etsi_en/302500_302599/302571/02.01.01_60/en_302571v020101p.pdf

19. Telecommunications Bureau of the Ministry of Internal Affairs and Communications: Frequency reorganization action plan (FY2023 version). Technical report (2023). https://www.tele.soumu.go.jp/e/adm/freq/search/actionplan/actionplan2023.pdf

20. ITU: Report ITU-R M.2445-0. Technical report (2016). https://www.itu.int/dms_pub/itu-r/opb/rep/R-REP-M.2445-2018-PDF-E.pdf

21. Sheriff, K., Moelter, H., Jandura, J., Kuka, E.: FCC approves C-V2X technology for connected vehicles ahead of final its rules. Technical report, Davis Wright Tremaine LLP (2023). https://www.dwt.com/blogs/broadband-advisor/2023/05/fcc-connected-vehicles-c-v2x

22. Lin, G.: China's latest regulation on 2.4 GHZ and 5 GHZ equipment - in compliance magazine. Technical report, International Product Compliance (2022). https://incompliancemag.com/chinas-latest-regulation-on-2-4-ghz-and-5-ghz-equipment/

23. Admin in South Korea: South Korea approves the 6GHZ band for unlicensed use. Technical report, ELEOS Compliance (2020). https://www.eleoscompliance.com/en/article/south-korea-south-korea-approves-6ghz-band-for-unlicensed-use

24. US Department of Transportation: Recent FCC public notices on the 5.9 GHZ safety band. Technical report, US Department of Transportation (2022). https://www.transportation.gov/safety-band/recent-fcc-public-notices

25. Federal Communications Commission, USA: Phase I testing of prototype U-NII-4 devices. Technical report (2018). https://docs.fcc.gov/public/attachments/DA-18-1111A2.pdf

26. Federal Communications Commission, USA: Order on reconsideration. Technical report (2024). https://docs.fcc.gov/public/attachments/FCC-24-32A1.pdf

27. MIC The Radio Use Website: Frequency assignment plan (as of December 2023). Technical report, MIC The Radio Use Website (2023). https://www.tele.soumu.go.jp/e/adm/freq/search/share/plan.htm

Runtime Norms Regulation Framework for Drones' Smart Cities Applications

Hana Gharrad[1]([✉]), Nafaâ Jabeur[2], Tarek Rahil Sheltami[3], and Ansar Ul-Haque Yasar[1]

[1] UHasselt, Transportation Research Institute, Martelarenlaan 42, 3500 Hasselt, Belgium
hana.gharrad@uhasselt.be

[2] Computer Sciences Department, German University of Technology in Oman (GUtech), Athaibah, Muscat 130, Oman

[3] Computer Engineering Department, Interdisciplinary Research Center of Smart Mobility and Logistics, King Fahd University of Petroleum and Minerals, Dhahran 31261, Saudi Arabia

Abstract. Norms establish safety standards and operational guidelines that ensure drones operate in a manner that minimizes risks to people and properties and with respect of privacy protection guidelines based on defined legislation. Today, the widespread use of drones in smart cities applications and in the urban environment requires the establishment of adaptive norms to address various operational, safety, and regulatory challenges. In this paper we suggest a runtime norms regulation framework for drones. The objective of this framework is (i) To design a system where different organizations have different access norms using a cloud of norms. (ii) To keep drones informed about the state of the norms they are interested in during their mission (iii) To allow the update of norms tolerance based on emergency situations.

Keywords: Norms · Smart Cities · Drones

1 Introduction

Drones play an important role in smart cities [1]. Many governments are already introducing drones in multiple functions like city monitoring, transportation and infrastructure protection [2]. However, the fixed nature of access regulations for different areas and regions restricts the wide deployment of drones, thereby limiting their utilization in areas where they might be required. Recently, there has been growing research advocating dynamic access control mechanisms, particularly in scenarios that require flexibility in response to real-time events such as emergencies and weather changes [3, 4]. Norms refer to the behavioral guidelines promoted by a social group or the majority of individuals within an ecosystem. The management of these norms facilitates the autonomous coordination among individuals or agents with homogeneous/heterogeneous objectives. This is particularly important in the evolving field of unmanned air vehicles, where regulatory frameworks are playing a crucial role in ensuring the real-time adaptability of drones to the changing environments, procedures, and situational requirements

A. Kocian et al. (Eds.): INTSYS 2024, LNICST 608, pp. 279–290, 2025.
https://doi.org/10.1007/978-3-031-86370-7_17

related to their operations. In smart cities, regulatory norms can change based on factors such as traffic conditions, weather, or emergency situations. Because of their dynamism, autonomy and flexibility of agent modeling, Multi Agent Systems (MAS) can be considered as one of the most promising approaches to model autonomous, decentralized, and adaptive operations. MAS enables drones to quickly adapt to these changes through real-time communication and negotiation among agents, ensuring compliance with current norms while maintaining operational efficiency. Within this context, in this paper we suggest a runtime norm regulation framework using MAS. Unlike pre-defined or static norms, this framework allows drones to autonomously adjust their behavior based on current conditions, which is crucial for the complex, unpredictable nature of smart cities. Access norms or access rules specify what geographical areas (spatial boundaries) agents are allowed or restricted to access based on pre-established geographical zones (attributes) or based on other additional criteria such as the dynamic factors like time, weather conditions, or special events. Also, it allows the regulation of access norms of regions based on emergency situations. In the first section we address the existing related work focusing on norm management and regulation. In the second section we present the proposed runtime norm regulation framework using a scenario as a prototype. In the third section we discuss the advantages and limitations and possible improvement of the current version of the suggested framework. Finally, a brief conclusion is presented in the last section.

2 Related Work

Norms are generally conceived as standards to specify good behaviours and guide individuals' activities [1]. They define the rights and duties of the members of a given society in terms of permissions, prohibitions, and obligations. Norms can be regarded as rules in the sense that each norm contains both a premise and a consequence. They can be interpreted as a special kind of soft constraints that a system can use to sanction the violations and reward the good behaviours.

Norms have been widely used as an effective approach for regulating open and heterogeneous Multi-Agent Systems (MAS) [2]. We are particularly talking about normative MAS which use norms as a mechanism for persuading autonomous and heterogeneous agents to behave according to the stated social order [3]. Norms are necessary in MAS to achieve agents' coordination and regulate their behaviours [4]. Normative systems are closely related to deontic logic which is a formal study of normative reasoning and norms (later called Standard Deontic Logic (SDL)). SDL has been a useful tool in the specification and reasoning of access control policies because the SDL introduce deontic operators.

Norms can be created by a single legislator, or they can also emerge spontaneously. In agent's societies two main approaches are possible for establishing norms which are the top-down approach and the bottom-up approach. In the first approach, norms could be static or dynamic, but they should be created by a specific authorized agent which act as norm recommender. In the bottom-up approach, a new norm will be merged when a considerable portion of agents follow it. Based on their observations, these agents should have the ability to choose to merge a new norm autonomously using their cognitive aspect. The second approach is suitable for systems with human-agent interactions whereas the first approach is suitable for regulating organizations in dynamic environment [3]. Time, place, context and risks are ones of the possible factors that could be taken in consideration in the norm emergence. The behaviour of majority of the other agents could also affect the emergence and immergence of norms. Different classifications of norms have been proposed based on different aspect, like their purpose and their scope. For example, norms have been classified in two main types: Essential norms and Conventional norms. Conventional norms emerge without enforcement and are not enforced by the entity representing the institution and no sanctions or rewards are defined for agents persuading these norms (example: greeting). Each agent expects other agents to conform to conventions because they are self-enforced. Conventions solve coordination problems when there is no conflict between the individuals and the collective interests [5]. Essential norms are used to solve or ease collective action problems when there is a conflict between an individual and the collective interests [6]. Another classification [3] groups norms as Substantive Norms and Procedural Norms. Substantive Norms define organizational relationships among members and the normative system itself by defining Regulative and Constitutive Norms. Regulative norms describe different sub-levels of ideal behaviour by means of obligations, prohibitions, and permissions while Constitutive Norms provide an abstraction to define the ontology used for describing the behaviour of the system and describe the legal consequences of actions in the normative system (for example it defines what is a restricted area and define that each flight altitude that exceed 40 m on a restricted area is counted as altitude violation).

Norm Management include the norms representation, regulation, emergence and enforcement (self-enforcement or third part enforcement). Which make it a complex system. To model normative multi agent system, logic formalization and different architectures have been proposed in the literature for the agents and the normative systems. One of the first formalization of norms is the SDL which consist of a classical propositional logic with deontic operators. Preference-Based Deontic Logic (PDL) which has been proposed to solve some paradox of SDL. Dyadic Deontic Logic (DDL) where deontic operators are dyadic deontic logics that contain binary deontic operators, and which has been also proposed to overcome some of DDL paradox. Defeasible Deontic Logic combined deontic logics (SDL or DDL) with defeasible logic. Defeasible logic is different from monotonic reasoning. It allows reasoning in the face of contradictions and allows revision of the obligations (overshadowing) by violations facts or by more specific obligations. Also, Defeasible logic has been also used to add temporal considerations for the norms (Normative Temporal Logic (NTL)).

The prementioned norms specifications has been used in normative systems to guide autonomous agent to interplay between their goals and the norms that they are trying to uphold. Norms also are behavioural guidelines imposed by social group which guide agents to achieve their goals in an acceptable manner within their social groups without compromising their autonomy [7].

Several normative agent architectures have been suggested like NoA, v-BDI, N-Jason and BEN (Behavior with Emotions and Norms). In [8] the authors suggested a formalisation to allow agents to plan for multiple goals and norms based on the utility gain of goals and utility loss of norm violations. The authors used the norms specification proposed in [9], to propose a practical reasoning approach in rescue operation scenario.

Due to the dynamic nature of the environment, norms and policies are related to contextual information. Therefore, the revision of the rules in normative multi agent system has been studied in the recent research works. Norms management become more challenging with on runtime and in open multi agent systems. In [10], the authors suggest three norm revision strategies for the agent. The first strategy is Synergy-based strategies which are based on the concept of synergy between the objective of the system and the norms. The authors define this synergy to be positive when it is likely to achieve the objective of the system when the norm is obeyed or not violated and negative when it is likely to achieve the objective of the system when the norm is violated. The second strategy is the sensitivity-based strategy which uses sensitivity analysis techniques of probabilistic reasoning aiming to make the set for norms more effective to a specific context by reducing the probability of norm violation for a given context. The third category is the category-based strategy. In this strategy, the norms are grouped based on their relations with the objective of the system that are discovered during the runtime and based on the violation of the norms.

Drones have already been an important component of transportation systems. Their variety of uses and benefits encouraged policy makers to consider the integration of this technology in transportation system. A variety of frameworks like EASA (European Union Aviation Safety Agency) aims to develop proposals to regulate drone operations based on risk, impact, performance, etc. The EASA framework specifies regulations per type of operation, define technical and operational requirements (entering a prohibited zone, pilots' qualifications...) and combine drone hardware legislation and aviation legislation. Drone also become more autonomous even in collaborative and swam systems. In collaborative multi agent systems and open multi agent systems (OMAS), in addition to aviation and hardware policies, collaboration norms [11] need also to be addressed. These norms are also named as society interaction rules. In [12], two main challenges have been identified for norms specification which are the dynamic modifications of norms (which require to interrupt or restart the collaboration) and the re-use of norms in different situations. The norms system will also allow agents to understand the impact of norm violation or obeyance on their goals and decide to adopt it or violate it [7]. In Multi-agents' system the norms management, emergency and revision have been addressed from different perspective. In the following some of the related research works will be addressed. To improve collaboration robustness between autonomous agent coalitions, the authors in [12] suggested to include normative control which specify permitted, prohibited, and obligatory actions as the relations between the agents in the same coalitions. Six subthemes have been addressed to manage norms in cooperative agents' group, which are the specification and the modification of the norms, the norms adoption, the conflict resolution, norms monitoring, norms enforcement and norms removal. The norms specification defines permitted, obligatory and prohibited actions. Norms adoptions aim to diffuse the norms in a distributed manner so that each agent will have local norms set. The monitoring aims to identify the agents that violate the active rules and identify the responsible agent and also evaluate the cost of the monitoring. In [7], the authors proposed a Utility-based Norm Synthesis (UNS) which elicits the suitable norm on the existence of unmatchable norms. Unmatchable norms are the norms that only one of them should be applied in the current context.

In [4], the authors suggest to automatically synthesis norms in online mode by modelling a norm generalisation mechanism. The proposed model aims to detect undesirable state and synthesises norms to avoid such states in the future. Norms synthesis consist of creating a set of norms which ensure that the success of the coordination which could be designed in an offline mode (at design time) or in an online mode (at run-time). Norms synthesis require state presentation and could be designed in a centralized or distributed manner. In the contrast, in norm emergence, agent choose their own norms in a collaborative way which means each agent will have a module that allow him to synthesis the norms and actively collaborate with the others agent in the synthesizing process. However, in norms synthesis, agent could passively collaborate in the synthesizing process (norms could be synthesised by observing agents' interactions).

Existing works focusing on the Dynamic Airspace Re-configuration (DAR) of Unmanned Aerial Systems (UAS) suggested to accommodate unmanned flights by offering automated services that are developed as a human-controlled process to be executed by an air traffic controller [3] or add a dynamism only on a single drone action like landing zone [4] or focus on modelling the norms management as an offline system [8]. In this paper we suggest a sort of automated DAR process modelled as a novel runtime norms regulation framework for drones only which can be applied in variety of smart cities applications. Unlike existing works, we define norm regulation as the automated real-time modification of access permissions and restrictions. This dynamic regulation ensures that agents can operate effectively within changing environmental and contextual conditions. The goal of this framework is to allow to change the access rules of regions based on the defined mission of the drone, the nature of the organization owner of the drone and the currents state of the region (events). To give a prototype the suggested framework, we use agent modelling with lightweight, publish-subscribe mechanism and relational database.

3 Norms Management Frameworks

The cloud of norms is a dimension of a collaboration framework that we have proposed in [17] which implements a five-dimensions (Mutuality, Autonomy, Norms, Administration, Governance) social model that mimics humans' reasoning and interactions enabling the drones to switch between selfish and collaborative behaviors. The cloud of norms refers to a cloud-based infrastructure that serves as a centralized repository for regulatory norms, which can be modified or accessed on-demand. This repository stores the information related to the access norms of the regions. The repository could be solicitated or/and updated on demand. This system allows real-time updates and adjustments of norms based on changing conditions, user demands, or operational requirements.

3.1 Cloud of Norms

The main idea of the cloud of norms is to allow the access rules of each region to be relaxed or tightened dynamically based on the mission of the drone, the organization owning the drone and the situation of the environment. The rules associated with each region are saved in the cloud, creating a cloud of norms and structured in SQL. This cloud stores information related to each region, type of drone, the organization's owner and the access rules. Each region is defined by a unique name and type. Each region has a set of norms with specific tolerance levels and thresholds. The tolerance refers to the permissible degree of deviation or flexibility allowed within the norm before it is considered as violated. To determine the applicability of a norm to different types of owners (organizations owning drones), each norm has an associated owner and can be in either an "active" or "inactive" state. The state of a norm can only be managed by the agent responsible for the region to which that norm belongs (NormMaster agent). Each drone aiming to access a region must send a request to the region's agent. The NormMaster agent will first log the drone's request to maintain a history of all received requests. In this request, the drone must provide details about its characteristics and mission, such as its weight, payload, speed, altitude, flight duration, and timing. All this information is essential for the norm master agent to determine whether the drone's request should be approved or denied, based on the norm's repository. Figure 1 give a detailed view about the used relational schema.

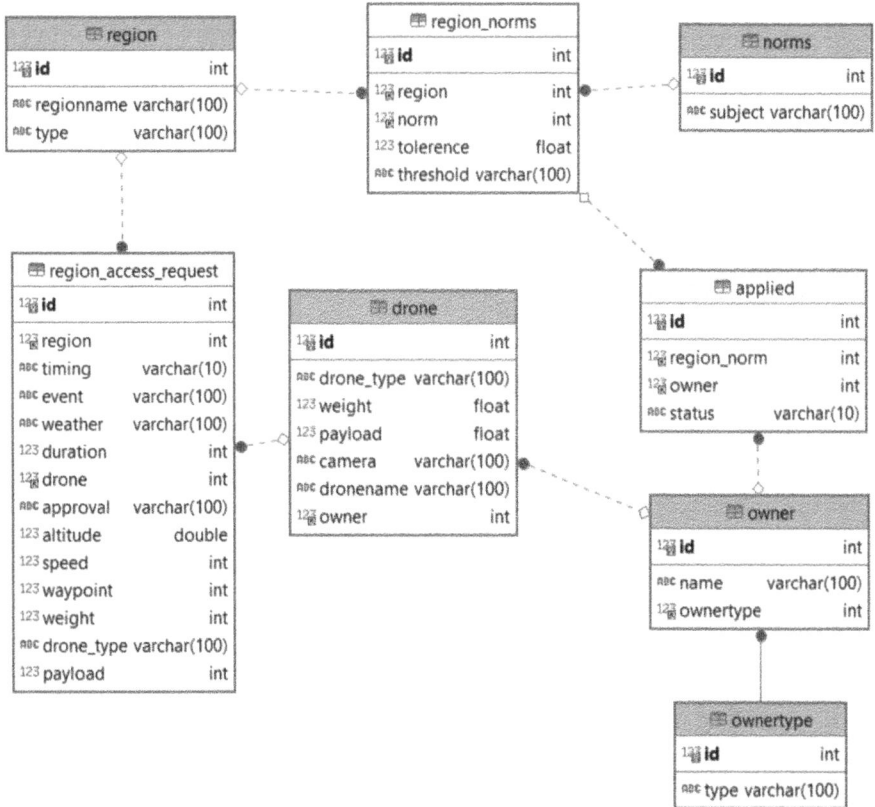

Fig. 1. Norm Master agent database schema.

3.2   Runtime Management

To simulate the concept of cloud of norms. We used Gama as agent platform. The two main type of agents are: Regions, Norms, NormsMaster and Drone. For a demonstration purpose four types of regions are defined (Farmland, Parks, Building and Residentials) where each region has a specific a set of rules that need to be applied in case of entering a region. We simulated 25 regions. Each region has a NormsMaster. The Fig. 3 shows the initial state of the simulation environment. A norm has a degree of tolerance. This degree of tolerance is defined based on the time, weather situation and context constraint as well as the type of the region, the properties of the drones and its mission. To solicit the required norms that need to be applied, the drone will send a norms specification request to the regions overlapping with his waypoint missions. In the realized simulation, the drones' behavioural norms were not modelled since the focus of the paper is not on the norm's synthesis but on norm regulation. The request includes the information about the properties of the drone (type, owner_type, battery level, camera…) and his waypoints mission overlapping with the region. The norm master agent (Region Agents) associated with the requested region will reply with a set of norms and their level of compliance which the drone should respect. The norm master agent identifies the level of compliance of each norm based on different dimension. Here, we consider drone properties and mission properties like time, space, weather, and context. This agent is also responsible for publishing the norms associated to the regions and identify its applicability to different type of owners. By requesting the norms, the drone agent subscribe to the norms of interest based on his mission. As a result, along his mission the drone agent will get notified in case of the change of the norm compliance levels. The tolerance level could be changed based on the request update trigged by the norm agent. This agent (NormAgent) fellow the state of the environment, in case of a critical event that require a relax or impose stricter access rules, this agent will send a request to the norm master to update the norm accordingly. The update concerns the change of the tolerance level which will be increased in case the rules need to be relaxed and will be decreased in case the rules need to be more tightened. For example, during emergency events the degree of tolerance of the access of the region where the event occurs will increase for emergency services allowing a flexible legal access only to dedicated drones. While during other events (like event where a crowd of people are expected: sport events) this tolerance may be reduced to increase safety. As the drone receive the sets of norms associated to the region to access and to his information, it can evaluate if his mission complies with the norms based on the norm threshold and tolerance. A drone will be able to start his mission only if it complies with all the norms requirements in all the waypoints of his mission. The Fig. 2 shows a detailed view of the communication between the agents.

This approach aims to add additional flexibility, when needed, to the mission of the drone based on their characteristics, their original organization, the nature of its mission and the current state of the environment. While it imposes more strict norms when more safety level is required.

For traceability purpose, the drone agent records all the received requests of access for his region following the schema shown in Fig. 1. After crossing the required region, the drone agent must send a mission report to the norm master agent. This report defines

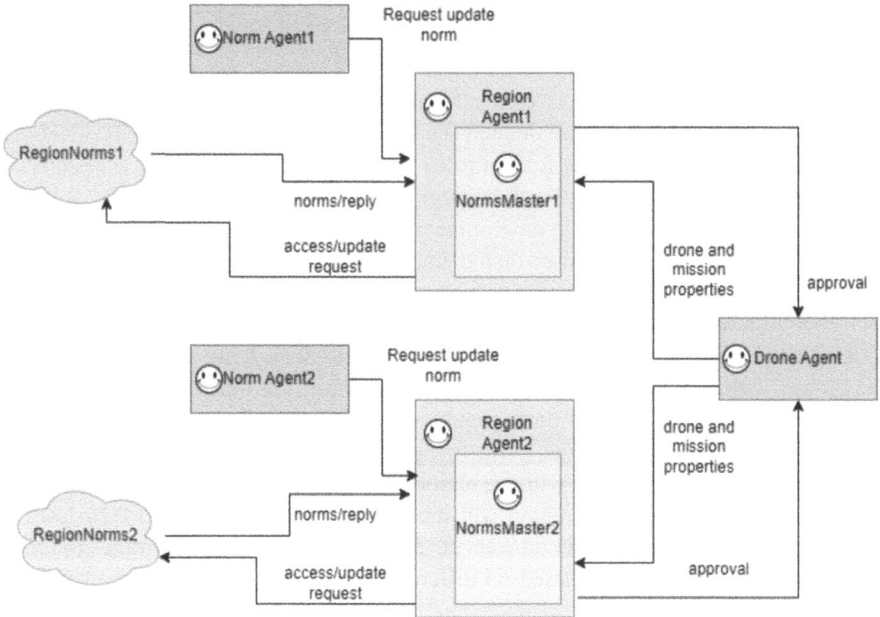

Fig. 2. Communication between agents.

to which level the drone complied with the specified norms of the region it gains access to. The mission report can contribute to identifying the reputation of the drone for future requests.

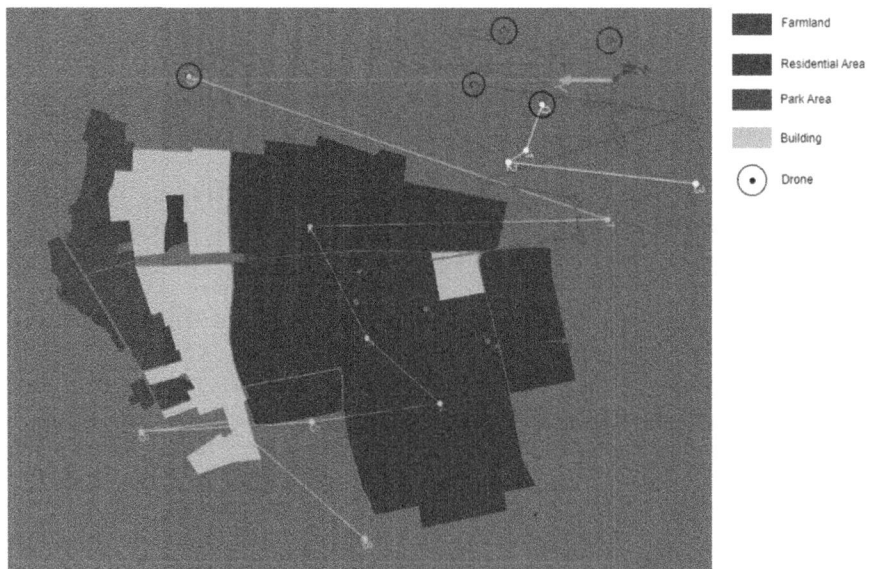

Fig. 3. Simulation Environment

3.3   Simulations Results

To evaluate the performance of the suggested norm regulation framework, 30 simulations were executed. Five drones and 25 regions were used in these simulations. Four regions of type "building", Five of type "park", 11 of type "farmland" and five of type "residence". The properties and the type of drones are detailed in the table below:

Table 1. Table of simulated drones

Drone	Organization	Type	Payload	Weight	Camera
Drone1	Police	Quadcopter	2.7 kg	6 kg	FPV (First-person view)
Drone2	Commercial Delivery	Quadcopter	10 kg	2.5 kg	FPV
Drone3	Traffic center	Quadcopter	0.8 kg	1.5 kg	PTZ(Pan-Tilt-Zoom)
Drone4	Commercial Delivery	Fixed Wing	4 kg	2 kg	NC
Drone5	Firefighter	Quadcopter	3 kg	2 kg	Thermal

For the evaluation, we will focus on two type of regions which are "Residence" and "Park". To demonstrate that our method provides a better balance granting and restricting access in response to different scenarios, we report the rigidity and flexibility ratio.

The flexibility is represented by the ability to adapt access as needed based on the change. The flexibility ratio is calculated using the Eq. (1) using the number of accesses granted (access granted to the request of the drone before starting the mission), the number of restored access events (number of accesses first non-granted but granted after events) and the number of totals of access events (Eq. (2)). More restored access indicates that the system can accommodate changes, allowing access when norms are more relaxed open an event.

The rigidity is represented by the ability to enforce restrictions. The rigidity ratio is calculated using the Eq. (3) using the number of accesses denied (access denied open the request of the drone before starting the mission), the number of access revocations (number of accesses first granted but revoked after events). A high number of revocations demonstrate that the system effectively enforces more restrictions open an event.

$$Flexibility\ Ratio = \frac{Number\ of\ Restored\ Access + Number\ of\ Granted\ Access}{Total\ Access\ Events} \quad (1)$$

$$Total\ Access\ Events = Access\ Granted + Access\ Denied + Restored\ Access \\ + Access\ Revocation \quad (2)$$

$$Rigidity\ Ratio = \frac{Number\ of\ Access\ Denied + Access\ Revocation}{Total\ Access\ Events} \quad (3)$$

As shown in Fig. 4, which summarizes the flexibility and rigidity ratio by organization, drones from emergency-related organizations (Police, Traffic, and Firefighter) experience lower rigidity and higher flexibility ratios, allowing them more adaptable access in restricted areas. In contrast, Commercial Delivery drones face higher rigidity and lower flexibility, reflecting stricter, less adaptable regulations in sensitive regions.

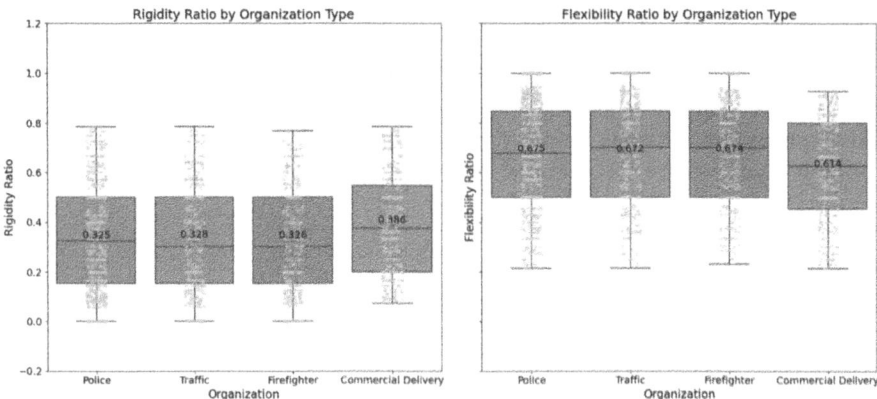

Fig. 4. Simulation results: (left: Rigidity Ratio by Organization type, right: Flexibility Ratio by Organization type)

4 Discussion

The suggest runtime norms regulation frameworks make the regulation of the norms or access rules to be managed dynamically which can unlock additional opportunities for drone application in smart cities and add more flexibility to legislation rules. One of the limitations of the proposed framework is that the drone will completely cancel its mission if one of the requested waypoints overlaps with a region which the drone does not comply with its norms. To solve this issue a possible option will be to revise the waypoint mission, like for example reducing the speed or changing the routing of the mission following the regions with more relaxed norms. This is applicable to some application contexts like for example delivery, while it is not applicable to other applications like person/car tracking.

In real smart city applications, the norm regulation can arise many challenges since the national aviation regulations establish strict, predefined rules that dictate drone operations based on static conditions like geographical zones, airspace classifications, and pre-authorized flight plans. For any change or update of the rules, an explicit regulatory approval should be obtained in real time which is not currently supported in many regulatory frameworks. Sometime, new rules are tested in a controlled environment to help the regulators to evaluate the impact of new rules on safety, privacy, and compliance before full-scale implementation. The proposed dynamic framework will need to include automated communication with regulatory bodies and air traffic control to update access permissions based on current conditions which should define permissible dynamic adjustments for specific scenarios. Such system has additional liability challenges in case of safety issues, where liability protocols need to distribute the responsibilities between different entities (drone operators, regulatory authorities, rule management systems).Also, to solve conflicts between norms, determine priorities and evaluate the rule, a real-time evaluation of rules based on the specific context using a dynamic risk assessment (drone could dynamically assess the risk of flying in a given area using define rules) or using a data-driven decision-making will be an important module.

In addition, in the current version of the proposed framework, the threshold was defined and fixed for each norm. As further improvement, the threshold could be learned from the repeated scenarios. The norms master agent will be able to identify the best level of threshold for each norm based on the required level of safety and the risk report which helps to update the threshold level from the previous experience. A simple neural network can be used to update the best threshold based on the risk report. However, we believe this approach can create additional legislative challenges since most of the current drone's legislations have fixed thresholds.

5 Conclusion

The use of drones in smart cities' applications opens a variety of valuable opportunities. At the same time, the access rules and regulations create a challenge in dynamic and complex environments. Although the proposed framework adds challenges to legislation and regional access rules. We think that the proposed framework opens a wide interesting application of drones in smart cities. The proposed framework will be a part of multi-dimensional collaboration architecture for drone collaboration proposed in previous work.

References

1. Dŭbravová, H., Bureš, V., Velfl, L.: Review of the application of drones for smart cities. IET Smart Cities 1–21 (2024). https://doi.org/10.1049/smc2.12093
2. Khan, N.A., Jhanjhi, N.Z., Brohi, S.N., Nayyar, A.: Emerging use of UAV's: secure communication protocol issues and challenges. In: Al-Turjman, F. (edn.) Drones in Smart-Cities, pp. 37–55. Elsevier (2020). https://doi.org/10.1016/B978-0-12-819972-5.00003-3
3. Singh, J., Adwani, N., Kandath, H., Krishna, K.M.: Real-time heuristic framework for safe landing of UAVs in dynamic scenarios (2022). http://arxiv.org/abs/2209.04805
4. Teutsch, J., Petersen, C.: Dynamic airspace re-configuration for manned and unmanned operations in shared airspace. In: Integrated Communications, Navigation and Surveillance Conference, ICNS (2024). https://doi.org/10.1109/ICNS60906.2024.10550738
5. Bulling, N., Dastani, M., Knobbout, M.: Monitoring norm violations in multi-agent systems. In: 12th International Conference on Autonomous Agents and Multiagent Systems 2013, AAMAS 2013, vol. 1, pp. 491–498 (2013)
6. Vasconcelos, W.W., García-Camino, A., Gaertner, D., Rodríguez-Aguilar, J.A., Noriega, P.: Distributed norm management for multi-agent systems. Expert Syst. Appl. **39**(5), 5990–5999 (2012). https://doi.org/10.1016/j.eswa.2011.11.108
7. Criado, N., Argente, E., Botti, V.: Open issues for normative multi-agent systems. AI Commun. **24**(3), 233–264 (2011). https://doi.org/10.3233/AIC-2011-0502
8. Mahmoud, M.A., Ahmad, M.S., Mohd Yusoff, M.Z., Mustapha, A.: A review of norms and normative multiagent systems. Sci. World J. **2014** (2014). https://doi.org/10.1155/2014/684587
9. Villatoro, D.: Self-organization in decentralized agent societies through social norms. In: Adaptive Agents and Multi-Agent Systems (2011)
10. Riad, M., Golpayegani, F.: Run-time norms synthesis in multi-objective multi-agent systems, pp. 1–15 (2021). http://arxiv.org/abs/2105.00124

11. Shams, Z., de Vos, M., Padget, J., Vasconcelos, W.W.: Practical reasoning with norms for autonomous software agents. Eng. Appl. Artif. Intell. **65**, 388–399 (2017). https://doi.org/10.1016/j.engappai.2017.07.021
12. Criado, N.: Using norms to control open multi-agent systems. AI Commun. **26**(3), 317–318 (2013). https://doi.org/10.3233/AIC-130560
13. Dell'Anna, D., Dastani, M., Dalpiaz, F.: Runtime revision of sanctions in normative multi-agent systems **34**(2) (2020). https://doi.org/10.1007/s10458-020-09465-8
14. Thomson, A.M., Perry, J.L.: Collaboration processes: inside the black box. Public Adm. Rev. **66**, 20–32 (2006)
15. Jin, D., Kannengießer, N., Sturm, B., Sunyaev, A.: Tackling challenges of robustness measures for agent collaboration in open multi-agent systems. In: Proceedings of the 55th Hawaii International Conference on System Sciences (2022). https://doi.org/10.24251/hicss.2022.911
16. Morales, J., López-Sánchez, M., Rodriguez-Aguilar, J.A., Vasconcelos, W., Wooldridge, M.: Online automated synthesis of compact normative systems. ACM Trans. Auton. Adapt. Syst. **10**(1) (2015). https://doi.org/10.1145/2720024
17. Gharrad, H., Jabeur, N., Yasar, A.U.-H., Al Abri, K.A.S., El-Hansali, Y., Kochan, B.: Enabling drones collaboration in ITS applications using a BDI architecture based on a 5-dimensional social model. In: Proceedings of the Future Technologies Conference (FTC) 2020, vol. 1, pp. 48–63. Springer (2021)

Autonomous Vehicles

A Data-Driven Integrated Framework for Virtual Testing of Autonomous Vehicles in Mixed Traffic Scenarios

Brunella Caroleo$^{(\boxtimes)}$ ⓘ, Javad Sadeghi ⓘ, Cristiana Botta ⓘ, Shadi Nikneshan ⓘ, and Maurizio Arnone ⓘ

Fondazione LINKS, Via P.C. Boggio 61, 10138 Turin, Italy
{brunella.caroleo,javad.sadeghi,cristiana.botta,shadi.nikneshan,
maurizio.arnone}@linksfoundation.com

Abstract. The increasing presence of autonomous vehicles (AVs) in urban environments introduces both opportunities and challenges, particularly regarding their interactions with traditional vehicles and other road users. This paper presents a comprehensive framework designed to assess the integration of AVs in mixed traffic scenarios. The framework is built upon real-world data collected from AV trials conducted in Turin, Italy. By leveraging traffic microsimulation along with machine learning techniques, the study proposes a framework aimed at assessing ex-ante the impacts on traffic of AVs introduction, thus constituting a relevant tool of virtual testing of CCAM (Cooperative, Connected, and Automated Mobility) trials before the physical introduction of autonomous vehicles on public roads. The integration of High-Performance Computing (HPC) ensures the efficiency of these simulations, enabling real-time analysis and testing. The proposed framework not only provides decision-makers with a tool for virtual testing of AV deployment, but also offers actionable insights into traffic management strategies. The study's findings contribute to a deeper understanding of the role AVs can play in future urban mobility systems, particularly as cities prepare for the broader adoption of CCAM technologies.

Keywords: Cooperative Connected and Automated Mobility (CCAM) ·
Autonomous Vehicles (AV) · Traffic Management · Traffic simulation · Virtual
Testing · Urban Transportation · Machine Learning

1 Introduction

Urban mobility is experiencing an era of transformation with the rise of Autonomous Vehicles (AVs) and Cooperative, Connected, and Automated Mobility (CCAM). While early research focused on private AVs, recent studies have shifted toward public and shared autonomous transportation, particularly autonomous shuttles using minibus technology. These shuttles are expected to become an essential element of future urban mobility, integrated within public transport systems.

© ICST Institute for Computer Sciences, Social Informatics and Telecommunications Engineering 2025
Published by Springer Nature Switzerland AG 2025. All Rights Reserved
A. Kocian et al. (Eds.): INTSYS 2024, LNICST 608, pp. 293–310, 2025.
https://doi.org/10.1007/978-3-031-86370-7_18

Current AV experiences, especially with shuttles, are often limited to controlled environments. The main challenge is to integrate these shuttles into mixed traffic, where they interact with pedestrians, cyclists, and traditional human-driven vehicles. Limited experiences with autonomous shuttles in mixed traffic conditions can be exemplified by initiatives such as the demonstrations within the European project SHOW (SHared automation Operating models for Worldwide adoption) [1], funded under the H2020 program. Transitioning from human-driven to autonomous vehicles requires careful planning to ensure safety, efficiency, and public acceptance. During this shuft, where autonomous trials are often geographically constrained (e.g. authorized routes), it is vital to evaluate their impact on urban traffic. However, the risk and feasibility analyses typically conducted by vehicle providers only partially address this need.

The city of Turin (Italy) serves as a vibrant environment for autonomous mobility studies, boasting a local CCAM ecosystem that has actively evolved in recent years. This ecosystem is a result of collaborative efforts, drawing on research funding from prominent initiatives such as the European SHOW project [1], the European IN2CCAM project [2], and the national ToMove project [3]. The city acts as a living lab, yielding insights into AV behaviour across various urban settings.

This work assumes a dual objective. Firstly, to provide a comprehensive framework that leverages actual data from urban infrastructure and autonomous vehicle trials, realistically simulating the interactions of these vehicles with other road users and infrastructure. Secondly, to provide decision-makers with a tool for virtual testing of AV trials before their physical deployment, thus preventing errors that may jeopardize urban mobility safety and assessing the impact of introducing AVs in specific areas before initiating live trials.

2 Related Works

The exploration of Autonomous Vehicles (AVs) and their integration into urban mobility is a multifaceted endeavour that has captivated the attention of researchers, engineers, and urban planners worldwide. Considerable research has been dedicated to understanding the implications of AVs in urban environments. Early studies primarily focused on the technological aspects, such as sensor fusion, perception algorithms, and decision-making processes of autonomous systems [4]. As AV technology matured, attention shifted towards assessing the impact of these vehicles on traffic flow, congestion, and overall urban mobility [5–7].

The specific domain of autonomous shuttle services, especially in public transportation, has garnered interest in recent years. Initiatives such as the European SHOW project [1] have explored the integration of autonomous shuttles into public transport systems [8–10], emphasizing their role in enhancing last-mile connectivity [11].

Traffic simulation has been used in numerous simulation research scenarios of AVs, highlighting its versatility and wide-ranging applications: it provides a helpful tool to answer complex research questions, to evaluate or test traffic management strategies and their impacts [12]. Simulation offers a safe and cost-effective method of testing and validating autonomous algorithms and control systems before real-world deployment. These simulations provide a crucial bridge between theory and practice, allowing researchers to refine AVs technologies in controlled virtual environments. Traffic simulators repli-cate situations and evaluate the consequences of different strategies for using AVs. In the majority of microscopic simulation research, AVs have been distinguished from human-driven vehicles based on their driving patterns, highlighting the pivotal role of driving behaviour in modelling AVs [13]. Understanding the AV driving behaviour is essential for creating realistic and effective simulations that mirror real-world conditions. Using microsimulation, some researchers studied the impact of different AVs penetration on traffic parameters [14] and on urban traffic flow and road capacity [7], highlighting potential risk that if AVs increase overall car use, they could strain traffic management. Additionally, microsimulation has emerged as a pivotal tool for understanding the com-plex interactions between AVs and other road users in realistic traffic scenarios. Existing works delve into the development of microsimulation environments for AVs, often uti-lizing platforms such as SUMO (Simulation of Urban MObility) [15]. The assessment of impacts related to autonomous services, safety, and overall traffic dynamics becomes feasible through this simulation, guiding the identification of optimal strategies in various contexts.

The safety of AVs and their interactions with pedestrians and traditional vehicles have been extensively investigated. Studies have utilized surrogate safety measures like Time to Collision (TTC) and Post Encroachment Time (PET) to evaluate and compare the safety of AV-pedestrian interactions with traditional vehicle-pedestrian interactions [16, 17].

Research efforts have also been made to integrate different simulation platforms to create comprehensive testing environments for AVs. The co-simulation of CARLA [18] (for the ego-AV simulation) and SUMO (for surrounding traffic microsimulation) has gained attention, allowing for more realistic testing scenarios [19, 20].

In summary, the landscape of AV research is vast and continually evolving, but research contributions in the field of virtual testing for autonomous vehicles have been sectoral, and an overall view is lacking. There are some scientific contributions that try to give an overview by cross-referencing the contributions that may come from different domains [21], but there is a lack of real data from connected/autonomous vehicles, and thus no concrete results from such integrated frameworks. In this paper, the authors propose to cover this gap by providing a comprehensive framework and testing it on real data collected in the field during autonomous driving experiments in Turin in recent years.

3 The Case Study

The City of Turin (Italy) serves as a dynamic setting for this study, with a robust CCAM ecosystem encompassing local institutions, research centres, the Traffic Control Center, and the public transport operator. In late 2022, as part of the H2020 SHOW project [1], two autonomous shuttles were tested in mixed traffic in Turin, making it the only Italian site among 20 European cities involved. These trials aim to innovate urban mobility and gather valuable data on autonomous vehicle behaviour in real-world traffic, guiding future autonomous experiments in the city [2, 3].

The Turin pilot was designed to offer a flexible, on-demand transport service with two SAE level 4 autonomous shuttles (provided by Navya [22]), which circulated on an authorized 5 km route near the City of Health and Science of Turin. The study's data analysed in this paper was collected during the pre-demonstration phase (August–October 2022), focusing on technical validation before the shuttles began carrying passengers. Navya's electric shuttle, capable of holding 15 passengers, uses LIDAR and localization technologies to navigate autonomously at speeds up to 18 km/h. To ensure safety, it operates in environments where traffic does not exceed 50 km/h. The shuttle slows or stops when an obstacle enters its "priority zone," typically positioned 1 m ahead of a checkpoint, and resumes only when the path clears.

During the test period, some videos were recorded across different days to observe interactions between pedestrians and autonomous shuttles at an unsignalized crosswalk with moderate traffic. This setup, free of traffic signal constraints (Fig. 1), allowed the study of natural interactions between road users, including pedestrians, conventional vehicles, buses, and the autonomous shuttle.

Fig. 1. Screenshot of the area chosen for video recording during the trial.

4   Methodology

The proposed framework is designed for adaptable use across various urban settings, adjusting to available data and traffic conditions, making it applicable beyond the specific case of Turin.

It consists of three main phases: data gathering, data analysis and modeling, and traffic microsimulation (Fig. 2). This modular structure allows each phase to function independently or integrate with others, providing flexibility across diverse urban contexts. In the Data Gathering phase, the framework adapts to a wide range of data sources, including AV sensors and infrastructure inputs. The Data Analysis and Modeling phase processes and validates this information, enabling machine learning applications to extract insights into AV behavior and interactions. The Traffic Microsimulation phase, using customizable models, simulates urban scenarios and can be implemented on various platforms, such as SUMO, tailored to project needs.

In the case-specific implementation for Turin case study, the framework incorporated local AV trial data, including sensor and traffic signal information, to create realistic microsimulations. This tailored approach accommodates Turin's unique urban characteristics, such as complex road networks and diverse traffic patterns.

By customizing each phase to align with specific data and technical resources, the framework offers a robust tool for assessing AV deployment impacts, applicable not only to Turin but also to other cities with similar data availability and mobility needs.

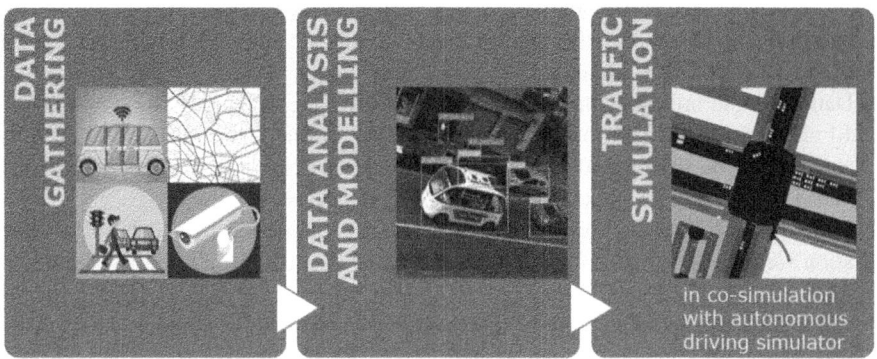

Fig. 2. The proposed framework.

4.1 Data Gathering

The foundation of the proposed framework lies in the extensive and detailed data collection process. Typically, the data sources of CCAM experimentations are:

1. Data from the autonomous vehicle itself, e.g. real-time location data, data from the IMU (Inertial Measurement Unit), current speed and acceleration, data of vehicle's steering and braking systems.
2. Data from the infrastructure, e.g. real-time traffic light phases (i.e. time to green, time to red).
3. Road network data, e.g. road network geometry, traffic demand, traffic signals, public transport routes and stops.
4. Sometimes, external camera captures (e.g. on the road) are available, and this data could be used to monitor behaviours of road users (i.e. traditional vehicles, autonomous vehicles and VRUs such as pedestrians and bikers) at critical road segments (e.g. pedestrian crossings). Keep in mind that vehicle providers often do not make available the videos taken by the cameras in the vehicle, so such information on interactions is not available unless external cameras filming the scenes are available.

In Turin case study presented in this paper the available data was the following:

1. Data from the autonomous vehicle itself: the Italian Smart Road Decree (regulating experimentations involving autonomous vehicles in Italy) asks at least for the following categories of data for autonomous experimentations taking place in Italy: date,

time, position in WGS84 coordinates; current operation mode (autonomous or manual); instant speed; instant acceleration; distance travelled since the beginning of the experimentation; activation of controls for the lateral dynamics of the vehicle; activation of controls for the longitudinal dynamics of the vehicle; number of revolutions per minute of the engine; gear ratio engaged, or other equivalent indicator; current value of yaw angle, roll and pitch; use of lighting and visual and acoustic signalling devices; acquired data of the sensors that are part of the system being tested; any V2V and V2I messages received and transmitted.

For each of the abovementioned category, data of the two autonomous shuttles has been collected for a period of three months (August–October 2022) for each second of the experimentation (data collected at a frequency of 1Hz).

2. Data from the infrastructure: all the traffic lights of the experimentation area (about 14 groups of traffic lights) were connected to the Traffic Control Centre of the City, and sent to the shuttle real-time traffic light phases (i.e. time to green, time to red) via SPATEM (Signal Phase And Timing Extended Message).

3. Road network data: the Municipality of Turin, in collaboration with the Traffic Operation Centre, put at disposal for the authorized zone: the road network geometry (crossed with Open Street Map), the traffic demand, information about traffic signals, and - thanks to the open data of the local Public Transport Operator – also public transport routes and stops were available via GTFS format.

4. An external camera has been installed at an unsignalized crosswalk and has recorded, in different days, about 10 h of interactions among different road users in the scene: traditional vehicles, autonomous vehicles, bikers and pedestrians, the last ones being free to cross that intersection without any traffic light regulation. The traffic scene was recorded by alternating two Garmin VIRB ™ Action Cams, with a resolution of 1080p HD and 30 frame/s. They were placed on the top of a carbon fibres telescopic pole at 10.80 m to the ground. The cameras were placed outside the roadway in a position that was difficult for drivers to detect.

4.2 Data Analysis and Modelling

Once data is collected in the previous step, the Data analysis and modelling phase includes the following activities:

- Data validation, pre-processing and exploration: this can be done by using statistical and machine learning techniques depending on the objectives of the data exploration. Included in this phase, if needed, compliance with legislative requirements is checked.
- Data visualization, to ease the interpretation of AVs data. This can be done -according to the objectives of the analysis- in real time (e.g. visualizing data of the autonomous vehicle collected via an API connection) or offline.
- Computation of distributions of parameters for next steps of analysis (e.g. speed profile for microsimulation setting and validation by vehicle type).
- If videos are available (source number 4 of the data in Sect. 4.1), data enrichment for a better comprehension of AVs behaviour with respect to the surrounding environment. In fact, in case of AVs circulating in mixed traffic and not reserved in dedicated lanes, it would be relevant to study AV behaviour with respect to other road users. This can be pursued by means of detection and tracking algorithms aimed to study the behaviours

of AVs and other road users in real traffic, and jointly with safety measures analysis of these interactions.

In Turin case study presented in this paper, validation of high-frequency monitoring data from AV sensors has been undertaken, ensuring the reliability of the dataset. Anomaly detection algorithms are implemented to uncover unexpected events, adding a layer of robustness to the dataset. The application of machine learning extends to unravelling hidden relationships among various features, providing valuable insights into the intricate dynamics of AV operations. Furthermore, compliance with legislative requirements has been systematically checked to ensure adherence to safety and operational standards.

A web dashboard in MS PowerBI has been created to visualize AV data, offering a user-friendly, interactive interface for both real-time (via API) and offline analysis (using.csv files from the vehicle provider). This setup allows analysts to check and interpret collected data. In this framework, data analysis (in Python) and data visualization/exploration (in PowerBI) serve distinct roles. Data analysis is used independently in Python to preprocess, validate, and analyze AV data, detecting anomalies and behavior patterns, such as outliers, speed changes, and potential traffic conflicts. The PowerBI dashboard, meanwhile, visualizes key metrics and trends, enabling stakeholders to explore data insights. Although data analysis results are not integrated in real-time, they are periodically uploaded to PowerBI as structured datasets (e.g., CSVs) for easy viewing. This setup ensures PowerBI is an accessible tool for insights derived from machine learning models, adaptable to both live and historical data analysis.

Given the absence of dedicated lanes for AVs in the case study area, understanding their behaviour in interaction with other road users is imperative. The methodology employs data enrichment by integrating AV sensors' data with information from cameras along the route. Due to the camera wide angle, the raw videos were affected by distortion error. The correction was performed according to the specific distortion matrix of the camera. Only the video sections including an interaction between pedestrian and autonomous/traditional vehicles were considered for further analysis. Video analysis, coupled with detection and tracking algorithms, offers a nuanced understanding of AV behaviour concerning the surrounding environment. Videos were collected across different days, and road users in the scene (i.e., pedestrians and vehicles) have been detected and tracked (Fig. 3). The object detection was performed using a customized YOLOv7 model [23] integrated with SORT algorithm [24]. This integration assigns each detected object a unique identifier that remains consistent across all frames, enabling seamless tracking of both pedestrians and autonomous/traditional vehicles in the video sequences.

Then, an algorithm automatically derived conflict measures to assess safety in conflicts, based on their spatial-temporal trajectories. The resulting distributions were compared through Kolmogorov-Smirnov (K-S) test for both traditional and autonomous vehicles. Notably, a specific emphasis is placed on studying surrogate safety measures (TTC-Time to Collision, PET-Post Encroachment Time) in AV-pedestrian interactions versus traditional vehicle-pedestrian interactions, revealing insights into the safety aspects of AV systems. Data distributions were modelled to understand differences regarding pedestrians' behaviours in front of the two vehicle types. The computation of distributions

Fig. 3. Example of the detection and tracking algorithm applied to the video.

of parameters for microsimulation setting and validation by vehicle type, particularly focusing on speed profiles, contributes to a deeper comprehension of road users' patterns.

4.3 Traffic Microsimulation

After data collection and analysis, the framework includes a traffic microsimulation phase, aimed to assess to what extent traffic in a zone selected for AV testing is impacted by the introduction of autonomous vehicles on public roads. Traffic microsimulation, rather than macro or meso-simulation, is needed to simulate individual vehicle movements and interactions. Commonly used microscopic simulators include VISSIM, AIMSUN, and SUMO, which can be customized for specific scenarios to assess various AV deployment strategies. This virtual testing environment enhances efficiency by reducing the need for extensive road tests, providing quantitative insights into AVs' traffic impacts. While traffic microsimulation can assess AV effects on traffic, it lacks the ability to model AV-specific features, like sensor positions. To address this, integrating traffic simulators with autonomous driving simulators like CARLA (Car Learning to Act) [22] through co-simulation creates a more complete testing environment, aiding in AV development, testing, and validation. This combined approach helps AVs handle complex real traffic scenarios safely and reliably, while also providing realistic traffic edge scenarios based on observed data. Such simulations accelerate AV technology's readiness for deployment on public roads.

In the Turin case study the open-source simulator SUMO (Simulation of Urban Mobility) [15] was selected for traffic microsimulation, partly due to its active user and developer community, which supports continuous advancements and knowledge sharing. Using TraCI (Traffic Control Interface) with SUMO allowed real-time control and customization of traffic scenarios, bridging Python with SUMO for enhanced flexibility. This approach enables a wide range of applications, from testing traffic management strategies to developing autonomous vehicle algorithms, making SUMO particularly effective compared to other simulators.

To integrate traditional and autonomous vehicles in simulation, the key differences lie in decision-making and sensory inputs. While humans rely on visual cues, which can be subjective, AVs use sensors like LiDAR, radar, and cameras to gather objective data and respond instantaneously. These differences influence AV simulation parameters, such as shorter reaction times and reduced minimum gaps, reflecting the faster response capabilities of AVs compared to human drivers. This distinction allows more accurate modeling of AV behaviors in mixed traffic environments.

For traffic simulation of the autonomous vehicles involved in Turin case study, the network of the testing area has been imported from Open Street Map by OSM Web Wizard, and then some adjustments have been performed to be in accordance with the real road network (e.g. the number of lanes, traffic signal cycles, speed limits). The autonomous shuttle, with its own characteristics (e.g. length, speed profile, etc.), has been modelled in SUMO, thanks to the analysis performed in the previous step (Data analysis and modelling) as well as SUMO's customizability. In order to test different traffic scenarios, traffic and pedestrian flows, public transport routes and stops have been added to the simulation environment. Additionally, different traffic management and control strategies have been tested to assess their impacts. In implementing traffic scenarios in SUMO, after creating the simulation network and traffic flows, the TraCI was used to define scenarios and their associated logic. TraCI continuously monitors simulation to execute these logics, specifying when an intervention starts, what will happen during interventions, where it is located within the network, and when it will end. These logics control characteristics of network elements, such as vehicle permissions on specific lanes or streets, intersection control management, and vehicle behaviours and routes. This simulation framework prepared a powerful environment to define complex and dynamic scenarios by TraCI. This enables detailed analysis and testing of various scenarios and analysis without extensive real-world testing, which can be crucial for further development and optimization of autonomous vehicles' technology.

High-Performance Computing (HPC) infrastructure was used to meet the computational demands of real-time analytics and high-traffic networks. HPC allows rapid processing of large simulations, completing in minutes what might take hours or days on standard computers.

The framework also implemented a SUMO-CARLA co-simulation to integrate realistic traffic flows into autonomous driving simulations. Running on HPC machines, this co-simulation combines SUMO's urban traffic modeling with CARLA's detailed AV simulations, creating a comprehensive platform for AV research. SUMO manages traffic flow, transforming background vehicles for CARLA, while CARLA's AVs interact with traffic to complete driving tasks. By distributing tasks between CARLA and SUMO, the framework evaluates AV algorithms and protocols on both individual and traffic levels. This integration enables realistic testing of AV control, perception, and localization in a simulated environment before actual road trials. It enhances AV safety and reduces development costs by completing most validations within a controlled virtual space.

The resulting integrated framework has several purposes. Firstly, it enables virtual testing of AV deployment in real traffic conditions, fostering safe and controlled experiments. The development process becomes cost-effective, and the deployment of AV demonstrations is accelerated. Furthermore, the integration enhances scalability and transferability, ensuring that insights gained from the simulation environment can be effectively applied to diverse urban contexts. In conclusion, the employed methodology reflects a holistic and meticulous approach, incorporating cutting-edge technologies and methodologies to address the challenges posed by the integration of CCAM technologies into urban mobility scenarios.

5 Results

The implementation of the proposed framework has yielded insightful results across various dimensions, ranging from the validation of collected data to the impacts of AV circulation on urban traffic. This section delves into the key outcomes derived from each phase of the methodology, shedding light on the efficacy and relevance of the researchers' approach.

The first result, coming from the data gathering phase, is the data itself: the extensive data collection process spanning three months has proven to be a valuable asset for the proposed work. The dataset, encompassing diverse parameters related to AV operations and the urban road network, offers a comprehensive snapshot of real-world scenarios. Ongoing projects (IN2CCAM [2], ToMove [3]) are poised to contribute additional CCAM data from real experimentations, ensuring a continuous and evolving dataset for future research endeavours. This wealth of data serves as a foundation for subsequent phases of the methodology, enhancing the robustness and applicability of the framework.

As regards the data analysis and modelling phase, a relevant result comes from the data visualization. The deployment of a web dashboard for data visualization (Fig. 4) enhances the interpretability of AV data, fostering a user-friendly interface for stakeholders and researchers. The primary purpose of the PowerBI web dashboard is to facilitate comprehensive data analysis and visualization, enhancing understanding and decision-making related to shuttle operations. Additionally, the dashboard provides real-time data monitoring capabilities with flexible filtering options such as date, operating zone, and shuttle identification. It has been designed with four key pages to provide insights into vehicle performance, sensor data, signaling devices, and overall fleet operations:

(1) Vehicle Dynamics: this section displays crucial metrics such as speed, steering rate and angle, bearing, and battery level. These parameters are analysed over time to understand the shuttle's dynamic behaviour. Additionally, the percentage of time spent in various operational modes is provided, offering insights into how often the vehicle operates in autonomous mode.
(2) Sensors: on this page, various sensor readings are visualized, including GNSS correction status, door status, vehicle mode, and battery status. Temperature data (engine, indoor, outdoor) is also displayed. This page helps in monitoring and assessing the shuttle's operational conditions and overall performance.
(3) Lighting, Visual, and Acoustic Signalling Devices: this section focuses on the shuttle's signalling systems, such as the state of blinkers, brake lights, and reverse lights.

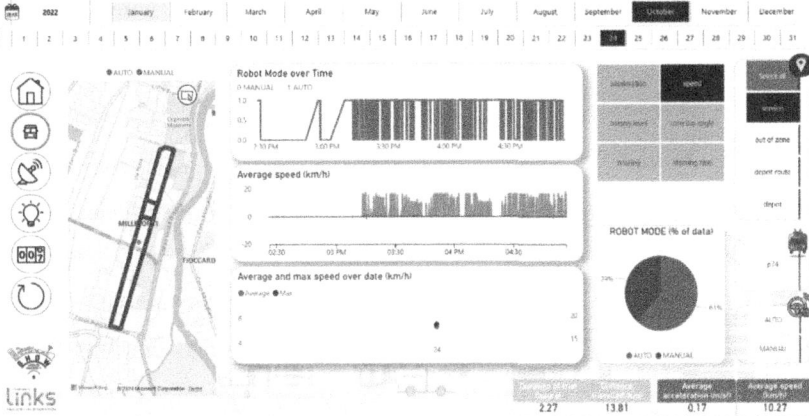

Fig. 4. Visualization and analysis of AVs data in PowerBI.

The analysis here aims to ensure that these critical safety components are functioning correctly, providing a statistical representation of their operation.

(4) Fleet Overview: designed for high-level insights, this page aggregates data across all shuttles in the fleet, showing key metrics like travel distance and duration for both manual and autonomous modes. It allows for comparisons across different shuttle IDs and operational modes, helping stakeholders to evaluate performance and compliance with legislative requirements.

Furthermore, the application of machine learning techniques in the analysis and modelling phase has yielded promising results, with anomaly detection activities mainly focused on detecting unusual behaviours in the data collected from autonomous vehicles' sensors. The main emphasis was placed on identifying abrupt speed changes (both acceleration and deceleration), which can indicate anomalies in vehicle operation. These anomalies are critical for ensuring the safety and efficiency of AVs in urban traffic. The primary method used for detecting these anomalies is the Median Absolute Deviation (MAD), a robust statistical technique that measures variability while resisting the influence of outliers. By applying MAD to the sensors' data, the framework successfully identifies significant deviations in speed that are marked as potential anomalies. This detected anomaly could point to an unexpected event, such as a vehicle malfunction or an external obstacle. The flexibility of the MAD method allows the threshold for anomaly detection to be adjusted, enabling both major and minor anomalies to be identified. This ensures that users can tailor the system to specific requirements, improving the detection of critical safety concerns or operational irregularities.

Additionally, camera data has been integrated into the analysis to further validate and understand such anomalies. Object detection and tracking methods, using YOLOv7 [23], have been employed to identify and track vehicles, pedestrians, and shuttles within the environment. These camera-based observations, when synchronized with the sensors' data, help explain the causes of detected anomalies, such as the presence of other vehicles or objects influencing the shuttle's behaviour. For example, a sudden deviation at a certain timestamp has been detected in the autonomous vehicle sensors' dataset, highlighting a significant drop in speed. This detected anomaly coming from the sensors' data has been combined with the corresponding video available from the external camera and has pointed to the reason behind the unexpected event, i.e. a vehicle overtaking the autonomous shuttle.

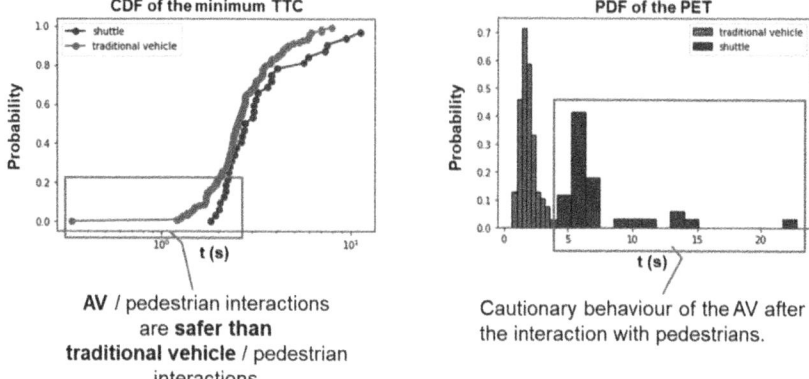

Fig. 5. Cumulative Distribution Function of the minimum TTC (left) and Probability Density Function of the PET (right): comparison autonomous shuttle (blue) vs. traditional vehicles (red) (Color figure online).

The study of AV behaviour in real traffic, especially in interactions with traditional vehicles and pedestrians, has unveiled nuanced patterns. This analysis was conducted using video data from an unsignalized crosswalk. The analysis focused on two surrogate safety measures (SSMs): Time-to-Collision (TTC) and Post-Encroachment Time (PET). These metrics were applied to assess conflicts between pedestrians and both types of vehicles (traditional and autonomous ones). A total of 33 AV-pedestrian interactions and 135 traditional vehicle-pedestrian interactions were analysed (main results displayed in Fig. 5). For TTC, which measures the time remaining before a potential collision, no statistically significant difference was found between the two types of vehicles. However, the tails of the distributions showed clear differences. In particular, pedestrian-human vehicle interactions exhibited a lower tail, indicating more dangerous situations compared to AVs. The PET, which measures the time elapsed between the vehicle and pedestrian passing through the same point, showed significant differences between the two cases. AV-pedestrian interactions had higher PET values, indicating a safer interaction compared to traditional vehicles. This is attributed to AVs stopping earlier and resuming movement more cautiously, increasing the overall safety margin during these interactions. In conclusion, while TTC did not reveal substantial overall differences, PET demonstrated that AVs create safer conditions for pedestrians by adopting more conservative driving behaviours. These findings suggest that AVs are more cautious in conflict scenarios, but they also highlight the potential for AVs to impact road network capacity due to their cautious nature. The results underline the importance of considering vehicle type in safety assessments and the potential of AVs to improve pedestrian safety in urban environments.

Fig. 6. Screenshot of SUMO environment in the case study.

As key outcomes of the traffic simulation phase of the proposed framework, the first result is the development of a 'baseline' to test further traffic management strategies: the testing area of the autonomous shuttle has been simulated in SUMO (Fig. 6), reproducing its real behaviour according to the sensors' data collected and analysed in the steps before. Shuttles' movement data derived from recorded shuttle data (step 1 of the framework) added into the simulation by TraCI, along pre-planned flows of passenger vehicles, public transportation, and simulated autonomous vehicles. The integration of recorded real-world data provides a high degree of authenticity and is valuable for assessing real-world scenarios and the impact of interventions or changes in traffic management with respect to the baseline, to be used as a reference scenario. Different traffic scenarios and control strategies have been tested and implemented, but -for reasons of space- they are not discussed in detail in this article and will be presented in subsequent publications. More recorded data from other real vehicles in addition to the shuttle dataset in future steps can increase the realism of the simulations.

Finally, as a result of the integrated framework, a simulation environment has been created to enable the virtual testing of autonomous vehicles. This environment is fed by sensor data collected in the field during real CCAM experiments, enriched with additional data from the surrounding environment, including infrastructure and interactions with other road users.

The simulation outcomes demonstrate the versatility of the microsimulation environment in assessing the impacts related to autonomous services, safety, and overall traffic dynamics. Optimal strategies in various contexts have been identified, contributing to the development of informed traffic management strategies. The utilization of HPC machines has significantly reduced computational time, making the simulation process efficient and scalable.

The integration of SUMO traffic microsimulation with CARLA autonomous driving simulator marks a significant achievement. Complex and realistic traffic scenarios have been provided to CARLA based on observed data, ensuring additional and customized scenarios tailored to the simulator's requirements. The co-simulation environment, operating on HPC machines, enables real-time analysis and simulation runs, reducing computational time and enhancing the overall efficiency of the testing process.

The cost-effective development process and accelerated deployment of AV demonstrations underscore the practical advantages of this integrated approach. The scalability and transferability of insights gained from the simulation environment ensure that the outcomes are applicable across diverse urban contexts.

6 Conclusions

The proposed framework is a comprehensive and versatile tool for advancing CCAM technologies in urban mobility. By leveraging real-world data, advanced machine learning techniques, and integrated simulation environments, the study contributes significantly to the understanding of AV impacts on urban traffic. The framework not only supports virtual testing of AV trials, but also provides actionable insights for urban planners and policymakers. As the development of autonomous technologies progresses, the findings and methodologies from this research will play a critical role in guiding the responsible integration of AVs into urban landscapes, ensuring both safety and efficiency in the transition to automated mobility systems.

The availability of real-world data is a vital aspect that enhances the robustness of the proposed framework. Unlike many previous studies that rely heavily on theoretical models or estimated data, this research integrates high-frequency AV data collected during real experimentations, which includes parameters such as speed profiles, interactions with pedestrians, and AV sensors' readings. The richness of this dataset allows for a more precise and realistic simulation of traffic scenarios involving AVs, making the results more applicable to real-world situations. This continuous data flow also ensures that the model remains adaptive and can be updated as more data is collected from ongoing trials.

The study's emphasis on data visualization through the PowerBI dashboard stands out as another key feature. This tool offers stakeholders a comprehensive, user-friendly interface to monitor vehicle dynamics, sensor data, and fleet-wide operations. Notably, this dashboard facilitates both real-time and offline data analysis, enabling users to gain a deeper understanding of vehicle behaviour in different traffic conditions. Such visualizations enhance decision-making processes by presenting data in a digestible format, which is particularly beneficial for stakeholders who may not have technical expertise in data analysis.

The application of machine learning algorithms for anomaly detection represents a major advancement in understanding AV behaviour. By focusing on identifying abrupt speed changes and other outlier behaviours, the framework ensures that potentially dangerous events are flagged early. This not only enhances safety but also provides valuable insights for improving AV operational efficiency. An important aspect of the anomaly detection system is its flexibility, allowing users to adjust thresholds based on specific operational needs, thus customizing the system for different urban settings.

From a traffic management perspective, the integration of the SUMO (Simulation of Urban Mobility) platform with real-world AV data creates a powerful microsimulation environment. The study examines how AVs interact with traditional traffic, including both human-driven vehicles and pedestrians. Through this simulation, the framework provides answers to crucial questions about how AVs will affect traffic flow, safety, and road network capacity in the future. By simulating various traffic scenarios may be explored, which helps urban planners and policymakers understand how the introduction of autonomous technologies might impact daily traffic patterns.

The adaptability and scalability of the proposed framework to different urban contexts are particularly noteworthy. While this framework was developed and tested using data specific to Turin, Italy, its modular design allows for adaptation to other urban environments with varying infrastructure, regulations, and traffic dynamics. Each phase of the framework, from data gathering to traffic microsimulation, is designed to be flexible and can be customized based on available data and the unique characteristics of the target city. For example, the Data Gathering phase can integrate local traffic data, AV sensor information, and infrastructure details from any city, allowing urban planners to substitute Turin's data with locally sourced inputs. The Traffic Microsimulation phase can then be configured to reflect local traffic laws, intersection designs, and typical driver behaviours by adjusting parameters to align with the new context. Moreover, the framework's reliance on widely used open-source tools, such as SUMO, facilitates adjustments for different traffic scenarios and control strategies, which can be adapted without extensive reconfiguration. Researchers wishing to replicate this framework can follow the structured methodology presented here and adapt each phase to their own data sources and computational resources, ensuring flexibility without sacrificing consistency. Future extensions of this work will aim to provide even more standardized datasets and modular code to facilitate reproducibility across diverse research environments. In addition to the technical aspects addressed in this framework, broader behavioural, regulatory, and ethical factors play a crucial role in the successful integration of AVs into urban mobility systems. From a behavioural perspective, the interactions between AVs and human road users—such as pedestrians, cyclists, and human-driven vehicles—pose unique challenges. These interactions are complex and can impact both the safety and public acceptance of AV technology. Future expansions of this framework could incorporate behavioural models to simulate and analyse how human road users react to AVs in various scenarios, which would improve the understanding of these dynamics and support more effective deployment strategies.

Regulatory challenges also affect the feasibility and scalability of AV deployment. Compliance with local traffic laws, adherence to safety standards, and adaptation to specific regulatory environments are all essential for real-world implementation. Different regions may have varying requirements for AV testing and deployment, which necessitates flexibility in the framework to accommodate such differences. Addressing regulatory requirements early in the deployment planning can help to streamline the approval process and ensure safer and more compliant AV integration. Finally, ethical considerations, such as data privacy and equitable access to AV technology, are paramount. The collection and use of AV data, especially in urban environments, must be handled with care to protect individual privacy and prevent unauthorized data usage. Additionally, ensuring that AV technologies are accessible and beneficial to all societal groups —rather than favouring specific demographics—will be vital for creating a truly inclusive mobility solution. These considerations highlight the importance of developing AV systems responsibly, with a focus on safety, inclusivity, and societal benefit.

Several challenges and limitations emerged during the study. A primary challenge was the computational demand required to run high-resolution, real-time traffic simulations, particularly when simulating complex scenarios involving interactions among diverse road users. To address this, high-performance computing (HPC) resources were employed, but the dependency on such resources may limit the applicability of the framework in contexts lacking similar computational capabilities. Future improvements could explore ways to optimize the framework to function efficiently on standard computing setups. Another limitation concerns the specificity of the data sources used in this study, which were tailored to the unique urban landscape and traffic conditions of Turin. Although the framework is designed to be adaptable to different urban contexts, its accuracy and relevance depend significantly on the availability and quality of local data, such as detailed traffic signal timings and high-frequency AV sensor data. In cities with less detailed traffic infrastructure or limited access to AV trial data, modifications to the data gathering and analysis phases would be required, potentially affecting the scalability and transferability of the framework's findings. Finally, ensuring accurate representation of human-driven vehicle behaviours and interactions with AVs remains challenging in a simulated environment. Capturing the nuances of human driving behaviour, including unpredictability and varied responses to AVs, would require additional refinements and possibly the integration of more advanced behavioural models. These challenges underscore the need for continuous development to enhance the framework's versatility and robustness across diverse urban mobility settings.

Acknowledgments. The authors would like to thank the collaborators of the Politecnico di Torino for their precious support: Prof. Silvia Chiusano, Prof. Marco Bassani, Prof. Francesco Deflorio, and Andrea Avignone. This paper is partially supported and funded by European Union's Horizon 2020 Research and Innovation Programme under Grant Agreement No 875530, project SHOW (SHared automation Operating models for Worldwide adoption), and by Horizon Europe Innovation Actions Programme under Grant Agreement No 101076791, project IN2CCAM (Enhancing Integration and Interoperability of CCAM eco-system).

References

1. SHOW project Homepage. https://show-project.eu/. Accessed 12 Sept 2024
2. IN2CCAM project Homepage. https://in2ccam.eu/. Accessed 12 Sept 2024
3. ToMove project Homepage. https://torinocitylab.it/to-move/. Accessed 12 Sept 2024
4. Anderson, J.M., Kalra, N., Stanley, K.D., Sorensen, P., Samaras, C., Oluwatola, T.A.: Autonomous Vehicle Technology: A Guide for Policymakers. RAND Corporation, Santa Monica (2016). https://www.rand.org/pubs/research_reports/RR443-2.html

5. Guériau, M., Dusparic, I.: Quantifying the impact of connected and autonomous vehicles on traffic efficiency and safety in mixed traffic. In: 2020 IEEE 23rd International Conference on Intelligent Transportation Systems (ITSC), pp. 1–8. IEEE (2020)
6. Rios-Torres, J., Malikopoulos, A.A.: Impact of connected and automated vehicles on traffic flow. In: 2017 IEEE 20th International Conference on Intelligent Transportation Systems (ITSC), pp. 1–6. IEEE (2017)
7. Yu, H., Tak, S., Park, M., Yeo, H.: Impact of autonomous-vehicle-only lanes in mixed traffic conditions. Transp. Res. Rec. **2673**(9), 430–439 (2019). https://doi.org/10.1177/036119811 9847475
8. Nemoto, E.H., Issaoui, R., Korbee, D., Jaroudi, I., Fournier, G.: How to measure the impacts of shared automated electric vehicles on urban mobility. Transp. Res. Part D: Transp. Environ. **93**, 102766 (2021). https://doi.org/10.1016/j.trd.2021.102766
9. Anund, A., et al.: Lessons learned from setting up a demonstration site with autonomous shuttle operation – based on experience from three cities in Europe. J. Urban Mob. **2**, 100021 (2022). https://doi.org/10.1016/j.urbmob.2022.100021
10. Antonialli, F.: International benchmark on experimentations with Autonomous Shuttles for Collective Transport. In: 27th International Colloquium of Gerpisa, Paris, France (2019). https://centralesupelec.hal.science/hal-02489797v2
11. Thorhauge, M., Fjendbo, J.A., Rich, J.: Effects of autonomous first-and last mile transport in the transport chain. Transp. Res. Interdisc. Perspect. **15**, 100623 (2022). https://doi.org/10.1016/j.trip.2022.100623
12. Alvarez, L.P., Meister, W.: Microscopic traffic simulation using SUMO. In: Proceedings of the 21st International Conference on Intelligent Transportation Systems (ITSC) (2018). https://doi.org/10.1109/ITSC.2018.8569938
13. Raju, N., Farah, H.: Evolution of traffic microsimulation and its use for modeling connected and automated vehicles. J. Adv. Transp. 2444363, 29 (2021). https://doi.org/10.1155/2021/2444363
14. Lu, Q., Tettamanti, T., Hörcher, D., Varga, I.: The impact of autonomous vehicles on urban traffic network capacity: an experimental analysis by microscopic traffic simulation. Transp. Lett. **12**(8), 540–549 (2020). https://doi.org/10.1080/19427867.2019.1662561
15. SUMO Homepage. https://sumo.dlr.de/docs/index.html. Accessed 12 Sept 2024
16. Parkin, J., Crawford, F., Flower, J., Alford, C., Morgan, P., Parkhurst, G.: Cyclist and pedestrian trust in automated vehicles: an on-road and simulator trial. Int. J. Sustain. Transp. **17**(7), 762–774 (2023). https://doi.org/10.1080/15568318.2022.2093147
17. Papadoulis, A., Quddus, M., Imprialou, M.: Evaluating the safety impact of connected and autonomous vehicles on motorways. Accid. Anal. Prev. **124**, 12–22 (2019). https://doi.org/10.1016/j.aap.2018.12.019
18. Dosovitskiy, A., Ros, G., Codevilla, F., López, A., Koltun, V.: CARLA: an open urban driving simulator. In: Proceedings of the 1st Conference on Robot Learning (CoRL 2017), Mountain View, United States (2017). https://doi.org/10.48550/arXiv.1711.03938
19. Li, P., Kusari, A., LeBlanc, D.J.: A novel traffic simulation framework for testing autonomous vehicles using SUMO and CARLA. CoRR, abs/2110.07111 (2021). https://doi.org/10.48550/arXiv.2110.07111
20. Yilmaz-Niewerth, S., Häbel, R., Friedrich, B.: Developing a comprehensive large-scale co-simulation for replication of automated driving in urban traffic scenarios. Transp. Res. Procedia **78**, 522–529 (2024). ISSN: 2352-1465. https://doi.org/10.1016/j.trpro.2024.02.065
21. Shi, Y., Liu, Z., Wang, Z., Ye, J., Tong, W., Liu, Z.: An integrated traffic and vehicle co-simulation testing framework for connected and autonomous vehicles. IEEE Intell. Transp. Syst. Mag. **14**(6), 26–40 (2022). https://doi.org/10.1109/MITS.2022.3188566
22. Navya Shuttles. https://navya.tech/en/solutions/moving-people/self-driving-shuttle-for-passenger-transportation/. Accessed 12 Sept 2024

23. Wang, C.Y., Bochkovskiy, A., Liao, H.Y.M.: YOLOv7: trainable bag-of-freebies sets new state-of-the-art for real-time object detectors. In: Proceedings of the IEEE/CVF Conference on Computer Vision and Pattern Recognition, pp. 7464–7475 (2023)
24. Bewley, A., Ge, Z., Ott, L., Ramos, F., Upcroft, B.: Simple online and realtime tracking. In: 2016 IEEE International Conference on Image Processing (ICIP). IEEE (2016). https://doi.org/10.1109/ICIP.2016.7533003

Federated Learning for Lane-Change Prediction

Lilit Yenokyan[1], William Lindskog-Muenzing[2], Christian Prehofer[3(✉)],
and Matthias Schubert[1]

[1] LMU Munich, Munich, Germany
schubert@dbs.ifi.lmu.de
[2] Flower Labs and Technical University of Munich, Munich, Germany
william.lindskog@tum.de
[3] DENSO Automotive, Eching, Germany
c.prehofer@eu.denso.com

Abstract. In this paper, we present a data-driven approach for predicting lane changes of vehicles in a highway scenario based on observing position, speed, and movements of surrounding vehicles. To train a prediction model, we employ federated learning (FL) with various locations acting as clients. The study employs Long Short-Term Memory (LSTM) networks that utilize 1 s of historical data to forecast lane changes over a 1, 3 and 5-s prediction horizon. We show that personalized FL performs well for a distributed setup without data sharing. The findings demonstrate FL's potential in automotive safety applications, nearly matching centralized performance while significantly improving data security and privacy across distributed locations. This study supports using federated learning as a viable and robust solution for privacy-preserving predictive tasks in dynamic environments.

Keywords: Federated Learning · Lane-Change Prediction · Automotive · Privacy

1 Introduction

Accurate prediction of lane-change scenarios is a crucial factor for highway safety. Research indicates that current adaptive cruise control (ACC) driver assistance systems can exhibit unpredictable behavior in irregular traffic conditions [2]. Furthermore, studies reveal that only about half of drivers use turn signals when changing lanes, with rates as low as 44% in China [29] and 52% in the United States [20]. This lack of turn signal usage significantly contributes to the number of incidents caused by lane changes. According to statistics from the National Highway Traffic Safety Administration (NHTSA), lane-change maneuvers result in up to 610,000 traffic accidents annually in the U.S., leading to at least 60,000 injuries [8].

W. Lindskog-Muenzing—Research carried out at DENSO Automotive.

© ICST Institute for Computer Sciences, Social Informatics and Telecommunications Engineering 2025
Published by Springer Nature Switzerland AG 2025. All Rights Reserved
A. Kocian et al. (Eds.): INTSYS 2024, LNICST 608, pp. 311–331, 2025.
https://doi.org/10.1007/978-3-031-86370-7_19

In this paper, we propose a data-driven approach for predicting lane changes of vehicles in highway scenarios by analyzing the position, speed, and movement of surrounding vehicles. A critical aspect of implementing data-driven solutions is addressing the privacy of driving data, particularly the need for data exchange among different organizations. This exchange involves gathering data from various highways and entities to develop collaborative, high-quality machine learning models. However, mobility data can be sensitive, raising concerns about confidentiality in light of privacy regulations.

To tackle these challenges, we utilize federated learning (FL) [9,16], a privacy-preserving machine learning framework that allows organizations to collaboratively train models without sharing raw data. In this approach, the raw data remain local, and FL enables model training across multiple clients by transmitting model updates after each training step. Research has shown that FL can lead to effective solutions while safeguarding sensitive information. By sharing only local model updates, FL not only protects individual data privacy but also has the potential to significantly reduce network traffic.

We demonstrate that federated learning can effectively leverage data collected from different vehicles to train robust predictive models for lane-change prediction. In our study, we utilize movement data from various highway locations, treating each location as a separate client within the FL framework. This approach allows us to train a global model on decentralized data without the need for raw data transfer.

In summary, our research contributions are as follows:

- We present a data-driven approach for lane change detection with well-defined steps, creating a reproducible framework that enables accurate comparisons for future studies.
- We demonstrate that federated learning achieves strong performance while preserving data privacy, making it a viable alternative for privacy-sensitive applications.
- We show that personalized federated learning improves accuracy by adapting models to specific locations, outperforming standard FL by effectively handling local variations.
- We highlight the benefits of FL over local models for data-scarce locations, providing a strong incentive for client participation in federated training.

In the subsequent sections, we review related work on federated learning and the dataset utilized for lane-change prediction. We then present our modeling and machine learning setup, followed by a comparative analysis of results from centralized and federated learning approaches. We identify federated learning methods and algorithms that are particularly effective for our use case, with data from different location. We focus on establishing a well-defined and reproducible data-driven framework for lane-change detection using federated learning.

2   Related Work and Lane-Change Definitions

Lane-change (LC) maneuver prediction tasks have been extensively addressed using machine learning approaches based on observed data. These methods typically categorize three fundamental maneuvers: changing to the left lane (LLC), changing to the right lane (RLC), and lane keeping (LK) [23,24]. Consequently, LC prediction can be treated as a classification task aimed at estimating the class or probability of the upcoming maneuver. In terms of data utilization, features commonly employed in LC prediction algorithms include geographic positioning system (GPS) traces, external camera or drone recordings, and vehicle sensor readings, such as those from cameras and radars [17,19,26].

In this section, we review related work and the state of the art in lane-change prediction.

Classification and Labeling. Regarding the research on lane-change prediction, definitions of lane-change vary. Some studies refer to the start of the lane-changing process, while others define it as the moment a vehicle crosses a lane marking. For example, [15] states "a lane change is fully executed if all points . . . lie within the observed section of the highway." On the other hand, [13] defines lane-change as "Crossing lane markings and staying in a new lane." A more precise definition is provided in [22]: "For the moment of the lane change, we are using the point in time when the vehicle center has just crossed the lane marking". Our work follows the actual Highway Drone (highD) [13] dataset's annotations, indicating when the vehicle crosses the lane marking (see [27] for more details).

Specifically, [15] introduces an automatic labeling approach that uses density-based clustering to detect lane changes. An SVM then learns the cluster boundaries to label new data, which is subsequently fed into an LSTM model for classification. Trained on the highD dataset, this model achieved 88% accuracy for a 3-s prediction horizon with only 1 s of historical data. However, the absence of a precise lane-change point complicates comparisons with other studies.

In a comprehensive analysis, [28] compares LSTM, SVM, XGBoost, and LightGBM methods for LC prediction, using the CitySim dataset with a 5-s input time duration. It achieves around 95% classification accuracy with LSTM and 98% accuracy with LightGBM. However, the report lacks clarity on the definition of lane-change, the prediction horizon, and the target value used in the modeling.

Other works define lane change as a process [3,13], concluding when the vehicle stabilizes in the new lane. This definition directly affects the prediction horizon, as the lane change must occur within that horizon, making comparisons across studies challenging.

Trajectory Prediction. In addition to maneuver classification, many studies adopt a two-step approach: first, they predict vehicle trajectories, and then they use classifiers to identify maneuvers. These maneuvers are classified either into aforementioned multiple categories or as a binary option (lane-change or lane-keep). For instance, [11] evaluates two kinds of ANN over two different datasets for trajectory prediction, followed by an SVM for binary classification of the vehicle's maneuvers. The lane-change point (LCP), defined as the vehicle's center crossing the line between two lanes, is predicted with an 85% F1 score for a 3-s prediction horizon and 93% for 1 s. There are also hybrid approaches based on both deterministic and probabilistic methods. [25] aims to detect the LCs by applying the potential field method for trajectory planning, taking into account the presence of surrounding vehicles to reduce false alarms caused by zigzag driving. Afterwards, SVM is used for vehicle intent classification. With the use of the Federal Highway Administration dataset, they detect LC on average 1.74 s before the vehicle crosses the center-line with a 98.1% accuracy.

Prediction of Time Until Lane-Change. Other studies aim to predict the precise time until the lane-change (TTLC). [22] develops a predictive model for estimating TTLC using LSTM-based RNNs. By using 3 s of historical data from the highD dataset, the authors claim that accurate predictions can be made as early as 3.5 s before the lane-change, with a median error of less than 0.25 s. This model's root mean squared error (RMSE) is later improved by 0.2 s by [18]. They propose a multi-task model to simultaneously predict the LC maneuvers and estimate TTLC for automated driving systems. The authors report that their model outperforms the SOTA on the highD dataset, achieving approximately 85% recall for a 3-s prediction horizon and a 60% recall for the defined maximum prediction horizon of 5.2 s. [5] offers a solution with a richer dataset, predicting the TTLC with an error of only 0.3 s at a prediction horizon of 3 s and a history of 3 s using LSTM. This method uses information about the driver's state along with general traffic information. While this information can be measured at many points in the scene, the driver state measurement makes the model only applicable to predict ego vehicle maneuvers.

Another relevant work, [12], conducts a comparative analysis of various machine learning approaches alongside a rule-based method for predicting lane-change maneuvers 2 s before a vehicle crosses the highway centerline. The results demonstrate that artificial neural networks (ANN) significantly outperform the MOBIL model. Additionally, the error rates in predicting LLC, RLC, and LK using ANN for 4 s in advance are 12.2%, 20.5%, and 0.5%, respectively.

Lane-Change Prediction in Federated Learning. Regarding LC prediction in the context of FL, there is limited research addressing this specific combination. The only notable study we found is by [7], which proposes a clustering-based personalized federated learning (CPFL) framework. It uses in-cabin driver monitoring data, such as head rotation, from 5 drivers in simulation scenarios to predict the intention to change lanes. However, its reliance on limited monitoring data does not capture the environmental factors influencing LC prediction, such as road conditions and traffic. Additionally, the small dataset raises ques-

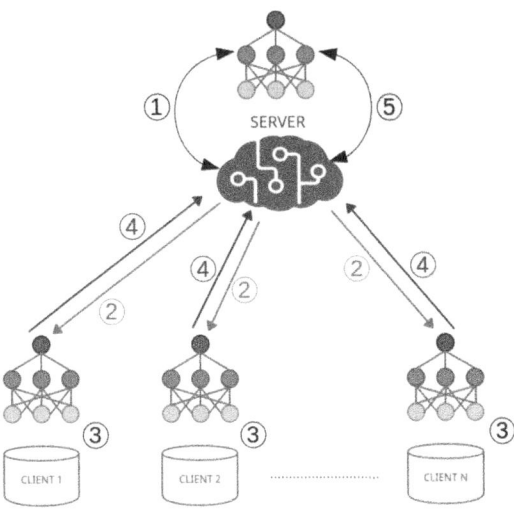

Fig. 1. Scheme of Federated Learning Approach. (1) server creates the model, (2) server sends the model to the clients, (3) clients train the model on local data, (4) clients send model parameters to the server, (5) server aggregates the parameters and updates the model. Adapted from [6].

tions about the generalizability of the results. In contrast, our work focuses on predicting lane changes of surrounding vehicles.

3 Federated Learning

Federated learning (FL) is a distributed, collaborative approach in machine learning that enables models to train directly on decentralized devices. Unlike traditional distributed learning, which aims to parallelize computation by distributing centralized data across nodes followed by aggregation, FL prioritizes privacy protection. In this framework, computation occurs on edge devices where the data is generated, and the centralized server only accesses and aggregates the parameters of locally trained models.

With the increasing emphasis on data privacy and security regulations, such as the General Data Protection Regulation (GDPR), there is a growing need for secure and efficient data processing methods. FL was introduced in 2016 by [16] as a solution to these challenges.

Key components of FL architecture, as shown in Fig. 1, are the **centralized server** and multiple decentralized devices called **clients**. The server acts as the central coordinator of the learning process. It manages the communication with the clients, handling the distribution of the global model and the collection of the local model updates. One of the server's key roles is to aggregate the model parameters from the local models trained on the client devices to get an improved global model.

Algorithm 1: Federated Proximal (FedProx) Algorithm

Input: Initial global model weights w_0, Number of communication rounds F,
   Number of clients K, Number of local epochs E, Learning rate η,
   Proximal term coefficient μ
Output: Trained global model weights w_F
for $t = 0, 1, \ldots, F - 1$ **do**
   // Server-side operations
   Select a random subset of clients S_t from K clients;
   Send the global model weights w_t to the selected clients;
   for *each client* $k \in S_t$ *in parallel* **do**
      // Client-side operations
      Receive the global model weights w_t from the server;
      Initialize local model weights $w_{t,0}^k \leftarrow w_t$;
      for $i = 1, 2, \ldots, E$ **do**
         for *each batch b in local data* **do**
            $w_{t,i}^k \leftarrow w_{t,i-1}^k - \eta \nabla \ell(w_{t,i-1}^k; b) + \mu(w_{t,i-1}^k - w_t)$ // Update
               local model weights with proximal term
      Send the updated local model weights $w_{t,E}^k$ to the server;
   // Server-side aggregation
   $w_{t+1} \leftarrow \sum_{k \in S_t} \frac{n_k}{n} w_{t,E}^k$ // Aggregate local updates to update global
      model

The clients' primary role is to perform the actual training on their local datasets. For privacy preservation, these datasets remain on clients' respective devices and are not shared with the server or other clients. Clients send their locally trained model updates (typically the gradients or updated weights) to the central server and receive the updated global model in return. This communication is typically done at the end of each training round.

The basic operation of FL is illustrated in Fig. 1. The training begins with the central server initializing the global model. During each communication round, a random subset (or all) of clients is selected to participate in training. These clients perform local training on their data and send the updated model parameters back to the central server, where the updates are aggregated to form an improved global model. In the simplest case, the aggregation process involves averaging the model parameters across clients, as in the FedAvg algorithm.

The **FedProx** algorithm (Algorithm 1) extends the classic FedAvg algorithm by introducing a proximal term to the local objective function [14]. This proximal term penalizes large deviations from the global model during local updates, thereby stabilizing the training process and promoting smoother convergence in heterogeneous data environments.

The **FedPer** strategy introduces a personalization layer within the neural networks, which is learned locally and allows for tailored model adaptation [1]. While federated learning (FL) mechanisms enable clients to benefit from knowl-

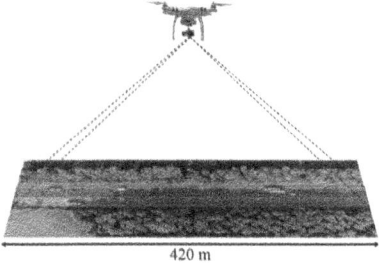 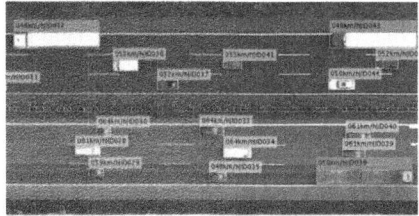

420 m

Fig. 2. Highway Drone Dataset. Adapted from [13]

edge shared among them, incorporating local personalization can also be advantageous. In the FedPer framework, the neural network is divided into two distinct components: the base layers and the personalization layers. During optimization, the learning process in clients must determine which aspects of the model should be treated locally in the personalization layer and which should be shared globally in the base layers. This distinction becomes crucial when clients have varying data distributions. In our setting, personalization is particularly important for adapting to different locations, each with its unique characteristics.

4   Lane-Change Dataset Overview

Two primary datasets commonly used in lane-change research are the NGSIM (Next Generation Simulation) Dataset [21] and the highD (Highway Drone Dataset) [13]. While the NGSIM dataset has been widely referenced, it suffers from limitations related to data quality and accuracy [4]. In light of these issues, we have chosen to focus our extensive analysis on the highD dataset.

The Highway Drone Dataset, called highD, is a comprehensive collection of naturalistic vehicle trajectories recorded on German highways and offers a detailed view of traffic patterns and vehicle behavior. Each recording spans a highway segment approximately 420 m in length, captured from an aerial perspective that eliminates occlusions, as illustrated in Fig. 2. The dataset encompasses traffic recordings from six distinct locations, including data from over 110,500 vehicles, covering 44,500 driven kilometers and 147 h of driving time. Vehicles are typically visible for a median duration of 13.6 s due to the high speeds on highways.

The data collection is conducted using drones with cinematic capabilities, which hover above the highway. The highD dataset includes four files for each of its 60 recordings, ensuring convenient data handling.

The **recordingMeta** file has general information about each specific recording, regardless of the individual vehicles captured. It contains entries for the recording's identifier, frame rate, location identifier, speed limit, date of the recording, day of the week, start time, duration, total distance driven, total time driven, the total number of vehicles recorded, and the y-coordinates of upper and lower lane markings. The **tracksMeta** file provides metadata about each recorded vehicle. It includes information such as the vehicle's identifier (id), width, height, initial etc. The **tracks** file comprises the actual movement data of the vehicles. Each row corresponds to a vehicle's position at a specific time frame, including data such as the frame index, vehicle identifier, coordinates (x, y), width, height, velocities, accelerations, front and back sight distances, distance headway, time headway, and time to collision with the leader vehicle.

Figure 3 shows an example of the trajectories from location 1 with three lanes for each driving direction. The x markings indicate lane-changes where the lanes are shown with dashed lines.

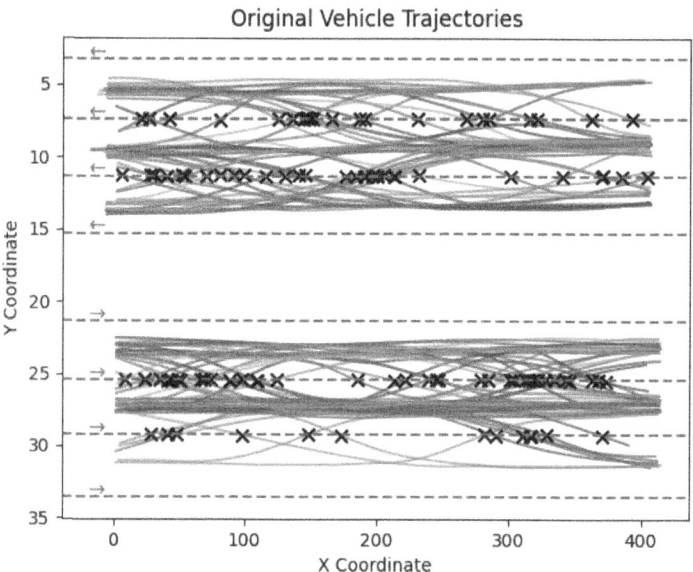

Fig. 3. Vehicles from Location 1

Next, we explore key descriptive statistics to understand the basic properties of the dataset. Table 1 provides a summary of the vehicle data collected at six different locations. It includes the number of recordings, trajectories, trucks, and cars observed at each location, along with the totals across all locations. The most significant observation is that the majority of the recordings (more than 60%) are from location 1. In addition, location 1 features 77% of recorded vehicles. Another noteworthy observation is that there are two types of vehicles, cars, and trucks, and the majority of the vehicles are from cars compared to trucks with a 4:1 ratio. Locations 2, 4, 5, and 6 have no speed limit, and locations 1 and 3 have 33.33 m/s (120 km/h) and 36.11 m/s (130 km/h) speed limits, respectively. This is already leading to some variations in the data distribution.

Table 1. Summary of Vehicle Data by Location

Locations	1	2	3	4	5	6	Total
# Recordings	37	3	3	4	10	3	60
# Vehicles	85962	3074	3747	4751	10079	2903	110516
# Trucks	16211	674	1037	952	1887	616	21377
# Cars	69751	2400	2710	3799	8192	2287	88939
% of vehicles	77.76%	2.78%	3.39%	4.30%	9.12%	2.63%	100%

Data Labeling

The dataset provides labeled *lane IDs* for each trajectory. We assign labels to frames where the *lane ID* changes as either *left lane-change (LLC)* or *right lane-change (RLC)*, while the remaining frames are marked as *lane-keep (LK)*. Figure 4 illustrates this process, using 1 s of historical data. The data is collected at 25 frames per second, enabling our predictions of lane-changes with a precision of 0.04 s. However, to accommodate the inherent variability in predictions, we extend the positive labels (*LLC, RLC*) by 12 frames before and after the original lane-change frame. This extension allows the model to predict lane changes within a broader 24 frames range (about 1 s).

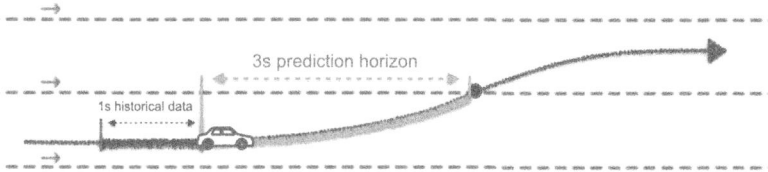

Fig. 4. Illustration of Labeling and historical Data

5 Model Development and Training

In this section, we delve into the development and training of our lane-change prediction model. A Long Short-Term Memory (LSTM) [10] network is chosen for lane-change prediction due to its capability to handle sequential data and capture long-term dependencies.

Before moving to the experiments and results, it is essential to understand the types of training setups used in this study. There are three learning configurations: centralized learning, federated learning, and local learning. The model trained in the centralized setup serves as a baseline to compare and validate the results of the federated learning. This comparison allows us to quantify the trade-off between privacy protection and prediction accuracy. Additionally, examining the model performance from local data learning is crucial to understanding the motivation behind collaboration.

Centralized Training. In the centralized setup, all training data is aggregated and processed on a central server. All sixty recordings are utilized to create the training, validation, and test sets. To ensure fair representation from each location, the data is first split into three subsets per location (see Fig. 5).

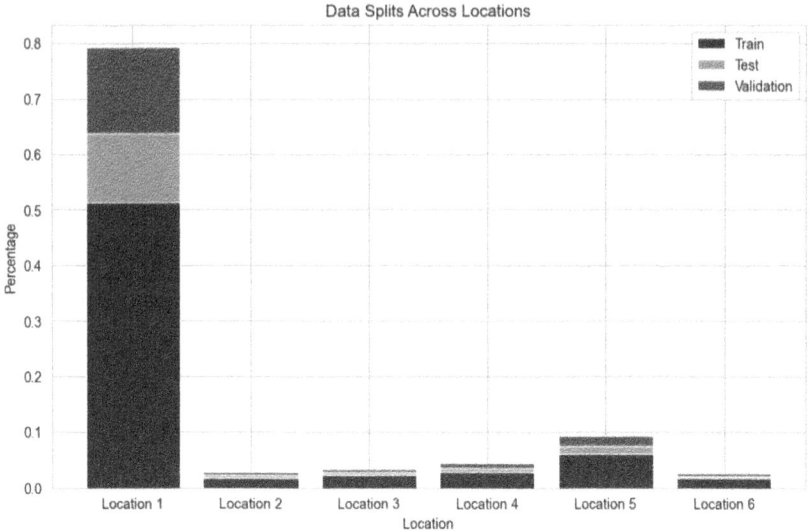

Fig. 5. Centralized: Data from all locations is merged into unified train, test, and validation sets. **Federated**: Train and validation sets are combined per location for training, with test sets remaining unchanged. **Local**: Each location uses its own train, validation, and test sets independently.

Each subset of sequences undergoes preprocessing before being vertically merged, shuffled, and divided into smaller batches. This method guarantees that approximately 20% of the data from each location is allocated for testing the model's generalization capability.

To mitigate overfitting, we employ early stopping alongside model-embedded regularization techniques. Training is halted if the model's performance on the validation set does not improve for a specified number of epochs, referred to as the *patience parameter*. This approach helps to maintain the model's robustness while avoiding unnecessary computation.

In summary, the centralized training in addition to the model-specific **hyperparameters** uses patience for early stopping, batch size, and number of training epochs. These hyperparameters are optimized to enhance overall model performance.

Federated Training. In FL, training data is distributed across multiple agents, and the model is collaboratively trained while preserving the data privacy for each client. In our case, the data is organically split between the six clients representing different highways. As introduced in Sect. 4, the samples per client vary significantly, with Client 1 providing almost 80% of the data. This creates inherent differences between the locations. In addition to quantitative differences, naturally, there are also variations in data distributions.

Similar to centralized setups, the FL training requires tuning **hyperparameters** such as learning rate, batch size, and local epochs to optimize performance. Additionally, determining the optimal *rounds* parameter is crucial, as it specifies the number of communication rounds between the server and clients. FL introduces specialized parameters for aggregation strategies, such as the *proximal* μ for **FedProx** and the partitioning of the neural network into base and personalization layers for **FedPer**.

Local Training. In local training, each agent independently trains its model using only local data, ensuring complete privacy and specialization to its location's characteristics, while following the same steps as the centralized setup without data sharing or model updates between agents.

6 Experimental Evaluation

This chapter presents the outcomes of our experiments, detailing the performance and evaluation of the FL approach for lane-change prediction. The subsections below cover the results of the experiments conducted across centralized, local, and federated setups, focusing on prediction horizons (PH) of 1, 3, and 5 s. The experiments were conducted using the hardware and software configuration as detailed in the Appendix. Further details on the evaluation can also be found in the thesis of the first author [27].

6.1 Centralized Training Results

Using the hyperparameter values outlined in the Appendix, Table 9, we trained centralized models for prediction horizons of 1, 3, and 5 s. The results in Table 2 and Fig. 6 demonstrate varying levels of accuracy, with the most notable performance observed in the 3-s prediction horizon, achieving an accuracy of 84.9% using only 1 s of historical data.

6.2 Local Training Results

The accuracy and F1 scores of local training on all 6 locations with prediction horizons 1, 3, and 5 s are presented in Table 3.

The first observation we make is that the prediction results significantly vary across different locations. The model performs exceptionally well in location 1, having the highest scores in all metrics. Compared to other locations, it also has the lowest validation loss and the most stable training process, indicating effective model performance and good data quality.

Table 2. Centralized Learning: Testing and validation results for 1 s, 3 s, and 5 s prediction horizons. The training values are in parentheses

Prediction Horizon	1 s	3 s	5 s
Testing			
Accuracy	0.941 (0.931)	**0.849** (0.836)	0.589 (0.648)
F1 Scores (LK, LLC, RLC)	0.910, 0.941, 0.938	0.798, 0.863, 0.858	0.587, 0.540, 0.644
Validation			
Accuracy	0.944	0.831	0.528
F1 Scores (LK, LLC, RLC)	0.921, 0.954, 0.939	0.787, 0.854, 0.837	0.499, 0.442, 0.626
Loss	0.190	0.428	0.901

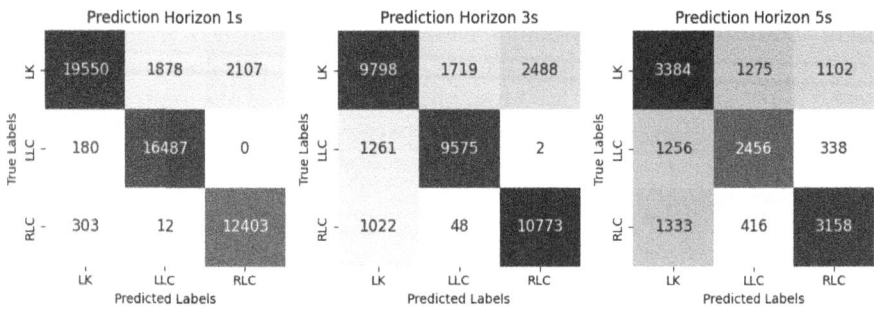

Fig. 6. Centralized Learning: Confusion matrices

Location 5 comes in second place, maintaining relatively good performance even for longer horizons, with smaller gaps between training and validation losses. The F1 scores for location 5 are also relatively high across all classes, showing its ability to make consistent predictions.

All locations perform fairly well for the 1 s PH according to the evaluation scores. However, the training plots show that the validation losses transition from horizontal lines to an upward trend throughout all 150 epochs, indicating the models' struggles to generalize. This pattern of increasing validation loss, indicative of overfitting, is particularly noticeable for longer prediction horizons.

For the 3 s PH, the gap between training and validation loss consistently increases in locations 2 and 3, highlighting overfitting and suggesting that the models are capturing noise in the training data. For the 5 s PH, the gap increases in all six locations with very large oscillations, demonstrating significant difficulties in making longer-term predictions. The confusion matrices validate our earlier observations. Notably, across all locations, the models exhibit almost perfect predictions when it comes to distinguishing between left lane-change and right lane-change. Across all locations, there are minimal instances where LLC is misclassified as RLC or vice versa.

Table 3. Local Learning: Testing results for 1 s, 3 s, and 5 s prediction horizons across 6 locations. The training values are in parentheses.

Location	Metric	1 s	3 s	5 s
Location 1	Accuracy	0.955 (0.945)	0.851 (0.825)	0.610 (0.672)
	F1 Scores (LK, LLC, RLC)	0.936, 0.950, 0.958	0.823, 0.880, 0.864	0.567, 0.577, 0.655
Location 2	Accuracy	0.860 (0.959)	0.546 (0.919)	0.630 (0.873)
	F1 Scores (LK, LLC, RLC)	0.858, 0.896, 0.860	0.453, 0.541, 0.678	0.534, 0.541, 0.802
Location 3	Accuracy	0.782 (0.934)	0.594 (0.93)	0.484 (0.885)
	F1 Scores (LK, LLC, RLC)	0.789, 0.781, 0.826	0.580, 0.551, 0.659	0.410, 0.490, 0.470
Location 4	Accuracy	0.821 (0.942)	0.677 (0.936)	0.402 (0.925)
	F1 Scores (LK, LLC, RLC)	0.800, 0.858, 0.820	0.661, 0.704, 0.675	0.257, 0.311, 0.579
Location 5	Accuracy	0.872 (0.943)	0.703 (0.896)	0.618 (0.800)
	F1 Scores (LK, LLC, RLC)	0.864, 0.855, 0.909	0.683, 0.726, 0.715	0.524, 0.637, 0.693
Location 6	Accuracy	0.792 (0.932)	0.615 (0.904)	0.409 (0.910)
	F1 Scores (LK, LLC, RLC)	0.788, 0.810, 0.784	0.644, 0.597, 0.555	0.498, 0.466, 0.097

Table 4. Accuracies of Federated Learning Using FedAvg, FedProx and FedPer: Testing results for 1 s, 3 s, and 5 s prediction horizons over all 6 locations

FL Algorithm	Accuracy for prediction horizon		
	1 s	3 s	5 s
FedAvg	0.927	0.818	0.576
FedProx	0.923	0.831	0.576
Fedper	0.931	0.841	0.567

6.3 Federated Learning Results

The federated learning was used to train one model per prediction horizon for three local epochs and 30 federated rounds. The training accuracy for all three algorithms, FedAvg, FedProx and FedPer are show in Fig. 4. Then, the models were evaluated on the client side at each location, and the results of these evaluations are presented in Table 5 for FedAvg, in Table 6 for FedProx and in Table 7 for FedPer.

For the main results of the three algorithms—FedAvg, FedProx, and FedPer, we refer to Table 4, which shows that FedProx and FedPer outperform FedAvg.

Table 5. Federated Learning Using FedAvg: Testing results for 1 s, 3 s, and 5 s prediction horizons across 6 locations, including F1 scores for each horizon.

Location	Metric	1 s	3 s	5 s
Location 1	Accuracy	0.935	0.824	0.575
	F1 Scores LK, LLC, RLC	0.907, 0.960, 0.956	0.739, 0.874, 0.891	0.539, 0.572, 0.618
Location 2	Accuracy	0.943	0.764	0.636
	F1 Scores LK, LLC, RLC	0.920, 0.973, 0.954	0.681, 0.854, 0.832	0.534, 0.652, 0.735
Location 3	Accuracy	0.823	0.804	0.453
	F1 Scores LK, LLC, RLC	0.783, 0.921, 0.793	0.734, 0.869, 0.854	0.585, 0.341, 0.472
Location 4	Accuracy	0.933	0.824	0.638
	F1 Scores LK, LLC, RLC	0.908, 0.962, 0.950	0.752, 0.885, 0.902	0.682, 0.541, 0.732
Location 5	Accuracy	0.939	0.829	0.695
	F1 Scores LK, LLC, RLC	0.912, 0.954, 0.966	0.757, 0.891, 0.893	0.638, 0.686, 0.742
Location 6	Accuracy	0.916	0.754	0.522
	F1 Scores LK, LLC, RLC	0.881, 0.916, 0.971	0.692, 0.790, 0.833	0.588, 0.423, 0.492
Overall	Accuracy	**0.927**	**0.818**	**0.576**

6.4   Discussion

Centralized models generally outperformed **local models** due to their access to a more diverse and comprehensive dataset, achieving a high accuracy of 94.1% compared to a weighted average of 91.4% from local models for the 1-s prediction horizon. For the 3-s prediction horizon, centralized models achieved 84.9% accuracy versus 79.1% from local models, and for the 5-s horizon, centralized models had an accuracy of 58.9% compared to 56.2% from local models. In contrast, local models, constrained to data from specific locations, often fail to capture the full spectrum of driving behaviors and conditions, leading to lower performance. This effect is especially pronounced in our case, as location 1 has substantially more data than the other locations, causing a notable drop in accuracy for less represented areas.

Centralized models typically achieve higher accuracy than **federated models** due to their direct access to a the full dataset. In our work, for the 1 s horizon, CL models reached an accuracy of 94.1%, compared to 93.1% from federated models (FedPer). Similarly, for the 3 s PH, centralized models achieved 84.9% accuracy compared to 84.1% from federated models, and for 5 s PH 58.9%, compared to 56.7%.

The accuracy difference between federated and centralized models is small, with federated models showing up to a 1% decrease in accuracy compared to

Table 6. Federated Learning Using FedProx: Testing results for 1 s, 3 s, and 5 s prediction horizons across 6 locations, including F1 scores for each horizon.

Location	Metric	1 s	3 s	5 s
Location 1	Accuracy	0.935	0.843	0.575
	F1 Scores LK, LLC, RLC	0.914, 0.962, 0.960	0.761, 0.887, 0.895	0.564, 0.563, 0.662
Location 2	Accuracy	0.926	0.755	0.585
	F1 Scores LK, LLC, RLC	0.900, 0.954, 0.954	0.658, 0.846, 0.786	0.453, 0.618, 0.750
Location 3	Accuracy	0.792	0.805	0.545
	F1 Scores LK, LLC, RLC	0.758, 0.893, 0.769	0.742, 0.854, 0.866	0.553, 0.464, 0.657
Location 4	Accuracy	0.917	0.815	0.565
	F1 Scores LK, LLC, RLC	0.891, 0.949, 0.943	0.725, 0.884, 0.867	0.571, 0.582, 0.609
Location 5	Accuracy	0.946	0.825	0.645
	F1 Scores LK, LLC, RLC	0.932, 0.961, 0.975	0.768, 0.885, 0.902	0.475, 0.679, 0.764
Location 6	Accuracy	0.909	0.765	0.495
	F1 Scores LK, LLC, RLC	0.881, 0.928, 0.958	0.684, 0.800, 0.836	0.577, 0.411, 0.505
Overall	Accuracy	**0.923**	**0.831**	**0.576**

centralized models for shorter PH. Although federated learning is often benchmarked against centralized solutions, in many cases, centralized solutions are impractical or unfeasible when data cannot be consolidated at a central location, often due to privacy or confidentiality requirements.

Comparing the results of locally trained models with those trained collaboratively in a federated setting is particularly interesting as it goes into the motivation behind local clients choosing to participate in FL. By doing so, clients contribute to and benefit from a collective intelligence that usually outperforms isolated local efforts.

Federated learning models (FedPer) demonstrate superior overall performance compared to the average performance of local models. The accuracies for FedPer and the average local accuracies are 93.1%, 84.1%, and 56.7% versus 91.4%, 79.1%, and 56.2% for the 1 s, 3 s, and 5 s prediction horizons, respectively. This indicates that FedPer models consistently outperform local models on average.

A more detailed analysis per location reveals that FL significantly improves short-term prediction accuracy (1 s and 3 s PH) for all locations besides 1. For example, locations 2, 4, and 6 see around a 10% increase in accuracy for the 1 s PH under FL. For the 3 s PH, the improvement is even more pronounced, with some locations experiencing up to a 15% increase. Specifically, location 2 sees an impressive 26% increase in accuracy for the 3-s PH. This substantial

Table 7. Federated Learning Using FedPer: Testing results for 1 s, 3 s, and 5 s prediction horizons across 6 locations, including F1 scores for each horizon.

Location	Metric	1 s	3 s	5 s
Location 1	Accuracy	0.939	0.860	0.581
	F1 Scores (LK, LLC, RLC)	0.901, 0.951, 0.960	0.775, 0.899, 0.895	0.312, 0.604, 0.694
Location 2	Accuracy	0.942	0.809	0.526
	F1 Scores (LK, LLC, RLC)	0.909, 0.957, 0.959	0.735, 0.903, 0.795	0.464, 0.435, 0.800
Location 3	Accuracy	0.767	0.749	0.476
	F1 Scores (LK, LLC, RLC)	0.720, 0.869, 0.724	0.672, 0.771, 0.822	0.356, 0.388, 0.589
Location 4	Accuracy	0.944	0.829	0.486
	F1 Scores (LK, LLC, RLC)	0.912, 0.955, 0.965	0.754, 0.892, 0.845	0.527, 0.431, 0.687
Location 5	Accuracy	0.928	0.831	0.599
	F1 Scores (LK, LLC, RLC)	0.885, 0.948, 0.944	0.758, 0.894, 0.832	0.113, 0.621, 0.759
Location 6	Accuracy	0.899	0.718	0.495
	F1 Scores (LK, LLC, RLC)	0.850, 0.909, 0.948	0.658, 0.794, 0.712	0.184, 0.642, 0.794
Overall	Accuracy	**0.931**	**0.841**	**0.567**

improvement likely results from the similarity in data across different locations, allowing the federated model to benefit from the shared information.

For the 5-s horizon, the overall performance of FL models is better than that of local models, but individual location results are mixed, with some locations showing slight increases and others slight decreases in accuracy. However, a notable advantage of FL is the more stable learning process, as evidenced by the accuracy plots. FL reduces the variability seen in individual locations, leading to more consistent performance improvements.

While the performance quality for the 1 s and 5 s horizons drops slightly in location 1, this decline is minimal. The slight decrease can be attributed to the aggregation of model parameters from all locations, which introduces a mix of diverse data characteristics. In a non-IID setup with significant quantity skewness, clients that carry the majority of data, such as location 1, may experience a minor reduction in performance. However, this reduction is marginal compared to the significant gains observed in locations with poorer data quality.

This indicates that FL is beneficial for all participating locations. Locations with poorer data and lower performance see substantial improvements, making the overall system more robust and reliable. At the same time, locations with better data quality, like location 1, do not experience significant degradation in their performance. This ensures that all participants benefit from the collaborative training process.

Comparison with Existing Literature. To validate our results for LC prediction, we compare them to existing works in the field. As existing literature does not apply FL for this specific task there is no direct comparison as machine learning for distributed data is more difficult. For reference, we compare both our CL and FL models to existing centralized works. The most comparable work is [15], which uses automatic labeling by clustering LC and LK maneuvers. They then train an SVM to learn the boundaries of these clustered labels, which are subsequently used as inputs for an LSTM model to predict the maneuver class.

This work also utilizes the highD dataset, predicting maneuvers using 1-s historical data with prediction horizons of 0.5, 1, 2, and 3 s. Their approach differs from ours in several ways. Firstly, they use only one recording from location 1 for training and sample additional trajectories from all locations for testing. In contrast, we train our models across multiple multilane locations, leveraging a more diverse dataset.

Another significant difference is in the feature set used for prediction. While they focus primarily on lateral velocity and acceleration, our approach incorporates both lateral and longitudinal values as well as features from surrounding vehicles. This difference in the feature set provides a more comprehensive understanding of vehicle dynamics in our model. Moreover, their model does not distinguish between left and right LC, whereas our approach explicitly accounts for the direction of LC.

Most importantly, the labeling process also differs significantly. They employ a complex clustering technique for automatic labeling, whereas we use a simpler approach by adding a 0.5-s tolerance around the exact LC frame. Their clustering and learning approach with SVM is heavily based on local data from a specific location, which might limit the generalizability of their model to other environments or datasets. In contrast, our approach uses a fixed ground truth for labeling, which can be applied universally across various locations and conditions, ensuring consistent and comparable results.

While there are major differences in privacy assumptions, lane change marking and data used, our FL models achieve competitive performance metrics compared to [15]. For instance, our centralized model achieves an accuracy of 94.1% for the 1 s PH, which is not far off the reported performance of 97.6%. This demonstrates that our simpler labeling approach and diverse dataset can effectively match the accuracy of more complex methods.

Our results demonstrate that both centralized and federated models are competitive with existing state-of-the-art approaches, with the added benefit that FL preserves data privacy and security. The minimal performance gap between centralized and federated models, coupled with the significant privacy advantages, underscores the potential of FL as a robust alternative for LC prediction tasks.

In summary, centralized models generally outperform local models due to a richer and more varied dataset, yet they may not always be optimal. High-performing locations might be disadvantaged when their specific high-quality data is diluted in a larger, more diverse dataset. FL effectively bridges this gap by leveraging diverse datasets from multiple locations while maintaining data privacy. This collaborative approach ensures that locations with poorer data and lower performance see substantial improvements, while high-performing locations experience only minimal performance degradation. This balanced and equitable solution enhances overall model accuracy and provides stability, making FL a compelling alternative that benefits all participants.

7   Conclusion

In this paper, we have presented a data-driven, federated learning framework to address the critical task of lane-change prediction, with the overarching goal of enhancing highway safety. After reviewing the existing approaches with different definitions of lane change and labeling, we started with a data-driven approach without trajectory prediction, AI-based labeling or similar. We developed and implemented a preprocessing pipeline tailored for handling multiple multivariate time series datasets, for both centralized and federated learning systems.

Our framework performs similarly to existing "classic" centralized learning approaches, where all data is centralized. As discussed, variations in definitions, labeling, and other factors underscore the need for standardized definitions and reproducible benchmarks. Specifically, we found that some local models degrade significantly due to limited amount of data. Additionally, differences in location characteristics, like speed limits or lane numbers, contribute to non-IID distributions [30], a known challenge in federated learning.

For the federated learning case, we have achieved the following main results:

- Federated learning performs, using all 6 locations, very close to centralized case, while preserving and protecting local data.
- Federated learning is able to improve the results for the locations with very little data. This clearly shows that federated learning enables the transfer the learnings between heterogeneous locations successfully.
- Personalization in federated learning, here applied to different locations, is shown to improve the results. This indicates that the differences in the locations can be handled better in this case.

In summary, our study demonstrates that federated learning can be effective for applications like lane keeping, representing an important step toward larger-scale use of AI-based, data-driven methods. This approach enables leveraging data from diverse, heterogeneous locations that cannot be centralized, often due to privacy, legal, or company confidentiality constraints.

A   Appendix: Hardware, Software and Hyperparameter Setup

Hardware and Software Setup

- NVIDIA GeForce RTX 4090 GPU with 24,564 MiB memory (Driver Version: 550.54.15, CUDA Version: 12.4)
- Operating System: Ubuntu 20.04
- Programming Language: Python 3.9
- Deep Learning Framework: PyTorch
- Federated Learning Framework: Flower
- Data Processing and Visualization Libraries: Pandas, NumPy, Scikit-learn, Seaborn, Matplotlib.

Flower orchestrated the client-server interactions in a synchronous manner, utilizing the server's GPU to accelerate training processes and manage the distribution, aggregation, and communication. This setup provided efficient and scalable FL, with consistent configuration across centralized, local, and federated models to maintain fairness in comparisons.

The following hyperparameters were varied across specified ranges (Table 8):

Table 8. Hyperparameter Ranges used in Grid Search

Hyperparameter	Values
Hidden Size	[32, 64]
Number of Layers	[2, 3, 4]
Learning Rate	[0.00001, 0.0001, 0.001, 0.01]
Batch Size	[16, 32]

The table below summarizes the best-performing models and hyperparameters selected through grid search for each prediction horizon based on their independent test set performance metrics. These exact values are used throughout our work for each prediction horizon regardless of the training setup to ensure fair comparisons of the model performance.

Table 9. Best Hyperparameters

Prediction Horizon(s)	Hidden Size	Number of Layers	Learning Rate	Batch Size
1	64	2	0.001	32
3	32	2	0.001	16
5	64	4	0.0001	32

330   L. Yenokyan et al.

In addition to the hyperparameters tuned through grid search, several other critical parameters were determined through a combination of literature review and empirical testing. These include a historical window size of 1 s, which was optimal after testing 0.5, 1, 2, and 3 s, the dropout rate of 0.3, weight decay of 0.01, patience for early stopping set to 10 epochs, and the FedProx parameter (proximal μ) of 0.7. While these parameters were not exhaustively tuned through grid search, they were carefully selected to complement the model's architecture and training regime.

References

1. Arivazhagan, M.G., Aggarwal, V., Singh, A.K., Choudhary, S.: Federated learning with personalization layers. arXiv preprint arXiv:1912.00818 (2019)
2. Carvalho, A., Lefévre, S., Schildbach, G., Kong, J., Borrelli, F.: Automated driving: the role of forecasts and uncertainty-a control perspective. Eur. J. Control. **24**, 14–32 (2015)
3. Chauhan, P., Kanagaraj, V., Asaithambi, G.: Understanding the mechanism of lane changing process and dynamics using microscopic traffic data. Phys. A: Stat. Mech. Appl. **593**, 126981 (2022). https://doi.org/10.1016/j.physa.2022.126981. https://www.sciencedirect.com/science/article/pii/S0378437122000735
4. Coifman, B., Li, L.: A critical evaluation of the next generation simulation (NGSIM) vehicle trajectory dataset. Transp. Res. Part B: Methodol. **105**, 362–377 (2017)
5. Dang, H.Q., Fürnkranz, J., Biedermann, A., Hoepfl, M.: Time-to-lane-change prediction with deep learning. In: 2017 IEEE 20th International Conference on Intelligent Transportation Systems (ITSC), pp. 1–7. IEEE (2017)
6. Díaz, J.S.P., García, Á.L.: Study of the performance and scalability of federated learning for medical imaging with intermittent clients. Neurocomputing **518**, 142–154 (2023)
7. Du, R., Han, K., Gupta, R., Chen, S., Labi, S., Wang, Z.: Driver monitoring-based lane-change prediction: a personalized federated learning framework. In: 2023 IEEE Intelligent Vehicles Symposium (IV), pp. 1–7. IEEE (2023)
8. Fitch, G., Lee, S., Klauer, S., Hankey, J., Sudweeks, J., Dingus, T.: Analysis of lane-change crashes and near-crashes. US Department of Transportation, National Highway Traffic Safety Administration (2009)
9. Hard, A., et al.: Federated learning for mobile keyboard prediction. arXiv preprint arXiv:1811.03604 (2018)
10. Hochreiter, S., Schmidhuber, J.: Long short-term memory. Neural Comput. **9**(8), 1735–1780 (1997)
11. Izquierdo, R., Parra, I., Muñoz-Bulnes, J., Fernández-Llorca, D., Sotelo, M.: Vehicle trajectory and lane change prediction using ANN and SVM classifiers. In: 2017 IEEE 20th International Conference on Intelligent Transportation Systems (ITSC), pp. 1–6. IEEE (2017)
12. Khelfa, B., Ba, I., Tordeux, A.: Predicting highway lane-changing maneuvers: a benchmark analysis of machine and ensemble learning algorithms. Phys. A **612**, 128471 (2023)
13. Krajewski, R., Bock, J., Kloeker, L., Eckstein, L.: The highd dataset: a drone dataset of naturalistic vehicle trajectories on German highways for validation of highly automated driving systems. In: 2018 21st International Conference on Intelligent Transportation systems (ITSC), pp. 2118–2125. IEEE (2018)

14. Li, T., Sahu, A.K., Zaheer, M., Sanjabi, M., Talwalkar, A., Smith, V.: Federated optimization in heterogeneous networks. Proc. Mach. Learn. Syst. **2**, 429–450 (2020)
15. Mahajan, V., Katrakazas, C., Antoniou, C.: Prediction of lane-changing maneuvers with automatic labeling and deep learning. Transp. Res. Rec. **2674**(7), 336–347 (2020)
16. McMahan, B., Moore, E., Ramage, D., Hampson, S., y Arcas, B.A.: Communication-efficient learning of deep networks from decentralized data. In: Artificial Intelligence and Statistics, pp. 1273–1282. PMLR (2017)
17. Morris, B., Doshi, A., Trivedi, M.: Lane change intent prediction for driver assistance: on-road design and evaluation. In: 2011 IEEE Intelligent Vehicles Symposium (IV), pp. 895–901. IEEE (2011)
18. Mozaffari, S., Arnold, E., Dianati, M., Fallah, S.: Early lane change prediction for automated driving systems using multi-task attention-based convolutional neural networks. IEEE Trans. Intell. Veh. **7**(3), 758–770 (2022)
19. Ozguner, U., Stiller, C., Redmill, K.: Systems for safety and autonomous behavior in cars: the DARPA grand challenge experience. Proc. IEEE **95**(2), 397–412 (2007)
20. Ponziani, R.: Turn signal usage rate results: a comprehensive field study of 12,000 observed turning vehicles. Technical report, SAE Technical Paper (2012)
21. U.S. Department of Transportation Federal Highway Administration: Next Generation Simulation (NGSIM) Vehicle Trajectories and Supporting Data. Dataset (2016). https://doi.org/10.21949/1504477
22. Wirthmüller, F., Klimke, M., Schlechtriemen, J., Hipp, J., Reichert, M.: Predicting the time until a vehicle changes the lane using LSTM-based recurrent neural networks. IEEE Robot. Autom. Lett. **6**(2), 2357–2364 (2021)
23. Wirthmüller, F., Schlechtriemen, J., Hipp, J., Reichert, M.: Teaching vehicles to anticipate: a systematic study on probabilistic behavior prediction using large data sets. IEEE Trans. Intell. Transp. Syst. **22**(11), 7129–7144 (2020)
24. Wissing, C., Nattermann, T., Glander, K.H., Hass, C., Bertram, T.: Lane change prediction by combining movement and situation based probabilities. IFAC-PapersOnLine **50**(1), 3554–3559 (2017)
25. Woo, H., et al.: Lane-change detection based on vehicle-trajectory prediction. IEEE Robot. Autom. Lett. **2**(2), 1109–1116 (2017)
26. Yang, X., Tang, L., Stewart, K., Dong, Z., Zhang, X., Li, Q.: Automatic change detection in lane-level road networks using GPS trajectories. Int. J. Geogr. Inf. Sci. **32**(3), 601–621 (2018)
27. Yenokyan, L.: Personalised federated learning: lane-change prediction. Master's thesis, LMU Munich (2024)
28. Yuan, R.: A comparative analysis of machine learning methods for lane change intention recognition using vehicle trajectory data. arXiv preprint arXiv:2307.15625 (2023)
29. Zhang, W., Huang, Y.H., Roetting, M., Wang, Y., Wei, H.: Driver's views and behaviors about safety in China-what do they not know about driving? Accid. Anal. Prev. **38**(1), 22–27 (2006)
30. Zhao, Y., Li, M., Lai, L., Suda, N., Civin, D., Chandra, V.: Federated learning with non-IID data. arXiv preprint arXiv:1806.00582 (2018)

Evaluating Traffic Control Strategies for Autonomous Shuttle in Different AV Penetration, Using SUMO Traffic Simulation

Javad Sadeghi$^{(\boxtimes)}$ ⓘ, Brunella Caroleo ⓘ, Cristiana Botta ⓘ, and Maurizio Arnone ⓘ

Links Foundation, Turin, Italy
{Javad.sadeghi,Brunella.caroleo,Cristiana.botta,
Maurizio.arnone}@linksfoundation.com

Abstract. The rapid growth of autonomous vehicles (AVs) and traffic strategies promises to transform urban mobility, necessitating a comprehensive investigation of their impacts on traffic. This study assessed the effects of different traffic control strategies on a network with an autonomous vehicles shuttle and varying levels of AV penetration. The simulation of Urban Mobility (SUMO) software was utilized as an open-source and flexible traffic microsimulation, creating a realistic simulation environment. Three traffic control strategies for shuttle movements were examined in a section of Turin, Italy: mixed traffic, dynamic lane, and separated lane strategies within the network. Each strategy was evaluated across five AV penetration levels.

The simulation results demonstrated that increasing the AV integration leads to reduced travel times and greater road efficiency. Both the separated lane and dynamic lane strategies improve travel times for the shuttle but have negative effects on other vehicles. However, the dynamic lane offers improvement for the shuttle while causing a lower negative impact on other vehicles compared to the separated lane strategy. Dynamic lanes offer a flexible and effective solution for modern traffic management, helping cities improve their mobility and reduce congestion. The findings highlight the importance of developing various control strategies and AV-compatible infrastructure to achieve traffic efficiency, reduced congestion, and an updated urban mobility framework.

Keywords: Traffic Control Strategy · Dynamic Lane · Autonomous Shuttle · Autonomous Vehicles (AVs) · Traffic Microsimulation · SUMO

1 Introduction

The research and development of traffic control strategies and AVs have seen rapid advancements in recent years, and simulations play a pivotal role in advancing development. Researchers and engineers rely on sophisticated simulation environments to model and evaluate the performance of autonomous systems in diverse and controlled scenarios. Simulations offer a safe and cost-effective means of testing and validating

© ICST Institute for Computer Sciences, Social Informatics and Telecommunications Engineering 2025
Published by Springer Nature Switzerland AG 2025. All Rights Reserved
A. Kocian et al. (Eds.): INTSYS 2024, LNICST 608, pp. 332–343, 2025.
https://doi.org/10.1007/978-3-031-86370-7_20

autonomous algorithms and control systems prior to real-world deployment [1]. Traffic simulation frameworks provide a helpful tool for answering complex research questions and evaluating traffic management strategies and their impact.

Many studies on the impact of AVs on Traffic parameters have focused on microscopic simulation. The detailed simulation of microscopic models is more precise, particularly when emissions or individual routes are simulated [2]. They can simulate a wide range of scenarios, from regular daily traffic patterns to uncommon events, such as accidents or road closures. Among microscopic traffic simulators, SUMO (Simulation of Urban Mobility) is a free and open-source package designed to handle large networks. SUMO enables the simulation of individual vehicles within road networks, thereby providing a platform for exploring a wide range of traffic-management topics.

While SUMO can run independently, complex traffic simulations with interactive control rely on the Traffic Control Interface (TraCI) library. TraCI serves as a bridge between Python and SUMO, enabling the definition of simulation scenarios, as well as control and dynamic interaction with the simulation through Python scripts.

This study aims to simulate the interactions between future autonomous shuttles autonomous vehicles, and human-driven vehicles under various traffic control strategies using SUMO, and to assess their impact to contribute to a deeper understanding of control strategies, AVs, and their roles in future urban mobility systems.

2 Related Works

In the context of impact of AVs on traffic flow, Nippold et al. studied the traffic flow and maximum capacity of signal-controlled intersections in Düsseldorf by using the SUMO traffic simulation tool in the presence of AVs. The results, integrated into the MATSim simulation, showed that AVs might decrease the maximum traffic capacity with a nearly linear reduction in capacity as AV penetration increases. Specifically, the maximum traffic flow rate decreased by more than 10% when comparing 100% conventional vehicles with 100% AVs [3].

In a study conducted by Lu, the impact of different penetration AVs on traffic parameters was investigated. The AVs were simulated in the SUMO traffic simulation suite with different driving parameters compared to conventional vehicles. Six scenarios with different AVs penetrations (from 0 to 100%) were simulated for grid and real-world networks. The results show that the capacity increases quasi-linearly with higher AVs penetration for both networks. In the grid network, the maximum flow increased by 16.01%, considering the 100% AVs penetration scenario with only conventional vehicles. For the real-world network simulation, the increase of maximum flow is around 25% from the 0% AVs penetration to purely AVs scenario [4].

Park et al. studied the impact of AVs on urban traffic flow and road capacity using a real-world network case study and VISSIM microsimulation. It simulates scenarios with varying AV penetration rates and traffic volume. The findings reveal that AVs significantly enhance traffic flow by reducing travel time and delay and increasing vehicle speed, especially at 100% penetration, with 17% time savings, 31% delay reduction, and 21% speed improvement. This study highlights the potential risk that if AVs increase overall car use, they can strain traffic management. Conversely, with all vehicles as

AVs, the current road network can handle 40% more traffic without additional road construction [5].

The dynamic control strategy is an advanced method of traffic management that adapts to real-time traffic conditions to optimize the flow of vehicles. This system often uses a combination of inductive loop detectors, infrared sensors, and cameras to detect vehicles. Advanced systems can be integrated with connected vehicle technologies, where vehicles communicate directly with the infrastructure, providing another data source for traffic management [6]. It reduced congestion, improved traffic flow, lowered emissions owing to reduced delays at intersections, and enhanced safety.

In another study, authors use Vissim, to compare the effectiveness of different bus lane management strategies at four selected locations in Rzeszów, Poland. These sites were chosen due to their similar length and traffic characteristics. The study evaluated three different options: no bus lanes, traditional exclusive bus lanes, and dynamic bus lanes. The dynamic bus lanes system was designed to activate only when buses were detected, allowing other vehicles to use the lane at other times, thereby optimizing lane usage. Results showed that dynamic bus lanes provided comparable benefits to buses as exclusive bus lanes but caused a much smaller increase in travel times for private vehicles. For instance, XBLs increased travel times for private vehicles by 12% to 25%, while DBLs only increased it by 1% to 12% [7].

Othman and Shalaby evaluated the effectiveness of Dynamic Bus Lanes compared to Exclusive Bus Lanes and mixed traffic operations under varying traffic demands and transit frequencies using AIMSUN simulations in Toronto, Canada. The results revealed that Dynamic Bus Lanes have the potential to improve the overall corridor performance over a wide range of traffic and transit service conditions, particularly under intermediate traffic demand levels. On the other hand, Exclusive Bus Lanes can be an efficient prioritization strategy that improves overall corridor performance under high traffic demand. Li et al. [8].

Optimized dynamic lane reservation for public transport, focusing on minimizing the impact on regular vehicles, while maximizing traffic efficiency for dynamic lane users. This approach utilizes bi-objective optimization and an improved evolutionary algorithm, featuring a hybrid crossover strategy for robustness and effectiveness. The proposed method was tested on a large-scale network. Their results showed that the dynamic lane approach is more effective for urban traffic efficiency than the previous models [9].

Scientific literature has investigated the potential impacts of AVs and traffic control strategies, such as dynamic lanes, on improving traffic capacity, and efficiency within existing mobility systems. Most research on AVs has focused on highway improvements, whereas only a few studies have addressed their impacts on urban transportation. Furthermore, the impacts of AVs and various traffic control strategies have not been fully explored.

3   Case Study

In the framework of the H2020 SHOW European project, [10] two automated shuttles were tested in real traffic in the Municipality of Turin (Italy) for future public transport. The shuttle can operate on both public and private roads with a high-performance guidance and detection system to adapt its navigation system to various situations. The shuttle can transport up to 15 passengers [9].

A fleet of automated shuttles can run along public roads, offering an on-demand transport service. Owing to the limited speed of the shuttles along the authorized route (speed limit is set to a maximum value of 18 km/h for safety reasons), congestion and slowdowns may occur when the shuttle are operating.

In this study, the shuttle path and outputs from the SHOW project were used as input data for the simulation. The simulation area was located at the center of Turin, which is the same area as the SHOW project. It covers the section bordered to the south by Corso Maroncelli, between the intersections of Via Ventimiglia and Via Genova, and to the north by Corso Spezia (Fig. 1). The shuttle is simulated along this route with 7 stop stations, where it stops for 30 s at each one. Ventimiglia has two lanes in each direction, from Corso Maroncelli to Corso Caduti sul Lavoro, while the rest of the street has only one lane. Therefore, a part of this section was selected to implement the traffic scenarios. Traffic control strategies were implemented on Via Ventimiglia, between Via Valenza and Corso Maroncelli, which includes two shuttle stop stations.

Fig. 1. Simulation area in Torino

The simulation was conducted using three distinct traffic-control strategies. These scenarios were defined and implemented using TraCI in SUMO.

In the first traffic control strategy, mixed traffic control was used for shuttles, AVs, and human-driven cars. This approach avoids prioritization or restrictions on any vehicle type. All vehicle categories shared road spaces, without any type receiving preferential treatment. In a mixed traffic environment, all vehicles interact with each other, which can create challenges for managing safety, predictability, and efficient traffic flow. This strategy was selected as the base scenario and served as a benchmark for comparing the effectiveness of the subsequent strategies.

The second traffic control strategy is a separate lane for shuttles in Via Ventimiglia, from Via Valenza to Corso Maronceli. A separated lane strategy involves creating lanes that are physically or visually separated from general traffic, and reserved for particular types of vehicles or purposes, such as bicycles or public transit. The consequence of this lane allocation is a reduction in lane availability for the other types of vehicles. The primary goal is to prioritize shuttle within the traffic network.

The third traffic control strategy involves the implementation of a dynamic lane system. A dynamic lane strategy refers to a flexible road lane management system in which lanes are reassigned dynamically based on priorities to serve specific vehicle types or purposes. Such as bicycles, or public transit vehicles. This was applied to sections of the network along Via Ventimiglia, from Via Valenza to Corso Maroncelli. This strategy aims to provide protection and prioritization for the shuttle, enhance user interest, and ensure smooth operation.

These scenarios were implemented using five different penetration levels of AVs and the defined AVs. In addition, 0%, 25%, 50%, 75%, and 100% penetration of the AVs.

4   Methodology

4.1   Traffic Behavior Models

Behavioral models in traffic simulations, such as lane-changing and car-following models, are essential components that define how vehicles interact with each other and navigate road networks. These models aim to replicate real-world driving behaviors, thereby enabling realistic and accurate traffic simulations.

Car-following models are mathematical representations used in traffic flow theory and simulations to describe how individual vehicles adjust their speed and spacing relative to other vehicles on a road. The Intelligent Driver Model is a car-following model designed to capture the behaviours of real-world drivers by considering factors such as the desired speed, minimum gap, time headway, and comfortable deceleration. It offers a realistic representation of how drivers adjust their speeds in response to traffic conditions [12]. IDM can be used to model a wide range of traffic conditions, from free-flowing traffic to congested scenarios. Its parameters can be adjusted to simulate various driving behaviours [13]. In this simulation, the IDM Car-following model was implemented for the vehicles.

Lane changing, as another model in traffic simulation behavior, is a crucial aspect of traffic flow and microscopic traffic simulations. These models aim to capture the complexity of the lane-changing dynamics and enhance the realism of traffic simulations. However, for AVs, lane-changing models are evolving owing to fundamental differences in decision-making between humans and machines. AVs rely on sensor data, environmental predictions, and safe execution, thereby introducing greater complexity. SUMO supports customizable vehicle behavior, enabling the implementation of various lane-changing models. In this article we use the LC2013 model, that incorporates psychological aspects such as impatience, making it a realistic model in simulating AVs and human-driven vehicle in lane-changing behavior.

4.2 Simulation Networks

The generation of road networks for SUMO can be accomplished in several ways, including manual creation, using Open Street Map (OSM), or importing maps from other simulation software, depending on the complexity of the network and the available data sources [14]. Complex Road networks often involve a combination of methods, owing to the differences between the input map details and real details. In this simulation, a combination of methods is used to create a more realistic network. The map imported by the "OSM Web Wizard" from the OSM was based on the road network. (Fig. 2) Due to differences between OSM and reality in details like the number of lanes, traffic signal cycles, shuttle stops, and speed limits, the imported map is reviewed and modified manually.

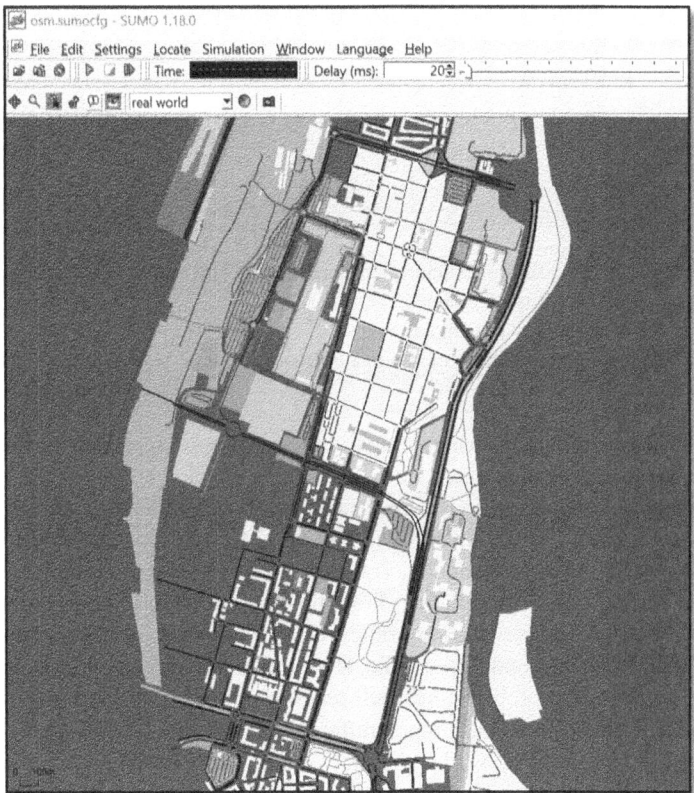

Fig. 2. Simulation Area in SUMO

4.3 Simulation Parameters

Humans primarily rely on visual cues, which can be subjective and sometimes influenced by cognitive biases or distractions. However, AVs use an array of sensors (LiDAR, radar, cameras, ultrasonic sensors, etc.) that provide objective and quantified data regarding their surroundings. This dataset is processed rapidly for decision-making. This affects the Reaction Times and AVs can react almost instantaneously. These differences change the parameters of the simulation models of AVs compared to those of human-driven vehicles. In the SUMO simulation, vehicle parameters are defined for each vehicle type and are pivotal for generating accurate and realistic traffic simulations. This definition represents different vehicles such as cars, trucks, and buses. The key attributes of these types include vehicle dimensions, speed limits, acceleration and deceleration rates, lane-changing behavior, fuel consumption, emissions, and preferred routes. SUMO offers customization to simulate the distinct behaviors of various vehicles ranging from passenger cars to autonomous vehicles. In this simulation, the SUMO parameters were modified based on Table 1 to define AVs and other vehicle types.

Table 1. Parameters of the driver model used in SUMO simulations [4]

Type Car	Min Gap (m)	Accel (m/s^2)	Decel (m/s^2)	Emergency decel (m/s^2)	Max Speed (km/h)
Human Driver	1.5	3.5	4.5	8	50
AVs	0.5	3.8	4.5	8	50
Shuttle	0.5	0.8	1.5	3	18

- Mingap: the offset to the leading vehicle when standing in a jam
- Accel: the acceleration ability of vehicles
- Decel: the deceleration ability of vehicles
- Emergency Decel: the maximum deceleration ability of vehicles

SUMO offers flexibility in customizing traffic flow types to represent various vehicle categories and their unique characteristics. This customization allows for the modeling of a wide range of scenarios and defines public transportation, emergency services, and freight transport. SUMO's flexibility in managing various traffic definition methods makes it a powerful tool for simulation. Traffic flows in SUMO can be defined and generated using several methods including direct flow definition, origin–destination (OD) matrices, turning percentages, random routes, flow distribution over time, public transport flows, and importing real-world data. These methods were chosen based on data availability. Combining or refining methods leads to more realistic and complex traffic simulations in SUMO.In this study, input traffic data were gathered through manual traffic counts at key intersections, while other network flows were assumed. Based on this, around 10,000 vehicles per hour inserted into the simulation network. Vehicle routes were generated using "jtrrouter," a Python script designed to randomly distribute traffic throughout the network. The selected route for the shuttle is defined in the routes file, which includes stops and their stop times.

The traffic scenarios in this study were designed and managed using TraCI in the SUMO environment. TraCI plays a central role in continuously monitoring and controlling the simulation by interfacing with Python scripts. This real-time interaction enables dynamic adjustments to traffic configurations based on simulated events.

To implement a dynamic lane in SUMO (Fig. 3), a specific point within the network is defined using TraCI. As the shuttle approached a predefined section, TraCI detected its presence and activated a dynamic lane in the upcoming segment until the next intersection. This dynamic lane assignment designated the first lane exclusively for shuttles, temporarily restricting access to other vehicle types. Once the shuttle traverses the dynamic lane section, allowing TraCI to revert the status of the first lane, the restricted lane becomes accessible to all vehicles, thereby restoring the standard traffic flow.

To implement the separated lane strategy, the properties of the lanes were modified using NetEdit, a graphical network editor within the SUMO. These modifications were made to restrict access to selected lanes and allow shuttles to operate in these lanes.

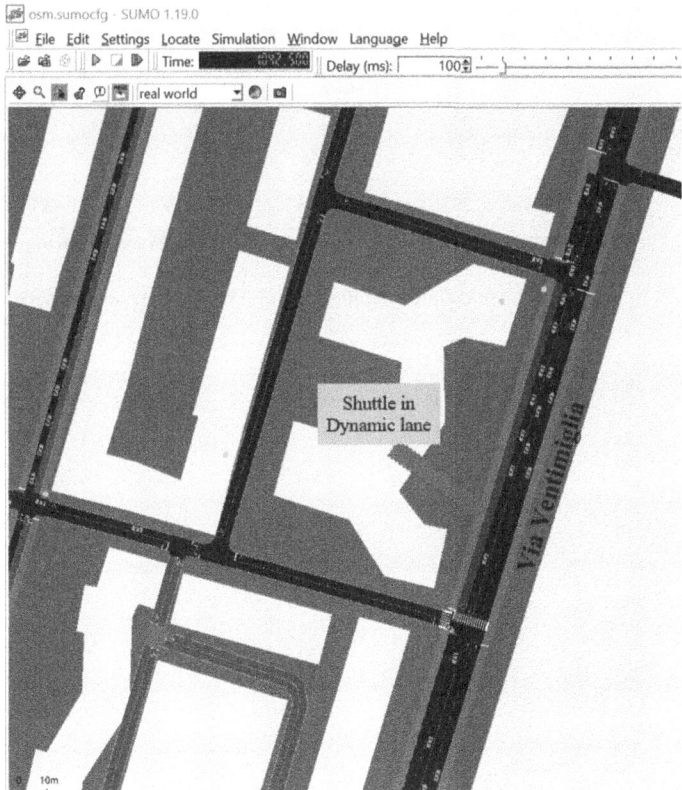

Fig. 3. Simulation of Dynamic Lane in SUMO

5   Simulation Results

Each scenario was simulated 10 times with different random seeds to account for variability in trip and route generation as well as simulation dynamics. The traffic efficiency of the vehicles was observed using the travel time in test sections of traffic strategies. The parameters were disaggregated by vehicle type to determine whether control strategies had a positive effect. The simulations were performed for a duration of 1 h. The results are aggregated and presented in Fig. 4 and Fig. 5 for various traffic strategies under different AVs percentages.

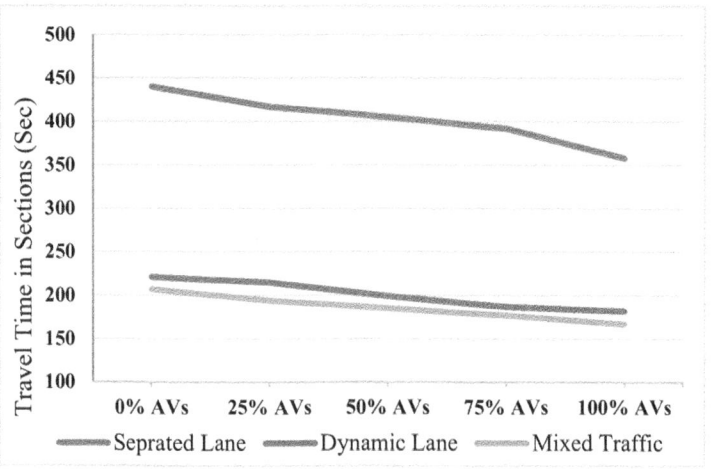

Fig.4. Travel time of vehicles in different strategies and AVs percentages in selected sections

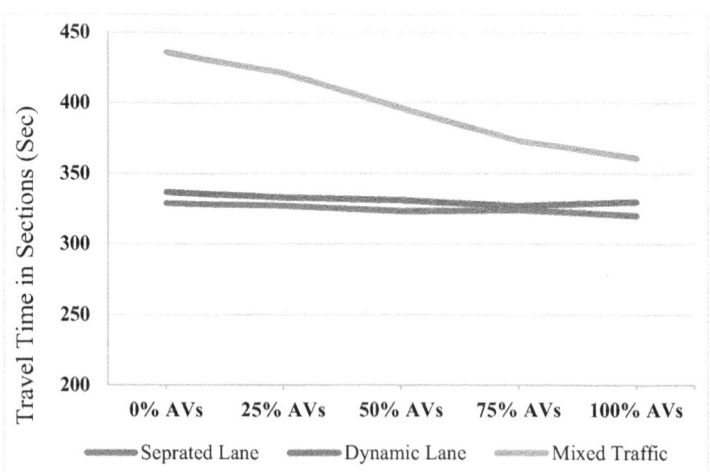

Fig. 5. Travel times of the shuttle in different strategies and AVs percentages in selected sections

In the Mixed Traffic Strategy, the travel time for both vehicles and shuttles decreased as the percentage of AVs increased. Vehicles showed a steady improvement, with decreasing 19.3% in travel times, from 207 s at 0% AVs to 167 s at 100% AVs. Similarly, Shuttle travel times start at 436 s in a fully human-driven scenario and progressively decrease to 361 s in a fully AV-based environment, it is around 17.6% reduction in travel time.

These results indicate that integrating AVs into a mixed traffic environment has a substantial positive effect on overall network performance. In mixed traffic, AVs can react faster to changes, maintain smoother acceleration and deceleration patterns, and effectively optimize space, all of which lead to reduced overall travel times. This behaviour not only improves the efficiency of general traffic but also enhances the reliability and punctuality of shuttle services, which is crucial in an urban setting where public transport plays a vital role in reducing congestion.

In the Dynamic Lane Strategy, vehicles also experienced decreasing 17.6% travel times by increasing AVs penetration to 100%. However, overall travel times increased by approximately 11.7% on average compared to the Mixed Traffic Strategy. For shuttle, travel times decreased by an average of 16.5% compared to the Mixed Traffic Strategy but remained approximately constant despite changes in the percentage of AVs.

The dynamic lane strategy benefits from its inherent flexibility, allowing lane allocation to change based on real-time traffic needs. The adaptability of dynamic lanes allows urban planners to adjust traffic flow patterns dynamically, which can be useful during peak hours or special events where shuttle reliability and consistency are key. The fact that shuttle travel times remained stable regardless of AV penetration highlights the robustness of dynamic lane strategies in supporting public transit without significantly disadvantaging other vehicles. This adaptability demonstrates a strong advantage of dynamic lane management, especially in the context of cities aiming to prioritize public transport while managing private vehicle congestion.

Similar patterns were observed for the Separated Lane Strategy. Travel time of vehicles improved 20.2% by changing penetration of AVs from 0% to 100% AVs. In comparison with the Mixed Traffic Strategy, there was an average increase of 126.7%. For shuttles, travel times decreased by the average of 18.2% compared to the Mixed Traffic Strategy but low reduction regardless of the proportion of AVs.

The results suggest that the implementation of separated lanes has both benefits and challenges. The advantage lies in its ability to provide a dedicated lane for shuttles, effectively eliminating interference from other vehicles, thus ensuring consistent and predictable travel times. However, this dedication of lanes also results in reduced road capacity for general traffic, leading to increased congestion in the remaining lanes. The increased travel time for regular vehicles implies that separated lanes may not always be the best strategy, especially when road space is limited, and it is essential to manage the flow of both public and private vehicles equitably.

A key insight from the simulations is that increasing AV penetration has a positive effect on overall network performance across strategies. The benefits were most notable in the Separated Lane Strategy, where the introduction of AVs led to a more reduction in travel time. The ability of AVs to travel more closely together and make quicker adjustments helps mitigate the bottlenecks created by the reduced road capacity associated with separated lanes.

The shuttle also benefits from the introduction of AVs. This improvement is the highest, by 17.2%, in the mixed traffic by changing AVs from totally human driven to fully automated vehicles.

The findings of this study highlight the influence of traffic control strategies on the effectiveness of urban networks. Among the strategies analysed, separated lanes offer substantial benefits for shuttle travel times but result in increased travel times for other vehicles. In contrast, dynamic lane strategies improve shuttle travel times with only a slight impact on general vehicle traffic. This makes dynamic lanes an attractive option for cities looking to optimize road usage while maintaining flexibility.

Dynamic lane strategies demonstrate advantages in their ability to respond adaptively to real-time traffic conditions. By prioritizing public transportation and optimizing the available road capacity, dynamic lanes offer a modern solution to urban traffic management. The flexibility in dynamic lanes allows for more efficient allocation of road space, improving the efficiency of public transit without unnecessarily affecting the travel times for other vehicles. As cities increasingly move towards smart and connected infrastructure, the use of dynamic lane strategies becomes even more relevant, providing adaptable solution that aligns with the goals of modern urban mobility.

6 Conclusions

AVs represent a frontier for innovation in urban mobility and promise transformational changes in urban traffic. This study focuses on evaluating various traffic control strategies under different AV penetration levels using the SUMO microsimulator. Across all strategies, as the AV percentage increased, there was a decrease in the travel time for vehicles. The greatest improvements for vehicles were observed with the implementation of separated lanes, where the implementation of the strategy led to an increase in the flow within remain lanes. This outcome demonstrates the significant impact of AVs under higher traffic congestion conditions that is due to their characteristic behaviours and reaction.

The results show that traffic control strategies have a significant impact on the effectiveness of urban networks. When comparing different strategies, separated lanes significantly improved the travel times for the shuttle but notably increased it for other vehicles. However, dynamic lane strategies improved the travel times for the shuttle compared with mixed traffic, with only a slight increase in travel times for both AVs and human-driven vehicles.

Dynamic lane strategies offer benefits by adapting to real-time traffic conditions, optimizing road usage, and providing adaptable solutions to traffic-management challenges. Changes in the traffic levels can impact the effectiveness of these strategies, due to delays at intersections.

This work also demonstrates the capabilities and flexibility of SUMO, as a free and open-source software, in implementing and simulating traffic scenarios. Although simulation studies provide useful insights, real-world testing is required to validate these results. Closing the gap between the simulation and real-world performance is crucial to ensure that the predictions are accurate and applicable in practical situations.

7 Future Work

In our upcoming projects, it will be pivotal to use real-time human-driven data sourced from AVs. The real-time data provided, stemming from connected vehicles and their continuous interaction with other vehicles, infrastructure, and even pedestrians, offer a more dynamic approach to simulating and managing urban traffic scenarios. The SUMO can be calibrated and validated using real-time data streams. The simulation outputs were continuously compared with the real-time data. This ensured that the simulation accurately reflected the current traffic scenario.

References

1. Paden, B., Cap, M., Yong, S.Z., Yershov, D., Frazzoli, E.: A Survey of Motion Planning and Control Techniques for Self-driving Urban Vehicles (2016). https://doi.org/10.48550/ARXIV. 1604.07446
2. Lopez, P.A., et al.: Microscopic traffic simulation using SUMO. In: 2018 21st International Conference on Intelligent Transportation Systems (ITSC), Maui, HI, pp. 2575–2582. IEEE (2018). https://doi.org/10.1109/ITSC.2018.8569938
3. Nippold, R., Wagner, P., Banse Bueno, O.A., Rakow, C.: Investigation of the effect of autonomous vehicles (AV) on the capacity of an urban transport network. In: SUMO Conference on Proceedings, vol. 2, pp. 53–65 (2022). https://doi.org/10.52825/scp.v2i.87
4. Lu, Q., Tettamanti, T., Hörcher, D., Varga, I.: The impact of autonomous vehicles on urban traffic network capacity: an experimental analysis by microscopic traffic simulation. Transp. Lett. **12**(8), 540–549 (2020). https://doi.org/10.1080/19427867.2019.1662561
5. Park, J.E., Byun, W., Kim, Y., Ahn, H., Shin, D.K.: The impact of automated vehicles on traffic flow and road capacity on urban road networks. J. Adv. Transp. **2021**, 1–10 (2021). https://doi.org/10.1155/2021/8404951
6. Alhajyaseen, W.K.M., Najjar, M., Ratrout, N.T., Assi, K.: The effectiveness of applying dynamic lane assignment at all approaches of signalized intersection. Case Stud. Transp. Policy **5**(2), 224–232 (2017). https://doi.org/10.1016/j.cstp.2017.01.008
7. Szarata, M., Olszewski, P., Bichajło, L.: Simulation study of dynamic bus lane concept. Sustainability **13**(3), 1302 (2021). https://doi.org/10.3390/su13031302
8. Othman, K., Shalaby, A., Abdulhai, B.: Dynamic bus lanes versus exclusive bus lanes: comprehensive comparative analysis of urban corridor performance. Transp. Res. Rec. J. Transp. Res. Board **2677**(1), 341–355 (2023). https://doi.org/10.1177/03611981221099517
9. Li, T., Wang, N., Jiang, B., Zhang, M.: A bi-objective lane reservation problem considering dynamic traffic flow. IEEE Trans. Intell. Transp. Syst. **24**(1), 367–381 (2023). https://doi.org/ 10.1109/TITS.2022.3212553
10. "Show Project". Show Project. https://show-project.eu/. Accessed 11 Dec 2023
11. "NAVYA." https://www.navya.tech/en/. Accessed 11 Dec 2023
12. Treiber, M., Hennecke, A., Helbing, D.: Congested Traffic States in Empirical Observations and Microscopic Simulations (2000). https://doi.org/10.48550/ARXIV.COND-MAT/ 0002177
13. Kesting, A., Treiber, M., Helbing, D.: Enhanced Intelligent Driver Model to Access the Impact of Driving Strategies on Traffic Capacity (2009). https://doi.org/10.48550/ARXIV.0912.3613
14. SUMO Website. "SUMO Online Documents" (n.d.). https://sumo.dlr.de/docs/index.html

Adaptive Video Bitrate Allocation for Remotely Operated Vehicles (ROV)

Eman Sarah Afi[1]([✉]), Ons Triqui[2], Sofiane Sayahi[3], Hichem Besbes[4], and Fethi Tlili[5]

[1] Mediterranean Institute of Technology, South Mediterranean University, Tunis, Tunisia
emansarah.afi@medtech.tn
[2] Higher School of Communication of Tunis, University of Carthage, Ariana, Tunisia
ons.triqui@supcom.tn
[3] Innovation Department, ACTIA Engineering Services, Ariana, Tunisia
sofiane.sayahi@actia-engineering.tn
[4] COSIM Lab, Higher School of Communication of Tunis,
University of Carthage, Ariana, Tunisia
hichem.besbes@supcom.tn
[5] GRESCOM Lab, Higher School of Communication of Tunis,
University of Carthage, Ariana, Tunisia
fethi.tlili@supcom.tn

Abstract. Establishing a stable and efficient connection between operators and remotely operated vehicles (ROVs) is essential for successful missions in challenging environments. Real-time video transmission is particularly critical, providing operators with visual feedback to navigate and control the vehicle effectively. This study aims to improve video transmission quality in a multi-camera ROV equipped with six cameras and various sensors. Our focus is to enhance the Quality-Aware Dynamic Rate Allocation (QADRA) system, which optimizes video quality by dynamically adjusting codec parameters like resolution and quantization parameters (QPs) based on expected peak signal-to-noise ratio (XPSNR) predictions. This enhancement addresses the unique challenges of achieving balanced video quality across multiple video streams.

The method involves developing a system that dynamically adapts codec parameters for each camera based on predefined bitrates, influenced by an assigned weight to each camera to control bitrate distribution and resulting video quality. By prioritizing certain video streams, this weighted system aims to optimize visual representation and thus improve the operator's situational awareness.

Results from theoretical exploration and analysis indicate that this approach can enhance the internal distribution of video quality across multiple camera feeds, contributing to more effective decision-making during teleoperated vehicle operations. In conclusion, this research advances the multi-camera video transmission capabilities for teleoperated vehicles, addressing limitations in video quality management and improving operational effectiveness in remote vehicle control.

Keywords: Video Bitrate Adaptation · Codec Parameters · Remotely Operated Vehicle

© ICST Institute for Computer Sciences, Social Informatics and Telecommunications Engineering 2025
Published by Springer Nature Switzerland AG 2025. All Rights Reserved
A. Kocian et al. (Eds.): INTSYS 2024, LNICST 608, pp. 344–360, 2025.
https://doi.org/10.1007/978-3-031-86370-7_21

1   Introduction

Remote Operated Driving Vehicles (ROVs) are a significant advancement on the path towards fully autonomous vehicles [1]. Even though autonomy is the ultimate objective, teleoperation provides a means for human operators to control vehicles in challenging environments where automation may encounter difficulties. In such situations, having a dependable real-time perception of the environment, chiefly through visual feedback, is crucial [1]. This ensures that operators can make well-informed decisions while overseeing vehicle operations from a distance. Clear and timely visual data empowers operators to navigate safely, evade obstacles, and carry out tasks accurately, underscoring the importance of video transmission in teleoperation.

Effective communication between operators and their machines is crucial for mission success in challenging environments. A key component of this communication is real-time video transmission, which provides operators with essential visual feedback. In this realm, several intricate challenges may arise, notably latency and cloud offloading. Latency, or the delay in communication between the vehicle and its control system, can impede real-time responsiveness, critically affecting operational efficiency and safety [1]. Meanwhile, cloud offloading, the process of relying on remote servers for data processing, can lead to unpredictable delays due to network variability, potentially disrupting seamless control and data handling [2]. Each of these issues underscores the importance of robust and adaptive systems to ensure optimal performance and reliability in teleoperated environments. Network latency can significantly affect teleoperation performance, hindering real-time perception and decision-making. Various strategies were reviewed to mitigate latency issues, underscoring the need for seamless communication systems to improve teleoperation effectiveness in CAVs.

The Quality-Aware Dynamic Resolution Adaptation (QADRA) framework is designed for adaptive video streaming, which predicts the average Extended Peak Signal-to-Noise Ratio (XPSNR) of VVC-coded bitstreams using spatiotemporal complexity features and an XGBoost-based model [3, 4]. QADRA maximizes XPSNR while keeping encoding and decoding times within acceptable thresholds for smooth and energy-efficient streaming, and it implements a JND (Just Noticeable Difference)-based representation elimination algorithm to remove redundant representations from the bitrate ladder [3, 4].

However, while QADRA is a good solution, it could benefit from enhancements, especially considering systems that need to transmit multiple video feeds, such as those with six different cameras, like in Remote Operated Driving Vehicles (ROVs). In such cases, a more advanced balancing of the bandwidth allocation across these video streams is necessary to ensure that the most critical visual information is transmitted at the highest quality, while less important feeds receive appropriate quality adjustments.

Our research delves into refining the QADRA solution by enhancing internal video quality distribution among various cameras in a remotely operated vehicle. Through dynamic adjustments of codec parameters like the resolution and the quantization parameter, along with assigning weight to each camera, the system strives to maintain video quality independently of network bandwidth considerations.

Our study will cover key sections such as a literature review, which delves into prior work on video transmission technologies and multi-camera systems, a detailed methodology outlining the solution to the research problem, and a conclusion offering insights into the implications of the findings, potential areas for future research, and the practical benefits of the improved system in real-world scenarios. Through comprehensive experimentation and analysis, this research advances multi-camera video transmission technologies and lays the groundwork for more effective visual feedback systems in remote vehicle operations.

2 Literature Review

Teleoperated systems have garnered significant attention in current research, with a focus on improving operator situational awareness and remote vehicle management through adaptive video streaming strategies. A notable contribution in this field is the "Quality-Aware Dynamic Resolution Adaptation Framework for Adaptive Video Streaming" (QADRA) [3, 4]. The QADRA framework optimizes video streaming quality by dynamically adjusting resolution based on XPSNR predictions, ensuring better operator situational focus and efficient vehicle control. By maximizing XPSNR while maintaining appropriate encoding and decoding times, QADRA aligns with the need for reliable and high-quality video transmission in teleoperated driving scenarios. This framework complements ongoing research aimed at enhancing video streaming techniques in teleoperated systems, addressing the challenges of balancing video quality and streaming efficiency [3, 4].

An adaptive video streaming machine for teleoperated driving emphasized the importance of low-latency video transmission to ensure operator safety in complex traffic situations [5]. The proposed system includes several components: a tele-driving machine, driver situational awareness evaluation, and traffic-aware multi-view adaptation to optimize video streams based on real-time traffic conditions [6]. Similarly, hardware limitations in autonomous vehicles were investigated, which proposed a preprocessing technique for individual quality adaptation using a single hardware encoder. This approach aimed to maintain high video quality while minimizing degradation for non-primary views [6].

In the realm of teleoperated driving, researchers explored the challenges posed by mobile networks and their impact on vehicle control [7]. They addressed the feasibility of teleoperated driving using current mobile networks, focusing on factors like latency, video stream compression, and bandwidth reduction for uplink video streams. It was found that while teleoperated driving is possible, network variability presents significant challenges. Strategies such as speed adjustments based on latency and video stream segmentation can help mitigate these issues, making teleoperated driving safer and more viable [7].

The framework for adaptive video streaming, which is designed for teleoperated automobiles, allows for the automatic reconfiguration of video streams from a couple of cameras in real-time, considering variable transmission carrier fines. The intention is to enhance visible exceptional by dynamically allocating bitrates and deciding on resolution scaling elements. The outcomes from deploying this framework on a teleoperated riding device are also offered [8].

The nuScenes dataset was introduced alongside its comprehensive series of records designed to facilitate improving and assessing autonomous car technologies, especially emphasizing object detection and tracking. The dataset includes a full suite of autonomous vehicle sensors and is annotated with 3-D bounding containers for diverse instructions and attributes. It extensively increases annotations and photos as compared to previous datasets like KITTI, supplying a precious aid for schooling and evaluating gadget studying algorithms for self-reliant driving. The authors introduce novel three-D detection and tracking metrics, in conjunction with cautious dataset evaluation and baselines for detection and monitoring techniques in the usage of lidar and photograph data [9].

Camera technologies play a crucial role in various applications such as vehicle detection, object recognition, and distance measurement. A comparison of different cameras reveals a wide range of sensor types, functionalities, technical specifications, and features. A camera showcases a horizontal FOV (field-of-view) of 90° and a vertical FOV of 60° [10]. It boasts a resolution of 1920 × 1080 pixels, real-time processing capabilities, and features such as vehicle detection and stereo vision techniques. This camera excels in distance calculation and employs geometric derivations for enhanced accuracy.

In contrast, a camera is presented with a variable FOV ranging from 60 to 120° and a longer range of up to 200 m [11]. This camera offers high-resolution imaging, object recognition, and lane detection capabilities. Additionally, it incorporates RADAR technology for all-weather functionality and LiDAR for precise distance measurement and obstacle detection.

In a related context, a camera [12] bears similarities with another camera [11] in the FOV range but is distinct in resolution, offering 1920 × 1280 pixels for superior imaging quality. This model supports multi-class object detection, real-time processing, transfer learning, and the evaluation of various deep learning models such as faster R-CNN and YOLOv3. Addressing the fusion of RGB cameras with LiDAR sensors, a comprehensive 360-degree FOV system was introduced alongside its highlights about heightened object detection accuracy for smaller targets through the combination of RGB and depth images, employing Siamese based on Yolov5. Notably, the system's efficacy is validated on the KITTI dataset, showcasing superior performance metrics [13].

Delving into the combination of AI technologies with image sensors, Cho et al. [14] highlight the integration of AI algorithms in image sensors to facilitate high-resolution imaging for long-range object detection. Leveraging YOLOv4 and DeepSort algorithms, this system enables real-time object identification and tracking while offering web-based visualization for multi-user support. Furthermore, a novel exploration by researchers [15] focuses on specific sensors like Sony IMX324 and Samsung S5K2G1, optimized for long-range forward-facing cameras. These sensors excel in traffic sign recognition up to 200 m, boasting high resolution, fixed-focus design, and athermalized features for consistent performance across varying temperature conditions.

Highlighting advancements in LiDAR and RGB camera integration, Arikumar et al. [16] emphasize a 3D LiDAR sensor with a 360-degree FOV and high angular resolution, capturing intricate 3D shapes, distance, and positional data. Furthermore, this system incorporates an RGB camera with a 120-degree FOV for high-resolution imaging and depth estimation leveraging principal component analysis (PCA). To focus more on CMOS technology innovations in night vision cameras, a scholarly work [17] introduces a camera with a 90-degree horizontal and 60-degree vertical FOV, equipped with night vision capabilities. This camera offers image stabilization, auto-focus, HDR capabilities, and high-resolution imaging suitable for diverse applications.

The evolution of LiDAR technology in object detection systems is examined by Kumar et al. [18], where laser-based sensors are employed for precise distance measurement and 3D mapping. This system is complemented by a camera with either CMOS or CCD sensors, providing high-resolution imaging, color information, and object detection functionalities. Conversely, a separate investigation [19] outlines a CMOS camera with infrared capabilities that was customized for night vision scenarios, boasting a 90-degree horizontal and 60-degree vertical FOV. This camera features auto-focus, image stabilization, HDR functions, and high-resolution imaging for optimal operational efficiency.

Object detection systems play a vital role in supporting these teleoperated applications, especially as the need to handle compressed video streams without compromising detection accuracy grows. Studies reveal that object detection accuracy significantly depends on the quality of the compressed video. For example, researchers analyzing video compression impacts on YOLOv5-based detection systems found that moderate compression (using a CRF of 37) maintains high detection accuracy while significantly reducing file size [20]. However, higher compression levels (CRF values of 42 and 47) led to noticeable detection performance degradation, particularly in poor lighting or when tracking fast-moving objects [21].

Further extending video compression strategies, researchers have proposed bit rate reduction methods in cloud gaming applications, using object detection techniques to eliminate non-essential scenes. By dynamically reducing the bit rate based on scene importance, the algorithm improves network efficiency and reduces latency, thus enhancing user experience without impacting essential visual elements [22]. Similarly, saliency-driven coding frameworks prioritize important regions in video footage, preserving essential areas for object detection while compressing less important regions more heavily. This approach, particularly effective for surveillance, achieves significant bitrate savings while maintaining high detection accuracy [23].

Additionally, the integration of federated learning and edge processing techniques offers promising solutions for managing privacy and computational efficiency across distributed networks. Federated learning enables collaborative model training on multiple devices without sharing raw data, enhancing privacy while maintaining effective machine learning capabilities. These benefits, particularly relevant for teleoperated and autonomous systems, underscore the need for further research into scalable and privacy-conscious AI applications [24].

Advances in object-detection-based video compression have utilized Versatile Video Coding (VVC) standards combined with saliency-driven approaches to focus on important video regions, thereby improving object detection even at high compression levels. Such frameworks help achieve a balance between high-quality video retention for key objects and overall file size reduction, proving advantageous in bandwidth-limited applications like teleoperated surveillance [25] (Table 1).

Table 1. Article comparison regarding video bitrate changes

Article	Similarities	Differences	Outcomes
Article [20]	• Focuses on object detection accuracy with compressed video • Evaluates different levels of compression (CRF values)	• Emphasizes the effect of compression on detection accuracy in surveillance • Uses YOLOv5 and tested on surveillance videos	Found that moderate compression (CRF 37) reduces file size with minimal detection accuracy loss; high compression (CRF 42, 47) drops accuracy, especially in low-light or fast-motion scenes. Retraining on compressed videos slightly improves results
Article [21]	• Studies the impact of video compression on object detection • Investigates video quality and its effect on detection algorithms	• Uses multiple deep-learning models for object detection • Proposes a new benchmark dataset for testing object detectors	Found that compression artifacts (blocking, blurring) degrade detection performance. Proposes that future research focus on the robustness of these distortions, highlighting the need for models that handle compressed video well
Article [22]	• Uses object detection to reduce video bitrate • Aims to reduce bitrate without significant loss of quality	• Focuses on cloud gaming and reducing bitrate for gaming experiences • Focuses on adaptive algorithms for cloud gaming scenes	Developed an adaptive algorithm that reduces bitrate by removing non-essential gaming scenes, decreasing encoding time by 14.6% and bitrate by 45.6% for some scenes. Improved network latency and gaming experience

(*continued*)

Table 1. (*continued*)

Article	Similarities	Differences	Outcomes
Article [23]	• Uses video coding techniques to improve object detection • Explores ways to compress less important regions while preserving object detection quality	• Uses Versatile Video Coding (VVC) and focuses on bandwidth savings • Targets video surveillance applications	Saliency-driven approach compresses unimportant regions more heavily, saving 29% bitrate without detection accuracy loss. Useful for surveillance where both video quality and detection accuracy are essential
Article [24]	• Discusses techniques to improve performance in data transmission • Highlights data privacy and machine learning across devices	• Focuses on federated learning, unrelated to video compression • Does not focus on video or object detection	Highlights benefits of federated learning for secure, decentralized machine learning while protecting data privacy. Does not address video compression directly but provides insights on data security and communication efficiency
Article [25]	• Uses object detection in video compression techniques • Aims to preserve important regions of the video while compressing others	• Proposes object detection-based VVC for video compression • Focuses on efficient data transmission for surveillance	Allocates more resources to key regions (detected objects) to maintain their quality, achieving significant compression while retaining clarity in important areas. Valuable for applications like surveillance where object clarity is critical

In conclusion, these studies collectively contribute to the development of robust, efficient, and adaptive teleoperated and autonomous systems by addressing video quality and object detection challenges in bandwidth-constrained environments. By leveraging advanced video compression, adaptive bitrate allocation, and federated learning, these innovations promise to improve situational awareness and decision-making capabilities for remote operators, paving the way for safer, more responsive, and more reliable teleoperated driving solutions.

3   Proposed Solution

Our methodology for adaptive video bitrate allocation in teleoperated vehicles involved two main chains: the Video Processing Chain, which is the QADRA framework that, as previously mentioned, is a solution to optimizing video streaming quality via dynamically adapting resolution based on XPSNR predictions [3, 4], and the Camera Weight Optimization Chain (Fig. 1).

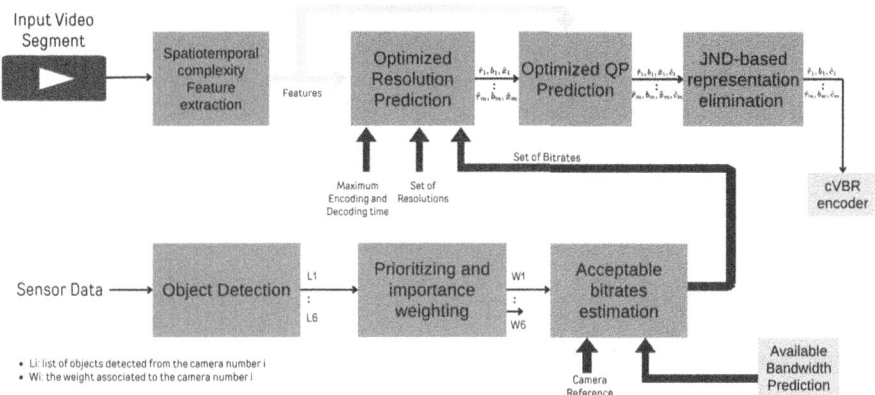

Fig. 1. Proposed solution for adaptive video bitrate allocation

The diagram illustrates distinct modules, each responsible for a specific task such as feature extraction, object detection, resolution and QP prediction, representation elimination, and bitrate estimation. These modules interact with one another but are separable, allowing for independent updates, testing, and maintenance. This modularity enhances flexibility and scalability, making it easier to adapt and extend the system.

The vehicle is equipped with 6 cameras (Basler acA1600-60 gc) that have a 12 Hz capture frequency and a 1600×900 region of interest (ROI), providing a surround view with one camera facing the back [26]. The system also includes a single LiDAR (Velodyne HDL32E) with a 20 Hz capture frequency, 32 beams, and approximately 1080 (± 10) points per ring. It can detect usable returns up to 70 m with ± 2 cm accuracy, providing up to ~1.39 million points per second. Additionally, the vehicle is outfitted with 5 RADAR units (Continental ARS 408-21) that capture at 13 Hz with a 77 GHz frequency [26]. These RADAR units can detect objects up to 250 m away and independently measure both distance and velocity in a single cycle using Frequency Modulated Continuous Wave technology [26].

For navigation, the system uses GPS and IMU sensors with a position accuracy of 20 mm [26]. Initially, all cameras have equal weights, but these weights are dynamically updated as driving scenarios change. The input video segment is provided by one camera, specified by a reference, and the weights are updated accordingly. A JND-based representation elimination technique reduces perceptual redundancy in the bitrate ladder; if the predicted quality difference between two representations is lower than a set threshold, the representation requiring a higher bitrate is eliminated. The proposed system focuses on the green blocks.

The available bandwidth prediction will simply be an input, but the module can be developed and appended to the system subsequently. Components like $\{b_1, ..., b_m\}$ represent the set of target bitrates, $\{\hat{r}_1, ..., \hat{r}_m\}$ the corresponding resolutions, $\{\hat{x}_1, ..., \hat{x}_m\}$ the perceptual quality in terms of XPSNR, and $\{\hat{c}_1, ..., \hat{c}_m\}$ the rate factors linking bitrate and QP.

3.1 Video Processing Chain

In the Video Processing Chain, the input video is segmented for real-time adaptation. Features related to the spatiotemporal complexity of the video content are extracted to predict optimal resolutions and Quantization Parameters (QP). A Just Noticeable Difference (JND) model is used to eliminate redundant video representations, optimizing video transmission. The constant Variable Bitrate (cVBR) encoder encodes the video using the selected parameters.

The input video segment serves as the initial data source for the entire process. It contains the raw video footage that will undergo various processing stages to optimize its quality and efficiency.

Spatiotemporal Complexity Feature Extraction

In this stage, spatio-temporal complexity features are extracted from the input video segment using a Video Complexity Analyzer (VCA). These features, including metrics like Average Texture Energy, Gradient of the Luma Texture Energy, Average Luminescence, Chroma Texture Energy, and Chrominescence, provide valuable information about the spatial and temporal characteristics of the video content.

Optimized Resolution Prediction

The optimized resolution prediction block aims to predict the optimal resolution for each target bitrate. This prediction is crucial in determining the appropriate resolution that balances video quality and bandwidth constraints. The perceptual quality (XPSNR) '$x_{(rt, bt)}$', encoding time '$e_{(rt, bt)}$', and decoding time '$d_{(rt, bt)}$' rely on video complexity features $\{E_Y, h, L_Y, E_U, E_V, L_U, L_V\}$, encoding resolution '$r_t$' and target bitrate '$b_t$' [3, 4].

The Optimization Function aims to maximize the perceptual quality $x(r, b_t)$, under the conditions imposed on $e(r, b_t)$, and $d(r, b_t)$. Hence, $x_{(r, bt)}$, $e_{(r, bt)}$, and $d_{(r, bt)}$ are the predicted XPSNR, which are used to encode and decode speeds of the representation (r, b_t) [3, 4].

Optimized QP Prediction

The optimized Quantization Parameter (QP) prediction block is responsible for determining the optimal quality of the video bitstream. The QP parameter plays a significant role in video compression, balancing the trade-off between video quality and bit rate [3, 4].

QP relies on video complexity features $\{E_Y, h, L_Y, E_U, E_V, L_U, L_V\}$, encoding resolution '$r_t$' and target bitrate '$b_t$' parameters: $q(r_t, b_t) = f_Q(E_Y, h, L_Y, E_U, E_V, L_U, L_V, r_t, b_t)$ [3, 4].

The loss function measures the deviation between the target and the predicted bitrate [3, 4].

JND-Based Representation Elimination
This block involves the elimination of JND-Just Noticeable Difference-based representation from the video stream. JND removal is essential to maintain video quality and reduce visual artifacts. Multiple representations of the video at different bitrates are generated. The module then calculates the JND between adjacent representations. If the JND between two representations falls below a certain threshold - meaning the perceptual quality difference is not noticeable) - the framework removes the representation with the highest bitrate.

This process ensures that the bitrate ladder contains only perceptually significant representations, optimizing bandwidth usage without compromising quality. Its output is given to the cVBR (Constant Variable Bitrate) encoder, which selects one of the represented video segments at different bitrates according to the available bandwidth, to ensure the best possible visual quality given the constraints.

3.2 Camera Weight Processing Chain

The Weight Optimization Chain processes sensor data from multiple cameras to detect objects in image frames. Camera views are prioritized based on the objects detected, and acceptable bitrates are estimated for each camera view to transmit critical information effectively.

The sensor data is the main input in the chain and plays a critical role in the video processing pipeline by incorporating object detection, prioritizing, and importance weighting. Object detection involves identifying and locating objects within the video frames.

This chain evaluates the potential loss of visibility for each detected object after compression. Hence, the evaluation shall determine how much the compression can downgrade the camera's overall view, thus concluding that the chain focuses on reducing compression-induced distortion.

3D Object Detection
The stage utilizes sensor data to identify objects captured by various cameras within the scene. The list of detected objects from camera i is represented as L_i, where $L_i = \{l_{i1}, l_{i2}, ..., l_{im}\}$ [3, 4]. Each l_{ij} corresponds to a detected object, such as a vehicle, pedestrian, or any other relevant entity.

The system processes each camera view. The primary purpose of this module is to identify the objects in the scene, which will then be used to assess the potential perceptual quality loss due to compression. The stage starts by detecting objects using 3D detection techniques (the used tool was mmdetection3d), which provide spatial awareness (specifically distance) of the objects in the scene.

Prioritizing and Importance Weighting
In autonomous and teleported driving systems, precise object detection is essential for

safe and effective operation. Image compression, employed to protect bandwidth, may compromise image clarity and delay detection performance.

To address the issue, a technique will be used to assess the impact of compression on detection accuracy and assign importance levels to key objects through a weighting mechanism.

A model shall then be established to quantify the decrease in detection accuracy due to compression, enabling real-time adjustments in response to fluctuating bandwidth conditions without sacrificing detection efficacy.

Dataset Destruction and Compression Methodology

To explore how compression influences object detection, the annotated front camera nuScenes mini dataset will be employed, since we need the object classes, their distance from the ego car and their bounding box coordinates.

Afterward, we will compress an image at five specific rates (R_1, R_2, R_3, R_4, R_5) using OpenCV, generating various degrees of image quality reduction. Subsequently, we will use an object detection model on the compressed images to detect objects within each compression level and assess detection accuracy at varying rates. Table 2 below is a sample table illustrating the detection outcomes at different compression rates:

Table 2. Distance and compression rates of the objects

Object	Distance (meters)	Coordinates	R_1	R_2	R_3	R_4	R_5
Object 1	10	$[x_{11}, y_{11}, x_{12}, y_{12}]$	Yes	No	Yes	No	Yes
Object 2	20	$[x_{21}, y_{21}, x_{22}, y_{22}]$	No	Yes	Yes	Yes	Yes
Object 3	30	$[x_{31}, y_{31}, x_{32}, y_{32}]$	Yes	No	No	No	No

Each object's detection success ("Yes") or failure ("No") should be documented for every compression rate. The loss attributed to compression will be calculated by determining the percentage of failed detections across the five rates.

Steps for Creating the Loss Calculation Model

The model aims to predict the reduction in detection accuracy caused by image compression; hence it will be crafted to intake object characteristics (such as class, coordinates, and distance from the ego vehicle) as inputs and generate the projected detection loss for detection loss after compression. The following actions were taken to construct this model:

1. *Initial Object Dataset Creation*

For every object, essential details like its category, distance from the ego vehicle, and spatial coordinates were considered as input features. These specifics were derived from the nuScenes dataset and played a crucial role in shaping the model's predictions.

The annotated front camera nuScenes mini dataset will be employed. Only certain categories will be accepted, so the objects should be filtered, and their categories will be converted the following way:

The rest of the categories will be ignored. Next, the following initial object detection with YOLOv5 will be performed and its categories will also be filtered the same

```
"human.pedestrian.adult": "person",
"human.pedestrian.child": "person",
"human.pedestrian.wheelchair": "person",
"human.pedestrian.stroller": "person",
"human.pedestrian.personal_mobility": "person",
"human.pedestrian.police_officer": "person",
"human.pedestrian.construction_worker": "person",
"vehicle.car": "car",
"vehicle.emergency.police": "car",
"vehicle.bicycle": "bicycle",
"vehicle.bus.bendy": "bus",
"vehicle.bus.rigid": "bus",
"vehicle.motorcycle": "motorcycle",
"vehicle.truck": "truck",
"vehicle.construction": "truck",
"vehicle.emergency.ambulance": "truck",
"vehicle.trailer": "truck"
```

Fig. 2. Filtered Objects & Converted Categories

previous way then we apply an object association algorithm based on an IOU threshold that needed to be superior to 0.5. This step is crucial because if we were to evaluate the perception of an object after downgrading the image quality, the same algorithm needs to be applied.

2. *Data Labeling*

For every object in the dataset, we will document the detection outcomes at five different compression rates (R_1 to R_5). Furthermore, we will determine the loss value O_{loss} by considering the failed detections across these rates. A detection loss score will then be allocated according to the following criteria [3, 4]:

$$O_{loss_i} = \frac{5 - \sum_{n=1}^{5} detected_{R_n}}{5} \tag{1}$$

The equation calculates the ratio of unsuccessful detections among the five compression settings. A greater loss value suggests that an object is at a higher risk of being overlooked at increased compression levels.

3. *Camera Weight Assignment*

The camera score S should be calculated as:

$$S = \sum_i O_{loss_i} \tag{2}$$

The scores will be pondered into weights to be utilized to adapt compression rates in real time and emphasize essential cameras when distributing bandwidth [3, 4].

4. *Model Training*

The dataset, which includes details about objects, detection outcomes, and computed losses, will be divided into training and validation sets. Subsequently, we will develop a regression model to forecast the object's loss by analyzing the input characteristics. This model will be trained to predict the loss for each object across different compression scenarios while considering the significance of each camera's perspective.

5. *Loss Prediction*

After being trained, the model could anticipate the potential loss of any novel object within a scene, considering its characteristics. This forecast would then empower the system to adapt the compression level in real time, minimizing detection loss for vital objects while permitting increased compression in less crucial areas.

6. *Evaluation and Iteration*

After the training, the model will undergo assessment using validation data. The anticipated losses will be juxtaposed with the real detection outcomes to gauge the model's precision. Adjustments need to be made to refine the model, like enlarging the dataset and exploring different predictive models.

Camera-Based Importance Weighting

By integrating weights specific to each camera into the model, the system could guarantee that significant objects observed by essential cameras received greater emphasis. This method enables a more efficient utilization of bandwidth without compromising the clarity of crucial objects. Cameras with elevated weights shall retain finer details, lessening the likelihood of overlooking vital detections, even when facing substantial compression.

Impact on Bandwidth and Detection

By incorporating object loss prediction and camera-based importance weighting, bandwidth is efficiently managed. High-priority objects captured by key cameras are preserved with minimal compression, while less critical views undergo more aggressive compression. This approach ensures that object detection remains reliable for safe vehicle operation, even when bandwidth is limited.

Acceptable Bitrates Estimation

In this phase, it uses the camera reference and its importance weights W_i, and the system estimates acceptable bitrates B_i for each camera view to ensure critical information is transmitted with higher quality. The system balances the need to preserve visual details in high-priority areas with the overall network capacity, optimizing both quality and bandwidth usage. Its input is available bandwidth prediction, whereas its output is a set of bitrates blocks representing the different bitrates that will be used in the video encoding process. The set is represented by $B = \{b_1, b_2, ..., b_n\}$, where b_i is a specific bitrate value. Moreover, it will be the input of the optimized resolution prediction block in the video processing chain.

Comparison

Table 3 shows the comparison of the proposed solution with existing video transmission frameworks from the articles:

Results

A preliminary version of the loss calculation model was tested once under simulated conditions. The primary goal was to assess the basic functionality of the model and gather

Table 3. Comparison of the proposed solution with existing video transmission frameworks

Framework	Focus Area	Optimization Strategy	Strengths	Challenges
Proposed solution	Adaptive video bitrate allocation	QADRA framework, camera weight optimization, and JND-based representation elimination	Flexibility, scalability, and enhanced quality distribution	The complexity in modular integration and updating
QADRA [3, 4]	Quality-aware dynamic resolution adaptation for adaptive streaming	XPSNR-based dynamic resolution adjustment	High-quality video streaming for teleoperated driving	Limited by resolution adaptation only
Teleoperated driving machine [5]	Low-latency video transmission in complex traffic	Situational awareness evaluation, traffic-aware multi-view adaptation	Low latency for operator safety	The complexity of real-time traffic adaptation
Single hardware encoder for autonomous vehicles [6]	Quality adaptation on hardware-limited systems	Preprocessing technique for individual stream quality adaptation	Reduces hardware dependency	Limited scalability for multiple views
Adaptive video streaming for teleoperated driving [7]	Mobile network latency mitigation	Speed adjustments, and video segmentation based on latency	Adaptability to network conditions	Inconsistent performance due to mobile network variability
Multi-camera adaptive streaming [8]	Real-time multi-camera stream adjustment	Dynamic bitrate allocation and resolution scaling	Enhanced video quality, adaptable to changing conditions	Limited to fixed carrier fine levels
nuScenes dataset [9]	Autonomous driving dataset for object detection and tracking	Comprehensive sensor suite, and 3D bounding box annotations	Supports advanced ML model training	Data size and resource-intensive for processing
Saliency-Driven Video Compression for surveillance [23]	Region-specific video compression for object detection	Prioritization of key video regions	Bandwidth-efficient, which retains high detection accuracy	Limited efficiency with rapid object motion
Federated learning for edge processing [24]	Distributed model training with privacy protection	Collaborative learning without raw data sharing	Privacy-conscious, which leads to it having efficient model sharing	Computational limitations at edge devices
Versatile video coding (VVC) with saliency approaches [25]	High compression with retained quality for important objects	Encoding that is object-detection-focused	High detection accuracy at reduced bitrate	Requires complex saliency modeling and tuning

insights for future improvements. The initial test of the model yielded suboptimal results, revealing significant limitations in the model's ability to accurately calculate detection loss at various compression rates. This outcome highlighted the need for further refinement, particularly in optimizing the model's handling of varying object distances and compression-induced artifacts. However, despite the unsatisfactory results, the testing phase provided valuable insights into the model's current limitations. It was clear that further adjustments were necessary to improve the model's performance. This test will serve as a foundation for future iterations and development.

Views of Improvements
To improve the model's precision and real-world relevance, one key enhancement is expanding the range of tested compression rates. Initially, only five rates were applied, leading to distinct loss values of 0, 0.2, 0.4, 0.6, 0.8, and 1—derived from the average success or failure of object detections. This limited granularity restricted smooth loss calculation, making it challenging to model the relationship between compression and detection performance accurately. Introducing a broader, more refined set of compression rates would provide smoother, more continuous loss values, enabling the use of advanced regression models and improving prediction accuracy across various network conditions.

Additionally, expanding and balancing the dataset is essential. The initial dataset, with 1,484 objects, was heavily skewed—1,085 were cars, while only 3 were bicycles. Such an imbalance limits the model's ability to generalize across different object types, which is critical for practical use. A more diverse and well-distributed dataset, including a wider range of objects like pedestrians, bicycles, trucks, and smaller vehicles, would significantly improve the model's robustness and predictive accuracy. This enhancement would ensure the system is prepared to handle a broader range of scenarios, thereby strengthening the teleoperation system's overall reliability and effectiveness.

4 Conclusion

Our research has laid the groundwork for an effective video bitrate allocation strategy in Remote Operated Driving Vehicles (ROVs), emphasizing real-time video quality adjustment through advanced methods like feature extraction and object detection. This approach optimizes bandwidth utilization and improves operator situational awareness and decision-making by delivering high-quality, real-time video streams. The system's adaptability and modular structure enable it to integrate seamlessly into various teleoperated vehicle setups, offering both versatility and ease of implementation.

The broader implications of our findings extend beyond the immediate application in ROVs. By addressing the bandwidth and video quality challenges specific to teleoperation, our approach can potentially inform video transmission strategies in a wide range of remote-controlled systems, such as aerial drones, underwater ROVs, and even telemedicine applications. The portability of our system is a crucial feature, allowing it to adapt to new and emerging technologies with minimal adjustments. Its modular design enhances reproducibility, making it feasible for deployment across diverse platforms and contexts while maintaining consistent performance standards.

We aim to build on this foundation by advancing perceptual quality loss models to better align with human visual perception and integrating more sophisticated object detection and tracking algorithms to address any existing limitations. Additionally, testing our system in controlled, simulated environments will allow us to evaluate its robustness and reliability under a variety of network conditions.

Future explorations will also involve real-world testing and integration with self-driving systems, where video transmission quality plays a key role in operational safety. This research represents a significant step toward enhancing the reliability and effectiveness of teleoperated vehicle technologies. By tackling video transmission challenges in dynamic network conditions, our proposed method paves the way for substantial advancements in remote control technology, bringing us closer to robust, resilient, and versatile teleoperated systems.

References

1. Kamtam, S.B., Lu, Q., Bouali, F., Haas, O.C.L., Birrell, S.: Network latency in teleoperation of connected and autonomous vehicles: a review of trends, challenges, and mitigation strategies. Sensors **24**(12), 3957 (2024). https://doi.org/10.3390/s24123957
2. Coronado, E., Cebrian-Marquez, G., Riggio, R.: Enabling computation offloading for autonomous and assisted driving in 5G networks. In: 2019 IEEE Global Communications Conference (GLOBECOM), Waikoloa, HI, USA, pp. 1–6 (2019). https://doi.org/10.1109/GLOBECOM38437.2019.9013490. https://ieeexplore.ieee.org/abstract/document/9013490
3. Premkumar, A., Rajendran, P.T., Menon, V.V., Wieckowski, A., Bross, B., Marpe, D.: Quality-aware dynamic resolution adaptation framework for adaptive video streaming. arXiv (Cornell University) (2024). https://doi.org/10.1145/3625468.3652172
4. Hofbauer, M.: Adaptive live video streaming for teleoperated driving. Ph.D. dissertation, TUM School of Computation, Information and Technology, Technische Universität München, Munich, Germany (2022). 1651626.pdf (tum.de)
5. Hofbauer, M., Kuhn, C.B., Khlifi, M., Petrovic, G., Steinbach, E.: Traffic-aware multi-view video stream adaptation for teleoperated driving. In: 2022 IEEE 95th Vehicular Technology Conference: VTC2022-Spring, Helsinki, Finland, pp. 1–6 (2022). https://doi.org/10.1109/VTC2022-Spring54318.2022.9860513. Available: (PDF) Traffic-Aware Multi-View Video Stream Adaptation for Teleoperated Driving (researchgate.net)
6. Hofbauer, M., Kuhn, C., Petrovic, G., Steinbach, E.: Adaptive multi-view live video streaming for teledriving using a single hardware encoder. In: 22nd IEEE International Symposium on Multimedia, Naples, Italy, pp. 1–8 (2020). https://doi.org/10.1109/ISM.2020.00008. Available: (PDF) Adaptive Multi-View Live Video Streaming for Teledriving Using a Single Hardware Encoder (researchgate.net)
7. Neumeier, S.: Enabling teleoperated driving in everyday's traffic scenarios. Doctoral dissertation, TUM School of Computation, Information and Technology, Technische Universität München (2023). 1695113.pdf (tum.de)
8. Schimpe, A., Hoffmann, S., Diermeyer, F.: Adaptive video configuration and bitrate allocation for teleoperated vehicles. In: 2021 IEEE Intelligent Vehicles Symposium Workshops (IV Workshops), Nagoya, Japan, pp. 1–6 (2021). https://doi.org/10.1109/IVWorkshops54471.2021.9669258. Available: Adaptive Video Configuration and Bitrate Allocation for Teleoperated Vehicles | IEEE Conference Publication | IEEE Xplore
9. Caesar, H., et al.: nuScenes: a multimodal dataset for autonomous driving. arXiv preprint arXiv:1903.11027 (2020). Available: [1903.11027] nuScenes: A multimodal dataset for autonomous driving (arxiv.org)
10. Zaarane, A., Slimani, I., Al Okaishi, W., Atouf, I., Hamdoun, A.: Distance measurement system for autonomous vehicles using stereo camera. Array **5**, 100016 (2020). Retrieved from: main.pdf (sciencedirectassets.com)
11. Parekh, D., et al.: A review on autonomous vehicles: progress, methods and challenges. Electronics **11**(14), (2022). https://mdpi-res.com/d_attachment/electronics/electronics-11-02162/article_deploy/electronics-11-02162.pdf?version=1657531632
12. Carranza-García, M., Torres-Mateo, J., Lara-Benítez, P., García-Gutiérrez, J.: On the performance of one-stage and two-stage object detectors in autonomous vehicles using camera data. Remote Sensing **13**(1), 89 (2020). https://doi.org/10.3390/rs13010089

13. Liu, H., Wu, C., Wang, H.: Real time object detection using LiDAR and camera fusion for autonomous driving. Sci. Rep. **13**(1) (2023). https://doi.org/10.1038/s41598-023-35170-z

14. Cho, K., Cho, D.: Autonomous driving assistance with dynamic objects using traffic surveillance cameras. Appl. Sci. **12**(12), 6247 (2022). https://doi.org/10.3390/app12126247

15. Sahin, F.E.: Long-range, high-resolution camera optical design for assisted and autonomous driving. Photonics **6**(2), 73 (2019). https://doi.org/10.3390/photonics6020073

16. Arikumar, K.S., Deepak Kumar, A., Gadekallu, T.R., Prathiba, S.B., Tamilarasi, K.: Real-time 3D object detection and classification in autonomous driving environment using 3D LiDAR and camera sensors. Electronics **11**(24), 4203 (2022). https://doi.org/10.3390/electronics11244203

17. Geng, K., Dong, G., Yin, G., Hu, J.: Deep dual-modal traffic objects instance segmentation method using camera and LIDAR data for autonomous driving. Remote Sens. **12**(20), 3274 (2020). https://doi.org/10.3390/rs12203274

18. Kumar, G.A., Lee, J.H., Hwang, J., Park, J., Youn, S.H., Kwon, S.: LiDAR and camera fusion approach for object distance estimation in self-driving vehicles. Symmetry **12**(2), 324 (2020). https://doi.org/10.3390/sym12020324

19. Zhang, K., Liu, Y., Mei, F., Jin, J., Wang, Y.: Boost correlation features with 3D-MiIoU-based camera-LiDAR fusion for MODT in autonomous driving. Remote Sens. **15**(4), 874 (2023). https://doi.org/10.3390/rs15040874

20. O'Byrne, M., Vibhoothi, V., Sugrue, M., Kokaram, A.: Impact of video compression on the performance of object detection systems for surveillance applications. arXiv (2022). https://arxiv.org/abs/2211.05805

21. Aqqa, M., Mantini, P., Shah, S.: Understanding how video quality affects object detection algorithms. In: Proceedings of the 14th International Joint Conference on Computer Vision, Imaging and Computer Graphics Theory and Applications (2019). https://doi.org/10.5220/0007401600960104

22. Baig, D., et al.: Bit rate reduction in cloud gaming using object detection technique. Comput. Mater. Continua **68**(3), 3653–3669 (2021). https://doi.org/10.32604/cmc.2021.017948

23. Fischer, K., Fleckenstein, F., Herglotz, C., Kaup, A.: Saliency-driven versatile video coding for neural object detection. arXiv (Cornell University) (2021). https://doi.org/10.1109/icassp39728.2021.9415048

24. Cai, Q., Chen, Z., Wu, D.O., Liu, S., Li, X.: A novel video coding strategy in HEVC for object detection. IEEE Trans. Circuits Syst. Video Technol. **31**(12), 4924–4937 (2021). https://doi.org/10.1109/tcsvt.2021.3056134

25. Kim, M.J., Lee, Y.-L.: Object detection-based video compression. Appl. Sci. **12**(9), 4525 (2022). https://doi.org/10.3390/app12094525

26. Advanced Navigation. "Spatial - MEMS GNSS/INS". https://www.advancednavigation.com/inertial-navigation-systems/mems-gnss-ins/spatial/

Model-Based Analysis for Cooperative Transportation under Uncertainty and Threats

Experimental Evaluation of Road-Crossing Decisions by Autonomous Wheelchairs Against Environmental Factors

Franca Corradini[1]([✉]) [ID], Carlo Grigioni[1] [ID], Alessandro Antonucci[1] [ID],
Jérôme Guzzi[1] [ID], and Francesco Flammini[1,2] [ID]

[1] University of Applied Sciences and Arts of Southern Switzerland, IDSIA,
Lugano, Switzerland
franca.corradini@supsi.ch
[2] University of Florence, Department of Mathematics and Computer Science
"Ulisse DiniâĂİ, Florence, Italy

Abstract. Safe road crossing by autonomous wheelchairs can be affected by several environmental factors such as adverse weather conditions influencing the accuracy of sensors based on artificial vision. Previous studies have addressed experimental evaluation of multi-sensor information fusion to support road-crossing decisions in autonomous wheelchairs. In this study, we focus on the experimental evaluation of its tracking performance against outdoor environmental factors such as fog, rain, darkness, etc. It is rather intuitive that those factors can negatively affect the tracking performance; therefore our aim is to quantify through a set of metrics how the performance of the single sensors and their information fusion changes when such external factors are present. This is a first step in designing warning strategies in a novel framework based on the MAPE-k feedback loop established for the sensor system. System reconfiguration to reduce the reputation of less accurate sensors can then be set, thus improving overall safety. The problem is analysed within the context of the European project REXASI-PRO which aims to design a trustworthy autonomous wheelchairs supported by drones in which security, safety, ethics, and explainability are entangled to improve autonomy for people with reduced mobility. Results have been achieved by using an available laboratory dataset realised for a simplified framework in a road-crossing scenario and by applying appropriate software filters to simulate different environmental conditions.

Keywords: Artificial Vision · Simulation and Modeling · Vehicle Safety Systems · Swarm Systems · Machine Learning

1 Introduction

Recent advances in AI have implied an increasing use of *Machine Learning* (ML) models in sensing systems for autonomous driving [11]. Images from multiple

A. Kocian et al. (Eds.): INTSYS 2024, LNICST 608, pp. 363–380, 2025.
https://doi.org/10.1007/978-3-031-86370-7_22

cameras can be processed through ML models to identify one or more obstacle, enabling obstacle avoidance strategies. Despite efforts to regulate these models, detailed procedures for their validation are still lacking, due to the difficulty of achieving adequate safety levels. The use of multiple sensors and cameras should increase the performance and robustness of the overall system providing additional safety.

In this context, *Autonomous Wheelchairs* (AWs) represent an interesting case of study. As the system is intended for people with severe physical or mental disabilities who have little or no ability to intervene, it must achieve higher levels of safety and be sufficiently robust against possible external disturbances. The research presented in this paper has been performed in the context of an international research project named REXASI-PRO (REliable eXplAinable Swarm Intelligence for People with Reduced mObility),[1] aimed at introducing an innovative engineering framework for safe navigation of AWs using trustworthy AI with the aid of drones. These provide a second point of view to the AW, providing additional information about obstacles or areas where it has partial or no vision.

Safe road crossing is a paramount concern for AW technology, particularly in the face of environmental challenges like adverse weather conditions. In the previous study [5] we explored the fusion of multi-sensor information to support road-crossing decisions in cooperative robotic systems made of AWs and flying drones. In such a context we proposed a mock-up system to simulate the scenario and collected a novel dataset for our tests. We used a set of sensors including cameras, supported by *Convolutional Neural Network* (CNN) models, to extract information on approaching obstacles. However, a structured approach for the safety level of the detection system and an in-depth study of the impact of environmental factors, such as weather conditions, on the performance of ML obstacle tracking was lacking.

In this study, we establish a novel framework for the sensor system based on the *Monitor, Analyse, Plan and Execute* over a shared *Knowledge* (MAPE-K) feedback loop [20] and aim to address the impact of environmental noises by focusing on the quantification of obstacle tracking performance and evaluating its robustness against outdoor environmental factors such as fog, rain, and darkness. By quantifying these effects, we seek to identify thresholds where tracking accuracy falls below acceptable levels, facilitating timely warnings and sensor reconfigurations that can be integrated in the MAPE-K framework. As a result, early warnings and sensor reconfigurations can be developed and integrated into the MAPE-K framework to improve overall safety, as required by international standards [1,4]. Through our research, we aim to contribute improving the trustworthiness [3] of AW navigation systems, ultimately empowering individuals with mobility impairments to navigate their environments with greater confidence and independence.

In order to evaluate performance for both single sensors and their information fusion, we apply appropriate environmental filters to the output coming from

---

[1] https://rexasi-pro.spindoxlabs.com.

the cameras, before applying a CNN model fine-tuned to our specific case. This analysis is a first step in the realisation of a model for the quantification of the uncertainty associated with one or more sensors.

The main original contributions of this paper are summarised as follows:

1) We experimentally evaluate the performance in video tracking and estimation of road crossing danger function after simulating adverse environmental conditions. Those are generated by applying appropriate software filters to a video dataset generated in a laboratory environment, which is equipped with wheeled robots, sensors, and optical tracking infrastructure [5].
2) We fine tune artificial vision performance compared to previous studies in order to improve video tracking performance by combining diverse modules and training datasets.
3) We set the specific contribution in the paradigm of autonomic computing through a general architectural framework for the sensing system based on the MAPE-K feedback loop supporting self-adaptation.

The remaining of this paper is structured as follows. In Sect. 2, related works are reviewed and summarised. Section 3 provides background information about the road crossing scenario with the related danger function, the laboratory dataset used for the experimentation, and the sensor fusion approach. In Sect. 4, the MAPE-K based approach for the sensing system is presented. Section 5 describes the tools and the implementation strategy for the simulation of the environmental factors and for the obstacle recognition. Section 6 provides and discusses the results of the experimentation summarising the main findings. Finally, Sect. 7 provides conclusions and hints for future developments.

2   Related Works

Fusing data from multiple and diverse sensors can overcome inherent limitations of single-sensor perception in object detection for autonomous driving [13,19]. However, severe weather conditions may compromise the sensors' ability to perform their original functions due to attenuation of signal strength and noise disturbances. Adverse weather condition represents for autonomous vehicles one of the main issue to gain level 4 of SAE standard [16] or higher autonomy for a long time [9].

With AI model implemented in the sensing system, new strategies have been studied to increase the level of safety and robustness in presence of adverse weather condition. The main efforts were made in building datasets and simulators to drive and validate ML models. In fact, most of the datasets commonly used for training do not contain many conditions other than clear weather [17]. Furthermore, datasets are limited by the meteorological conditions common to the area where they are collected. Therefore, simulators capable of recreating various weather conditions with different intensities are now of great interest to test the performance of autonomous systems.

In [14] is presented a novel full-scale rain simulation system, developed to quantifying Advanced Driver Assistance Systems sensor performance when driving in the rain. The simulator can recreate a wide range of dynamic rain intensity experienced by the vehicle at different driving speeds, along with the corresponding droplet size distributions.

A Polarized Object Detection Benchmark is introduced in [15], consisting of a benchmark dataset that incorporates the physical dimension of optical polarisation imaging to tackle object detection challenges in complex road scenes under adverse weather conditions.

Reference [17] introduce a new large-scale simulation dataset which is generated by an automated pipeline from a high realism video game with the focus on simulating weather conditions. While in [10], a novel dataset of U.S. road markings is used for the training of an ensemble deep learning model. The collection is realised also applying data augmentation to simulate several atmospheric condition, resulting in the achievement of a more robust model against weather disturbances. We decide to adopt this strategy with the dataset previously recorded and presented in [5]. From the dataset recorded in optimal condition, we apply data augmentation through the library Automold,[2] created specifically to introduce various real-world scenarios for road images that pose challenges for the training of autonomous vehicle neural networks. More details are given in Sect. 5.

3   Background

In urban vehicular traffic environment, pedestrian and wheelchair users are among the most exposed subjects [6?]. The road-crossing scenario is therefore an essential situation to analyse in terms of pedestrian-vehicle conflict to prevent accidents [2]. In this context, wheelchair users may encounter further disadvantages, due to a possible lack of reaction, or inability to analyse the danger.

In reference [5], we proposed a danger evaluation approach for road crossing using a sensor system based on multiple, diverse, and redundant components. Information fusion was applied at different levels of information processing and to test the method we created a novel dataset recorded in our laboratory using a simplified scenario, where laboratory devices were used to simulate the crossing scenario. The results highlighted the advantages of using diverse sensors to take safer road crossing decisions, especially when information fusion is applied at the lowest level of data processing.

In this section we provide a brief description of the danger evaluation approach and the laboratory setup of the existing work.

3.1   A Danger Function to Support Road-Crossing Decisions

According to the scope of the project where this experimentation has been performed, the reference system for the road-crossing scenario is composed of an AW and a drone, as depicted in Fig. 1.

---

[2] https://github.com/UjjwalSaxena/Automold–Road-Augmentation-Library.

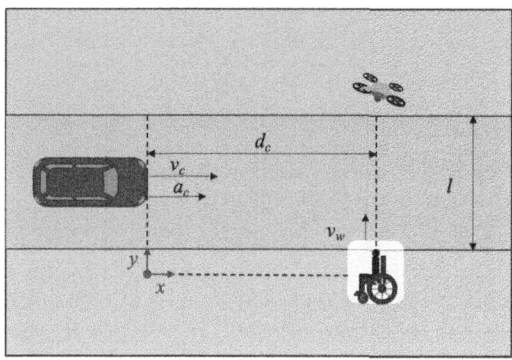

Fig. 1. Diagram illustrating a road crossing scenario with a car, a drone, and a person in a wheelchair. The car is on the left, moving right with velocity (v_c) and acceleration (a_c). The drone is above, and the wheelchair is on the right, moving upward with velocity (v_w). The relative distance between the car and the wheelchair is labeled (d_c), and the road width is labeled (l). Coordinate axes (x) and (y) are shown at the bottom left.

The *Time To Collision* (TTC) is a well established approach to quantify the danger of collision in driving and road-crossing contexts, described in the ISO 23376:2021 as the seconds that will take to two vehicle to collide if their relative speed is constant. In the road-crossing situation represented in Fig. 1 it is defined as $TTC = d_c/v_c$. For our analysis we wanted to include more information related to the kinematics of the car including its acceleration, and to significantly increase the danger value for short distance d_c. We designed a continuous function g, called *Danger Function* (DF) reflecting a kinematic analysis of the road-crossing scenario at a particular instant of time t. For decision-making, the crossing is considered dangerous when the value $g(t)$ exceeds a given threshold $g^* = 1$. The DF and safety condition are defined as:

$$g(d_c, v_c, a_c) := \frac{k_v \cdot h(v_c) + k_a \cdot f(a_c)}{\log(d_c + \epsilon)}, \tag{1}$$

$$g(d_c, v_c, a_c) < 1, \tag{2}$$

where d_c, v_c and a_c are respectively the distance, relative speed and relative acceleration between the vehicle and the pedestrian at instant t. k_v, k_a and ϵ are set following heuristics related to the geometry and kinematics of the scenario, whereas h and f are linear transformations with threshold applied on the components v_c and a_c.

The linear transformation of the speed is

$$h(v_c) := \begin{cases} 0 & \text{if } v_c \leq \underline{v}_c, \\ \frac{v_c - \underline{v}_c}{\overline{v}_c - \underline{v}_c} & \text{if } \underline{v}_c < v_c \leq \overline{v}_c, \\ 1 & \text{if } v_c > \overline{v}_c, \end{cases} \tag{3}$$

368   F. Corradini et al.

and, for the acceleration

$$
f(a_c) := \begin{cases} -1 & \text{if } a_c \leq -\bar{a}_c \\ \frac{a_c + \underline{a}_c}{\bar{a}_c - \underline{a}_c} & \text{if } -\bar{a}_c < a_c \leq -\underline{a}_c \\ 0 & \text{if } -\underline{a}_c < a_c \leq \underline{a}_c \\ \frac{a_c - \underline{a}}{\bar{a}_c - \underline{a}_c} & \text{if } \underline{a}_c < a_c \leq \bar{a}_c \\ 1 & \text{if } a_c > \bar{a}_c. \end{cases}
\tag{4}
$$

Such transformations have been chosen to prevent contribution by low speeds (i.e., $v_c \leq \underline{v}_c$) and low accelerations (i.e., $|a_c| \leq \underline{a}_c$) to the DF, and at the same time places a normalised upper limit on the contributions of high speeds ($v_c \geq \bar{v}_c$) and accelerations ($|a_c| \geq \bar{a}_c$). Furthermore, only positive speed values are included since vehicles are not expect to go backwards and the acceleration contribution is significantly reduced. In our experience, these limitations improved the results of the danger analysis in part to reduce the effects of noisy sensors measures. Detailed information on the coefficients and parameters design can be found in the above-mentioned work [5].

We would like to point out that such DF is a simplification of a real road crossing scenario, where other factors as the danger perception of the individuals or environmental elements might play an important role. Some of these factors might be considered by varying the values g^*, however, some situations may require a more complex model. Nevertheless, such representation results to be quite straightforward to use in the context of information fusion since just kinematic properties are required without any evaluation or hypothesis of the conductor capabilities.

3.2 A Laboratory Dataset for Simulated Road-Crossing

In order to build a dataset for the reference scenario, we used three wheeled ground robots named *RoboMasters*[3] (RMs) equipped with cameras and distance sensors. This allows to evaluate system performance in the simplified experimental setup depicted in Fig. 2. A dataset has been recorded in the *IDSIA Autonomous Robotics Laboratory*.[4] We collected ground-truth poses from a very accurate motion tracking system, which were used to evaluate the performance of the system. We shared the dataset with the scientific community by making it available on a publicly accessible repository.[5]

It should be noted that we did not use a real drone in the simulated environment, as for the proof-of-concept we only needed to acquire an additional view of the scene, a bit higher and from a different perspective. In future experiments, we plan to use a more realistic setting with a real drone.

For each experimental run, we recorded data from two cameras and a set of range sensors located on the two RMs acting as the AW (RM_w) and the drone (RM_d), together with the information of the motion tracker. In conclusion, we

---

[3] https://www.dji.com/ch/robomaster-ep.
[4] https://idsia-robotics.github.io.
[5] https://huggingface.co/datasets/carlogrigioni/safe-road-crossing-aw-dataset.

Fig. 2. Example of data collection scenario. Three RoboMasters devices are positioned on the laboratory floor where the dataset has been recorded. The device on the left acting as the wheelchair is labeled "W," the one on the right representing the obstacle is labeled "C," and the one at the bottom labeled "D" represents the drone. A red arrow runs horizontally from the left to the right show the trajectory of the obstacle. Blue chevrons pointing left near the bottom vehicle are equivalent to the pedestrian crossing. Blue lines run parallel to the red arrow, indicating the boundaries of the obstacle trajectory. (Color figure online)

collected three main streams of information from the sensors (i.e. two from the cameras and one from the range sensors block) that were used to derive the distance of the RM acting as the approaching vehicle (RM_c). No particular transformation is required for the range sensors measurements, whereas each frame of the recorded videos were elaborated through a ML model to obtain the RM_c distance.

Overall, twelve runs were recorded with some variations of the experiments setup and the kinematics of the RM_c. In particular, two different laboratory setups were adopted: scenario A (for the experiments $1 - 6$) consisted in shorter tests with RM_c running along a brief path. On the other hand, scenario B consisted of a longer run. Furthermore, the background of scenario B was a plain white wall, instead in scenario A there were multiple objects as shelves, devices and boxes. This aspect proved to be relevant for the analysis of the results in Sect. 6.

Additional information on the devices, the laboratory and the experimental setup can be found in reference [5], and in the associated repository.[6]

3.3   Sensor Fusion

When sensors data are combined, among the various aspects to consider, an important one is to define the default value when the obstacle is not detected. This may be due either to the actual absence of the obstacle or to the inability of the sensor to perceive it. In the work [5] only a partial discussion was made, considering the contribution of each sensor absent until the first obstacle detection. At this point, when the sensor no longer sees the obstacle, the last value detected is kept constant. This choice proved to be inadequate for the data coming from the cameras, which do not have an automatic reset procedure, such as the range sensors.

---

[6] https://github.com/IDSIA/rexasi-pro/tree/main/DECSoS_Workshop.

Information fusion from sensors and cameras can be done at different levels. We can directly average the distances measured by the sensors or perform the fusion only after the evaluation of the DF for each sensor or even at the level of the binary road-crossing decisions (e.g., by a voting procedure). Here we focus on the combination of the distances, which, according to [5], is the one providing best performances when a trivial average of the sensors data is applied without considering whether the sensor detects an obstacle or not, as described in the Subsect. 3.2.

4   Sensing System Framework

To improve safety and enable future certification against relevant standards, we propose a multi-agent, multi-modal, self-adaptive sensing system to achieve reliable event detection, where sensor outputs are combined to provide a common result for a specific task [1]. Multi-modal fusion has become a paramount task in the context of autonomous driving systems [13], and can be achieved through the use of multiple sensors diverse by software, hardware or position. Self-adaptation is achieved by combining a *Managed System*, consisting of the swarm system under consideration (i.e. AW and drones), with a *Managing System* based on the MAPE-K feedback loop, as depicted in Fig. 3. The *Managing System* elaborates the strategy for the autonomous safety logic over the *Managed System*. This is monitored together with the environment through the sensing system and implements the actions decided by the managing component.

The swarm system may consist of one or several autonomous systems working together as subsystems of the *Managed System* to achieve a given purpose. In general, autonomous vehicles can be expressed through logical or functional blocks defined by the information flow and processing steps performed. We adopt the architecture presented in [12], where the main functional blocks identified are: *Perception, Planning and Decision, System Supervision* and *Motion and Vehicle Control*. Information regarding the environment and the system itself are collected through the *Perception* block composed of the sensors on-board the autonomous system and the pre-processing elaboration of their raw data. Elaborated data together with actions outlined by the *Managing System* are processed by the *Planning and Decision* block to evaluate the navigation plan for the vehicle. This is finally implemented by the *Motion and Vehicle Control* by means of the propellers. The *System Supervision* monitors the overall functioning of each components and detects any possible errors.

For the entire system, we identify as 'Sensing System' the sum of all the *Perception* blocks of the single autonomous systems with the MAPE-K loop of the *Managing System*. In the monitoring phase, the sensor data are further processed, applying alignment, resampling or other operations as required [18]. In the monitoring and analysis phases, data information is analysed and combined appropriately, taking into account any discrepancies between sensors and the degree of reliability of each one. All relevant information is then extracted in order to make appropriate planning choices. Finally, the overall strategy for the swarm system is planned and actions are sent to the managed subsystems.

In the context of the road crossing carried out by a swarm system composed of an AW and an autonomous flying drone, these two devices represent the subsystems of the *Managed System*. The *Managing System* might be a separated elaboration unit on-board the AW able to communicate with other systems, such as multiple autonomous drone, AWs or smart systems around the city. The data from the sensors on-board the two autonomous systems are combined in the monitoring phase of the *Managing System* and a danger level for the road crossing is calculated in the analysis phase. In the planning phase, the behaviour to be performed by the swarm system is decided, i.e. whether to cross the road or not according to predefined requirements. Finally, the single actions are sent to the two systems to be executed.

In the remaining part of the paper we analyse by means of metrics how the performance of individual sensors on-board the *Managed Subsystems* and their information fusion varies in response to weather disturbances. This is a first approach to define appropriate strategies to be applied at the *Managing System* level in the *Monitoring* and *Analysis* phase.

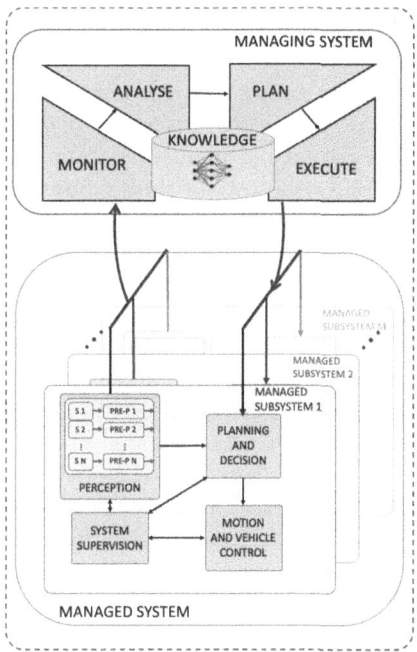

Fig. 3. Diagram illustrating the reference architecture of the self-adaptive swarm autonomous system framework composed by a managing system and a managed system. The managing system is based on the Monitor, Analyse, Plan and Execute over a shared Knowledge (MAPE-K) feedback loop. The managed system consists of multiple subsystems, with Managed Subsystem 1 highlighted. This includes the blocks Perception, Planning and Decision, System Supervision, and Motion and Vehicle Control. Arrows indicate the flow of information between the managing and managed systems, emphasising the interaction between knowledge processing and subsystem management.

5 Simulation and Obstacle Recognition

This section provides information about the approach used to simulate specific environmental condition, to implement the obstacle detection and for the information fusion.

To study how environmental (i.e., exogenous) factors affect road-crossing decisions, we simulate relevant outdoor and environmental disturbances by means of appropriate *filters*. Those filters, applied to the frames recorded by the video cameras, can mimic the presence of adverse conditions such as darkness, rain and fog.

Raw data from cameras are split into frames using the OpenCV library.[7] The environmental factors are simulated at the frame level by the Automold library for data augmentation. We use the library to simulate four different effects with different intensity that can be set through coefficients:

- *fog* with coefficient 0.3, 0.5 and 0.7 (Fig. 4a);
- *rain* of type *drizzle, heavy,* and *torrential* (Fig. 4b);
- *bright* with coefficient 0.3, 0.5, 0.7, and 0.9 (Fig. 4c);
- *dark* with coefficient 0.3, 0.5, 0.7, 0.9 (Fig. 4d).

The application of most filters on a frame of our dataset is shown in Fig. 4. We refer to the unfiltered images and sequences as the *original* ones.

For obstacle detection, original and augmented frames are processed by YOLO (*You Only Look Once*).[8] YOLO is a state-of-the-art object detection architecture, widely used for its real-time performances, generalization and adaptability capabilities. YOLO's pre-trained deep neural networks are based on the COCO image dataset [8], consisting of 80 categories including person, bicycle, car, motorcycle, bus, train, and truck. Together with the recognition of the object class in the frame under elaboration, YOLO provides the pixel coordinates of the bounding box of the recognised object. If the focal length of the camera is known, the distance between the object and the camera can be derived.

In [5], YOLO v5—the latest version available at that time—is adopted for the obstacle detection elaboration from the cameras videos. Such model does not have a dedicated class for the RM, however, it recognises the device always under the *motorcycle* class. In conclusion, unfortunately this version did not provide high performance for distances longer than a couple of metres. As an alternative to this pre-trained model, we implement the fine-tuning of the new YOLO v8 architecture by means of a dataset of RM images[9] whose results can be seen in Fig. 5. This model demonstrates to have better performance for long distances of the obstacle RM_c. Instead, for short distances we encounter similar or worst results with respect to YOLO v5. Furthermore, the new fine-tuned model provides enlarged bounding boxes, therefore the focal length has to be modified by a constant factor to overcome this distortion. In the following, we refer to the pre-trained architecture as Y5 and to the fine-tuned one as Y8.

---

[7] https://docs.opencv.org/4.x/index.html.

[8] https://github.com/ultralytics/yolov5.

[9] https://universe.roboflow.com/godwyll-aikins/robomaster-i5ydd.

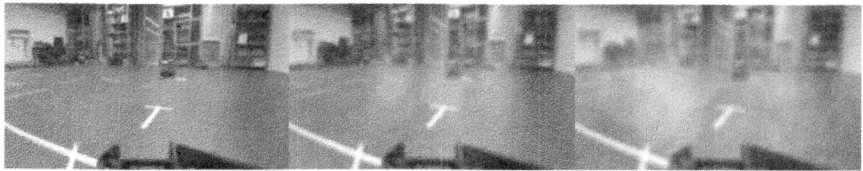

(a) Fog filter at level 0.3, 0.5 and 0.7.

(b) Rain filter at level drizzle, heavy and torrential.

(c) Brightness filter at level 0.3, 0.5 and 0.7.

(d) Darkness filter at level 0.3, 0.5 and 0.7.

Fig. 4. A frame of the recorded dataset processed with multiple filters simulating diverse environmental conditions. Each row demonstrates the impact of the respective filter on the visibility of the obstacle. 1. Top row: Fog filter at levels 0.3, 0.5, and 0.7, progressively increasing fog density. 2. Second row: Rain filter with effects of drizzle, heavy rain, and torrential rain. 3. Third row: Brightness filter at levels 0.3, 0.5, and 0.7, showing increasing brightness. 4. Bottom row: Darkness filter at levels 0.3, 0.5, and 0.7, showing increasing darkness.

To guarantee redundancy and diversity during the information fusion, we consider both Y5 and Y8. Both models are therefore applied to all the frames of all the experiments to identify the bounding boxes of the obstacle (identified as a *motorcycle* by Y5 and as a *RM* by Y8). Therefore, a total of four data flows for the information fusion can be defined: two processed from the RM_d camera

(a) Original frame without and with the bounding box.

(b) Frame with filter rain without and with the bounding box.

Fig. 5. Examples of environmental filters applied on a frame of our dataset before and after the application of the bounding boxes elaborated by the fine-tuned model of YOLO version 8. (a) Top row: On the left the original frame and on the right the same frame with the green bounding box generated by the model around the obstacle. (b) Bottom row: On the left the frame with a rain filter and on the right the same frame with the rain filter and the green bounding box generated by the model around the obstacle generated by the model.

using the two different YOLO models, and, processed in the same way, another two from the RM_w camera. It can be noted that in this approach redundancy and sensory diversity are obtained through software thanks to the use of different ML models. The distance sensors introduced in Subsect. 3.2, are not included since artificial noises can not be applied to reproduce the above-mentioned environmental factors. The distance of the obstacle is computed from the bounding boxes obtained by the YOLO models [7].

For each sequence, we have four signals generated by the two cameras. We can combine these by a trivial sensor fusion approach using the arithmetic average of the position measurements for a given frame as discussed in Subsect. 3.3. We denote such a procedure as *A-Fusion*. As an alternative approach, denoted in the following as *W-Fusion*, we consider an arithmetic fusion of the distance measurements that removes the signal that are not based on actual measurements but on imputations. In case of missing data, due to the absence of obstacles or sensor malfunction, a *reference* maximum distance value is imputed. This equates to the maximum detectable distance of interest, which in the case of our tests is 4 m. This strategy correctly identifies situations where the sensor has never seen an obstacle or it is no longer visible in the sensor field of view. If all the four measures are based on an imputation, we just consider the *reference* maximum distance.

6   Experimental Results

In this section, we present the results of our experimental analysis. As discussed in the previous section, we apply relevant filters to the video sequences to simulate environmental conditions. The original, unperturbed, video sequences are also considered for comparison.

As performance descriptors, we consider the percentage of frames where the target has been recognised by YOLO (Table 1), the *Root Mean Square Error* (RMSE) of the DF based on the sensors measurements, or the sensors fusion procedures, compared against the ground-truth measurements provided by the tracker (Table 2). We similarly proceed for the road-crossing decisions, based on the DF value compared against the threshold levels described in Eq. 2, by reporting accuracies (Table 3) and F1 measures (Fig. 6). As quantitative descriptors we provide mean values over the different sequences and, in parentheses, the standard deviations. The only exception is the F1 score. For the sake of simplicity, we prefer to present the aggregated results of the two scenarios as box plots. These data are reported separately for the two datasets scenario as a large discrepancy in performance was found. This is probably due to the difference in backgrounds between scenarios A and B, described in the Subsect. 3.2, which can influence the obstacle detection of the two YOLO models.

Regarding the frame recognition rates in Table 1, the filters simulating adverse weather conditions typically induce rates that are lower than those in the original sequences. In extreme conditions (i.e., fog with coefficient 0.7 and heavy rain) those rates are close to zero, resulting in very low performance. The corresponding results are not reported for the sake of space.

As expected, the Y8 model results to work better with respect to the Y5 model, especially for highly adverse conditions (e.g., *heavy rain*). However, there is a clear difference in performance between the data from RM_d and RM_w. Indeed, the best performance is achieved using the videos recorded by the RM_d, probably due to the fact that in these shots the RM_c has poses similar to those of the dataset used to fine tune the Y8 model.

Unexpectedly, the brightness and darkness filters with low coefficient levels (i.e., 0.3 and 0.5) induced higher recognition rates. In practice, such filters act as an image preprocessing improving the performance of obstacle recognition. Probably this is due to the blurring of background elements, so that the RM_c is better recognisable from the YOLO models. For *bright* and *dark* filters, the rates are quite similar for the different values of the coefficients, and we therefore report only the data for a single coefficient for each filter.

Regarding the RMSE and accuracy values in Table 2 and Table 3, similar observations to Table 1 can be obtained. Adverse environmental filters generally lead, with a few minor anomalies, to a deterioration in performance with the exception of the *bright* and *dark* filters, which keep them constant or even improve them. The two fusion *W-Fusion* and *A-Fusion* do not differ significantly in terms of RMSE. On the other hand, *W-Fusion* is definitely better considering the accuracy values in Table 3. This means that although the two fusion methods

Table 1. Means and deviations of the frame recognition rates of YOLO pre-trained (Y5) and fine-tuned (Y8) for the two videocameras of RM_d and RM_w.

Sc.	Cam	YOLO	Original	Fog		Rain		Bright	Dark
				0.3	0.5	drizzle	heavy	0.5	0.5
A	RM_d	Y5	20.52 (4.04)	21.11 (4.94)	7.61 (4.31)	27.33 (4.03)	0.82 (0.72)	18.10 (3.97)	17.28 (4.06)
		Y8	**73.41** (9.21)	**52.30** (10.37)	**28.16** (9.25)	**73.11** (9.52)	**69.00** (7.99)	**75.32** (8.49)	**76.10** (7.95)
	RM_w	Y5	35.96 (18.16)	31.53 (15.96)	6.44 (6.34)	25.82 (13.24)	0.20 (0.50)	31.73 (16.56)	36.61 (5.87)
		Y8	41.63 (5.45)	8.12 (9.92)	6.13 (1.57)	29.30 (14.07)	24.83 (13.80)	46.56 (11.28)	52.31 (10.90)
B	RM_d	Y5	38.03 (12.22)	35.59 (10.75)	11.12 (4.33)	38.27 (10.80)	0.16 (0.39)	42.23 (12.69)	43.42 (12.74)
		Y8	**47.39** (8.87)	**52.02** (4.66)	**19.09** (6.22)	**40.53** (3.56)	**26.16** (2.61)	**81.42** (6.95)	**81.17** (6.10)
	RM_w	Y5	31.86 (10.03)	27.10 (14.29)	18.53 (10.54)	15.53 (5.63)	0.20 (0.32)	27.41 (11.31)	26.66 (11.44)
		Y8	25.51 (5.45)	12.44 (4.31)	4.59 (1.62)	15.02 (5.31)	14.16 (5.12)	58.31 (5.95)	64.70 (9.63)

Table 2. Means and deviations of the RMSE for the danger function of YOLO pre-trained (Y5) and fine-tuned (Y8) for the two video cameras of RM_d and RM_w and for the two fusion strategies *A-Fusion* and *W-Fusion*.

Sc.	Cam	YOLO	Original	Fog		Rain		Bright	Dark
				0.3	0.5	drizzle	heavy	0.5	0.5
A	RM_d	Y5	1.44 (0.40)	1.39 (0.38)	1.52 (0.45)	1.46 (0.38)	1.55 (0.47)	1.40 (0.41)	1.38 (0.34)
		Y8	1.15 (0.45)	1.33 (0.39)	1.54 (0.37)	**1.13** (0.42)	1.26 (0.46)	1.15 (0.42)	1.15 (0.43)
	RM_w	Y5	1.35 (0.35)	1.40 (0.38)	1.55 (0.45)	1.44 (0.39)	1.55 (0.47)	1.37 (0.36)	1.35 (0.35)
		Y8	1.43 (0.44)	1.53 (0.44)	1.54 (0.46)	1.46 (0.40)	1.49 (0.42)	1.41 (0.43)	1.50 (0.42)
	A-Fusion		1.22 (0.46)	1.29 (0.44)	**1.40** (0.44)	1.23 (0.41)	1.32 (0.43)	1.20 (0.45)	1.25 (0.43)
	W-Fusion		**1.09** (0.41)	**1.15** (0.41)	1.49 (0.37)	**1.17** (0.40)	**1.22** (0.46)	**1.07** (0.41)	**1.07** (0.35)
B	RM_d	Y5	1.26 (0.32)	1.25 (0.29)	1.16 (0.30)	1.28 (0.35)	1.13 (0.34)	1.27 (0.35)	1.28 (0.27)
		Y8	1.06 (0.29)	1.03 (0.19)	1.39 (0.28)	1.02 (0.27)	1.10 (0.33)	0.90 (0.16)	1.11 (0.29)
	RM_w	Y5	1.08 (0.22)	1.20 (0.19)	1.23 (0.22)	1.11 (0.31)	1.13 (0.34)	1.17 (0.25)	1.07 (0.24)
		Y8	1.01 (0.29)	1.07 (0.31)	1.12 (0.33)	1.05 (0.30)	1.06 (0.30)	0.93 (0.28)	1.09 (0.31)
	A-Fusion		**0.88** (0.27)	**0.88** (0.28)	**1.06** (0.34)	**0.93** (0.29)	1.01 (0.31)	**0.82** (0.28)	**0.97** (0.29)
	W-Fusion		1.00 (0.13)	1.12 (0.18)	1.36 (0.22)	1.13 (0.24)	**1.01** (0.29)	1.01 (0.23)	1.12 (0.16)

do not differ much from each other in terms of risk evaluation, the *W-Fusion* method is more precise for road-crossings decisions. For a deeper analysis of the quality of the road-crossing decisions provided by our system, we also consider the F1 performance. The boxplots in Fig. 6 for the original sequences and for two filters clearly show the advantages of the *W-Fusion* procedure we proposed with respect to the trivial arithmetic average *A-Fusion*. Notably, the performance of our fusion procedure is superior to that of individual sensors, with few exceptions, advocating the advantages of adding redundancy and diversity to the sensor system equipment. The cases where this is not observed are special situations where one sensor outperforms the others. Since we use a majority voting system, in this particular case, the fusion tends to worsen the results. As a solution to this problem, performance indicators can be imputed to each sensor and then combined by averaging their contributions appropriately.

Table 3. Means and deviations of the accuracy for road-crossing decision of YOLO pre-trained (Y5) and fine-tuned (Y8) for the two video cameras of RM_d and RM_w and for the two fusion strategies *A-Fusion* and *W-Fusion*.

Sc.	Cam	YOLO	Original	Fog		Rain		Bright	Dark
				0.3	0.5	drizzle	heavy	0.5	0.5
A	RM_d	Y5	44.64 (7.98)	48.45 (6.35)	36.63 (7.28)	46.04 (8.21)	35.55 (8.15)	44.74 (7.04)	49.75 (5.47)
		Y8	69.55 (4.55)	59.06 (13.94)	46.23 (13.90)	**69.56** (5.59)	**63.76** (4.73)	**73.92** (6.12)	68.90 (4.86)
	RM_w	Y5	57.29 (6.94)	51.85 (7.29)	36.65 (8.43)	49.10 (5.37)	35.55 (8.15)	54.29 (7.05)	58.04 (6.72)
		Y8	48.61 (2.66)	37.77 (7.24)	37.08 (7.75)	46.01 (8.91)	41.59 (4.29)	48.06 (3.92)	43.26 (5.51)
	A-Fusion		43.43 (3.92)	43.58 (5.12)	35.55 (8.15)	42.06 (5.10)	35.55 (8.15)	44.53 (4.25)	44.17 (4.52)
	W-Fusion		**69.37** (5.10)	**63.53** (10.09)	**53.44** (13.28)	64.39 (5.20)	62.19 (5.36)	71.39 (4.95)	**70.09** (2.53)
B	RM_d	Y5	67.95 (11.02)	68.75 (9.60)	62.62 (18.12)	68.04 (9.43)	62.34 (18.89)	70.94 (6.69)	66.01 (11.26)
		Y8	63.22 (15.09)	65.23 (12.42)	62.26 (16.10)	66.45 (12.49)	63.09 (17.41)	75.17 (5.25)	62.90 (16.70)
	RM_w	Y5	68.49 (11.52)	65.61 (14.55)	63.16 (15.88)	64.50 (16.78)	62.34 (18.89)	64.01 (13.72)	68.65 (12.12)
		Y8	72.18 (10.20)	66.26 (15.51)	62.73 (18.68)	67.73 (13.11)	66.99 (14.75)	71.90 (8.53)	65.19 (15.54)
	A-Fusion		64.49 (14.93)	66.32 (14.17)	62.35 (18.53)	64.02 (16.41)	62.34 (18.89)	66.84 (12.71)	64.07 (15.74)
	W-Fusion		**72.30** (5.54)	**70.98** (5.89)	**63.60** (13.97)	**72.16** (6.67)	**68.58** (11.49)	**74.49** (4.48)	**70.03** (9.22)

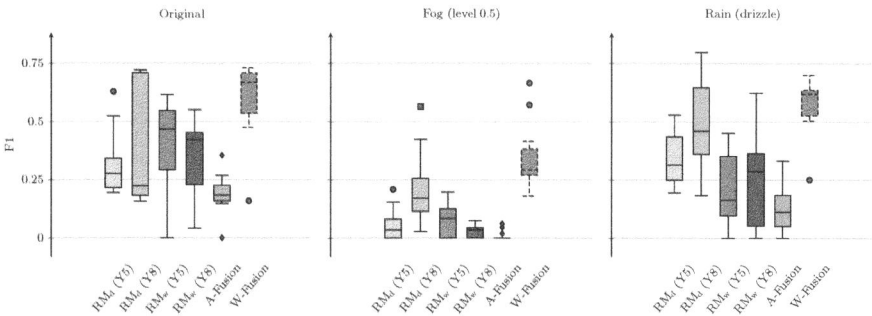

Fig. 6. The image displays three box plots comparing F1 scores across different conditions: Original, Fog (level 0.5), and Rain (drizzle). The plots illustrate the impact of weather conditions on model performance for the two video cameras of RM_d and RM_w processed with the two models YOLO version 5 and the fine tuned YOLO version 8 and for the two fusion strategies *A-Fusion* and *W-Fusion*.

Both generic Y5 and fine-tuned Y8 are negatively influenced by adverse weather as expected, with the exception of the *bright* and *dark* filter. However, Y8 appears to be more robust against environmental disturbances. The new *W-Fusion* outperforms the simpler *A-Fusion* and all single sensors in terms of accuracy and F1 performance for the road-crossing decision.

7 Conclusions

Our study addressed the crucial aspect of road-crossing decisions by autonomous wheelchairs, supported by flying drones, in the face of various environmental factors. By focusing on the refinement of obstacle detection performance through artificial vision and its evaluation against outdoor conditions like fog, rain, brightness and darkness, we aimed to quantify the impact of these factors on tracking accuracy of both single sensors and information fusion approach. This analysis was conducted in the perspective of a future integration of safety strategies into the novel framework for the sensory system we proposed in this work.

Adverse environmental conditions were found to significantly challenge video tracking performance. However, our approach facilitated a systematic assessment of these effects within the specific operational context. By leveraging available laboratory datasets and employing tailored software filters, we demonstrated the feasibility of evaluating video tracking robustness against environmental variables in reference scenarios. Our findings underscore the importance of proactively addressing environmental challenges in autonomous wheelchair navigation systems. We also established that different types of sensors are affected differently by environmental factors. This highlights the importance of using an information fusion approach between multiple sensors.

In future works, we plan to identify instances where tracking accuracy falls below acceptable thresholds, enabling the issuance of timely warnings and the potential reconfiguration of sensor priorities to enhance overall safety. In addition, the incorporation of supplementary sensors, such as light and rain sensors, will provide additional layers of detection for critical situations.

The approach presented in this study can be generalised and therefore applied to a larger class of cooperative autonomous robots and self-driving vehicles in order to test their robustness against environmental factors. In the future, we plan to extend the experimentation in multiple operating conditions and more realistic scenarios, also including real sensors on-board the autonomous wheelchair that can be affected by different disturbances.

Acknowledgment. This work was supported by the Swiss State Secretariat for Education, Research and Innovation (SERI) under contract no. 22.00291 (REXASI-PRO project). The project has been selected within the European Union's Horizon Europe research and innovation programme under grant agreement ID: 101070028 (call HORIZON-CL4-2021-HUMAN-01-01). Views and opinions expressed are however those of the authors only and do not necessarily reflect those of the funding agencies, which cannot be held responsible for them.

References

1. Corradini, F., Flammini, F., Antonucci, A.: Probabilistic modelling for trustworthy artificial intelligence in drone-supported autonomous wheelchairs. In: Proceedings of the First International Symposium on Trustworthy Autonomous Systems (TAS 2023), Article no. 52, pp. 1–5. Association for Computing Machinery, New York (2023)
2. El Hadmani, S., Benamar, N., Younis, M.: Pedestrian support in intelligent transportation systems: challenges, solutions and open issues. Transp. Res. Part C: Emerg. Technol. **121**(3), 102856 (2020)

3. Flammini, F., Alcaraz, C., Bellini, E., Marrone, S., Lopez, J., Bondavalli, A.: Towards trustworthy autonomous systems: taxonomies and future perspectives. IEEE Trans. Emerg. Top. Comput. **12**(2), 601–614 (2024)

4. Flammini, F., Marrone, S., Nardone, R., Caporuscio, M., D'Angelo, M.: Safety integrity through self-adaptation for multi-sensor event detection: methodology and case-study. Futur. Gener. Comput. Syst. **112**, 965–981 (2020)

5. Grigioni, C., Corradini, F., Antonucci, A., Guzzi, J., Flammini, F.: Safe road-crossing by autonomous wheelchairs: a novel dataset and its evaluation. In: Computer Safety, Reliability, and Security, SAFECOMP 2024 Workshops: DECSoS, SASSUR, TOASTS, and WAISE, Florence, Italy, 17 September 2024, pp. 47–60. Springer, Heidelberg (2024)

6. Henje, C., Stenberg, G., Lundälv, J., Carlsson, A.: Obstacles and risks in the traffic environment for users of powered wheelchairs in Sweden. Accid. Anal. Prev. **159**, 106259 (2021)

7. Lee, J.M., Hwang, K., Jung, I.H.: Real distance measurement using object detection of artificial intelligence. Turkish J. Comput. Math. Educ. (TURCOMAT) **12**(6), 557–563 (2021)

8. Lin, T.-Y., et al.: Microsoft COCO: common objects in context. In: Fleet, D., Pajdla, T., Schiele, B., Tuytelaars, T. (eds.) ECCV 2014. LNCS, vol. 8693, pp. 740–755. Springer, Cham (2014)

9. Zhang, Y., Carballo, A., Yang, H., Takeda, K.: Perception and sensing for autonomous vehicles under adverse weather conditions: a survey. ISPRS J. Photogramm. Remote. Sens. **196**, 146–177 (2023)

10. Ng, M., Jagetiya, D., Gao, X., Shi, H., Gao, J., Liu, J.: Real-time detection of objects on roads for autonomous vehicles using deep learning. In: 2022 IEEE Eighth International Conference on Big Data Computing Service and Applications (BigDataService), Newark, CA, USA, pp. 73–80 (2022)

11. Sellat, Q., Ramasubramanian, K.: Advanced techniques for perception and localization in autonomous driving systems: a survey. Opt. Mem. Neural Netw. **31**, 123–144 (2022)

12. Velasco-Hernandez, G., Yeong, D.J., Barry, J., Walsh, J.: Autonomous driving architectures, perception and data fusion: a review. In: 2020 IEEE 16th International Conference on Intelligent Computer Communication and Processing (ICCP), Cluj-Napoca, Romania, pp. 315–321 (2020)

13. Wang, Z., Wu, Y., Niu, Q.: Multi-sensor fusion in automated driving: a survey. IEEE Access **8**, 2847–2868 (2020)

14. Li, L., et al.: An investigation of ADAS camera performance degradation using a realistic rain simulation system in wind tunnel. Presented at the WCX SAE World Congress Experience, SAE International (2024)

15. Zhu, Z., Li, X., Zhai, J., Hu, H.: PODB: a learning-based polarimetric object detection benchmark for road scenes in adverse weather conditions. Inf. Fusion **108**, 102385 (2024)

16. SAE International Recommended Practice. Taxonomy and Definitions for Terms Related to Driving Automation Systems for On-Road Motor Vehicles. SAE Standard J3016_202104 (2014)

17. Liu, D., Cui, Y., Cao, Z., Chen, Y.: A large-scale simulation dataset: boost the detection accuracy for special weather conditions. In: 2020 International Joint Conference on Neural Networks (IJCNN), pp. 1–8 (2020)

18. Khaleghi, B., Khamis, A., Karray, F.O., Razavi, S.N.: Multisensor data fusion: a review of the state-of-the-art. Inf. Fusion **14**(1), 28–44 (2013)

19. Cui, Y., et al.: Deep learning for image and point cloud fusion in autonomous driving: a review. IEEE Trans. Intell. Transp. Syst. **23**(2), 722–739 (2022)
20. Arcaini, P., Riccobene, E., Scandurra, P.: Modeling and analyzing MAPE-K feedback loops for self-adaptation. In: 2015 IEEE/ACM 10th International Symposium on Software Engineering for Adaptive and Self-Managing Systems, Florence, Italy, pp. 13–23 (2015)

Impact of Network Delays on Edge-Assisted Platooning Systems in 5G Networks: Addressing Latency Challenges

Christian Quadri[1]([⊠])[ID], Salvatore Pedone[2][ID], and Adriano Fagiolini[2][ID]

[1] University of Milano, Milan, Italy
`christian.quadri@unimi.it`
[2] University of Palermo, Palermo, Italy
`{salvatore.pedone,adriano.fagiolini}@unipa.it`

Abstract. The low latency offered by 5G mobile network and edge computing paved the way for a new approach to platoon control. Moving the controller to the edge overcomes the scalability issues and the limited radio coverage of the vehicles, typical of traditional distributed platoon controllers based on dedicated short-range communication (DSRC) solutions. However, mobile operators must provide a suitable level of quality of service (QoS), offering good radio coverage, but also preventing congestion at the base station level, to guarantee a low latency control loop for sending motion data to the controller and getting the desired acceleration instruction back from the controller, within a short time. In this paper, we investigate the influence of uplink and downlink network delays on an edge-assisted platooning system. We simulate specific scenarios of network congestion by saturating the physical radio resource of the base station, which leads to an increase in communication latency. Through a simulation campaign, we analyze the performance of the platooning system in terms of target distance preservation and string stability.

Keywords: Platooning · Mobile network · Simulation

1 Introduction

The advent of 5G mobile network, combined with the edge computing paradigm, has opened new opportunities for autonomous driving supporting services. In particular, vehicle platooning is getting new attention with the possibility of controlling the vehicle remotely, exploiting the combination of low latency offered by the new radio standard [1] and the availability of computation capabilities close to the radio access network [7].

Traditionally, platooning control is realized through a distributed system supported by dedicated short-range communication (DSRC), using 802.11p, C-V2X, and VLC [2,4,16,17]. Recently, edge-assisted platooning has been proposed [3,6,9,11], to overcome the poor scalability of DSRC platooning, due to limited radio coverage of the vehicles, and to facilitate the integration with other ITS

© ICST Institute for Computer Sciences, Social Informatics and Telecommunications Engineering 2025
Published by Springer Nature Switzerland AG 2025. All Rights Reserved
A. Kocian et al. (Eds.): INTSYS 2024, LNICST 608, pp. 381–393, 2025.
https://doi.org/10.1007/978-3-031-86370-7_23

systems running at the edge, thanks to the centralized control of the platoon. This approach to platooning requires full mobile network coverage to operate and mobile operators have to guarantee suitable quality of service (QoS) levels to preserve the correct behavior of the platoon system, i.e., distance policy and string stability. Some previous works have investigated the impact of network delays on platooning performance. In [11] has shown that the system can tolerate round trip time delays up to 70 ms. However, the results were obtained by modeling network latencies as probability distributions, neglecting congestion phenomena and realistic radio channel conditions. In another work, Nardini et al. [9] analyzed the case of platoons involving vehicles from different network operators, considering realistic radio channel using the popular Simu5G [10] framework. Nevertheless, the analyses do not consider uplink and downlink delay separately. In [6], Hidayatullah et al. presented a complete analysis of delay impact on platoon considering both distributed and centralized platoon management and investigating the platoon system performance under realistic power-train and network models. Also in this case, the evaluation does not split uplink and downlink channel delays.

In this paper, we investigate the influence of uplink and downlink network delays on an edge-assisted platooning system. Differently from the previous works, we consider uplink and downlink delays separately, by investigating the centralized platooning system reactions in the presence of delays in data and instructions. We simulate specific scenarios of network congestion at the mobile base station level, leading to an increase in communication latency due to the saturation of the physical radio resource of the base station. We run a preliminary simulation campaign considering different levels of congestion severity to evaluate the performance limit of the platoon system. From the results it has emerged that the edge-assisted platooning system is more sensitive to downlink delay as increases misalignments in vehicle motion, while can tolerate moderated delays in uplink without compromising the platoon maneuvers.

2   Edge-Assisted Platooning

A simplified architecture of edge-assisted platooning proposed in [11] is depicted in Fig. 1. Each vehicle is directly connected to a radio base station, which provides the vehicle with uplink and downlink connectivity towards the edge computing platform. Differently from the traditional platooning supported by the dedicated short-range communication (DSRC) paradigm, the access to radio medium is completely under the control of the base station scheduler, eliminating the contention overhead and minimizing signal interference. The platoon vehicles communicate with an edge server where an instance of the platoon controller is deployed. Each vehicle periodically sends motion data (e.g., position, speed, acceleration) to the remote controller, which computes the control law and sends back the acceleration instruction to the vehicle.

In traditional DSRC-based platooning, the platoon control is realized in a distributed fashion, in which each vehicle is responsible for the computation of its

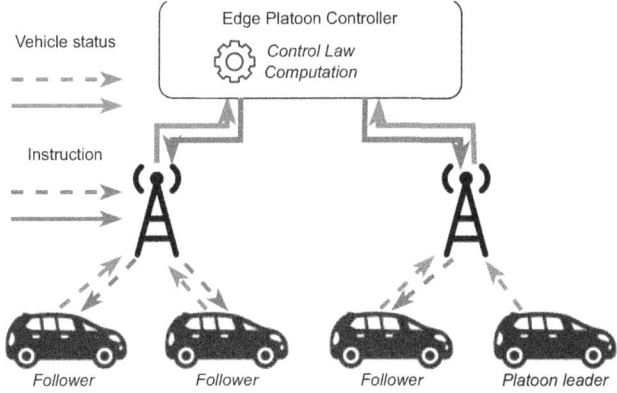

Fig. 1. Edge-assisted platooning architecture.

instructions. Conversely, edge-assisted platooning offers a centralized approach to controlling the entire platoon. As discussed in [11], the centralized control allows the controller to have a unified view of the platoon by recreating a virtual representation of the physical platoon on the edge. Moreover, long platoons can be easily managed without the limits of vehicle radio coverage and additional delays due to multi-hop transmissions. However, moving the platoon control remotely introduces new delay components. In addition to the delays caused by uploading the motion data to the edge server through the base station and the backhaul network, edge-assisted platooning introduces the instruction delay, caused by the delivery of the instruction messages from the edge server to the platoon vehicles. In the following sections, we present in detail the different components of the centralized platoon control system.

2.1 Network Delay Schema

In Fig. 2, we report the schema of the delay components of edge-assisted platooning.

T_{OBU1}	T_{RAN_UL}	T_{BS_UL}	T_{BH_UL}	T_{MEC}	T_{BH_DL}	T_{BS_DL}	T_{RAN_DL}	T_{OBU2}	T_{ACT}
	Total uplink delay				*Total downlink delay*				

Fig. 2. Schema of the delay components.

The components in grey are delays caused by onboard computation (T_{OBU1} to read motion sensors data and T_{OBU2} to instruct the onboard actuators), and edge server computation of the control law (T_{MEC}), while T_{ACT} refers to the actuation lag due to physical inertia of the vehicle. The other delay components are directly induced by the mobile and edge networks. More specifically, the uplink is made of three parts:

1. T_{RAN_UL} represents the transmission time of a message between the vehicle and the base station that is serving it. This component considers the whole uplink communication process, that is the actual message transmission and the acknowledgment from the base station.
2. T_{BS_UL} is the time spent by the base station to receive, decode and process the message and send it to the edge server through the backhaul network. This component includes the control plane overhead for granting the transmission, performed by the uplink scheduler of the base station.
3. T_{BH_UL} is the transmission time of the message between the base station and the edge server. Being the backhaul network equipped with optical fiber offering high data rate, the delay is mainly caused by the geographical distance between the base station and the edge server where the platoon controller is deployed. According to previous studies [9,11], the remote controller can be easily deployed on an edge facility at the access ring of the telco operator network. This solution allows the edge facility to serve directly a large group of base stations, maintaining backhaul delay to a negligible level.

Analogously, the downlink delay is composed by:

1. T_{BH_DL} is the transmission time of the message between the edge server and the base station across the backhaul network.
2. T_{BS_DL} is the time spent by the base station to receive, decode and process the message and schedule it for sending to the vehicle. This component includes the control plane overhead for informing the vehicle that a message is going to be transmitted.
3. T_{RAN_DL} represents the downlink transmission time, i.e., the actual transmission and the final acknowledgment.

The most critical delay components are the ones that involve the base station processing and radio transmissions, i.e., T_{RAN_UL}, T_{RAN_DL}, T_{BS_UL}, T_{BS_DL}. This is because the radio channel quality is highly variable, directly affecting the transmission time and amount of consumed physical layer resources[1]. Moreover, the base station represents a bottleneck when is overloaded, because the transmission requests are queued by the base station scheduler due to the lack of available physical resources, causing extra delays [13]. In this work, we focus on T_{BS_UL} and T_{BS_DL} delay components, investigating the impact of the congestion of the base station on the performance of the platoon.

---

[1] The base station adopts the so-called Adaptive Modulation and Coding scheme approach, by dynamically changing the coding and modulation parameters according to the quality of the radio channel. The higher the quality, the more efficient the modulation and coding scheme, resulting in fewer physical resources consumed for transmitting the same quantity of data.

2.2   Cooperative Adaptive Cruise Control Control Law

The standard definition of Cooperative Adaptive Cruise Control (CACC) [12] is

$$\ddot{x}_{i\_des} = \alpha_1 \ddot{x}_{i-1} + \alpha_2 \ddot{x}_0 + \alpha_3 \dot{\varepsilon}_i + \alpha_4(\dot{x}_i - \dot{x}_0) + \alpha_5 \varepsilon_i \tag{1}$$

$$\dot{\varepsilon}_i = \dot{x}_i - \dot{x}_{i-1} \tag{2}$$

$$\varepsilon_i = x_i - x_{i-1} + l_{i-1} + d_{des} \tag{3}$$

$$\alpha_1 = 1 - C_1 \tag{4}$$

$$\alpha_2 = C_1 \tag{5}$$

$$\alpha_3 = -\left(2\xi - C_1 \left(\xi + \sqrt{\xi^2 - 1}\right)\right) \omega_n \tag{6}$$

$$\alpha_4 = -C_1 \left(\xi + \sqrt{\xi^2 - 1}\right) \omega_n \tag{7}$$

$$\alpha_5 = -\omega_n^2 \tag{8}$$

on of the i-th vehicle. $\ddot{x}_0$ and $\dot{x}_0$ are the acceleration and the speed of the platoon leader, respectively. x_{i-1}, $\dot{x}_{i-1}$, $\ddot{x}_{i-1}$ and l_{i-1} represent the position, the speed, the acceleration and the length of the preceding vehicle, respectively. $\dot{\varepsilon}_i$ is the delta speed between the i-th vehicle and the preceding one. ε_i is the distance error with respect to the target distance d_{des}. CACC has three parameters: the weighting factor between the accelerations of the leader and the preceding vehicle C_1, the damping ratio ξ and the controller bandwidth ω_n. The output of the control law is the desired acceleration the vehicle i-th ($\ddot{x}_{i\_des}$) should implement to maintain the target inter-vehicle distance, (d_{des}) and the string stability property.

2.3   Control Loop and Age of Information Schema

In traditional DSRC-based platooning, each vehicle periodically computes the control law onboard using the data read from its sensors and the ones obtained by other vehicles through V2V communication. The constant availability of fresh data from onboard sensors and other platoon members usually sent every 100 ms [2], allows the vehicle to finely adjust the acceleration at any time. Under low radio medium contention and low interference, the communication delay is below 1 ms [5,15], bounding the age of information of the data of other vehicles around 100 ms. Under these settings, the OBU can compute the control law synchronously at fixed time intervals and pass the computed acceleration instruction to the actuators immediately.

On the contrary, in edge-assisted platooning, the computation is performed asynchronously, every time the remote controller receives updated motion data from a platoon vehicle. As proposed in [11], the edge controller builds a dependency graph telling which vehicles depend on the update sent by a specific vehicle. The graph topology is strictly based on the control topology *Leader-and predecessor-following* that is often proposed for the Cooperative Adaptive Cruise Control control law. For example, suppose that the edge controller receives data

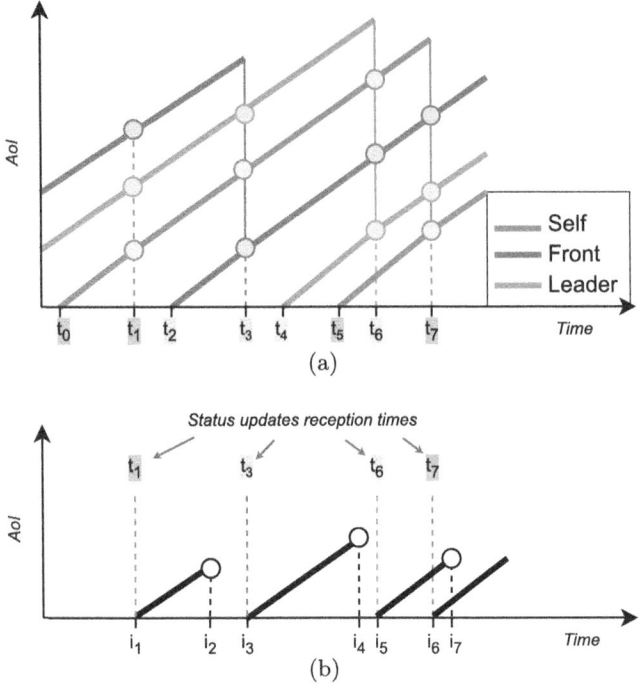

Fig. 3. Age of the information schema.

from the vehicle i. According to the Cooperative Adaptive Cruise Control control law (see Sect. 2.2), the data of the vehicle i are used to compute the instruction of the follower vehicle, $i + 1$, and the vehicle itself. Therefore, the reception of the data of vehicle i triggers the computation of two instructions that will be sent unicast to the vehicles. In case leader data are updated, the instructions are computed for all the followers, since all the followers depend on the platoon leader.

The paradigm shift of the control loop from onboard-synchronous to remote-asynchronous introduces new delay components that affect the age of the information (AoI) model of the platoon system. The Fig. 3 shows the evolution of the AoI of the vehicle data (Fig. 3a) and the instruction (Fig. 3b) for a generic i-th follower ($i > 1$). At t_0, the vehicle i reads the data from the onboard sensors and sends them to the edge controller. The uplink message is received at t_1 and triggers the computation of the desired acceleration instruction ($t_1 = i_1$ in Fig. 3b[2]), using the new data of vehicle i and the previously received data of the other platoon members, i.e., leader and front vehicle. The colored dots in the figure indicate the AoI of the vehicles' data. For example, at t_1, the oldest information is the one of the front vehicle, while the freshest is of i-th vehicle.

---

[2] In this work, we assume that the computing time of the control law, T_{MEC} in Fig. 2, is negligible.

Similarly, at t_2 and t_4 the front and the leader vehicles send their updates that will be received at t_3 and t_6, respectively, leading to instruction computation at i_3 and i_5.

Differently from DSRC-based platooning, the remote platoon controller always deals with delayed data, whose delay is determined by the uplink delay components (see Fig. 2). Therefore, the platoon controller builds its virtual delayed representation of the platoon, of course, the lower the uplink delay, the more precise the computed instruction. Moreover, the data update time interval could significantly vary due to radio link quality, serving base station scheduling policy, and its congestion. Another key difference compared to DSRC approach is the extra control loop delay introduced by the delivery of the instruction message to the vehicles. In Fig. 3b, timestamps i_2, i_4 and i_7 represent the time when the instruction message is delivered to the vehicle. This is particularly critical because instructions are directly responsible for the synchronization and safety of the vehicles. Indeed, a delay in instructions leads to misalignments in vehicle motion by increasing the risk of collision and the platoon efficiency. Instead, data can tolerate small delays without compromising the platoon maneuvers.

For the aforementioned reasons, the mobile network has to be able to guarantee a suitable level of QoS in both uplink and downlink, to minimize the error with respect to the target distance and to preserve the string stability. In the following, we will show the impact of the delays caused by the congestion of base stations on the platoon performance.

3   Simulation Setup

To evaluate the impact of the network delay components, we simulate a highway scenario with a fleet of 8 light-duty commercial vehicles. We develop a simulator framework using OMNeT++ on top of the SUMO simulator [8]. In particular, we rely on the Veins [14] and Simu5G [10] frameworks to model vehicles and 5G mobile network, respectively. In Table 1, we report the main simulation parameters and mobile network configuration. The mobile network consists of 8 base stations, each deployed 1000 m apart from one another along the highway. This guarantees suitable radio coverage for the whole platoon journey. Each base station offers 3 physical resource blocks (RBs) every 1 ms, leading to an offered gross data rate between 1.5 and 3.5 Mbps, depending on the radio channel quality (see 5G standard [1]). The offered data rate by a single base station is sufficient to handle all the data traffic of the platoon, which is around 500 kbps for an 8-vehicle platoon.

3.1   Background Traffic Generation Scenarios

To generate congestion at the base station level (see T_{BS_UL} and T_{BS_DL} in Fig. 2), we simulate background traffic, generated by mobile devices that do not belong to the platoon. We consider three scenarios of traffic generation: *(i)* *uplink background*, where most traffic is generated in uplink (uplink packet size

Table 1. Simulation parameters.

General parameters	
Simulated road	Straight 3-lane highway
Simulation duration	300 s (100 s of warm-up time)
Simulation scenario repetitions	20 random seeds
Platoon parameters	
Number of platoon members	8
Leader speed pattern	Sinusoidal
	90 km/h ($\pm$ 5 km/h), 0.1 Hz
CACC parameters (see [12])	
Weighting factor (C_1)	0.5
Damping factor (ξ)	1
Controller bandwidth (ω_n)	0.2 Hz
Target distance (d_{des})	15 m
Mobile network configuration	
Number of base stations	8 (along the highway)
Inter-Base station distance	1000 m
Base station physical resource	3 RBs per TTI (1 ms)
UE Tx power (gain)	26 dBm (+0dBi)
Base station Tx power (gain)	46 dBm (+18dBi)
Carrier frequency	800 MHz
Base station model	ITU-Urban macrocell
Pathloss model	Free Space with $\alpha = 3.5$
Base station scheduler	Max Channel Indicator
Background network traffic	
Number background device (N_{bg})	0, 30, 60, 90 UEs
Application type	UDP Constant Bit Rate
Packet size (UL/DL)	10, 500 byte
Packet frequency (UL/DL)	20 pkt/s
Generation starting time	120 s–140 s
Generation ending time	220 s–240 s

of 500 bytes, downlink 10 bytes); *(ii) downlink background*, where the traffic is concentrated in the downlink (uplink packet size of 10 bytes, downlink 500 bytes); and *(iii) symmetric background*, which is the combination of the two previous scenarios (uplink and downlink packet size of 500 bytes). For each scenario, we consider 4 levels of background traffic, simulating 0, 30, 60 and 90 background devices that generate traffic for 100 s. These four levels of background traffic allow us to generate different congestion levels at the base station, in which the base station resources are reserved for platoon vehicles, i.e. no-background, and situations in which resources are shared among other vehicles or devices that do not belong to the platoon.

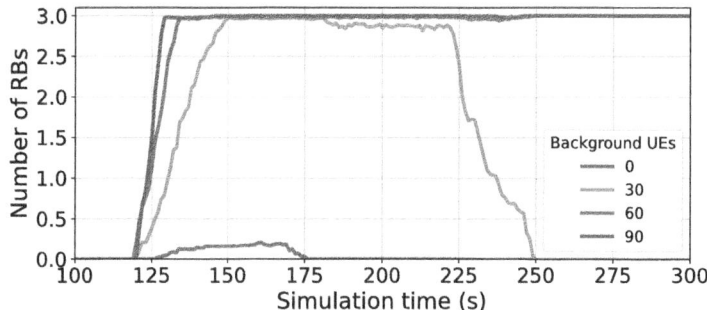

Fig. 4. Example of base station physical resources utilization considering different numbers of background devices. (Color figure online)

In Fig. 4, we show the utilization of the uplink physical resources of the base station that serves the platoon vehicles. The blue line represents the case of no background traffic, from which we can observe that the platoon traverses the base station coverage area between 125 s and 175 s, using a limited amount of resources. With 30 background devices (orange line), we observe a mild level of saturation, but still, the base station is able to manage all the generated traffic. However, as the number of background devices increases to 60 and 90, network congestion becomes severe. The base station, overwhelmed by the high volume of traffic, cannot process transmissions efficiently, resulting in increased latency, causing an increase in the transmission time. In particular, in the case of 90 background devices, the level of resource saturation rises very fast and it is maintained constant until the end of the simulation. In the next section, we show the performance of the edge-assisted platooning system under the different background scenarios.

4   Results

In this section, we present the results of the simulation campaign. For each background scenario, we repeat the experiment 20 times, by varying the initial random seed. To ensure our analysis focuses on the platoon's steady-state behavior, we excluded the first 100 s of simulation data, eliminating initial transient effects.

In Fig. 5, we report the overall results, considering the distance error as a quantitative metric for the evaluation of the platoon performance. On the left of the figure, we show the box plot[3] of the distribution of the distance error for

---

[3] The whole box plot shows up to 90th percentile, largest boxes represent the 2nd and 3rd quartile, as a classical box plot.

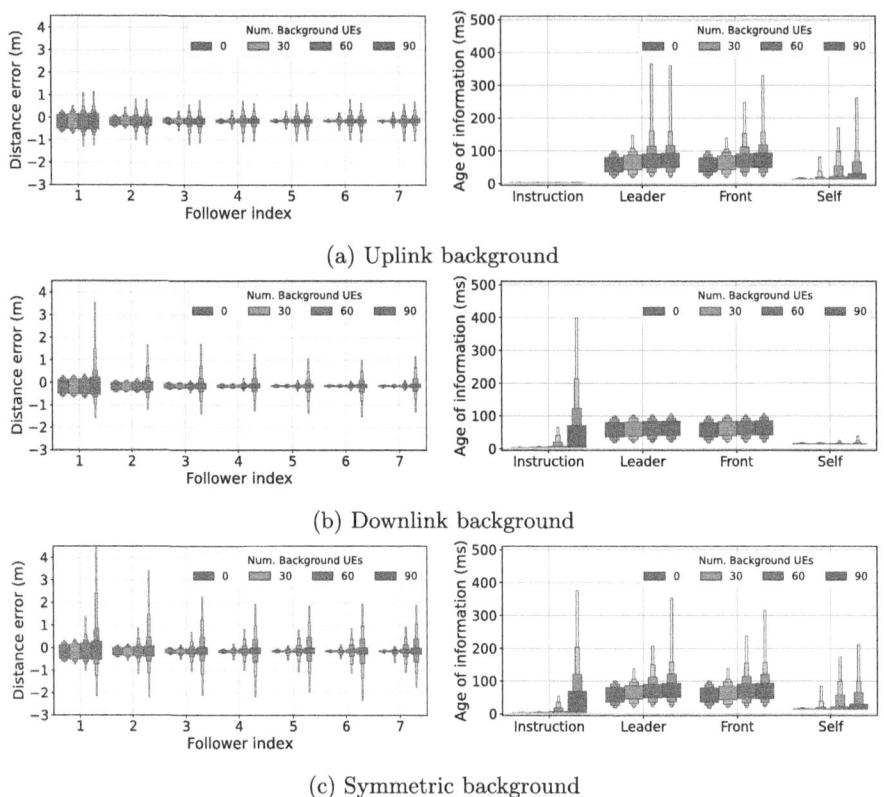

(a) Uplink background

(b) Downlink background

(c) Symmetric background

Fig. 5. Box plot of the distribution of distance error for all the followers (left) and box plot of the distribution of the age of the information of data and instruction (right), under different levels of base station congestion.

all the followers, while, on the right, we report the box plot of the distribution of the age of the information of motion data and instruction. As we can observe, the platoon system is able to guarantee low distance error and string stability for up to 30 background devices, this is because the mobile network can guarantee a suitable level of QoS, maintaining the age of the information of motion data up 100 ms and less than 15 ms for the instruction. The performance level significantly drops considering the scenarios with 60 and 90 background devices. As shown in Fig. 4, in these cases the base station is unable to handle the whole traffic in time, causing extra delays, which significantly affect the age of the information. However, the system behaves differently in the case of *uplink background* (Fig. 5a) and *downlink background* (Fig. 5b) scenarios. Although string stability is lost in both these cases, the downlink case exhibits larger distance errors, demonstrating that the edge-assisted platooning system is more sensitive to instruction message delays. This increased sensitivity results in vehicle motion misalignment, confirming our analysis in Sect. 2.3.

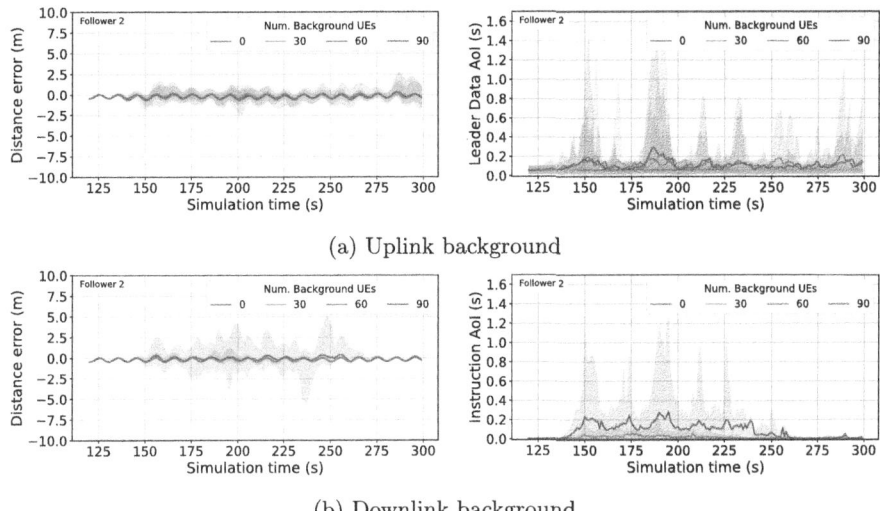

(a) Uplink background

(b) Downlink background

Fig. 6. Evolution of distance error (left) and age of the information of leader data and instruction (right) over time in uplink and downlink background scenarios.

This aspect is more evident when focusing on a single vehicle. In Fig. 6, we report the evolution of the distance error (on the left) and the age of information of leader data and instruction (on the right) over time for the second follower. The solid lines represent the median values, while the areas cover the 90th percentile. As we can observe, although the peaks of the age of information (on the right) reach similar high values, the impact on the platoon system is significantly different. In particular, the distance error in the case of the uplink scenario is bounded between -2.5 and $2.5\,\mathrm{m}$, for all the background traffic levels. On the contrary, in the downlink scenario, the error peaks are below/above $-5/+5\,\mathrm{m}$. As for the *symmetric background* scenario (Fig. 5c), the performance is worse than the other two cases, as it combines the effects of both scenarios.

The results have shown the high sensitivity of the edge-assisted platooning system to the delay of the instruction computed by the remote controller. While the system can tolerate moderately long delays in transmitting the motion data to the remote controller, even for a prolonged time, the downlink delay must be kept low, and delay peaks should be only temporary and sporadic, avoiding congestion at the base station level. These preliminary results provide indications for mobile operators to tune the base station scheduler to reserve resources for critical services and prevent congestion by limiting the number of critical services that can be safely managed. Moreover, these findings can be the starting point for designing and tuning specific control laws tailored to remote and centralized platoon controllers, accounting for the intrinsic and unavoidable network delays.

5   Conclusion

In this paper, we have presented an evaluation of the impact of mobile network delays on edge-assisted platooning system. In particular, we analyze the sensitivity of the system to uplink and downlink delay separately. What has emerged from the preliminary simulation results is that downlink delay components are more critical than the uplink ones.

The follow-up of this study is twofold. First, to provide the network operator with specific QoS requirements for uplink and downlink channels; second, to formulate and test control law specifically designed to tolerate non-negligible delay components.

Acknowledgments. This work received funding from the European Union - NextGenerationEU - National Recovery and Resilience Plan (NRRP) - MISSION 4 COMPONENT 2, INVESTMENT N. 1.1, CALL PRIN 2022 PNRR D.D. 1409 14-09-2022 - FORESEEN: FORmal mEthodS for attack dEtEction in autonomous driviNg systems, Grant: P2022WYAEW, CUPs: G53D23006720001, B53D23026280001

References

1. TS 38.214 (Rel-18); Physical layer procedures for data. Technical report, 3GPP (2024)
2. Balador, A., Bazzi, A., Hernandez-Jayo, U., de la Iglesia, I., Ahmadvand, H.: A survey on vehicular communication for cooperative truck platooning application. Veh. Commun. **35**, 100460 (2022). https://doi.org/10.1016/j.vehcom.2022.100460
3. Dabbene, S., Lehmann, C., Campolo, C., Molinaro, A., Fitzek, F.H.P.: A MEC-assisted vehicle platooning control through docker containers. In: 2020 IEEE 3rd Connected and Automated Vehicles Symposium (CAVS), pp. 1–6 (2020). https://doi.org/10.1109/CAVS51000.2020.9334658
4. Gonçalves, T.R., Varma, V.S., Elayoubi, S.E.: Performance of vehicle platooning under different v2x relaying methods. In: 2021 IEEE 32nd Annual International Symposium on Personal, Indoor and Mobile Radio Communications (PIMRC), pp. 1018–1023. IEEE (2021)
5. Hassan, M.I., Vu, H.L., Sakurai, T.: Performance analysis of the IEEE 802.11 mac protocol for DSRC safety applications. IEEE Trans. Veh. Technol. **60**(8), 3882–3896 (2011). https://doi.org/10.1109/TVT.2011.2162755
6. Hidayatullah, M.R., Juang, J.C.: Centralized and distributed control framework under homogeneous and heterogeneous platoon. IEEE Access **9**, 49629–49648 (2021). https://doi.org/10.1109/ACCESS.2021.3068968
7. Kekki, S., et al.: MEC in 5G networks. ETSI White Pap. **28**(28), 1–28 (2018)
8. Lopez, P.A., et al.: Microscopic traffic simulation using SUMO. In: IEEE International Conference on Intelligent Transportation Systems (ITSC) (2018)
9. Nardini, G., Noferi, A., Stea, G.: Platooning-as-a-service in a multi-operator ETSI MEC environment. IEEE Access **11**, 60040–60058 (2023). https://doi.org/10.1109/ACCESS.2023.3286023
10. Nardini, G., Sabella, D., Stea, G., Thakkar, P., Virdis, A.: Simu5G-an OMNet++ library for end-to-end performance evaluation of 5G networks. IEEE Access **8**, 181176–181191 (2020). https://doi.org/10.1109/ACCESS.2020.3028550

11. Quadri, C., Mancuso, V., Ajmone Marsan, M., Rossi, G.P.: Edge-based platoon control. Comput. Commun. **181**, 17–31 (2022). https://doi.org/10.1016/j.comcom.2021.09.021
12. Rajamani, R.: Vehicle Dynamics and Control, vol. 7. Springer, New York (2012)
13. Singh, U., Dua, A., Tanwar, S., Kumar, N., Alazab, M.: A survey on LTE/LTE-A radio resource allocation techniques for machine-to-machine communication for B5G networks. IEEE Access **9**, 107976–107997 (2021). https://doi.org/10.1109/ACCESS.2021.3100541
14. Sommer, C., German, R., Dressler, F.: Bidirectionally coupled network and road traffic simulation for improved IVC analysis. IEEE Trans. Mob. Comput. **10**(1), 3–15 (2011). https://doi.org/10.1109/TMC.2010.133
15. Wang, B., Zheng, J., Ren, Q., Li, C.: Analysis of IEEE 802.11p-based intra-platoon message broadcast delay in a platoon of vehicles. IEEE Trans. Veh. Technol. **72**(10), 13417–13429 (2023). https://doi.org/10.1109/TVT.2023.3274688
16. Won, M.: L-Platooning: a protocol for managing a long platoon with DSRC. IEEE Trans. Intell. Transp. Syst. **23**(6), 5777–5790 (2022). https://doi.org/10.1109/TITS.2021.3057956
17. Yang, C., Kwong, C.F., Chieng, D., Kar, P., Yau, K.L.A., Chen, Y.: Navigating the road ahead: a comprehensive survey of radio resource allocation for vehicle platooning in C-V2X communications. IEEE Commun. Surv. Tutorials (2024). https://doi.org/10.1109/COMST.2024.3440033

A Model-Based Approach for Analysis of Data-Alteration Attacks in Co-operative Vehicles

Cinzia Bernardeschi[ID], Maurizio Palmieri[ID], Marta Sanguinetti, and Alessio Vivani[(✉)]

Department of Information Engineering, University of Pisa, Pisa, Italy
{cinzia.bernardeschi,maurizio.palmieri}@unipi.it,
alessio.vivani@ing.unipi.it

Abstract. This work presents a modular approach for modelling and analysing the effects of data-alteration attacks in co-operative vehicles applications. The approach exploits multi-model simulation and Functional Mock-Up Interface (FMI)-based co-simulation tools. The system model is extended with an attacker Functional Mockup Unit (FMU) which implements a strategy for the injection of the attack. Co-simulation results can be analysed to show the behavioural traces of the system under various attacks. The approach is applied to a platoon of vehicles.

Keywords: Cyber-physical systems · Co-simulation · Cybersecurity

1 Introduction

Co-operative vehicular systems are complex Cyber-Physical Systems (CPSs) where a co-ordination algorithm interacts with the vehicles, consisting of the controller of the movement of the vehicle and the dynamic model of the vehicle. With increased connectivity, modern vehicles have become more susceptible to cyber-security attacks [1,5]. A case is reported in the work [13], in which it is shown how to gain control of a Jeep multimedia Electronic Control Unit (ECU) remotely over the Wi-Fi connection and successively, to access inner vehicle communication system (the CAN bus), listening to the traffic on the CAN bus,

This work received funding from the European Union - Next-GenerationEU - National Recovery and Resilience Plan (NRRP) - MISSION 4 COMPONENT 2, INVESTMENT N. 1.1, CALL PRIN 2022 PNRR D.D. 1409 14-09-2022 - FORESEEN: FORmal mEthodS for attack dEtEction in autonomous driviNg systems, CUP N.I53D23006130001; from the project SERICS (PE00000014) under the MUR National Recovery and Resilience Plan funded by the European Union - NextGenerationEU - UNTWISTER: UsiNg digital TWIns to enable SecuriTy in cybER-physical ecosystems, CUP J33C22002810001; and from the Italian Ministry of Education and Research (MIUR) in the framework of the FoReLab project and of the CrossLab project (Departments of Excellence).

A. Kocian et al. (Eds.): INTSYS 2024, LNICST 608, pp. 394–410, 2025.
https://doi.org/10.1007/978-3-031-86370-7_24

and also sending commands over the bus to safety critical units, e.g., the braking ECU. A review of industrial cyber-physical systems from a cybersecurity perspective is in [7].

To protect vehicles from attacks, possible solutions adopted are Intrusion Detection Systems (IDSs), which identify system attacks by watching the CPS for irregularities in network traffic or system behaviors [8,12,14,19].

The modelling of a CPS is complex due to inherent multi-disciplinary issues, in particular CPSs are characterized by the co-existence of discrete behaviors (the controller), and continous behaviour (the physical laws), which may exhibit different aspects, such as mechanical or electromagnetic ones. Therefore CPSs can benefit from the availability of different modeling languages and tools, each tailored to different components or aspects. For this reason, in CPSs co-simulation technique is widely used [6]. Co-simulation enables the global simulation of a coupled system via the composition of various simulators. System's components can be modelled by different formalisms and exported as simulation units. An orchestrator then co-ordinates the execution of the units. A generally recognized standard for co-simulation is the *Funtional Mock-Up Interface (FMI)* [4]. Many modelling and simulation tools export the models as FMU, that can be run under the supervision of an FMI-based orchestration engine.

In this work, a method is proposed to analyse the beahaviour of co-operative vehicles systems under attacks, assuming vehicle to vehicle communications. The method is based on model-based attack injection and co-simulation technique. We assume that an attacker has gained access to the communication network; and we consider alteration of data sent through the communication network, which are input to the co-ordination algorithm. The effect of such an attack is that the output computed by the co-ordination algorithm (executed locally at the vehicle) is based on corrupted inputs and wrong commands can be sent to the physical system. The INTO-CPS co-simulation framework [21] is used, which offers an integrated "tool chain" for comprehensive model-based design of CPSs. The approach is applied to a platoon of vehicles [18].

The paper is organised as follows: Sect. 2 briefly presents co-simulation technique, and platooning application. Section 3 introduces the Attack FMU, which is in charge of implementing attack injection in the CPS. Section 4 presents the application of the proposed approach to a simple platoon of vehicles. Section 5 reports the conclusions.

2   Background

2.1   Co-simulation

An extensive survey on co-simulation has been published by Gomes et al. in [6], providing definitions of the fundamental concepts and a taxonomy of the literature based on the discrete events and continuous time computational models.

The standard most widely used for co-simulation of dynamic systems is the Functional Mockup Interface (FMI) [15]. It has as key components, elements called Functional Mockup Units (FMUs), that represent a part of the system to

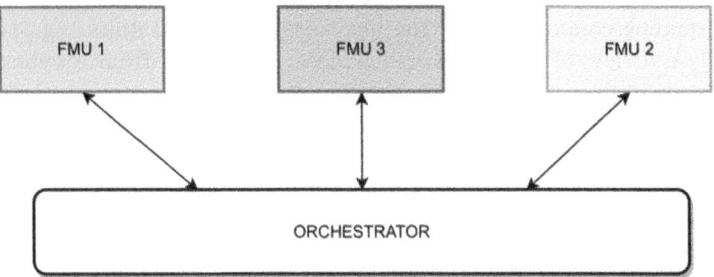

Fig. 1. Co-simulation architecture.

be modeled. Each of them is responsible for simulating the element that it is modeling and is independent from the other ones. The models are all connected, via an Interface, to a co-simulation Orchestrator which is in charge of the communications between FMUs. A co-simulation schema with three simulation units is shown in Fig. 1.

When a co-simulation starts, the Orchestrator (Master) will initialize the models of the FMUs (Slaves) by calling the functions **fmi2Instantiate** and **fmi2SetupExperiment**. Then it will call the **fmi2DoStep** which will increase the simulation time by a time step, that can be set at simulation design time, and then will pass data between FMUs via *set* and *get* methods called **fmi2Set<type>** and **fmi2Get<type>** (*type* ranges over data types, *set* is used to output data at the interface and *get* is used to read data at the interface). The **fmi2DoStep** method will call another function that will simulate the behavior of the model, in the language used to develop such model. At the end of the run, it will free the allocated resources by calling **fmi2Terminate** and **fmi2FreeInstance**. An example of simulation FMI-compliant is provided in Fig. 2.

In our work, we will use the INTO-CPS framework [9] for co-simulation of the cyber physical system. INTO-CPS is a collection of tools developed to aid the development of CPSs. INTO-CPS supports FMU obtained from models developed with Modelica, Simulink, Python and other various modeling tools. After the generation of the FMUs, it is possible to create multi-models by defining the components, the interconnections between each other and the values to be assigned to each parameter. The Orchestrator has a Graphical User Interface that allows to create and modify multi-models and run simulations, together with the possibility to visualize the results obtained from a run inside a graph and on .csv files that get generated after the co-simulation. We use a fixed co-simulation step. The simulator reads input data available at the Orchestrator FMI interface, executes for a time equal to the co-simulation step and produces output data that are made available at the Orchestrator interface.

Co-simulation has been applied extensively in different application fields. For example, co-simulation has been used by some of the authors in [2] for space coverage tasks of drones; and in [16], for the comparison between a vehicle-

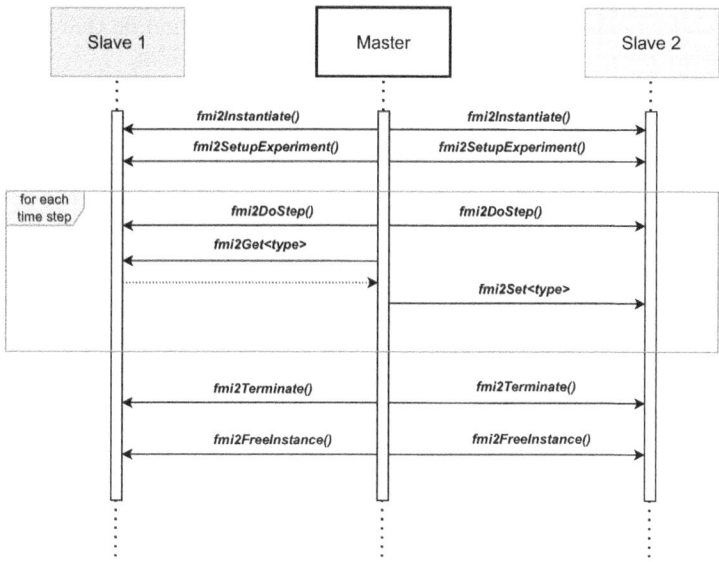

Fig. 2. Example of Simulation FMI-compliant.

to-vehicle communications against a centralised multi-access edge computing paradigm in vehicle platoons.

2.2 Platoon of Vehicles

Platooning has been a subject of research for almost four decades as a promising area in automotive engineering, in particular for improving safety and efficiency [11,18].

Simple platooning is the coordinated movement by two or more autonomous vehicles, with each following vehicle maintaining a safe distance from the preceding vehicle. The vehicle at the front of the line is the `leader` of the platoon. As the leader moves, the vehicles behind (`followers`) move and adjust their position.

In our case study, we consider a platoon of 4 cars, see Fig. 3: the leader and three followers. The leader moves with a variable speed, depending on an acceleration function, which is implemented as a function, e.g., a sinusoidal function, with amplitude, frequency, phase and offset taken as input parameters of the co-simulation. Varying the previously mentioned parameters it is possible to model different system's behaviours. For the algorithm to work vehicles need to communicate with each other, the network is modelled to be an ideal network with no delay and no noise. Each vehicle has a co-ordination module that is wirelessly connected with the other cars, leader included. In particular,

- every car receives from the leader its speed, position and acceleration, called v_leader, x_leader and acc_leader;
- a car i+1 that is behind another car i receives from the preceding one its speed, position and acceleration, called v_i, x_i and acc_i;
- each car will have to notify to its co-ordination module, locally, at which speed it is moving, and its actual position, obtaining in return the desired acceleration (acc_des) to have in order to obtain a steady state in which every car has the same speed of the leader, while being at a specific distance one to the other, in our case, the safety distance (d_safe).

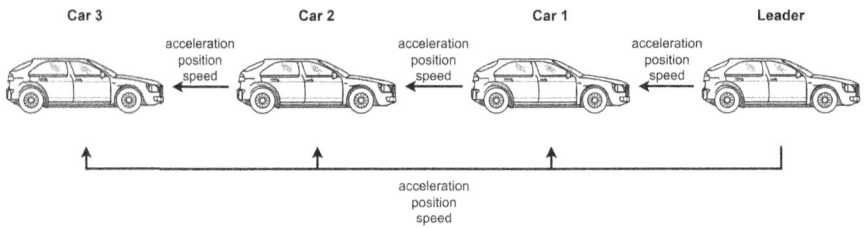

Fig. 3. A simple platoon.

The main goal of a platoon co-ordination algorithm is to maintain a specific inter-vehicle space and to guarantee *platoon stability* [20]. One of the most popular control law is Cooperative Adaptive Cruise Control (CACC) [17]. In the CACC algorithm, a car adjusts its velocity using information coming from the preceeding car and the leader. The desired acceleration (accdes) of each follower is computed locally to the vehicle as follows:

```
accdes_ego = C1 acc_leader + (1-C1) acc_front - K1 (v_ego - v_lead)
- K2 (x_ego - x_front + L)
```

where ego identifies a generic follower, front is the car behind it, K1 and K2 are gain parameters of the controller, C1 is the weighting factor between the acceleration of the leader and the acceleration of the preceding vehicle and L includes the the vehicle's length and the safe distance d_safe.

In our case study, we assume safety distance d_safe = 15 m and vehicles of the same length: L = 4 m.

A simple block diagram of such system is shown in Fig. 4, where LEADER is the leader and the $i - th$ follower car is named CAR i; the coordination module local to CAR i is named CACC i.

In absence of attacks, Fig. 5 and Fig. 6 report the speed and the position of the vehicles during co-simulation generated by the INTO-CPS tools. The results show the stability of the platoon.

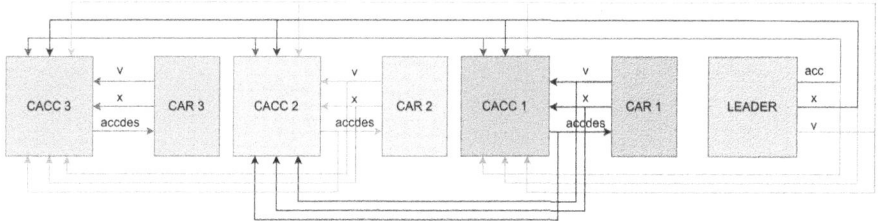

Fig. 4. Block diagram of the system.

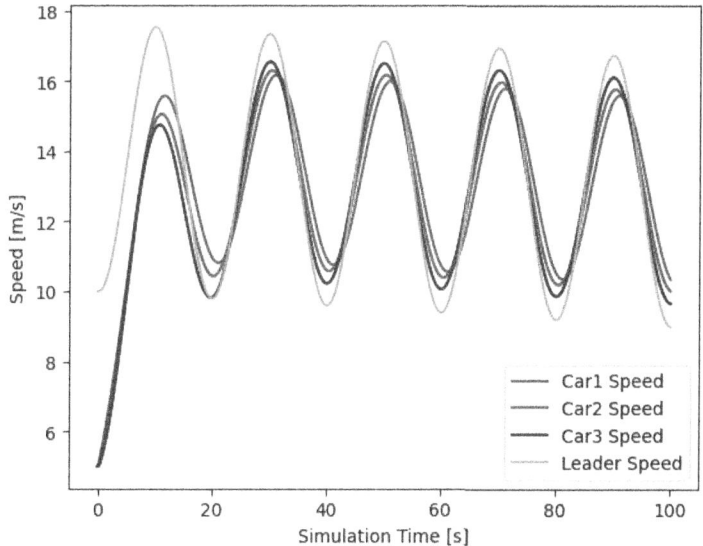

Fig. 5. Graph of the speed of vehicles in the platoon.

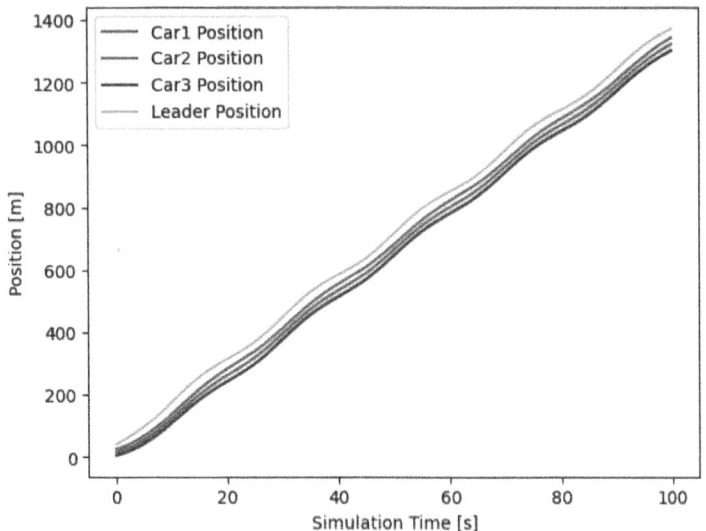

Fig. 6. Graph of the position of vehicles in the platoon.

3   Model-Based Attack Injection: The Attack FMU

In the following we concentrate on the effect of data alteration attacks. These data are used in the co-ordination algorithm to compute commands to be sent to the vehicle. As a result vehicle's acceleration can be wrong, causing a wrong movement of the vehicle, too low or too fast.

The Attack FMU receives as input a signal, and produces as output the same signal. In case of no attack, the value of the output is equal to the value of the input; in case of attack, the output is changed accordingly to a function specified by the designer, e.g., increment by a constant.

The FMU models an attack that at a certain time, `attack_time`, chosen by a parameter of the system, the value received in input will be changed by adding a constant `attack_value`, that is yet again a parameter. We assume permanent and periodic attacks. Variable `attack_type` is used to specify a permanent attack (`attack_type = 1`) or periodic attack (`attack_type = 2`). In case of `attack_type` different from 1 and 2, we assume that the attack is not active. Variable `period` is used when triggering periodic attacks. Variable `current_time` is the current simulation time. The system evolves every cosimulation step (`step_size`). A periodic attack starts at `attack_time`; it lasts `period` time; then it is triggered again after `period` time. Setting the period appropriately, an attack that is executed only once can be modeled.

The Attack model is described in Python, and exported as an FMU using UniFMU toolbox [10] which allows exporting models in various languages into an FMU. The code is shown below: in case of triggered attack, the output value is assumed to be equal to the input value summed with a constant (the `attack_value`):

```
1    def do_step(self ,current_time ,step_size ,no_step_prior ):
2        if self.attack_type == 1 and self.attack_time <=
    current_time :
3            self.output = self.input + self.attack_value
4        elif self.attack_type == 2 and self.attack_time <=
    current_time :
5            if current_time >= self.attack_time + self.
    counter * self.period :
6                self.output = self.input + self.attack_value
7                if current_time >= self.attack_time + (self.
    counter + 1.0) * self.period :
8                    self.counter = self.counter + 2.0
9            else :
10               self.output = self.input
11       else :
12           self.output = self.input
13       return Fmi2Status.ok
```

Listing 1.1. Attack FMU example (Python code).

Function do_step is invoked by **fmi2DoStep** to simulate the behaviour of the attacker in the co-simulation. We note that, using the Attack FMU, only data input to vehicles are altered, while the code executed by vehicles is not changed.

Figure 7 shows a continuous attack in the case in which the signal is the position of CAR 1 that is received from CAR 2. In this type of attack, we make CAR 2 believe that the first car is in a different position with respect to the actual one. Increasing the position seen by the second car will cause an increase of its speed in order to reach the preceding one.

Figure 8 shows an example of a periodic attack, assuming a period equal to 1.5 s.

4   The Platoon Case Study

We decided to perform various attacks in different positions using the Attack FMU, this allowed us to deeply understand how the system was working in all those cases. For each attack we ran tens of simulations in order to determine its impact and the range of values under which the attack would be safety-threatening. In particular, we focus on the three cases described below. For each of those cases we kept the following initial values:

```
-LEADER: v0 = 10 m/s x0=40 m
-CAR 1: v0 = 5 m/s x0 = 25 m
-CAR 2: v0 = 5 m/s x0 = 15 m
-CAR 3: v0 = 5 m/s x0 = 5 m
```

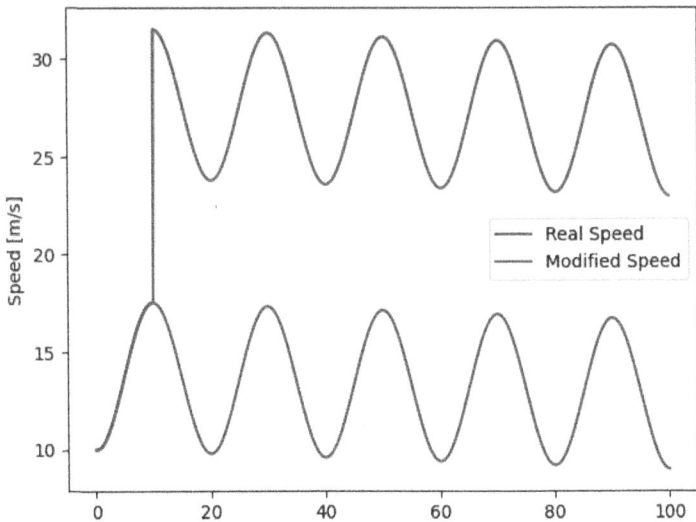

Fig. 7. Example of continuous attack.

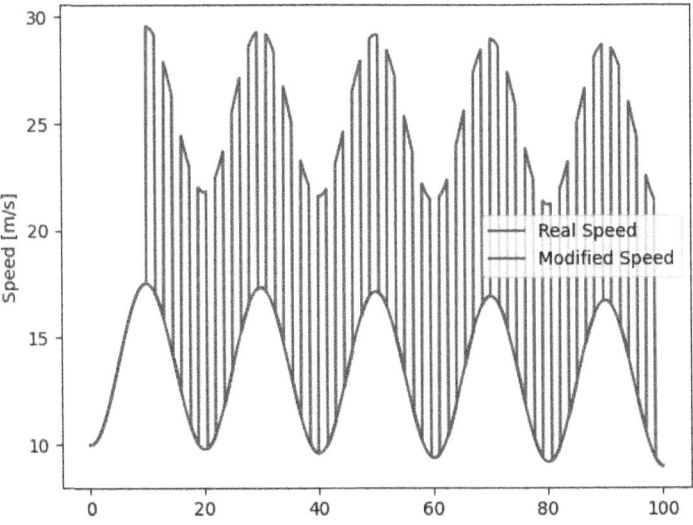

Fig. 8. Example of periodic attack.

Then we tried to discover the minimum values required to have a crash and we compared the periodic case and the continuous case in terms of time-to-crash using the same values. When deciding the attack values, we choose them in order to not exceed the physical limits. For example, we tried to select attack values that changed the speed and the acceleration in a reasonable way, neither increasing nor decreasing them too much.

4.1   Attacks on the Speed

The first attack that we chose to analyze was an alteration of the v_leader input, from LEADER to CACC 1, as we can see from the block diagram in Fig. 9.

In particular, if we use a positive attack_value, the first car will increase its speed and will move towards the leader, in order to keep the spacing at 15 m, while if we use a negative attack_value we will make CAR 1 slow down, because it believes that the leader is moving at a lower speed. For each scenario we used both the periodic and the constant attack FMU.

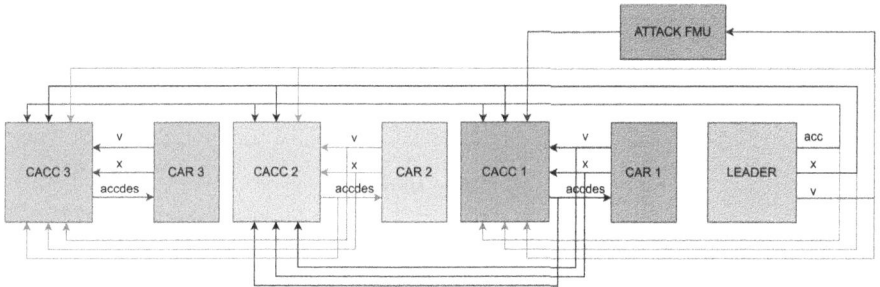

Fig. 9. Block diagram with an attack on the speed.

Positive Attack Value. Here we tried different values depending on the attack FMU used. For both of them we found out that, depending on the attack_value, the alteration of the data may lead to a crash between CAR 1 and the LEADER. Moreover, we have seen that for the periodic attack the minimum value to use to get an impact is 12 m/s, while for the constant attack we only need 7 m/s. We remark that the attack values add to the basic speed of the car. If we use values below that threshold there will be no impact, but the safety distance constraint is not respected, since the first car and the leader will not have a safe spacing. The CAR 2 and CAR 3 will not be directly affected by this attack, they simply will be following the CAR 1, meaning that they will be accelerating, but the algorithm will make them stay at a distance of 15 m from the preceding car. Here we show an example of impact. The simulation used attack_value = 14 and constant attack FMU. Figure 10 reports the position of vehicles in case of the previous attack. As it can be seen, after some simulated time CAR 1 and the LEADER will crash. The simulation will still continue as there is not a mechanism for early stopping, for this reason we see that CAR 1 will also surpass the LEADER during the simulation. In some of the other Figures provided later in the paper we will see similar behaviours as the one shown in Fig. 10, except for Fig. 14 where there is no crash at all.

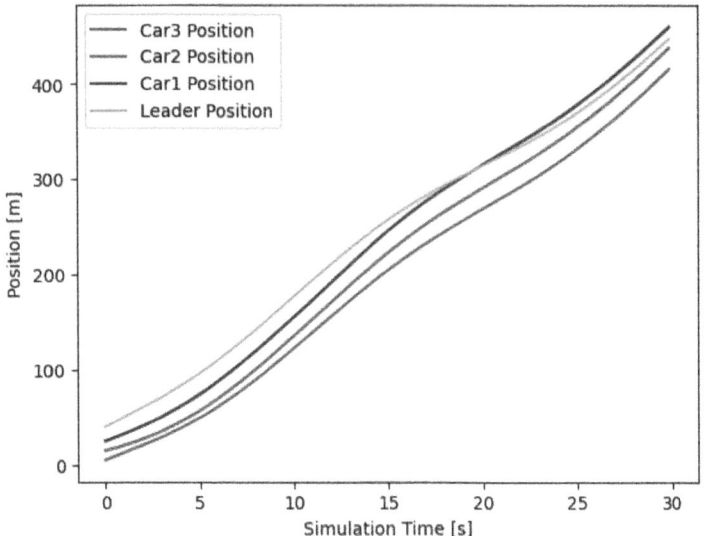

Fig. 10. Graph of the positions in the continuous case.

Negative Attack Value. The attack value we used is $-8\,\mathrm{m/s}$. For this value we obtained, for both periodic and constant attack FMUs, that there is no impact between the CAR 1 and the CAR 2, that's because the first car doesn't slow down fast enough to make it impossible for the algorithm to avoid the collision. Even though there won't be a crash between cars, the system will still be broken, since the first car will always believe that the leader is going slower than it actually is, meaning that it will stay further away from it, making the following cars do the same, with respect to the leader. Of course, when using the periodic attack, we will observe a smaller spacing between the platoon and the leader, but the effects are still pretty significant, since we have a distance of 25 instead of 15 (we have to remember that each car is assumed to be 4 m long). Figure 11 reports the position of vehicles in case of the previous attack.

4.2   Attacks on the Acceleration

Here we model a data alteration between CACC 1 and CACC 2 considering the transmission of information about the acceleration of the CAR 1. The concept of this attack is simple, by increasing the actual acceleration of the first car, the following one will try to catch up and will increase its speed to do so and that may lead to a crash, while giving negative values as inputs to the attack, the second car will think that the preceding one is going to stop, causing issue on the platoon since the last two cars will slow down to avoid impact. Figure 12 show the block diagram in case of the previous attack.

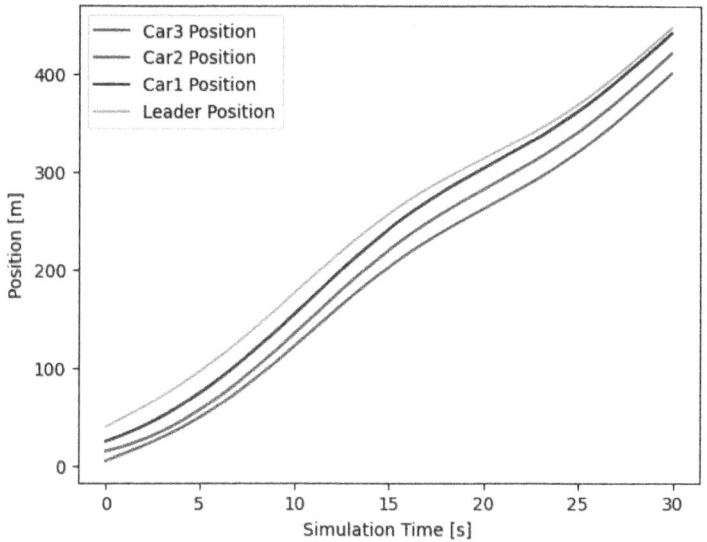

Fig. 11. Graph of the positions in the periodic case.

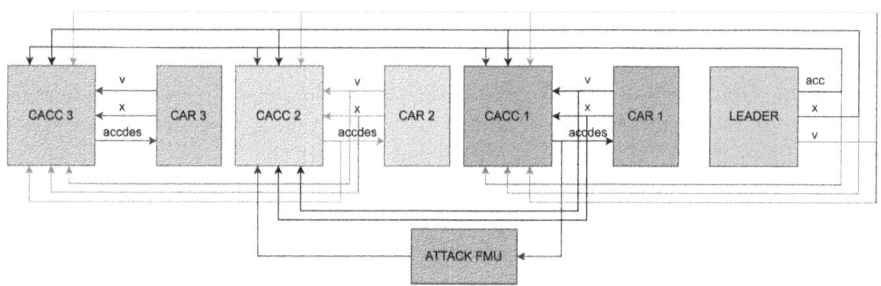

Fig. 12. Block diagram in case of an attack on the acceleration.

Positive Attack Value. In this case we tried a couple of values. In particular we determined which were the minimum values for attack_value that can lead to a crash. For the periodic attack it's $2.5 \, \mathrm{m/s^2}$, with an impact after 25 s, while for the constant attack it's $1.5 \, \mathrm{m/s^2}$. With lower values we only break the platoon because CAR 1 and CAR 2 will be too close one to the other. Then we tried the attack value at $2.5 \, \mathrm{m/s^2}$ for the constant attack FMU as well, obtaining a crash in 5 s. Figure 13 reports the position of vehicles in case of the previous attack.

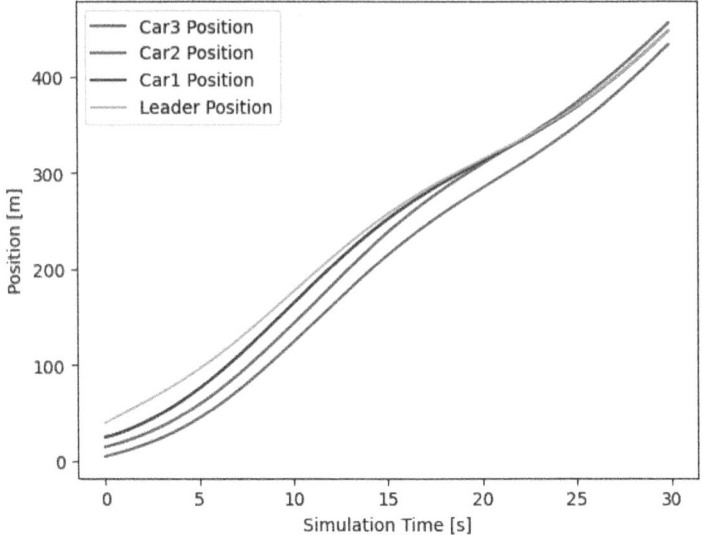

Fig. 13. Graph of the positions in the continuous case, positive attack value.

Negative Attack Value. Here we chose to check the lowest acceptable acceleration value, that is -9 m/s^2. We obtained that for the periodic attack we heavily break the platoon, making cars 2 and 3 keep a very long distance from CAR 1 and the LEADER. The constant attack led instead the system to a crash, in fact the second car braked too fast for the algorithm to handle it, so the last car hadn't been able to stop in time to avoid the impact. We can also easily observe that for smaller values for the attack we won't have any crash, but we will still break the overall system by separating some cars from the others. Figure 14 reports the position of vehicles in case of the previous attack.

4.3 Attacks on the Position

In this type of attack, we want to make the CAR 2 believe that the first car is in a different position with respect to the actual one. Increasing the position seen by the second car will cause an increase of its speed in order to reach the preceding one, in the other case it will slow down to avoid an impact. Figure 15 shows the block diagram in case of the previous attack.

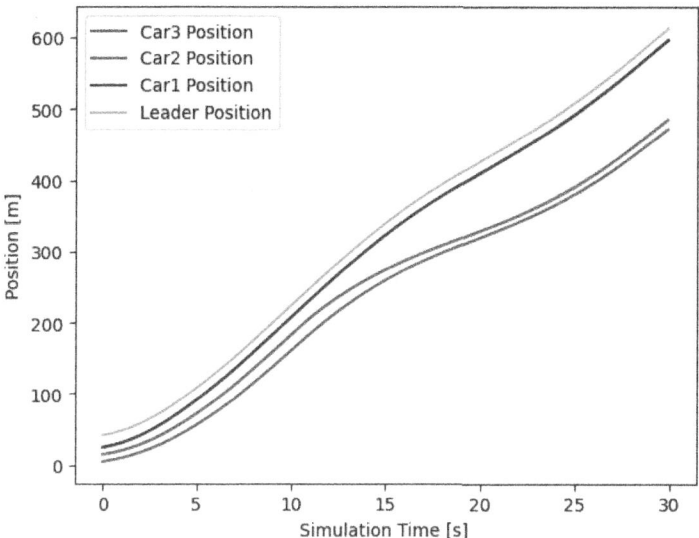

Fig. 14. Graph of the positions in the continuous case, negative attack value.

Positive Attack Value. Again, we firstly looked for the minimum value that led the system to a catastrophic event. We determined that for the periodic attack it is 35 m, while for the constant one it is 17 m. It's important to note that the attack_value must be greater than 15 m if we want to cause an accident, in fact in this way we are sure that the car will accelerate since it will try to reduce the spacing leading it to be 15 m. Then we tried both attacks with a value of 40 m, obtaining a crash in 16 s for the periodic FMU, and in 4 s for the constant one.

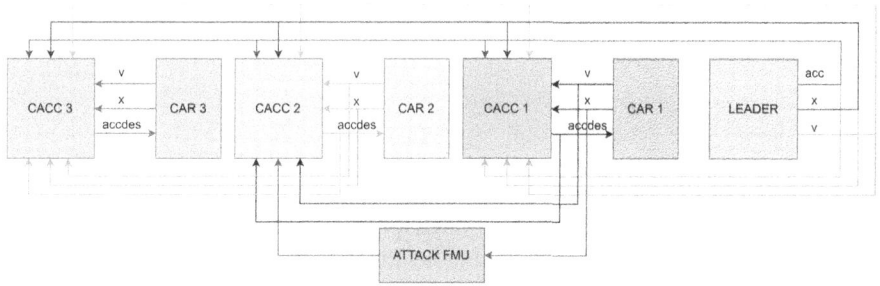

Fig. 15. Block diagram in case of an attack on the position.

Negative Attack Value. In this case we have a limitation in the value that we can put as input, in fact, since the system expects to stay in a steady condition in which each car is at 15 m of spacing, obtaining a value for the position of the preceding car that is less or equal to the one of the Car 2 might make the attack easily detectable by a simple sanity check of the input data. For this reason, we tried the lowest possible value, that is $-14\,m$ and we obtained in both cases that the platoon gets broken without leading to a crash.

4.4 Analysis of Results

First of all, we noticed that the attacks that impact the most on the system are those in which we make the controlled car accelerate, since the precedent car has no information on the parameters of the following car. If instead we perform an attack in which we make the controlled car brake, we have a crash only if the safety distance between the controlled car and the following one is violated as a consequence of an immediate slowdown. Anyway, in these kinds of attacks even if we don't have a crash, we always cause breaking since the platoon is divided, without making it possible to achieve the desired constant spacing. Another result that we obtained is that performing different simulations with different initial values, the behavior of the system consequently to the attack didn't depend a lot on the initial position and initial speed of the vehicles. This is probably because the desired accelerations depend on the differences of speed, position and acceleration, which should be independent from the initial values once the system has stabilized.

We have also observed that putting the attack FMU on analogous connections the behavior of the attack is the same and change only the cars involved. For example, an attack between the desired acceleration sent from the CACC 1 to the CACC 2 will be similar to the one performed between CACC 2 and CACC 3.

5 Conclusions

This work presents a modular approach for analysis of attacks in CPSs based on co-simulation technique and the development of the Attack FMU, which is added as a simulation unit in the co-simulation. The approach has been applied to a simple platoon of vehicles as case study. In our previous work [3], an approach to inject faults in a co-simulation is proposed that modifies the behaviour of the attacked component by introducing functions that simulate the effects of attacks. The approach has been applied to a line follower robot case study. The main advantage of Attack FMU is modularity, the Attack FMU is simply added to the co-simulation multi-model, and flexibility, the condition and effects of attacks can be easily changed in the Attack FMU. Moreover, the Attack FMU can be also applied in case of system's components with intellectual property (IP) protection. As future work, new classes of attacks could be modeled and the use of the design space exploration tool of the INTO-CPS framework could be exploited to generalize the observations on the effects of the attacks.

References

1. Alladi, T., Chamola, V., Zeadally, S.: Industrial control systems: cyberattack trends and countermeasures. Comput. Commun. (2020). https://doi.org/10.1016/j.comcom.2020.03.007
2. Bernardeschi, C., Domenici, A., Fagiolini, A., Palmieri, M.: Co-simulation and formal verification of co-operative drone control with logic-based specifications. Comput. J. **66**(2), 295–317 (2023). https://doi.org/10.1093/comjnl/bxab161
3. Bernardeschi, C., Domenici, A., Palmieri, M.: Formalization and co-simulation of attacks on cyber-physical systems. J. Comput. Virol. Hacking Tech. **16**, 63–77 (2020). https://doi.org/10.1007/s11416-019-00344-9
4. Blochwitz, T., et al.: The functional mockup interface for tool independent exchange of simulation models. In: Proceedings of 8th International Modelica Conference, pp. 105–114. Dresden, Germany (2011). https://doi.org/10.3384/ecp11063105
5. Checkoway, S., et al.: Comprehensive experimental analyses of automotive attack surfaces. In: 20th USENIX Security Symposium (USENIX Security 11). USENIX Association, San Francisco, CA (2011). https://www.usenix.org/conference/usenix-security-11/comprehensive-experimental-analyses-automotive-attack-surfaces
6. Gomes, C., Thule, C., Broman, D., Larsen, P.G., Vangheluwe, H.: Co-simulation: a survey. ACM Comput. Surv. **51**(3), 49:1–49:33 (2018). https://doi.org/10.1145/3179993
7. Kayan, H., Nunes, M., Rana, O., Burnap, P., Perera, C.: Cybersecurity of industrial cyber-physical systems: a review. ACM Comput. Surv. (2022). https://doi.org/10.1145/3510410
8. Khraisat, A., Gondal, I., Vamplew, P., Kamruzzaman, J.: Survey of intrusion detection systems: techniques, datasets and challenges. Cybersecurity **2:20**, 1–22 (2019). https://doi.org/10.1186/s42400-019-0038-7
9. Larsen, P.G., et al.: The INtegrated TOolchain for Cyber-PhysicalSystems (INTO-CPS): a Guide. Technical report, INTO-CPS Association (2018). http://into-cps.org/fileadmin/into-cps.org/Filer/INTO-CPS-Manifesto.pdf
10. Legaard, C., Tola, D., Schranz, T., Macedo, H., Larsen, P.: A universal mechanism for implementing functional mock-up units, pp. 121–129 (2021). https://doi.org/10.5220/0010577601210129
11. Maiti, S., Winter, S., Kulik, L.: A conceptualization of vehicle platoons and platoon operations. Transp. Res. C: Emerg. Technol. **80**, 1–19 (2017)
12. Metzker, E.: Reliably detecting and defending against attacks: requirements for automotive intrusion detection systems. VECTOR (2020)
13. Miller, C., Valasek, C.: Remote exploitation of an unaltered passenger vehicle. Black Hat USA, vol. **2015**(S 91), 1–91 (2015)
14. Mitchell, R., Chen, I.R.: A survey of intrusion detection techniques for cyber-physical systems. ACM Comput. Surv. **46**(4) (2014)
15. FMI Standard. https://fmi-standard.org/
16. Palmieri, M., Quadri, C., Fagiolini, A., Bernardeschi, C.: Co-simulated digital twin on the network edge: a vehicle platoon. Comput. Commun. 35–47 (2024). https://doi.org/10.1016/j.comcom.2023.09.019
17. Rajamani, R., Tan, H.S., Law, B.K., Zhang, W.B.: Demonstration of integrated longitudinal and lateral control for the operation of automated vehicles in platoons. IEEE Trans. Control Syst. Technol. **8**(4), 695–708 (2000). https://doi.org/10.1109/87.852914

18. Sheikholeslam, S., Desoer, C.A.: Longitudinal control of a platoon of vehicles. In: 1990 American Control Conference, pp. 291–296 (1990). https://doi.org/10.23919/ACC.1990.4790743
19. Son, M.: Cybersecurity IDS - MICROSAR intrusion detection system (IDS). VECTOR (2020)
20. Swaroop, D., Hedrick, J.: String stability of interconnected systems. In: Proceedings of 1995 American Control Conference - ACC 1995, vol. 3, pp. 1806–1810 (1995). https://doi.org/10.1109/ACC.1995.531196
21. Thule, C., Lausdahl, K., Gomes, C., Meisl, G., Larsen, P.G.: Maestro: the INTO-CPS co-simulation framework. Simul. Model. Pract. Theory **92** (2019). https://doi.org/10.1016/j.simpat.2018.12.005

A Preliminary Approach to Verify Platoon Behaviour Using Execution Traces and Model Checking

Simona Correra[✉], Valeria Sorgente, Giulia Varriano, Vittoria Nardone, Francesco Mercaldo, and Antonella Santone

Department of Medicine and Health Sciences "Vincenzo Tiberio", University of Molise, Campobasso, Italy
s.correra@studenti.unimol.it,
{valeria.sorgente,giulia.varriano,vittoria.nardone, francesco.mercaldo,antonella.santone}@unimol.it

Abstract. The rapid advancement of autonomous vehicle technology has significantly changed Intelligent Transportation Systems. Cooperative Cruise Control increases the efficiency of connected and autonomous vehicles by improving road safety, reducing fuel emissions and increasing traffic flow. By allowing vehicles to work together, Cooperative Cruise Control addresses key problems that cause road accidents, such as inadvertent braking, rear-end collisions, and driver error. This technology will enable vehicles to respond almost instantly to changes in speed and distance. Improve communication and coordination between vehicles and promote safe human distancing - reducing the chance of errors - new verification methods are needed to ensure the reliable performance of these platoon systems. This paper presents a preliminary approach to analyzing platoon system behaviors through execution traces. The aim is to develop an abstract model that reflects operations performed by platoon systems. Then, verifying the model using rigorous mathematical verification techniques, *i.e.,* model checking. The study ensures that the system consistently exhibits the desired behavior.

Keywords: Platoon · Formal Methods · Autonomus Veihcle

1 Introduction

With the rapid growth of driverless vehicle technology in recent years, Intelligent transportation systems (ITS) face significant changes. The Cooperative Adaptive Cruise Control (CACC) [1] is an innovative example of connected and autonomous vehicle technology. It aims to improve road safety, reduce fuel emissions and increase traffic flow. The CACC-supported vehicle category presents a important option to address the high rate of road accidents worldwide. By allowing connected vehicles to cross in a coordinated manner, CACC solutions can reduce some of the most common causes of accidents, such as inadvertent

A. Kocian et al. (Eds.): INTSYS 2024, LNICST 608, pp. 411–423, 2025.
https://doi.org/10.1007/978-3-031-86370-7_25

braking, rear-end collisions and driver error. A platoon is a group of vehicles that travel together, coordinating their speed and maintaining a safe distance from one another. CACC-based platoons advance vehicle coordination and communication by allowing vehicles to respond almost instantly to changes in speed and distance. Furthermore, CACC supports a safer space between cars and reduce the chance of human error, which often leads to accidents. The use of such advanced automation can reduce accidents on the road network. As a result, CACC could define an essential step in creating safer and more efficient roads around the world.

Several works have been proposed in the literature to develop and verify various aspects of platoon systems. Some considerable examples include research on platooning protocols [13,18], which focuses on the rules and procedures governing vehicle coordination; existing testbeds that evaluate platooning protocols and messages [4,5,22], providing practical insights into real-world applications; and studies on cybersecurity in platooning [11,12,23], addressing the potential vulnerabilities and threats that these systems may face. These studies provide valuable insights into the comprehensive understanding of platoon systems and their operational dynamics.

Considering the critical role these emerging technologies play in increasing road safety, it is necessary to develop new methods to verify the reliable performance of the platoon system [2]. Rigorous verification processes are required to ensure these systems perform reliably and as intended in various real-world conditions [6]. Thus, to ensure better safety for all road users using comprehensive testing and inspection methods is needed. A comprehensive assessment confirms that CACC-based class control meets accuracy standards, reliability, and safety standards at a high level.

For the above reasons, we propose a preliminary approach to verify platoon systems' behaviour. Specifically, we aim to analyze the execution traces of a platoon system to develop an abstract model depicting its behaviour. By applying model checking– a rigorous mathematical verification technique–, we want to assess the system's behaviour to ensure that it consistently exhibits the desired behaviours while avoiding any unwanted ones.

The remainder of this paper is organized as follows: Sect. 2 briefly describes the model checking technique and outlines CACC and platooning, Sect. 3 overviews the current literature and contextualizes our work in the existing literature. Section 4 presents the workflow of the proposed approach, and Sect. 5 shows preliminary results. Section 6 discusses challenges and limitation of the proposed approach. Finally, Sect. 7 concludes the work.

2 Background

This section provides an overview of Cooperative Adaptive Cruise Control (CACC) and Platooning to contextualize the context of this work better. Moreover, in the following, we briefly describe the Model Checking technique workflow to provide the reader with preliminary notions about the technique used in this work.

2.1 Platoon and CACC

Cooperative Adaptive Cruise Control (CACC) [1] is an extension of Adaptive cruise control (ACC) [24]. CACC is an on-board system designed to maintain a minimum safe distance from vehicles directly ahead in the same lane. This distance can be either fixed or dynamic, depending on the vehicles speeds, and is typically aligned with a specified time interval that reflects a minimum reaction time. To guarantee a safe and efficient drive, CACC incorporates several components. It collects real-time data regarding the environment using various onboard sensors, such as radar, LIDAR, and cameras. Communication V2X, where X can be either another vehicle (V) or local roadside units (I), allows vehicles to share their data with others. Through V2X communication, every vehicle will receive and send information concerning traffic conditions and potential risks. The onboard unit processes sensor data and V2X communications and computes safe inter-vehicle distance. This analysis will allow the vehicle to adapt its driving strategy appropriately using acceleration and brake commands.

A group of vehicles that move together by synchronizing their speed and maintaining a safe distance between each other is called a platoon. The communication within the vehicle improves their cooperation toward any agreements over the manoeuvres and driving speeds, improving traffic safety through the prevention of collisions. Furthermore, the reduced gap between the vehicles shortens the body-dynamic drag against the following cars, lowering their energy consumption and, therefore, their $CO2$ emissions. Platooning indicates the coordinated driving of connected vehicles in a line, based on wireless communication, to manage functions such as platoon creation, joining, and leaving. Platooning holds two primary architectures: centralized, wherein a leader or a server makes operational decisions, and distributed, with each vehicle autonomously deciding on its position by using V2X and sensor data for maintaining safety distances and performing manoeuvres collaboratively.

2.2 Model Checking

Model Checking [7] is a technique within Formal Methods, which are rigorous mathematical approaches commonly employed to specify and verify complex systems. Owing to their precision and reliability, such techniques are particularly well-suited for the development and verification of safety-critical systems. Model Checking involves exhaustively exploring all possible states of a system and verifying whether specific properties hold in each state using a Model Checker tool. This tool requires two inputs: a formal model of the system and temporal logic formulas that specify the desired behaviors. The Model Checker evaluates these properties against the system model and provides a binary outcome: it returns true if the system satisfies the property and false otherwise. If the system fails to satisfy a property, the Model Checker can generate a counterexample—a sequence of events demonstrating how the property is violated. This feature is especially valuable for diagnosing and addressing the root cause of the violation.

The Formal Model of the System. The behavior of the system, as defined during the specification process, can be described using a formal model. This behavior is typically represented as a *Labeled Transition System (LTS)*. An LTS is composed of a set of states, transitions between these states, and labels that annotate the transitions. Additionally, one state is designated as the initial state. Formally, an LTS is defined as a quadruple $T = (S, \mathcal{A}, \longrightarrow, s)$, where S represents the set of states, $\mathcal{A}$ denotes the set of transition labels (or actions), $s \in S$ is the initial state, and $\longrightarrow \subseteq S \times \mathcal{A} \times S$ specifies the transition relation.

Processes are used to algebraically represent the elements of an LTS. One of the most notable process algebras employed for modeling complex systems is Milner's Calculus of Communicating Systems (CCS) [14]. This formalism provides a set of fundamental operators for defining finite processes, operators for communication and concurrency, and a mechanism for recursion to represent infinite behaviors. The syntax of *processes* behaves as follows:

$$p ::= \mathrm{nil} \mid \alpha.p \mid p + p \mid p|p \mid p \backslash L \mid p[f] \mid x$$

where α ranges over a finite set of actions $\mathcal{A} = \{\tau, a, \bar{a}, b, \bar{b}, ...\}$. Processes can perform input actions labeled as "unblocked", denoted by a, while output actions are considered "blocked", represented by $\bar{a}$. When a process is ready to execute an action a, it can synchronize with another process performing the corresponding blocked action $\bar{a}$. This is why these are called *complementary actions*.

An action $\tau \in \mathcal{A}$ is a generic *internal action*. This allows processes to be described abstractly, hiding complex sequences of operations, and keeping details private. The sets of *visible actions* $\mathcal{A} - \{\tau\}$ are included in the set L, which can be used to create communication between processes through internal actions. Visible actions are those used to define the system properties.

The relabeling function f, in processes of the form $p[f]$, is a function such that $f : \mathcal{A} \to \mathcal{A}$, such that it satisfies the constraint $f(\tau) = \tau$. In addition, each constant x is defined by a definition of constant $x \stackrel{\mathrm{def}}{=} p$.

The semantics of CCS by induction on the structure of processes is very rich:

- The nil process allows no action to be performed;
- The process $\alpha.p$ can execute α and later become the process p;
- The $p + q$ process can act as either process (p or q);
- The | operator expresses parallel composition, while the \ operator expresses action restriction. If visible actions are in the set L, then $p \backslash L$ is a process that acts like p but cannot execute any of the actions (even blocked actions) found in L. This is true even though any pair of complementary actions can be executed for communication;
- The $[f]$ operator guarantees relabeling of actions: if p executes α and becomes the new process p', then $p[f]$ can execute $f(\alpha)$ and become $p'[f]$.

The behavior of the process x where $(x \stackrel{\mathrm{def}}{=} p)$ is that of its definition p.

Temporal Logic Formulas for Properties. Temporal logic formulas provide a formal way to specify that certain properties will hold in all states at every step, or that a specific event will happen at some point in the future. Two simple instances are the *safety properties* and the *liveness properties*. The first one expresses that an undesirable situation will never happen, while the second one declares that some reactions will always follow some actions.

In our study, we adopt *mu-calculus* logic [20] as the temporal logic framework. The syntax of mu-calculus is presented below, where Z represents variables, and K and R denote subsets of actions from $\mathcal{A}$. $\phi ::=$

$$\texttt{tt} \mid \texttt{ff} \mid Z \mid \phi \vee \phi \mid \phi \wedge \phi \mid [K]\,\phi \mid \langle K \rangle\,\phi \mid \nu Z.\phi \mid \mu Z.\phi$$

The satisfaction by a state s in a transition system of the formula ϕ, written as $s \models \phi$, is outlined as follows:

- **Basic cases:** Every state satisfies $\texttt{tt}$, while no state satisfies $\texttt{ff}$;
- **Logical Connectives:** A state satisfies $\phi_1 \vee \phi_2$ ($\phi_1 \wedge \phi_2$) if it satisfies ϕ_1 or (and) ϕ_2.
- **Modal operators** $[K]\,\phi$ **and** $\langle K \rangle\,\phi$:
  i. A state satisfies $[K]\,\phi$ if, for every action in K, it transitions to a state that satisfies ϕ.
  ii. A state satisfies $\langle K \rangle\,\phi$ if it can transition to a state that satisfies ϕ by performing an action in K.

Formal Verification Environment. Model Checking techniques [7] require a formal verification environment to validate the properties defined on the system model. Concurrency Workbench of New Century (CWB-NC) [8] is one of the most widely used environments for verifying software systems, supporting various specification languages such as CCS. In this study, we use CWB-NC as the formal verification environment.

3   Related Work

This section reports on the current literature on verifying platoon behaviour. In [21], it has been proposed to control vehicle platoon with collision-safety and efficiency measures based on the platoon behaviour. It uses a local model predictive control (MPC) formulation to separate safety from tracking control. Furthermore, a braking hold-back strategy has been defined to improve the efficiency of the platoon with smaller inter-vehicle distances. A corridor-based reference shaping and V2V communication strategy have been introduced to have a behaviour based on the situation, providing excellent performance with traffic disturbances and low communication effort.

Various projects have been designed and implemented in the past years to improve safety, emissions reductions, and driving comfort. For example, COM-PANION (Cooperative Dynamic Formation of Platoons for Safe and Energy-optimized Goods Transportation) was developed to define a cooperative system for truck platooning management to reduce fuel consumption and improve

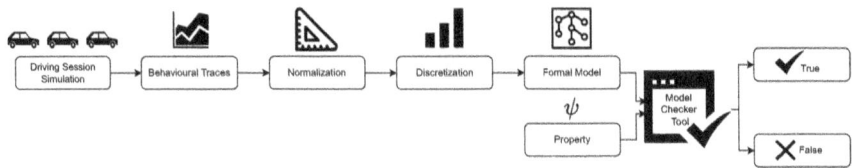

Fig. 1. Our preliminary approach workflow.

safety. Communication among vehicles is performed using V2X communication and ACC. Due to the different parties involved in the platoon (for example, sensors and inter-vehicle communication), it can be vulnerable to attacks. In [17], a strategy is proposed to improve the protection of the platoon. The authors introduce a protocol validated through theoretical analysis and experimental simulation using the PLEXE simulator. This allows the enhancement of platooning resilience by incorporating mechanisms such as real-time voting, which enables vehicles to detect and mitigate malicious attacks.

4   Preliminary Approach

The Fig. 1 depicts the workflow of our preliminary approach to verify a platoon system. The process begins with collecting traces from a simulated platooning driving session. These traces capture time-series data on vehicle parameters such as velocity and acceleration.

Initially, the collected data are subject to normalization using the min-max normalization technique [3]. Once normalized, the data is then discretized through two different methods:

- The first method identifies maximum and minimum values and discretizes the data into three intervals.
- The second method applies a sliding window to the samples, assessing their stationarity within the interval using the Augmented Dickey-Fuller (ADF) test [9]. For non-stationary samples, the slope of the interpolated data curve is computed to determine whether the trend is increasing or decreasing.

The discretized values are then used to construct formal models of the system. More in detail, we define two transformation functions, *i.e.*, f_1 and f_2, used on data produced by both discretization methods. Table 1 shows a simple example of execution traces for three vehicles, simplified to include only three moments in time. Note that for both Acceleration and Velocity, we use the following notation: $FeatureName_{XY}$, where $FeatureName$ corresponds to a string indicating a discretized value for the feature, X indicates the vehicle ID and Y is the instant of time when the discretized value occurs.

As stated in Sect. 2.2, to build the formal model, it is necessary to transform traces into an LTS using processes algebraically. To do so, we define two transformation functions producing two distinct formal models. The first transformation

Table 1. Example of Discretized Traces.

Vehicle ID	Time	Acceleration	Velocity
V_1	1	Acc_{11}	Vel_{11}
V_1	2	Acc_{12}	Vel_{12}
V_1	3	Acc_{13}	Vel_{13}
V_2	1	Acc_{21}	Vel_{21}
V_2	2	Acc_{22}	Vel_{22}
V_2	3	Acc_{23}	Vel_{23}
V_3	1	Acc_{31}	Vel_{31}
V_3	2	Acc_{32}	Vel_{32}
V_3	3	Acc_{33}	Vel_{33}

function defined is f_1. It takes as input all discretized traces of one vehicle and produces as output sequential processes able to mimic in each state the parallel composition of features. For this objective, we need the following definitions (as shown in Milner [14]).

Definition 1 (Well-terminating process). A CCS process is considered well-terminating if it performs the action $\bar{\delta}$ exclusively when it terminates immediately afterward.

The δ can be found in the definition of the operators $\|$ and ";" (see Table 2), and it is introduced to synchronise processes on termination. The two operators represent the sequentialization and parallel execution of two well-terminating processes, and the resulting processes from their application remain well-terminating.

Table 2. Operators for well-terminating processes.

$$p\|q = (p[\delta_1/\delta] \mid q[\delta_2/\delta] \mid (\delta_1.\delta_2.DONE + \delta_2.\delta_1.DONE))\backslash\{\delta_1, \delta_2\}$$
$$p; q = (p[\delta_3/\delta] \mid \delta_3.q)\backslash\{\delta_3\}$$
$$DONE \stackrel{\text{def}}{=} \bar{\delta}.nil$$

From the semantic CCS algebra:

- The constant $DONE$ represents a process that terminates immediately without performing any further actions;
- The ";" operator is used to enforce the sequential execution of two processes, p and q. In this way, p must terminate before q can begin its execution;
- The process "$p\|q$" models the parallel execution of p and q, terminating only when both processes have completed.

From this point forward, only CCS programs in which the operator | has been consistently replaced by | are considered.

More precisely, p_{ij} process has the following definition:

$$p_{ij} \overset{\text{def}}{=} (Acceleration \parallel Velocity) ; p_{ij+1}$$

where p_{ij} process represents the parallel composition of the vehicle i features at each time instant j, spanning from 1 to n. Therefore, for vehicle i, there will be a series of processes at each time instant j, mirroring the parallel composition of all trace features at each timestamp. Roughly speaking, the f_1 transformation function generates a process able to reproduce the sequential alternancy of features for a specific vehicle. Thus, it reproduces how the vehicle dynamics change during the trip.

The second transformation function is f_2, and it produces a formal model that mimics the parallel composition of the vehicles during their trip by synchronizing their evolution at each instant of time. More in detail, we define a synchronization process $sink$ coordinating all vehicles at each timestamp, $i.e.$, all vehicles are scheduled by the orchestrator process $sink$ having the following definition:

$$sink \overset{\text{def}}{=} sync_1.\dots.sync_n.\overline{go}_1 \dots \overline{go}_n.sink$$

Thus, this formal model comprises the parallel composition of each vehicle, each modelled as a process of features, with an embedded synchronizing process that, at each moment, can coordinate the vehicle evolution during the trip. More in detail, we show in the following a simple example of the complete formal model.

$$p_{00} \overset{\text{def}}{=} (increasingAcc0.DONE \parallel increasingVel0.DONE); (\overline{synk_0}.go_0.p_{01})$$

$$\vdots$$

$$p_{n0} \overset{\text{def}}{=} (increasingAccN.DONE \parallel increasingVelN.DONE); (\overline{synk_0}.go_0.p_{n1})$$

$$sink \overset{\text{def}}{=} sync_1 \dots sync_n \overline{go}_1 \dots \overline{go}_n.sink$$

$$All \overset{\text{def}}{=} (p_{00} \parallel \dots p_{n0} \parallel sink) \backslash \{syc_0, \dots sync_n, go_0, \dots go_n\};$$

The above definition involves n processes, one for each vehicle, and a $sink$ process synchronizes vehicles at each timestamp. The process ALL allows the parallel composition of all vehicles synchronized through the sink and all restricted synchronization actions.

Finally, these models jointly with specific behavioural properties of interest are inputs to the Model Checker tool. This tool verifies if the formal model meets the specified properties. If the property holds, the tool returns a true value; otherwise, it returns false.

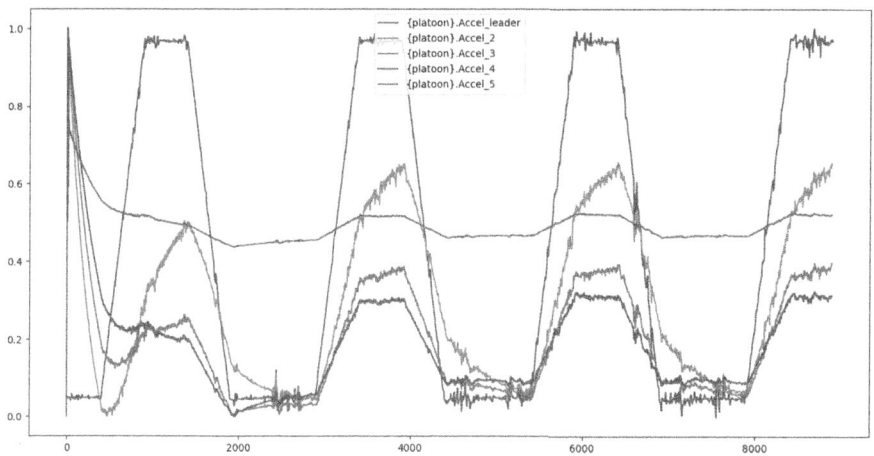

Fig. 2. Normalized acceleration trends.

4.1 Our Case Study

We used traces generated using the approach proposed by Palmieri *et al.* [15]. Traces comprise 8,899 velocity and acceleration samples collected every 0.01 s from 4 cars in a platoon to evaluate our methodology. First, we normalized the samples with the `scikit-learn` [16] method MinMaxScaler: this allowed us to obtain data comprising 0 and 1. Once data had been normalized, and since formal methods require non-numeric samples, we performed the discretization. Observing the nature of the samples, we noticed that trends were repeated cyclically. For velocity, we had a trend formed by constant and increasing velocity that repeated itself. Instead, the acceleration trend comprises four repeating parts: low-level stationary, increasing, high-level stationary, and decreasing. Figure 2 and Fig. 3 show normalized trends of acceleration and velocity, respectively.

We performed two types of discretization. One type was made using the `cut` method from `NumPy` library [10], and a bin equal to three was applied on each sample. The second discretization was performed in two phases: firstly, we used the Augmented Dickey-Fuller test to evaluate if the sample in a window were constant, and in the case of non-constant results, we assessed the slope to define if there were an increasing or decreasing. To apply the statistic test, the `adfuller` method from statsmodel library [19] while the slope was defined using `polyfit` method from `NumPy` library [10]. To determine the best size of the window, we tried several widths (50, 100, 150, 200, 250, 300, 350, 400, 450, 500, 550)

5 Preliminary Result

Table 3 shows two possible formulas that can be verified on the formal models created with our approach. Specifically, the first formula checks that when the

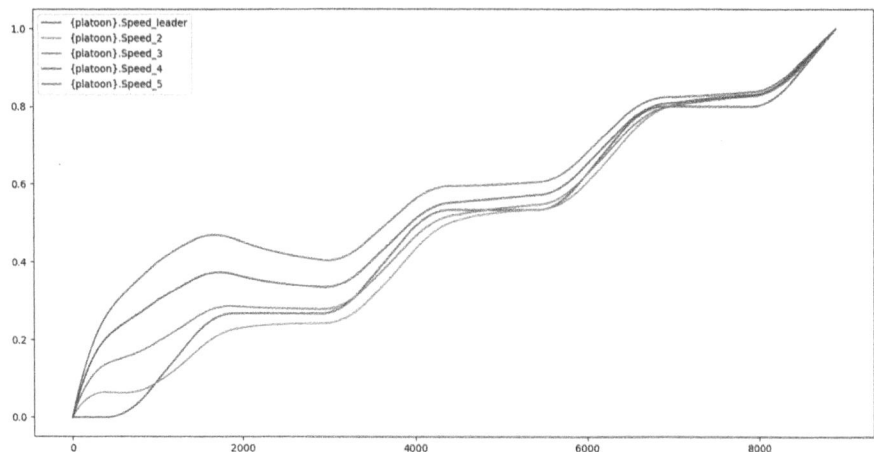

Fig. 3. Normalized velocity trends.

Table 3. Two formulas for checking normal behaviours.

$\varphi_1 \;\; = \mu X. \langle increasing Acc0 \rangle\; \varphi_{1_1} \vee \langle -increasing Acc0 \rangle\; X$
$\varphi_{1_1} = \mu X. \langle increasing Acc2 \rangle\; \varphi_{1_2} \vee \langle -increasing Acc2 \rangle\; X$
$\varphi_{1_2} = \mu X. \langle increasing Acc3 \rangle\; \varphi_{1_3} \vee \langle -increasing Acc3 \rangle\; X$
$\varphi_{1_3} = \mu X. \langle increasing Acc4 \rangle\; \mathbf{tt} \vee \langle -increasing Acc4 \rangle\; X$
$\varphi_2 \;\; = \mu X. \langle decreasing Acce0 \rangle\; \varphi_{2_1} \vee \langle -decreasing Acce0 \rangle\; X$
$\varphi_{2_1} = \mu X. \langle decreasing Acce2 \rangle\; \varphi_{2_2} \vee \langle -decreasing Acce2 \rangle\; X$
$\varphi_{2_2} = \mu X. \langle decreasing Acce3 \rangle\; \varphi_{2_3} \vee \langle -decreasing Acce3 \rangle\; X$
$\varphi_{2_3} = \mu X. \langle decreasing Acce4 \rangle\; \mathbf{tt} \vee \langle -decreasing Acce4 \rangle\; X$

lead vehicle accelerates, all following vehicles subsequently accelerate in a cascading manner. Conversely, the second formula verifies, in a dual manner to the first, that if there is a deceleration, it propagates throughout the entire platoon.

Table 4 displays the results of verifying two logical formulas, φ_1 and φ_2, across our formal models. More in detail, column **Model ID** indicates the identifier for each model, where each ID corresponds to a sample window size used during model construction. The other two columns, labelled φ_1 and φ_2, represent the outcomes of the formula verifications, with a check mark signifying that the formula is satisfied for that model. From the Table 4, it is evident that both formulas, φ_1 and φ_1, hold for all the tested models, regardless of the sample window size. This result suggests that the behaviour being checked remains consistent across these preliminary models. However, it's important to note that this represents an initial, simplified analysis. In future work, we plan to verify more complex formulas using traces that include data from real-world vehicles and scenarios involving potential attacks. Results will allow for a deeper exam-

Table 4. Results for φ_1 and φ_2 properties reporterd in Table 3.

Model ID	φ_1	φ_2
50	✓	✓
150	✓	✓
200	✓	✓
250	✓	✓
300	✓	✓
350	✓	✓
400	✓	✓
450	✓	✓
500	✓	✓
550	✓	✓

ination of the system's robustness and security under varied and more realistic conditions.

6   Challenges and Limitations

Although our preliminary approach shows promising results in verifying platoon behaviour, it also presents several challenges and limitations. Overcoming these issues is crucial to enhance our method's robustness, scalability, and practical applicability.

The model-checking process inherently faces the "state explosion" problem, where the number of system states grows exponentially with the addition of each vehicle or behavioural parameter. The verification process can be computationally prohibitive in large platoons or complex environments, limiting its use in real-time applications or more extensive networks. Abstraction techniques can be employed to simplify the model by focusing only on critical states or transitions. Techniques such as symbolic and bounded model checking can reduce the number of states by analyzing only a subset of behaviours or time intervals. Additionally, compositional verification, which verifies each component or vehicle independently before integrating the results, can help manage complexity in larger systems.

Furthermore, our method discretizes the continuous data, such as velocity and acceleration, into categories of trends. It makes the analysis task easier but might lose important information and slight deviations or subtle behavioural changes that could indicate problems. Adaptive discretization can address the issues where granularity changes dynamically with real-time data trends. Another helpful method could be the application of multiresolution discretization, using finer granularity in the most critical sections, *e.g.*, during rapid acceleration or braking-in, to avoid missing essential details without overwhelming the verification process.

Finally, verification based only on traces of simulated executions cannot truly capture real-world conditions, such as variable road conditions, environmental considerations, or unexpected interactions with human-driven vehicles. This limitation makes the verification outcome for platoon behaviour less representative of performance in diverse environments. A hybrid testing approach that combines real-world sensor data with simulated scenarios could improve the accuracy of execution traces. Additionally, using digital twins that mirror real-time conditions from live environments could yield more realistic simulations of actual platoon behaviour. This approach would likely strengthen the model's robustness by enabling verification across a broader range of potential scenarios.

7   Conclusion

Given the wide spread of driverless vehicle technology and the critical role these emerging technologies play in increasing road safety, it is necessary to develop new methods to verify the reliable performance of these autonomous systems. For these reasons, our work proposes a preliminary approach to verify vehicle platoon behaviour using its execution traces. More in detail, we propose a preliminary model checking-based approach aiming to rigorously verify a platoon's abstract model built from its execution traces and using behavioural properties expressed in temporal logic. The results achieved seem promising. In the future, we plan to improve platoon modelling jointly with its property specifications to guarantee and verify the security aspects of platoon systems.

Acknowledgment. This work is partially funded by the European Union - Next-GenerationEU - National Recovery and Resilience Plan (NRRP) - MISSION 4 COMPONENT 2, INVESTMENT N. 1.1, CALL PRIN 2022 PNRR D.D. 1409 14-09-2022 - FORESEEN: FORmal mEthodS for attack dEtEction in autonomous driviNg systems, CUP N.I53D23006130001.

References

1. ISO: 20035:2019, Intelligent transport systems - Cooperative adaptive cruise control systems (CACC) - Performance requirements and test procedures (2019)
2. Accelerate safety measures to reduce road traffic deaths: Who (2024). https://www.who.int/southeastasia/news/detail/02-09-2024-accelerate-safety-measures-to-reduce-road-traffic-deaths-who
3. Ali, P.J.M.: Investigating the impact of min-max data normalization on the regression performance of k-nearest neighbor with different similarity measurements. ARO-The Sci. J. Koya Univ. **10**(1), 85–91 (2022)
4. Alvarez, L., Horowitz, R.: Safe platooning in automated highway systems part i: safety regions design. Veh. Syst. Dyn. **32**(1), 23–55 (1999)
5. Bergenhem, C., Huang, Q., Benmimoun, A., Robinson, T.: Challenges of platooning on public motorways. In: 17th World Congress on Intelligent Transport Systems, pp. 1–12 (2010)

6. Braiteh, F.E., Bassi, F., Khatoun, R.: Platooning in connected vehicles: a review of current solutions, standardization activities, cybersecurity, and research opportunities. IEEE Trans. Intell. Veh. (2024)

7. Clarke, E.M., Grumberg, O., Peled, D.: Model Checking. MIT Press, Cambridge (2001)

8. Cleaveland, R., Sims, S.: The NCSU concurrency workbench. In: CAV. Springer (1996)

9. Hamilton, J.D.: Time Series Analysis. Princeton University Press, Princeton (2020)

10. Harris, C.R., et al.: Array programming with NumPy. Nature **585**(7825), 357–362 (2020). https://doi.org/10.1038/s41586-020-2649-2

11. Ju, Z., Zhang, H., Li, X., Chen, X., Han, J., Yang, M.: A survey on attack detection and resilience for connected and automated vehicles: from vehicle dynamics and control perspective. IEEE Trans. Intell. Veh. **7**(4), 815–837 (2022)

12. Kim, H., Jeong, Y., Choi, W., Lee, D.H., Jo, H.J.: Efficient ECU analysis technology through structure-aware can fuzzing. IEEE Access **10**, 23259–23271 (2022)

13. Lee, G., Jung, J.I.: Decentralized platoon join-in-middle protocol considering communication delay for connected and automated vehicle. Sensors **21**(21), 7126 (2021)

14. Milner, R.: Communication and concurrency. PHI Series in computer science, Prentice Hall (1989)

15. Palmieri, M., Quadri, C., Fagiolini, A., Bernardeschi, C.: Co-simulated digital twin on the network edge: a vehicle platoon. Comput. Commun. **212**, 35–47 (2023)

16. Pedregosa, F., et al.: Scikit-learn: machine learning in Python. J. Mach. Learn. Res. **12**, 2825–2830 (2011)

17. Petrillo, A., Pescapé, A., Santini, S.: A collaborative approach for improving the security of vehicular scenarios: the case of platooning. Comput. Commun. **122**, 59–75 (2018)

18. Schwab, A., Lunze, J.: Vehicle platooning and cooperative merging. IFAC-PapersOnLine **52**(5), 353–358 (2019)

19. Seabold, S., Perktold, J.: Statsmodels: econometric and statistical modeling with python. In: 9th Python in Science Conference (2010)

20. Stirling, C.: An introduction to modal and temporal logics for CCS. In: Concurrency: Theory, Language, and Architecture, pp. 2–20 (1989)

21. Thormann, S., Schirrer, A., Jakubek, S.: Safe and efficient cooperative platooning. IEEE Trans. Intell. Transp. Syst. **23**(2), 1368–1380 (2020)

22. Tsugawa, S.: An overview on an automated truck platoon within the energy its project. IFAC Proc. Vol. **46**(21), 41–46 (2013)

23. Wang, Z., Wei, H., Wang, J., Zeng, X., Chang, Y.: Security issues and solutions for connected and autonomous vehicles in a sustainable city: a survey. Sustainability **14**(19), 12409 (2022)

24. Winner, H., Danner, B., Steinle, J.: Adaptive cruise control. Handbuch Fahrerassistenzsysteme: Grundlagen, Komponenten und Systeme für aktive Sicherheit und Komfort, pp. 478–521 (2009)

Author Index

The manufacturer's authorised representative in the EU is Springer
Nature Customer Service Centre GmbH, Europaplatz 3, 69115 Heidelberg,
Germany. If you have any concerns regarding our products, please
contact ProductSafety@springernature.com

Printed and bound by CPI Group (UK) Ltd, Croydon, CR0 4YY
28/04/2026
02098521-0013